A Finger in the Wound

A Finger in the Wound

Body Politics in Quincentennial Guatemala

Diane M. Nelson

UNIVERSITY OF CALIFORNIA PRESS

Berkeley   Los Angeles   London

University of California Press
Berkeley and Los Angeles, California

University of California Press, Ltd.
London, England

Library of Congress Cataloging-in-Publication Data

Nelson, Diane M., 1963–.
    A finger in the wound : body politics in quincentennial Guatemala
/ Diane M. Nelson.
        p.   cm.
    Includes bibliographical references and index
    ISBN 0-520-21284-3 (alk. paper). — ISBN 0-520-21285-1
(pbk.: alk. paper)
        1. Mayas—Ethnic identity.   2. Mayas—Civil rights.   3. Mayas—
Politics and government.   4. Body, Human—Political aspects—
Guatemala.   4. Body, Human—Symbolic aspects—Guatemala.
6. Ladino (Latin American people)—Guatemala—Social conditions.
7. Mestizaje—Guatemala—Social conditions.   8. Popular culture—
Guatemala.   9. Sex role—Guatemala.   9. Violence—Guatemala.
11. Guatemala—Ethnic relations.   12. Guatemala—Politics and
government.   I. Title.
F1435.3.E72N45   1999
305.897′4152—dc21   98-35061
                                                                CIP

Printed in the United States of America
9 8 7 6 5 4 3 2 1

Portions of chapter 5 originally appeared in *Anthropology Today* 10, no. 6 (1996): 3–7.
Reprinted by kind permission of the Royal Anthropological Institute of Great Britain
and Ireland. Portions of chapter 7 originally appeared in *Cultural Anthropology* 11,
no. 3 (August 1996): 287–308. Reprinted by kind permission of the
American Anthropological Association. Not for further reproduction.

*For Mark
and for Myrna*

July 4, 1989

I love to feel the mountains alive in my veins, complete with their rivers, their coolness, their torridity. And I am inspired by their people who survive amid such poverty and grief. Of course, all this is only part of the picture; there is still the frustration of not knowing what to do.

December 16, 1989

My last trip was to a village in Chajul. . . . We stayed eight days and again it was a very rich experience. By the time we left, the people in the community appeared to be growing attached to us (we had been there once before) seeking us out and inviting us to visit them in their houses. They have such an enormous need for someone to listen to them. I can't stop feeling frustrated at my inability to offer more concrete help.

Excerpts from letters Myrna Mack Chang wrote while researching what would become *Dónde Está el Futuro?* (AVANCSO 1992). Elizabeth Oglesby's translation (1995).

CONTENTS

ILLUSTRATIONS

ACKNOWLEDGMENTS

Sitting on her spring-entranced, tree-shaded front porch in May 1985, just before sending us on our first trip to Guatemala, Beatriz Manz warned Paula Worby and me that there was something about Guatemala that got into your blood, that stayed with you. Now it is October 12, 1998, and I am still writing about Guatemala and thinking about blood. It has been a central concern in writing about the country and the catastrophe of war and counterinsurgency, but it is also metaphoric for the kinlike ties that have made possible the knowledge I have. I want to acknowledge here the relationality of those ties and that knowledge. It somehow doesn't seem strong enough to say that this document is only meaningful in its relation to the interactions, flows, transfusions, spills, and donations of many, many other people to whom I am deeply indebted (of course, the blood metaphorics also rightly conjure the vampirism of transnational research).

Much of my relation with Guatemala has been mediated gynocentrically through many Sweet Sisters of Solidarity. First in many ways is Paula Worby, who has shared so much for so long; from those first six months of round-the-clock work in 1985, she has challenged me and laughed with me. I still rely on the friendship and critique we began with Emily Schnee at the Charlie's Tap jazz bar—a mutual support that continues as we struggle to find ways to be political in this world. I feel enormous gratitude to a wise big sister, Marcie Mersky, who has given me careful advice and trust in myself and continues to teach me about commitment. Also a gift from that first project was working with Jennifer Harbury, whose walk across her own bridge of courage and tragedy has inspired me and many others. I am deeply grateful to Beatriz Manz, gifted researcher, political activist, and teacher, who made it possible to go to Guatemala. Paula and I met Myrna Mack on that first trip, and she remains a vibrant inspiration. Her death is a still-aching loss that structures this work. The flying hands, the never-ending cigarettes, the golden gifts of whispered gossip that brought ever-larger networks of violence and resistance into focus, the deep support for the value of "taking time out" to train, the bloody knife, and finally the broken wall.

Central to the sane-making circle in the chaos of Guatemala City was Claire Creelman, mistress of the ribald political insight. I offer many thanks to Rachel Garst, who accompanied me in "discovering" the Mayan movement, and to friends and important supports for my pregraduate work in Guatemala, including Father Ricardo Falla; Father Ron Hennessey (best joke-teller in the western hemisphere); Madre Raquel; the folks at CEIDEC, IOCE, and COMADEP in Mexico City for teaching me how to read silences; Pancho Cali for sharing Eisenstein; Judith Feaster for chocolate cake and venting frustration; and my colleague on the Development Poles project, Dixie (Humberto Samayoa). Rolando Lopez is a matchmaker from heaven, and I have learned a great deal from him about delight amid commitment and the power of good food, film, and friends.

In thanking those who made some three years of fieldwork possible, I owe songs of praise and appreciation for generous donations to the women and men working for indigenous and human rights in Guatemala. I hope that there is some value in this book that can in a small way return the enormous investment of time and energy of the Mayan activists who agreed to be interviewed. Dr. Demetrio Cojtí has been overwhelmingly generous with time, insight, and critique, as has Andrés Cus. Narciso Cojtí, Marcial Maxian Simacox, Ricardo Cajas, and members of COCADI, COINDI, and CISMA were most helpful. I would also like to thank Julio Ixcamej, Marcelino Nicolás, and Pedro Gaspar González from the ALMG and Alfredo Copil of the Delegation 169. Much of my understanding was developed through long-term wrangles and exchanges with Alberto Esquit, Miguel Angel Velasco (of the "Comalapa gang"), Victoria Alvarez, Francisca Alvarez, Fidelia Teleguaro Siguen, and the powerful sisters, Delia Tujab and Gloria Tujab. I thank them for all their time and patience! Patience and insight were also given by Angel Arturo González, a most organized and energetic informant to whom I am most grateful, and I sincerely thank the other men and women who took time out from their busy schedules in "the state" to aid me in this project.

I spent long hours over coffee and lemon meringue pie, slowly developing perspective on the intricacies of modern-day Guatemala, with Edeliberto Cifuentes, Julia González, Ramón González Ponciano, Mario Loarca, Carlos Fredy Ochoa, Olga Pérez de Lara, Gustavo Porras Castejón, and Linda Asturias de Barrios and her very promising students. Thanks to them and all the people who agreed to share with me their busy lives. A very warm and special thank you to Tasso Hadjidodou and to Concha Deras, who, among many other gifts, told me my first Rigoberta joke. To Nobel laureate

Rigoberta Menchú, thanks for being an inspiration and for giving me the chance to participate in the Indigenous Summits.

Luís Solano is a friend who explained many things (like economics) with never ending patience, nursed my brother back to health, and introduced me to the best steak restaurants in Guatemala. The staff of Inforpress and Central America Report provided invaluable assistance, and I am deeply indebted to everyone at AVANCSO who shared their intelligence, challenges, humor, and bright courage during hard times of surveillance and threat, giving me an intellectual as well as a physical and emotional home. Special thanks to Ruben Nájera and Clara Arenas and my structural adjustment team.

The fieldwork would have been not only less rich but well-nigh impossible without the friendship and accompaniment of José Fernando (Pepe) Lara—film connoisseur, fan of Amici pizza, DJ, translator, companion in the deep sense—as friend and fellow traveler in trying to understand Guatemala. I owe many of my readings here to our long discussions. Another important part of the fieldwork (along with shopping the informal sector and watching B movies on Sexta Avenida) was my community of "gringos." From Judith Turbyne, I learned the truth of the saying "If it's not Scottish, it's crrrrap!" Ron Strochlic, supermodel and genius at So jokes, is absolutely essential in the Guatemala survival kit, as is Fernando Bances. Kevin Robinson and David Holiday were enablers in my addiction to the mind-numbing details of state functioning. I thank Matthew Creelman, Gladis, Tomás, and Pilar for Gloria Trevi and sweet friendship. For a social life, deep emotional support, and music, I thank *Las Bufis*—especially Trish O'Kane and Debbie Katzman. I thank Karen Brandow for amazing courage, second-generation *chavas* Liz Oglesby and Ana Pérez for friendship and enthusiasm, and Joanne Eccher, Derrill Bazzy, and Sonia Lipson for teaching me how to be in solidarity. Finally, I have been given a great gift in Abigail Adams, whom I met during fieldwork and who is an invaluable, inspiring, and challenging *compañera* in the "field" of anthropology.

I learned much of the thrill of theory and the political work it can do when applied with commitment and a sense of humor from members of Sit.Com.: Avery Gordon, Jeremy Granger, Sandra Joshel, and Stephen Pfohl. And I continue to be inspired by the fearless challenger of everything sacred, Jackie Orr.

My first and best "diss" buddy is Bill Maurer, bureaucracy warrior, *Star Trek* fan, and theory guide, and I also want to thank the members of my cohort (perhaps fittingly, we were the earthquake class), who were vitally important teachers. Amy Borovoy, Suzie Sawyer, Donald Moore, Aida Hernández, Donna Daniels, and Stefan Helmreich make anthropology glisten and purr and unsheathe its claws.

At Stanford, the Stanford Central American Action Network helped me merge politics, theory, and guerrilla theater and gave me Marcia Klotz, partner in theory crime, ground-zero survivor, and sex rebel. Thanks to all the members of our postmodern, porno, post-Fordism, pop-culture, and panic-theory reading group: essential to my theoretical conditions of possibility are Fernando Luera, Carol Jones, Kim Gillespie, Ben Robinson and Lee Medovoi, with extra special thanks to Rob Latham for science fiction, Asian Trash Cinema, and much more. Central to this book has been the kitchen table at 128 Trinity Street, especially for day-to-day talk, challenge, and exploration with Scott Mobley and Valerie Kaussen. Jon Hunt, Catherine John, Douglas Fogel, Gabe Brahm, Pam Bailey, Jennifer González and Warren Sack all helped me Cruz through. A special Vulcan salute to cyborg anthropologist Crystal Hables Gray. Finally, the years of writing this were made physically bearable by martial arts, and I want to thank Master Song and the inhabitants of the "House of Discipline and Respect."

As a Marxist, I am deeply aware of the importance of material support, and here I want to thank Stanford Latin American Studies for summer fieldwork funding and the anthropology department of Stanford University for fellowships and assistantships, as well as funding for fieldwork in 1991 and 1992. The National Science Foundation grant number DBS-9209825 allowed me to spend the year in Guatemala researching this book, and this support is gratefully acknowledged. This work has also been supported by a Mellon dissertation write-up grant, and funding for follow-up fieldwork was graciously provided by Lewis and Clark College.

Finally, I sincerely thank my dissertation committee members, Akhil Gupta, Carol Delaney, and George Collier, for seeing me through this book and many other kinds of education. I feel truly blessed to have had such challenge and support from these and my other wonderful teachers at Stanford—especially Jane Collier, Ben Paul, Renato Rosaldo, and Gail Kligman. They have left me bereft of the horror stories most people carry from their graduate careers, and I hope I come to merit their patience and investment. Carol Smith and Kay Warren have been amazing supports and, with an anonymous reader, gave this book the tough and smart read it needed toward the end. At Stanford, fundamental support was constantly provided by Beth Bashore in all areas of need, and by Jeanne Giaccia, Ellen Christiansen, and Shannon Brown.

My colleagues at Lewis and Clark College in Portland have also been invaluable helpmeets. I thank Deborah Heath and her embrace of the artificial, Alan Cole for his ex-centric takes on things, Todd Little-Siebold and Christa Little-Siebold for material, psychic, and emotional lifelines, Rishonna Zimring for serious levity, and Jack Hart, Clayton Morgareidge, Bob Goldman, Dick Adams, Anne Meneley, and Carol Wilson.

For making all these relations into the material reality of this book I warmly thank Stan Holwitz, Rose Anne White, Carolyn Hill, and Cynthia Bertelsen.

My mother, Lois Nelson, and my father, Donald Nelson, patiently and lovingly made the solid ground I stood on to do this work. They have encouraged me at every step, and none of my little triumphs felt real until they were shared with them. There is no way I can adequately thank them for their sacrifices and love, but I hope they know that I am grateful. I especially acknowledge all my mother endured to give me an education. The same is true of my sister, Erika Zachman, and my brother, Brian Nelson.

To them I dedicate this small work, and to Mark Driscoll, who is so fully imbricated in it and in me that in many ways this book is a gift we've given each other. He is a landmark in all the geographies charted here, my *compañero*. More than anyone else, he made this possible.

This work is the outcome of the fluidary intermixing of all these blood lines and relations. I hope it is not in vain. What is good has come from them, what is wrong or missing is mine.

ABBREVIATIONS

AAA	American Anthropological Association
AEMG	Guatemalan Mayan Writers Academy
AGG	Business Association of Guatemala
ALMG	Guatemalan Mayan Language Academy
APM	Assembly of the Pueblo Maya
ASC	Association of Civil Sectors
ASIES	Association for Social Investigation and Studies
AVANCSO	Association for the Advancement of Social Science in Guatemala
CACIF	Coordinating Committee of Agricultural, Commercial, Industrial, and Financial Associations
CCPP	Permanent Commissions (representatives of the refugees in Mexico)
CECMA	Center for the Study of Mayan Culture
CEDIM	Mayan Center for Research and Documentation
CEEM	Military Center for Strategic Studies
CEIDEC	Center for Integral Studies of Community Development
CERJ	Council of Ethnic Communities "Everyone United"
CIEDEG	Guatemalan Protestant Church Conference
CISMA	Center for Research and Mayan Studies
COCADI	Kaqchikel Coordinator of Integral Development
COINDI	Indigenous Cooperation for Integral Development
COMG	Guatemalan Council of Mayan Organizations
CONAVIGUA	National Coordinating Committee of Guatemalan Widows
CONDEG	Guatemalan Council for the Displaced
CONIC	National Indigenous and Campesino Coordinator
COPMAGUA	Coordination of Organizations of the Pueblo Maya of Guatemala
CPR	Communities of the Population in Resistance

CUC	Campesino Unity Committee
DARPA	Defense Advanced Research Project Agency
DCG (or DC)	Christian Democrats (Presidency, 1986–1990)
EAFG	Guatemalan Forensic Anthropology Team
EC	European Community
ECOSOC	Economic and Social Council (United Nations)
EGP	Guerrilla Army of the Poor
ESTNA	School for Strategic National Studies
FAR	Rebel Armed Forces
FDNG	New Guatemalan Democratic Front
FIN	National Indigenous (or Integration) Front (now defunct)
FIS	Social Investment Fund
FLACSO	Latin American Faculty of Social Sciences
FMLN	Farabundo Martí National Liberation Front
FODIGUA	Guatemalan Indigenous Fund
FONAPAZ	National Peace Fund
FONAVIVIENDA	National Housing Fund
FRG	Guatemalan Republican Front (led by General Efraín Ríos Montt)
GAM	Mutual Support Group for Families of the Disappeared
GATT	General Agreement on Tariffs and Trade
IIN	National Indigenist Institute
ILO	International Labor Organization
IMF	International Monetary Fund
INAEH	National Institute for Anthropology and History
INC	National Consensus Group
INGUAT	Guatemala Institute for Tourism
INIAP	Institute for Research and Political Training
IRIPAZ	Institute of International Relations and Research for Peace
IUCM	Mayan Unity and Consensus Group
Majawil Q'ij	Mayan Coordinator "New Dawn"
MAS	Solidarity Action Movement (Presidency, 1990–1993)
MINUGUA	United Nations Mission to Guatemala (Verification of Peace Treaty)
MIR	Revolutionary Indigenous Movement
NACLA	North American Congress on Latin America
NAFTA	North American Free Trade Agreement
NGO	nongovernmental organization
ORPA	Revolutionary Organization of the People in Arms
PAC	Civil Self-Defense Patrols
PAN	Party of National Advancement (Presidency, 1996–present)
PGT	Guatemala Workers' Party
PLFM	Francisco Marroquín Linguistic Project
PRODERE	Program for the Displaced, Refugees, and Returnees
PRONEBI	National Program of Bilingual Education
RUOG	United Representation of the Guatemalan Opposition

SIL	Summer Institute of Linguistics (Wycliffe Bible Translators)
UASP	Unity for Labor and Popular Action
UCN	National Union of the Center
UNDP	United Nations Development Program
UNESCO	United Nations Education, Science, and Culture Organization
UNHCR	United Nations High Commission on Refugees
UNICEF	United Nations Children's Fund
UNSITRAGUA	Guatemalan Union of Labor Unions
URNG	Guatemalan National Revolutionary Unity
USAC	University of San Carlos (National University)
USAID	United States Agency for International Development
WCIP	World Council of Indigenous Peoples

Map 1. Guatemala.

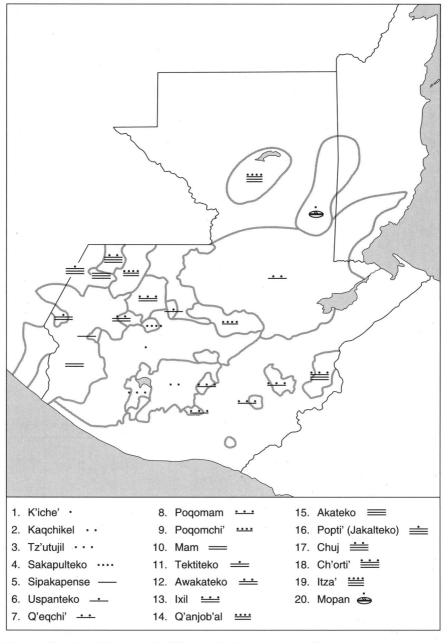

1. K'iche' ·	8. Poqomam ·–·	15. Akateko ═
2. Kaqchikel ··	9. Poqomchi' ····	16. Popti' (Jakalteko) ═·
3. Tz'utujil ···	10. Mam ══	17. Chuj ═·
4. Sakapulteko ····	11. Tektiteko ═·	18. Ch'orti' ═··
5. Sipakapense ——	12. Awakateko ═··	19. Itza' ═···
6. Uspanteko –·–	13. Ixil ═···	20. Mopan ◓
7. Q'eqchi' ·–·	14. Q'anjob'al ═····	

Map 2. Peoples of Guatemala. "Guatemala is composed of four peoples who are linguistically, culturally, and historically distinct: the Pueblo Maya (approximately 60 percent of Guatemalans), the Pueblo Ladino (approximately 39 percent of Guatemalans), the Pueblo *Garífuna* (less than 1 percent of Guatemalans), and the Pueblo Xinka (in danger of extinction). Within the Pueblo Maya there are various linguistic communities because they speak [these] specific languages" (Cholsamaj Press). Map used with kind permission of Cholsamaj Press.

ONE

Introduction

Body Politics and Quincentennial Guatemala

In interviews Guatemalans speak of their nation as a wounded body.[1] When asked about Mayan cultural rights activism, both nonindigenous Guatemalans (ladinos) and Maya say that it is a "finger in the wound" (*un dedo en la llaga*), suggesting that attempts to address ethnic difference are painful proddings, irritating interventions. The metaphor was frequently deployed in conversations and in the press in the years surrounding 1992, the Columbus Quincentennial, a watershed for indigenous organizing. An editorialist in the newspaper *La Hora* warned against "enthusiasm for indigenous languages . . . because this is a dangerous political game against national unity. . . . It is a finger in the wound" (11 August 1990).[2] The Mayan activist Pop Caal makes a similar point: "The ladino [nonindigenous] tries to erase and put a veil over the problem, not because he is convinced that discrimination does not exist, but because he is afraid that putting a finger in the national wound will stir up conflicts between both groups" (Bastos and Camus 1993, 27).

This metaphor suggests that the wound afflicts a body politic, a nation that exists but is not whole or complete.[3] Is the wound ethnic difference

1. I have identified some people by their generic position rather than their name, usually at their request. Whenever I quote someone without a citation, this was a personal communication in an interview or informal conversation. I rarely taped formal interviews, instead taking handwritten notes, which were later transcribed and fleshed out. For less formal talks, I typed up notes from memory. All of the interviews with Guatemalans were conducted in Spanish, and all translations of spoken and written words are mine unless otherwise noted, with copious translation assistance from José Fernando Lara, especially with the jokes.

2. Enrique Sam Colop (1991) has analyzed this editorial, as has Kay Warren (n.d.).

3. It is a nation which is not one—a term I borrow from Luce Irigaray (1985b) to mean it is not one in the sense of singular and undivided, nor is it necessarily a nation at all. The met-

draining the body politic of its vitality, and is Mayan organizing a finger in the wound because it reminds that body of its racism? Or is racism itself the finger in an always existing wound caused by stress fractures along gender, class, geographic, and cultural lines (lines, I argue, that are necessary for the body's very intelligibility)? Because there is a body in the metaphor, but a body that is deeply contradictory—scarred and wounded by violence—I think the metaphor is useful for describing the body politic of the Guatemalan nation. Guatemala is emerging from a civil war that displaced one-eighth of the population and left some one hundred and twenty thousand people dead or disappeared: the wounded body is thus also terribly material.

Now, the transnational system that undergirds current processes of globalization is grounded in the building blocks of whole, homogeneous, and functioning "modern nations," and Guatemala cannot be understood outside this framework. Where such a body politic is lacking (as in ethnically diverse postcolonial countries), this lack is blamed on "primordial" identifications that hark back to the premodern era. Tradition and ethnicity are found guilty of holding nations back, denying them the benefits of civilization and modernization. Or worse, these timeless and apparently irrational identifications rip the nation apart through the actual wounding of bodies in civil war and counterinsurgency.[4]

This book critically examines such notions of the nation and of ethnic identification. I argue that ethnicity and tradition are not always already there, nor are they naturally opposed to the modern nation relying on the homogenizing state to repress these differences. Instead, in the wounded body politic of Guatemala, modernity and tradition, nation and ethnicity are interpenetrated on every side—and the state, rather than trying to erase multiple identifications, is a productive site for their articulation.

This term *articulation* condenses many of the concerns of the book. I use it to mean a relation, a joining that creates new identifications and social formations (as in the *relational* identifications of Maya and ladino—a.k.a.

---

aphor of the wounded body is also deployed by Chicana(o) theorists to discuss the nation which is not one (neither singular nor technically a nation) of border cultures. Gloria Anzaldúa says, "1,950 mile-long open wound dividing a *pueblo*, a culture, running down the length of my body. . . . The US-Mexican border *es una herida abierta* where the Third World grates against the first and bleeds. And before a scab forms it hemorrhages again" (1987, 2–3). Similarly, Guillermo Gómez-Peña, writing on border culture and deterritorialization, signs off "from the infected wound" (1987). The Nigerian writer Wole Soyinka (1996) also evokes the metaphor of the wounded body to describe his postcolonial nation.

4. Guatemala, Peru, Northern Ireland, Yugoslavia, Rwanda, and Sri Lanka form a short list of world "hot spots" where, despite nods to histories of colonization and class-based antagonisms, popular (and too often social-scientific) understandings rely on the notion of primordial hatreds.

non-Maya).[5] Articulation is recombinant. As Ernesto Laclau and Chantal Mouffe argue, it changes as it joins, creating "a relation among elements such that their identity is modified as a result of the articulatory practice" (1985, 105). What I am naming Quincentennial Guatemala might also be termed "postcolonial" in the sense that after five hundred years we have no access to a moment before the articulations among Europe, the Americas, Africa, capitalist modes of production, *milpa* (corn) culture, Christian god, Mayan gods, Spanish and the array of indigenous languages, and so on: in another word, all of the relations joined into Columbus's mistaken coining of *Indian*. There are no identifications in Guatemala that were not formed *in relation*. In chapter 2, I suggest that an analytics I call "fluidarity" may be appropriate for dealing with such identifications in flux.

To articulate also means to join words together to make sense (common and otherwise), a meaning that foregrounds the struggles over representation that so engage Maya and ladino in Guatemala. In turn, *to be articulate* means to speak well, to express oneself clearly, a characteristic that many ladinos find quite uncanny when wielded by the traditionally disempowered: for example, Mayan women represented by Nobel Peace Prize winner Rigoberta Menchú.[6] *Articulation* also carries the sense of "coupling": with all the pleasures and dangers of such an intimate activity—as well as the generational hopes and fears of miscegenation or "race improvement" that link the coupling of individual bodies with the reproduction of the body politic. In Quincentennial Guatemala, the state is increasingly engaged in articulating these various processes.

This book is an ethnography of that state as it emerges from thirty years

---

5. Stuart Hall says,

> By the term "articulation," I mean a connection or link which is not necessarily given in all cases, as a law or a fact of life, but which requires particular conditions of existence to appear at all, which has to be positively sustained by specific processes, which is not "eternal" but has constantly to be renewed, which can under some circumstances disappear or be overthrown, leading to the old linkages being dissolved and new connections—re-articulations—being forged. It is also important that an articulation between different practices does not mean that they become identical or that the one is dissolved into the other. Each retains its distinct determinations and conditions of existence. However, once an articulation is made, the two practices can function together, not as an "immediate identity" . . . but as "distinctions within a unity." (1985, 113–114)

See also Gramsci 1989; Hall 1986; Morley and Chen 1996; Slack 1996; Althusser 1971; and Laclau and Mouffe 1985.

6. Ms. Menchú received the Nobel Peace Prize in 1992, an honor announced just a few days after October 12, 1992—hour zero of the Columbus Quincentennial. She is well known for her testimonial, *I, Rigoberta Menchú,* written in collaboration with Elizabeth Burgos-Debray (1984), and for her tireless efforts for human and indigenous peoples' rights (discussed in chapters 2 and 5).

Figure 1. "*Encuentro de Dos Mundos, 1492–1992*" (Clash of two worlds, 1492–1992). Postcard. Copyright Daniel Hernández Salazar. Published with kind permission.

of civil war and military dictatorship, and as it relates to—and thus helps to constitute—an emerging ethnic identity: the Maya. But the book is also about the emerging *ladino* identity. Traditionally defined only negatively— as not-Indian—and assumed to control the state and the economy, this identity cannot help but change as the Maya transform what it means to be Indian and as the state increasingly becomes a site and stake of struggle.

So what I am calling Quincentennial Guatemala is the sickening fear, the fierce exhilaration, and the doggedly persistent hope of these intricately articulated emergings. *Quincentennial Guatemala,* a term that refers to the five-hundred-year anniversary of Christopher Columbus's 1492 voyage, encompasses these anxieties and aspirations in the context of the country's recent history while emphasizing the still painful wounds of the Conquest. *Quincentennial Guatemala* is a condensed way of talking about complex processes like the election of a civilian government in 1985, the decade-long peace process that culminated in December 1996 with signed peace accords, struggles on the terrain of the state over what postwar Guatemala will look and feel like for non-Maya and Maya alike, and the explosion in organizing around Mayan identity—galvanized in part by global reactions to 1992, which produced a flurry of hemispheric meetings, Rigoberta Menchú's Nobel Peace Prize, and the United Nations declaring first a Year and then the Decade of Indigenous People.

Twenty years ago, the only Maya in Guatemala were on thousand-year-old glyphs and in tourism literature. Until about the mid 1980s, the word *Maya* was primarily used in archaeological discourses to refer to the builders of Tikal (the "Classic" Maya city, probably abandoned by the ninth century A.D.), in linguistics (referring to Maya trunk languages), and in government tourism campaigns designed to lure foreigners carrying hard currency with the promise of an exotic ancient past. *Maya* was not used popularly, or by those self-identifying, to refer to existing indigenous people. But in Quincentennial Guatemala, indigenous activists are redeploying the term *Maya* to refer to members of Guatemala's twenty-one distinct ethnic-linguistic communities, who have traditionally identified primarily with their communities of origin, secondarily with their ethnolinguistic group, and only distantly if at all as indigenous. The term has been appropriated to claim everyone related to the linguistic trunk that unites such disparately identified groups as the pre-Conquest K'iche's, Kaqchikeles, and Tz'utujiles, whether or not these groups descended directly from the builders of Tikal. Mayan organizers refer to the work of creating activists and of salvaging their culture from five hundred years of destruction as to *formar* (to create). The new and increasingly hegemonic use of the term *Maya* is part of this practice of *formando,* making or forming this new, pan-indigenous identification.

However, I quite emphatically want to differentiate the sense of making—encapsulated in the words *formar* and *articulate*—from a facile view of identity as easily taken on or willfully discarded. Though I argue that identification is produced rather than primordial, this production occurs through the slow accumulation of the minute effects of orthopedic change. I use the term *orthopedic* in Foucault's (1979) sense, from the Greek *ortho* (straight) and *paideia* (the training of children), to suggest the ways that powerful practices such as the law, schooling, and the use of language work with individual bodies to produce the body politic rather than simply repress an already-existing self. Thus identification is produced through constant repetition in sites of power that themselves are historically overdetermined, as well as through unconscious investments and resistances. The current success of the Mayan movement is not the result of a few people waking up one morning and deciding to become Maya. It grows out of half a century of organizing around linguistic rights (impossible to foretell back in the 1940s, when the indigenous activist Don Adrián Inés Chávez began his work); out of the crucible of five hundred years of Conquest and the last thirty years of catastrophe—civil war, earthquakes, and grinding poverty; out of political struggles, reversals, and shifting strategies; out of unexpectedly passionate attachments; and out of changes in the global information economy that produce employment for Mayan intellectuals and technological innovations now turned to Mayan ends (like high-speed networking with transnational solidarity). In turn, there is no guarantee of the effects of these articulations.

Nor is my emphasis on the production of identifications (and I mean *all* identifications—Maya, ladino, Guatemalan, gringa [North American], and so on) meant to support the frequent and insidious suggestion that the Maya are duped or easily manipulated. Ladino discourse (of the left and right) is full of images of Indians as empty-headed, asleep or just waking up, or a sack of potatoes waiting to be hauled around. In the model villages (army-run resettlement areas), military intelligence officers told me that their job was to "change the cassettes" in indigenous peoples' heads through hours of reeducation. Such discourses obviously seek to delegitimate Mayan demands by suggesting their inauthenticity and their external sources, and they also set up the ladinos who articulate them as saving the gullible Maya from those who would lead them astray. These discourses in turn mesh contradictorily with similarly popular images of primordial indigenous identity: the inherent Mayan backwardness that limits the nation's modernization. As I explore throughout the book, such apparent contradictions often work simultaneously, in this case, perhaps, to assuage ladino anxieties about Mayan empowerment.

The pan-Mayan cultural rights movement is one of the most vibrant sectors of the Guatemalan body politic, able to cajole and pressure the government to sign accords guaranteeing them rights to cultural difference. Their organizing acknowledges that the violence and erasures of the catastrophic colonial past make it impossible to trace a clean line to any primordial identity. Instead, I examine how the colonial process itself, even as it yearned for assimilation, has created Mayan activists, and how the state, as it responds to the Maya—and itself attempts to deploy culture to *formar* the nation—is itself changed in the process. Quincentennial Guatemala offers a case study of how national, ethnic, and gender identifications are constantly transformed through processes of articulation, and I suggest that the instability of these identifications—rather than their "primordial" nature— incites ambivalence and attempts to "fix" them (in both the sense of to stabilize and to repair). I am especially interested in those sites and processes of fixing—like the school, the law, the household, and the production of sexual desire—that link or articulate individual bodies with the body politic. For example, competing efforts to form a "whole" national body politic often lean on material bodies for their proof—on what those bodies wear, on their cultural practice, on their "racial" and "sexual" markings, and in the case of continuing counterinsurgency, on materially wounding those bodies.

However, unlike in many parts of the world, Guatemala's war is ending, Mayan demands are being recognized, and ladinos and indigenous peoples are finding ways—complex, fear-filled, and often violent—to live together.

This book examines the roles in forming Quincentennial Guatemala played by transnational organizations, gringa anthropologists, Mayan activists becoming state officials, and ladino government functionaries studying to become Mayan shamans, and by events like the 1992 Nobel Peace Prize, the founding of the Ministry of Culture and Sports, the legalization of the Guatemalan Mayan Language Academy (ALMG), and the ratification process of the International Labor Organization's Convention 169.[7] Drawing from these examples, I suggest that ethnic, gender, and nation-state identities are mutually constitutive, meaning that they do not exist outside their relation to each other, and that at this historic moment the Guatemalan state is an important matrix through which these relations occur.

AN INTRODUCTION TO QUINCENTENNIAL GUATEMALA

History as Catastrophe

The largest and most industrialized country in Central America, Guatemala has been at war for over thirty years. The country's indigenous population (estimated to be from 45 percent to over 70 percent of a population of around eleven million), itself divided among some twenty-three ethnolinguistic groups (twenty-one Maya and two others), has historically been disempowered on the national political and economic scene.[8] Non-Indians, commonly called "ladinos" (although this is not a homogenous category either), tend to hold the institutionalized positions of power in the country.[9]

Like its present, Guatemala's past can be described as a traumatic wound,

---

7. "Convention 169" is the abbreviation for United Nations International Labor Organization's Convention 169 on the Rights of Indigenous and Tribal Peoples in Independent Countries.

8. Guatemala is ethnically more diverse than is suggested by the categories of "Indian" and "non-Indian" (ladino). The Guatemalan Mayan Language Academy (ALMG) counts twenty-one Mayan linguistic groups in addition to non-Mayan indigenous peoples like the Xinka. In addition to the ladinos, there are the African-Caribbean *Garífuna* as well as vibrant Chinese and German communities.

9. *Ladino* is a complex term in Guatemala (see chapter 6) and has been employed for centuries of ambivalent border crossings. In the Roman Empire, it was applied to conquered peoples who learned Latin and began "passing" into roles of translators, as middle men and women. The term also applies to the Sephardic Jewish language of the Diaspora, a mixture of Spanish, Hebrew, Arabic, and other influences added in exile. Victor Perera, a Guatemalan novelist and journalist, brings together this strand with the common usage in Guatemala (*ladino* as "non-Indian") in his book *The Cross and the Pear Tree* (1994b). In Colonial Guatemala, *ladino* first meant those indigenous people who learned Spanish and left the community to live in the borderlands between Criollo colonizer and indigenous colonized. John Watanabe puts it quite concisely: "While the subtleties and ambiguities of actual relations between Maya and Ladinos belie such stark oppositions, these racist stereotypes pervade—and shape—Guatemalan life" (1995, 30).

an unsutured opening on the body politic. Since the pre-Colombian period, a series of catastrophes has time and again erased the material documentation of the past—the stories as well as the storytellers. The openness and allure of this unfinished history is materialized in the great ruins of Tikal, Quirigua, Kaminaljuyu, and others, which the "mysterious fall" of the Classic Maya civilization left with their memories erased. Few can resist the magic pull and melancholic thrill of loss evoked by an encounter with the ancient past at these ruins—a feeling I call "ethnostalgia."[10] This ruptured history has engendered passionate debates over the meaning of the archaeological record—debates with charged political effects.[11]

Likewise open and fiercely debated are understandings of the lifeways of post-Classic but pre-Colombian inhabitants of Mesoamerica. The heroics and tragedies of internal wars among the pre-Conquest K'iche's, Kaqchikeles, and Tz'utujiles were just barely preserved in post-Conquest chronicles like the *Popul Wuj*. The Spanish Conquest brought blood and dislocation and the burning of the Mayan books, a deeply traumatic memory (see Hill 1992; Carmack 1983; Clendinnen 1987) frequently invoked by Mayan cultural rights activists.

Not only the indigenous past has been buried in ruins. In addition to the unnatural disaster of colonization, earthquakes destroyed the colonial and postindependence (1821) capital cities time and time again, so that today the catastrophe of the colonial past is evinced in the ruins of the abandoned capital of Antigua, and there are few buildings in Guatemala City that pre-

---

10. I borrow the term *ethnostalgia* from Mario Loarca, to mean the sense many ladino state officials expressed in interviews when they enthused about their Mayan roots—felt most keenly when they go to Tikal. One government tourism brochure, in English and distributed at the airport to all entering foreigners, reads,

> Visitors nowadays feel a strange thrill when they stand in front of the impressive legacy of Mayan science, art, and magic hidden in the depths of the jungle and protected by thousands of species of plants and animals. The Maya's magnificent cities, their structures, sculptures, bas-reliefs, friezes and paintings stand proudly . . . waiting to be discovered again and again. . . . History and nature come together in Guatemala in a way that simply marvels its visitors. (INGUAT n.d., 5)

George Lucas even used the legendary Tikal as a set in *Star Wars* (see chapter 7).

11. For some of these representations, see Coe 1993; Carmack 1981; Stuart and Stuart 1977; Schele and Miller 1986; and Freidel, Schele, and Parker 1993. For the effects of these debates on the "modern-day Maya," see Sam Colop 1991; Pop Caal 1992; Taller J'a C'amabal I'b 1989a and 1989b; Fischer and Brown 1996; and Cojtí 1995. This is a fascinating polemic, which unfortunately cannot be addressed adequately here. Actors in the transnational grid of foreign "scientists," besieged ladino bureaucrats, Mayan intellectuals, army officers, and gringas in fluidarity seize hold of different stories about this open past in complex ways that I will trace fleetingly throughout the book. Please see Quetzil Castañeda's lovely history of the production of this "museum of Mayan culture" (1996) in Chichen Itzá, Yucatan Mexico, and the way it variously works for local residents, state officials, and gringos.

date the 1920s.[12] Politically, over a century of postindependence dictatorships gave way to a progressive government in 1944 that enacted land reform and laws that protected labor. But 1954 brought the CIA-backed coup that overthrew the elected government of Colonel Jacobo Arbenz and tried to erase the memory of reform by murder, exile, and censorship—setting up the military governments that would rule until 1985.[13]

These in turn midwived the most recent catastrophe, which overdetermines my entire discussion here: the ferocious counterinsurgency war of the early 1980s, with its scorched-earth attacks on highland villages, mass murder, and disappearance of tens of thousands of people. Between 1978 and 1984, an estimated seventy thousand (primarily indigenous) people were killed, forty thousand disappeared, and over one million displaced out of a population of eight million. Most of these acts were perpetrated by the Guatemalan army. The beginnings of Guatemala's civil war, called part of the country's "national folklore" by one state official (Walsh 1996, 1), are usually traced to 1963 when army officers rebelled against the U.S.-supported regime (in place since the 1954 coup). They formed the Rebel Armed Forces (FAR) and, inspired by the Cuban revolution and drawing on the cadres and experience of the Communist Party (PGT), organized primarily ladinos in the capital city and eastern Guatemala. A brutal counterinsurgency campaign disarticulated the movement by the early 1970s (Jonas and Tobis 1974; Melville and Melville 1971), but by the mid-1970s the FAR and PGT were regrouping, and indigenous peoples were being organized by two new guerrilla forces: the Guerrilla Army of the Poor (EGP) and the Revolutionary Organization of the People in Arms (ORPA). In the early 1980s the violent government responses to these challenges—including the consolidation of the armed struggle under the aegis of the Guatemalan National Revolutionary Unity (URNG)—resulted in some four hundred highland villages being completely destroyed (wiped off the face of the earth and of official maps); a Guatemalan diaspora with over a million people displaced within the country (Fabri 1994; AVANCSO 1992), and tens of thousands of refugees crossing the border into Mexico; bloody crackdowns on all sectors, ranging from labor to the church to academics to journalists to prominent government officials; and the destruction of almost every organization working for social change, from the indigenous political party National Indigenous Front (FIN) to credit cooperatives and church study groups (Simon 1987; Manz 1988a; M. McClintock 1985; Falla

12. I am indebted to Mark Driscoll's work on the similar loss and nostalgia incited by the frequent destruction of Tokyo, especially "Apoco-Elliptic Japan" (1994).

13. Many fruitful histories of this event detail the interests of U.S. companies and political figures in getting rid of Arbenz and his land and labor-law reforms (Kinzer and Schlesinger 1983; Gleijeses 1991; Handy 1984).

1984, 1988, 1992). Guatemalans live among the eloquent ruins left by the war: model villages built on the charred remains of burned houses, clandestine cemeteries (EAFG 1995), holding cells for the disappeared built into houses, and military and civil patrol installations throughout the cities and countryside.[14]

By 1984 the revolutionary guerrilla army of the URNG, which in 1981 seemed poised to follow in the footsteps of the Nicaraguan Sandinistas and take power, was brutally smashed, withdrawing to isolated strongholds in the mountains and lowland jungles. Though seldom mentioned in the national press, or even among friends as a result of the silencing accomplished by terror, the URNG maintained guerrilla columns in many parts of the country and until the cease-fire of 1996 engaged the army in skirmishes, undertaking daring acts of sabotage. Only with the peace process heating up in 1995 did the URNG become a fixture in the news, a major change in status forcefully marked by a guerrilla captain inviting a television news team to cover the peaceful occupation of a town in June 1996. This was a truly historic shift from 1993, when people still used elaborate code to keep from even mentioning the guerrillas during informal discussions in their own homes. Although the URNG carried enough international prestige for the United Nations and U.S. government to back the peace talks, for the past decade there has been little hope that they will take power, and their negotiating position has been correspondingly weak.[15] Despite internal and external critiques of their strategies, the loss of what the revolutionaries represented in terms of hope for a radical change in Guatemala's political and economic structure is to many a catastrophic and traumatic loss. New Year's Eve 1996 saw the official return to Guatemalan territory of the URNG commanders, with full demobilization beginning soon afterwards.

The way indigenous peoples in particular were affected by the killing, uprooting, and subsequent resettlement policies of the civil war led many anthropologists to fear that the country's distinctive indigenous culture would disappear (Carmack 1988; Jonas, McCaughan, and Martínez 1984; Fried et al. 1983). And yet the past ten years have witnessed the emergence of a vibrant indigenous rights movement expressed in a wide array of organi-

14. The Central Square in Guatemala City is bounded by the cathedral, palace, and the Bank of the Army. Just behind the palace, and covering several square blocks, is a major army installation. Even the "Zona Viva" in Zone Ten, with five-star hotels, nightclubs, and fancy restaurants, is right next to the old Politécnica, still a major army base. This was the site, ironically enough, of one of Jennifer Harbury's hunger strikes as she pressured the government for information on her missing husband, the guerrilla leader Efraín Bámaca Velásquez (see chapter 2).

15. The Group of Friend Countries, an international coalition composed of Colombia, Spain, Norway, Mexico, Venezuela, and the United States, politically and financially supported the peace process (INFORPRESS 1996).

zations, ranging from human rights activism to rural development agencies, and from associations of Mayan writers and painters to the recently state-recognized and state-funded ALMG (Bastos and Camus 1993, 1995; C. Smith 1990b; Fischer and Brown 1996; Tedlock 1992; Warren 1992, 1996; Wilson 1995). This movement, in turn, has been energized by the hemispheric organizing around the Columbus Quincentennial and the 1992 Nobel Peace Prize, as well as struggles for representation in the peace process.

This book looks at both Mayan organizing and state-sector responses to it, as well as ladino and Maya struggles to form state policy. I also explore the imagi-*nations* that surround and inform these struggles over state power at the national level: the complex histories, erotic investments, and deep-seated fears articulated through colonially inflected fantasmatics of race, sex, and gender. The intensity of the counterinsurgency war—with massacres and scorched-earth campaigns radically out of proportion to the threat of the guerrilla army of the URNG—suggests that political-economic analyses of the violence must take into account the overdetermination of fantasy and paranoia. All of the efforts of the Mayan cultural rights activists as well as state officials and ladino organizers occur under the threat of bodily harm. Their efforts are imbricated with race, class, and gender as expressed in jokes, stereotypes, representations on the national and international scenes, and in the imaginary communities that activists, government officials, and transnational actors are trying to make real.

I focus here on the Quincentennial because it served as a node for articulating these imagi-nations, for making sense of thirty years of bloodshed in a larger historical context. All the epistemic murk and pain and rage and desire for change coalesced around it like cotton candy condenses around a cone of paper. For example, a poster distributed by the organization Majawil Q'ij during October 1992 shows the Maya-K'iche' hero Tecún Umán fighting a Spanish conquistador, only the fearsome figure on the rearing horse is a twentieth-century soldier armed with an M-16—an economical representation of five hundred years of power-drenched relations. To briefly introduce the Quincentennial setting of this book and the myriad relations I hope to evoke through the term, I describe similar condensations circulating in the press and in conversations during that historic October.

The Quincentennial resonates powerfully for both Mayas and ladinos because strategies for the post–Peace Accords future rely heavily on what Max Weber called the "authority of the 'eternal yesterday'" (Gerth and Mills 1958, 78). Struggles over the meanings of these yesterdays are often over blood—both its mixing and its shedding—and thus who has contributed most to the future. Official discourse complacently remembers a "meeting of two worlds," with Spain contributing the cultural treasures of civilization and white "blood" to the (now shared) traditions and folklore of the "brown" Indians, creating the new "mestizo" (mixed) nation. Drawing on eugenics discourses, these mestizos claim to have improved the race with their blood and to have sacrificed that blood in struggles against external enemies—first in winning independence from Spain and then saving the nation from either communism or yanqui imperialism (depending upon their politics). The Maya contest this version of yesterday, emphasizing the violence of that "meeting," the rapes that produced the racial mixing of *mestizaje,* the appropriation of their culture (Classic Mayan ruins, indigenous ritual life, and traditional clothing) to identify Guatemala, and they question the entire logic of *blanquemiento* (whitening).[16] They also claim to have shed more blood for the nation, in constant uprisings against the Spanish, and as the foot soldiers and primary casualties in war—especially the most recent catastrophe, which many Maya call genocidal. Focusing on the intensity of their suffering in Quincentennial Guatemala is not, as many ladinos denounce, an indication of Maya desires to live in the past (in "Mayassic Park" as one pundit put it), but a powerful strategy of seizing "hold of a memory as it flashes up in a moment of danger" as Walter Benjamin says (1969, 255), a way of laying claim to the future.

The Quincentennial as a Moment of Danger

The Quincentennial, which foregrounds issues of culture and identity, ethnicity and the nation's history, was experienced as a moment of danger and a promise for projects attempting to make sense of Guatemala's past as catastrophe—some striving to close over those wounds and others insisting that only by opening them up would the body politic heal, be "fixed." Mayas and ladinos in the civilian government, army, and guerrilla organizations seized on the Quincentennial in attempts to "fix" (both to hold still and to repair) Guatemalan-ness, culture, and the role of indigenous people in the nation's future.

The Government and Press   In the summer of 1992, Spain sponsored an exposition on the five hundred years, attended by Guatemala's President Jorge Serrano Elías, who spoke with pride of Guatemala as an "Indian nation." Guatemala's pavilion at the exposition excited controversy in Guatemala, however, because it was considered "too Indian," with its diorama of a highland market day and figures of indigenous women with baskets of

---

16. Carol Hendrickson addresses the practice of ladinos who "wrap themselves in traje and embrace or 'become' the Indian as an expression of what it is to be Guatemalan" (1995, 80) (more ethnostalgia). In chapter 5, I address the role of *traje* in marking national identity.

corn and squash for sale. So it was changed to a display of Guatemala's "national products" (exports): coffee, rum, bananas, and so on.[17]

The official responses to October 12, 1992, usually celebrated in Guatemala as the "Day of the *Raza*" (race) were ambivalent and subdued. Plans for a major celebration were scaled back as local and international critiques of the Conquest heated up. In general, however, government pronouncements echoed the many ladino newspaper editorialists who lauded the creation of a new world and a new people (*raza*) in the joining of Europe and the Americas. The editor of the daily *Prensa Libre* (Guatemala's highest circulation newspaper) said, "It was the most amazing human adventure of our time. It was both glorious and painful, but it began a new race, our race. . . . We must celebrate and commemorate the fusion of Spanish, Indian and Negro that created us all" (12 October 1992). The secretary of public relations for the president of the republic took out full-page ads in the major newspapers that read simply, "*Un Solo Pueblo* [one single people]: October 12." Surrounding the phrase are photos of indigenous *cofradía* members in traditional garb, an indigenous campesino wielding a hoe, and ladinos wielding high technology—working at telephones and computers, thereby reiterating the "natural" relation of ladinos with modernity and Maya with tradition.[18]

In other official pronouncements, however, Guatemala became isomorphic with the indigenous past in a nationalist contrast to an imperial Europe. The Archbishop Prospero Penados de Barrios chastised the Spanish ambassador for plans to celebrate October 12 rather than mourn the effects of the Conquest and said, "You are Pedro Alvarado and I am Tecún Umán." Tecún Umán, the mythic K'iche' warlord who fought the Spanish invaders to the death, figured prominently in discussions of the Quincentennial, and his story condenses stereotypes and ambivalence over Guatemalan national identity. Legend has it that he mistook the Conquistador Alvarado's horse for part of the man, attacking the animal and leaving himself open to the lance. It is said that when he died the brilliant green quetzal bird rested on his chest and to this day carries his blood in the flash of red on its breast.

Like other memories, that of Tecún Umán can be seized in various ways. Enrique Sam Colop discusses the racism of the story of his death and how it misreads the chronicles (Sam Colop 1991). Kay Warren says, "Stories of

17. In the various reactions to Rigoberta Menchú winning the Nobel Peace Prize in October 1992 (see chapter 5), many ladinos expressed pride that Guatemala had another Nobel winner (Miguel Angel Asturias had won for Literature in 1967), but also concern about being represented to the world as "a country of Indians."

18. The *cofradía* is a brotherhood charged with caring for a particular saint (Rojas Lima 1988; Vogt 1990; Cancian 1965; Warren 1989; Wilson 1995).

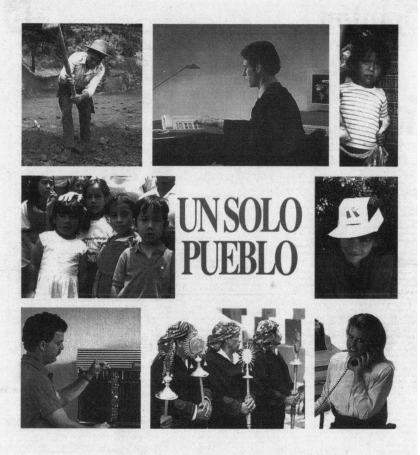

Figure 2. "One Single People, October 12." Presidential Office of Public Relations. Paid newspaper advertising, *La Hora*, 12 October 1992.

Figure 3. Mural *La Conquista* (The conquest) by Galvez Suárez, National Palace.
Postcard Collection "Welcome to Guatemala" by Diego Molina. Pedro Alvarado
kills Tecún Umán as the quetzal bird flies overhead.

Pedro de Alvarado's defeat of the Mayan leader Tecún Umán have been
given legendary status in national schools and state-sponsored histories. . . .
Maya simply do not believe this story, which they feel has been created to
assert Maya stupidity and ignorance" (1996, 96–97). Tecún Umán's memory also rises up in moments of hybrid ritual. Many indigenous communities perform "The Dance of the Conquest," which was imposed by or borrowed from Spain, where it is still performed (Tedlock 1992, Hendrickson
1995). Its original form retells the story of the Reconquest against the
Moors, and in Guatemala the blackfaced masked figures are still called
"*moros*," whereas the blond white-skinned masks adorn Spanish "*Cristiano*s"
(Christians). In the Guatemalan highlands, however, the leader of the
Moors has been rechristened Tecún Umán and wears a stuffed quetzal in his
elaborate headdress, whereas the leader of the Christians is Pedro Alvarado.
I first saw the dance performed in Nebaj in 1985, when only a few of the
burned-out villages had been rebuilt, refugees were still being brought
down against their will from the mountains into militarized "model villages," and the earth was still fresh in the clandestine cemeteries. The dance
is performed over a week, enacting skirmishes between the two armies as
Tecún Umán's lieutenant and diviner spies on Alvarado with the help of his

Tecún
Myth as a
retelling of
victory of
Spain over
Moors

son, foretells the future, and humiliates the Spaniards in a variety of ways. After the final catastrophic battle, however, Tecún Umán is killed and placed in a coffin with glass panels so he can be seen when he is paraded through town. At the moment of his death, and throughout the day as the coffin moved through the streets of Nebaj, a torrent of grief accompanied it. People fell upon the coffin shrieking and crying, some cursed the army and called out the names of dead friends and relatives, and family members carried away those overcome with mourning.

In other more official identifications with the legend, the quetzal mythically marked with Tecún Umán's blood is both the nation's currency and Guatemala's national bird, which reportedly cannot live in captivity. A large mural in the National Palace commemorates the moment of Tecún Umán's death, his statue adorns many town squares, and he is commemorated every February 20. The army's spokesman, Yon Rivera, described the conquest as a result of the Spaniards'

> evident technological superiority over the National Army, represented at that time by Indians who valiantly defended their country.[19] . . . We should not talk of celebrating, but instead of commemorating. That defeat changed world history. What must be celebrated is the National Army, headed by Captain Tecún Umán, who offered his life fighting for his nation. Today's National Army has many Indians among its troops who have decided to continue to defend their national territory. If the National Army back then had had similar advanced technology, Guatemala would never have been conquered. (*La Hora,* 12 October 1992)[20]

A third reading, which seems, in contrast, to set up the indigenous population as clearly other to the "nation," informed the cover of the weekly

---

19. In 1978, as the counterinsurgency war was heating up and indigenous issues were making news with the formation of an indigenous party—the National Indigenous (or Integration) Front (FIN)—Belize was negotiating for its independence from Great Britain. In response, on Tecún Umán Day, the defense ministry made a similar speech celebrating Tecún as a defender of the nation against a foreign invader—here to be understood as England (Falla 1978, 456).

20. Just as in the United States, the military offers a job and possible route to advancement for poor and indigenous youths. Some families decide to "sacrifice" one son to military service in return for the portion of his wages sent directly "to the mother." However, the majority of indigenous soldiers are forcibly recruited, grabbed off buses, taken from school dances, or picked up walking down the street. As one ladino state worker said, "If it weren't for the Indians, there would be no army. No city ladino would allow their child to be grabbed, and no ladino schoolboy from the capital could survive the training." The National Coordinating Committee of Guatemalan Widows (CONAVIGUA), a primarily indigenous organization headed by Rosalina Tuyuc, has worked for several years to end forced recruitment, appearing at army bases to retrieve youths, agitating for the army to observe its own age limits, and trying to get legislation through the Congress to make forced recruitment illegal.

Figure 4. Tecún Umán enters his coffin. Dance of the Conquest,
Nebaj, August 1985. Photo by author.

newsmagazine *Crónica*. In capital letters, next to an extreme close-up of
Rigoberta Menchú's face, it reads, "INDIGENOUS POWER: What Are Its
Goals? Integration or Division? Revenge or Justice? Peace or Conflict?"
(16–22 October 1992). The lead story quotes state officials, congressmen,
and army staff, warning that indigenous demands could lead to a race war

→ Similar to Brazil's case of Indigenismo

and the balkanization of the country. This is a common refrain.[21] Expressing this fear, and intimacy, the ladino Congressman Francisco Reyes complained to me, "The Indians are a scorpion in our shirt!" In a similar but
slightly more sensationalist vein, the front-page headline in the second
largest daily newspaper, *El Grafico* (which is not a tabloid), screamed, "They
are selling human heads!" over a photo and text coverage of the indigenous
demonstrations around the Quincentennial. The story inside, which has
nothing to do with the Quincentennial, claims that graves were being
robbed in the highlands and suggests that this barbarous enterprise was an
instance of Indian witchcraft (14 October 1992).[22]

The URNG In a paid advertisement on October 12, the General Command of the URNG declared:

> Indigenous Peoples and the popular sectors have maintained a powerful and
> invincible resistance in defense of their rights, their identity, their history, and
> their cosmology. The might of other civilizations is not sufficient to bend, as-
> similate, or uproot this powerful identity. . . . Indians are victims, along with
> campesinos and the poor, of atrocities, the loss of their land, and displace-
> ment, but they are waking up and are part of a new future for Guatemala. . . .
> Our peace proposal demands full recognition of the identity and rights of the
> indigenous population, their culture, language, free association, their cus-
> toms and forms of worship, which converge with other values of universal civ-
> ilization and make our nation a harmonious and rich mosaic. We share this
> struggle, we identify with it as brothers against oppression, discrimination,
> and exploitation. This is a struggle that forms part of the great national un-
> dertaking of the Guatemalan people to end the disgraceful and bloody crisis
> that has kept us in great misery and underdevelopment, but whose solution
> we can now see forming in our future. (*Prensa Libre* 12 October 1992)[23]

Warring attempts to "seize hold" of the Maya (in this case to best represent or speak for them) were on view when two days later the government

21. Accusations of indigenous divisionism were especially fierce surrounding the ratification of ILO Convention 169, as I explore in chapter 8.

22. Another ambivalent attitude toward the memories rising up in 1992 positions the
ladino as simultaneously guilt-ridden oppressor of the Indian, victim of transnational exploitation, and innocent betrayed by the Indian to international interests. One ladino editorialist wrote: "Celebrate? No! It is best not even to remember. Such shame, disgrace, it is better to forget, to seek amnesia. In these five hundred 'tears,' the Indian has barely changed his
status or his disastrous lifestyle. Liberty raises her torch in New York, but in her backyard—or
better said, her Hispano-American toilet—the Indian, on his knees, kisses the boots of Saint
Wall Street. Yesterday it was Spain and the criollos, today the corrupt, the exploiters, and the
gringos" (*Crónica*, 16–22 October 1992).

23. Note that despite claiming that indigenous people are part of the URNG, the distinction between "us" and "them" is grammatically retained. This may be a sign of respect but also
marks a salient division, an issue I address in chapter 2.

of the republic used their "right of reply" in a full-page ad saying that the URNG's "supposed struggle for the full recognition of the identity and rights of indigenous peoples is a lie and clear evidence of the political and ideological manipulation of the indigenous issue for hidden aims." It claimed that whereas the government builds clinics and schools and provides essential services to all the population, the URNG only destroys, and that there is nothing in the URNG proposal that is not already included in the Constitution.

Indigenous Organizations

The Popular and Cultural Rights Divide   Although such boundaries are constantly blurred, indigenous activism tends to divide between cultural rights groups—which focus on rights to difference based on an identity position of "Maya" (Bastos and Camus 1993, 1995)—and what is called the "popular" sector—human rights groups, many with a more Marxist analysis of the situation and a more openly antagonistic relation with the government. The dividing line between these is a fraught and emotion-laden place, and because most of these groups are quite new—many formed in the late 1980s and early 1990s—their positions should not be reified.

Participants in the popular movement, both ladinos and indigenous people, have found class to be their most salient identity category, a position seen to resist the divide-and-conquer tactics of colonial racioeconomic organization. In *Patria del Criollo,* the Guatemalan historian Severo Martínez Peláez argues that the category of Indian was created during the colonial era to designate those most exploited by the hacienda system (1990). The book is required reading at the National University (Universidad de San Carlos, or USAC), where many of those who now work in the state, in the research community, and in Mayan organizations studied. As such, this book colors many peoples' understandings of nation and ethnicity. As I discuss later, Martínez Peláez argues that there is no such thing as authentic indigenous identity—what is now called "*indio*" is a product of the Colony, a racialized legitimation of class exploitation, and ethnic markers like the *cofradía* (saint society) and traditional clothing (*traje*) were imposed as Spanish counterinsurgency. It is hard to capture how many times *Patria del Criollo* was cited directly and indirectly in interviews and in the press. Though hegemony construction is a project fraught with multiple valences, I would call this a hegemonic book. Rereading it after conducting field interviews, I was constantly struck by how often informants expressed views from the book as their own. The result of this class identification has been a tendency to downplay issues of racism, presupposing that once the class structure was overturned such discrimination would melt away.

Many of today's popular groups have roots in historical processes like

Catholic Action (beginning in the 1950s) and the labor movement, or in the Campesino Unity Committee (CUC, founded in the late 1970s), but most are "Sectors Arising from Repression and Impunity"—organized in the 1980s to respond to the counterinsurgency war. They include organizations of widows and orphans (National Coordinating Committee of Guatemalan Widows [CONAVIGUA] and the Mutual Support Group for Families of the Disappeared [GAM]), refugees (the Permanent Commissions [CCPP]), internally displaced (Guatemalan Council for the Displaced [CONDEG] and the Communities of the Population in Resistance [CPR]), and human rights organizations (Council of Ethnic Communities "Everyone United" [CERJ], which resists forced recruitment into the army-run civil patrol system). The CUC, to which Rigoberta Menchú belongs, is part of this sector and was formed in the 1970s to struggle for land and labor rights. CUC was decimated by the counterinsurgency war and only began to reconstitute in the late 1980s. Even as the civil war has wound down, these groups have faced continuing army repression, with leaders killed and disappeared, surveillance and intimidation of members, and bombings of their offices. These popular indigenous organizations have been closely linked to the student and union movements through different umbrella groups like the Unity for Labor and Popular Action (UASP) and they have a major presence in national life, often heading demonstrations in traditional indigenous clothing (*traje*), taking over the Congress, making statements to the press, and demanding demilitarization, land reform, and restitution for their losses during the war. Although the majority are indigenous, issues of ethnic identity or cultural rights have in general been secondary to demands based in their positions as poor people and as victims of state violence.

The cultural rights groups, which are the focus of this book, have taken the name Maya for themselves and have concentrated their efforts around linguistics, education, and development issues. Mayan groups include the Guatemalan Mayan Language Academy (ALMG), the Guatemalan Mayan Writers Academy (AEMG), the Mayan Center for Research and Documentation (CEDIM), the Mayan Cultural and Educational Center Cholsamaj, and the Center for the Study of Mayan Culture (CECMA). Some of these Mayan activists were involved in religious, popular, and even revolutionary movements but say they often encountered racism within the very groups claiming to represent them. Many concluded that struggles for economic justice did not adequately address their multiply oppressed positions. Instead, they say, it was necessary to develop Mayan-led organizations to struggle for political, economic, and cultural rights. The ALMG first served as an umbrella group for these organizations and later joined with fourteen others to form the Guatemalan Council of Mayan Organizations (COMG), which in turn has joined a larger federation, the Mayan Unity and Consensus Group (IUCM).

Although the Mayan groups have been accused of being elites, intellectuals unconnected with their bases, and not representative (claims I address subsequently), their discourse—including the use of the word *Maya* to name themselves—has been growing in appeal. This trend is quite clear in the names of the "popular" Mayan Coordinator Majawil Q'ij, which was formed in the early 1990s, and the Coordination of Organizations of the Pueblo Maya of Guatemala (COPMAGUA), created to implement the peace accord on indigenous identity. Member organizations send delegates to Majawil and COPMAGUA and several of these representatives—who had previously identified only as popular—said that interacting with international indigenous organizations and with the cultural rights leaders had made them aware for the first time of the specificity of their indigenous identity. The very use of the term *Maya* in their titles shows that this process was already underway. Though by the end of 1998 many groups were employing the term *Maya,* in the early 1990s it was still used almost exclusively by groups with a specifically culturalist agenda.

Indigenous Responses to the Quincentennial   Struggles over the meaning of the Quincentennial and how best to deal with its scars were fierce at the Second Intercontinental Congress held in Quetzaltenango, Guatemala, in 1991 to plan indigenous and popular responses to 1992. Delegates from twenty-seven countries throughout the Americas attended, and issues of identity and representation became central to their discussions. I did not attend the meetings, and those who did still disagree about what occurred and why. My understanding is that similar issues to those that divide the Mayan cultural and the popular movements within Guatemala were involved. Many indigenous delegates felt they were not adequately represented either in numbers or in their views being taken into account, and they finally walked out. Nonindigenous activists claimed there was no racism intended, but that many ladinos at the conference had years of organizing experience that made it easier for them to dominate the proceedings.

In part because of these disagreements, the indigenous response in Guatemala to 1992 was also relatively subdued. There was a small march in Guatemala City that stopped at the Congress and National Palace and demanded approval of the International Labor Organization (ILO) Convention 169. The biggest demonstration was held outside the capital, in Sololá, where Rigoberta Menchú, generating enormous enthusiasm as a candidate for the Nobel Prize, was greeted by some ten thousand people.

However, indigenous peoples are seizing hold of memory around the

Quincentennial in ways that destabilize any reified division between the "popular" and the "Maya." A foreign researcher who had expressed strong reservations about the Mayan movement in 1990 (mainly because she felt it vindicated an identity that did not exist, something the Maya were "making up") was forced to change her mind. She told me in October 1992 that she couldn't believe how all her friends in CUC and CONAVIGUA were "going over to the Mayan thing. There seems to be something there that really affects these people, that is meaningful for them."

Although on the ground (and in some recent scholarship on the ethnic rights movement) divisions still exist between the more class-based groups and the Mayan cultural rights organizations, there are also convergences.[24] The International Indigenous Summits sponsored by Rigoberta Menchú and the peace talks, especially the round addressing "Identity and Indigenous Rights," have mobilized articulations across this divide. I think it is worth quoting at length from the Majawil Q'ij reaction to the Quincentennial, in part to show the way new identifications are articulated, the Majawil Q'ij view of the state, and the growing convergences among the discourses of popular indigenous groups and those of the Mayan culturalist organizations.

"Life, Resistance, and the Future:
After Five Hundred Years a New Dawn for our People,"
Maya Coordinator Majawil Q'ij

For us, October 12, 1492, means the violent destruction of our history. The invaders and their descendants sought only gold, riches, land, and slaves. We know very little of this history, only what our elders have told us and what researchers have revealed. Our Mayan grandfathers knew the stars, developed the calendar we still use today, and worked the land together. Their spiritual and material wealth was destroyed by the invaders. They burned our codices and built churches over the temples of our ancestors. The Calvary of the indigenous peoples of America began in 1492.

The invaders massacred entire villages, stole our mother earth, and distributed her and our peoples as forced labor. With Independence in 1821, the tribute and fruits of indigenous labor went to the criollos rather than to Spain. In 1871, they undertook the liberal reforms. Indigenous peoples lost their communal lands so the powerful could plant coffee. Some peoples were

24. Cross-communication between the "popular" and Mayan groups was mobilized by the Serrano "auto-coup" of May 1993 and the subsequent organizing around the return to constitutionality (creating the National Consensus Group [INC]), the purge of state institutions, and the creation of the Association of Civil Sectors (ASC). This cooperation between popular and culturalist groups has extended to shared participation in the ASC, which was the official representation before the government-guerrilla peace talks.

Figure 5. "After 500 Years We Are Here! Sing, Rise Up, America!" Banner carried in Quincentennial procession, Guatemala City, October 12, 1992. Photo by author.

forced by law to become ladinos. In 1944 the democratic revolution began. It ended the dictatorships, built schools, and distributed some land, but the rights of the indigenous peoples were not taken into account. In 1954 the direct persecution began of indigenous campesinos and poor ladinos who had received land. In the seventies there were massacres in Sansirisay and Panzós. The 1980s began with the massacre in the Spanish Embassy, and in the next years there continued the transformation of 440 indigenous villages into ashes by the military. Today, poverty forces our peoples to spend up to six months working on the plantations for starvation wages.

They clearly want to destroy our culture. Through the schools they try to make us change our *traje* and forget our languages. They propose laws to "protect" us, while the civil patrols and the military control in our communities destroy trust, unity, and community life. We have suffered massacres just as our ancestors suffered the destruction of the cities of Gumarkaaj and Iximche in 1524. This is a policy to finish off the Indians with the same cruelty and savagery of the Spaniards during the invasion, only now this is carried out by the new lords of Xibalbá.[25]

25. The "lords of Xibalbá" refers to the underworld of the *Popul Wuj*.

It has taken five hundred years for them to recognize our values. How much longer will it take before they recognize us as human beings and as peoples?

As indigenous peoples, we have always resisted, and now we are struggling within the framework of dialogue and negotiation. The state must recognize our human rights and our specific rights as indigenous populations, because we are the majority. These include the right to our archaeological heritage, the right to own communal land, and the rights to resources and to recuperate our culture. We reject the use of Mayan names for repressive groups like the Army Battalion Caibil Balam and the folkloric use of our culture while we die of malnutrition. We have the right to elect our own authorities, and the state must recognize our laws and include them in the laws of the country. Perhaps our struggle is more clearly recognized internationally, with the candidacy of our sister Rigoberta Menchú for the Nobel Peace Prize and initiatives like the ILO Convention 169. These will help us end the racism and discrimination that still weigh so heavily in our own country.

After five hundred years, Guatemalans seek to change the terrible situation affecting our country. Though Indians have suffered this Calvary of discrimination most, now Indians, ladinos, *Garífunas,* campesinos, workers, students, professionals, and so on are all suffering from hunger and the lack of land, work, fair wages, education, and health services.[26]

Though the government says it respects the law, it does not respect our rights to our culture, or the rights of our youth not to be forcibly recruited into the army, or the rights of refugees to return to their lands. On top of this, we suffer the impunity, corruption, and drug trafficking of the powerful. The state must recognize our human rights and our specific rights as indigenous populations. We must all look to the future to create a Guatemala without ethnocide, without colonialism, without oppression and death. (condensed from *La Hora Supplement,* 12 October 1992)

Echoing the sense of hope and "new times" expressed here, a Mayan friend said she had a pre-Quincentennial child and a post-Quincentennial baby. She had been very involved with Catholic Action and the CUC, and her first child was named in good Catholic fashion for his saint's day. Her post-Quincentennial baby, however, is named Bailam, from the *Popul Wuj.*

---

26. The *Garífuna* are the peoples of African descent living primarily on the Miskito or Atlantic Coasts of Central America (N. González 1989). They are the black people or "Negroes" extolled in some accounts of the new Guatemalan *"raza."* *Garífuna* representatives participated in the 1991 Quetzaltenango meetings, raising awareness of their situation and leading the organizing group to change its name to the National Maya, Black, and Popular Resistance Movement. One way that many ladinos I interviewed attempted to discredit the Mayan cultural rights movement was to claim that they in turn were racist and exclusionary because they acted like they were the only ethnic group in Guatemala. These ladinos would thus set themselves up as the defenders of black people (in other words, as light-brown people saving black people from brown people).

"My mother is horrified," she said. "She thinks I've become a pagan! But this is an historic change for us, a new dawn after so many years of war."

Ladino Reactions   Much of this book is devoted to ladino reactions to Mayan cultural rights organizing and the Quincentennial. Like whiteness in North American discussions of race, ladino identity has often been invisible in Guatemalan struggles over ethnicity and nation. As Renato Rosaldo (1988) suggests, the powerful tend to feel they have no culture, save for the universal culture of civilization. But this comfortable position is disrupted by Mayan organizing, which forces ladinos to think critically about their own identifications, a process that makes many people quite cranky. For example, Carlos Figueroa Ibarra, an exile visiting Guatemala in October 1992 to check out the possibility of returning, said,

> The worst part of all this Five Hundred Years stuff is the Maya saying that the ladinos have no culture. How ignorant! I am ladino, petit bourgeois, and they tell me I have no culture! We have our literary tradition and a history of resistance! Without us there would have been no 1944, or the resistance of the 1960s. We have a valiant history. We have our own Nobel Prize winner in Miguel Angel Asturias!

The unsteady mixture of class, practice, and "high" culture through which he and many others define ladino ethnic identification may lead to the many attempts to "fix" or hold the Maya still—as a "self constituting other": as traditional to the ladino's modernity, as domestic labor to support that petit bourgeois home, and as folkloric in contrast to ladino literary pretensions.

The Quincentennial's unprecedented challenges to ladino identifications produced a range of uncertainties and irritations. The Guatemalan anthropologist Celso Lara decried the cynicism and melancholia pervading the ladino character. "We have no happy cultural expressions. Look at Guatemala's *Semana Santa* [Holy Week]. It has no Easter, no resurrection. We put all our energy and passion into Good Friday, celebrating death, not rebirth." Similarly Diego Molina, a well-known photographer, described his fellow ladinos as "liars, traitors, charlatans, thieves, hypocrites, cowards, murderers, machos, drunkards, co-opted, negative, petty politicians, sold out, and always taken advantage of."

Attempts to fix things were often expressed through metaphors of the family and the conviviality of home (often as a counter to Mayan emphasis on historic antagonism). For example, Mr. Molina prides himself on creating positive images of the country, which he displays in postcards, magazines, books, and large-scale exhibitions lavishly funded by both the state and private interests; he calls these images "a beautiful family album." Responding to Mayan organizing by saying "we all have to live in one house," as Alvaro Colón of the government agency FONAPAZ (National Peace

Fund) did, or describing ladinos and Mayas as a heterosexual couple, are metaphors that concisely evoke their terrible intimacy, as well as the power asymmetries embedded in the patriarchal nuclear family. As I explore throughout the book, the Indian is often coded as female. Discussing the emergence(y) of Mayan organizing and possible autonomy, many ladinos echoed the state official who complained, "But this is like a wife leaving her husband. She already has a home, a family, a legal bond, she can't just up and leave!" At other times, the Indian is coded as a problem child. As Congressman Jorge Skinner-Klee wrote in an editorial, "The Indian is like a family member we want to hide" (*Siglo XXI,* 3 August 1992). Couching ethnic relations in this metaphor of the family seems to be a way of dealing with the weirdness of the Quincentennial, the way modes of ladino identification—being that which everyone else aspired to because of its attachments to whiteness, the modern, and the future—are suddenly under question and rendered uncanny. From the German *unheimlich* (un-homelike), *uncanny* suggests the feeling of being cut off from something that was once intimately part of the self, a sense of eerie alienation.[27]

So Quincentennial Guatemala is an uncanny site for ladino identification, where the ladino body politic is acknowledged to be wounded, just as the national family is dysfunctional. A popular joke during the Quincentennial went, "They say that Fidel Castro invited President Serrano to Cuba. While Serrano was there he attended an enormous rally in Havana. Hundreds of thousands of Cubans were there, and Castro led them in a cheer: 'Who is the mother of the Nation?' he called, and the crowd roared, 'Cuba! Cuba!' 'Who is the father of the Nation?' he asked, and they said, 'Castro! Castro!' 'And what do you want to be?' 'Communists! Communists!' they replied. Well, Serrano was very impressed and decided that he had something to prove about Guatemala and capitalism, so he invited Castro to come to Guatemala. When Castro arrived, Serrano had them truck in thousands of

27. The Quincentennial also evoked many wildly clever and quite sincere attempts to deal with its uncanny demands. One of the most popular plays in Guatemalan history was *Epopeya de las Indias* (Epic of the Indies), which was performed for several years in the National Theater and reversed the story of discovery while constantly adding references to current events in the Quincentennial years. The play is a wonderful mix of high and low culture. The main character is a Maya named Cristóbal Culón—a name that plays on the Spanish for *Columbus* (*Colón*) and *ass*—who goes off to "discover" Spain. There he and his mates are horrified to find the living standards far lower than home, the Spaniards believing in only one god, and Isabel and Ferdinand speaking the stereotypical Indianized Spanish, the ungrammatical forms of which are ripe for obscene word play. This ladino mimicry of how Indians supposedly speak (in other words, badly—they are inarticulate) is a major form of comic diversion and essential for the sense of many of the jokes about Rigoberta Menchú analyzed in chapter 5. The play ends with a call on the audience to acknowledge the violence of the Conquest and to attempt to imagine a different past that might lead to a more peaceful future.

Civil Patrollers for a rally in front of the National Palace.[28] He also went out and asked, 'Who is the mother of the Nation?' And they rather halfheartedly replied, 'Guatemala, Guatemala.' 'Who is the father of the Nation?' Serrano asked. 'Serrano, Serrano,' they said. 'What do you want to be?' And the great shout went up, 'Orphans! Orphans!'"

THEORIZING DOUBLE BIND(INGS)

Ladinos seem caught between the cozy image of the nuclear family (with the Maya as wife and mother in a presumably petit bourgeois home) and the uncanniness of national domesticity that makes them long to escape family ties altogether, as orphans. Guatemalans in general seem similarly ambivalent about the state. As Serrano's Presidential Advisor Juan Daniel Alemán put it, "The state is a piñata. Everyone hits us and everyone expects us to give them sweets." Too, when I asked Guatemalans about a national project, many said that the country is "schizophrenic," based in a fundamental split between Indian and ladino, between poor and rich, and whose plans for the future are constitutively contradictory. Dr. Demetrio Cojtí, a prominent Mayan intellectual, describes the ambivalence of the ladino toward the Indian: "They hate them and they love them simultaneously. They admire them for their glorious past, but they treat those of the present with disdain and violence. . . . They consider the Indian a treasury of 'national authenticity,' but they either treat them as slaves or try to force them to assimilate" (Cojtí, 1990, 9). Richard Adams describes the relation as "a fear-laden embrace" (1990, 159). This emotional double bind informs the complex work of the Maya and the complex reactions of the state and ladinos, and also suggests the way they are "doubly bound" to each other in the contradictory process of nation building.

In attempting to understand Quincentennial Guatemala, I have been strongly influenced by the work of Carol Smith and the contributors to her collection *Guatemalan Indians and the State, 1540–1988* (1990b), and by Brackette Williams (1989) and others who insist that ethnicity and nation cannot be understood without also investigating the state. Of course, when one goes looking for the state it tends to become rather elusive—its aims contradictory, its long arms hard to trace back to a point where someone shoulders the blame. Guatemalan state policy seems to be both to wipe out

---

28. The Civil Self-Defense Patrols (PAC) were instituted by the army throughout the highlands as part of the counterinsurgency war. Local men were forced to patrol and surveil their villages, often in twenty-four-hour shifts. At the height of their deployment, over half a million men were recruited. One of their duties has been to show up for government rallies. For accounts of abuses of the patrol system and the disruption it has created in community life, see Manz 1988a; Simon 1987; Paul and Demarest 1988; and Nelson 1990.

the Maya through assimilation or even genocidal counterinsurgency and to maintain them as workers and tourist attractions, even responding at times to their demands for representation. I have borrowed the theoretical tools developed by Antonio Gramsci, Louis Althusser, Stuart Hall, and Michel Foucault to analyze these contradictory effects of state power. I use Foucault's notion of the "governmental state" as shorthand for the ways many theorists have articulated these ideas and to mean the state as productive of subject-effects rather than repressing already existing identities.[29]

The state, represented by "ideological apparatuses" and orthopedic practices such as the school, legal kinship, hygienic infrastructure, and economic regulation, is not a clear-cut set of interests that gets what it wants through repressive apparatuses. In Guatemala it has been and still is extraordinarily repressive—that is why there is so much attention to wounded bodies in this book. But it is also, and simultaneously, a set of relations: a structure of domination, yes, but one which in turn forms the conditions of possibility for all political work.

Rather than repressing or homogenizing, this state "fixes" in both the sense of holding steady and the sense of repair. In Foucault's theory of governmentality, disciplinary and regulatory powers fix—in other words, hold people in the gaze of power and in their designated place—but the liberal state is also legitimated by fixing in the sense of mending and invigorating. Wendy Brown says:

> As the social body is stressed and torn by the secularizing and atomizing effects of capitalism and its attendant political culture of individuating rights and liberties, economic, administrative, and legislative forms of repair are required. Through a variety of agencies and regulations, the liberal state provides webbing for the social body dismembered by liberal individualism and also administers the increasing number of subjects disenfranchised and deracinated by capital's destruction of social and geographic bonds. (1995, 17)

This sense of fixing, of ameliorating and improving, may be one of the sweets that keep people coming back for the "piñata effect" of the state, de-

---

29. For example, it may not be useful to think of the state and public life as opposite and inimical to the privacy of the home. Instead, theories of governmentality help us see that the distinction between public and private is a boundary internal to capitalist production and bourgeois legality: in other words, rather than the state encroaching on the already existing (primordial) home, domestic experiences of intimacy and comfort in contrast to the alienation and competition of the outside world are effects of and produced by a larger formation. As Jane Collier suggests, citizenship requirements and bourgeois law require people to obey an inner voice: "[T]he ideal of a 'free' market for jobs and commodities—which accompanied, and was made possible by, the spread of bourgeois legal concepts and institutions—required competitors for employment and sales to have inner capacities and desires that distinguished them from rivals" (1997, 207).

scribed by Presidential Secretary Alemán. The wounded body politic of Quincentennial Guatemala may need all the fixing it can get.

But how are individual bodies linked to this body politic that is fixed, regulated, and produced by the governmental state? How do bodies come to matter, as Judith Butler asks, with some mattering more than others? These questions are fundamentally about identification, about fantasy and desire, and they have drawn me to use the theoretical tools of feminism and psychoanalysis.[30] These tools help elucidate the role of gender in producing the bodies of men and women and of ladino and Maya, as well as the imagi-nations of larger bodies politic, and I deploy them here in hopes of understanding the fear-laden embrace, the simultaneous love and hate that Dr. Cojtí sees in ladino relations to the Maya. How else to explain the explosion of jokes told about Rigoberta Menchú when she won the Nobel Prize, or the primal contradiction that Indians are seen by ladinos as both "the same," in that they are Guatemalans and mestizos, differentiated only by such folkloric effluvia as handmade clothing, *and* as primordially "different," racially distinct, a frightening mass of ignorant savages always ready to revolt? Diana Fuss suggests that "identification is the detour through the other that defines the self. This detour through the other follows no predetermined developmental path, nor does it travel outside history and culture. Identification names the entry of History and culture into the subject" (1995, 3).

I have also found the concept of the "body image" very useful in tracing the strange journeys of identifications through history and culture. I borrow the notion from neurophysiology and psychoanalysis via the work of Elizabeth Grosz in *Volatile Bodies,* who suggests that the body image is the way in which a person's corporeal exterior is psychically represented and lived, an imaginary anatomy—it is what gives a subject her sense of place in the world and her connection to others (Grosz 1994, xii). The body image is necessary for posture, movement, and tactility and is linked to the model that the subject has of other bodies and that other bodies have of the subject's body (1994, 68). For example, the experience that an amputee has of a "phantom limb" is caused by the body image. Psychically the wounded body does not give up the limb—although often, over time, the imaged

---

30. As Ann Stoler says,

Saying "yes" to Foucault has not always meant saying "no" to Freud. . . . Despite Foucault's rejection of the repressive hypothesis, there are surprising ways in which their projects can and do converge. . . . Both were concerned with boundary formation, with the "internal enemy" within. . . . If Foucault has led us to the power of discourse, it is Freud that has, albeit indirectly, turned us toward the power of fantasy, to imagined terror, to perceived assaults on the European self that made up the anxious and ambivalent world in which European colonials lived. (1995, 168–169)

limb changes shape. In the case of an arm, after several years the psychical body image of the hand may nestle close to the physical stump. Doctors treating amputees have found that some control of the phantom limb is possible, and people can learn to extend the limb into the prosthesis to facilitate maneuverability.[31] In fact, according to Grosz, the body image is necessary for the manipulation of any prosthetic. The image extends to include external objects and implements like cars and surgeon's scalpels and, perhaps, allows wounded bodies politic to function by enfolding (in fear-laden embraces) other bodies.

Embraces can also be pleasurable, and despite the emphasis here on war, wounding, and power-saturated relationalities, this book is also concerned with pleasure—with how necessary it is to identification and to the functioning of the state, and with laughter as a (sometimes nervous) symptom of body politics. That is in part why the book is so fascinated with popular culture, including jokes, movies, fashion, and science fiction. It is also why I have used as illustrations the postcards that circulate among Guatemalans and between Guatemala and the rest of the world, creating and maintaining relations. These are all ways that we make sense of the world.

To conclude this brief overview of the book's theoretical framework, I note that any understanding of wounded bodies politic and of subject constitution as fluid must take into account the way identifications are overdetermined by transnational political economy. Without denying the powerfulness of certain blocs in the world economy (Guatemala *is* far from God and close to the United States), I try to follow Regulation School theorists (Boyer 1990; Lipietz 1987) who not only take seriously world systems theory (Wallerstein 1974, 1983) and Gunder Frank's notion of the development of underdevelopment (in Rhodes 1970) but also question their fatalism—what Lipietz calls "pessimistic functionalism." The identifications I am exploring in Guatemala are formed in relation to multiple transnational flows—ranging from anthropologists, tourists, and indigenous representatives moving around the world to the imposition of structural adjustment economic policies and to the effects of consumer preferences in the United States and Taiwan on the lives of Mayan farmers. But if subjects (Maya, ladino, state officials, and, I argue, economic actors) are understood to be produced through interactions, articulations, resistances, and countermaneuvers, then, as with the governmental state, perhaps even United Nations mandates and World Bank neoliberalism are not imposed unilaterally and homogeneously by western powers. Instead, these are the effects of constant

31. According to Allucquere Rosanne Stone (1995b), the body image is quite malleable. Paraplegics working with neurophysiologists have managed to transport certain portions of their body image so that they rub together where there is feeling on the physical body, allowing them pleasurable sensations otherwise denied.

hegemony work (including, of course, capitulations), they are unevenly applied, and they are in complex relation with other interlocutors (for example, Guatemala is involved in trading blocs with other Latin American countries, has special relations with Mexico, Spain, Israel, and Taiwan, and receives increasing direct foreign investment from South Korea and Japan).

METHODS

It is a well-known joke that the longer a foreigner stays in Guatemala the harder it is to write about it. Whole books can come out of a three-week sojourn, whereas those who have lived there several years are gradually overcome by such a sense of complexity and contradiction that it becomes increasingly difficult to write (Francisco Goldman captures this perfectly in his novel *The Long Night of White Chickens* [1992]). After my first fieldwork in Guatemala in 1985, in which I spent six months traveling through the highlands, southern coast, the cities of Guatemala, and the refugee camps in Chiapas, Mexico, my knowledge was so superficial that I was able to sit down and write hundreds of pages of description and analysis.

Thirty-five months spent in Guatemala over the past fourteen years have humbled me. Guatemala is extremely complex, a space of terror as well as laughter, of horrific violence as well as bravery. So much of the information available there has been multiply encoded and recoded, filtered through rumor and personal histories, and encased in a hard veneer derived from political antagonisms, that it is a truly perilous claim I make in trying to represent it at all. Though never with the intensity the Guatemalans suffer, I have experienced the "epistemic murk" that Michael Taussig discerns in the "space of death," of "the great steaming morass of chaos that lies on the underside of order and without which order could not exist" (Taussig 1987, 4). In Guatemala, there are constant border crossings between order and chaos, and I have tried to acknowledge this experience by focusing throughout on contradiction and ambivalence.

My tactic in writing about years of conversations, events, written and spoken polemics, and observed and experienced emotions is to acknowledge that the interrelations of ethnic, gender, and national identities in Guatemala are quite fluid and always in recombinant articulation with me, the gringa anthropologist. As I explore in more detail in chapter 2, these not very solid identifications may call for a methodology of fluidarity: a practice and analytics that combine solidarity—being partial to, as in on the side of, the people I work with—with an acknowledgment of how partial, how incomplete, my knowledge and politics have to be.

I have been involved as a gringa researcher, journalist, and solidarity activist with Guatemala since the mid-1980s. I was very fortunate in my first sojourn there in 1985 to work with several gringas who had long histories of commitment to the Guatemalan cause. Their willingness to vouch for me, despite my inexperience and naïveté, allowed me to meet and form relationships with a wide range of Guatemalans, including many living in exile in Mexico City and in refugee camps in southern Mexico, as well as those working in Guatemala City and the highlands in research, human rights, church-based organizing, and development efforts. These contacts, and the trust they in turn graciously and courageously placed in me, allowed me and the gringas I was working with to interview Guatemalans from many different backgrounds—from those involved in clandestine work to powerful elites.

This first field trip was followed by a research project on the army-run resettlement areas known as Development Poles or model villages (see chapter 3 and Nelson 1987, 1990), with field research lasting from July 1996 to January 1997. I later worked with Guatemalan exiles in Mexico on development projects in Chiapas and made three return trips to Guatemala before the year-long stay (October 1992 to October 1993) in Guatemala City that forms the basis of this book. While there I was invited to work as a translator at the three International Indigenous Summits called by Rigoberta Menchú as part of the United Nations Year of Indigenous People, which gave me a glimpse of the enormous energy and commitment of the transnational indigenous rights movements. Finally, I returned for two months in the summer of 1996 for follow-up fieldwork. Limited as it is, this background, the contacts, and the basic knowledge it has afforded me (like knowing jokes about all the presidents since Lucas García), and the modest reputation afforded by the research projects I've worked on, have made me part of the communities I "partially" limned in the acknowledgments. I have kept in touch with many of these people: witnessing their responses to historic changes in the past twelve years; rejoicing and commiserating with many, met in exile, who have now returned home (some taking on major responsibilities in the civilian governments); talking over ways that senses of self change with people who were peasants when I met them and now newly identify as Maya; mourning the death of friends like Myrna Mack and working to support the struggle for justice of her colleagues (I was based at AVANCSO, the research institute that Mack founded). Although twelve years is a short time to understand the complexities of Guatemala, I have had the honor and privilege of forming deep and lasting friendships with people who have been generous in helping to explain those complexities.

All this by way of explaining how I "got" the information herein, some of which is quite intimate ("How in the world did you get people to tell you their sexual fantasies?" I've been asked), and why I'm willing to try to explore the Guatemalan imagination. These explorations are always "partial," of course—both incomplete and interested—and there's "not a very generalizable recipe" for an appropriate methodology (Geertz 1973, 416), but I have tried to interview a wide range of participants and to observe a number of the interactions I elaborate on here.

I was based in the capital, Guatemala City, interviewing city-based Mayan intellectuals and as many state officials as would see me (including members of the government ministries, the Congress, judges, and the executive branch). I called on friends and acquaintances for contacts in the state and among ladino elites, researchers, and Mayan activists, and asked for feedback and clarification from people I've known for a long time in these circles. Where possible I held multiple conversations with people. Interviews were conducted in offices; in waiting rooms (where I spent an inordinate amount of time); in walks through Zone One; in restaurants and cafés (I had an unofficial office in a downtown hotel's restaurant); in cars and buses; in people's homes and in my home; in the aisles of movie theaters and marketplaces, and in the lobbies of government buildings, of hotels where conferences were going on, of the National Theater, and of the martial arts gymnasium where I worked out; and in bars and nightclubs (although these were kept to a minimum as they tended to get a bit sticky). Fieldwork was greatly complicated by the failed "auto-coup" of May 1993, when then-president Jorge Serrano Elías tried to institute martial law. He was deposed and went into exile, and many of my contacts in the state went underground, while entirely new faces inhabited the palace and ministries as part of the congressionally selected government of Ramiro de León Carpio.

The book is principally concerned with the Mayan cultural rights organizations and in no way claims to represent the popular movement nor the range of indigenous strategizing (urban and rural) vis-à-vis the state (or vice versa). This is not a book about all indigenous organizing, but a book that focuses primarily on Mayan professionals—in general, people with a sixth-grade education and higher, who hold nonmanual-labor jobs (teachers, secretaries, translators, development specialists, and so on) and who work in urban areas, primarily Guatemala City. Although there are many Mayan-identified organizations that want nothing to do with the Guatemalan state, here I am primarily interested in those who have decided, for historic and strategic reasons, to struggle for representation in that state. But this is not an in-depth study of "The Maya" or so-called Mayan Nationalism as an isolated phenomenon. Rather it is an attempt to understand Mayan cultural rights activism in relation to the Guatemalan state and ladino sectors, investigating the ways these interactions articulate, or fix, identifications in the short term.

I should also make clear that a structuring but absent presence of the book is the role of the Guatemalan army. I did not focus on the military in my fieldwork, in part because it is difficult and in part because it would limit my contacts with other sectors. I believe, based on my own experiences and those of my friends and informants, that there has been a qualitative change in the way power works in Guatemala, given the change to civilian government in 1985 and the recent Peace Accords. However, the army remains an extremely significant force in the city as well as the countryside. I explore this issue in chapter 3, but emphasize here that, although things are different than when I began fieldwork in 1985, fear of the arbitrary power over life and death held by the army overshadows all the work done by Guatemalan state officials, Mayan activists, and gringa anthropologists. Without giving the army total power—which it never had, even at the height of counterinsurgency in the early 1980s—it should not be forgotten that despite many important and structural changes, Guatemalan society remains heavily militarized.

Although I briefly discuss the recombinant relations between the Maya and the URNG, I cannot explore the revolutionary movement in depth in this book. This is because during all of my fieldwork it was almost impossible for me to talk to or about members of the movement. Their recent emergence into public life, the discussions mobilized by the findings of the Truth Commission, and the URNG's transformation into an aboveground political movement will make for exciting work in that field in the years ahead. Some of the harshest critiques of the revolutionaries, however, have come from Maya who question the clear-cut binary between how the army and the guerrilla treated indigenous people. Some claim that both sides in the war used them as cannon fodder.

In Quincentennial Guatemala, many previously clear-cut boundaries are becoming crosscut, interpenetrated. For example, the limited (but expanding) openness of the current moment has created vicious struggles over what counts as political. Charges of being "co-opted," "manipulated," "sold out," "a demagogue," "inauthentic," or of not representing those you claim as followers are frequently lobbed at every target imaginable, including Mayan rights activists, the guerrillas, popular leaders, human rights groups, nongovernmental organizations, researchers, and the government. During my fieldwork I had to constantly remind myself that the boundaries of the political are flexible and that it was dangerous to assume that I always already knew what constituted a progressive, feminist, or antiracist project. Obviously, although I frequently forgot it, this means refusing to romanticize or to demonize either ladinos or Mayas. It means giving up both heroes and villains (see chapter 2). For those, indigenous and ladino, who have sacrificed family, friends, and home and risked their lives in the struggle for a more equitable future (and even for those who risked little, working in solidarity), Mayan critiques of racism in the guerrilla and popular movement are hard to hear and too easily evoke a violent disavowal. Total immersion in the world of the Maya, however, can blind one to the important history of the ladino (anthropologists and tourists tend to have little interest in nonindigenous Guatemala). Casual references to a "ladino state" ignore the enormous costs borne by the majority of ladinos who are not represented there. In turn, overemphasis on the struggles over culture—such things of beauty as *traje,* mountain shrines, and incense-laden ritual—can cover over the ugliness of desperate poverty and internal divisions among the Maya.

Toward the end of a year in the field, in 1993, one of my ladino friends (who went on to play a major role in the peace process) said, "I have met with you many times and we have talked about many things. In return, I want you to promise me one thing about your research. Please, *please* do not be tempted by caricatures." I think that keeping open these tensions and contradictions, refusing to assume that any one position is unproblematically liberatory or unremittingly pernicious, is one way I can respond to his concern. As Charles Hale suggests, we need to devote attention to the different sides of a conflict so we can portray each side as fully constituted, complex, knowledgeable actors, while simultaneously stepping back and viewing them from a distance in order to highlight the structural determinations of their consciousness (1994, 216).

Throughout this book I try to make this double move and to retain the power differentials and the fear and uncertainty that undergird life in Guatemala, without forgetting that people lead "normal" lives. Despite the fact that many Guatemalans live in extreme poverty (Jonas 1991), most people do go to work and school and church, formulate plans and see them through, march in protest and go shopping, hang out in parks, consume greasy *Pollo Campero* (fried chicken), and tell jokes, play games, listen to Madonna, dance the *son,* and watch B movies.

I did all those things, too (although my *son* dancing is barely serviceable), and I try to keep myself present in the following chapters, along with the other transnational power vectors that frame these debates within Guatemala. I work against my own erasure both by analyzing my problematic position as gringa, Lizard Queen, translator, and possible baby snatcher, and by deploying overt and possibly inappropriate tropes. My textual strategies of using the metaphors of Maya-hacker, Rigoberta Menchú as transvestite, and bodies that splatter are meant to remind you of the representational labor occurring, while they problematize categories like "Maya," "Guatemala," "identity," and "authenticity."

Finally, as my acknowledgments make clear, this book is a relational project and deeply partial, both in the sense of incomplete and extremely subjective. I have tried to be as respectful as possible of all of those who were so generous with their time and analyses, and I take full responsibility for all the errors and limitations here contained. Although anything I can give will be hopelessly small in comparison to all I have received, I hope this book contributes to an always emerging project of waging peace in this constitutively wounded land.

A MAP TO PRECEDE THE TERRITORY

The book folds around the themes of bodies and bodies politic, beginning with the vulnerable body of a North American woman hurt in a highland village and ending with the laboring body of the Mayan woman prosthetically supporting Guatemala's insertion into the global economy. I open with the transnational bodies politic expressed in relations of solidarity and counterinsurgency between the United States and Guatemala, and in succeeding chapters slowly head toward the individual body itself—a body stripped down, desiring, and marked by race, class, and gender. We get there by moving through discussions of body politics in the state and Mayan organizing to the hieroglyphic veil of clothing and the attempts of smutty jokes and the discourses of eugenics and *mestizaje* to penetrate it, to reach the body. Then we move back out to bodies politic through Mayan organizing and its relation with modernity and the cyberspatialized nation-state to the effects of transnational forces like UN Conventions and neoliberal economic packages.

In the second chapter I concentrate on the almost fatal beating of a North American tourist because of rumors that she had snatched a baby in order to sell its organs. I take this incident as a starting point to investigate my own position in the transnational flows that affect identifications in Quincentennial Guatemala and in the United States, exploring the relational term *gringa,* which means being somehow involved with Latin America. Guatemala's geographic and political position—as a site for human rights and solidarity activism, international sanctions, *maquila* (foreign-owned assembly plants) production, UN peacekeepers, and increasingly as a tourist destination—deeply affected my fieldwork, and Guatemala's history of civil war has also politicized anthropological work there in ways different from more settled fieldsites, linking analysis to solidarity. In chapter 2, I interrogate these aspects of the field and the contradictions of trying to produce a critical and politically aware ethnography of the Guatemalan state when that state is in flux and when many Guatemalans identify gringas as baby-snatchers.

The organ-harvesting rumors and the various attempts to explain them condense issues central to this book: the production of meanings in a space overdetermined by violence and uncertainty, and the ubiquity of transcultural and transnational interactions for this account of identifications. Through critically investigating my own relation to the solidarity movement that first motivated my academic work, I develop the concept of fluidarity as a way of thinking about Quincentennial Guatemala—where "the *pueblo*" is heterogeneous and identities are not solid. Fluidarity is a practice and theory of identity-in-formation, aware of its own investments, the pleasures of intervention, and the erotics of relational subject-making. It is historically specific and knows that it is very hard to give up solid bodies, clear-cut enemies and friends, but that this may be the most responsible way to approach the current conjuncture in Guatemala.

Chapter 3 provides a brief history, focusing on both the state's institutional attempts to deal with the indigenous population and with the "piñata effect"—how, despite the delegitimation of the war and rampant corruption, people turn to the state for sweets and as a site of struggle. I discuss the Ministry of Culture and Sports, founded with the civilian government in 1985, its role in the context of the Quincentennial, and the way officials there deploy the concept of "culture" as a commodifiable product, something to be seized hold of. For example, culture was described as a solution to Guatemala's disadvantageous economic positioning in the world system and as a central component in constructing a new, legitimate nation-state. In opposition to the traditionally held belief that the indigenous population was a hindrance to economic development that must be eradicated, I explore this emerging vision of the state vis-à-vis Mayan culture, which is now seen as a renewable, clean, "national" resource to be sold as tourist imagery and as material goods like "traditional" weavings. I suggest that this vision marks a shift toward the more governmental state that can support the ratification of ILO Convention 169 and the Accord on Indigenous Rights.

The historic shifts that the Culture Ministry tries to address have also opened a space for indigenous participation in the state, the subject of chapter 4, which explores the struggles to consolidate the Guatemalan Mayan Language Academy (ALMG) as a state-funded agency. The ALMG's mandate is to standardize the alphabets of the twenty-one Mayan languages, create materials for bilingual education, and promote the revitalization of traditional Mayan lifeways. I suggest that the ALMG activists are seizing hold of memories of community and "culture" as part of the process of being "community-bound," of heading toward a community based in new identifications and commitments. I am especially interested in the historical production of these activists as Mayan "middle men and middle women," people trained as teachers and catechists who have become leaders in the struggle for cultural rights. I focus on an historic moment when colonially inflected markings of subordination (hostile markings such as the Mayan languages, clothing, and religion) are being taken for empowering use in producing identifications.

Two days after Rigoberta Menchú won the Nobel Peace Prize, a friend asked if I'd heard the latest joke. "Why," she asked, "did Rigoberta really win the Nobel Prize? Because she's an *indita desenvuelta!*" (she's an articulate little Indian, or a naked little Indian). *Desenvuelta* means both "articulate" and "well-spoken," and also "unwrapped"—referring to taking off an indigenous woman's traditional skirt: in other words, Rigoberta had slept her way to the prize. Within a week I had heard this joke (and many others) several times from a wide range of people, ladino and Maya. Within a month I knew I had to write about it, because the joke condenses so many issues around identification, gender, language, and national identity in a transnational framework. Chapter 5 analyzes the responses to Rigoberta Menchú's Nobel Peace Prize through the prism of jokes, which foreground gender and sexuality as sites of ambivalence in identity formation and emphasize the uncanny effects of multiple boundary crossings. Mayan women's *traje* figures prominently in the jokes and marks a place of particular challenge to notions of ethnic-national identity. The highly polemical responses to the Peace Prize (the "positively hostile and cruel" content of these jokes) suggest that because representations of both Mayan-ness and Guatemalanness depend heavily on images of indigenous women in *traje,* and because Rigoberta Menchú who uses *traje* challenges many of the stereotypes of indigenous women, her image also challenges the naturalness of these identities. In exploring the mutual constitution of ethnicity and nationalism, I address the ways gender is mobilized to structure and give force to these emerging and multiply contested identities. The fascination with clothing leads me to read the jokes as situating Ms. Menchú as a sort of transvestite in Marjorie Garber's (1992) sense, as a marker of more general cultural anxieties. Ms. Menchú is not what she seems (a powerless Maya woman) and therefore rips at the seams that are meant to bind identities such as powerful, ladino, and masculine.

Chapter 6 further explores the social regulation of race, gender, and sexuality in Guatemalan ladino discourse about indigenous bodies—a sort of "biopolitical economy" that draws on a complex set of stereotypes, fantasies, ideals, notions of home, and eroticized imaginaries. Examining the book *Guatemala: Linaje y Racismo* (Lineage and Racism) by the Guatemalan anthropologist Marta Casaus Arzú in relation to my own interviews, I explore how gender and sexuality are constitutive of ladino discourses on "Indians." I pay special attention to two apparently contradictory notions of race and ethnicity. One is *mestizaje* (racial mixing), which proposes that differences between Indian and ladino are cultural, not genetic; ethnic, not racial. The other views difference as racial, leaning on notions of blood purity and "objective" phenotypic marks of difference. I suggest that these apparently opposed discourses are similar in that they both carry eugenic promises of progress through the social regulation of desire, both call on the body as proof, and both, by "racing" the body in different ways, simultaneously erase the constitutive gendering and sexualizing of those bodies.

In Quincentennial Guatemala, forms of information manipulation like those found in science fiction are changing the role of the Maya in relation to discourses of modernity, technology, and the imaginary bodies politic of cyberspace and the national community. In chapter 7 I explore how Mayan activists appropriate "modernity" in order to prove their appropriateness for the nation, and how state sectors respond to this strategy. I build on the way Mayan activists rename identity-positions as "Maya-K'iche'," "Maya-Kaqchikel," and so on, to develop the metaphor of the "Maya-hacker." This term, mixing the ethnic and the high-tech, attempts to capture the uncanny effects of Mayan efforts to undermine the colonial binary of identity that consigns the Indians to the premodern and defines ladinos as those with access to the modern in terms of language, technology, and knowledge. Historically, any indigenous person who spoke Spanish or held a desk job was redefined as ladino. But, by appropriating "modern" technology and knowledge while refusing to be appropriated to this redefinition, the Maya-hacker is, in Trinh Minh-ha's words, the "inappropriate(d) other" (Trinh 1986). I argue that this "inappropriate" presence on the national scene and in the state is creating ambivalent realignments of various identities and forcing a rethinking of the nation's future. But in chapter 7 I also explore how gender, often read as "tradition," prosthetically supports this political strategy.

Chapter 8 moves back out from the nation-state as the site of these struggles to the transnational terrain of international law as the site of complex interactions among the United Nations, the Guatemalan state, and local, national, and international indigenous organizations over the ILO's Convention 169. The Convention—which was ratified by the Guatemalan Congress in March 1995—contains potentially radical provisions concerning self-determination, limited legal autonomy, and territorial rights for indigenous peoples. It stipulates indigenous participation in the development and implementation of national laws that affect them and requires national respect for *derecho consuetudinario* (customary law). The Convention also calls for recognition of the special importance and spiritual relationship that indigenous peoples have to the land—here understood as territory—which will include lands they occupy or use in other ways.

The struggles surrounding ratification of Convention 169, including disseminating and discussing these provisions, are part of the processes of Quincentennial Guatemala that constitute identifications. These struggles in turn reveal deep fissures in the state itself, as some see the Convention threatening state sovereignty and the very existence of the Guatemalan nation, whereas others—including three Guatemalan presidents—have actively supported ratification. I will focus on the apparent contradictions of a racist state apparatus ratifying a juridical instrument that could potentially redefine its entire relation to the governed. This is linked in turn to the question of why the ILO, member agency of the United Nations, an international organization deeply invested in territorially defined nation-states, is pushing a convention that contemplates nations without states and states without territorial boundaries.

The conclusion contextualizes struggles over Convention 169 and the contours of the more governmental state in a period that has been labeled "post-Fordist." Here I return to the role of the body in Guatemala's late capitalist body politics, suggesting that transnational power relations—from the ILO to World Bank structural adjustment to gringa anthropology to *maquila* production—are laying the groundwork for a new flexibility in national and ethnic incorporations. Not only may Mayan articulations of cultural identity be in the interests of national and multinational capital, but, simultaneously, these national and multinational regimes may form some of the conditions of possibility for Mayan identity formation and (in)corporation. This brings me back to the larger arguments in the book: that neither the state nor transnational capital is a monolithic power that always gets what it wants; that power works in multiply territorialized interstitial places, often through bleeding boundaries; and that ethnic, gender, and national identifications are produced through mutually constitutive and always contingent relationships.

"A finger in the wound" refers to these messy boundaries, their interpenetrations, and the lack of a coherent, seamless national or ethnic identity in Quincentennial Guatemala. Attempts to fix such identifications lean on the body and function as a sort of orthopedics, a way of articulating selves. But these attempts also fail, as constant appropriations unsettle these struggles to stabilize ethnic and national identities. Mayan, ladino, Guatemalan, gender, and other identifications are "community bound": they are headed toward a future and never fully finished community, and also bound together, constantly rearticulating those identifications.

TWO

Gringa Positioning, Vulnerable Bodies, and Fluidarity

A Partial Relation

There can be no pure opposition to power, only a recrafting of its terms from resources invariably impure.

JUDITH BUTLER

What are we if we do not protect our children?

Maya-Q'eqchi' man, describing his reaction to purported gringa baby-snatcher

A GRINGA IN RELATION WITH GUATEMALA

This book is concerned with the formations of, and the conditions of possibility for, identity. To begin, I explore how being a gringa anthropologist is both power-filled and a wounded body politic, and how that identity is formed in relation with multiple others.[1] Abigail Adams argues that the term *gringo* necessitates a relationship with Latin America—a North American is not a gringo until she crosses a border (A. Adams 1997). Thus *gringo* is an articulation in the sense described by Ernesto Laclau and Chantal Mouffe: "Any practice establishing a relation among elements such that their identity is modified as a result of the articulatory practice" (1985, 105). "Gringo" is a category produced through interactions, and as such, it works on a variety of borders including but not limited to national frontiers, stereotypes of phenotypic difference, sartorial codes, and—as "gringa" (marked by the Spanish feminine)—gender boundaries. In turn, the gringa changes the places she goes.

I am arguing that all identity is formed through articulation, a notion that problematizes traditions of solidarity that lean on "solid" identities and clear-cut divisions between victim and victimizer.[2] Taking the articulatory

---

1. I owe the insight that being a gringa anthropologist is formed in relation with others to Abigail Adams, with whom my work on Guatemala is complexly "in relation." She has deeply influenced my thinking about gringa-ness.

2. As I discuss in the following, I am speaking of solidarity as a praxis of identifying in struggle. Etymologically, *solidarity* suggests unity of opinion, purpose, interest, or feeling. In la-

notion of identity seriously, along with the relationality of gringa identity, I develop the concept of *fluidarity* as a practice of necessarily partial knowledge—in both the sense of taking the side of, and of being incomplete, vulnerable, and never completely fixed (Clifford 1986).[3] This neologism plays with the idea of *solid*arity in an attempt to keep its vitally important transnational relations open and at the same time question its tendency toward rigidity, its reliance on solid, unchanging identifications, and its often unconscious hierarchizing. Gringa identification, like all identification, is here understood as "the play of difference and similitude in self-other relations[,] . . . the detour through the other that defines the self" (Fuss 1995, 2–3).

Since 1985, in my fieldwork and in writing this book, I have understood my relation to Guatemala as being *in solidarity* as a researcher and activist. This has meant forming alliances with Guatemalans and like-minded gringos and producing "partial" accounts that take the side of the oppressed. Here I explore my own investments in solidarity and suggest that a different politics may be necessary to relate to Quincentennial Guatemala. ·

My introduction to the field of "partial" Guatemala studies was as a student and research assistant for an inspirational and politically committed professor who insisted that knowing about the carnage in Guatemala carried the responsibility of working to stop it. In 1985, while Guatemala was under military dictatorship, I first went there to assess the effects of the civil war in highland indigenous communities and in the refugee camps in Mexico. I and another young gringa, Paula Worby, started out in Mexico City, visiting the makeshift and overcrowded offices of Guatemalan exile and refugee organizations that were buzzing with activity: fund raising; sending out denunciations; aiding recent arrivals; collecting, sharing, and trying to make sense of rampant rumors; disbursing funds; planning delegations to Europe and the United States to publicize the war; meeting with foreign solidarity delegations; and (although this was never specified) recuperating

---

bor history, it has been a way of talking about hanging together so that one does not hang separately and of understanding that one's interests are best served by worker unity against the power of capital. In practice, at least in the 1980s with Central America, it meant that North Americans solidly identified with the struggle of revolutionary and popular organizations against murderous U.S.-backed regimes in Guatemala or El Salvador. These struggles shared our interests or feelings vis-à-vis the U.S. government. Although North Americans were usually not tortured or killed for trying to change government policies, we could identify with the oppressed in other countries, in part out of guilt at the use of "our" tax dollars. Solidarity organizations are usually composed of alliances among exiles and gringos also often active in the civil rights, antiwar, nuclear disarmament, tax resistors, Sanctuary, labor, gay and lesbian, and other "social movements."

3. *Fluidarity* is Mark Driscoll's term. He is attempting to both theorize and practice this concept (Driscoll 1998).

for a return to armed combat.[4] Each contact led to another, until we were
suspended in webs of people and organizations that gave meaning to what
we would find in Guatemala—and, looking back, to my entire *formación*
(education) as a solidarity gringa. Priests, nuns, lay churchworkers, journalists, peasants, indigenous people, haggard and desperately thin delegates from the Chiapas camps, university professors and students, labor
unionists, people who had left jobs and family because of threats or in a
miraculous escape from an army death squad, people fleeing the destruction of their entire family and village, all were struggling to survive and to
do political work in the megalopolis. They were uniformly warm and welcoming to two young (and in retrospect, rather ignorant) gringas. They
shared their experiences, passed on the stories of the dead, and generously
gave us a wealth of contacts and letters of introduction to people in Guatemala. They emphasized, through their practices and their remonstrations,
the importance of publicizing the brutality of the human rights abuses.

In Guatemala we encountered similar, almost shocking openness (except, of course, as regarded guerrilla affiliation) from almost everyone we
met. We were put up in people's homes and often by the Catholic Church,
which gave us automatic access to many villagers; constantly told we should
"talk to so and so and you can use my name"; driven around in jeeps, tractors, and motorbikes, loaned horses, and accompanied on grueling walks
up mountains and through jungle mud, to make sure we got to places and
talked to key witnesses; and given endless hours of time as people told their
stories, often leaving us weeping together. We were mostly outside of the
city, living for several months in northern Huehuetenango and the Ixil area
around Nebaj. We also interviewed in the Petén, in the Atitlán region, the
southern coast, and San Marcos. We talked to the owner of the biggest coffee plantation in the country, who admitted he treated his workers better
now because the guerrillas killed his neighbor. We lived with Guatemalan
nuns who had buried more people than they could count and who feared
for their lives at all times. We talked to Maya-Chuj men about the massacres
in their villages and what it was like to serve twenty-four hours every four
days in the Civil Patrol.[5] After interviews conducted almost clandestinely in
the back room of the church or the kitchen of a hastily rebuilt house in a
model village (see chapter 3), people would thank us for risking the trip

4. I certainly don't mean to imply that everyone in the limbo of exile in Mexico City was a
guerrilla. As mentioned in chapter 1, suggesting this was tantamount to calling for their murder. In 1985 the Guatemalan army was making incursions into Mexican territory to kill refugees, and the Mexican military and police were picking up exiles in Mexico City who were often never seen again.

5. The term *Maya-Chuj* is a bit anachronistic because this form of address came into use in
the late 1980s.

there and for informing "America" about their lives. All of these people seemed to feel it was worth their time to talk to us, and everyone from the coffee *finquero* (plantation owner) to the refugee expressed the sense that they lived in relation to transnational forces and that the body image other countries had of Guatemala mattered. In turn, when I represented the lives of Guatemalans, in the sense of creating a picture of their experiences through my writing, I felt I was adequately representing them in the sense of speaking for them, of serving as a mouthpiece for their stories.

After returning to the United States, and in between working with the other members of the research team to write up our results (Manz 1988a), we took every chance we could get to talk and write about the situation in Guatemala. And since then I have tried to combine research in Guatemala with work in the United States to create awareness of that situation and to link it to politics at home. In the mid-1980s, there seemed to be a clear antagonism between the Guatemalan military government and the civilian population and, with the Reagan wars in Central America, between the U.S. government and struggles for peace and justice at home and abroad.[6] This antagonism and these transnational parallels, or similarities, made the mixing of research and solidarity work seem relatively straightforward. Because the United States was so directly involved in worsening the situation—the antagonism was overt—political work at home was also straightforward (stop supporting genocide), if always difficult and under constant discussion. Spurred on by reading what seemed like blatant lies in the U.S. press and sitting in packed auditoriums listening to Noam Chomsky talk about "turning the tide" (1985), I believed that if other gringos only knew what was *really* going on (the personal tragedies behind the anticommunist rhetoric), they (as I had) would do something to change it. This may sound hopelessly naive in today's cynical climate (is it already time for eighties' nostalgia?!), but it was a different historic moment. Both solidarity with the peoples of apartheid South Africa (including the divestment movement's focus on finance capital's world reach) and of Central America (which was wondrously emboldened by the Sandinista victory of 1979 and highly focused on the fragility of "democracy" in the United States as homeless-

---

6. What I am calling *Reagan wars* were a complicated combination of covert operations, supply lines, training, psychological operations, propaganda, arms sales, vote rigging, terror tactics, selective murder, support for military coups d'etat, and some outright intervention, which has been termed low intensity conflict (McClintock 1985: 1 and 2; Amnesty International 1987; Bermúdez 1987; Klare and Arnson 1981; Dean 1986). These wars ranged from arming, training, and fighting with the Nicaraguan "contra" (as in counterrevolutionaries) against the Sandinista government (Sklar 1988), to siding with the military governments against powerful revolutionary forces—the URNG in Guatemala and the Farabundo Martí Liberation Front (FMLN) in El Salvador (Gettleman et al. 1986).

ness exploded, the Sanctuary Movement challenged national boundary-maintenance, and the Iran Contra scandal grew) were about linking lives and struggles transnationally in relatively black and white ways.

Despite the fact that the 1986 inauguration of a civilian government in Guatemala changed the political landscape, government-sanctioned human rights abuses continued. Six months in the highlands that year researching the army's "Development Pole" resettlement strategies convinced me that although the violence was more selective, there was still a solid line between the oppressive state run by the venal military and elite and the victimized *pueblo*. Of course, much of the rationale for solidarity work and "partial" anthropology is based on taking the side of the *pueblo* in this binary. Here the gringo can most comfortably intervene as concerned witness, chronicler, translator, and, through the accompaniment of our invulnerable bodies overtly marked by ethnicity and nation, as shields.[7] Relying on the Caucasian gringo phenotype and its meaning within transnational political relations, I could boldly go where Guatemalan nationals would fear to tread, interviewing soldiers and civilian paramilitary leaders in highland villages, coaxing testimonials of human rights abuses, and photographing the sites of massacres.

Though I felt like I had almost magical power at the time, the experiences of Coalition Missing members grimly remind us that gringos are not superhuman (GHRC/USA 1996). Coalition Missing is a mutual support and activist network composed of nineteen U.S. citizens who have been victims of Guatemalan state-sponsored repression—like Sister Dianna Ortíz, who was abducted and tortured in 1989; Carol Devine, whose husband Michael was murdered by members of the army in 1990; and human rights observer Meredith Larson, who was stabbed in 1990. The coalition's important work occurs right on that line between the state and the *pueblo* where solidarity works best. The struggle of Jennifer Harbury, a member of Coalition Missing, is perhaps the most stunning example. After her hus-

---

7. The U.S. Central America Solidarity movement is primarily white and middle-class. The sense of gringo invulnerability is heightened by the knowledge of the extreme violence suffered by Guatemalans compared with only a few cases of gringos killed for apparently political reasons in Guatemala in the past twelve years. This solid, invulnerable foreign body is key to the vitally important accompaniment movements organized by Witness for Peace and Peace Brigades, where foreign volunteers spend twenty-four hours a day with leaders at risk. The very presence of these gringo bodies—as potential witnesses, or as possible victims who would claim international attention (as when Ben Linder was killed by the contra in Nicaragua)—shielded many activists. There is even a joke about Rigoberta Menchú that plays on this practice. Why is Rigoberta like a *chile relleno*? Because she always comes between two *francés* (she's like a sandwich, with *francés* playing on French bread and French people: before her return from exile in 1994, she was always accompanied by foreigners).

band, guerrilla commander Efraín Bámaca Velásquez (Everardo) was captured by the army, Ms. Harbury positioned herself against both the Guatemalan and U.S. states, demanding information on his whereabouts. Through excruciating years of lobbying and heroic hunger strikes, she (in alliance with hundreds of gringos and Guatemalans) forced public acknowledgment that not only had the army tortured and killed him, but the Guatemalan responsible, Colonel Julio Roberto Alpírez, was on the CIA payroll as an "asset" (Harbury 1997). These revelations created a major shakeup in the Guatemalan military and led to unprecedented public acknowledgment in the United States of CIA malfeasance as described in the Intelligence Oversight Board report. Harbury's struggle shows the enormous power of gringo solidarity. The similarity of her personal tragedy to those of so many Guatemalan victims of state repression, combined with her difference—she's a Harvard-educated lawyer and a gringa—makes for an extraordinarily effective intervention on the side of the *pueblo*.

This divide between state and *pueblo is* powerful (and transnational: Harbury's life has been threatened in both Guatemala and the United States, and her lawyer's car was bombed in Washington, D.C.). When gringos do feel vulnerable in the field, as Linda Green so powerfully evokes (1995), it is precisely because of this divide. Siding with the *pueblo* makes us potential victims of the state. This binary, the basis for the political engagement of anthropologists partial to their subjects, assumes (often correctly) that when we gringos position ourselves with "the people," they'll be glad to have us on their side.

In working on this book in Quincentennial times, however, I have found "the people" to be rather more heterogeneous, "the state" less clearly bounded, gringas less magically welcome, and my accounts to be far more "partial"—in the sense of incomplete –than I had acknowledged. As I became involved, even tangentially, in passionate internal divisions within the *pueblo* (divisions inside popular and revolutionary organizations, between Mayan and popular organizations, among Mayan communities, and between men and women), as I witnessed the state becoming a site of struggle rather than an enemy to be smashed, as my work encountered suspicion from Maya scholars and others increasingly empowered to represent themselves (Fischer and Brown 1996; Warren 1992; Watanabe 1995), and as I watched the wave of violence against gringas that was not state-sponsored, I have had to confront the instability of my previously solid representations.

The vulnerability of this position as a gringa in solidarity was most shockingly brought home by recent assaults on gringas in Guatemala by that *pueblo*. In the most damaging incident, June Weinstock was attacked in a highland indigenous community in March 1994. She was beaten for hours and left for dead. Rumor had it that she had stolen a child to sell its organs in the first world. Neither the police nor the army intervened.[8] Here my body image of a gringa as solid, guilty perhaps but powerful, was suddenly confronted with the gringa as wounded, open.

In the following, I analyze these experiences, including the brutal beating and varying accounts of it, as quilting, or condensation points for a number of the issues involved in this book: the production of meanings in a space overdetermined by violence; the articulation of the problematic categories of "gringo," "solidarity," and "anthropology"; and the complexity and ubiquitousness of transcultural and transnational interactions for this book's account of ethnic, national, and gender body politics. Fluidarity is a way of trying to respond in a responsible way to these complexities while trying to avoid what Gayatri Spivak calls "the ferocious standardizing benevolence of most US human-scientific radicalism (recognition by assimilation)" (1988a, 294). My benevolence (and comfortable position) as an anthropologist in solidarity hits a snag with this violence against another gringa. The highland Maya peoples usually coded as victims are suddenly perpetrators. I struggle to construct a story to rationalize this and have to think about my benevolence, discomfort, and rage.[9]

8. In early March 1994, a similar rumor caused a riot in the south-coast town of Santa Lucia Cotzumalguapa. A North American woman, protected by the police, escaped the "lynch mob." The police station was burned, and the army occupied the town. I thank Pepe Lara for keeping me up to date.

9. The internal complexity and even violent division within indigenous communities should not come as a surprise to anthropologists, having been well documented (Carmack 1988; Brintnall 1979; Warren 1989; C. Smith 1990b)—even if, to anthropologists drenched in ethnostalgia, it sometimes does. In turn, a fear of foreigners is not new: Maud Oakes was accused of witchcraft in Todos Santos (1951), and Richard Wilson suggests that among the Q'eqchi' of Alta Verapaz (where Weinstock was attacked), foreign anthropologists (*kaxlan*) are categorized as "hot" and along with ladinos and drunk men as able to cause severe illness (1995, 145). When Linda Green began fieldwork in Chimaltenango people would run away and hide when they saw her coming, and her Kaqchikel assistant was frequently asked "if it was true that I wanted to steal their children and if *gringos* ate children" (1995, 114).

Beliefs in witchcraft have recently caused other sorts of problems for gringas. The UN verification team (MINUGUA) charged with investigating reports of human rights violations received an anonymous denunciation of a murder, and after hiking for more than four hours to reach the highland village, the MINUGUA team was surprised to find that the entire town calmly admitted to killing the man because he was a witch. A member of the team later called me to ask what I thought: Could this be true? Could they really believe this? As we talked, she was quite open to an Evans-Pritchard-esque account, saying that their investigation had found many people dying of respiratory diseases compounded by malnutrition in the area and that it would make sense if the people explained these anomalous deaths by witchcraft, which they could do something about, rather than dire poverty, which seemed pretty entrenched. But she said she thought the *real* reason was that the military had come through in the early 1980s, killed people, and told the others that if there were anyone bad in the village that person should be killed. The MINUGUA official in charge of indigenous affairs stated emphatically

Rather than being "solid," a gringa in relation to Guatemala is overdetermined by complex plays of identification and difference over what Liisa Malkki terms "bleeding boundaries" (1992, 26). Anthropology has been justly critiqued for being a handmaid of colonialism, and even the best intentions have been revealed as far from innocent, so I have been trained to think of myself as powerful when I go, as a gringa, to the field. However, I feel intensely vulnerable when I contemplate Weinstock's deeply wounded body, a material example of bleeding boundaries. My ethnic and national identifications feel brutally crosscut by my gendered subject-position, and I am reminded that no body politic is whole and unchanging: they are all open and contingent, wounded. This chapter explores these contradictory articulations of gringa identity as a site that is neither innocent nor transcendent (Visweswaran 1994), that is both complicitous and inescapable, but that through its very relationality and vulnerability—its unstable, desire-driven articulation—may be the only site from which to launch a fluidary analysis.

SOLIDARITY

The work and affect of solidarity, as in participant-observation, are precisely about the interplay of identity and difference, intimacy and distance, over transnational and other boundaries. Like many North Americans, my first "orientation" to Guatemala was through Rigoberta Menchú's testimonial (1984).[10] Originally directed at the international solidarity audience to explain why a people would legitimately rebel against the state, it is a com-

---

that it was the army's fault. She said, "Traditionally Mayan communities had ways of dealing with these problems, their customary law, norms, but now the military rules these communities, not Mayan law. It was the military commissioner and the Civil Patrol who incited it." These readings of the murder echo our solidarity attempts to explain the attack on June Weinstock. The Civil Patrol is one of the most nefarious of the army's counterinsurgency apparatuses; in the patrol's heyday, all highland men and boys were forcibly recruited to police their communities. The patrol is a militarized institution, armed, usually run by ex-soldiers, and reporting back to the army, but it is also isomorphic with village men, making the line between victim and perpetrator difficult to see.

10. The autobiography recounts her childhood in the highlands near Chajul, where people eked out a living farming and traveling as migrant workers to the plantations of the southern coast (where malnutrition and pesticides killed her younger brother). She also describes their indigenous culture, her parents' struggles for land, and the family's involvement in Catholic Action and the CUC. The book ends with her younger sister joining the guerrillas and Ms. Menchú going into exile in Mexico.

The relation of Ms. Menchú's testimonial to gringo audiences could be a book in itself, including the debates over the CIV track (required first-year course) at Stanford University, writings on the issue of teaching testimonial as a genre, and the politicized rejections of her book (and her Nobel Peace Prize) by Dinesh D'Souza (1991) and others.

pelling text. The book movingly describes how her brother was killed in the Chajul town square, how her father died in the Spanish Embassy massacre in 1980, and how her mother was tortured to death, all at the hands of the Guatemalan Army. It evokes a complex play of similarity: one of the uses of testimonial is to incite identification with a struggle, a position that is not one's own yet to which we are linked—because we are women, because we have felt pain, because we can imagine the trauma of losing a mother, a brother, and so on. Yet testimonial is also about difference. It is directed toward people who have not experienced these things.[11] To do this, it relies on a certain amount of exoticism, or ethnostalgia, consciously wrought or not.[12] Menchú's book is an intriguing interweaving of the invitation to identify with her experiences of loss and consciousness raising and the denial of such identification as she highlights the constitutive difference of indigenous lifeways from those of the reader and refuses to reveal the secrets of her community.

As I explore in chapter 5, Ms. Menchú is an important nodal point in national, ethnic, gender, and transnational relations as an exiled "representative of the Guatemalan opposition," a spokeswoman for indigenous peoples before the United Nations (see chapter 8), and Nobel Peace Prize winner in the Quincentennial year.[13] As such, it has been her job to incite solidarity— in other words, identification with the Guatemalan situation—among an international audience, primarily through repeated invocations of her experience (D. Stoll 1991). Ms. Menchú has been in constant relation with the international community for close to twenty years and, like the Mayan organizing I describe in chapter 4, this relation is community-bound. It is consciously aimed toward producing a community, a body politic of solidarity.

My work as researcher, writer, translator (for Ms. Menchú and others), and now teacher has been bound (articulated and attached) to this (imagined) community, to the *pueblo* of Guatemala, and to international solidarity, which are all potent spaces of gringa self-fashioning (Clifford 1988).

11. Elaine Scarry (1985) discusses the difficulty of translating pain across the membrane between bodies. Carolyn Forche's poetry is one of the few places that explores how this membrane allows for the play of horror and pleasure in those of us who read human rights reports and then find their scenarios popping up in our fantasy spaces. The boundaries between the sadomasochistic images that saturate our pop culture repertoires and the bodily experiences of torture victims in Guatemala are, frighteningly, not particularly solid.

12. I suggest later that Ms. Menchú's story is particularly powerful because of the way she condenses many meanings and emotions around gender and ethnicity as a *mujer maya* (Mayan woman). I explore the double bind of what I call ethnostalgia, as both tool and limit to ethnic mobilization, in chapter 7.

13. Ms. Menchú was affiliated with the five-member United Representation of the Guatemalan Opposition (RUOG), an exile organization that coordinated international solidarity work. Thanks to the peace process, most of its members now live and work in Guatemala.

This identification in turn includes solidarity among gringos, a collective identity of sameness that partly absorbs the shock of relating with so much difference. Much of my relation with Guatemala has been mediated and accompanied by gringa *compañeras* (companions, or comrades): from the intrepid mentor who first gave me the opportunity to go there (and who would hate being called a gringa), through solidarity committees and action networks, to the writing of this book in constant dialogue with women whose lives and work include Guatemala. Journalists, solidarity activists, development workers, human rights professionals, and anthropologists of several generations, these gringas are smart, committed, political, and savvy women, and most of them have a great sense of humor. That is in part why we can laugh at and identify with Francisco Goldman's (1992) term for us, "The Sweet Sisters of Solidarity."

Solidarity, like *gringa*, is about articulations across different borders and about the constitution of such borders (Gupta and Ferguson 1992).[14] *Solidarity* is a term that has been theoretically contested and heavily negotiated in practice, and as a consequence it is deeply and emotionally resonant. Solidarity to me has meant making self-conscious alliances, of trying to be aware and respectful of difference while striving to find common ground as the basis for a radical politics. It was and continues to be an attempt to confront local politics transnationally and valiantly, what Beatriz Manz and Ricardo Falla call "committed anthropology": "*antropología comprometida*, to opt for, to side with" (Manz 1995, 261).

Solidarity as Political

As I explore the limitations of solidarity and problematize the notion of sides, I don't want to lose the ways in which solidarity is politically productive and the fact that the antagonisms do exist. In a different vocabulary, solidarity might be called consciousness-raising about power asymmetries. It is a process that—although shot through with problematic assumptions—articulates subject-positions to oppositional projects, an aspect I would want to save for my project of fluidarity. For example, my political awareness of imperialism, racism, and exploitation was evoked through solidarity with

---

14. Mary Pratt calls these *contact zones,* referring to the

space of colonial encounters, the space in which peoples geographically and historically separated come into contact with each other and establish ongoing relations, usually involving conditions of coercion, radical inequality, and intractable conflict. . . . I aim to foreground the interactive, improvisational dimensions of colonial encounters so easily ignored or suppressed by diffusionist accounts of conquest and domination. A "contact" perspective emphasizes how subjects are constituted in and by their relations to each other. . . . It treats relations in terms of copresence, interaction, interlocking understandings and practices. (1992, 6–7)

Figure 6. Gringos in Solidarity. Fundraiser, consciousness-raiser, and spirit-raiser. Cambridge, Massachusetts, October 1988. Photo courtesy of Sonia Lipson.

Guatemala. While studying in Spain during 1983 and 1984, I began reading reports of the massacres and scorched-earth policies of the Guatemalan government's counterinsurgency campaigns from a less U.S.-centric point of view, and many of my middle-American notions of U.S. history bit the dust. It was a shock to learn that "my" government had overthrown democratically elected governments, like that of Jacobo Arbenz in 1954.

After those first six months in Guatemala in 1985, I became very involved with solidarity work in the Boston area. Solidarity meant politics at home, at a time of arrests, break-ins and government intimidation of activists (Gelbspan 1991). We worked to create awareness that Guatemalan workers, peasants, and indigenous people had risen up against a repressive military government, installed by the United States to maintain the most unequal distribution of resources in the hemisphere, and that they were slaughtered indiscriminately with tacit U.S. support.[15]

The power of *traje* (traditional clothing) to represent Mayan indigenous

15. Of course, people in many different countries were active in solidarity with Guatemala and the rest of Central America, especially during the high tide of U.S. aggression.

identity was used strategically to excite interest in the darker side of those bright colors of "ethnic" crafts so popular in the United States. Through beautiful photographs, exuberant folk art, and descriptions and enactments of Mayan dance and ritual (including gringa transvestism), we strove to make people care that the creators of these "cultural treasures" were being killed and forced into exile. We organized speaking tours by Rigoberta Menchú and other Guatemalan activists to allow them to speak for themselves and to use the authenticity of their presence to incite awareness among "gringos-in-formation"—people beginning to relate to Guatemala. In the United States, we held fund-raisers for popular organizations, lobbied Congress, participated in marches and got arrested, performed guerrilla theater, and held weekly vigils. We ran local papers, wrote for any national press that would print us, and filled church basements, union halls, high school gymnasiums, streets, and parks with meetings, dances, and demonstrations. In Guatemala, we carried out research that Guatemalans were unable to do in isolated areas (published in English and Spanish) and accompanied Guatemalans at risk for their activism, protecting them with the gringo *güera* phenotype backed by the eagle passport.[16]

The Flows of Solidarity: Technologies of Gringa Self-Fashioning

Solidarity, like anthropology, is a specific sort of body politic, formed not only through supportive relations with Guatemalans in struggle and with (more or less) like-minded gringos, but also through differentiations.[17] One identity against which we define ourselves is that of the Guatemalan ladino (unless they're members of the popular movement)—especially the middle-class and wealthy. We seldom talk to them, except as figures to be mocked, and accept unquestioningly that we have a right to expect access to Mayan organizations, indigenous villages, or popular movement representatives, whereas they may not.

In Guatemala, gringo-ness is also constituted through sometimes uncomfortably subtle internal differentiations. As solidary researchers, activists, or anthropologists, we like to believe that we are obviously different from the other kinds of gringos, such as the military advisors, embassy people, journalists (seen as trafficking in the same information without the commitment [Malkki 1997]), and especially the dreaded tourist.[18] In fact,

16. *Güera* is slang for "fair" or "light-skinned."

17. Elder nuns and Sparticist League punks may be on the same side but rarely converge except at large demonstrations.

18. For the debate on tourism and anthropology, see MacCannell (1976), Gewertz and Errington (1991), and O'Rourke (1987). Claude Lévi-Strauss in *Tristes Tropiques* caught this ambivalence nicely, as he often does: "I hate travelling and explorers. Yet here I am proposing to tell the story of my expeditions (1977:3)." The international tourists caught going up the

we feel that part of our mission is educating the tourists we meet while "taking a break" at beautiful Lake Atitlán or those we (disgruntled) find in out-of-the-way places that we struggle to get to.

Attempts to dissociate ourselves from gringo tourists may be part of a disavowal that the Quincentennial is a different moment than that of my first fieldwork in 1985, when I was one of the only white people around and Guatemalans would thank me for interviewing them. Guatemala, because of its proximity to the United States, its physical beauty and cultural traditions, the buying power of the dollar, the ease of acquiring visas, and the pathos and emotion of the war, has become intensely crowded with foreigners. This may come as a shock to gringa colleagues who work in more isolated areas, but Guatemala is crawling with tourists, journalists, students, UN workers, researchers, and Peace Corps volunteers (over two hundred— the largest contingent in the world). As a politically committed anthropologist, I want to think I am different from these foreigners, but in the eyes of Guatemalans, my self-representations are folded into complex and overdetermined understandings. I am "confused" with tourists, hippies, missionaries, faceless consumers who reject "imperfect" snow peas that go to feed pigs rather than children, exhumation teams whose work implicates community members in histories of violence and brutality (EAFG 1995), hundreds of students who want an interview and are never heard from again, well-meaning political tourists who have read Menchú's book and want to learn about suffering, New Agers who hope to apprentice with a Mayan shaman (Castañeda 1996), National Guardsmen and women (A. Adams forthcoming), and so on.[19] Thus, my body image as a helpful North Ameri-

---

Sepik river of Papua New Guinea in Dennis O'Rourke's film *Cannibal Tours* clearly came for the experience of authentic tradition (condensed into the awe and slight risk surrounding cannibalism). They're rather shocked at the lack of modern amenities, however, and would like to help the "natives" modernize, a path, after all, they must inevitably walk. Of course, by the time the tourists arrive, the natives are already what Dean MacCannell calls "ex-primitives" (1994), problematizing that strange simultaneity of the modern and the traditional. Inderpal Grewal (1996), Quetzil Castañeda (1996), and James Clifford (1997) also complicate the relations among travel, power, and writing.

Of course, we may be unwise to disdain the role of tourists in these transnational articulations. For example, an army spokesman in 1986 admitted to me that the rebellious town of Santiago Atitlán on the volcano-lined Lake Atitlán had escaped scorched-earth annihilation and subsequent resettlement as a "model village" because of the many tourists in the area (see also Simon 1987). Tourist dollars—which are earned at underpaid service jobs in the United States (Guatemala is not a high-end tourist destination)—are important in helping families survive the devastation of the war and, as I explore in subsequent chapters, to value indigenous identity markers (see also Hinshaw 1988).

19. The deployment of the U.S. National Guard in the highlands of Guatemala is part of low intensity conflict. As in the model villages, these soldiers in uniform perform "humanitarian" projects, road building, vaccination campaigns, and other "development work."

can academic must include the image other bodies have of me, which includes bundles of stereotypes, images, and histories. As such, I am always already participating in identificatory processes informed by my own imaginings and fantasies, and at the same time, I figure in the fantasies of others.

It is also unpleasant to acknowledge that all of us gringos are drawn to Guatemala through the attractions of similar imaginings—of traditional Indian culture, unpaved roads, dangerous hygiene practices ("Don't drink the water!"), war, poverty, and a weak currency that makes it really cheap.[20] Guatemala is rife with the signs of third-world backwardness that allow us to deny coevalness (Fabian 1983) and thus give us the magic frisson of going back in time, the hope of maybe lending a hand as they step over into modernity, and, of course, the winning of our anthropological fieldwork spurs.[21] But Guatemala is complexly articulated to modern transnationalism, and part of what I am trying to evoke here are the multiple strands linking Guatemala with the rest of the world. These strands complicate "home" and "the field" (Gupta and Ferguson 1997; Kearney 1996) and serve to situate me and this project as part of much larger, on-going relationships. These interconnections mean that there is no clear arrival scene for the solidarity worker or the anthropologist. We find tourists hanging out in isolated war-torn field sites and indigenous kids home from migrant work in the United States who have a better grasp of popular culture than the anthropologist—who makes a disappointing informant on the intricacies of Metallica lyrics. "My" informants show up at the American Anthropological Association meetings (AAA) as Ph.D.s wielding Derridean theory, or I find I'm the fourth interviewer of the day for a well-known Mayan intellectual. These aren't just the jokes of postmodernity (although this book is fascinated with jokes): they are important in complicating the field situation and the sorts of analyses that are possible. Power and counterpower become diffuse, and the self-fashioning going on in these busy and crowded postcolonial encounters is riddled with contradictions.

What may seem like uncanny boundary crossings (Mayan Ph.D.s, and U.S. popular culture penetrating remote villages) can also reassure us that we already live in a hybrid world (see chapter 6 on *mestizaje*) and that apparent differences have been domesticated. The very parallels that make solidarity so powerful (similarities between U.S. and Guatemalan government repression) may also lull us into assuming that this is a homey place. Solidarity and gringa self-fashioning may too often assume the humanist

20. Part of the attraction of risk is often its simultaneity with privilege (like tradition's relation to modernity). Our insurance plans include the provision for air lifting us out.

21. The first question at my first job interview was "Can you explain to us how this is fieldwork? It sounds like you lived in the city and did interviews in offices."

We may also be susceptible to the romantic spell of the intrepid gringa, an adventuress braving harsh and dangerous conditions for a good cause. Crossing crocodile-infested jungle rivers, climbing mountains, enduring squished-tight bus rides, outsmarting the military and Civil Patrol who try to keep areas off limits, bringing back tales from the militarized highlands, and going weeks without a good cup of coffee—these are experiences unavailable outside of movies for most gringas. Highly pleasurable, too, are the positive responses from territorially incarcerated Guatemalans unable to travel so freely (at least before the early nineties) and from exiles stuck in Mexico thankful for information. Such stories return high yields in cultural capital back in the United States and legitimate our social science through the vividness of participant observation's "being there."

In a similar mode, it is also extremely pleasurable to be the object of Guatemalan solidarity work: to be the addressee of testimonial, to have people thank you for listening to their stories, and to have Rigoberta Menchú repeat her story on your college campus with the object of winning over your identification. Being hailed, or called out in this way functions like a seal of approval in these days of intense critique of the white first-world I-eye (Kondo 1990). Recourse to the politics of solidarity can offer a space of innocence for the gringa, a site cleansed by good intentions and activist "politics," from which we can still speak unproblematically of the Other.[26]

Pains   The instability of this position, however, became clear when I confronted the unexpected heterogeneity of the *pueblo* expressed in splits in the popular movement along lines of political strategy, ethnic identity, and racism. As I explore throughout the book, the struggles over unity and difference within the field are fierce and problematize any attempt at a solid intervention. The webs of meaning that situated my then-solid understandings of nation and ethnicity in Guatemala (including Menchú's testimonial and the genealogies in Arias 1990; Frank and Wheaton 1984; Harnecker 1984; Andersen 1983; and Payeras 1983) posit a teleology of revolution and indigenous consciousness-raising and organizing. In these "partial" stories (our partiality incited through the careful hegemony work of testimonial, and of course, partially true), the Maya are understood to form a tributary in the mighty river of solid revolutionary unity (*El Pueblo Unido Jamás Será Vencido* [the people united will never be defeated]). The tremendous cost in lives both Maya and ladino in pursuit of this goal gives this narrative a terrible, historic weight.

Of course, this unity was always contested (if not always publicly), but in

---

26. I thank Marcia Klotz for continuing discussions of how to simultaneously do politics and admit our complicity.

the mid-1980s there was a major split in the EGP (Guerrilla Army of the Poor), a member of the umbrella guerrilla group the URNG, when Commander Benedicto (Mario Payeras) left with many indigenous (and ladino) cadres.[27] The split was about many things, but the ethnic issue seems to have played an important role. Suddenly indigenous identification was seen as dangerous by many of my friends. The split felt like a betrayal to revolutionary Guatemalans and to many gringos involved in solidarity who sided with the EGP. For the URNG, it must have seemed an atomization they could ill afford given the disastrous currents of the war.

The fault lines and what was at stake were not especially clear to me as a benighted young gringa. Although there was clear competition to woo foreign solidarity workers to the different sides, the space of terror meant that no one was willing to talk openly about the guerrillas in general, much less the split. I realized only later that if I talked to or worked with certain people, then lines of information and of friendship with others, including other gringos in the solidarity movement, would be cut. Attempts to understand why were often met with silence or a curt, "You don't ask those questions!" Gaps in my understanding of these events may have been unavoidable given my concern to maintain solidarity and my discomfort in suggesting I knew better than a Guatemalan about their internal issues. A fluidary practice might be more willing to question but cannot evade these problems.

Charles Hale confronted similar issues as an *internacionalista* (solidarity activist) in his work on the Atlantic Coast of Nicaragua, although less fettered by secrecy and in a situation where the differences were quite clear between Sandinista and Miskitu. "The expectation was that *internacionalistas* acted in accordance with cadres' assessments of the revolution's needs and priorities, rarely dissented, and in the case of political disagreement always deferred. The more immersed in my research I became, the more these assumptions began to chafe" (1994, 10). Thanks to the extraordinary flexibility of Sandinista leaders (at the time, of course, a triumphant revolution) and his own ability to convince both sides of the usefulness of his project, Hale was able to conduct shuttle fieldwork, moving between the two in a "tension-ridden research endeavor" that was ultimately successful. This could also describe fluidarity that attempts, as Hale did, to work closely yet be constantly critical.

When I began interviewing members of the emerging Mayan cultural rights movement in 1988 and 1989, many emphasized their Mayan identity

---

27. They formed what would later be called *Octubre Revolucionario* (Revolutionary October). For their analysis, see the journal *Otra Guatemala,* published in Mexico, and *Opinión Política;* see also C. Smith (1990b and 1992).

but reiterated strongly that their projects paralleled the demands of the popular movement. However, some of them expressed anger and frustration at the ladino-dominated Left because of its exclusion of Mayan demands and representations, because the guerrillas used the Maya as cannon-fodder in ways similar to the army, and, as one or two suggested, because the guerrillas themselves had massacred indigenous people.[28] These claims have yet to be documented in full. However, David Stoll (1993) details guerrilla murders of suspected army spies in the Ixil area, and the demobilization, with its accompanying increase in public discussion of the war's seamier engagements, is giving weight to stories once scoffed at as army propaganda (*New York Times,* 4 September 1997).

The testimonials of Rigoberta Menchú and others, and the large number of indigenous combatants in the guerrilla organizations, suggest that many Maya found them a hospitable site of struggle. In turn, the revolutionary organizations were pushed by the incorporation of so many indigenous people (C. Smith 1990b, 271) to theorize the relations among class, ethnicity, and nationalism and to create more equal relations among Maya and ladino, supporting Mayan customs as much as possible given their mobility and attacking racism in self-criticism sessions (Simon 1988; Díaz-Polanco 1987; Harbury 1994; author interviews). However, many other indigenous people left the organizations, some as part of larger splits, some fed up with what they perceived as ongoing racist discrimination. What is undeniable is that despite the large numbers of Mayan combatants, there were no indigenous commanders representing the guerrillas in the peace talks, and there are few ranking officials who are Maya.[29]

Unlike the Sandinistas, the URNG was losing the war. Combined with the ferocity of the army's counterattack, the dispersal of organization, and the paranoia of a hunted exile, the URNG has not been particularly flexible in dealing with ethnic difference. This is in part because the official positions rest on a species of class reductionism. Though guerrilla organizations— the ORPA and the EGP especially—have published sophisticated analyses acknowledging racism as an axis of exploitation, class remains the primary and solid antagonism in the last instance (C. Smith 1990b). In turn, au-

28. The army, which now boasts several Mayan generals, makes similar claims in its counterinsurgency propaganda.
29. An exception was the murdered Commander Everardo, Harbury's husband. When the journalist Joel Simon queried Rolando Morán, high commander of the EGP, on this issue, Morán sidestepped: "There are many indigenous commanders, just no high commanders. The EGP has total respect for indigenous culture and each ethnicity's rights and customs. . . . The Guatemala of the future will be multiethnic, and we will absorb all the elements of indigenous culture. There are indigenous commanders; they head up columns and units" (from an unpublished interview transcript, October 1994, with thanks to Joel!).

tonomous Mayan organizing often elicits powerful resistance. As Miguel Angel Reyes Illescas, URNG advisor, said in 1994, "We have learned from the experience of Nicaragua. Indigenous issues are just an opening for the CIA. We are very afraid that this will end up just like in Europe, with fratricidal conflicts that tear us apart."[30] Carol Smith asks, "What kept Guatemalan Marxists so orthodox?" and answers, "Mainly because they too fear a 'race war' unless cultural 'difference' is controlled by some other form of solidarity—and for Marxists the best candidate for solidarity is class solidarity. Otherwise, the ladino nation risks becoming a Maya nation" (1992, 13).

Despite often very conscientious efforts to attack internalized Mayaphobia, the ladinos who control the Guatemalan Left maintain many of the categories, stereotypes, and fantasies that motivate ladino politicians and state bureaucrats.[31] They are nationalist, and that nation is imaged as modern (Chatterjee 1990; J. Collier 1997). This is very similar to what Hale found in Nicaragua:

> [Despite their] emphasis on democratic participation and empowerment, Sandinistas did not dispense with a deeply ingrained association of Miskitu consciousness, identity, and demands with cultural backwardness. And despite great commitment to egalitarian economic change, they found it little easier than their Somocista predecessors to fathom Indian economic organi-

---

30. He is referencing the CIA arming and training of indigenous Miskitu contras (counterrevolutionaries) against the Sandinista government. Reyes Illescas has written thoughtfully elsewhere (1985) of the questions around nation, agrarian reform, ethnicity, and the "*indio nuevo*" (new Indian). His written analysis of the different historic and revolutionary theories is nuanced: "Class and ethnicity entail specific properties that are not antagonistic; recognizing that these specificities create different rights for indigenous people" will help us better understand the ethnic-national question and why indigenous people are participating in the revolution (1985, 63). However, he notes with apprehension "the 'racist' ideologies of one strata of indigenous youth who deny class struggle" (1985, 63).

In turn, indigenous issues have also been a site for articulation and at least partial reconciliation. In 1988, the Center for Integral Studies of Community Development (CEIDEC), an exile organization then based in Mexico City, began monthly meetings to address the "Ethnic-National Question." The meetings were open to all, although CEIDEC was identified with the Payeras contingent. Each month, a guest speaker (including Severo Martínez Peláez, Héctor Díaz-Polanco, and Gustavo Porras Castejón, later the government representative in the peace talks) would lecture in the morning. Then participants would break into small groups to discuss the issues before returning to a plenary discussion. I was able to participate for six months in this extraordinary undertaking, which continued through 1992 and produced several volumes of collected papers (CEIDEC 1992).

31. Some of this class reductionism may be attributed to the omnipresence of Severo Martínez Peláez's analysis in *Patria del Criollo,* which, as noted, is required reading at the National University and in many secondary schools. Carol Smith (1991) suggests that the book is read under both right-wing governments and in left-wing study groups.

zation as anything more than traditional forms badly in need of modernization. Most important, a radically new version of Nicaragua nationalism . . . retained a Mestizo standard of cultural homogeneity. (1994, 35–36)

This seems similar to Guatemalan revolutionaries' hopes: that the Maya will
be freed from their chains when they take off their distinctive *traje* and unite
behind battle fatigues (C. Smith 1991).

Even in the late 1990s, it is still seen as a betrayal by some Guatemalans
and gringos to appear to side with different tendencies, and it is still
difficult—in terms of the reactions of friends, and in terms of my self-
definition as a gringa in solidarity—to suggest that the lines between
friends and enemies are not always clear and that the efforts to form unitary, solid identities from wounded body politics can be violent, exclusionary, and disfiguring in their own right. This in turn has forced me to examine the deep investments that I and many gringas have in particular stories
about Guatemala (like the *pueblo* united against the state) and our unwill-
ingness to listen to certain voices. The Quincentennial has pushed me to listen to the Mayan experience of unity and to contest (in part through this
book) the class and "race war" reductionism of *compañeros* on the Left (as a
result, some of them no longer speak to me).

However, I must also confess to enjoying a compensatory pleasure in
making arguments in favor of valuing diversity (listening to Mayan demands
or, alternatively, to the points of view of state workers). I began working with
the Maya movement in 1988. In 1989 I went to graduate school, where I was
confronted with powerful critiques of my race and sexuality privilege and
my blindness to that privilege. My Marxist feminism and solidarity work
around Central America did not save me from racism or homophobia. Demands from fellow students and the texts of feminists of color and others to
shut up and listen, to let them represent themselves, closely echoed the demands I was hearing from Mayan activists—except that in Guatemala, these
critiques were directed at Guatemalan ladinos, and at me only tangentially.[32] In fact, they called me out, in similar ways to my hailing as a solidarity activist: as a North American, I was encouraged to speak these truths to
the ladinos and gringos I had access to. Though I have felt shocked and
horrified by the overt racism of many of my ladino *compañeros,* in seeking
ways to be in fluidarity I have to admit that it is comfortable to displace such
critiques from me to them, where I once again am allowed to inhabit the
pleasant place of benevolence.

32. The list of texts that demanded I listen is very long. I have been very influenced by
Mohanty et. al. (1991), Trinh (1989), Spivak (1987), Anzaldúa (1987), Moraga (1983), Lorde
(1984), Said (1978).

Part of the difficulty of writing this book has been giving up the pleasure of pure heroines and villains and realizing how much my sense of self as a "nice gringa" was dependent on those clear-cut boundaries. In the 1980s, Central America became a space of utopic possibilities for many gringas, especially after the Sandinista triumph in 1979. The revolutionary movements promised, through enormous sacrifice and pain, to realize the hopes for justice, equality, and a fair distribution of wealth that seemed so distant in the Reaganite United States. The subsequent defeats of the revolutionary movements on the battlefield, in the voting booth, and at the negotiating table are painful blows.[33] As Rey Chow suggests for socialist scholars of the People's Republic of China (PRC), "now disillusioned with the China they sanctified[,] . . . the[ir] grief is tremendous" (Chow 1993, 12). Many gringos, myself included, try to disavow this grief and hold on to the belief that the sides are still clearly opposed.[34] This book is an attempt to come to terms with this loss of a certain future and an exploration of the struggles to fashion a different, more contingent one.

So I want to be very clear that solidarity is in part about enjoyment and about forms of self-fashioning that may not be very self-reflexive. As gringos, we rely on heroes and villains. We feel more content with ourselves when we are positioned as moral subjects against the voracious and unjust power structure and as the vehicles of justice for the victims whose side we take. Gayatri Spivak's shorthand for such positions vis-à-vis these self-consolidating others, "white men saving brown women from brown men," is taken from the British intervention in *sati* (widow burning) that served as a justification for colonialism (1988a, 297). We need to rigorously explore the ways our interventions as "white people saving brown people from slightly less-brown people" may maintain colonialist-style relations, may blind us to difference among these people, and are integral to consolidating a subject-position as gringa.

Fables of Imperfect Rapport and Violent Disruption   The fables of rapport (Visweswaran 1994, 29) that undergird solidarity are increasingly revealed as imperfect. Open-armed welcome may be more pragmatic than personal,

33. For courageous description of a personal reaction to the Sandinista defeat, see Lancaster (1992).

34. There has been a mass exodus of solidarity, journalist, and anthropological gringos from Nicaragua and El Salvador—where to outside observers it appears that revolutions have ground down into depressing in-fighting and drawn-out autopsies on the corpse of the good struggle. These gringos have relocated to Guatemala (and now Chiapas), where the wars are just recently over and there is an apparent new historical subject stepping onto the stage in the form of indigenous struggle.

more tied to historically specific tactical needs than one's "niceness." We often fail in attempts to identify with the Guatemalan people and to differentiate ourselves from our government, from tourists, and so on. Quincentennial Guatemala offers special challenges for gringa self-fashioning, which is no more solid than the *pueblo*.

Abigail Adams suggests that this failure of rapport may inhere in the very ambivalence of the term *gringa* (A. Adams 1997). It is generally a negative term, and few Guatemalans would be so churlish as to call you a gringo to your face.[35] (The exception is men's running commentary on city streets, which is deeply concerned with lighter skin and hair color, as evidenced in the wolf calls of *"canche"* or *"güera,"* which meld national, phenotypic, and gender identities.) *Gringo* is defined as "disparaging" in the dictionary and carries a burden of hatred. A possibly apocryphal origin story attributes Mexican coinage during the U.S. invasion, as a way to tell the green-uniformed yanquis to go away ("green-go!"). (For other valences, see A. Adams 1997.) People would often laugh, surprised, if I self-identified as gringa. They might say, "Oh no, you're not really a gringa. You're not like those others," which would always please me. It seems to mean "ugly American" and imperialist, condensing many highly charged emotions around global inequalities, wealth, color, cultural capital, commodity access, military aid, rude tourists, and complex imaginaries of Rambo and Madonna. Friends from Canada and Europe working in Guatemala strongly resisted inclusion in the term, even as a joke.[36] Very close Guatemalan friends might use it as a term of endearment, but so powerful is the word that it was some-

---

35. Children in highland villages, who in general do not know much Spanish, have run after me shouting the word *gringo* (or simply, "foto!"—thus situating me as a technologically mediated spectator). I don't know what they think when they use this term. Army counterinsurgency has attempted to depict the guerrilla as a foreign presence, as outside agitators rather than a response to local injustice, by using the terms *canche* (blonde) and *gringo* for combatants. Subcommander Marcos of the Zapatista National Liberation Army in Chiapas was accused by the Mexican press of being a gringo (and a gay). His lyrical and fluidary response— that he was a gay in San Francisco, a Catholic in Northern Ireland, a Palestinian in Israel, and so on—is one of the reasons the Zapatista rebellion has been labeled the first postmodern guerrilla uprising.

36. While in Guatemala, I sang with a musical group composed of foreigners. We performed mainly covers of *nueva cancion* (new song), with some pop, doo-wop, and international folk songs, at *peñas* (music clubs), parties, and benefits. Several of the U.S. citizens thought *"Gringas Satánicas"* (Satanic Gringas) would be a fun name that would lampoon the term while (although I did not theorize it this way at the time) differentiating ourselves from those "other" gringas—at least the ones who couldn't laugh at themselves. Fortunately, given recent events, the suggestion was vetoed in favor of *"Las Importaciones No Tradicionales"* (Nontraditional Imports), a play on IMF-supported cash crops, or nontraditional exports, and our position as outsiders.

thing of a rite of passage when someone used it directly. It seems to be used extensively in referring to foreigners who are not present.

Despite my growing awareness of the U.S. imperial relation to Guatemala encoded in the term, when I encounter "imperfect rapport" with Guatemalans I consider friends and colleagues (with whom I was in solidarity), it is still a shock. One of my first contacts upon arriving in Guatemala in 1985 was the Chinese-Guatemalan anthropologist Myrna Mack Chang. Her enthusiastic support enabled our first research project, and she was a vital resource, guide, and mentor for me. She was a strong woman, a careful and avid anthropologist, and a scholar committed to social and political change, and I strongly identified with her. Despite her friendship and support, however, I was a gringa to her and to my other Guatemalan friends, an always problematic identification for those living daily the effects of thirty years of U.S.-backed dictatorship. In one-on-one discussions, or in overheard conversations, I was often startled at their anti-Americanism. For Guatemalans, my "gringo-ness," my marked identification with a hated government, bled through my self-identification as the friendly, politically committed researcher. Myrna especially chafed at our nationally marked privilege to go anywhere in the country and inquire about anything, when she felt trapped in the city. This difference, of course, was brutally re-marked by the government assassination of Myrna Mack Chang in September 1990. She was killed for doing the research and writing that gringas have done all along (Oglesby 1995). Her murder made clear that a Guatemalan anthropologist (despite her family's wealth and her international connections) was vulnerable in ways that gringas have not been. I am not necessarily easily distinguishable from the state that both protects me (to a point) against such violence and is feared and hated by my friends.

This does not mean Myrna's or any other Guatemalan's friendship is not sincere. The enormous energy that she and countless others give to forming transnational solidary body politics suggests a powerful similarity of purpose. But gringas may resist acknowledging the differences that lead people to respond to our good intentions with ambivalence or even violence, as in the almost fatal lynching of June Weinstock in 1994. She is a gringa fifty-something environmental activist who was using her vacation to study Spanish in Guatemala. In the months before her trip, the Guatemalan press (newspapers, magazines, and radio) was full of macabre stories of fattening houses and children's bodies found without organs, the body cavity stuffed full of dollars and a thank-you note in English. Guatemalan public discourse, which runs on rumors in the best of cases, was raging on speculation and hearsay about baby trafficking, child snatching, organ transplants, and the nefarious gringos behind it all.

Ms. Weinstock was strolling through San Cristobal in Alta Verapaz with the resident gringo Evangelical missionary. She patted a child on the head.

When the child's mother claimed soon after that the child was missing, suspicion fell on Weinstock. Apparently, a crowd formed and went through her things, finding nothing. She took refuge in the courthouse, which was stormed by townspeople who dragged Weinstock outside and began to beat her, an exercise that would continue for some three hours, including raping, stoning, and stabbing her, and later torching the courthouse. Community members finally left her for dead,[37] despite the attempts of the mother, child found, to intervene and stop the violence. The indigenous men beating June Weinstock said, "What are we if we do not protect our children?" (Kadetsky 1994, 26). The Evangelical pastor left her to her fate, claiming there was nothing he could do. He later told the U.S. television news team from *20/20* that he wished the army had come in and gunned down every man, woman, and child in the town. Five hours of the attack were filmed by local amateurs, the spectacle broadcast in its entirety on Guatemalan television. The U.S. press, generally silent on Guatemala, was full of spectacularizing stories in the dailies, *Time* magazine, and TV's *20/20*.[38]

Around the time of the attack, gringas living throughout Guatemala felt a sudden chill surround them when they went out in public. Neighbors with whom they'd had cordial relations became hostile, and white women with children—even when those children were clearly (phenotypically) their own—were accosted with hostile comments and often felt physically at risk. Many changed their habits, never going out alone. One friend was threatened with a machete after attending a christening in the department of El Quiché.

My first reaction to the Weinstock attack and these stories was to talk to as many gringas as I could. We tended to agree that the Mayan villagers were not to blame—a view echoed by solidarity organizations and in the progressive press. Instead, we pointed our fingers at the usual suspects: the army and right-wing elites. As Victor Perera wrote in the *Los Angeles Times* on May 1, 1994: "The mob attacks . . . may be part of a right-wing strategy to create a climate of instability hostile to human rights monitors. . . . The assailants were egged on by state road workers and unidentified outsiders" (1994a). In this reading, the military (through its journalist accomplices) stoked "national hysteria" through strategic placement of the sensationalist stories of baby snatching, thereby laying the groundwork for just such an outbreak. This strategy was meant to discourage the presence of solidarity foreigners (especially the newly deployed United Nations Mission to Guatemala [MINUGUA]) who were supporting popular organizations, monitor-

37. She was in a coma for months, although at last report she is slowly recuperating.

38. For a fuller description of the attack and its context, see A. Adams (1997). Adams has worked in a neighboring community.

ing the peace talks, and preparing evidence for the planned truth commission. "Military spokesmen claim they had no authority to intervene in a civil disturbance; with circumstantial but persuasive evidence, human rights activists accused the military of engineering the attack and hiring the road-workers to carry it out" (Kadetsky 1994, 26).

Because this was the real cause (the army as solid enemy), then, as an experienced Guatemalanist, I could read the reports on the beating in the U.S. press as straightforwardly racist. The indigenous people were portrayed yet again as savages, a representation that has historically served to justify state oppression. In making this argument, I could position myself as a white woman saving brown people from white interpretation.

In this quest to refuse a representation of the Indian as nasty and brutish and the gringa as a threat rather than a helpmeet, I also sought proof of a rationale underlying the attacks. Some newspaper accounts linked the rumors directly to the boom in international adoptions, often shady enterprises in which birth mothers are paid pittances to give up their children and gringos take for granted the *disponibilité* (availability) of the child—of course it's better to be raised in the United States than to sell Chiclets in the streets of Guatemala City.[39] Stories of babies being taken by powerful people and put to macabre uses (in cannibal feasts, vampiric rituals, and as magical mortar to make their buildings strong) have long histories and are transnational in scope.[40]

In a "third-world country" like Guatemala, which suffers from neoliberal policies imposed by the International Monetary Fund (IMF), and where infant mortality among the Maya is over fifty per one thousand births, how metaphorical *is* it to claim that a child has died because North Ameri-

39. Claudia Castañeda (personal communication) has carefully deconstructed these assumptions.

40. Victor Perera claims that "when the Spanish conquistadores invaded the Guatemalan Highlands in the 16th Century, Mayan mothers believed the men with pale complexions and blond beards were anemic and required the blood of brown-skinned infants to become well" (Perera 1994a). Vampire stories have traditionally carried such anxieties about gender, nation, ethnicity, technology, and age (see Latham 1995a). Although these stories are similar to the blood libel cases brought against Jews throughout Europe well into the twentieth century (Bacal n.d.), the fact that Jews were less powerful than the purveyors of the libels (as opposed to the less powerful Maya telling stories about gringa baby snatchers) suggests that these tales resonate more with the "race war" discourse that ladinos deploy against the Maya.

The disavowal of the baby-snatching rumors is also transnational: the U.S. State Department travel advisory following the attack warns citizens that the "*unfounded* rumors that foreigners are involved in the theft of children for the purpose of using their organs in transplants have led to threats and incidents of mob violence. . . . Travelers should avoid contact with children." The report reassures us that attacks have not occurred in "traditional tourist areas" (U.S. State Dept., Guatemala—Travel Warning, June 24, 1994; emphasis added). I thank Don Nelson for passing this advisory on.

cans stole its organs? As Guha (1983), Taussig (1987), Tsing (1993), Warren (1993), and others have discussed, such rumors are often extremely
clear readings of neocolonial transnational power relationships. Guatemala
is the third largest exporter of children for adoption among developing
countries. Guatemala's marginality in the world system and rural poor
people's marginality to the light-skinned urban elites who may earn thousands of dollars through facilitating such adoptions (and the rest of their
wealth from exploitation along similar axes) are foregrounded by these
rumors. Of course, the children of poor and indigenous people are also
"snatched" by the army's forced recruitment and by plantation labor con-
tractors for migrant work. These children are often returned dead: victims
of the war, malnutrition, or pesticides. Finally, another marginality that is
articulated through these rumors is that of women. It may be cliché to speak
of the triple oppression, but most Guatemalan women's lives are deeply
constrained by the multiple orthopedics of poverty, racism, and misogyny.
At the same time that they are accused of overproducing children and thus
undermining national progress, they enjoy limited access to information,
material methods, or the domestic relations of reproduction that would allow them control of their fertility.[41] As a gringa in solidarity, who grasps
these marginalities, I have a political stake in explaining the attack as in
some ways rational. Violence on the periphery is not a natural phenomenon, I want to insist, nor is it irrational. Its roots are deep and historical and
ineluctably linked to the world system, whether manifested in CIA coups,
M-16s in soldiers' hands, *maquila* production, transnational reproductive
politics, or the presence of tourists in highland villages.

I want to assign a rational reading to these rumors, one that resists reading the "natives" as savage. I want to read the rumors as Daniel Rothenberg
does, as an "extraordinary narrative, a vicious, poetic vision of exploitation,
marginality and fear. . . . The children of the poor are transformed into
commodities whose circulation yields enormous profits for the middlemen
and extended lives for the rich foreigners whose bodies now contain their
young, healthy organs" (Rothenberg 1994). But a great deal more must be
said about the work of condensation in these rumors, as I keep returning,
revulsed and fascinated, to the body on the ground, the wounded, no
longer solid body of that white woman—the gringa.

---

41. Dr. Carlos Pérez Avendaño in the daily *La Hora* recounts getting stuck in a traffic jam
and having to confront a pickup truck loaded with people, including an indigenous woman
with a child. He feels ashamed at the six square meters he has alone in his Mercedes. Arriving
late at his meeting, he comments on the traffic to his coworkers, who respond, "You're so
right—it's really unbearable: They need to stop having so many kids. APROFAM [the state-run
family planning organization] needs to hand out condoms and put IUDs in the *indias*, there
are already enough *indios*" (15 October 1993).

FROM SOLIDARITY TO FLUIDARITY

My desire for rationality keeps running into the spectacular violence of the attack—it is unnerving, uncanny, an elaborate public display of ambivalence and its effects. The attack condenses much of my ambivalence about doing fieldwork in and writing about Guatemala. I was in the United States, trying to write about Guatemala, when the attack occurred. Being at such a distance and reading and hearing about it from friends forcefully reminded me of my role as spectator—once out of the field, what happens to *participant*-observation? Spectatorship, as we know from film theory, is a fraught realm involved in meaning production and the very formation of the subject, as well as the guilty pleasures and terrors of voyeurism and passivity.[42] I am positioned through the North American eyewitness, the Evangelical missionary who left the white woman to her fate. I want to be a white woman saving a white woman from brown men. Instead, I am limited in my power both to intervene and to make sense of an action that seems to overflow with significance.

What does it mean when gringos are taken for baby snatchers, when members of a community beat and rape a gringa for three hours in what they take to be self defense? How am I to understand the dissonance between what I think I am doing (whether it be social science or solidarity) and what we are understood to be doing? I think the attack, part of the Quincentennial's complexity, is difficult for us gringas to deal with because it brings home the fact that we have to give up both our innocent victims and our clear-cut enemies. After fifteen years of the compromises and dirt of "democratization," the incorporation of terror and violence, the way repressive and ideological state apparatuses course through the body politic in the forms of the Civil Patrol and lynch mobs (making state and *pueblo* hard to tell apart), victims and enemies are not solid or timeless. As I argue throughout this book, they are formed in relation to each other, constantly in process, fluid. The *pueblo* we are in solidarity with is revealed as split, heterogeneous, asymmetrically gendered, and sometimes violent.

In turn, making the people of San Cristobal out as only dupes of an army misinformation campaign seems to miss much of what is happening there (see A. Adams 1997) and elsewhere in Guatemala. It recapitulates the denial of coevalness by positioning them as stupid, superstitious, easily manipulated, innocent victims of false consciousness and media propaganda. As such, it may well be a last-ditch attempt to save them for our own use (as brown people needing to be saved from black information). In turn, blaming the army for spreading the organ-stealing rumors both makes it magi-

(handwritten marginal note: good)

---

42. See Mulvey (1989), Silverman (1983), de Lauretis (1987), and Clover (1992), among others.

cally capable of creating any desired effect and is a way to hold on to a "bad guy" (although this story also *blames* the army for not intervening).[43]

Instead, we are forced to confront the possibility that the motivations of everyone involved are more complex and that perhaps we cannot account for them. Indeed, my attempts to instrumentalize the rumors of baby snatching as a military strategy disavow the fact that the account of army responsibility is itself a rumor. In fact, much of our understanding of Guatemala, our documentation, participant-observation, guided interviews, surveys, and so on is based on hearsay and rumor, on partial stories—both interested and incomplete. Meaning is endlessly deferred through the multiple and on-going decodings of news stories, official pronouncements, leaks, long discussions over drinks, and rumor, for Guatemalans and for anthropologists. This is always a condition of knowledge, especially in the space of death that Guatemala continues to inhabit, but admitting that rumors may be our only access to meaning forces us to question our hold on truth and problematizes our understandings and identifications.

I hope that by analyzing the disavowals that surround the attack on June Weinstock we can move toward what I have termed "fluidarity." Part of this move consists in acknowledging how partial, how incomplete, gringa subject-positions are. It means acknowledging a historic shift in the U.S. Left and in academia, where white feminists are critiqued by women of color, well-meaning liberals find ourselves called racists and homophobes, and Marxists are questioned by identity claims more complex than class. This situation may lead us to escape to an Other place, where we can be benevolent again, or to demand that other identities be stable and solid so that we can lean on them (as in saving a victim from a victimizer). Acknowledging that none of these identities are solid or a-historical may also help us to think beyond the responding white-guilt genre (without, of course, merely heaving a sigh of relief and going on with business as usual). This is vital because the self-flagellation of the "mea culpa move" deeply reinscribes the power of white North Americans and the powerlessness of everyone else. The critiques of power essential to fluidarity must go beyond these simple

43. This supposed capability of the army is not unlike the magic power many of us impute to the IMF and World Bank, or to U.S. foreign policy. They have massive and violent effects, but they have to work to get what they want—as do we.

Similarly, ruptures in some of these victim-perpetrator positionings tend to be rather violently rejected by solidarity gringos. The anthropologist David Stoll has earned a number of enemies by questioning a historiography of indigenous victims of state exploitation joining the guerrilla forces en masse because they are seen to unproblematically represent indigenous interests. In *Between Two Armies* (1993), he represents Maya-Ixil responses to the EGP guerrillas as ambivalent and criticizes the strategies of the guerrillas themselves. Although Mr. Stoll's style is a bit confrontational, I would suggest that the almost total rejection of his position (and often of him) points in part to the resistances discussed here.

binaries. As Gyan Prakash (1992) reminds us, to only condemn Western society as repressive runs the risk of muting heterogeneities within both sites and bolsters the Western versus third-world contrast that underpins the very power relations that anticolonial studies seek to destabilize.

One way that an account of identities as mutually constituted helps here at the outset is by making untenable the clear-cut self-versus-other relation that too often leads to the rut of guilty navel-gazing (which, of course, offers a certain enjoyment). I want to retain a notion of the positive and complex valences of fluidarity as a transnational and anthropological practice, while deeply questioning the disavowed technologies of self that are involved. I do not want to let gringas off the hook, nor do I want to ignore the complicity of solidarity in the on-going production of relations of oppression. One way of interrogating this position is to ask what sort of subject is constituted and what are the enjoyments of solidarity and anthropological work? How do identification and disavowal work in this transnational scene? However, although we must be aware of the paternalism of first-world benevolence, we also need activism, as well as strategies of writing that flow from a self-consciousness of, and political resistance to, the privilege that makes that benevolence possible.

The coming chapters are an attempt at fluidary analysis that holds on to the deep involvement of the global scene in Quincentennial Guatemala. As fluidary anthropologists, we cannot withdraw from these transnational relations, despite our carefully thrashed-out critiques of the power asymmetries that we produce, and that produce us, as we work within them. A major concern of my work is the porousness, and even lack, of clear-cut boundaries between the transnational and the national, between the nation and ethnic identity, between the state and civil society, between the modern and the authentically traditional, even between male and female. I will argue that this lack, this wounded body politic, necessitates the continuous production of such identities. Rather than assuming that I know an Indian, or a woman, or an enemy when I see one, I will focus here on the relations that continually produce such identifications. It is precisely at the sites of struggle and of production—the state, the school, and the family—that identifications are both reiterated and appropriated (as in the ALMG appropriating space in the state educational system). Fluidarity looks to these spaces and relations, rather than to any solid identity positions, in order to discern and support democratizing work. As Judith Butler suggests,

> The critical task for feminism is not to establish a point of view outside of constructed identities; that conceit is the construction of an epistemological model that would disavow its own cultural location and, hence, promote itself as a global subject, a position that deploys precisely the imperialist strategies

that feminism ought to criticize. The critical task is, rather, to locate strategies of subversive repetition enabled by those constructions, to affirm the local possibilities of intervention through participating in precisely those practices of repetition that constitute identities and therefore present the immanent possibility of contesting them. (Butler 1990b, 147)

I explore these reiterations and contestations throughout, seeking fluidary ways to describe state-indigenous, ladino-Maya, male-female-transvestite, and other relationalities.

For example, the work of solidarity to articulate a hegemonic narrative of Guatemala as "an international pariah" (with the corresponding pressures of trade sanctions, reductions in U.S. aid, and so on) includes complex articulations among the desires, resistances, manipulations, seductions, and lobbying of many Guatemalans, gringos, officials of various states, and UN workers (see chapter 8). The negotiations and repetitions involved in making a particular story into common sense—like the one I recounted about justified rebellion and counterinsurgency terror, or about the cultural rights of the Maya within the nation-state—are about articulations that momentarily constitute identities.

It can feel like a grievous loss to find that identities are contingent, that the *pueblo* is not united or the enemy solid and easily identifiable, that radical social change is not around the corner, and that our understandings are deeply partial—limited and incomplete. Friends in Guatemala call this mourning *revolucionostalgia,* and its powerful emotions are part of fluidarity (as are the pleasures I discussed—which we need to acknowledge, not repress). But discarding the idea of unified and homogeneous agents and of power uni-directionally deployed from the first world, or from the Guatemalan state, does not preclude struggles for justice and peace. I hope instead that it allows us to analyze frequently contradictory positions and the overdetermined nature of different struggles.[44]

This is the move that makes what has come to be called poststructuralism seem threatening to some kinds of politics—including those based on identity. If the subject of feminism, for example, does not exist as woman but is instead the effect of institutions and practices that produce the category of "woman" (and then never as a fixed identity), then how does one fight women's oppression? Laclau and Mouffe respond that, although there is

44. When I say *overdetermined,* I do not just mean multicausal—for example, that all the various accounts of the beating are partially true, each containing a kernel of "realness." Instead, I want to gesture toward the surplus of meaning that gives an event its symbolic power. Louis Althusser's (1971) sense of *overdetermination* is about the incomplete, open, and politically negotiable character of every identity and thus the constant (because never fully successful) attempts to "fix" that identity—to both hold it still and to repair it.

no original sexual division, there is overdetermination among diverse sexual differences that produces a systematic effect of sexual division. This in turn opens up an immense field of action (1985, 117–118). I argue that the same overdetermination affects national, ethnic, and gender differences—in that there *are* relations of oppression that are understood as such—but that such relations are not natural, timeless, given, or solid. Instead, they are produced through the struggles described in this book.

With the peace treaty signed in December 1996, it is surely appropriate to mourn the diminished prospects for rapid revolutionary change. However, some Maya now ask what would have happened if the revolution, without a single indigenous high commander, had won? Would this have unified and healed the wounded body politic, or would it have recapitulated historic exclusions and millenarian pain? Perhaps this very failure has created the conditions of possibility for what Rosa Luxemburg might call a more "mature" struggle, one in which the Maya are articulated in both the sense of "formed in relation to" and "represented," one that would have been impossible without the relations created by that struggle.[45] So, even though Quincentennial Guatemala may demand that we give up last instances and final guarantees, I think it is also about new forms of antagonism, because it opens up *every* place as a site of struggle, including the ter-

45. Slavoj Zizek cites Rosa Luxemburg, arguing against Eduard Bernstein's fear of seizing power too soon, and suggests that "the first seizures of power *are necessarily 'premature:'* the only way for the working class to reach its 'maturity,' to await the arrival of the 'appropriate moment' for the seizure of power, is to form itself, to educate itself for this act of seizure, and the only possible way of achieving this education is precisely the 'premature' attempts" (Zizek 1989, 59). Ernesto Laclau and Chantal Mouffe relate this to Luxemburg's theory of "spontaneism":

> [T]he working class is necessarily fragmented and the recomposition of its unity only occurs through the very process of revolution. . . . [Spontaneism] affirms the impossibility of *foreseeing* the direction of a revolutionary process. . . . What is at stake is not merely the complexity and diversity inherent in a dispersion of struggles . . . but also the constitution of the *unity* of the revolutionary subject. . . . We must concentrate not only on the plurality of forms of struggle but also on the relations which they establish among themselves and on the unifying effects which follow from them. . . . [This analysis multiplies] the points of antagonism and the forms of struggle . . . up to the point of exploding all capacity for control or planning of these struggles by a trade-union or political leadership. . . . The very logic of spontaneism seems to imply that the resulting type of unitary subject should remain largely indeterminate. (Laclau and Mouffe 1985, 10–11; emphases in original)

The Maya may not form a tributary in the great river of class-based revolutionary consciousness to be controlled by ladino commanders (and supported by solidarity gringas), but this does not mean that the struggle and the tremendous loss it entailed were in vain, or that it is over.

rain of the state. It is a moment bright with the promise and peril of unintended consequences.[46]

Fluidarity is a practice, not a recipe. As a writing strategy it does not follow a predetermined path but swerves, detours, and enfolds, as a way of embracing the multiple flows of identifications. Its practice includes supporting struggles like Jennifer Harbury's and the Guatemalan popular movement that line themselves up against the state, at the same time that it acknowledges such alignments as articulatory practices, changing both activists and the state (and thus I hope to escape the self-righteous binary of clean versus co-opted). Fluidarity must also identify with the wounded body of June Weinstock, a gringa imagined, for a wealth of material and fantasmatic reasons, as a threat. Fluidarity understands that Guatemala's counterinsurgency state is powerful but insists that it is not all-powerful. In turn, fluidarity refuses to see the people of Guatemala as only victims or dupes but suggests that nodes of power (both resistive and destructive) are scattered throughout Guatemala's wounded body politic. Similarly, I am not arguing that gringas in solidarity are dupes or victims of propaganda. This would ignore the complex productivity of the gringa-formed-in-relation that I've suggested here, the often unconscious processes of identification. Not only gringas but Maya, ladino, state politician, and revolutionary fighter—all of these bodies politic—are formed through identifications that Diana Fuss describes as "erotic, intellectual, and emotional. They delight, fascinate, puzzle, confuse, unnerve and sometimes terrify. They form the most intimate and yet the most elusive part of our unconscious lives" (1995, 2). Thinking of these as wounded bodies politic foregrounds the pain of a politics of affiliation that must recognize "the sacrifices, reversals, and reparations involved in every imaginary identity formation" (Fuss 1995, 7).

46. I refer the reader to Stuart Hall's brilliant "The Problem of Ideology: Marxism without Guarantees," where he discusses the impossibility of the economic as determinate, in terms of a final closure on the domain of ideology.

Understanding "determinancy" in terms of setting of limits, the establishment of parameters, the defining of the space of operations, the concrete conditions of existence, the "givenness" of social practices, rather than in terms of the absolute predictability of particular outcomes, is the only basis of a "marxism without final guarantees." It establishes the *open horizon* of marxist theorizing—determinancy without guaranteed closures. The paradigm of perfectly closed, perfectly predictable, systems of thought is religion or astrology, not science. . . . "Determination in the last instance" has long been the repository of the lost dream or illusion of theoretical *certainty*. And this has been bought at considerable cost, since certainty stimulates orthodoxy, the frozen rituals and intonations of already witnessed truth. (1996, 45)

THREE

State Fetishism and the Piñata Effect

Catastrophe and the Magic of Culture

We all know the fascination which the love, or horror, of the state exercises today.
MICHEL FOUCAULT

The state is a piñata. Everyone hits us and everyone expects us to give them sweets.
JUAN DANIEL ALEMÁN, presidential secretary

STATE FETISHISM

A fluidary analysis has repercussions for how we understand and interact with that apparently most solid of entities, the state. Here my "partial" ethnography takes us from the personal to the political, from the status of gringa self-fashioning to a fascination with the state, and from the state as a bounded thing that homogenizes and hegemonizes to the state as dreamwork.[1] I examine state functioning and its relation to the Maya through theories of power, drawing on Karl Marx, Michel Foucault, and psychoanalysis to investigate its contradictory, fetishlike qualities. Though some hold that the state is identified with economics—in other words, that it represents the interests of one class (Poggi 1978, 130)—I suggest that, given the catastrophic situation of countries like Guatemala, much of the state's power comes from the way it links the power of the modern with the magic of "culture."

In Guatemala, as elsewhere in Latin America, Africa, and Asia, "the state" is the primary actor in "democratization"—a body image presented to both internal and external audiences. For example, if "it" is elected and civilian, then the entire country is legitimate on the world stage and benefits from foreign aid, higher credit ratings, increased tourism, and "most favored nation status."[2] Most classical theories of the state describe it as Sovereign (the

---

1. In chapter 8, I link this dreamwork to framework (in the sense of a frame as both context and also an internal structure that gives shape and support).

2. A billion dollars of foreign assistance has been promised for implementation of the Peace Accords in Guatemala; the aid is to come primarily from the United States and the European Community (EC).

Figure 7. National Palace, Guatemala City. Postcard. Copyright Thor Janson.

State with a capital S), with a reason of its own, speaking the language of law, and actively making decisions (in other words, as solid). This sovereign State has been described by Thomas Hobbes as Leviathan (1985), by Georg Hegel as performing the necessary function of unifying an inherently fragmented society (in Poggi 1978, 121), and by Max Weber as claiming "the monopoly of the legitimate use of physical force within a given territory" (in Gerth and Mills 1958, 78).[3] These theories—along with various forms of Marxism that seek to smash the state—reify it into a thing that acts, speaks, responds, and can be broken. Thus "the state" functions as a fetish. Though actually composed of many charismatic and bureaucratic individuals, institutions, interest groups, laws, enforcers, and time-encrusted rituals, it appears to be a unitary entity with a will of its own.

In Guatemala, with the return to civilian rule, "the state" is increasingly the site of demand for Mayan and popular groups. It is expected to fix past injustices and to repair economic and political dysfunctions, and it thereby carries a certain legitimacy. To draw on psychoanalytic theory, this state is like the manifest content of a dream. It has a material presence in the pal-

3. For a far more thorough overview of theories of the state in relation to historically situated analyses of the Guatemalan state than I can gloss here, please see Carol Smith (1990b).

ace, where people demonstrate; in the Congress, where people lobby; in the press, where it acts; and in the army, which people try to avoid. Classic theory sees the state as clearly separate from civil society—which it seeks to represent, protect, or, in Marxism, ruthlessly exploit in the interests of economic elites. The continuing sturdiness of this division is manifest in Guatemala, where the parties to the peace process were the state and the guerrillas (pretenders to the state). Everyone else was represented by the Association of Civil Sectors (ASC), which could make suggestions but could not participate directly in discussing the accords.

Fetishes function to cover over a trauma or a wound and to hide a latent content. I argue in this chapter that Guatemala's catastrophic history—including Conquest, foreign intervention, the civil war, and the scramble since 1985 to constitute a functioning civilian government—demystifies this sovereign subject of the State (as clearly differentiated from Civil Society). Although the state obviously retains power, in Quincentennial Guatemala people seem to see through the manifest content of a State wielding "legitimate violence" to its latent workings: its illegitimate repressive apparatuses, the bumbling bureaucracy, and the corruption. Though there is constant discussion of the division between "state" and "civil society" (as in the ASC)—and among gringo analysts about a "strong" or "weak" state (C. Smith 1990b)—in practice Maya and ladino seem to find those boundaries to be porous. This porousness encourages struggles for representation with the state as a site of struggle. And in turn the state is responding in discourse and practice to the demands that it ensure rights and support "development" and "culture" (including bankrolling the development of Mayan cultural difference). These struggles, paradoxically, legitimate the state as both the site of demand and the stake of the struggle. These contradictions were nicely summed up by Juan Daniel Alemán, President Serrano's secretary, who said, "The state is a piñata. Everyone hits us and everyone expects us to give them sweets."

Though I retain the useful fetish-effect of "the state" in the following chapters, I also argue that the political work around ethnic, national, and gender identities is demystifying the state and reminds us, as Foucault says, that "power is exercised from innumerable points in the interplay of nonegalitarian and mobile relations" (Foucault 1980, 96). By examining the history of the Ministry of Culture here (and other Maya-state interactions throughout the book), I argue that the state is not a solid, repressive power that acts unilaterally on an already constituted "civil society" but that these "spheres" are mutually constitutive. I suggest that Guatemalans are able to pull apart the weave of the state to examine, as well as act on, enter into, and contest, its individual strands of ministries, secretaries, Congressional offices, monies allotted and misspent, and so on. Struggles over culture and history, over modernity and tradition, and over Mayan and national identity articulate the state, modify its identity, and penetrate the apparent bound-aries between state and civil society. This is in part because of the chronic legitimation crisis caused by decades of civil war, an inferiority complex as-sociated with being "so far from God, so close to the United States," and the openness engendered by the democratization process (as limited as that process may be).

However, there is more to the work of the fetish than merely seeing through to the latent content. Playing detective and getting down to how the fetish "really" works completely misses the magic act. Given that Guate-malans, like many peoples, see through the legitimation claims of their states, how are we to understand the "piñata effect"—the contradictory but simultaneous moves of hitting the state and expecting sweets? How are we to understand the state's continuing aura, its power—what Michael Taussig calls "Maleficium: State fetishism"? As he suggests, pulling the state apart—marking it with a small *s,* or dismissing it as a fiction—does not account for "the peculiar sacred and erotic attraction, even thralldom, combined with disgust, which the State holds for its subjects." It is this "double helix of at-traction and repulsion" in Quincentennial Guatemala that I explore in this chapter (Taussig 1992, 111).

THE NATION-STATE IN RUINS

First I'd like to explore the repulsion and disgust occasioned, I argue, by the many antagonisms condensed into the Quincentennial. One of its most po-tent effects has been to denaturalize the relation between ladino and na-tional identity combined with control of the state. Analysts concerned with ethnic issues often call Guatemala's government a "ladino state" (C. Smith 1990b; Fischer and Brown 1996), but those who prefer class analysis (Jonas 1991) emphasize the often violent exclusion of most ladinos from state decision-making. It is vital to remember that historically those with access to state power have been both ladino and rich (in other words, "ladino" is not a homogenous category).

The struggles of the last fifty years, including "the longest-running civil war in Latin America," have coalesced around class antagonism—but it is also vital to remember that these struggles have been about *which* ladinos will control the state apparatus. The Quincentennial exposes how class is constantly interpenetrated by ethnicity. As Carol Smith suggests, there are class differences between Guatemalan Indians and ladinos that depend on ethnicity as well as income and control of the means of production. These differences were "reinforced by a linear reading of Guatemala's political history, which 'blamed' culture rather than real political relations for the continued existence of two separate and unequal groups" (C. Smith 1990b, 72). Verena Stolcke (n.d.) has argued that unequal class relations in supposedly free, democratic states are often inextricably linked to racism, both to explain why groups of people fail, despite the so-called level playing field, and to support the self-image of those who, despite membership in a favored "race," are still in bad shape. This is the old "we may be poor, but at least we're not . . ." ploy, in which the wounds of class division are bandaged by identification along ethnic lines. The Quincentennial is strangely marked by state violence against ladinos of all classes and by ladinos (many of them former exiles) holding all of the positions of power in the state. In turn, many ladinos, regardless of whether they're Right or Left, rich or poor, unite against Mayan demands for power-sharing through fearsome warnings of a "race war." This suggests that although many are excluded from state power, the Quincentennial challenges their shared sense that the state is their rightful terrain.

I think this is in part because most ladinos are nationalists, like Nicaragua's Sandinistas described by Charles Hale and India's independence activists described by Partha Chatterjee. They associate a successful state with "rationalizing and reforming the 'traditional' culture of their people," including "science, technology, rational forms of economic organization, [and] modern methods of statecraft" (Chatterjee 1990, 237). As I discuss in chapters 6 and 7, ladino identity is closely tied to notions of modernity. Speaking Spanish, wearing "western" clothing, and enjoying access to advanced technology has historically defined ladinos as against the tradition, superstition, and backwardness of indigenous culture. As Renato Rosaldo (1988) points out, the powerful tend to represent themselves "without culture," except of course for "high" or "universal" culture (which is one of the sites of struggles in the Ministry of Culture). It is frequently suggested that ladinoization, or assimilation to the "modern" and "universal" (either through education and "development" or the violence of ethnocide) is the "ladino state's" policy toward the Maya (Fischer and Brown 1996; Wilson 1995; C. Smith 1990b; Carmack 1988).

However, the Quincentennial—with the Nobel Peace Prize, Mayan organizing, and Convention 169, which all point to the blood on those "modern," "civilized" hands—has increasingly revealed ladino culture as a problem. The sudden fashionableness of indigenous identity is pushing ladinos to frame a reply, a culture of their own as a counter. Rather than assuming that the ladinos represent national culture to be emulated by nonnational ethnic people, new language informed many responses to the Quincentennial ("All the ethnicities must be involved in forming Guatemala's national future, and that means the *ladino ethnicity* as well" [*Prensa Libre,* 13 October 1992; emphasis added]). In fact, I suggest that the term *culture* is taking on a different meaning in the context of the Quincentennial. It is becoming the concern of an increasingly governmental state, extending a promise of

Figure 8. Tikal, a Nation in Ruins. Photo by author.

identity and simultaneously undergirding historic antagonisms (an issue I take up again with *mestizaje* in chapter 6).

If culture was once a mark of powerlessness, Mayan organizing is re-articulating *culture* as a sign of power, throwing previously unproblematic ladino identifications into question. Edeliberto Cifuentes, professor of history at the National University, admitted, "What can the ladinos do? Our own identity is suddenly in crisis. Indians have their own organizations, their organic cultures, and ladinos want to be a part of this, but they have not developed their own project of what the country should be like. We can no longer teach a history that erases difference or talk of a unity that doesn't exist. We do not have a nation yet." The editorialist Mario Roberto Morales wrote, "The mestizo is pathetic, an imitator, full of complexes, a schizoid personality. He hates his Indian mother and lives on fantasies of his Spanish father. His is a divided conscience" (*Prensa Libre,* 15 December 1992). A ladino social scientist echoed this sort of melancholia in an interview with me: "Ladinos reject Rigoberta's Nobel Prize so strongly because she is a symbol of the unification of the Maya, that they are flourishing, strong, homogeneous, everything that the ladinos are not. They have culture, but the ladinos are completely disenchanted."

This crisis of cultural identity is mapped by many ladinos as a crisis of the nation-state. I asked a recently returned ladina exile how it felt to be back, and she said, "I wish I were an archaeologist." When I asked why, she said, "Because it's all a ruin." The theme of the annual seminar of the Business Association of Guatemala on October 30, 1992, was "Does Guatemala Have a National Strategy?" The ministers of finance and defense participated in the seminar, along with the president of the Coordinating Committee of Agricultural, Commercial, Industrial, and Financial Associations (CACIF) and a Catholic bishop involved in the peace process, and they agreed in general that Guatemala did not. The moderator, Francisco Pérez de Antón, editor of the weekly newsmagazine *Crónica,* summed up the proceedings by joking, "We sound a lot like Columbus. We don't know where we're going, we don't know where we are when we get there, and we're doing it all on borrowed money!"

This sense that Guatemala is a disaster grows out of both the effects of its unenviable position in the world economy (as a small export-oriented country) and the deep illegitimacy of the elites and the state. For thirty years, the state was the army, and the dividing line between the military and the civilian is still quite porous, at times indiscernible.[4] Although elections

---

4. General Alejandro Gramajo, who was defense minister during the government of Vinicio Cerezo and has been indicted in the United States for torture and murder, was also a presidential candidate for the 1995 elections. General Ríos Montt became president of the Congress in 1994 and hoped to change the Constitutional ban on former de facto leaders running

were held periodically (and one civilian was elected in 1965 after signing a secret pact with the military), the results were often ignored, or power changed hands through coups d'etat (in 1982, General Ríos Montt; in 1983, General Mejía Víctores).[5] By the mid-1980s, the counterinsurgency war had touched almost every family in Guatemala. Although the brunt of the violence fell on inhabitants of rural areas, neither the rich nor the powerful were spared, and the military's move to constitutionality in 1984 and civilian elections in 1985 was clearly in response to legitimation crises at both the national and international levels.[6]

Despite the continuing war and human rights violations, in 1985 there was a palpable sense of hope and optimism surrounding the first civilian elections in twenty years. The elected president, Christian Democrat Vinicio Cerezo Arévalo, warned upon taking office that the army retained at least 60 percent of the power in the country but that he would do what he could to expand what he calculated to be his 30 percent. Cerezo himself, and many in his cabinet, had survived assassination attempts and had been forced into exile. Part of his government's popularity was based in the fact that people who had suffered army repression themselves now held power. In turn, and despite massive limitations, civilian rule opened a space for

---

for president of the Republic. Though he was unsuccessful, his proxy ran a close second in the 1995 elections, losing to Alvaro Arzú in the second round of voting.

5. Ignoring the vote occurred even when *military* men won, as when the Christian Democrat candidate Efraín Ríos Montt (a figure who still haunts the political landscape) was denied the presidency in 1974 (D. Stoll 1988).

6. Although human rights abuses have radically declined since the mid-1980s, they continue at alarming rates and still claim even high-ranking people like judges and the army colonel investigating the Myrna Mack assassination. The "epistemic murk" surrounding such violence has allowed the Guatemalan government and the U.S. State Department to retain "plausible deniability" regarding army and governmental responsibility. However, human rights activists in Guatemala have confessed that the current figures for violations may conflate the victims of "common" or drug-related crimes with state or army-sanctioned violence. Though I do not want to underestimate the extent of human rights violations, an important part of everyday life in Guatemala is the alarming increase in nonpolitical violent crime and the government's delegitimation as a result of its inability to control this crime. Just as in the United States, rising crime is linked to increasing poverty, urbanization, and police corruption. Of course, citizen insecurity, as in the United States, justifies increased expenditures on police-state paraphernalia and decreases resistance to surveillance. In a recent case, a university professor was killed, and her murder was attributed to death-squad activity directed against her husband, a prominent journalist. Her friends, however, blame drug traffickers because she refused to let them use her land for an airstrip. Others suggest the murderers were disgruntled former employees. Thirty-five years of militarization means that not only are the weapons easily available, but so are the techniques. So many civilians are ex-military that the telltale sign of political killings, the coup de grâce, is now hard to read. Who knows how many of the battered corpses appearing in Guatemala were the victims of personal vendettas, drunken brawls, or the bureaucracy of death? This uncertainty is part of the power of terror.

popular and Mayan organizing. New newspapers and magazines began to publish, allowing the exchange of different points of view, and a number of research institutions were inaugurated and embarked on studies of everything from *maquila* production and the internally displaced to indigenous "customary law."

Now boasting an internationally legitimate government, Guatemala enjoyed the economic effects of loosened international trade restrictions and increased foreign aid. The new Constitution mandated that 8 percent of the national budget be distributed directly to the newly autonomous municipalities to support development work at the local level. Shocking violence still occurs, like the massacres of San Andrés Ixtapa (1988) and Xamán (October 1995) and the assassination of anthropologist Myrna Mack (1990; her convicted assassin was part of Cerezo's Palace Guard), presidential candidate Jorge Carpio Nicole (1993), and Catholic Bishop Juan Gerardi (1998), but there has been an undeniable democratic opening since 1985, culminating in the Peace Accords of December 1996.

The failures and limits of this opening are legion (as documented by Painter 1987; Jonas 1991; AVANCSO 1992; and others), and no one in Guatemala harbors illusions that Guatemala's democratic project is a done deal. Little of the aura of the "State with a capital *S*" surrounds state officials whose human failings are all too familiar. The new money flowing through, including fortunes associated with drug trafficking, has been too tempting for many state officials to resist. Cerezo left office sailing into the sunset on a new yacht, and Serrano's "auto-coup" of May 1993 was partly a proactive response to threats to try him on corruption charges.[7]

The clear understanding of this situation informs a popular joke I heard told about both Presidents Cerezo and Serrano. "President Carlos Salínas de Gortari of Mexico invited Vinicio Cerezo to visit, and he took him on a tour of Mexico City. They first went to a new high school with computers in the classrooms and everything up to date. Cerezo was very impressed, and Salínas winked at him and patted his pocket. '10 percent,' he said (meaning he had skimmed it off the top). Cerezo was more impressed. Then Salínas took him to a new hospital, with the latest equipment, fully staffed, a fleet of ambulances, and so on. Cerezo oohed and aahed, and Salínas patted his pocket again and said, '15 percent.' Cerezo's eyes widened. Finally Salínas showed him a public housing project with gardens, swimming pools, tennis courts, everything. Cerezo expressed his admiration, and Salínas patted his pocket and said, '20 percent.' When Cerezo returned home to Guatemala, he was very depressed and spent many days trying to think how he

7. In October 1992, Cerezo had the temerity to publish a long meditation on Columbus written from the deck of his new yacht.

could impress his friend and neighbor. Finally he invited Salínas de Gortari to visit Guatemala. He took him to the top of the highest building in Guatemala City and said, 'Look at our new beltway around the city.' Salínas peered out the windows, he looked all around, he took out some binoculars and looked again. Finally he turned to Cerezo puzzled and said, 'But Mr. President, I don't see any highways.' And Cerezo smiled and patted his pocket. '100 percent,' he said."

Jokes like these are ways of making sense of "epistemic murk," of getting a semiotic handle on why things don't seem to work. They are ways of dealing with the regular scandals that reveal the government's inability to deal with even its most basic infrastructural responsibilities, like providing roads or mail service, and the government's fundamental distrust of its "subjects." For example, phone tapping is so widespread that people say, "When I tell a joke on the phone, three people laugh." The facts and figures that dribble out concerning amounts embezzled and official support for surveillance, violence, and continuing death squad activities suggest that such macabre humor, like rumors of baby snatching, may be only too appropriate to the situation. Lily Tomlin's great line, "No matter how cynical I get, I just can't keep up," captures Guatemalans' attitudes quite well.

The state is further demystified in the generalized sense that no one in it seems to know what they are doing. One of President Serrano's advisors admitted, "The Serrano government has never managed to get beyond improvisation." Serrano's vice-minister of culture, Estuardo Meneses, said, "I hate to say this, but I make most of my decisions by the seat of my pants. There is no policy, there is no discussion. Things have to get done, so I do them." A man who had worked in the Finance Ministry under Cerezo, run a development agency, and accepted a job with the de León government in late 1993, said when I interviewed him: "I went to a talk the other day on how strong the Guatemalan state was. Well, I stood up and said, 'I have worked in the state for years and I don't know what you're talking about. There isn't even really a state! The ministries don't do anything, everyone is corrupt. The government has no plan, no money, and no clue. How can you say it is strong?'" A recently returned exile who was working in the vice president's office under Serrano echoed this sentiment. "There is incredible chaos within the state. I would never have believed it until I started working there. It's much worse than just bureaucracy. There is no imagination, no interest in resolving problems, no creativity. Policy is set by the international donors who give us money." The Maya-Ixil former Congressman Diego Brito said he was also shocked upon entering the Congress to learn how unconcerned members seemed with law making or nation building. "All they care about is *fama, lana, y dama,* [getting famous, rich, and laid]."

Foucault suggests that "perhaps the state . . . does not have this unity, this individuality, this rigorous functionality, nor, to speak frankly, this importance" (1991, 103). Although most agree that the Guatemalan state is politically exclusive, ethnically discriminatory, and economically monopolistic, it may be precisely because of this insecurity, this tenuousness, that the state is also open in some ways. It is the subject of demand, the "piñata," the space in which diverse groups are struggling for representation. Guatemalans express shame and despair about their dysfunctional state, but they still claim it as theirs, the site and stake of the struggles around the newly problematized ladino identity and of both the Mayan and popular movements. As a ladino priest said, "The state is being questioned as never before, but what can take its place? There are more and more initiatives on its margins, organizing to negotiate with the state. The state knows it is weak, that it has to change." In the following, I explore the state's relations to these struggles, describing past and emerging policies toward the indigenous population and culture, and how these relations are historically situated, internally rent, and productively contradictory.

THE STATAL VILLAGE

In one interview after another, ladino and indigenous Guatemalans spoke of the country as "schizophrenic," "deeply divided," "pulverized," "fragmented at its core by ethnicity," and of ethnic identity as a "finger in the wound" of the body politic. For these people the Guatemalan state clearly does not function adequately as "a symbol for unity, something transcendental, symbolizing the inescapable unity of a people on one soil" (Mitchell 1991, 81). From the finance minister to union leaders, from the secretary of presidential affairs to Mayan activists, many Guatemalans speak of the need for unity, for a "national project that can include everyone," but in the next breath they often accuse everyone else of being "manipulated," "interested," "co-opted." Even the army, considered by many to be the most stable institution in the country, with the most developed "national project," is deeply divided, as evidenced by frequent coup attempts and internal purges.

I found these discourses of divisionism reminiscent of studies describing the "closed corporate community" rent by *envidia* (envy) and fear of the neighbors' Evil Eye (Wolf 1957, 1986). For North Americans, it is important to remember that Guatemala is a very small country, extraordinarily centered on the capital city, and that the numbers of educated urbanized people there are relatively low, making the "national scene" rather like a village.[8] The warp and weft of personal and kinship ties tightly weave state

8. In fact, my field methodology depended on this metaphor. I presumed to "study the state" by basing myself in Guatemala City, where "it" would be available through my visits to networked offices. My emerging sense that this worked (I did get a sense of the manifest and

structures together and, as Marta Casaus Arzú describes (1992), tend to exclude nonladinos.[9] A single generation of a family may be represented in the army, the clergy, the academy, and the guerrillas.[10]

These family monopolies and the sense of Guatemala as a "city-state" contribute to the feeling of many urban ladinos that the city, and even certain zones within it, is an island.[11] Given gringos' anthropological (and ethnostalgic) fascination with the Indian, and given that even skewed government statistics place Indians at 40 percent of the population, it is shocking the extent to which the Maya have been absent from the national scene: from news coverage, from government, from the professions, and even from the forums that address indigenous issues and the peace talks held in their name. Despite the optimism and material changes that I am charting, ladino popular imaginings and state structures are struggling to "keep Indians in their place." Indigenous issues may flash up at the moment of the Quincentennial—in press coverage, in the chants and graffiti of a Unity for Labor and Popular Action (UASP) march, and in presidential speeches, but it is a constant and brutal struggle to win every small space of Mayan repre-

---

latent contents of the "state" through interviews) but also did not work (so how come the "state" still works and has power?) has led to my attempts here to theorize some of the fantasies and pleasures of "state fetishism."

9. This fact, however, joined to the history of extraordinary violence and uncertainty about how to face the current global conjuncture, also tends to feed a claustrophobic, incestuous relationality fissured in multiple ways. I examine these familial ties and their relation to identity in chapter 6. My thinking about family, incest, and identity has been strongly influenced by Fernando Luera's work on this topic (1997).

10. I remember being invited to eat Sunday dinner with Myrna Mack's family. Assuming that because it was her family, they must be cool, I started to talk rather openly about my work on counterinsurgency in the highlands and in the model villages. I suddenly felt shooting pain up my shin as Myrna kicked me expertly (and hard) under the table. It took two more blows for me to understand that I should shut up, because her face remained calm. Afterward, she told me that her siblings were plantation owners and real estate brokers and very right-wing, and that there had been an Opus Dei priest at the table as well. After Myrna's assassination, her sister, Helen Mack, was transformed from a right-wing businesswoman into a self-taught lawyer and human rights activist struggling to have Myrna's killers—including the intellectual authors of the crime—captured and tried. She has said that part of the impetus for this radical change in her identifications was awareness that her sister's murder was condoned and planned by people whom she knew and had considered friends.

11. Many of my ladino interviewees were shocked and horrified that I lived in Zone One. Although the cathedral and National Palace are there, it has a reputation something like the Casbah in French colonial fantasies of the Maghreb (see the 1937 film *Pepe le Moco,* which captures this beautifully—I thank Jon Hunt for showing it to me!). The U.S. Embassy Human Rights officer even warned me that I should move because they advised Americans to not even venture into Zone One. He seemed primarily concerned about the high levels of crime there. Strangely enough, this same official has been recently implicated by the Internal Oversight Board for supporting and later covering up criminal activities by Guatemalan military "assets" (informants) for the CIA.

sentation.[12] This almost total historical erasure of the Maya (except for positions of servitude and in images of Guatemala's past) suggests both the traumatic nature of the "ethnic question" and the shock caused by the Quincentennial, Rigoberta Menchú's Nobel Prize, and the emergence(y) of the Mayan movement in general.

However, the villagelike nature of the nation-state also makes the borders of the "state" rather fluid, as Timothy Mitchell suggests about states in general: "Societal elements seem to penetrate it on all sides" (Mitchell 1991, 88). Within this community and through the democratic opening, the same people may go from living in exile, endangered by their political beliefs, to being vice-ministers; directors of nongovernmental organizations (NGOs) who have denounced state policies may be called on to head up government projects; academic critics may find themselves presidential advisors when a former schoolmate is elected; a Maya-Ixil orphan from Nebaj may be elected to the Congress; and Mayan activists may become minister and vice-minister of education.[13] The novelty and porousness of the civilian governments since Cerezo's inauguration in 1986, and the need to call on various talents including former exiles and Mayas, has created hope for change and certainly questions an analysis of the Guatemalan state as a monolithic structure. What we need to explore is the magical thrall in which it holds people—why they struggle for representation there.

STATE POLICY

As with the reactions to the Quincentennial, state policy regarding the indigenous peoples is multiple, ambivalent, and apparently contradictory.[14]

---

12. Over breakfast at the planning meeting for the UN Decade of Indigenous Peoples in May 1994, a month before peace treaty negotiations on the indigenous issue were to begin, Rigoberta Menchú complained about the lack of indigenous representation on either the government or guerrilla negotiating team. "Our people have struggled for them," she said. "They have been killed for this struggle, massacred, and then if they see that they are ignored, now that they are seeking peace, they will not be happy. It is not right that they sacrifice and sacrifice as a people, as our indigenous brothers and sisters, and then find they are still not taken into account."

13. Although Mayan activists were named ministers in 1993 by President de León Carpio, the government of President Arzú, elected in 1995, has not appointed any Maya to ministry posts.

14. Arcadio Ruiz Franco, former director of the National Indigenous Institute, identified an aspect of this contradiction in 1972. He claimed that the non-Indian man knows nothing of the Indian; he is "immersed in his personal horizon, chained to his prejudices, traditions, ignorance," and sees nothing in the Indian of value, yet he is completely dependent on the Indian as the labor force of the nation (Ruiz Franco 1972, 320). In that time period, Guzmán Böckler and Herbert (1970) were also exploring, as I and many others continue to do, this rich contradiction.

On the one hand, there is the sense that Indians have a specific place where they belong, where they are appropriate. Many of the policies, attitudes, and jokes I explore throughout this book are ambivalent responses to escapes from such spatial incarcerations. On the other hand, there is the pervasive sense that Indians must be brought out of those spaces, assimilated into a larger community and national project, and "rationalized and reformed" as Chatterjee suggested. Similarly, the state and urban ladinos in general exhibit a profound ignorance and contempt for indigenous culture and life. "We are tourists in our own country," said an employee of the vice president's office. Driving with a ladino friend past the Central Park where a demonstration was going on, I remarked that many of the Maya there were from Nebaj. He asked how I knew that, and I said because of their *traje*. He was surprised because he had not known that clothing styles are specific to regions. And yet, powerful ladinos whom I interviewed exhibited a driving will to know, a pleasure and fascination in exploring indigenous cultural difference. At least since the popularly elected governments of Arévalo and Arbenz (1944–1954) the state has sponsored a plethora of studies and research.

Chatterjee suggests that this contradiction lies in the very constitution of the nation-state, which must exhibit "modern methods of statecraft . . . [but this] could not mean the imitation of the west in every aspect of life. . . . [T]he self-identification of national culture would itself be threatened" (1990, 237). If the west stands in for "modernity" with its science and rationality (eagerly sought out and paid for with IMF loans), Guatemalan national culture also needs "tradition"—historic depth, origins, a proud link to an ancient Golden Age that may return again. The deep, affecting bond of an imagined community needs more support than military parades and shopping trips to Miami. The national body image needs a relation with sincerity, with moral rectitude, and with the ardor and mystery of home. The Mayan past, represented both by pre-Columbian ruins and by contemporary indigenous rural life (clothed in ancient garb, genuinely religious, and authentically observing "millenarian" practices without a hint of irony), serves as this prop for Guatemala, an extension that overcomes the distances between glorious past, degraded present, and hoped-for future.[15] A case in point: while working in a small indigenous village near Lake Atitlán during a recent presidential campaign, I was sitting in on a Catholic mass when a candidate on a flesh-pressing tour pulled into town with his entourage and tried to enter the church. After waving from the back, the candidate withdrew under the dour gaze of the priest, but several of his ladino

15. Quetzil Castañeda (1996) eloquently shows the modernity of the "tradition" inscribed on such ruins and on contemporary practices.

aides remained, and I overheard one say, "My God! This is just like ancient times! See the women all on one side of the church, their heads covered? It's like going back in time!" His companion concurred, saying, "They're all in costume! We really should get out here more often. This is the real Guatemala."

Here it seems that the past, rural village life, and the nation itself, get condensed into the figure of the Mayan woman, a point I return to in chapter 5. I suggest that many of the contradictions and much of the ambivalence expressed in state relations with the Maya have to do with this necessary simultaneity of modernity and tradition, what Jane Collier calls an impossible task. "Modern nationalists have to find traditions that distinguish them from other nations without marking them as traditional or backward" (J. Collier 1997, 207). Keeping in mind this double bind of the nation-state may help us better understand what is too often analyzed as merely a paradox: that "the state, in its desire to obliterate ethnic identity has at times strengthened it" (Wilson 1995, 29). Though I cannot address in detail the state's indigenous policy of the past forty years (see C. Smith 1990b), I briefly outline manifestations of these contradictions and various attempts to seize hold of the distinguishing traditions of the indigenous population while remaining modern (if only disappointingly).

The "Democratic Spring"

Within the framework of the Patzcuaro Accords (1938) that initiated the hemispheric International Indigenous Institute as part of the Organization of American States, Guatemala created the National Indigenist Institute (IIN) in 1945.[16] Its first director, Antonio Goubaud Carrera, explained its assimilationist genesis thus:

> How many Guatemalans are there who speak languages strange to the national language, wear fantastic outfits that set them apart from the rest of the population, are tormented by beliefs that a tidbit of enlightenment would eliminate, and chained to technologies that date from thousands of years ago? How many, we must ask, believe that Guatemala is no more than the mountains that limit their vision and their community? To confront this problem the government has created the National Indigenous Institute. (In González Ponciano 1991, 396)

The governments of Presidents Arévalo and Arbenz (1944–1954) promulgated many changes that positively affected the indigenous population, including land and labor reforms. Initiatives aimed directly at the Maya,

---

16. Most Latin American countries created such institutes, perhaps the best known being Mexico's Instituto Nacional Indigenista (INI).

however, seem informed by ambivalence and contradiction. For example, declaring that he cared more about living Indians than dead ones, the minister of the interior gave the go-ahead for dozens of acres of the pre-Colombian site of Kaminaljuyu to be bulldozed and paved over for government housing.

The government of President Arévalo, concerned about the loss of authentic indigenous *traje*, promulgated a law in 1947 to "fix" textile designs that were being "adulterated."[17] The law created three categories of authenticity to be administered and guaranteed through the IIN. "Autochthonous Indigenous Textiles" were made and used by indigenous people since before 1940, "Authentic Indigenous Textiles" expressed indigenous peoples' own artistic conceptions, and "Guatemalan Textiles" had typical designs but were mass-produced and could not claim to come from a specific region.[18] The IIN was charged with conducting a careful study of the specific designs and quality of each community's production and then issuing patents for each area, as well as protecting this production by limiting the importation of textiles similar to those produced nationally.[19] The Office of Tourism was to be "intimately connected" with the IIN for this project (Decree 426), a connection that suggests that local body politics

17. I think the double meaning of *fix* is useful here and reveals the contradictions at play in state-indigenous relations. The government wanted to pin down, to control, the rapid changes in textile production—those fantastic outfits so symbolic of ethnic difference. Yet even though the IIN was intent on fixing, or repairing, those suffering Guatemalans in need of a tidbit of Enlightenment—which would presumably strip them of their distinctive clothing—this policy seems designed to repair the damage that modernity has done to "authentic" textile production.

18. On a trip to Nebaj in 1990, I was horrified to see bored Civil Patrollers crocheting the traditional shoulder bags in soft pastel colors rather than the "usual" dark reds and greens. When I asked them why they had changed the colors, they said it had been by order of a gringo development worker who claimed they would sell better, which they did. I floundered for awhile in Tristes Tropiques mode. That summer, however, I finally made my way to the Ixchel Traje Museum and found to my surprise that the "authentic" Nebaj *huipiles* from the 1930s looked nothing like those of today, either in color scheme or design. Although I cannot go into the productive debate over tourist art, authenticity, and identity, this was one more reminder that indigenous peoples are not outside history and that tradition is not particularly solid. In her ethnography of *traje*, Carol Hendrickson (1995) discusses the intense hybridity of *traje* design and production as well as the complex relation among historical changes, gender relations, and ethnic identifications.

Current ladino and government interest in "customary law" looks like a similar attempt to surveil and "fix" indigenous expressions. Though customary law works through its very flexibility, based on personal knowledge of those involved and sensitivity to context, many researchers and advocates suggest that it be reduced to and fixed in written and immutable laws in order to save it. Of course, this is a hotly contested site (see chapter 8).

19. *Traje* design and color schemes tend to be specific to each indigenous community (see chapter 5; Hendrickson 1995; Asturias de Barrios and García 1992).

(regarding women's work and what covered their bodies) were already articulated to local and transnational images of those bodies.

These governments also legally supported the unification of four Mayan alphabets (gaining state support for such unification was the first project of the ALMG in the late 1980s). According to the 1950 law:

> Literature is being printed in as many alphabets as there are people to invent them, creating confusions among the indigenous people who read in their maternal language and do not know which one to abide by; as it is the duty of the state to limit irregularities, disorders, and confusions created if an official alphabet for each language were not adopted; the IIN adopts as the official instrument the graphic symbols cited below for the four majority languages of Guatemala: Quiché, Cakchiquel, Mam, and Kekchi [*sic*]. (Accords of August 3, 1950, on alphabets for four indigenous tongues)

Yet this is the same government that both declared Spanish the official language and proclaimed that "it is of urgent necessity to focus from every point of view on the ethnic problem that confronts the country in its social constitution in order to incorporate the indigenous people into national culture, relieving them of the inferior situation they have maintained" (Decree 269 8/1946). Thus, governmental attempts to "fix," or to repair that culture by assimilating it into national, ladino culture should also be viewed as attempts to hold it in place or to regulate it.

The Militarized State

The IIN was not especially effective in the impossible task of confronting this "problem," but after the 1954 coup that deposed President Jacobo Arbenz, the military governments seemed to maintain the goal of assimilation. In 1956 an IIN document declared that "the Indian with more buying power and with national culture will be a better producer and consumer and a more active citizen. To achieve this we must adapt him scientifically through our acculturation program" (in González Ponciano 1991, 402). These programs were to be carried out by the newly formed Guatemalan Seminar for Social Integration. Strategies included showing U.S.-made films, but the seminar primarily organized research and publishing on indigenous themes (which of course "fix," as in holding in their scholarly gaze), with emphasis on anticommunism, business opportunities, and tourism.

Although the military governments' policy toward the indigenous population appeared to be outright extermination after 1978, either through massacre and starvation or by using indigenous boys as cannon fodder in the army and Civil Patrols, many observers admit that the army seems to have a policy of cultivating integration by seizing hold of and deploying indigenous culture.[20] One military use and abuse of culture (identified here as indigenous lifeways)sets it up as the antithesis to the soldier male the army wants to produce. Through forced recruitment, they seize hold of boys in a moment of danger and remove them from their communities. Deterritorialization is a conscious strategy of the army, as General Otzoy admitted in a 1993 public debate over involuntary army recruitment with CONAVIGUA's Rosalina Tuyuc: "It is of vital importance for the nation to get Indians out of their communities, so they understand they are part of Guatemala." Reports of the brutal barracks training suggest that internalized racism is a tool used to break the boys down so they can be remade as soldiers, in part by promising them marks of the ladino (modern, bourgeois practices like wearing shoes and eating meat) and of masculinity. Mayan men are often feminized in relation to traditional practices and in their limited power vis-à-vis the ladino.[21] Richard Wilson suggests that the hypermasculinizing techniques of the body to which young Mayan men are subjected through training may be "designed to inculcate . . . the state's regulatory norms and values" (1995, 253) and leave their marks on the boy's hair, gait, posture, hygiene, and sexual practices—in part through the links between barracks and brothel (see Enloe 1983).

In a rather cynical move, army spokesman Yon Rivera responded to depictions of the army's counterinsurgency campaigns as genocidal by saying, "These people need to read their dictionaries. The Royal Academy of the Spanish Language says that genocide is the extermination of an ethnic group, but as we know, in Guatemala the majority of our population is indigenous" (*La Hora,* 12 October 1992). Ethnocide, erasing the memories of cultural identification, *does* seem to have been an army goal, however. As a former finance ministry official said, "Because they can't kill everyone, they try to kill what is Indian and leave the bodies." In fieldwork in 1985 and 1986, I found that the army bombed sacred sites in the mountains and bulldozed pre-Conquest ruins in building the resettlement areas known as model villages (Nelson 1990). The model villages, built for the resettlement of displaced war survivors on the ashes of villages destroyed by the army, were organized into six so-called Development Poles in the northern departments of Huehuetenango, El Quiché, Alta Verapaz, and Petén. The area around Nebaj, Quiché, known as the Ixil Triangle (for the three towns of Cotzal, Chajul, and Nebaj) was one such pole. Throughout the high-

20. A brutal counterinsurgency campaign was also directed primarily against ladinos in the 1960s.

21. Hendrickson suggests that "the values manifested by the colorful, hand-woven shirts and the calf-length pants of some male *traje,* for example, do not match those of, say, blue jeans and T-shirts or suits and ties. Men in *traje* are therefore seen as 'less' masculine, serious, and competent" (1996, 162).

lands, the army targeted traditional authorities, including shamans and di-
viners. A young diviner in Nebaj told me that before the war there had been
thirty Mayan priests (the preferred term) in the town, but by 1988 there
were only ten, several of whom, like him, had only recently begun to practice. "The army killed a lot of the priests because they can foresee troop
movements and would warn the guerrillas. They also helped people change
into their animal spirits so they could escape the army sweeps," he said. A
young K'iche' man in Chichicastenango said, "There used to be a lot more
shamans around here but many were killed in the violence. They are very
wise. They know who did things to people here, and there are some who
don't want that kind of knowledge around."[22]

You are objectifying the army!

However, indigenous culture is also part of the army's arsenal in their
"power over life," productive as well as destructive. As in their reactions to
the Quincentennial, the army _claims_ the indigenous past, identifying itself
as a national institution with indigenous histories of resistance. In its state
project of creating a national identity, it has a sophisticated understanding
of the necessity of simultaneous modernity (like high-tech counterinsurgency weapons) and tradition. For example, it uses figures and names from
Mayan mythology and from contemporary Mayan social organization for its
institutions. Statues and murals on the army bases represent indigenous
warriors and gods, and the names of divisions and elite fighting groups like
the Kaibiles commemorate figures from the _Popul Wuj_. As a ladino who
worked for the army-controlled National Reconstruction Committee in the
mid-1980s said, "The army and the church are the only nationwide institutions with networks that extend throughout society to its very roots. Because
of this, the army really understands the Indian. The army's symbolic expressions, their images, these are symbols of the Indians—in their campaigns, their uniforms, their chants, their training. Their perceptions are
close to indigenous expressions."

I have been told that some unit subdivisions are named after the various
levels of _cofradía_ hierarchy for the area the army base is in and that the army
employs Mayan priests to "cleanse" army bases and mark important days in
the Mayan calendar. In their publication propagandizing the Development
Pole and model village resettlement areas, the army quoted liberally from
the _Popul Wuj_ (Government of Guatemala 1985). As Gustavo Porras, a long-

22. The science-fictional aspects of these comments do not mean that army strategists do
not believe them, or at least believe they have efficacy among the indigenous villagers and the
indigenous soldiers whom the army seeks to control. In their incursions into indigenous territory, the army seems quite willing to take on the mantle of horror accorded such "space
invaders." In a popular joke that plays on the Spanish abbreviation for Unidentified Flying Object (_Objeto Volando No Identificado,_ or OVNI), those responsible for massacres and disappear-
ances are OMNIs (Un-Identified Military Objects).

time ladino observer of the army, said, "To the chagrin of the Left, the army has been in the vanguard of working with the Indian. They really know the communities, whereas most Guatemalans are totally ignorant. They know the Indians because they live and work side by side. Most Guatemalans don't give a damn about our prehistory, and progressives may be the worst, as if the world started with the Colony. But the army knows this history, they know it is still important."

Similarly, Richard Wilson describes how among the Q'eqchi's of Alta Verapaz the army is appropriating the "authoritarian symbolism" of the *tzuultaq'a* (mountain spirit). He argues that the *tzuultaq'a* is central to all "Q'eqchi' collective imaginings" (1995, 53) and thus their appropriation by the military has heightened army control. Army headquarters is called "Home of the Soldier Tzuultaq'a," and Wilson quotes Col. Homer García, head of army information, saying "'We liken ourselves to the mountain spirits because like them, we dominate the land, we command over all who are in our territory.' As this Ladino officer spoke of Q'eqchi' symbolism so comfortably, I thought to myself that the army has become the Guatemalan state institution with the most profound understanding of indigenous culture" (1995, 242).

The army seizes hold of indigenous culture with extraordinary cynicism, and Mayan groups are now demanding that the army cease using Mayan names for the very organizations that terrorize them. However, both Maya and ladinos admit that the army is one of the few state institutions with a national project that takes the Maya into account. The orthopedic powers of military training may be polyvalent, creating unexpected effects. For example, the army teaches their recruits to read. Being a member of a division named after the hero of the *Popul Wuj* may be the first time the boys have experienced any valorization of their culture at all. Before it was politically correct, the army deployed the discourse of deference to indigenous culture, as in the Civil Patrol Code of Conduct: "I will respect community customs and traditions as well as the Civil and Military authorities" (in Wilson 1995, 241). Some commanders make the effort to learn the language of the areas where they're based. The infamous Lucas García brothers (Romeo, de facto president from 1978 to 1982, and Benedicto, now patron of the national *Rabina Ajau* Maya queen festival) already spoke Q'eqchi' from growing up in Alta Verapaz and flaunted their fluency.[23] Finally, the army is one

23. In fact, Lucas García presented something of an anomaly. As head of the state during the worst years of counterinsurgency, he was the representative of ladino and upper-class interests. Yet his rural origins, dark complexion, and command of a Mayan language suggested how unsolid his ladino identity was. There are many jokes that play on his boundary crossings. One such joke goes: Lucas García was on a tour around the world, visiting a lot of different countries. He seemed to enjoy every place he went, but his staff was shocked when the plane

of the only institutions in the country where indigenous men and even some women can consistently attain positions of authority. There is now a Mayan general, Otzoy, who was a member of the Army High Command from 1993 to 1996.

These are chilling issues to confront, but they are vital to understanding why, despite the violence, the army enjoys some ideological as well as repressive control and why the *pueblo* is not entirely united against them—why counterinsurgency has been effective.[24] In part, of course, forced recruitment and militarization through the Civil Patrol mean that many members of the *pueblo* either are part of the military or love someone who is. But young men are not *only* forced or duped into performing military service. The army has managed to mobilize them through discourses that were already drenched in power (gender systems, tradition, and so on).

Foucault suggests that racism is not just the assignment of hierarchical value to a range of phenotypic expressions such as hair, skin color, and nose shape. As Ann Stoler explains, Foucault sees racism instead as a grid of intelligibility, a grammar that is not necessarily about any particular group of people but about a more generalized division within a body politic. He connects racism to a pervasive sense of threat from internal enemies whose identities vacillate. Racism, understood as the constant war against these threats to the health and happiness of this body politic, promises a common good—it is not merely a negative or repressive discourse. "It establishes a *positive* relation between the right to kill and the assurance of life. It posits that 'the more you kill [and] . . . let die, the more you will live.' It is neither racism nor the state that invented this connection but the permanency of war-like relations inside the social body" (Stoler 1995, 84; emphasis in original).

If, in some cases, indigenous people saw the revolutionaries killing them, and the larger effect of guerrilla presence as army massacres, it may have been a form of racism in Foucault's sense—a desperate struggle for the common good of their communities—which in part mobilized their par-

---

touched down in Indonesia. Lucas García ran down the gangplank and stretched out on the ground, kissing the earth and crying, "Finally I'm home!" His aide ran over and said, "Mr. President, General, what are you doing? You aren't from Indonesia!" Lucas García looked surprised, "But my mother was always calling me *Indio necio, Indio necio.*" The joke reflects the practice of calling bad ladino children *"indios,"* and *necio* means "naughty," suggesting that not only is García an Indian but he's stupid (see also S. Hill 1992).

24. I hope it is obvious that that there is constant and persistent resistance to this militarization. Paul and Demarest (1988) document how the people of San Pedro la Laguna forced the army to rein in the violently corrupt military commissioners there, and after the massacre in Santiago Atitlán, townspeople forced the army to remove their base. Returning refugees and the Communities of the Population in Resistance (CPR) have been especially effective in mobilizing international support for creating demilitarized resettlement zones.

ticipation in the army and Civil Patrols. In turn, the war has been called genocidal in its ruthlessness and brutality, but it was not always Indians who were killed. The counterinsurgency discourse that justified killing off peoples "to the last seed" targeted indigenous people, but primarily as they were seen as subversives and thus subsumed in the larger category of adversary to the health of the body politic. The army, well aware of the importance of location to indigenous identity, played up the "foreignness" of "the subversive," calling them *canche* (blonde, fair skinned), gringo, and *kaxlan* (foreigner). But these "reeducation lectures" would not have worked so well if they had not been couched in an already comprehensible racist grammar that suggested that indigenous people had to kill to preserve life (Wilson [1995] highlights the discourses of the sacred and sinfulness also woven into this grid).

"What does racist discourse do? For one, it is a 'means of introducing . . . a fundamental division between those who must live and those who must die'" (Foucault in Stoler 1995, 84). When we call Guatemala's counterinsurgency war genocidal, we are taking for granted that the fundamental division is between Maya and ladino.[25] Why, then, were so many ladinos killed both in the early 1980s and in the 1960s? Why is the army supporting (within very clear limits) indigenous culture? Why have indigenous people actively engaged in counterinsurgency? If we understand the fundamental division to be class, that the war is about control of the means of production (regardless of whether you believe the *tzuultaq'a* or Dupont's fertilizer is responsible for a good crop), we miss the almost biological meaning assigned to subversion and cannot explain the horrific extent of the violence. If we assert that the army is only repressive and that indigenous people were forced and duped into participation, we drain the Maya of *all* power. The Guatemalan army held and holds enormous power over death, a terrifying constraint on Mayan and ladino action. But I think we also need to think about their power over life—the way counterinsurgency folded discourses of class and race, discourses of insider and outsider, and that positive relation between the right to kill and the assurance of life, to create a grid of intelligibility for indigenous (and ladino) participation in counterinsurgency.

In no way do I mean to bestow on the army a unity of purpose that does

25. Denouncing the war as genocidal or ethnocidal is a very powerful solidarity discourse and was effective in the mid-1980s in raising consciousness about the brutality of the war. In Quincentennial Guatemala, however, we have to think carefully about what we assume to be the *genos* (race, species, origin) or *ethnos* (people, nation) that is under attack. Are we positing an already existing solid identification with a presumed biological component? Is that what the Guatemalan army targeted? Is it inefficiency that accounts for the army's utter failure to wipe out the Maya? Awful as it is to admit, army spokesman Yon Rivera may be right when he says that the army's plan was not genocide. The fundamental division was around "subversion."

not exist, much less condone their practices. But as with any strategy of power, to resist it we must see how it is productive as well as repressive. In turn, it is never all-powerful—we cannot assume that it will always produce the desired end. As Carol Smith suggests, none of the military state's attempts to "'penetrate and centrally coordinate the activities of civil society through its own infrastructure' [have] been entirely successful. . . . The corporate Indian community has reformulated them along its own lines, making them work for the community rather than for the state" (1990b, 17). Again, the army was the state for some thirty years, and this position was not maintained only through violence and repression. In reviewing "state" policy toward the Maya, we must be alert to the contradictory ways this militarized power also incites, induces, and seduces Guatemalans, including the Maya, during this period and into the present—ways that I try to suggest in a brief history of the army's model village program. Ann Stoler argues that Europe used their colonial holdings as "laboratories of modernity" (1995, 15; see also Rabinow 1991). Rather than assuming a space-time continuum in which the further we go from the capital the more traditional it gets (see chapter 7), I would suggest the same for the army's work in remote model villages, where that power over life that is increasingly part of state policy was tried out.

Model Villages as State Policy   The system of model villages, developed since 1982 in the areas hardest hit by the counterinsurgency war, provides an example of the complexity of the militarized state's relation to the Maya. Joined with the intensity of counterinsurgency violence, and more selective repression following 1983, the model villages constituted a highly developed Foucauldian panopticon (Foucault 1979 and 1988), employing surveillance, documentation, confession, techniques of "pastoral power," and dividing practices.[26]

In 1986, I spent six months visiting these Development Poles, and even though all were under overt and constant military control, they diverged widely from one another.[27] In the Ixil area, people were eager to get out

26. This describes the situation at the height of army control. As army control relaxes, many people have begun to move back into more scattered settlement patterns. Popular organizations like CERJ, which oppose forced participation in the Civil Patrols, have had little luck organizing in these areas, however, and as the army moves to disarm the Civil Patrols as part of the Peace Accords, the Development Poles will be among the last places freed from their weight.

Richard Wilson also reads the Development Poles in Alta Verapaz through Foucault, although I think he misses some of the productivity of these army regimes (Wilson 1995, 250–255).

27. I felt most like a solidarity prosthetic on this project. I was hired by a group of Guatemalan exiles in Mexico who had received Ford Foundation funding. Though they were not safe

of the sprawling refugee camp right outside Nebaj and desperate to start planting again; they waited for the army to gain territory back from the guerrillas and thus open that land for resettlement. Army engineers were building wide roads and bridges to connect the new consolidated villages that were sprouting up, and army PR agents were helicoptering in foreign journalists and diplomats to marvel at the "comfort" and progress of the infrastructure. *Progress* in this case meant running water, a school, a Civil Patrol post, and housing. At the other end of the spectrum, the only places I was denied access to were the newest villages at the time, Acamal and Saraxoch in Alta Verapaz (see Wilson 1995), which were receiving newly captured members of the Communities of the Population in Resistance (CPR). Viewed from the gate and based on very guarded talk with the Civil Patrols there, it seemed that people barely had the minimal housing of plank walls and tin roofing, many families were piled in together, and food was scarce. In contrast, the new village of Chisec, also in Alta Verapaz, boasted a hostel, several restaurants, a "video-salon" that showed two or three movies a day (I saw Chuck Norris and a slasher film), and a coffee harvest. The term *Development Pole* covered tiny Yanahí, where six lonely families lived a stone's throw from the Usumacinta River and Mexico, waiting for refugees to return. It also referred to the tremendous diversity of the entire Ixcán area, where thousands of internally displaced and returning refugees mingled (often explosively) with new arrivals invited by the army from land-poor areas throughout Guatemala, mixing dozens of languages, religions, and attitudes toward the state in new communities split by suspicion and fear (see also AVANCSO 1992; Manz 1988a and 1988b; and Falla 1992).

These varied sites share the new geography of the model villages (most explicitly deployed in the Ixil area around Nebaj), which was designed to make the inhabitants as visible as possible. The original buildings destroyed by the army were quite spread out, but in the new villages the houses are arranged in compact grids. Each house is a simple block with large windows and bounded on two sides by wide streets, so that any passerby has full access to the contents of the house. Until 1988, every model village had an army post on an overlooking hill with anywhere from thirty to one thousand soldiers stationed there. According to village residents, the army maintains a system of spies among them and has conscripted every male fourteen years or older into the Civil Patrol—such that, in the diabolical calculus described by Foucault, every (male) prisoner becomes a warden (1979, 201).

Many of the current residents of the model villages had fled into the

---

anywhere in Guatemala, I could extend their reach by getting into some of the most militarized parts of the country. Copies of my field report were circulated in the exile community as quickly as I could write up, and excerpts were published in the EGP internal newsletter.

Figure 9. Acul, model village in Ixil Triangle Development Pole. "450 houses for that number of families, a total of 2,700 beneficiaries. Living areas amid a comfortable infrastructure. Wide streets and a two-way main street, which includes the access road to Nebaj" (Government of Guatemala 1985, 45). Photo by author, 1986.

mountains and jungles of northern Guatemala to escape army massacres (for these experiences, see Falla 1988 and 1992). Although the "population in resistance" (CPR) as they call themselves has dwindled, in 1992 and 1993 the army continued to sweep these areas, capturing those it could and re-settling them.[28] Combined with the "development" work designed to keep people in the highlands rather than let them swell into the urban areas, these forms of discipline perform precisely as Foucault suggests: to "fix and regulate movements[,] . . . it dissipates compact groupings of individuals wandering about the country in unpredictable ways, it establishes calculated districts" (1979, 219).

Of course, *to fix* also means "to repair," and in the 1980s, as these refugees were brought in, they were forced to undergo a process of questioning and "reeducation" that might last several months, living either inside the

28. In 1996, within the context of the peace talks, the CPR signed several agreements with the government and nearby municipalities to formalize their by-then de facto settlements. David Stoll (n.d.) suggests this is often a fraught resettlement as well.

military compound or in special receiving centers. They were often questioned for days or even weeks on their ties to the guerrillas and the location of other refugees. Many were coerced into leading army patrols in search of their companions, or to broadcast in their Mayan languages from army helicopters that those remaining "in resistance" should turn themselves in. Dossiers were opened on each returnee, and they were issued identification papers that were necessary to travel, because the Civil Patrol of each village checked people's papers as they entered and left the village.[29] Refugees were usually forced to sign (or thumb print) a confession of being duped by the guerrillas and to receive "psychological counseling" and twice-daily reeducation lectures. Living in the villages, everyone was under the surveillance of the Civil Patrol, which signs the documents necessary to leave town and reports weekly to the local army base.

Then began the phase of "development," or what Foucault calls "pastoral power": "salvation meaning health, well-being . . . standard of living, security" (in Dreyfus and Rabinow 1983, 214). The army distributed food and seeds in the villages and engaged in road building and irrigation projects. Posters were stapled to every house, depicting a soldier with a smiling Ixil girl in *traje*. Signs were posted at the entrances to villages, street corners, and along the roads, bearing legends such as "Welcome to Saraxoch, a village that is ideologically new" (Alta Verapaz); "Welcome to Pulay, a village that builds what others have destroyed"; "People and army united will never be defeated"; and "The people of Salquil support their army" (Ixil area). Posters were also put up showing heroic-looking Civil Patrollers in full *traje*, or a cartoon of an evil-looking Fidel Castro trying to climb out of Nicaragua into Guatemala but being smashed by an army boot. The fact that all of these signs were in Spanish suggests they were put there more for people like myself or other members of the army than for residents' benefit. David Stoll (1988) details how salvation discourse infused the rebuilding work in the Ixil area under born-again Christian dictator Ríos Montt, with the help of Evangelical church aid (including the Summer Institute of Linguistics). Wilson (1995) also describes how religious discourses of sin, punishment, and redemption were mobilized through army rebuilding campaigns. The army was quite proud of their accomplishments in these areas. Most officials I talked to on site and in the capital were effusive about their aid for the deprived Indians and how they were rebuilding the nation. Without any apparent irony, they handed out a glossy book of more than one hundred pages on the progress made in the Development Poles (Government of Guatemala 1985).

29. On what would normally be a seven-hour journey by bus in 1986, my papers were perused twenty-three times, which stretched the trip to thirteen hours.

In the Ixil area, the army tried to prove its cultural sensitivity by providing modified *huipiles* (traditional blouses) rather than the secondhand western clothing provided by local nuns and by building a ritual steam bath (*temascal*) in the refugee receiving area, which they named *Xemamatze* (New Dawn) in the Ixil language. As Foucault says, "This formidable power of death . . . now presents itself as the counterpart of a power that exerts a positive influence on life, that endeavors to administer, optimize, and multiply it" (1980, 137).

Many have denounced the "development" work in the poles as the misuse of international food aid for military purposes, unconscionable intervention into local affairs, and blatant public relations without any foundation—denunciations that all carry weight. This development work definitely functions as an "anti-politics machine" (Ferguson 1990), but, although some poles received far less attention than others and service among villages varied widely, almost all villages were provided with roads, water systems, *pilas* (communal laundry basins), schools, seeds, and development aid in the form of hundreds of teachers, agricultural extensionists, accountants, and health promoters. These aid providers included government agencies and members of the Army Civilian Affairs units (which employed quite a few Mayan women) as well as gringos, and they opened schools, set up demonstration plots to introduce new crops and organic farming methods (including fish farms and raising rabbits), provided and helped distribute materials that facilitated artisanal production, pulled teeth and handed out medicines (many of them long expired and with instructions only in English), tried to introduce more efficient stoves to reduce deforestation, promoted hygienic practices, taught cooking classes, campaigned to get more little girls to attend school, and furthered a range of other initiatives.[30] These projects hired Maya, many for their bilingual capacities, and young ladinos from more urban areas—many of whom said they endured the privations of the sites and distance from their families in the hopes of contributing to the less fortunate in their country. Though many of these projects were laughably ineffective (like the Taiwanese development experts living in Chacaj, Huehuetenango, who spoke no Spanish, much less Mam, Q'anjob'al, or Chuj), they represent a very different form of state interaction with these far-flung, formerly "forgotten" areas. Here "state institutions foster and draw on . . . micro-fields of power as they permeate the body politic at large" (Stoler 1995, 28).

The "New" Army   Similarly, at the national level, the de facto Ríos Montt government (1982–1983) created the State Council, which for the first

---

30. Many of the gringos were brought in through religiously connected NGOs and later through the U.S. National Guard (D. Stoll 1988; A. Adams 1997).

time in Guatemala's history included indigenous representatives. This State Council was to offer policy advice and was run by the man who would be president (1990–1993), Jorge Serrano Elías. It surprises many that Ríos Montt's party, the Guatemalan Republican Front (FRG), is so popular with indigenous voters (several of the seven indigenous congresspeople [1990–1994] were elected through the FRG). Although his short reign is infamous for massacres and secret tribunals, many explain his party's popularity as caused in part by this support for indigenous representation.[31]

By 1985 the army said that, as a result of personnel rotation, it was a completely different institution from the early 1980s, and it claimed full credit for the Constitutional Congress and return to civilian rule. As it did after the Serrano auto-coup in 1993, the army now proclaimed itself the safeguard of democracy and economic development.[32] As a disciplined institution, it had discharged its responsibility to the nation, the state of emergency was lifted, and a new regime could take its place.

As part of its continuing national project, this "new" army developed the School for Strategic National Studies (ESTNA), which brings together community leaders, teachers, journalists, government officials, artists, writers, Mayan activists, labor unionists, NGOs, and army personnel for short courses on national identity and culture. A priest who participated said, "In 1986 they began to hold seminars and discussion groups, and there they laid out the ethnic line very clearly, with a firmness that has never been expressed by the civilian government." Participants represent a wide range of political positions; the more leftist ones attend, they say, because it would be impolitic to refuse the invitation. I interviewed seven people who had participated in seminars, and they all said they had very positive experiences. They listened to talks by experts, including Mayan activists and anthropologists, held discussions with each other, and worked on a group research project that they then presented to the other participants. The "ethnic-national problem" was frequently discussed. Participants also uniformly expressed surprise at how open the army members were to listening and discussing options for the country's future. "People shouldn't be so afraid of the army. If you are willing to argue with them, they will come around. I

---

31. His "Bullets and Beans" program, which did bring direly needed aid to counter-insurgency-hit areas, is also remembered as a relief, especially in areas decimated under the Lucas García regime.

32. Victor Perera reports that in 1995 the Guatemalan Army "paid half a million dollars to a U.S. public-relations agency, Robert Thompson, to clean up the military's abysmal international image. Newspapers have published scores of ads showing a new, kinder and gentler Guatemalan army concerned with its indigenous citizens' poverty index . . . and with preserving the northern rain forests" (1995, M2). Some of this concern with image is governmental in Foucault's sense and is evoked in part by the attention of transnational observers like the United Nations, as I discuss in chapter 8.

made a lot of friends through ESTNA. They occupy a structural position, yes, but they are also very open to change. They really want to develop a national project and they are clear on their goals," said a ladino development worker.

I suggest that the model villages may be useful models for the more governmental regime now in place with "democratization" (Burchell, Gordon, and Miller 1991; Foucault 1991). In Foucault's historical overview of "governmentality," the society of sovereignty seems to be displaced by the disciplinary society and then by the society of government, but in truth there is a "triangle, sovereignty-discipline-government, which has as its prime target the population. . . . [It is] the ensemble formed by the institutions, procedures, analyses and reflections, the calculations and tactics that allow the exercise of this very specific albeit complex form of power which has . . . as its principle form of knowledge political economy, and as its essential technical means apparatuses of security . . . resulting on the one hand, in the formation of a whole series of specific governmental apparatuses, and, on the other, in the development of a whole complex of *savoirs* [knowledges]" (1991, 102–103). Foucault suggests that the governmentalization of the state is productive, both allowing the state to survive and also forming "the only real space for political struggle and contestation" (1991, 103)—thus the piñata effect. Democratization and nation building out of ethnic difference in Guatemala comes complete with internalized discipline and structures of surveillance (all of those development workers in the model villages were constantly writing reports, and as I outline later, current ladino "ignorance" of the Indian is accompanied by intense scrutiny). Critics of ESTNA, for example, complain that it is an excellent way to keep tabs on many different sectors. I suggest that "democratization," and the new techniques experimented with in the model villages (as laboratories of modernity), have opened the way for a proliferation of discourses and productive struggles, waged in part (at ESTNA, through development initiatives throughout the highlands, and elsewhere) over memory and culture, modernity and tradition.

The point of talking about the productivity of these powers along with their repressive effects is to avoid the sense that "democracy" is only a mask for military rule. Such an analysis of manifest (false) versus latent (true) content does little to explain either the power of the state or the many effects of contestatory practices. I try to avoid the notion that the state and civil society are separate, enclosed entities (the former corrupt and repressive, the latter noble and liberatory); instead, I argue that they are interpenetrated at every point. As Mitchell suggests, "The boundary of the state never marks a real exterior, it is a line drawn internally. . . . Producing and maintaining the distinction between state and society is itself a mechanism that generates resources of power" (Mitchell 1991, 90; see also Gramsci

1989; Hall 1986; and Maurer 1997). I do not suggest that the civilian government and the military apparatus are completely separate. However, I hope to avoid the limited critique that there is no difference at all between military and civilian rule. In turn, I also resist the optimistic suggestions that it is only a matter of time till democracy wins out and the military is put in its place, curbed like a well-trained pit bull (see U.S. State Department discourse; Fauriol and Loser 1991). A certain magic may need to be invoked to think these relations in all their complexity, something like dreamwork or jokework. But first we must finish the analysts' initial task of describing the body politics of the nation-state and ethnic relations in democratizing, post-1985 Guatemala.

Civilian Rule

According to a member of Serrano's presidential staff, the civilian government was not as clear in its goals regarding the indigenous peoples or the nation as the army has seemed to be. He said, "We are more lost than the children of La Llorona." La Llorona is a mythic woman who can be heard crying in the night as she searches for her missing offspring.[33] A man working in the Ministry of Culture said, "In terms of the indigenous issues, we've really been caught with our pants down." Many people I interviewed said merely, "There is no Indian policy. There is no national project." It seems quite meaningful that these issues ("Indians" and the nation) would be perceived as relatively isomorphic. Until (and even after) the Quincentennial, state policy and funding tended to be directed at indigenous people only as they were lumped into another category: as the poorest of the poor, as displaced, and so on, as if assimilationist policies had already worked.

Yet there have been a number of initiatives aimed directly at (and developed in response to the demands of) the indigenous population. The Constitutional Assembly of 1984 included indigenous representatives, and the new Constitution contains, for the first time in history, specific (if limited) rights for indigenous peoples. There was a great deal of dissension in the assembly regarding the indigenous languages, and disagreements were so bitter regarding Article 70—on indigenous issues in general—that it was left blank, to be filled in at a later date(!). Other initiatives include the Ministry of Culture and Sports, set up under the Christian Democrat government, and the ALMG, originally associated with the Ministry of Culture, which became legalized as an autonomous state agency (see chapter 4). By 1993, several governmental funding agencies had been created to channel money

---

33. As I suggest in chapter 6, this may be a story of *mestizaje*. La Llorona is said to be an indigenous woman who drowned her children fathered by a Spanish man. In some versions, La Llorona is also a baby snatcher, which links her to the rumors explored in chapter 2.

directly to indigenous organizations and municipalities, and several proposals were being considered to create a state institution for indigenous people along the lines of a ministry. ILO Convention 169 was supported by top administration officials and finally ratified in April 1995. The National University formed the Inter-Ethnic Studies Center, and all of the major ladino research institutions devoted resources and attention to indigenous issues, publishing books and monographs and organizing forums and discussions. Seven Maya were elected to the Congress, and the Human Rights Ombudsman Office set up a special defense section to protect specific indigenous rights. The government has undertaken a major tourism initiative as part of the multinational, UNESCO-sponsored Mayan World project (see Castañeda 1996). Finally, Mayan groups have struggled for and won a place in the National Dialogue and in the ASC for representation in the peace talks, achieving recognition of their rights through the Accord on Identity and the Rights of Indigenous Peoples, part of the peace treaty signed in December 1996.[34]

So, along with the sense articulated by so many ladino state workers of being lost (like the children of La Llorona)—of being tourists in their own country, of having no indigenous policy and no national policy, of being ignorant of the Indians, and of wanting them to disappear—there is also a great deal of energy and interest directed from in and around the state toward indigenous issues. Although each of these initiatives deserves closer scrutiny, I think we can gain a general sense of the manifest and latent content of post-1985 indigenous policy by focusing on the Ministry of Culture and Sports. First, to give a sense of the context of work around culture in 1992—part of the Quincentennial production of *savoirs* that Foucault talks about—I outline Guatemalan research projects that focus the intense interest incited by indigenous culture and organizing.

The Maya as Object of Study   As Myrna Mack and others have ruefully remarked, unlike gringo colleagues who must publish or perish, Guatemalan scholars have faced the threat of "publish and perish" (Oglesby 1995). However, as I explore in the next chapter, just as the Maya have found culture to be a site where they can struggle and survive in Quincentennial Guatemala, indigenous issues seem to be a safe site for research and publication. Since the late 1980s, there has been an explosion in research on the Maya. In addition to the underfunded work of government institutions like the Department of Sociocultural Studies and Research, the Institute for An-

34. The National Dialogue was a stage in the peace process in which various sectors of "civil society" created proposals to be discussed at the negotiating table. The organization grew into the ASC.

thropology and History, the Center for Folklore Studies, the Seminar on Integration, the increasingly vestigial National Indigenous Institute, and other dependencies of the Ministries of Education and Culture, many private agencies are keenly interested as well. These ostensibly nongovernmental organizations are often deeply interpenetrated with the state (as think tanks for parties, and so on), and governmental workers say they draw frequently on private research, in its published form as well as through consulting with investigators from the following organizations.

The Association of Social Investigation and Studies (ASIES) was founded as a policy think tank by members of the Solidarity Action Movement (MAS; Serrano's party, president 1990–1993), the Christian Democrats (DC; Vinicio Cerezo's party, president 1986–1990), and the National Union of the Center (UCN; runner-up in the 1985 and 1990 presidential races). Directors and researchers frequently serve in the government or in advising capacities. ASIES is currently involved with projects on the Maya, focusing on changing power in the municipalities, customary law, bilingual education, and rural development.

The Association for the Advancement of Social Science in Guatemala (AVANCSO), where I was based, has been working on an ethnic identity project, research on the effects of *maquila* production and the war in indigenous areas, and on the situation of Mayan women. The experiences of AVANCSO grimly remind us that research into cultural issues is political. Myrna Mack, one of the founders, was killed outside their offices. During much of my fieldwork, the office was under surveillance, and the staff and directors were threatened and frequently followed.[35]

The Latin American Faculty of Social Sciences (FLACSO) has published a great deal recently on the Mayan movement, of which *Quebrando el Silencio* (Breaking the silence; Bastos and Camus 1993) and its follow-up *Abriendo Caminos* (Breaking paths; Bastos and Camus 1995) seem to have had the most impact. These are respectful books that clearly define the split between the political and the culturalist indigenous movements and are careful not to overwhelmingly endorse either one. FLACSO also organized a series of seminars beginning in 1988 that were edited and published as *Estado Nacion: Las Demandas de los Grupos Etnicos en Guatemala* (Nation-state: The demands of ethnic groups in Guatemala; 1993). Its editor was Dr. Jorge

---

35. The surveillance and threats increased dramatically in 1993, during the trial and sentencing of one of Mack's murderers. Though they hung around the park across the street and sometimes took photos or called in threats, in a show of pathetic cowardice the perpetrators only directly confronted one member of the staff, the small, middle-aged cleaning woman. As Myrna's sister, Helen Mack, presses to indict the intellectual authors of the crime, who were in the upper echelons of Cerezo's government, the intimidation continues. In February 1997, AVANCSO's messenger was beaten and interrogated by armed men.

Solares, a dentist and autodidact anthropologist who was also the go-between for the Mesa Maya in the National Dialogue and runs the Inter-Ethnic Institute of the National University (USAC). FLACSO also published the very popular study *Guatemala: Linaje y Racismo* by Marta Casaus Arzú (see chapter 6).

The Institute for Research and Political Training (INIAP) is a think tank that has a relatively schizophrenic reputation: both avowed orthodox Marxists and returned exiles work there, but it also has close ties to the government, and one of its founders, Héctor Rosada Granados, was the architect of the de León Carpio government's peace plan (although the plan was not signed, it formed a rough draft for the existing accords). INIAP also held a series of diagnostic meetings on the indigenous question attended by many of the same people as the FLACSO seminar and has conducted fieldwork on rural expressions of the indigenous movement. Their book, a very slight edition, was written by Humberto Flores Alvarado, who obviously abhors the Mayan cultural rights movement and describes it as "paternalist, individualist, centralizing, opportunist, utilitarian, and egotistical" (INIAP 1992, 57). At the book's presentation, a Mayan activist who had participated in the seminars said, "I wonder what happened to all the information they generated through those meetings? I guess it's in the 'archive.'"[36]

The Institute of International Relations and Research for Peace (IRIPAZ), whose director has both lived in exile and was the vice-minister of foreign relations under President Serrano, is researching the "ethnic reality" in Guatemala. IRIPAZ publishes the results of team research and training projects, including *Historias de Nuestra Historia* (Histories of our history); (García Ruiz 1991).

In addition, the many ladino-run NGOs that have maintained close relations with indigenous communities for decades maintain archives and print short studies and diagnostic reports on their projects. Most of the private universities (especially Rafael Landívar and Mariano Galvez) have research projects on indigenous issues, many with special emphasis on linguistics. Then, of course, there are the hundreds, perhaps thousands, of foreign researchers like me working in Guatemala on this intriguing topic.

So, despite repeated confessions and denunciations that ladinos and the state are completely ignorant of the Indian, there is plenty of surveillance occurring and large amounts of information available.[37] At the same time,

36. He was making a grim joke, because *archive,* meaning "files," is also the name of the infamous army intelligence wing.

37. Of course, such "ignorance" frequently includes a great deal of stereotypic information along with its fascination. As Judith Butler suggests, such exclusions are not indifferent:

When they were debating gays in the military on television in the U.S. a senator got up and laughed, and he said, "I must say, I know very little about homosexuality. I think I

these projects have multiple effects. Many are employing and training indigenous people, in some cases even producing Mayan activists (see chapters 4 and 8). The results of the research have also been very useful for Mayan aims, both in the sense of valorizing their culture and in providing information and theoretical frameworks. Also, the effects of such work in producing ladino activists in antiracism work should not be underestimated. Several people I interviewed spoke of a coming to consciousness through their research. For many it represented the first time they had left the capital for the interior for more than a touristic sojourn at Lake Atitlán, and the first time they had spoken with indigenous people about more than the price of their labor. Mayan activists have encountered many stalwart allies among these ladino researchers, and the ladinos suggest that they now have very different concepts of the future nation for which they are struggling.

Ministry of Culture and Sports

The Ministry of Culture and Sports was initiated in the waning days of military rule (under the de facto Mejía Víctores government), set in motion under the regimes of Cerezo and Serrano, and was supposed to be disbanded by de León Carpio in late 1993. In 1996 it was limping along, overseeing "high culture" events and under constant threat of dissolution. The Ministry of Culture and Sports brought together state agencies previously grouped separately as Fine Arts, the IIN and related agencies charged with indigenous issues, and departments concerned with national heritage (the Institute of Anthropology and History, parks, museums, and so on).

Vice-Ministry of Culture and the State of Emergency   The ministry's prototype was the Vice-Ministry of Culture instituted in the late 1970s under the state of emergency of General Lucas García's military regime. According to Angel González, who has worked with the Ministry of Culture on and off since this inception in 1978, the government was faced with a deepening legitimation crisis and turned to culture, principally in its Arnoldian sense of "high" culture ("the best that has been thought and written"), but with a nod toward the more anthropological ideas that would be institutionalized

---

know less about homosexuality than about anything else in the world." . . . Then he immediately launched into a homophobic diatribe which suggested that he thinks that homosexuals only have sex in public bathrooms, that they are all male, etc. So what he actually has is a very aggressive and fairly obsessive relationship to the homosexuality that of course he knows nothing about. At that moment you realize that this person who claims to have nothing to do with homosexuality is in fact utterly preoccupied by it. (Butler 1994, 34)

in 1986. Human and financial resources were earmarked for "high" cultural events like the ballet and symphony, to be performed in the newly inaugurated National Theater overlooking the Civic Center in Zone Four, Guatemala City.[38] At a time when any gatherings were suspect, the vice-ministry organized two Cultural Coordination Meetings (1980 and 1982) to plan infrastructure and future projects, all the better to "dignify the Guatemalan in his different cultural expressions, stimulate creative freedom, contribute to the formation of a national identity, and support the recognition as well as the distribution of and high esteem for the multiple cultural expressions of the country" (Ministry of Education 1981, 9).

In the early 1980s under military rule, *indigenous culture* came to signify a way of dealing with the insurgent rural population in the model villages. In the capital, the term seemed to be developing a sense of what was lacking in national identity, a bandage for the wounded body politic. In reports on these coordinating meetings and in the memories of participants, the term *culture* began to be deployed in a more reified sense, as something that could strengthen or "fix" national identity in relation to both internal and external difference. Since 1944, government concern with integration viewed culture as an epiphenomenon that would be swept away by the winds of modernity and nationalism, but in the 1980s, culture began to be viewed as a "thing" with political use and as something everyone, not just Indians, "had."[39]

The final report on the first of these coordinating meetings sounded themes that would be reiterated through the next decade in state documents and public speeches. Whereas the vice-ministry's goals include increasing participation in the arts and improved maintenance of the nation's cultural heritage (at this point mainly buildings), the report highlights the need for increased understanding and respect for "the artistic, artisanal, linguistic, festive, and religious expressions of the indigenous and popular ethnicities in order to contribute to an authentic appreciation of the autochthonous *cultures* of the country" (Ministry of Education 1981, 24; em-

38. The National Theater, named in honor of Guatemala's "other" Nobel Prize winner, the novelist Miguel Angel Asturias, is one of my favorite buildings in the rather tawdry urban landscape of Guatemala City. The architect Efraín Recinos says that he wanted to create a geography of *mestizaje*, combining elements of Classic Mayan architecture with western motifs such as Art Deco (the dominant form in the central zones of Guatemala City) and honoring indigenous philosophy through the building's harmonious relation to the landscape.

39. Attempts to maintain the "authenticity" of textiles, as well as current attempts to legislate aspects of indigenous culture (as in customary law), suggest both the desire to fix a moving and troublesome target and the view that "culture" is a "thing" amenable to such control. These meetings are part of the conditions of possibility for the far more widespread emergence(y) of ladino culture as a problem—a symptom, I argue, of a wounded body politic.

phasis on plural mine). This strengthening of internal identity was to be accompanied in turn by vigilance and "regulation of the mass media so that their programming does not introduce foreign patterns that would alter our national cultural identity" (1981, 25).[40] In the project of democratization and nation building, the role of culture would be central and should receive the appropriate attention from the state (including a Ministry of Culture):

> Culture is the foundation that creates all of our activities as a collective, based in our being and historic destiny, and the State of Guatemala has at times neglected its vital importance, leading to the deterioration of the cultural identity of the urban population and the marginalization of the majority rural population. We feel that any program for National Development cannot function in Guatemala if it has not first fully identified, for each of the cultural groups that form part of our nation, who they are, what they feel, and what they do. A Ministry of Culture is of transcendental importance for the future development of Guatemala because an understanding and recognition of cultural identity will consolidate all of the vital structures of the nation. (1981, 28).

Formation of the Ministry   Once the official state of emergency was lifted in 1986, the Ministry of Culture and Sports was created and placed under the direction of Elmar Rojas, a well-known painter and architect. As with the different notions of *culture,* informants had varied attitudes regarding the role of sports in the ministry. Some proclaimed that sports are the one thing that unites all Guatemalans, and even Rigoberta Menchú seemed to agree. Arriving late to a program in her honor in October 1992, she apologized and said, "I have been at a soccer game and feeling quite patriotic!" Others felt it was a monumental mismatch, the sports side draining resources from culture, creating conflicts of interest and internal strife. Bending over backwards to justify the relation, the official report on the ministry's "Policies, Goals, Strategies" proclaims, "For a long period of time the country has been torn apart for different reasons, creating a climate of aggression, violence, mourning, and social indifference. To change this situation, sports and recreation should be organized and developed in such a way that they return the Guatemalan man to his social activities, supporting peace, happiness, and human solidarity" (Ministry of Culture 1986, 14).

40. In the classic double bind of the "third-world" country, however, the goal immediately following reads: "We must seek out and coordinate international cooperation to consolidate Guatemalan culture." (As a fan of the Material Girl, I found it interesting that in my interviews with men, this concern about external penetration was usually condensed into the figure of the singer-actress Madonna. Several Mayan fathers in particular seemed deeply concerned about her effects on their daughters.)

Nancy Leys Stepan, tracing the history of eugenics in Latin America, suggests a more historical rationale for linking culture and sports. In Latin America, early-twentieth-century biology tended to be neo-Lamarckian, holding that inherited traits could be passed down. Although neo-Lamarckianism was discarded in favor of Darwinian evolutionary theory in the United States and Europe, Stepan suggests that for Latin Americans it held progressive possibilities denied by social Darwinism, which sees poverty, criminality, and other forms of "degeneration" as genetically determined. In contrast to social Darwinism, neo-Lamarckianism was linked to images of progress through state intervention in sanitation, hygiene, and family and reproductive health. Although creepily fascinated with the notion of "racial improvement" ("an aesthetic-biological movement concerned with beauty and ugliness, purity and contamination" [Stepan 1991, 135]), the doctors, activists, and state officials involved in the "hour of eugenics" linked "general hygiene, anti-alcohol campaigns, *sports education,* a minimum-wage law, and a reduction in the cost of living" as ways to improve the miserable conditions of their nation's citizens (Stepan 1991, 100; emphasis added). Just as I argue for culture, Stepan suggests that "through eugenics, gender and race were tied to the politics of national identity" (1991, 105).

Beyond these conceptual issues, the ministry has been plagued with problems from the beginning, with frequent changes of director and address, lack of funding, labor-management struggles complicated by the fact that employees are represented by seven unions, charges of corruption, and over-identification with the Christian Democrat government that has spurred attacks by successor regimes.

Much of the ministry's first year was devoted to infrastructure, setting up offices, hiring people, and buying cars. The elite notion of culture definitely held: most ministers and vice-ministers have been lawyers, and there has only been one anthropologist employed in the upper echelons (Flavio Rojas Lima, who was vice-minister for less than a year). However, the policy statements of the first years emphasize the broader notion of *culture.* Along with decentralizing cultural services and "dignifying the Guatemalan," the ministry is to "research and enrich the ethnocultural groups," "rescue, conserve, and promote folklore, artisanry, and popular art," and "increase internal tourism" (Ministry of Culture 1986, 2–11).

Rather than insist, as in earlier documents, that national identity means homogenization, a different language—of unity with diversity—is deployed in the documents of 1986. "Our goal is to strengthen the national identity of the Guatemalan, so that the different social groups of the country will be coparticipants in integral development. We must research and enrich the cultural values of the country's different ethnicities, their language, their customs, artisanry, art and folklore, rituals, ceremonies, religion, and their own forms of organization." Angel González said that "along with the architects and other artists, the Indians were there, with a very decisive presence." This discourse seems to echo Mayan demands, perhaps because the Ministry of Culture housed the ALMG as the Academy struggled for legalization.

In early 1986, a group of primarily ladino citizens concerned about culture and identity, many of whom had participated in the Coordinating Meetings in 1980 and 1982, held a Conference on Culture. Participants claimed this conference had a powerful effect in making them rethink Guatemalan identity. "It revolutionized me," said one. "It also made me decide, along with many others, that the new Culture Ministry was a possible place to work." Most of the people I interviewed about the conference continue to work on cultural issues, either in the ministry, in NGOs, or in transnational organizations like the United Nations Education, Science, and Culture Organization (UNESCO).

The 1986 conference included members of Congress, bureaucrats, artists, labor unionists, popular movement activists, development workers, municipal officials, and army representatives from all over the country. The Mexican anthropologist Guillermo Bonfil Batalla opened the proceedings, providing a theoretical overview for the discussions of identity.[41] Conference participants discussed the history of cultural policy, what worked, and what did not. They analyzed racism toward the indigenous population and criticized ladinos dressing up as Indians, especially when used in political campaigns or as waiters. As one participant said, "For the first time I realized what an insult it is to have waiters dressed as *cofradía* [traditional saints societies] members! Why aren't there restaurants with waiters dressed as army generals, or folklore performances in the National Theater of Catholic ceremonies? I realized that only the Indian is folklorized, and that is racism."

Although some resisted this talk, many participants said the discussions were refreshing. "We saw how Indians exist in the social consciousness, but also how we as ladinos are afraid to manifest this identity," said one. Discussion also centered on the pernicious effects of foreign cultural imposition on national identity. "With all this discussion," said another participant, "some really interesting things happened. For example, as organizers we

41. In part because of this conference, at least five state officials I interviewed cited Bonfil Batalla and his theories of acculturation—several pulled out pen and paper and drew the chart he had taught them to describe the interactions of foreign and domestic cultural attributes. Though I cannot explore it here, Mexico seems to serve as an Ego Ideal for many Guatemalan state officials in terms of its purported advances in national identity formation around the *mestizaje* project, its indigenous policy, and especially the power and longevity of the PRI (although this may be changing!).

had gone around getting private funding for the conference, and we had talked McDonalds into donating food. But after so much talking about identity and nationalism, everyone ended up refusing to eat the hamburgers. It was seen as cultural imperialism. They said they wanted *pan con frijol* [bread with refried beans] for lunch."

Even though most participants have undoubtedly returned to the Golden Arches, these experiences of the conference suggest that Guatemalan and ladino identifications, like Mayan identity, are produced through time and articulated through struggle, discussion, and praxis. The process of forming the Ministry of Culture (which was simultaneously a space of corruption and even counterinsurgency) served as a quilting point for such articulations and perhaps small changes in ladino body image.

The Christian Democrat Years   Elmar Rojas quit the ministry in 1987 in a dispute over hiring practices; in an interview, he said that he was particularly concerned about the ruling Christian Democrat party using jobs in the ministry as political favors.[42] Under the reign of his successor, Minister of Culture Anaisabel Prera Flores, the ministry became more overtly concerned with indigenous issues and actively supported the ALMG in its demands for a unified alphabet and for legalization. The ministry provided the ALMG with an office, telephones, and funding for a secretary, and ALMG members say that Prera was an important ally in their Congressional fights. Additionally, in 1989, the ministry brought thousands of members of indigenous *cofradías* to a march in Guatemala City, where President Cerezo received them in the National Palace. Although it is often considered to be falling into disuse, the *cofradía* is a civil-religious organization that cares for saints and sponsors festivals and is conceptually linked to maintaining traditional indigenous culture. The *cofradía* march was a major news event, and several people said it was formative in their understanding of the Mayan movement. Many said they felt deterritorialized in their "own" urban space by the sudden influx from the countryside, through thousands of Indians in full regalia ("All those elders with their *trajes,* their staffs of office, their incense, their food," said one ladina) filling the streets of the capital. Many said they were also surprised at how strong indigenous identity was, in both numbers and in tradition. "I still don't know much about these things, but I had thought that all that *cofradía* stuff died out long ago," said one ladino. "To

42. Rumor has it that this is precisely how one minister came to power. It is said that, implicated in the disappearance of impounded drugs from the Justice Ministry's safe, she would enjoy immunity if given a minister's position, and thus she was. One former minister was accused—but never indicted—of misusing several million dollars of UNESCO money for Christian Democrat projects and of turning the ministry over to party politics, using it as a Christian Democrat campaign office.

see them all in the streets, to think they have maintained these beliefs and customs for so long, after so much violence, it really opened my eyes." Some saw the move as crass and cynical: "They just wanted to create the public image of having political backing, that they were popular among the Indians," said Angel González.[43] However, it also served to get money into the communities; in return for their presence each *cofradía* (seven hundred participated) received one thousand quetzales, a significant sum when daily minimum wage was three quetzales.

Some of the ministry's multiple and contradictory policies, goals, and strategies toward culture (such as self interest, surveillance, and attempts to respond to popular needs) are suggested by the *cofradía* march. Leticia de Martínez, planning director at the ministry from 1992 to 1993, said,

> We seek to maintain these identities, to preserve them. We cannot impose, we must be clear that the role of the state is to facilitate, to advise. We need to help them understand how to get access to the state's resources. We need to do a lot more for the ethnicities, and our point of entry has been the *cofradía*. They are part of the traditions of the country and they are a way the ministry can penetrate, can communicate with the communities. We met our goal. We now have contacts among them, we are able to support them a little, and they say the money helps pay for festivals, clothes for the virgin, liquor, fireworks.

In 1988, the ministry published a new overview of its goals, which proclaimed "The Right to Culture" (and which was illustrated with Mayan glyphs and photos of indigenous people in *traje,* as well as the National Theater and murals from the National Palace, including those of Tecún Umán). As part of integral development and democratization, this right would allow the "people of Guatemala to be able to say with pride, 'I am part of this nation'" (Ministry of Culture 1988, 2). In this document, culture is seen as integral to the existence of the state, to identity, and national defense. This occurs in part, the document argues, because when the Guatemalan man feels part of the nation, the "transformative energy of his creativity begins to surge." Concomitantly, the loss of his heritage weakens him. According to the document, given Guatemala's increasing transnational interdependence, this solidified national identity with its accompanying energy reserves is necessary to confront the galloping changes in technology and world history.

The fundamental goal of the ministry's work plan contained in this state-

---

43. Richard Wilson concurs: "Such cynical manipulation of indigenous culture was accompanied by a profusion of utterances about the value of the indigenous heritage of the nation" (1995, 263). My fluidary analysis wants to ask if such cynical manipulation always gets what it wants, and indeed, how manipulated are those *cofradía* members accepting four hundred dollars from the government? Unfortunately Wilson does not suggest what this trip meant to people from the communities.

ment is to get beyond the traditional elitist and exclusionary model concerned primarily with fine arts and based in the notion of a homogeneous national culture and replace this with an understanding of Guatemala as a multicultural country, whose unity as a nation rests on ethnic multiplicity. Errors of the past are based in paternalism and ignorance of these populations—ignorance regarding who they are, their aspirations, their real needs, and their motivations (Ministry of Culture 1988, 28–29). Instead, it is the state's responsibility to promote all cultural expressions. The document reviews the legal and political bases for the ministry's work contained in the Constitution and the government's National Plan. The Constitution (Art. 58) recognizes the right of persons and communities to possess and maintain their cultural identity and holds the state responsible for preserving and promoting culture (Art. 65) and for opening national and international markets to free trade of national artistic and artisanal production (Art. 62). The National Plan seeks to decentralize (see chapter 8) and democratize state services, "promote Central American integration and the international struggle against cultural colonialism," and "determine the characteristics of the different cultures that compose the diverse reality of the country so that development plans are incorporated by the communities" (Ministry of Culture 1988, 18–20).

Here again is the concern that not enough is known about the indigenous population, a situation that limits state penetration. The ministry's plan calls for an ethnographic inventory of indigenous cultural expression (such as artisanry, architecture, painting, literature, and weavings) and of production, including technical information. This is where the notion of culture as market value begins to be deployed.[44] Some of the language suggests an import substitution model, with protection for domestic production, under the rubric of preventing a dangerous cultural alienation. The ministry's plan calls for a new rationalization in cultural development, based on scientific facts and figures.[45] For example:

44. Through 1992 and 1993, *Prensa Libre* published a monthly series called "Let's Get to Know Guatemala." Each book-size, fifteen-page pamphlet detailed one of Guatemala's departments, with sections on geography—including a pull-out poster-size map—history, the municipalities, local festivals and myths, hospitality, and a personal account of getting to know the department. The series was underwritten by the Granai and Townson bank, and the back cover of each pamphlet was a full-page ad for the bank with a poem and the tag line "conserving our values." Similarly, in 1996 the think tank ASIES began a nationwide ethnographic project to survey the entire country and produce reports on each municipality, including its population, resources, development needs, and so on. In addition, the Socioeconomic Accord of the Peace Treaty calls for a cadastral survey (of land use and boundaries), another example of the sense that the country is not integrated and that the population is ignorant of itself, a situation the Ministry of Culture was supposed to "fix."

45. Foucault (1991) reminds us that statistics are the science of the state.

Once the facts are gathered and analyzed we can begin to apprehend the cultural potential of the country, to systematically inventory cultural organisms, their publics and their costs, which will allow us to define rules and assess efficiency criteria, profitability, and the efficient intervention of public powers. This will require statistical studies, analysis of public expenses in this area, cost benefit analyses, and what one could call the *cultural accounting of the nation.* (Ministry of Culture 1988, 39; emphasis added)

Just as the work of the ministry was justified through claims that a strong national cultural identity was necessary to compete in the postindustrial transnational world, the document suggests the corresponding utility of indigenous cultures. In a section extolling the rich and ancient multiplicity of cultures that configure the ethnological map of Guatemala, the ministry asserts that "the public is segmented into subpublics, products of the fragmentation of the population in diverse subcultures (*known in marketing parlance as market segments*)" (Ministry of Culture 1988, 29; emphasis added). As I analyze below, this instrumental notion of culture is both useful for a developing governmentality of the democratizing Guatemalan state and appropriatable by Mayan activists deploying their own notions of culture.

Though suggesting an important shift, this discourse is also, of course, about marketing the ministry. As a new (and always underfunded) state institution, the ministry was called upon to justify its existence. This became especially true after the Christian Democrats lost the presidency to President Serrano Elías in 1990.

1990 to Planned Dissolution   The new Serrano government, in austerity mode following a tightening in their World Bank structural adjustment package, called for dismantling the ministry, denouncing it as a Christian Democrat breeding ground for corruption. In the months surrounding the election, the ministry went through a series of ministers and vice-ministers before finally the powers that be were convinced of its value. Angel González said that the man whom Serrano sent in to close the ministry "fell in love with what we were doing. He said he had no idea of all the valuable things we did, and he came out saying its mandate should be expanded." Serrano named as minister Eunice Lima, a lawyer and diplomat, who had headed the Fine Arts Office under the military dictatorships of the 1970s and was minister of education under General Mejía Víctores (1993–1996).[46] Minister Lima cleaned up the ministry's image—by paying off

46. According to Julia Becker Richards and Michael Richards, in this capacity she was responsible for creating the National Program of Bilingual Education (PRONEBI), which "assumed a vanguard position in a growing Mayanist movement that cast the Mayan languages as central to the cultural heritage of the nation and a national treasure to be fortified and preserved" (1996, 213).

debts and reorganizing previously chaotic institutional relations—and organized a series of high-profile festivals (principally music and theater) and international summit meetings. The ministry also energized its publishing activities, putting out dozens of titles by national authors, including several books on indigenous themes like a reprint of Flavio Rojas Lima's study of the *cofradía* system (1988) and a novel by the Maya-Kanjobal writer Gaspar Pedro González (1992), who is also a member of the ALMG. In the words of Angel González, "The ministry was finally getting going."

Some complain, however, that the minister was still far more interested in theater and ballet (high, universal, "ladino" culture) than culture in the anthropological sense. The Guatemalan anthropologist Flavio Rojas Lima, who was vice-minister for nine months before Eunice Lima took over as minister, complained, "Now they don't care about the Indians at all! When I was vice-minister, I tried to reanimate it, but I left because I could not work with Serrano. He was totally arrogant. I told him that the Ministry of Culture had better deal with the ethnic policies, but there was no response." Angel González would agree: "On the Indians?" he said. "Nothing. Really, since Serrano they have done nothing."

Minister Lima also agreed that there had not been adequate attention paid to what she said should be

> the primary function of the ministry: the ethnic groups and popular cultures. This shouldn't really be a Fine Arts Ministry, the private sector can deal with that. I have been thinking about this for a long time; the state cannot leave it unattended any longer. We must acknowledge the reality that there are many cultures. For too long we have maintained an official culture, the mestizo, abandoning the ethnic cultures. But we need more equality. We can no longer impose culture, instead we must work with the communities, do what they want.

She said she was personally working to create a new division within the ministry to do precisely that, a General Direction of Ethnic, Indigenous, and Popular Culture.[47]

The ministry's planning director, Leticia de Martínez, was enthusiastic about the ministry's emerging focus on indigenous issues. She consulted with anthropologists and Mayan activists, including members of the ALMG, on the best way to set up the division. The idea was to create a Mayan-run agency within the ministry. As Vice-Minister Estuardo Meneses said, "They can come and tell us what their projects are and we'll give them money. Our

47. The ministry's planning officer, Ms. Martínez, said they had first thought to call it the Direction of Mayan Culture, but then she was reminded by the anthropologist Celso Lara that the Maya are not the only indigenous people in Guatemala, thus the rather unwieldy title.

priorities, of course, are national needs, but now the Indians are participating in the national project as never before. The General Direction would be a way to analyze their needs and respond. It will help us concentrate on the nation, on creating Guatemalan-ness."

Martínez said that although the ministry was focusing more on indigenous issues, it was still a struggle to convince other branches of the government that culture in general was an important issue and that indigenous culture needed attention, even though external pressures like the International Year of Indigenous Peoples were helping to change people's attitudes. She mentioned that a talk given by the Mayan Manuel Salazar Tetzagüic (named vice-minister of education by de León Carpio and later made president of the Guatemalan Indigenous Fund [FODIGUA]) at the palace in October 1992 had helped them in their struggles to create the new division:

> I was amazed. All the ministers and vice-ministers were there, listening to this indigenous man. I had never seen anything like it. There is a lot of controversy on this issue, but they came and they had to think about it. He gave a very careful, measured talk. He was very serious. The government people know that there is a lot of talent, that the Maya are much more qualified now. They are well prepared, and we know we have to listen to them. We used that talk to help raise consciousness about our role, that our ministry could be the most important for the development of our nation. Culture is basic to everything—health, education, development.

Despite this knowledge and enthusiasm, the disjunction between culture as fine arts and culture as "basic to everything" continues, even during the ministry's press conference to announce an internal reorganization and the new focus on indigenous and popular culture. The press conference was basically a party for the cultural "elite," with an open bar held in a salon of the National Theater in January 1993. Writers, musicians, painters, actors, radio personalities, and ministry officials mingled with journalists. Copies of the reorganization plan were distributed in folders covered with indigenous textiles, and plastic plaques with fake jade Mayan figurines were distributed as tokens of appreciation to journalists and artists who had contributed to the work of the ministry in the past year. Little mention was made of the proposed General Direction, and there were no Maya in attendance. Libations flowed liberally, people schmoozed, and finally a piano was rolled out and the country's most famous composer serenaded Minister Lima. He also played a medley in memory of Audrey Hepburn, who had died that day, and general conversation turned to the influence of her work. When I told a ladino friend about attending the fete, she first said she was jealous that I had had the chance to hang with those national stars, and then laughed and said that I had found a little piece of the "state" that I was looking for. "That's where it happens," she said. "It's not an accident that there weren't any indigenous people there!"

One way the government has tried to respond is by creating a Social Cabinet to coordinate the efforts of various ministries (including Education, Rural and Urban Development, Agriculture, Health, Planning, Finance, and the Tourism Institute), with specific attention to ethnic issues. Ms. Martínez said she feels that in this cabinet the Ministry of Culture is finally being listened to. "At that level I think they are beginning to understand the importance of culture, but that understanding is not reflected in the budget yet." In 1992 the ministry was allotted sixty-two million quetzales (about twelve million dollars), approximately three-quarters of 1 percent of the national budget (compared to a whopping 20 percent that went to debt payments, 28 percent to education and transportation, and 8 percent to defense).

Vice-Minister Meneses spoke at length about the ministry's uphill battle to work within the government. "The government does not have a policy on culture, which makes it hard for us to work. There is no continuity (we've had seven ministers in seven years); there is no development, no coherence. . . . We are trying to win a space in the government, to convince the president and other sectors of the importance of culture." Meneses also saw the monthly meetings of the Social Cabinet as a step forward and mentioned various initiatives of the Serrano government to address the ethnic sector, including the Social Investment Fund (FIS) and National Peace Fund (FONAPAZ), as well as plans to create a National Indigenous Fund and a secretary of indigenous affairs to be based in the palace. He claimed that the ministry was instrumental in inciting this work. (These funds seem to be a direct result of the modeling work done in the Development Poles, as ways to intervene directly into areas seen as most "in need.")

Meneses cited two major reasons for this increase in government interest. First is the impact of indigenous organizing. "In the last few years we've seen a major increase, around a whole set of demands, and it is getting stronger and stronger. Their political organization is growing, and we can't stop it. But the government needs to respond, we need to channel it." Secondly, he said, some people are finally beginning to realize that indigenous culture is a "productive resource":

> I could get fired for saying this because officially it is coffee, but the major moneymaker for Guatemala now is tourism. Some billion quetzales come into the country through tourism, and those tourists come for culture. No one wants to see the Chamber of Commerce, the Finance Ministry, the army! No, they come for culture. And how much do we, the Culture Ministry, receive? Some sixty million quetzales. That's all! Our cultural heritage is a major money-earner. It could be our entry into the global economy. We have a ma-

jor industry to develop here, one that is not vulnerable to trade sanctions, to quotas, to tariffs, to rain or frost or drought. It can compete with any product on the world market and requires very little investment.

Apparently there was a growing agreement about the importance of culture, because the ministry's budget was more than doubled for the 1993 fiscal year, to 160 million quetzales.

Simultaneous with complaints about the lack of government interest in indigenous issues, there was a turf war going on among different government agencies over who could mark out terrain with the indigenous banner. The Ministry of Culture was working to create their General Direction of Indigenous, Ethnic, and Popular Culture, and the presidential secretary for political affairs was developing plans for a Secretariat of Indigenous Affairs. According to one of the architects of this planned secretariat, there was disagreement regarding the appropriate level for the agency—General Direction, secretary, ministry, and so on. (There are similar disagreements among the Maya in terms of what to ask for [NACLA 1996c].) The idea, she said, would be to create a space within the state for indigenous people, but there was concern about it becoming bureaucratized and politicized. A secretariat was seen as powerful enough—as a member of the cabinet, it would have access to the president—but also small enough to be agile and responsive. Serrano's secretary for political affairs, Juan Daniel Alemán, said that the new organization was needed to "construct a national identity, one that works for the nation's welfare."

There were also rivalries over the administration of the proposed National Indigenous Fund, part of an international effort to channel money directly to indigenous projects. The Ministry of Culture insisted that it was an appropriate home for the fund, as did the secretary for political affairs and FONAPAZ.[48] Some of these arguments over which ministry or section

48. FONAPAZ is associated with FIS, and both channel national and international (including World Bank) monies to NGOs and local community groups. They are both autonomous entities assigned to the presidency and meant to bypass inefficient bureaucracies. FONAPAZ is specifically oriented toward areas most affected by the war and has been relatively successful in funding grassroots work. Mayan activists and ladino NGO workers spoke highly of its director, Alvaro Colón. He in turn spoke of his efforts with FONAPAZ, of physically visiting rural areas, working closely with indigenous people, and gaining insight into the power of traditional communities, as a revolutionizing experience. "Most ladinos still believe that they are the only civilization here. For too long they have believed that the Indians are responsible for the backwardness of this country, but I have realized that on the contrary, the Maya are the main factor in whatever civilization we have."

Although, as Colón said, the conflict zones that are the responsibility of FONAPAZ correspond almost isomorphically to the indigenous zones of the country, the FODIGUA is contemplated as an alternative way to raise funds for projects of a specifically cultural nature. Colón said, "I refused to have anything to do with planning it until they promised to turn it over entirely to Mayan leadership." In July 1994, the fund was renamed the Guatemalan Fund

should be in charge of which indigenous project were probably about job security and which "indigenist" initiative would have access to state and international funds (and their accompanying graft opportunities). But these struggles over culture, both in terms of bureaucratic jurisdiction and in being listened to within the larger state, also seem to be struggles over access to the emerging "cultural capital" of the indigenous movement. This is both about personal gain (Prera parlayed her position as minister into a Paris-based job with UNESCO) and also, I would suggest, about the hopes for the nation as unified and the state as legitimate, which were expressed by all of these state officials when they discussed culture.

Vice-Minister Meneses suggested, however, that these rivalries contributed to the decision to dissolve the ministry after the Serrano coup in May 1993. Promising to clean house and get rid of corruption, the new president, Ramiro de León Carpio, immediately called for the dissolution of the ministry, setting off a rather heated debate in the press about its role. Both sides agreed that culture was vitally important to the nation, with the pro-ministry side arguing for expanding its role, and anti-ministry forces contending that the ministry did nothing for culture, being too bureaucratic and corrupt, and that it should all be swept away, its tasks delegated either to a newly cleaned up and more agile state agency (which would also mean breaking the unions), or turned over to the private, "more efficient" sectors. Vice-Minister Meneses said of this suggestion, "This is because tourism—based in our cultural heritage—is the wave of our future, where the money is. Certain sectors know this and they want to control it absolutely. They want to be making the dollars off of it. That's why they want to privatize it and get the state out of it. This is why there is so much animosity toward the ministry."

The de León Carpio government set up a state commission to investigate the ministry, under the auspices of the seventy-year-old vice president. It was headed by the writer Mario Monteforde Toledo and included the Mayan activists Dr. Demetrio Cojtí and ALMG member Gaspar González. The commission's final report strongly recommended retaining the ministry and greatly expanding its mandate to deal more explicitly with Mayan affairs. This recommendation was ignored, and the ministry was supposed to be downgraded to a directorate within the Ministry of Education, to become an umbrella for the fine arts and the National Institute for Anthro-

for Indigenous Development (FODIGUA) and signed into existence by President de León Carpio, to be headed by the Maya-K'iche' Manuel Salazar Tetzagüic. Money was to come from external sources, as agreed in the Iberoamerican Summit of 1994, but has not been forthcoming. Promised twenty million quetzales at its initiation, by late 1995 only five million had been disbursed (Bastos and Camus 1995, 147).

pology and History (INAEH). Plans for both the General Directorate of Indigenous, Ethnic, and Popular Cultures as well as the Secretariat for Indigenous Affairs in the Palace were scrapped, although the National Indigenous Fund (now FODIGUA) has become a reality. Interested parties and bureaucratic inertia seem to have saved the ministry, at least in its high-culture manifestation. It continues, in rump form, to support museums, dance, music, and theater productions into the era of President Alvaro Arzú, who has also called for its dissolution.

In his inaugural speech, which angered and frustrated many of my informants in the bureaucracy, de León Carpio signaled a major shift away from the emerging articulation of culture and indigenous issues that I have been charting here. Rather than deploying a unity in diversity discourse, de León Carpio attempted to suture over the effects of Guatemala's catastrophic history by suggesting that national unity was already achieved and that any special attention to Indians would be discriminatory to everyone else. This position shocked many who had been ecstatic about human rights ombudsman de León Carpio's ascension to the presidency.[49] As ombudsman, he had spearheaded the definition of and respect for "collective rights" in addition to individual human rights, forming a general legal rubric for attention to indigenous issues. He had also personally pleaded with the Guatemalan United Nations specialist on indigenous rights, Agosto Willensen, to return to Guatemala after years in exile to start up a new ombuds section for indigenous issues. Although de León Carpio made the historic move of naming the first Maya to a ministry position (Dr. Alfredo Tay as education minister), his attitude toward culture and indigenous issues was seen as a major retrenchment.[50]

49. The Congress met on June 5, 1993, to choose a successor to Serrano, who had left the country in disgrace. That was my birthday, and between spending most of the day at the assembly called by Mayan leaders to respond to the crisis (which became the Assembly of the Pueblo Maya [APM]) and preparing for my party, I was only partly keeping up with the goings-on. At about eleven that night, we went outside for the customary birthday firecrackers in the street in front of the house, and one of the neighbors came out on her balcony. I thought she was going to yell at us for waking her up, but she started shouting "*derechos humanos! derechos humanos!*" (human rights! human rights!). That's when we found out that de León Carpio had been chosen. She thought we were celebrating his election and came out to celebrate with us.

50. There was a great deal of speculation about whether de León was acting as a spokesman for such a retrenchment within the army. His cousin, Jorge Carpio Nicole, head of the National Union of the Center (UCN) party, two-time presidential runner-up and influential newspaper editor, was assassinated soon after de León took office. The crime has not been solved, and many saw it as a direct message to de León Carpio. He did, however, finally have to concede to PR demands to acknowledge indigenous difference. After his inauguration, he went on a national tour and transvestited as a Todos Santos indigenous male while in the highlands.

A member of the team preparing the Secretariat of Indigenous Affairs in the Palace expressed shock and disbelief that more than a year of work was being thrown out with total disregard. "They don't understand how important this is. I feel responsible to all the people who worked with us on this. We have let them down. There were so many expectations. What is it all for, if so much work and effort and hope can be erased so easily? Don't they realize that we could end up like Bosnia if these demands are not attended to?" Vice-Minister of Culture Meneses suggested that the dissolution of the ministry was a mistake because it closed down a governmental way to channel the growing power of the Mayan movement:

> There are many interests behind closing the ministry. They realize that it is a site with political potential, a place where artists and writers with international stature like Mario Monteforde come together, and then there are the indigenous sectors. This could be an important place for them, and there are those who understand that this could be dangerous[,] . . . but the state must deal with this. I've said this to many people, but they are not taking it as seriously as they should.

I left the field a week after the decision was taken to disband the Ministry of Culture, so I cannot detail here the developments in the indigenous policy of the de León Carpio and Arzú governments, although under Arzú Convention 169 was finally signed, as was the Accord on Identity and Indigenous Rights, which in late 1998 was engaging the Congress in wrangles over how to make it into national law (including, a decade late, writing the famous empty Constitutional Article 70 meant to deal with the Maya).

STATE FETISH AS SYMPTOM AND CULTURE AS MAGICAL CURE

So what do these contradictory policies, strategies, and goals of the Guatemalan state tell us? The state is "more lost than the children of La Llorona," and yet there are scores of studies and initiatives dealing with the indigenous issue. One part of "the state" struggles to make the others "listen" to its concerns about the importance of culture. Whereas some state sectors warn that the Maya are a danger and even warn of a race war, others insist that the Maya are already fully integrated and need no "special treatment." Meanwhile, there is still no functioning state institution concerned specifically with indigenous demands (the ALMG described in the next chapter is state-funded but autonomous, although FODIGUA is beginning to provide funds for various projects). The Maya in turn disagree on whether they even want such an institution, worried that it might become a ghetto. State workers and ladinos in general are characterized as completely ignorant of the Indians, and yet I encountered a number of well-informed ladinos throughout the state structure who are dedicated, politically and emotionally, to indigenous causes (Alvaro Colón, who runs FONAPAZ, is even training to become a *sacerdote maya* [a Mayan priest]!). Within all of the institutions where I worked, there are individuals who seem wholeheartedly (and not just for my benefit) supportive of Mayan issues, who in both formal interviews and more relaxed social contexts treat Mayan people respectfully and deploy the most politically correct of rhetorics: as one said, "This is an indigenous country, and we will never advance until we give the indigenous peoples their full rights as equal citizens with the right to diversity, so they can maintain their culture." State policy seems to be to "fix" Mayan culture by "rationalizing and reforming," homogenizing and hegemonizing it (making it ladino). Yet it often "fixes" it, stabilizes and repairs it, by, for example, supporting Mayan language unification, or writing Mayan rights into law. This in turn supports the *formación* (creation of) Mayan activists through the ALMG or Delegation for the Ratification of Convention 169 (see chapters 4 and 8).

Does the state as fetish help us understand these "paradoxes?" In its manifest content, the Quincentennial Guatemalan state seems powerful and legitimate: it gets international loans, signs peace accords, hands out money, is looked to for justice, represents Guatemala to the world, and regulates relations between the global and the local.[51] Many Guatemalans, however, view it as a nation-state in ruins. In attempting to map the manifest with this latent content, I have taken you through the inner workings of one site within the state. There we saw petty bureaucratic rivalries, party politics, absconded funds, meetings, memos, kitschy faux-jade plaques, concerts, soccer matches, and people rethinking their identities.

So, what is the allure of the piñata effect? As the presidential secretary said, people "hit" the state, slam it for being corrupt and inefficient. But they also hit it in a dereifying move parallel to the fluidary analysis I've tried to practice here—they break it open to get at the sweets that somehow, magically, await them inside. They hit it up for money, power, and other goodies, and this move, like the party game, is both violent and playful.

But why does it work, when people "know very well" that Guatemala is a nation in ruins, when they have a clear-eyed analysis of the state as corrupt, clueless, counterinsurgent, and still possibly murderous? Given the disenchantment, the terror, why are ladinos and Mayas working so hard for representation there, in tiny civic committees battling over municipal control,

51. In September 1996, President Arzú addressed the UN General Assembly: "Now is the time for reconciliation. Now is the moment to get back to development . . . for seeking effective formulas for linking our villages with the World Trade Organization, for connecting the impoverished families of our neighborhoods with the international financial institutions, for relating the decisions of our indigenous communities with the major development agencies" (GNIB 1996b, 1).

in the popular movement's political party (the New Guatemalan Democratic Front, or FDNG), through the reincorporation of the URNG, and the ALMG's struggles for state recognition? Are they dupes?

Both Karl Marx and Sigmund Freud analyzed the fetish as a cover for something else. In Marx's notion of commodity fetishism, the thing being exchanged covers over and hides the human relations of production embedded therein. The magic of the commodity is in part the way social relations among people are hidden by the apparent relations among things (the commodity's value seems based on the accidental interplay of supply and demand rather than the value of labor). For Freud, the fetish conceals a lack, a castration, that is too terrifying to contemplate and so is hidden by the fetish object. It is around this lack, in turn, that the symbolic network is articulated.

At this Quincentennial moment, the state as fetish may be a symptom of the wounded body politics of Guatemala's catastrophic history. As a fetish, it covers over the lack of solid identifications and becomes powerfully invested with all the energy attempting to leap over, disavow, and close that wound. The energy filling the space between manifest and latent content may give the state its power to incite, induce, and seduce people into struggling over the site and stake of the "real" state. It is this always lacking and yet power-filled nation-state that Taussig identifies as the "maleficium."

As Slavoj Zizek reminds us, it is not enough to analyze the latent content. Our task is not only to unmask these hidden meanings; "we must also examine the process—homologous to the 'dream-work'—by means of which the concealed content assumes such a form. . . . There is definitely more at stake than the commodity-form itself, and it [is] precisely this 'more' which exert[s] such a fascinating power of attraction" (Zizek 1989, 15–16). In this chapter and the rest of the book, I argue that Maya and ladino relations on the terrain of the state are overdetermined, structured by what Zizek calls "ideological fantasy." This is a process, like the dreamwork and jokework, through which social relations take on their contingent forms and which exerts a fascinating power of attraction for my analytic work.

So, although I agree with Philip Abrams (1988) on "the difficulty of studying the state," I argue that we must add this dimension of fantasy to understand his description of it: "not the reality which stands behind the mask of political practice as it is. [The state] is itself the mask which prevents our seeing political practice as it is" (Abrams 1988, 58). I find the image of the mask suggestive but too quiescent; the mask image misses the fantasy work, the process involved in constantly articulating this form, the state, that seems so real. It also retains a sense of "the people" being duped by the mask (the manifest content), whereas we analysts might see latent political practice as it really is. I think Taussig goes one better with Abrams's "dazzling and disturbing representation" of the state as mask, saying that "it not only implicates the State in the cultural construction of reality but delineates that reality as inherently deceptive, real and unreal at one and the same time—in short, a thoroughly nervous Nervous System" (Taussig 1992, 113).

In Quincentennial Guatemala, this system has sustained many blows and is getting panicky at the hemorrhaging, even verging on anaphylactic shock.[52] Culture looks like a magic bullet that can heal this wounded body politic, ease its nervousness, perform the dreamwork that maintains it as simultaneously real and unreal. Culture has often served as a "therapeutic myth, meant to explain why we fall ill and why we get well" (Borch-Jacobson 1996, 1)—in Guatemala, poverty, backwardness, and other social ills have been blamed on indigenous culture. But now the army deploys Mayan culture in creating soldier males and in exerting its power over death and life throughout the national territory. Rather than a backwater, the "traditional" Mayan highlands become "laboratories of modernity" where governmental strategies are tried out before becoming state policy. The Ministry of Culture calls for a "cultural accounting of the nation" and claims that culture will create "Guatemalan-ness," which will in turn magically bring with it "integral development," a surge in creativity, and the ability to compete in the transnational realm. Vice-Minister Meneses calls culture (and he repeated this in all our interviews) a productive resource, a commodity, reified as an industry immune to tariffs, needing very little investment. This magical industry will produce without consuming (mimicking capital in its most mysterious form, money breeding money in interest). It draws gringos (and ladinos as "tourists in their own country") with a similar promise: "The touristic ideal of the 'primitive' is that of a magical resource that can be used without actually possessing or diminishing it" (MacCannell 1994, 102).[53]

---

52. Webster's definition of anaphylactic shock is "a condition of hypersensitivity to substances caused by previous exposure to the substance and resulting in shock or other physical reaction." Fetishism is about a trauma that is disavowed, that people do not want to deal with—for example, that ladino identity is not solid, or that the modern state needs the magic of culture. But disavowal is not the same as psychotic foreclosure. The pain of these wounds is available because the body politic retains trace memories of "previous exposures" and physically reacts. The fetish acknowledges the history of bodies politic, the results of the hostile markings I explore in the next chapter. As Emily Apter suggests, "Fetishism fixes in time and place—commemorating a founding moment in the etiology of consciousness, harking back as a 'memorial' (Freud's expression) to an unrepeatable first form—[however,] it is hardly immune to repetition compulsion" (Apter 1993, 4). The double helix of attraction and repulsion exerted by the state as fetish is itself a symptom of these memorials, of these founding and repeated traumas in the catastrophic history of the national body politic.

53. The image of entire indigenous villages joining the URNG and the sense that once "awakened" this majority would carry the revolution to victory—without insisting on leading their own organizations—suggests that the URNG had a similar magical reading of culture.

Culture here suggests the power of the romantic fantasy of "the nation" as well as promising a magic solution to that task that Jane Collier suggests is "ultimately impossible": "Modern nationalists have to find traditions that distinguish them from other Nations without marking them as traditional or backward[,] . . . [and] the impossibility of the task does not relieve [them] from the obligation to attempt it" (1997, 207).

Until the pan-Mayan movement emerged, ladinos could both define themselves as modern against Mayan tradition and appropriate Mayan tradition as their own past. Mayan activism in Quincentennial Guatemala troubles this move; it exposes the way relations between national and ethnic identities are not natural or whole but instead are created and contingent, stumped. On a smaller scale, this may be similar to the crisis William Pietz describes in fetishistic systems in which "the political economic reality of capitalist society suddenly appears in public culture *as fetishistic* (that is, as an alien and perversely unnatural reality)" (1993, 149). I don't want to push this optimistic simile too far, but Mayan organizers insist that they remain Maya while appropriating the markers of modernity, at the same time that they demand that ladinos stop exploiting the image of the Maya, especially of the Mayan woman, for their own identity purposes (COMG 1991; Cojtí 1994; Majawil Q'ij 1992). These demands are being written into national law through the peace treaty with the Accord on Indigenous Rights and through international law in the Congressional approval of the ILO's Convention 169. Because the Maya claim to be both the past and future of Guatemala, ladinos have to adjust their body image. Suddenly, in organized seminars and study groups, as well as informal gatherings and conversations in barrooms, beauty salons, and soccer matches, people are discussing that previously unmarked category: ladino body politics.

Uncannily, what had been national, modern, and natural now shows up as a crisis in ladino identification. Although Mayan traditions previously appeared vestigial, marked for extinction as modern Guatemalan and ladino identities rushed toward the future, the Quincentennial reminds us that tradition is "not modernity's opposite, . . . [it] is modern as well" (J. Collier 1997, 215).[54] State fetishism and the piñata effect may be magically charged by the promise that the state—representing modernity par excellence— and culture—standing in for tradition, community, and sincerity—will provide this simultaneity and overcome this crisis. Identification, as Diana Fuss reminds us, is "both voluntary and involuntary, necessary and difficult,

---

54. As Jack Amariglio and Antonio Callari (1993), William Pietz (1993), and Anne McClintock (1995) point out, the etymology of the term *fetish* betrays the ambivalence of imperialism—although the term was coined to describe "primitive" practices, fetishism actually organizes modern, imperial identity.

dangerous and effectual, naturalizing and denaturalizing. Identification is the point where the psychical/social distinction becomes impossibly confused and finally untenable" (1995, 10). The fetish, as "a critical, materialist theory of social desire" (Pietz 1993, 129), helps us see the state linking body and body politic, the intimacies of identification and the macro of political economy, "the dialectical unity of the voluntary and the violent" (Pietz 1993, 151), and what Taussig calls a "praxis, of the maker making him/herself" (1992, 126).

In my fluidary attempts to analyze the state as terrain and praxis, I look at the ways "real" Mayas and ladinos articulate ethnic, class, gender, and national identifications in relation to one another (through the Ministry of Culture and Sports, the ALMG, and so on), and I try to understand the ways the "fear laden embrace" (R. Adams 1990, 156) in which they are locked resists appeals to "reality," the ways that embrace is overdetermined by fantasy. Zizek suggests that "the fundamental level of ideology . . . is not of an illusion masking the real state of things but that of an (unconscious) fantasy structuring our social reality itself" (1989, 33).

Which brings me to the Maya.

FOUR

Hostile Markings Taken for Identity

Questions of Ambivalence and Authority in a Graveyard inside Guatemala, October 1992

The Spanish invasion broke the process of our own evolution. . . . Because of the huge differences between one world and another, this experience was highly traumatic for the Pueblo Maya. . . . We are not only oppressed, but mutilated and atomized. . . . The long centuries of oppression have placed the Pueblo Maya in a clear position of subaltern disadvantage.

Document of the Guatemalan Mayan Language Academy

Identity [under colonialism] is a hostile marking. The work is to turn it into a process of liberation.

DONNA HARAWAY

IDENTITY AS COMMUNITY-BOUND

Mayan culture may now function as a magical treasure for the state (and for Mayan organizations), but under Guatemala's various colonialisms, the "Indian" has also been identified—by ladinos and the state—through the hostile markings of stereotypes: as lazy, stupid, brutal, backward, superstitious, uncivilized, illiterate, rebellious, and, in the clearest case of projection, hostile (González Ponciano 1991).[1] Mayan cultural rights activists are

---

1. The chapter title mimics Homi Bhabha's "Signs Taken for Wonders: Questions of Ambivalence and Authority under a Tree outside Delhi, May 1817" (1985). I use the term *graveyard* to refer in general to the effects of the civil war, although the term also has special relevance for the ALMG; in addition to the way counterinsurgency targeted Mayan villages, the ALMG office building is specifically haunted by this past through the clandestine holding cell found there when the Academy moved in. "October 1992" obviously refers to the Quincentennial. I would like to thank Mary Pratt for her help in thinking through the arguments of this chapter.

Freud describes projection in "On the Mechanism of Paranoia" thus: "An internal perception is suppressed, and, instead, its content, after undergoing a certain degree of distortion, enters consciousness in the form of an external perception" (1963c, 36). For example, instead of "I love him," the paranoic perceives that "he hates me." Instead of "I depend on Indians," the postcolonial paranoic perceives that "Indians hate me." The frequent warnings from ladinos that Mayan organizing will lead to a race war seem symptomatic of this.

attempting to create a body politic in part out of the body images that others have of them. Much of what they have to work with is post-colonial—namely, the identities that, over the past five hundred years, have been hostilely marked through the orthopedics of church, school, army barracks, courtroom, and land registry, through relations with the state. As such, Mayan identifications are caught in the double helix of attraction and repulsion. They are also, in part, formed through active Mayan petitions to that state.

Here I explore one such petition: efforts to legalize the Maya-controlled but state-supported Guatemalan Mayan Language Academy (ALMG) (chapter 8 explores a similar process around Convention 169). The positions of middlemen and middlewomen (those who work between the state and their communities as translators, teachers, and so on) have historically led to ladinoization, the erasure of Mayan identification. In the years leading up to the Quincentennial, however, these very positions have produced Mayan cultural rights activists. Short biographies of several middlemen and middlewomen struggling for legalization of the ALMG suggest that the process of articulating the magic of culture to this political struggle—an organizing strategy they call *formación* (creation)—serves to constitute Mayan identifications. I will also address the role of gender in these articulations and suggest that there are problematic attempts to bind, or fix, certain identities, even within a project bound for community understood as equal and just.

"Mayan Identity": In Search of . . . the Authentic Indian

The question of how much original "pre-Colombian" culture is retained by present-day indigenous peoples has fascinated historians and anthropologists, gringo and Guatemalan, for years (for an excellent overview of this question, see C. Smith 1990b). Some argue that there are idols behind the altars, timeless beliefs camouflaged in acceptable clothing (the hostile markings of Catholicism or obedience to the Spanish Crown). "Fierce resistance" and the "closed corporate community," developed (and later critiqued) by Eric Wolf (1957 and 1986), which function to protect and maintain identity through time (even as the communities incorporate external elements), are key images in these readings and in the contests over culture.

An alternative reading of ethnic identity suggests that there is *no* difference, only hostile markings: that ethnic identity is only an ideological cover to justify class inequalities. The Guatemalan historian Severo Martínez Peláez suggests this in *Patria del Criollo* (1990), a book that, as I have mentioned, is the standard text at the National University and many secondary schools and was frequently quoted in my interviews. Martínez Peláez argues that the category of "Indian" was created during the Spanish colonial period to designate those most exploited by the hacienda and later plantation systems. This economic reductionism downplays racism, arguing that once the class structure was overturned, such discrimination, along with ethnic identification, would melt away (see also Friedlander 1975; Díaz-Polanco 1985 and 1987). Martínez Peláez has suggested, in a much-repeated formulation, that *traje* (traditional clothing), singular for each community, was instituted by the Spanish colony as a form of counter-insurgency.[2] This understanding of indigenous identity as imposed informs some of the extremely hostile responses Mayan organizing has encountered from the Right as well as the Left, because Mayan claims for "special rights" are thus seen as false, based on nothing, or worse yet, based on false consciousness.

Most accepted now (at least by gringo academics) is an understanding of indigenous identity as syncretic, hybrid, and firmly ensconced in history, as in Oliver LaFarge's notion of a "sequence of cultures" (1940) or Richard Adams's much-maligned indigenous-ladino continuum (1956).[3] As Kay Warren says, "It is no longer a process of assimilation or of a lost identity, but rather the fashioning of a new and plural personality" (1992, 6). These readings acknowledge that both the form and content of Mayan identity have been shaped in relation to nonindigenous orthopedic technologies, which hostilely mark this body politic through religious proselytizing, sumptuary codes, Spanish-monolingual education systems, labor extraction regimes, and violent displacement. Even the term for the new pan-ethnic identity, *Maya,* is hybrid, formed in relation. One effect of these relations (such as colonial separation of indigenous communities [*pueblos de indios*] from Spanish towns, state-regulated land tenure arrangements, and government paternalism) is the importance of community to identity. Most ethnography, foreign and Mayan, agrees that indigenous identity is community-bound. It is based in, bound to, a special relation to a territory, with

2. After my first sojourn in Guatemala, recovering from a near fatal attack of "típica fever" (see chapter 5), I read *Guatemala!* (Jonas and Tobis 1974). The book quotes Martínez Peláez on the origin of *traje* as colonial imposition—a quote that I accepted with shock and cited unquestioningly in an earlier version of this chapter (presented at the AAA meetings, 1991). I thank Robert Carlsen who very kindly pointed out the much more careful historical work that he and others have done (Carlsen 1993; Pancake 1992; Asturias de Barrios and García 1992; Otzoy 1991 and 1996; Arriola de Geng 1991; Hendrickson 1995 and 1996).

3. The contributors to Fischer and Brown (1996) are especially sensitive to the impact that gringo academic theory has on Mayan organizing. A common refrain among anti-Mayan ladinos is that there are gringos behind the movement—that Mayan issues are being manipulated by outsiders. Mario Roberto Morales writes, "Mayan theories of identity are not their own; they are from the United States. . . . They are *Maya agringado* [gringoized]" (*Siglo XXI,* 29 July 1995).

shared premises, endogamous kin groups, municipal politics (Tax 1937), and local production relations (C. Smith 1984, 1988, 1989, and 1990b). John Watanabe (1992) and Richard Wilson (1995) eloquently describe how the relation to a specific landscape is more than economic, or even political. It is a sacred tie that links fertility, gender, food, ethnicity, relations to the dead and the living, the unseen world, and right living and forms the basis for the categories and "cognitive mapping" that make sense of lives. It is the basis of cooperation and thus survival in an uncertain world.

But what happens when people are no longer bound to (tied to) the community? Historic changes culminating in the Quincentennial, including labor imperatives, opportunities to study, colonizing projects, forced and voluntary army recruitment, itinerant government jobs as teachers and development specialists, and the massive and brutal displacement of the war, have taken many indigenous people away from their villages. Is ladinoization the only alternative?

These understandings of identity as locally bound, as tied to a specific landscape, can also bind people to a particular identity—as rural or old-fashioned. Viewing "Indian-ness" as bound to a particular place can become an incarceration and a double bind, so that any indigenous person who leaves their community, the rural area, and the manual labor associated with the village is vulnerable to accusations of inauthenticity and ladinoization. This rejection can come from village-bound indigenous people, gringos, and ladinos. For example, a ladino journalist (who considers himself very progressive) told me that he had learned at ESTNA (the army's School for Strategic National Studies) that "if you take an Indian out of his village, he stops being an Indian. He immediately starts changing. He realizes his position and decides he doesn't want to be poor, so he changes his clothes and changes his name. Look at Demetrio Cojtí. He works for a big international organization, he never goes to his community, he doesn't eat beans anymore." Here, authentic indigenous identity is tied to being traditional, rural, and poor (eating beans), which in turn marks ladino identity as modern, urban, and economically better off (as Carlos Figueroa Ibarra put it, "I am ladino, petit bourgeois, and they tell me I have no culture!").

Mayan activists resist this simple binary that makes an indigenous person who leaves their community or steps out of *traje* into a ladino. But they acknowledge that the effects of colonialism, and particularly the rapid changes of the past thirty years, have left Mayan culture broken, "mutilated," and "atomized" (ALMG 1990), a culture in pieces, a wounded body politic. As Ricardo Cajas, president of the Guatemalan Mayan Writers Academy (AEMG) put it, "We have to understand that the Conquest has done great harm to our pride, destroying our sense of ourselves. No one wants to be an Indian. They have left us with the culture of destruction. We are destroying ourselves. This is the true catastrophe of the Conquest. Colonialism lives inside us." The goal of many Mayan activists is to fix, in the sense of *repair,* this culture, to renew people's pride in their indigenous identity. There are many and often fierce disagreements over what constitutes the culture that cultural rights activists are fighting for. However, the Maya I interviewed seem to agree that it is not necessarily "fixed" or bound to a specific practice or to a single place.[4] So even though they might contest the notion that identity is community-bound and assert that one can, indeed, be a Maya in Guatemala City, I suggest that their work *is* community-bound in the sense that they are headed toward, moving in the direction of, a future community.[5]

This community-bound work is specific to the Quincentennial moment I have been exploring here, including the horrors of the counterinsurgency war, the destruction of the revolutionary movement, and the emergence of a critical (in both senses of the word) mass of educated indigenous people. Mayan activists emphasize culture, which has led to accusations that this community-bound work is apolitical and that their determination to work within the state is co-opted. Such criticisms, however, must take into account the army campaigns in which hundreds of indigenous villages were destroyed "down to the last seed" (which I condense into the graveyard of the chapter's subtitle).[6] This all-too-recent history overdetermines the mode in which Mayan cultural rights activists have decided to work. The Maya argue, fluidarily, that Manichaean allegories that posit a clear and never-breached opposition between colonizer and colonized, between inauthentic and authentic identities, and between politics and culture (just like those between rural and urban and between traditional and modern) are colonial strategies of rule that cover over the historicity of identities. This is why Sam Colop calls the Quincentennial "five hundred years of cover up [*encubrimiento*]" rather than discovery (*descubrimiento*) (Sam Colop 1991, 9).[7]

4. As I stated above, this research focuses primarily on Mayan professionals, who in general have some education, tend to hold information-processing jobs (teachers, secretaries, lawyers, development workers, lobbyists, and so on), and work in urban areas, primarily Guatemala City.

5. I borrow these different senses of *bound* from N. Katherine Hayles's work, *Chaos Bound* (1990). I hope they also retain a sense of contingency. Community is something we are always striving for, a horizon, rather than a fixed, solid thing.

6. A Guatemalan army commander describing the scorched-earth campaign said, "We're not going to leave a single seed, we are going to make a clean sweep" (in Falla 1984, 116). As I suggested in the last chapter, the "people" (*genos*) being wiped out may have been more "subversives" than indigenous people per se, but the Maya definitely feel that far more of their blood was sacrificed in the war.

7. I apologize for the imposition of Arabic numbers on Sam Colop's Mayan pagination, but my computer still lacks the program. Perhaps a sympathetic Maya-hacker can help me out?

Attention to hostilely marked identifications and hybrid subject-positions—ones formed in relation with the state—suggests (with apologies to Audre Lorde) that the master's tools may be the only way to make the master's house livable for all its inhabitants. Mayan activists are insisting on participating in the state and in using the hostile markings of identity. Although they deploy notions of Mayan culture, tradition, history, and language as timeless, ahistorical elements, the discourse of Mayans who are community-bound centralizes their struggle to salvage and create (*formar* in Spanish) Mayan identity. The very terms of the debate, like the use of *Maya,* are part of the appropriative-resistive dialectic of their work, which wants to maintain difference but organize a more pan-indigenous identity.

The Fraughtness of Fluidarity

The notion of identity I deploy here—that it is in part an appropriation of hostile markings—is meant to serve as a defense of the Mayan cultural rights movement against detractors who claim that this movement is apolitical. But this is a fraught attempt at fluidarity. As Kay Warren (1992), Jean Jackson (1989), and Jane Collier (1997) have pointed out, what indigenous peoples in struggle may want from scholars, especially foreigners, may not be what we want to give. Warren has confronted the demand that she use her anthropological know-how and her position at a prestigious U.S. university to excavate and publicize links between the Maya of today and the glorious Mayan past. This contrasts with her own sense that contemporary Mayan identity is a processual, creative task (1992). Making arguments for hybrid identities, no matter how well supported by the U.S. academy's currently hip theory, may feed right in to anti-indigenous arguments that it is all made-up, inauthentic hogwash.[8] As in the case of identity in Mashpee (Clifford 1988) (where in order to recover their land, the Mashpee Wampanoag were forced to prove they had "solid" identities—which they failed to do), such arguments made by academics can have negative effects on indigenous claims for specific rights and material compensation. We have been critiqued for offering ammunition to the enemy, and it is difficult to respond with an anti-identity politics argument from our relatively privileged position of gringos.

8. I look more closely at these hostile reactions in chapters 7 and 8, but it may be worthwhile to quote some of the unpleasant spleen excreted in response to Mayan efforts: Mario Alberto Carrera, an editorialist for *El Grafico,* writes: "I fear these so-called professional Maya are falling into a tearful and dreadful past-loving nostalgia, exactly like the Italians fell into with Mussolini or the Spanish with Franco. They are ethno-authoritarians! They want to pull us away from the mestizo present into the times of the classic Maya. But this has been lost to the dusts of time. They are not even Maya! They are Toltec-Quichés and 90 percent are mentally mestizos"(21 January 1995).

In contingent defense of the project, my analysis here charts the violent exclusions and fixings involved in essentialized notions of identity as they are deployed against the Maya. As Judith Butler asks, how do we keep the instrumental uses of identity from becoming regulatory imperatives? (1991, 16). I suggest that we do so by insisting on both the importance of such identities and their historic situatedness. Otherwise, the search for some ahistorical "truth" of identity is very like the blood and phenotype discourse I discuss in chapter 6: fertile ground for racism and the erasure of gender, sexuality, class, and other power differentials.

The way power demands authentic difference from its others (the way some ladinos need "real" Indians, and the way modernity needs tradition) seems to be a disavowal of the tenuousness of its own identification—as not-Indian, as male, as modern, as legitimate, and so on. Attempts to think through indigenous identity in its relation to ladinos and the nation-state— and vice versa—may help explain the hostility, projection, and paranoia (as well as acquiescence) that greet indigenous demands for representation. In turn, such an analysis may unsettle the powerful positions from which such accusations come.

Besides, given the degree to which these reactions so overshoot their target, what proof of authenticity would be adequate? Some Jurassic Park–like reincarnation of Tecún Umán from the blood of a living Maya to prove their Indian-ness? History often has less to do with how things "really were" than with the ability to articulate the past to a political project in the present. It is the current struggles of the Maya to create such an articulation that I want to support here. Finally, I have tried to listen to the Maya I interviewed who acknowledge the porousness of identities and, although they value its magic, understand the process and work of "culture." They are well aware of the ways that identity politics can exclude, and, as a fledgling movement, they know that they can ill afford to lose supporters through too-strict identity categories.

However, this is not to underestimate the hostile atmosphere in which the Mayan cultural rights movement is attempting to work—an atmosphere that may occasion hostile reactions on their part to even the best-intentioned gringa in fluidarity. After interviewing ALMG leaders and other Mayan activists in the summer of 1991, I wrote an article for a solidarity newsletter (Nelson 1991) and a very preliminary version of this chapter; I thought that the chapter's title, which I have retained in this book, played cleverly with the theories of Donna Haraway and Homi Bhabha. Returning the next summer to Guatemala, I showed the English versions of both to Guatemalan friends, ladino and Mayan, and, not trusting my written Spanish, asked one of the ladinos to help me translate so I could give copies to the ALMG members I knew. Time got away from us and we never got around to the translation.

When I returned to Guatemala to do my dissertation field work, I imme-diately looked up the Academy, which had in the intervening year and a half been legalized and now occupied its own office building, rather than the closet on the roof of the Ministry of Culture where it had been before. The entire executive council had changed, and most of the people I knew were working at other jobs. After giving the secretary my card, I waited for over an hour before I was shown up to the president's office and confronted by two Academy members. They had the two articles I had written in English on the desk, and they really laid into me. As a "nice gringa" who had usually been received as such, I had never had such an experience in Guatemala, and it was very upsetting. In part they were angry that I had mentioned that women were underrepresented in the Academy, but I finally realized that what they most resented was the chapter's title, which they understood to mean that I thought *they* were hostile.[9] They adamantly were not hostile to anyone, particularly ladinos and the Guatemalan nation, and how dare I suggest it? I realized then the fear that undergirds their work, and that it was distinctly more fun to read about the "natives talking back" in a classroom than to actually experience it. I rather lamely endeavored to explain the title in terms of projection and colonial paranoia. Needless to say, I imme-diately found a translator and, although I admit to experiencing a severe re-luctance to face them again, gave them copies.[10] Afterward we got on well enough and they were very generous with their time and analyses. They later told me, "We thought that since the one article you wrote was so posi-tive, they had made you write one against us for balance." The "they" was never specified, although I assume they meant the popular movement, with which I had been identified through the solidarity publication.[11]

The issue of gender critique is also a fraught one for a feminist gringa in fluidarity. What if feminism is not an operative category for the people I am working with? As the ALMG president said as he bawled me out: everyone

9. I had actually said very little about women's issues in the paper, and when I presented it at the AAA, I was criticized for ignoring gender oppression. Poor anthropologists, caught be-tween our various audiences!

10. I ended up presenting a translated version at the ALMG's fifteenth workshop in the Petén in July 1993. Paranoia seemed to be a useful concept, because it became something of a catchphrase during the conference.

11. In fact, I heard through the grapevine that the article caused internal problems at the Guatemalan News and Information Bureau (GNIB) because it was considered too "pro-Indian," which points to the intense ambivalence around the issue and the rationale for the ALMG president's reaction. U.S. solidarity's resistance to Mayan organizing—previously viewed as reactionary and divisive of the popular movement—seems to be changing, probably in part because of the hegemony work I have been describing. A recent issue of GNIB featured an interview with a Mayan *sacerdotiza* (priestess), an article on peasants reclaiming "Mother Earth," and an update on the Indigenous Rights Accord (1995).

critiques them for talking about Mayan identity and Mayan equality and then going home where they have refrigerators and western goods and "stay-at-home" wives who take care of their children. But who are we to judge? Do people judge your work by how you live your life at home? He is right, of course, and ours is an easy critique to be made from outside. Here and in chapter 7, I will try to describe gender issues involved in the work of the Academy, including how Mayan women's identifications are being produced at that site.

INDIGENOUS ORGANIZING—REPEATING WITH A DIFFERENCE

The Guatemalan state has made repeated attempts to assimilate the indigenous populations through various forms of ladinoization—both the repressive state apparatuses of massacre and occupation, and the ideological state apparatuses (Althusser 1971) that I am calling "hostile markings" (such as religion, clothing, and language).[12] The Maya have often resisted colonial and postcolonial imposition and deterritorialization with arms, but I do not want to posit them as an always already revolting subaltern subject (Nelson 1997). Many have ladinoized, making the choice to give up the markings of indigenous identity like *traje* and language. Indigenous resistance, much less identity, is not a given, and the ALMG openly acknowledges that ladinoization is a threat to indigenous identity and that many Maya experience an identity crisis: "The Spanish language is a symbol of superiority. . . . Their lives are saturated by the invasion of the dominant system, and they try to imitate the ladino or foreigner. . . . They believe that they will overcome prejudice by imitation" (ALMG 1990, 41).

However, just as the ruses of ladinoization are multiple, so are the responses to it. In fact, I will argue that it is precisely at the points where nonindigenous "nation-state" identity most insistently repeats itself—the school, the church, and the legal system—that Maya are working, repeating but with a difference.[13] Judith Butler suggests that regulatory norms materialize identities through forcible reiteration. "That this reiteration is necessary is a sign that materialization is never quite complete. . . . Indeed, it is

12. Of course, the failure of these assimilation attempts smacks of the Foucauldian penitentiary's inability to "reform" its subjects (1979), which thereby produces criminality.

13. In exploring the relationality of "hostile markings" projected from the state and nonindigenous sites with emerging Mayan identifications, I only glancingly treat issues that have been richly analyzed elsewhere. On the law, please see Carmack (1995) and R. Hill (1992); on schooling and language, see Fischer and Brown (1996), CECMA (1992), COCADI (1985), and Englund (1992 and 1996); on religion, see Warren (1989), Wilson (1995), Watanabe (1992), Tedlock (1992), Falla (1978), D. Stoll (1990), and Brintnall (1979); and for general overviews of the Mayan movement as a whole, see Bastos and Camus (1993 and 1995). (This is, of course, a short list.)

the instabilities, the possibilities for rematerialization, opened up by this process that mark one domain in which the force of the regulatory law can be turned against itself to spawn rearticulations that call into question the hegemonic force of that very regulatory law" (Butler 1993, 2).

This repeating with a difference has also been termed colonial hybridity and ambivalence by Homi Bhabha, terms that retain the mixing of syncretism but insist on the violent ways that culture clashes and disciplinary encounters leave their orthopedic marks: most brutally on the colonized, but also on the colonizer. Hybridity works in Guatemala as both imposition and as rearticulation, as the Maya insist on inclusion and participation. As I argue throughout this book, the Maya are not fighting for withdrawal. They want representation—with difference. For example, in deploying Mayan identity, the ALMG evokes the timelessness of something inborn, but also acknowledges the role of hybridity and invention. They say we must "affirm our identity through strengthening the values of the Mayan culture through the research, institutionalization, and systematization of a desire to be different in language, external identification (clothing), cosmology, and other factors. . . . We desire a better future without losing our identity, and, as far as possible, to maintain a dignified politico-cultural position from which to construct a new and just economic-cultural project that will revise the structures of the invasion" (ALMG 1990, 41).

Bhabha says that hybridity and mimicry are "produced at the site of interdiction" (Bhabha 1984, 129)—*interdiction* carrying the double meaning of "an official prohibition or restraint" (what colonialist authority desires, the aim of its orthopedics) and "to speak between" (the upsetting of that authority). In the following, I briefly explore several such sites of interdiction.

The Hybridity of Identity

Clothing   Traje, perhaps the most recognizable of indigenous markings, is clearly a hybrid product. Although few agree with Martínez Peláez that the different styles for each town, which continue to exist, were designed and imposed by the Spanish colonizers (Asturias de Barrios and García 1992; R. Hill 1992; Pancake and Annis 1982; Pancake 1988), there were limits that were imposed through sumptuary codes, and new materials, techniques, and designs were assimilated. Some of these assimilations were based on attractiveness, others were in mimicry of the fashion of the powerful, and there continues to be constant change in form, design, and content (including the recent incorporation of ancient calendar glyphs or the logo for Pepsi Cola).[14]

Contrary to Martínez Peláez's analysis, state orthopedics of the last one

14. I thank Paula Worby for reporting the Pepsi incorporation.

hundred years have been aimed at stripping indigenous people (especially men) of distinctive *traje*. In most towns throughout the highlands, where the bulk of the Maya still live, many and sometimes all women wear some form of traditional dress—the wrap skirts, belt, *huipil* (blouse), or shawl—whereas men wear "western" clothes—jeans, button-up shirt, and boots or sandals (Hendrickson 1995). In only a few towns, those renowned for their traditionalism, do men continue to wear traditional clothing—often brightly colored woven shirts with similar color and design patterns to women's *huipiles,* short pants, sometimes a poncho, or head-scarf for ceremonial occasions. Among urbanized Maya, many women retain *traje* (although often only after struggling with discrimination and their own reluctance), but *no* Mayan men wear *traje* in public. In my interviews, most Mayans say that indigenous men do not wear *traje* because their contact with the ladino world has exposed them to more racism than women have faced and more pressure to blend in to survive. Irma Otzoy, a Mayan anthropologist, agrees:

> Mayan men involve[d] themselves in the economic and administrative matters of the country but . . . [i]n 1836 . . . a government order stated that "no Indian may hold the office of *regidor, alcalde, síndico,* nor any other parish position, without wearing shoes or boots, a shirt with a collar, long trousers, a jacket or coat, and a hat that is not made from straw or palm leaf" (Carrillo Ramírez 1971, 49). These restrictions forced some Maya men to reduce the use of or totally abandon their aboriginal dress.

She suggests that the Mayan woman retains her *traje* because she is more valiant than men (Otzoy 1996, 146–147).

Even Mayan men from towns where masculine *traje* is maintained feel this pressure when they leave. A friend from Todos Santos has mastered the acrobatic trick of changing his clothes on a packed Bluebird school bus. As he heads into town on vacation from studying in Guatemala City, he slips into his *traje,* and on the way out of town, he squeezes into "western" clothing. "I can't wear that clown outfit outside," he says. Carol Hendrickson insists that there is a gender component to this passing, that ladinos tend to see a man in *traje* as "one who is less masculine (even less adult) in a world dominated by non-Maya values" (1995, 89). Thus it is not just exposure to ladino racism that leads Mayan men to abandon *traje,* but ladino sexism as well, which pressures them to conform to particular configurations of masculinity.

So what these orthopedics produce is a gendering of ethnic identifications, because it is primarily Mayan women who wear *traje* (see chapter 5). In turn, what was left of colonial fashion has been constantly refashioned and appropriated, because the women who weave it and wear it use it as a signifying practice—mixing and matching with the *traje* of other towns and with *ropa usada* (cast-offs from the United States).[15] The production of these "typical" weavings has meant survival for many families, thanks to the tourist trade. More important, wearing traditional dress is often synonymous with indigenous female identity. Many indigenous women say they would rather be naked than wear western clothing. A friend told me that during the war she fled her village for Guatemala City, where she disguised herself by transvestiting in ladino clothing. She was miserable and terrified and very lonely. But when she saw two friends from her village on the street, rather than run to greet them she hid out of shame because she felt so naked without her *traje.*

For others, the *formación* work of Mayan activism is encouraging the use of *traje,* in turn supporting women's identifications. To paraphrase Cynthia Enloe (1983), *traje* becomes her—it is, of course, beautiful (becoming), but the use of *traje* is also productive: women become Maya to both external observers and themselves when they put it on. A woman leader of the ALMG said, "I had stopped wearing *traje,* because there was a great deal of discrimination against me where I used to work. But when I began to reflect, to work with the [Mayan] organization, I realized that my culture was very valuable. My identity now is stronger. I will always identify with what I am. I will never leave my *traje* again. Women are the ones who have resisted more, who maintain the culture."

Religion   The battery of colonial Catholic proselytizing was also deeply synthesized, so that now what is considered traditional religion (as opposed to orthodox Catholicism) is organized around *cofradías* (brotherhoods) that care for saints, and advancement through the politico-religious hierarchy requires "paying dues" by cleaning the church and sponsoring festivals for these saints (Rojas Lima 1988; Cancian 1965; Vogt 1990). Many people retain the "Mayan calendar" and pray to an amalgam of ancient and Catholic deities at sacred places in the mountains marked by crosses (Tedlock 1992; Colby and Colby 1981). This syncretism (believers, but not quite) has been attacked by various waves of purifying movements within the Catholic church, the most recent being Catholic Action, which involved Rigoberta Menchú and her family, large numbers of people in the popular movement, and many of the people who are now working with the ALMG.

Since the 1950s, the role of these catechists in the community has been ambivalent (Brintnall 1979; Warren 1989; Wilson 1995). In mostly Maya-monolingual towns, they have a great deal of control in the dispersion of Church doctrine as the translators for the priest. As some Mayan activists

---

15. What *traje* means to these women may vary widely, as Sheldon Annis found among Catholic and Protestant women weavers (1987).

suggest, however, the catechists were often instrumental in undermining the same traditional practices and authority that they now are trying to salvage as members of the ALMG. In any case, it would be hard to overestimate the importance of the catechists' work, deeply embedded in Liberation Theology, in the constitution and in the constitution of activists in the popular, revolutionary, and Mayan movements (Falla 1980). Kay Warren, witness in the 1970s to this Quincentennial prehistory, describes a "new identity" emerging from the Church's work among the Kaqchikel of San Andrés Semetabaj (1989).

Although many Mayan activists have left the Church to pursue what they consider more traditional means of worship ("we *are* pagans," they proudly declare), there is a growing movement within the Catholic Church, the *Pastoral Indígena*, which is working for full participation with indigenous difference. Their demands include the integration of Mayan languages and Mayan spiritual symbols in the mass, respect for specific forms of Mayan religiosity, and indigenous representation in church decision-making. There are increasing numbers of Mayas studying in the seminary and being ordained as priests and nuns. The influence of the *Pastoral Indígena* was clear in the extremely apologetic tone of the Church's official "Pastoral Letter on the Five Hundred Years." As a Jesuit priest said, however, not everyone in the Church is open to syncretism going in the other direction. At the mass in the Cathedral in celebration of Rigoberta Menchú's Nobel Prize—a fine affair with most of the Church hierarchy in attendance—it was fine to burn *pom* (traditional incense) and to have Rigoberta carry in a cross made of corn, "but when she started to talk about *dioses* [gods] you can bet that fell like a bucket of cold water on many of the people there!"

Mayan relations with the Church are also ambivalent in the terrain of language and history. Despite efforts like the *Pastoral Indígena* to work within the Church, the institution's history of violent proselytizing is well remembered. The screams of Indians burned alive as idolaters, the horrors of de Landa's inquisition and the vast destruction of life and literature it incurred, are frequently invoked. At the same time, it is only through the anthropology of early Spanish priests—the ethnography of Sahagún (Clendinnen 1991) and the transcription and translation of the *Popul Wuj*—that much remains at all of the history of conquest and its antecedents.

The Maya have a similarly ambivalent relation to the growing power of Protestant (usually fundamentalist) Christianity—close to 35–40 percent of Guatemalans now claim this faith. Though some analysts reduce this explosion in conversion to an instrumental response to the counterinsurgency attacks on Catholics, the rapid spread of Protestantism is based in many factors (D. Stoll 1988 and 1993; Annis 1987; Wilson 1995). The promise of redemption through personal discipline, including resistance to alcoholism, is a powerful force, as is the openness of the form to indigenous participation. The monetary and temporal expense demanded by the years of study to become a Catholic priest, the renunciation of family life it calls for, and the rigidity of the hierarchy contrast markedly with the ease of becoming a Protestant pastor.[16] In turn, Mayan pastors like Vitalino Similox now play an important role in indigenous organizing.[17]

Protestant missionaries, primarily through the Wycliffe Bible Translators, or Summer Institute of Linguistics (SIL) (D. Stoll 1982 and 1988), have offered both opportunity and limits to the Maya, especially in relation to their languages. In the late 1940s and early 1950s, linguists and missionaries with SIL moved into remote highland villages and began to "reduce" the spoken indigenous languages into written form in order to translate the Bible. They trained local people as translators and teachers and have encouraged the production of literature in the indigenous languages, which they print and distribute. I would argue that these texts can be "signs taken for wonders" (Bhabha 1985), which open up sites for resistive redeployment. Bhabha cites the East Indians, proclaiming, "It is THEIR book; and they printed it in our language, for our use" (Bhabha 1985, 164). I would rewrite this, just as the U.S. bible translators rewrote the Mayan books. The Mayan Indians might say, "It is OUR book; and they printed it in our language for THEIR use." The ALMG translators are not accepting this invitation to convert to (U.S.-funded) Protestantism and assimilate (use literacy in one's mother-tongue as a stepping-stone to literacy in Spanish). Instead, the ones trained to be translators—to maintain the distinctions between languages—are speaking and writing in-between and interdicta.

Many indigenous people trained by the SIL are now involved in the ALMG and argue that language is the clearest link to the past. "Despite attempts to exterminate the Mayan languages, beginning with the tragic 'burning of the books,' they continue to operate as the fundamental element in the identity of the Mayan community" (ALMG 1990, 43). Here, the hybridity of the colonial encounter surfaces, because these languages are partly "available" and their proponents "formed" by the missionary's enterprise, and the SIL in turn has become a sort of common enemy against which a generalized pan-Mayan identity is being organized.

This is because the SIL's attention to specificity led it to place individual

16. On the role of women and long-standing traditions of ecstasy and the word in Protestant practice in Alta Verapaz, see Abigail Adams (1998).

17. The Guatemalan Protestant Church Conference (CIEDEG) has become an important site for the defense of Mayan and human rights. Perhaps as a result, in August 1994 Pascual Serech, a president of the organization, was killed in Chimaltenango by the local military commissioner, and in June 1995 Manuel Saquic Vásquez, minister and coordinator of CIEDEG's Maya defense committee, was also killed.

translators in villages deemed linguistically different, which led to various alphabets and some confusion. Beginning with the work of Adrián Chávez in the 1940s, Maya have worked to unify the alphabets of their languages, in part to make cross-linguistic communication easier.[18] The development of a unified alphabet by Mayan and ladino linguists and the struggle for it to be accepted and implemented at the national level was an important step in developing Mayan activists and in planning for the ALMG. Although supported by some SIL linguists, the new alphabet has met with impassioned resistance from many, who feel that their life's work is being superseded. In turn it has made it hard for some literate Maya to read. The alphabet is now legally the national norm, but implementation has been another story: much like the term *Maya,* its use tends to mark those sympathetic to the Mayan movement against those who oppose it or are merely ignorant of the legal changes.

The Law   As I discuss in more detail in chapter 8, legality is also a terrain of struggle for Mayan rights, both in efforts to create laws (changing the Constitution, unifying the alphabet, legalizing the Academy, ratifying ILO Convention 169, and writing Article 70) and to use those that exist (see Richards and Richards 1996). Many communities retain practices of "customary law" that Mayan activists are working to support against the encroachments of militarized local power structures like the Civil Patrol and military commissioners.[19] Although colonial and postindependence law has denied indigenous people personhood (the famous justifications for empire), reduced their villages, and forced them to labor, it has also been used to defend community, land, and individual rights (R. Hill 1992). Popular and Mayan activists now carry copies of the Constitution and the Peace Accord under their arm to back up arguments, and law is the most popular university career for indigenous students.

The School   Education in indigenous communities is primarily in Spanish, but since 1980, government schools have become nominally bilingual through the third grade in a system that has employed and trained Mayan teachers (although in secondary, lower-paying jobs). Mayan activists claim that, although it is a step forward, the bilingual program is still primarily

18. Adrián Inés Chávez founded the Academy of the K'iche' Language in Quetzaltenango, developed a K'iche' alphabet, and translated the *Popul Wuj.* As Falla (1978) describes in his history of the indigenous movement of the late 1970s, Chávez's renown was such that various projects tried to seize hold of his memory as he reached his seventieth birthday, including the indigenous political movement Patinamit, the national teachers' union, the Rabina Ajau national indigenous queen committee, and even the Masonic lodge (see also Fischer 1996).

19. The December 1996 Peace Accords officially disbanded the Civil Patrols, but the patrols' effects linger in community power structures and memories of hurt.

aimed at teaching Spanish rather than literacy and competence in their own languages. The National Program of Bilingual Education (PRONEBI), originally funded by the USAID, has been in charge of implementing the bilingual curriculum. The program originally targeted the four majority languages of K'iche', Kaqchikel, Q'eqchi', and Mam, but by 1988 they were beginning to work with other languages.

Besides providing a paying job dealing with cultural issues, PRONEBI offers some of its Mayan workers a useful place to raise consciousness about cultural politics. As a bilingual teacher said,

> At first it was very hard to work with the indigenous teachers. They are products of the colonial system. It's not their fault. When they went to school, there were signs up prohibiting them from speaking their languages; they were punished. Children remember this; they keep these colonial ideas inside them and then they teach the same thing. But there are more and more bilingual teachers, and we are feeling strong, supported. With the new Constitution, with the ALMG, we have legal recourse.

A PRONEBI worker, Manuel Ortíz García, told me,

> The program is meant to *castellanizar*—make the children into Spanish speakers—and parents accept this. When we first went into the villages to talk about culture, identity, language, people did not like what we said. They did not want to be Indian. They wanted to be like westerners. But now they are demanding bilingual education. It is hard work because the parents think their kids should learn Spanish, what use is it to speak their language? So we try to explain our history, why it is important.

PRONEBI employs several of the founders of the ALMG, who explain their involvement:

> It is difficult for the Academy to work in the sewer waters of a structure of social and economic exploitation. But this does not mean that we cannot carry out dignifying activities within the political and economic ladino hegemony. However, it must be clear that this is not the only solution, but an historical contribution in the struggle for Mayan demands that must follow many paths. (ALMG 1990, 61)

Being Rendered as Fit Vehicles

So it is precisely at the sites of the enunciation of power that hybridity proliferates and where the Maya are working. Right where state-colonizer identity was most insistently repeated, the Maya repeat with a difference: what was meant to fix (ladinoize) is being used to fix or hold on to Mayan culture. Many of the current Mayan activists were involved in the routes to advancement that neocolonialism left open to them: as school teachers, catechists, or working with missionaries. They were playing, in fact, the parts set forth under British colonization for natives in India by Macauley's "Minute on Indian Education" of 1835: "We must at present do our best to form a class who may be interpreters between us and the millions whom we govern; a class of persons, Indian in blood and colour, but English in taste, in opinions, in morals, and in intellect. . . . We must render them by degrees fit vehicles for conveying knowledge to the great mass of the population" (in Spivak 1988a, 282).

But in Guatemala, the indigenous people supposedly being "rendered fit" were not merely the passive receptors of colonialist and neocolonist culture. The ALMG says, "Many activists come from the education field: they often find in their students the best mirror to reflect their own frustrations. . . . [From the inside,] schools are revealed to be great prisons for mental castration, true advance troops for colonial domination" (ALMG 1990, 60). In drawing the following biographical sketches of Mayan activists based on interviews, I suggest that it is in the very sites meant to render indigenous people "fit" (to fix them, or make them ladinos, to "fit in" to the homogenizing nation-state) that Mayan identity is partially produced, is being repaired.

Narciso Cojtí said that he worked as a catechist with his father in Catholic Action. "I went to Catholic high school, and we would go out on campaigns against the Mayan religion. Because I knew both the Mayan religion and Catholicism, I carried a double-edged sword. I knew a lot, and I was a destroyer of my own religion. Now that I am more involved [in Mayan organizing], I understand the barbarity I've committed and the need to support our traditions. We can be the worst destroyers of our own meaning." He later worked for twelve years with the Francisco Marroquín Linguistic Project (supported by a private university), for which he traveled throughout the country. He said that he was somewhat involved in the effervescence of organizing in the mid-1970s, the community responses to the 1976 earthquake, and the meetings that led to the formation of an indigenous party and the Campesino Unity Committee (CUC), "Although when they became clandestine, I lost sight of them."

Because of his linguistic work, he had some trouble with the army, but he said that he always tried to be as open as possible so as not to draw suspicion. He said that he was approached by the guerrilla to do work for them, and that when he refused, they became angry. "I don't trust those groups. Their leaders are ladinos, they are not interested in the indigenous people. They were also involved in ethnocide. If you look at the violence and see who was being killed, on both sides it was the indigenous people. The leaders, the ladinos, held back. We were the cannon fodder. I don't think the guerrillas are against the Maya, no, but I do not think they are willing to deal with the indigenous situation."

He said that he thought he understood racism pretty well, until, as part of his reflection on identity in 1988, he decided to begin to wear a modified *traje*.

> Then I began to understand! I suffered a series of barbarities! I was told that
> hotels were full and then watched them give rooms to ladinos, people tried to
> overcharge me for meals, bus tickets, and other things. I went to a friend's
> wedding and heard people exclaim, "Dirty Indian!" under their breath as I
> went by. And everyone there was Indian, just dressed in different clothes! I be-
> gan to understand the situation suffered by indigenous women, that men
> don't understand. Most men don't wear *traje* and we can lose ourselves in the
> other society, but now I see why the women say we cannot know what they suf-
> fer. These reactions don't bother me so much now because I am involved in
> the indigenous question. I understand that it is discrimination.

He has continued his work as a linguist with private projects and at
PRONEBI and was on the provisional executive council of the ALMG after
legalization. He attended the 1990 meeting in Ecuador to plan for the
Quincentennial, and said that he was very impressed with the unity of the
movement there, that they were able to mobilize a strike that shut down
the entire country.[20] "This is a big problem in Guatemala: unity. There are
many problems around individual interests. People are becoming more and
more prepared, capable, but we are not united, not as individuals, nor as
ethnic groups, and there are class divisions. Even indigenous leaders come
to our meetings and say that discrimination doesn't exist, but this is only because they have entered the other world. We have to remember that as indigenous people we still do not have the right to many things." When asked
about the future, he said, "We have a lot of work to do now. Very difficult
work, to strengthen ourselves, to help people to valorize their identity, what
they are. We have to use all the resources at our disposal, including
PRONEBI, the Academy, and so on, to do these things."

Delia Tujab is a lawyer and was active in the legalization drive for the
ALMG. She was also in charge of the national forums and workshops on the
ILO Convention 169 described in chapter 8. She was raised in Tactíc, Alta
Verapaz, speaks Q'eqchi', and both her parents were well-known artisans,
her father a silversmith and her mother a weaver. She said that they were
both involved in community development work, lobbying for roads and
schools, and through them she learned the importance of patience when
you want something from the government. Her parents insisted that all of

20. Of course, Ecuador has not suffered the sort of massacres and civil war whose scars run
so deep in Guatemala. The work of Suzana Sawyer on indigenous organizing in Ecuador makes
clear the very different conditions of possibility in that country, the sort of audacious imagination possible there that is still foreclosed in violence-prone Guatemala, despite the Peace Accords (Sawyer 1996a, 1996b, and 1997).

the children get an education, girls as well as boys, sending them all to Guatemala City to study. "My parents said we must always remember we were indigenous. That is why I have never stopped wearing *traje,* even when people would tease me all the time." She said that through her work as a lawyer she has learned the ins and outs of lobbying and the importance of personal relationships. "I have met a lot of the 'important people' of Guatemala, and I've learned how to lobby them. It is not a question of a few days, and it's not work you can get emotional about. You have to be very patient. Lobbying is listening. Carefully, over the years, we have slowly developed friendships with people in Congress, in the palace and ministries, in the private sector. As indigenous people, we need to learn how to do that kind of thing. It is how the ladinos keep power."

She has been working with the Supreme Court in the development of the new penal code (see chapter 8), arguing about the need for translators in the regional courts. "Many lawyers are opposed to the new rule about the translators, but I told them we needed them. It is necessary for the indigenous peoples who have never been represented in the courts, for over five hundred years! If they are worried about expenses, then take money from the defense budget. We hardly need an army of fifty thousand soldiers when we can't get justice in our communities!"

Ms. Tujab acknowledged, however, the extent to which the country remains militarized. "This is a militarized society, and if we want to change it, we have to deal with that." She said that this was the reason she accepted the army's invitation to give a course at the military school, ESTNA. She felt it was an important place to make an intervention by using her status as a professional and a lawyer. She said that people there say "that they have no problems with Indians, they get along fine with them, and the proof of this is that they have Indian maids! That they let them in their houses! I told them that that is not what I am talking about. Valuing someone for their labor is not the same as valuing them as a full human being with respect for all the different aspects of their culture."

She also tries to use her professional status to help children, especially girls, value and retain their culture. She gives lectures in elementary schools on Mayan culture and *traje.* "I think it helps for them just to see an 'Indian' who is successful and wears her *traje* with pride. I have even gone to visit the women's prison because there are indigenous women there. They are supposed to wear uniforms, but we are fighting so that they can wear their *traje* there, so even if they are in prison, they are not being robbed of their identity."

Andrés Cus was trained as a teacher in Alta Verapaz. There he began to work with a Catholic priest who was creating a Q'eqchi' dictionary and from there moved to work for PRONEBI. He was president of the provisional board that set up the ALMG and was in charge of their linguistic research department in the Quincentennial years. Even before he began to work with the languages, he confronted the drawbacks of "westernization" in his daily life:

> Personally, I like to wear *caites* [traditional sandals]. *Now* I realize that they are a symbol of our identity. Without these markers, especially with men, you don't even see that they are Maya; they disappear. It is important to strengthen these symbols, but it also makes sense. I went barefoot until I was twelve, with no problems, but the first money I ever earned, do you know what I used it for? To buy some shoes. They were awful, way too big for me, and very expensive, and they weren't even leather. They were plastic! I could hardly wear them, but I thought I needed them to go to the teachers' school. When I realized I was going to teach out in the hamlets, however, I saw that the shoes were not going to survive. So I thought, "I wore *caites* before," so I even wore *caites* to our graduation. They go best with the simple clothing, which is all you can afford as a teacher! When I went to work at PRONEBI, they'd ask me why I was wearing them, they all teased me. And I'd said, "I'll tell you why! They hold up, they let your feet breathe, they're economical, and they show humility. You are going out into the villages where our brothers are barefoot and hungry, and you're going to be wearing nice shoes!?" As I work more on issues of identity with the Academy, I realized there are so many things they tell us we need, like perfume, makeup, a big car, jewelry, suit, tie, name-brand shirt, but that's all so we'll look ladino. Even TV. What does it give us, besides unreal images of women, so that people no longer value the women of our countryside, women who can work. Now the ideal is a skinny woman on the beach! Do we need that stuff? It is just creating the mentality that will fit us into our economic roles.

Ricardo Cajas says he was also formed in the Catholic Church. When I first spoke with him in 1989, he was president of the Guatemalan Mayan Writers' Academy (AEMG), member of the ALMG-in-formation, and running for mayor of the country's second largest city, Quetzaltenango, a race he very nearly won. On his loss, he said, "I couldn't believe how much money they spent to beat me—on newspaper ads, commercials, billboards, and on gifts. I'd go into areas and people would ask me what I had brought them because the ladino candidate had handed out T-shirts, hats, uniforms for their soccer team, basketballs! It was over the top!" The reactions of ladinos to Cajas's candidacy horrified a ladino friend of mine from Quetzaltenango, who said, "He was definitely winning, and at the last moment all the ladinos pulled together. Their differences didn't matter as much as the fact that they did not want an 'Indian' elected."[21]

Cajas said that he had been involved in the worker and student move-

---

21. In 1995 a Maya-K'iche' candidate, Rigoberto Quemé Chay, won the Quetzaltenango mayoral elections.

ment for twenty-five years, and for those twenty-five years had been working to create an indigenous movement within it. He was a student activist
and a leader in the teacher's union, for which he was imprisoned in 1974.
"At that time there was a convergence between the indigenous movement,
the teachers' organization, and the popular movement. The earthquake in
1976 strengthened us; it led us to coordinate our work."

The convergence between the three led to a national indigenous coordination that held a series of seminars with indigenous people from around
the country. Several organizations came out of this coordination, including
the National Indigenous Front (FIN—also sometimes called the National
Integration Front), which attempted to work as a political party, the CUC,
and what he called the Revolutionary Indigenous Movement (MIR).[22] He
said that by 1981, during the third seminar, which was held clandestinely
because of the war, they were beginning to question the lack of indigenous
leadership in the popular movement. "Where were the indigenous people?
we asked ourselves. If the popular movement wins, if Lucas García falls,
where will we be? We are still in a submissive position within the popular
movements. Why are there always ladino leaders and indigenous soldiers
out there dying?" He said that this awareness led some to leave the movement altogether. A friend of Cajas said, "He used to be very involved in the
popular movement, but we pulled him over to the Indians." Cajas smiled
and agreed:

> I became more and more aware of how the indigenous people are excluded
> from having any say. It's as if they still believe we're *no son para cargos sino para
> cargar* [not made for holding positions, only for carrying things]. I've come to
> realize that we cannot liberate the people of Guatemala without internal de-
> colonization. This is the first step. It is not contrary to the class struggle, but
> we cannot allow the majority to be excluded from this struggle, and we can-

22. The history of FIN is complex and tragic and deserves much closer attention than I can
give it here. Beginning in 1976 as an indigenous rights organization, the group quickly con-
ceded to charges of racism by changing its focus from an indigenous to an integration front.
Members (including some who later formed the ALMG) began the long, slow work of collecting signatures and lobbying to be officially recognized as a political party. They both tried to
use, and were used by, the different parties, and after splitting over the issue, the FIN officially
backed the candidacy of General Lucas García for the 1978 elections (Falla 1978). The history of his tenure is well known, and many of the FIN members were assassinated. Though the
party is considered a failure by many in the present-day Mayan movement, its very failure may
reflect Rosa Luxemburg's understanding of the necessary prematurity of social movements
(discussed in chapter 2). Their "maturity" depends on the ways identities are formed in process—through the differences in the subsequent repetitions of such struggles. In Quetzaltenango, Cajas's failure may have been a condition of possibility for Quemé winning the mayor's
seat. The ALMG's "working differently" is a repetition with difference from earlier struggles for
Mayan rights.

not participate as long as the colonial situation persists. We will no longer accept other people speaking for us.

The struggle, Mr. Cajas said, is not going to be won with arms. The Maya are familiar enough with graveyards. Instead the indigenous people must work in every space they can:

> We are not against anyone. It is an error for the popular movement to think that we reject them, but they must recognize that the Maya people are different.[23] We respect the convergences with them, with the church, with political parties. For example, the SIL has worked in this area. The people went to them to learn the language, how to translate, and so on. That's how the AEMG was started. We used what they had to give us, and then we became independent. We can't be enemies with anyone. That is why for our last anniversary we invited the head of the military base, so he could see we had nothing to hide. We have more people in the university, even organizing with the indigenous queen contests. Although this is only a copy of our culture, even there we are able to extract some concessions. We are pursuing our project even in the belly of the beast.

No Assassination without Representation

As Professor Cajas suggests, indigenous people are working in sites of power throughout the nation. Like him, they have also been instrumental in the sites of counterpower, including the overt resistance movements. In the mid-1970s, indigenous people were important participants in the various social movements coalescing around struggles for radical change. I have already mentioned the importance of Liberation Theology and Catholic Action in indigenous communities, and Rigoberta Menchú testifies to the power of these discourses in her own coming to political consciousness (Menchú 1984). Untold numbers of indigenous people participated actively and clandestinely in the popular and revolutionary movements. Accounts of the armed struggle (Fried et al. 1983; Frank and Wheaton 1984; Concerned Guatemala Scholars 1982) and personal testimonials (Harbury 1994; Hooks 1991) show the deep identification of many indigenous people with these movements.

The critiques Professor Cajas makes, however, were frequently repeated in my interviews with Mayan activists and even with some ladino participants in the struggle. When asked how they became involved with the Mayan cultural rights movement, several Mayans I interviewed cited the case of the Revolutionary Indigenous Movement (MIR), an attempt to create an

---

23. The previous quotes were taken from an interview in 1990, whereas this quote is from 1992. Notice the change in identity terms.

indigenous-led guerrilla front. As one person said, "The end of MIR is very painful to remember. It seems that the leadership of the guerrillas could not stand indigenous leadership, the ladinos would not accept it. They wanted a committee of campesinos, not a revolutionary movement. That is why they eliminated the MIR. The guerrilla wiped them out because they thought they were divisive, revisionists." This story was confirmed by several people, but we will have to wait for the Truth Commission findings to learn more.

The continuing power of counterinsurgency throughout the period of my fieldwork does not lead me to expect that people will express support for the revolutionary movement. I also would never demand that the URNG be more than human, expect them not to make mistakes, or insist that they should have foreseen the massive brutality of the army's response in the war. However, this story of the guerrillas eliminating an indigenous revolutionary front circulates widely and informs the reactions of many Mayan activists. Many believe that Mayan bodies in the graveyards and clandestine cemeteries were victims of ladinos of both the Left and the Right, beliefs that overdetermine their struggles to work differently.

Of course, after the declaration of Iximché in 1981, when the coordination of indigenous groups publicly supported armed struggle, many of their members were killed by the army, as were tens of thousands of Maya working throughout the country as middlemen and middlewomen. The Maya are quite clear that the army is their worst enemy. However, on top of the loss and horror of the army's scorched-earth campaigns and massacres, many Maya say that they feel they were used as cannon fodder by both the army *and* the guerrilla (D. Stoll 1993).

These experiences are essential to Mayan cultural activists' decisions to work differently, to function within the "belly of the beast," and to concentrate on culture. They argue that coding resistance merely as an armed or explicitly "political" challenge to the dominating system is too limiting and ignores the multiple fronts of their struggle. Although they insist that they share the concerns and struggles of the popular movement, in being strategic the Maya are attempting to see to it that indigenous people are not sacrificed in struggles that represent their interests but in whose decision-making processes they are not represented. As Mayan activist Dr. Demetrio Cojtí put it, "Where are the indigenous people in the executive councils of the unions, of GAM [Mutual Support Group for Families of the Disappeared], of UASP [Unity for Labor and Popular Action]? They are clearly in the organizations, but when we ask them why there are no Maya making decisions we are told, 'We are not racist, we do not differentiate between Indians and ladinos, so we do not need Indians on the board.' We say that having representation is not racist!"

A simple binary coding of resistance denies the hybridity and heterogeneity of the oppressed and denies, as the ALMG insist, that cultural work is implicitly political. As Narciso Cojtí said,

> There was so much violence because the army was not in control of the situation. That is why the thing was so brutal, so bestial, totally excessive. It was meant to scare people. We continue to fight, but we have learned from the mistakes of the past. We are working differently now. We have to work in nonviolent ways. It's the only thing possible right now. We have seen what has happened, who has the money and the technology, and we know who will win. We must begin with our identity because we are disfigured by the education system and other violent means. We must work this way now, to become stronger.

As another ALMG founder put it, "The ALMG looks just cultural, but inside we are very political. We are defining different models of development. We are struggling to regain our culture, the languages, but it is the organization that is difficult to regain. Many of us have lost our identity." Similarly, Demetrio Cojtí, when asked if the Maya want land, replied that first they need culture. "The first thing you do when you're bleeding is you try to staunch the flow. We are bleeding to death, and the blood is our culture. We need to deal with that first."

As I have mentioned, the reaction of much of the Left to the Mayan movement is often quite hostile, ranging from critiques that they are "sold out," and "the enemy," to claims that they are "racist, resentful, and want to get rid of all the ladinos." As one Mayan leader said, however,

> We are not trying to take anything away from the URNG or the popular movement. We are one facet of the same struggle. We are just dealing with an issue they have not attended to, that perhaps they overlooked. Some people say that we are counterrevolutionary. They accuse us of being spies, of working for the CIA, all sorts of terrible things, just because we care about the ethnic question. But I try to tell them they are mistaken; that there is difference there. I, as a man, cannot tell you what it's like to be pregnant, or what a woman suffers, I just can't. It's the same with the ladinos. They just can't understand.

Ernesto Laclau and Chantal Mouffe suggest that resistance exists wherever there is power, but that this resistance is only sometimes political. They argue, for example, that women have always been resisting male domination, or that workers have been resisting capitalist domination for centuries, but the work is to identify the discursive conditions for the emergence of collective action—of a feminist movement or labor organizing. Such collective action is based on a rearticulation of relationships, often through the intervention of an external discourse (like human rights or the Quincentennial) that interrupts the discourse of subordination so that a difference previously stabilized as subordination becomes instead a site of antagonism.

Thus, indigenous peoples have always resisted their subordination to the Spanish and the wealthy ladinos through the manifold mechanisms of everyday life, ceremonial and ritual responses, and the closed corporate community (Warren 1989). But those relations must be rearticulated for the antagonism of the relationship to become meaningful in a different way—the symbolism changes, which then changes the discourse of resistance into another form (Laclau and Mouffe 1985, 142–165). Indigenous interpellation as "middlemen and middlewomen" through the hostile markings and orthopedics of school and church has articulated new forms of indigenous identification. So, too, the participation in the political movements of the 1970s and 1980s intervened to change the discourse of resistance, giving rise, for some, to identifications newly articulated as Maya. These struggles in turn open up new terrains for these repetitions with a difference. As a member of the *Pastoral Indígena* said, "The indigenous involvement with the guerrilla was important; it helped us leave off our passive resistance and begin to participate actively. It was a vital expression of our people. But we must be very careful and work very thoughtfully. We want to be heard, to be understood and taken into account. We need recognition for the organizations of the Mayan People, not just incorporation into another struggle." As with state fetishism, in Quincentennial Guatemala what was once naturalized (if resented)—Maya incorporation into ladino-led struggle—is increasingly revealed as alien and untenable. Here too culture may offer a powerful remedy for a wounded body politic striped with hostile markings and struggling for identification.

MAYAN ORGANIZING

Legalization of the ALMG

The legalization of the Academy was a seven-year struggle for recognition. Even after so long, its legalization took some observers, and even members, by surprise. "I'm not sure those Congressmen even read the legislation before they passed it," said Andrés Cus. Most ALMG members attribute their success with the Academy and with the unified alphabet to constant lobbying. As one member said:

> We could not wait for the ladinos to wake up and realize we have rights. We had to force them to listen to us. And that didn't happen with a couple of street demonstrations or a few meetings, but instead working like flies. The fly doesn't really hurt you, but it's always there. It bothers you, it pesters you, until you can't stand it anymore and you have to do something about it. We have to learn from the politicians, how they do things. It's all through the back door, through family members. We would do anything to get in and talk to Congress members. If they closed the door, we acted like we worked there to get in. If they closed the window, we'd say we were related to some bigwig and get in that way.

They acknowledge the help of ladino allies like Culture Ministers Anaisa-bel Prera and Marta Faisen, and said of then-President Vinicio Cerezo, "I'm not sure he understood it very well, but he behaved himself." Cerezo of-fered to create the Academy through a presidential decree, but members decided they wanted full Congressional approval so they would not be overly identified with any one political party or administration. A ladino re-searcher at FLACSO said, "It was just a political maneuver of the Christian Democrats, but the Maya were very astute in using the opening and the help of supporters." A member active in the lobbying effort said, "We were very careful about the political moment, using the elections in our favor. We would go in and act like we could deliver the votes, and everyone is inter-ested in the 'Indian votes.' Of course, we didn't own those votes, but we promised them anyway. We talked to everyone, made them live up to their slogans about supporting the indigenous people."

On November 15, 1990, the Academy was made into a legal state entity. As the ALMG says in the introduction to the pamphlet containing this law, "The Guatemalan state recognizes an autonomous state agency of a techni-cal, scientific, and cultural nature that will promote the knowledge and dif-fusion of the Mayan languages and culture. This recognition is not the gift of the government, but is the result of the efforts of an entire People, the Mayan People, who are seeking the construction of a fully multilingual and multicultural society in Guatemala" (ALMG 1991, 1). The legal designation of autonomy was an important political concession. It means that even though the state is responsible for financially supporting the Academy, it has no other rights over the organization. The ALMG must account for ex-penditures but has full administrative and political independence. Only a few entities enjoy this status, including the National University and the municipalities.

The law defines the tasks of the Academy as to

(a) Carry out scientific research to stimulate and support the development of the Mayan languages of the country, within the integral framework of the na-tional culture. (b) Plan and carry out programs of educational and cultural development based in this linguistic, anthropological, and historical research. (c) Create publications to promote the knowledge and use of Mayan lan-guages and to strengthen Guatemalan cultural values. (d) Normalize the use of Mayan languages in Guatemala. (e) Provide technical and scientific advice to the government and other state agencies. (ALMG 1991, 9)

The Academy is also supposed to research and propose legislation related to cultural issues; create Mayan language schools in the linguistic commu-nities and promote the study of Mayan languages throughout the republic; translate and publish all the legal texts pertaining to these issues; provide technical training in linguistics and research to members of the different linguistic communities; and rescue languages in the process of extinction (ALMG 1991, 9). The law provides a yearly budget of five million quetzales for this work.

Organizationally, each of the twenty-one Mayan linguistic communities elects a council, which in turn elects one member to the national executive council (*Consejo Superior*).[24] This council, elected every three years, directs all of the Academy's work and elects the seven members of the board (*Junta Directiva*), who in turn oversee the day-to-day running of the Academy. Board members serve for one year and cannot be reelected. The first board contained two women and represented almost exclusively the three majority language groups: Kaqchikel, K'iche', and Q'eqchi'. No women were elected in the 1992 elections, but there was a "revolt of the minorities" in which representatives of the Poqomam, Achi, Sakapulteka, and other smaller linguistic communities were elected.

Though critics of the Mayan movement have called the Academy members an "elite," many of these members have only a sixth-grade education (although to be on the executive council, some university training is preferred). In 1993, full-time workers in the central office received a salary of approximately 2200 quetzales a month (about 450 dollars), and those who work full-time in the communities earn about 1200 quetzales (250 dollars).[25] These are excellent salaries compared to the minimum agricultural wage (less than 500 quetzales a month), but they hardly afford a luxurious lifestyle, especially given the fact that many board members maintain two households, one in the city and another for their families in their communities of origin. Many commute weekly between their two homes and retain their other work as teachers, traders, and so on, taking sabbaticals for the year they are on the board.

The first year of legal status, 1991, was spent renting and outfitting the building for the office, hiring personnel, and creating the different departments. Organizing and settling in were greatly hampered by the foot-dragging of the Finance Ministry in allotting them their legal budget (a foot-dragging that FODIGUA has also experienced). It took until August 1991 for the first 10 percent of the Academy budget to be released. Since then, financing has been a continual struggle. The Academy does have a few other resources—since it was formed in 1986, it has received support for its linguistic and organizing work from foreign donors and

24. The Mayan linguistic communities are listed as Achi, Akateko, Awakateko, Ch'orti', Chuj, Itza', Ixil, Jakalteko, Kaqchikel, K'iche', Mam, Mopan, Poqomam, Poqomchi', Q'anjob'al, Q'eqchi', Sakapulteko, Sipakapense, Tektiteko, Tz'utujil, Uspanteko. See map 2.

25. Thanks to Paul Kobrak for this information from Aguacatan.

NGOs, the Academy was paid for the Maya language supplement it wrote for the newspaper *Siglo XXI* (now produced by CECMA), it sells its publications, and members pay dues—but the Academy depends on state monies to undertake its nationwide training and research plans. For 1992, the Academy received only three of the five million quetzales promised, and by June of 1993, they had received only seven hundred thousand quetzales for that year. The Academy president at that time, Marcelino Nicolás said, "They won't give us the five million, and that's not even one quetzal for every Maya! They spend a lot more on dead Maya than on live ones." Despite these problems, by mid-1993 the Academy had organized the local councils, set up offices in twenty linguistic communities, and were working on programs of descriptive and applied linguistics, sociocultural and socioeconomic research, and bicultural education.

Culture and Identity: Salvage and Formation

The aims of the Academy's research work are dual: both salvage (*rescate*) and formation (*formación*, a term carrying the sense of "to train or educate," but also the more constitutive notion of "to give form to"). This work is meant to both recover and uncover (Sam Colop 1991) cultural and linguistic practices that may not have received systematic treatment (making them available for general use) or that may be practiced by declining numbers of people. As mentioned above, Academy members feel that they are in a race against time and against ladinoization, which includes the "internal colonialism" that moves Mayan peoples to devalue their own practices and to mimic western ways.

As part of this double move of salvage and *formación,* members of the ALMG say, "We must begin to form Elders' Councils, learned people of the Pueblo Maya who, supported by their communities, by linguists, professionals, and anthropologists, can begin the work of restoring and developing the Mayan languages. This will be an arduous task, but if it is not begun, what might have been recuperated will be lost forever" (ALMG 1990, 48). This merging of the old and the novel is apparent in the prayers and offerings to the supreme being, the Creator and Shaper of Man, with which they begin their meetings. One leader of the ALMG says that this practice surprises many observers, but "The Maya give thanks for food, for air, for the tools that serve us, the office machines, and the computers."

Promotores   The Academy is training volunteers from the different communities in basic linguistic and interviewing skills so that they can compile lists of vocabulary words in their languages. In consultation with members of the community, these *promotores* detail definitions and usage, then the lists are revised by the Academy's local councils. The aim is to formalize the information, create dictionaries for each language, and increase the vocabularies of everyone involved. These groups work to create vocabularies for new things (computers, Big Macs), rather than borrow words from Spanish or English. The Academy also trains researchers for fieldwork on cultural issues, with the aim of writing a monograph for each cultural area. (This work parallels but also intervenes interdicta in the investigations of private and state research organizations described in chapter 3.)

This process is meant to involve as many people as possible, inciting interest, forming skills, and creating cultural promoters while drawing on other sites involved in this work (such as the Francisco Marroquín Linguistic Project [PLFM] and PRONEBI). The idea is to provide opportunities for people to get involved through short-term paying jobs and thus to *formar* activists. As Mr. Cus said, "Our method is participative, we want people involved in planning and carrying out the projects. This is a very slow process. The results are not obvious right away, but it is part of our work of rescuing communal organization and creating leaders."

The Board   The Academy's board, which draws in community members for a year of responsibility in the capital, is also part of this *formación* work. It is modeled in part on the *cofradía* system, in that it rotates responsibilities while incorporating and training people. There was some grumbling inside and outside of the Academy over the inexperience of the new board in 1993 and their lack of formal linguistic training. Even some of the original founders complained that "the democracy issue is all well and good, but the Academy needs to prove itself as a professional, technical institution that can hold its own among the universities."[26] However, the Academy is strongly committed to creating and strengthening activists and leaders—especially from the less-represented linguistic groups—through such a system.

The Fifteenth Workshop   This commitment was expressed in the Academy's fifteenth workshop, which I attended in San Luís Petén. The site was chosen to support (*animar*) the recently organized Mopan community, an ethnolinguistic group that many people think is disappearing. The site was quite remote from Guatemala City, entailing some eight hours on a bus, much of it on unpaved roads into the jungles of the Petén, which was

26. Miguel Angel Velasco said in 1993, "I appreciate the way the Academy is committed to democracy, and having every group represented, but they have to accept that the Kaqchikeles, for whatever reason, are better educated, better prepared, for some of these roles. But there isn't one Kaqchikel on the board of directors right now. They insist on minority representation, but that is not always best for the functioning of a new bureaucracy." These remarks are interesting because in the same interview he expressed ambivalence about the stability of his own Kaqchikel identity.

reputed to be full of bandits, guerrillas, drug runners, and rogue army units.[27] These annual workshops have become important events in Guatemala, drawing national and foreign academics, a variety of NGOs, Mayan activists, and the curious. The choice of San Luís drastically cut down the number of ladino and foreign supporters and researchers who attended, to the disappointment of many Academy members. "Where are the gringos?" asked one organizer. However, hundreds of Mayan activists had come from all over the country to listen to talks and participate in three days of workshops and training sessions. Almost all of the twenty other linguistic communities had sent representatives. Many of them had never traveled so far, and they commented on the importance of getting to know different parts of the country. Many of the participants took advantage of the trip to visit the archaeological site of Tikal for the first time.

Though they said that the level of academic exchange was not as high as at other workshops, most of the organizers were very pleased with the results. Many more Maya participated actively than usual, feeling more comfortable, they said, to ask questions and work through uncertainties. The organizers felt that the work of the Mopan was exemplary in setting up the infrastructure, which in turn stimulated the Mopan sense of pride and identity. The gala events of the workshop, the ritual of the opening and closing ceremonies, the lectures and training sessions, the theater and musical events, and the exchange among Maya from all over showcased indigenous identity in the region and contributed to an understanding of the continuing power of ethnicity throughout Guatemala for both the Mopan and nearby Itza' (generally quite isolated from highland organizing), and their ladino neighbors.

Becoming Maya   As individuals become articulated (linked) to these projects—through friends, because there was a position open, or because they heard about it in the news—they begin to articulate (express) themselves differently. The young woman working as a receptionist at the Academy said, "I have learned so much here! I am from Sacapulas, and before I didn't even know we had a different language! Now I am trying to learn it." Olga Xicox, who works with the affiliated Center for Research and Mayan Studies (CISMA) in Quetzaltenango, said:

> When I went to high school, I stopped wearing *traje*. There was a lot of pressure on us. But now that I am working with CISMA, I am sure I will never take it off again. I may not be pure Maya, but I am a descendent. I was like so many

27. The last two are not clearly separate categories. San Luís is about an hour away from Poptún, where the gringo Michael Devine was killed by the army in 1990, supposedly because he had evidence of army involvement in drug trafficking.

of the young people today. I didn't care about the past; it seemed too hard to learn about it. But when we start to do research, to understand the Mayan world, when we see that this is something we have inside, then we become interested, we see it has a lot to offer.

Miguel Angel Velasco is a young Kaqchikel man who says his father, a *milpa* (corn) farmer, decided the children would be better off learning Spanish, so they did not learn Kaqchikel. Mr. Velasco worked for five years in the public relations office of the National Palace and was doing quite well, he says, in charge of his own radio show, earning a lot of money, and working with the president and other important people. "But I just felt I couldn't go on. It was going against something inside me." While living in Guatemala City, he had become involved with the Center for the Study of Mayan Culture (CECMA), which was run by Kaqchikel friends from his hometown of Comalapa.[28] Because of his work with CECMA, he started to study the Kaqchikel language. When he was offered a job at the Academy, he took it "without a second thought. I had seen so many people grow old doing the work I was in with nothing to show for it but money. I wanted more than that. I am realizing there is a lot of potential in the Academy, they can do a lot with the budget, with state support." The job has made him reflect a great deal about his identity, however:

28. In fact, we joked about the *mara de Comalapa* (the Comalapa gang) because so many Kaqchikel people from there have risen to national prominence, including army General Otzoy, Rosalina Tuyuc of CONAVIGUA, the Protestant pastor Vitalino Similox, most of the people at CECMA, and the anthropologist Irma Otzoy. Comalapa is a very special place, but in general the Kaqchikeles hold many prominent national positions. As Mr. Velasco said, they consider themselves better educated and better prepared. In part this is because of their proximity to the capital and the educational and development opportunities this provides. There are an extraordinary number of foreign-funded development projects in the Chimaltenango area: foreign workers can live in the city and still do their work in the countryside. Vice versa, Kaqchikeles can commute in to the university or jobs without the prohibitive expenses of living in Guatemala City.

This brings home the multiple heterogeneity out of which the Maya are trying to construct a pan-Mayan identification. People are acutely aware of supposed slights and perceived unequal representations among ethnolinguistic groups. Linguistic differences, lack of personal ties, and even centuries-old resentments sometimes flare up and limit cross-ethnic organizing. A K'iche' activist said he still has a hard time trusting Kaqchikeles because they had betrayed the Maya and joined with the Conquerors to defeat the K'iche' kingdom (on attempts to overcome this division, see Warren 1996). Intervillage differences also surface. A Tz'utujil advisor to an indigenous congressman said that he did not trust the ALMG because the man who said he represented the Tz'utujiles was not from his side of Lake Atitlán. "Friends from Solola know him, but I don't know him. I didn't vote for him. How can he say he represents me?" For the First International Indigenous Summit, it was clear that Rigoberta Menchú's office had made carefully considered choices in inviting a balance from both the popular and cultural rights groups among the Guatemalan delegates. Though some saw this as an important olive branch, a Q'eqchi' activist said, "They are from different tendencies, but they are all Kaqchikeles!"

Sometimes I don't know how I most identify. I think in Spanish, I write best in Spanish, I have a lot of ladino friends. My father is not very happy that I have taken this job. He does not like the "Indian stuff," as he calls it. For him, I had the signs of success, I wore a suit and tie and I hung out with ladinos. I knew famous politicians, and he was very proud. He has been trying to get me to quit. I still won't wear those clothes, the *caites* and things, because I don't like them. My father would kill me if I did! But I do wear the *chumpa* [jacket].[29]

Even second- and third-generation ladinos have been moved to rethink their identity through their work with Mayan issues. A member of the staff of the presidential secretary for political affairs in the National Palace who was instrumental in planning the Secretariate for Indigenous Affairs (dropped after the Serrano coup) said:

I have been horrified at the racism among the ladinos. I never realized it until I began to work on indigenous issues like the ALMG. Because I was working on these things, I have experienced a great deal of rejection here in the office; they treat me very badly. I am ladino. I don't speak a language; I don't wear the *traje*. Maybe my grandmother was indigenous, but I am ladino. Nonetheless I am beginning to feel the part, I feel a bit like an indigenous person. Since I've been working with them, experiencing this hatred from the people in the office, it has made me feel indigenous.

Seizing Hold of Identity   Given the emphasis on *formación,* on the struggle to reverse ladinoization, and on the (re)membering of indigenous identity, what is the difference for which the Maya demand respect? Hostile identities can be indefinite, ambivalent, difficult bases on which to build authority. Because of the porousness of phenotype and stereotype and the ease with which *traje* can be taken off, language has taken on a special power as a marker (Fischer and Brown 1996; COCADI 1985; Englund 1992 and 1996).[30] Its relation to the pre-Conquest past, its role in identifying ethnic

29. This jacket was originally created for tourists—with a denim base and quiltwork pieces of *huipiles* and *cortes* sewn on. It has become an unofficial *traje* for many Mayan men (see Hendrickson 1996). It can be both dressy and casual, is pan-Mayan, and carries the extra cachet of being worn by foreigners. Mr. Velasco said that he and his sister were starting a small business to make and sell them. "I think it's good that there's a sort of compromise thing for men to wear, because they certainly aren't going back to wearing the old traditional clothing," he said. In fact, the dearth of male *traje* created a semiotic problem for the New Guatemalan Democratic Front (FDNG) and their publicity posters. Juan León, a Maya-K'iche', ran for vice president on the ticket in the 1995 elections, and to represent his Mayan identity, he had to transvestite in men's *traje* from Todos Santos, a village and ethnolinguistic group not his own.

30. As Andrés Cus and Narciso Cojtí suggested, without *traje* Mayan men disappear, a theme I explore in more detail in the next chapter. This remark has a double sense, of course, because *disappear* as a transitive verb was coined in Guatemala—one more way in which the graveyard haunts Mayan organizing.

groups, and its opacity to outsiders all give it power as a positive identity-marker. Prelegalization ALMG documents suggested a linguistically based hierarchy for membership, with Maya-speakers given first priority, bilingual Maya-and-Spanish-speakers second, and finally, as observers, those who identify with or support Mayan culture (but these must learn a Mayan language within two years of joining). Currently, anyone who shows interest and can pay the dues can join. The laws governing membership in the executive council state that one must be "Guatemalan and of the Maya ethnicity, cannot be a member of the executive committee of a political party or hold a religious position, and preferably hold a university degree and speak, write, and understand any of the Mayan languages" (ALMG 1991, 12).

However, like any marker in the hostile environment of colonialism, language is also a problem. Mr. Velasco is not alone in having parents who think it best to grow up speaking Spanish.[31] Especially in the Quetzaltenango area, language is not a clear marker of indigenous identity, because many families are second- and third-generation Spanish speakers but retain *traje* among the women and consider themselves indigenous.

This was the case with Dr. Alfredo Tay, a K'iche' raised in Quetzaltenango. He identifies as Maya, works with the ALMG, and teaches communications at the National University (where he is studying K'iche'). In June 1993, he was named minister of education, the first indigenous minister in Guatemalan history. Dr. Tay admits that it is hard to define indigenous identity: "When Dr. Cojtí talks of a Mayan nation, I guess that means unity. It is something we need to develop. We need to seek out what we have in common, our similarities. For some people, it may only be a history of suffering, of experiencing racism. But it is also a question of becoming conscious, of coming together, of developing a commitment." He has been attacked by ladinos both for not being Indian enough and for being "too Indian"—an antiladino racist. "I admit that at times it has been hard to claim my indigenous background. It was not like it is today. I was trained by the church, studied in the United States, and I do not speak a language. But I have always been an Indian." He admits that the ministry is a double-edged sword. Education is traditionally one of the hardest posts to fill, because the ministry is chronically underfunded and racked by teachers' strikes and student walk-outs. "This is an important opening for the Maya," said Tay,

31. This doesn't always work, of course. A Kaqchikel friend says proudly that his parents tried desperately to make him learn Spanish as a baby, but he would have nothing of it. Finally, he says, his grandfather intervened and told his parents he was Kaqchikel and they were going to have to face it. "You're trying to teach him Spanish, but he isn't speaking anything. Let him learn Kaqchikel and get the Spanish later."

"but the same people who question my indigenous identity will be the first to claim that Indians are good for nothing if we make any mistakes." This "paradox" suggests the way that fantasy structures identification and hostility.

In his speech at the ALMG workshop in the Petén, Andrés Cus emphasized the importance of consciously claiming identification as he outlined the Mayan rights contained in the Constitution and in the pamphlet on Specific Rights issued by the Guatemalan Council of Mayan Organizations (COMG 1991). To achieve these demands, he said, "We need to consolidate the identity of the people. The Mayan people are sick and we need to make them better. We need to respect our elders, respect our traditions. . . . These are the bases of our Mayan culture: respect for life, human life and the natural world, participation in the community, solidarity, working for equilibrium."

Part of this work of simultaneous salvage and formation of identity is the invocation of a harmonious communitarian history, sourced in part from the post-Conquest "Mayan Bible," the *Popul Wuj,* and (selected) documents of anthropology. The ALMG says, "If we remember our ancestors, they were perfectly able to get along; there is anthropological and archaeological proof of this. Like them we know our world, we have full mastery of our environment" (ALMG 1990, 62). In our discussions Mr. Cus reiterated that a sense of confidence and security in oneself as a Maya, and identification with the community, were the marks of identity:

> What we see is a destruction of our values at a terrible pace. People must be conscious of this. If you know who you are, it is not destructive to learn Spanish, English, French, whatever, but otherwise this can hurt you. We are working in the communities, and people are beginning to understand. Five or six years ago, if we spoke of the Pueblo Maya people laughed or they got very embarrassed. But this is changing; even the press has had to change the way they talk about us.

Dr. Demetrio Cojtí also reiterated the centrality of consciousness and commitment to Mayan identity rather than any one cultural trait. "Maya need to know how to defend themselves. Being Maya is not enough. We must know about indigenous rights, educate ourselves, communicate. If someone calls you a racist, you need to know how to respond, know the legal arguments."

Thus Mayan identity seems to be precisely the *process* of being community-bound: the work itself of education, *formación,* and (re)membering. With these markings, they are constructing a postcolonial identity and seizing hold of a mythic past to serve as a utopic future. Given the span of five hundred years and the hostility of colonial identity formation, it thus seems reductive to posit a simple Manichaean allegory of a "true" difference distinct from an imposed "otherness" or a pure, uncorrupted space from which to confront power. Instead, identity is produced through hostile markings and state orthopedics and through the way Mayan middlemen and middlewomen repeat with a difference between the interdictions of power: in the state, the school, the church, the courtroom, the Congress, and so on. In those sites meant to "fix" them, to turn them into ladinos, the Maya are repairing their communities, *formando* activists. (And this is only paradoxical if we insist on holding on to "solid" identifications.)

The Maya, a wounded body politic, haunted by massacres and grave-yards, are working differently. They are walking the halls of power wearing *caites*, learning from ladinos how to lobby, deploying the law to authorize their authority, and using state funds for salvage and *formación*. They are "alike but not quite." This is Bhabha's description of mimicry, which he links to colonial authority's narcissism—to the attempts to form Macauley Minute-like middlemen and middlewomen. He links its contra-diction of menace (not quite alike) to colonial paranoia. "The place of difference and otherness, or the space of the adversarial . . . is never entirely on the outside or implacably oppositional. . . . It is a pressure and a presence that acts constantly, if unevenly, along the entire boundary of authorization" (Bhabha 1985, 171). The projection of hostility onto the Maya, the overreaction of many ladinos to the elaborately legal and extraordinarily careful organizing of the Mayan cultural activists, suggests just this colonial paranoia.

Perhaps the ladino reactions I examine throughout this book overshoot their mark so often because the hybridity and mimicry of Mayan identity in *formación* is not reducible to something solid like clothing, diet, skin color, or language. This more fluid identity poses, as Bhabha says, "a *question* of colonial authority, an agonistic space. To the extent to which discourse is a form of defensive warfare, mimicry marks those moments of civil disobedience within the discipline of civility: signs of spectacular resistance" (Bhabha 1985, 181). Ladino identification thought it was solid, modern, civilized, and rational and that Indians were fixed—bound to rural areas or bound for ladinoization. The Quincentennial reveals how dependent ladino identity is on the Maya, how dependent modernity is on tradition, and that, as Emily Apter says, "the subliminal contamination of the colonial mind by the very belief in a 'magical essence' that it so abhorred in the native subject . . . undermines the myth of Western cultural superiority" (1993, 8). In the next chapter, I explore how this moving target, particularly as incorporated by Nobel Peace Prize winner Rigoberta Menchú Tum, questions identification, undermines the myth of ladino superiority, and calls out the hostility and cruelty of jokes. Here I briefly introduce the issue of gender within the Mayan cultural rights movement, a subject I return to in chapter 7.

THE DOUBLE BIND OF THE COMMUNITY-BOUND

Of course, Mayan efforts toward being community-bound encounter double binds, like the critiques that they are not really representative or truly authentic. The need for unity when confronting powerful antagonists with the demand for inclusion may limit a movement's flexibility in acknowledging internal difference, as the revolution based on class unity resisted Mayan specificity. The pan-Mayan movement is bound and determined to create a critical mass out of the twenty-one language communities and thousands of municipalities in which Mayan identifications are based, and it sometimes resists acknowledging the specificity of, for example, "minority" linguistic communities (leading to the 1993 "revolt" within the ALMG).[32] Too, despite the emphasis on inclusion, some members of the ALMG complain of being policed for not being Mayan enough: in their clothes, their religious practices, or their friends. One member who asked not to be named said, "I was out with one of the leaders, and we saw some of my ladino friends. They waved and started to come toward us, and the leader pulled me aside and told me not to talk to them, that they didn't respect the Maya. That seemed paranoid to me."

Mayan women may also find themselves in a double bind. Though I have tried to suggest the political nature of Mayan activism that is community-bound and to valorize their work vis-à-vis what I find to be too-simple analytical categories (co-opted or clean), I do not want to romanticize them. Pan-Mayan strategies of *formación* and seizing hold of memory posit complex and heterogeneous identities. However, questions of gender tend to be displaced by class and ethnic identification in their literature and in interviews with both men and women members.

As I suggest in the next three chapters, gendered identifications are vital if unacknowledged in forming national and ethnic bodies politic (creating a fetish effect around the *mujer maya* [Mayan woman]). Gayatri Spivak describes how the solidarities of the subaltern community are built on kinship and clan that are themselves structured predominantly through sexual differences in which "the figure of the woman moving from clan to clan and family to family as daughter/sister and wife/mother, syntaxes patriarchal

---

32. Indigenous communities are internally rent and relate unevenly to each other. For example, the internal age and status hierarchies are often resisted by the young through adherence to new social movements like Catholic Action. In turn, Carol Hendrickson says, "Asymmetries of all sorts exist throughout Maya culture and society—from dialect status to relative merit of *costumbre* [religious practice]." The "borrowing of *traje* pieces across town lines is often asymmetrical[, which] . . . hints at a valuation of *traje*—a ranking of one as 'better' or 'worse.' . . . The judgment on *traje* also reflects a more general evaluation of the town" from which it comes (Hendrickson 1995, 63). Carmack (1995) is especially sensitive to wealth differentiation within and among Mayan communities.

continuity even as she is herself drained of proper identity" (Spivak 1988b, 220). Similarly, my interviews are full of remarks that "it is the women who retain their Mayan culture"—through the *traje,* the languages, and in their roles as mothers responsible for the physical and social reproduction of indigenous people.

This is an empowering discourse for women, as some of the interviews quoted previously suggest. Part of this empowerment emerges from seizing hold of memories encoded with the authority of the "Mayan Bible," the *Popul Wuj.* In an almost universal trope when asked about women in the Mayan movement, both male and female organizers claimed that gender relations are equal among the Maya. This is illustrated, they claim, in the *Popul Wuj,* in which, unlike the Christian Bible, men and women are formed at the same time from the same material. This is a powerful discourse of equality, which the Maya deploy against the ladino model of unequal gender relations. Similarly, when one Mayan woman mentioned issues of domestic violence in Mayan homes, she quickly amended her remark, saying, "This might exist, but it is an effect of the ladinoization of our people."

In fact, many of my interviews with Mayan women involved such amendings, which suggests the double bind of intense loyalty to the Mayan struggle and awareness of the specificity of Mayan women's issues.[33] There are Mayan women working throughout the urban and rural networks of cultural rights organizations. Increasing numbers of women are getting university degrees in subjects ranging from linguistics to law and engineering. However, although there were two women on the ALMG board before 1992, from then until 1995 there were none on the board or the executive council, and there are few women leaders in the urban-based Mayan organizations.[34] During my fieldwork, the only women working in the ALMG main office were employed as secretaries, cleaning women, and accountants.

The terms of the cultural activists' empowering discourse can also contribute to the exclusion of women from these spaces. When identity boundaries, even as appropriations of hostile markings, are patrolled, it is often

33. There is also the double bind of being interviewed by a foreign woman, which may be overdetermined by a reluctance to criticize one's organization to an outsider. Interviews were often held in office situations, where any complaints might be overheard, and, of course, I was asking questions informed by my concerns with the specificities of gender identification—concerns that may not resonate with their experiences and consciousness, an issue I return to in chapter 9.

34. Interestingly enough, there are several Maya and ladina women in prominent positions in the popular movement, although primarily in positions associated with their identities as widows. Two examples are Rosalina Tuyuc of the National Coordinating Committee of Guatemalan Widows and Ninéth García of the Mutual Support Group for Families of the Disappeared.

Figure 10. *"Tres mujeres haciendo tortillas, Santa Catarina Palopó, Solola"* (Three women making tortillas). Postcard. Copyright Gianni Vecchiato. Published with kind permission.

women who are chastised for failing to uphold their roles as the guardians of tradition.[35] One leader of the ALMG said, "A woman is not a woman unless she makes tortillas. Some women say they don't have time, but this is part of a woman, she cannot leave it behind. My wife would be too ashamed if she did not make tortillas, she would lose the dignity of being a woman." The small, fat traditional tortillas of Guatemala are patted out by hand (unlike in Mexico where a press is often used). It can take several hours to prepare the corn and roll the tortillas for each meal. Even the most outlying villages now boast at least one *nixtamal* (mechanical corn grinder), which has immensely shortened women's time devoted to tortillas, but there are many men who claim that the only authentic tortilla is made of corn ground by hand and rolled out in hours of painstaking labor.

Discussion of the genocide suffered by the Maya and emphasis on the

35. One can find this chastisement in the resistive text of the Conquest-era indigenous chronicler Guaman Poma (Guaman Poma de Ayala 1980) of Peru, who both critiques the Spanish conquerors for besmirching the virtue of native women (the seeds, so to speak, of the *mestizaje* examined in chapter 6) and lays into the indigenous women for their promiscuity.

role of women in passing on the culture to their children have resulted in a marked pronatalist stance among the Mayan rights movement. In interviews, Mayan and ladino men emphasized the importance of children for indigenous women's identity, claims that I examine in the next two chapters. Of course, Mayan pronatalism is also inflected with the Catholicized upbringings of many activists. Many strongly rejected the 1993 "Population Law" legislation, which was denounced by the Church as "the abortion law" although abortion was nowhere mentioned, and which primarily provided funds for education on reproduction and contraception (Fabri 1994). Similarly, a Mayan woman activist said, "Indigenous women use only natural methods of birth control. They would never abort a child! You have the children God gives you, and you accept it. Using contraceptives causes birth defects, and in the Maya cosmology it is viewed as a sin." In another interview, however, she asked me what kind of contraception I used and if I could supply her with information. She said that her husband had left her five years ago with one child and that abstinence was her form of birth control. "If I had stayed with him I would have had many more children and I would not be involved the way I am now, in the Mayan organizations, and going to school. It would have been impossible!"

Another Mayan woman was more explicit about problems with Mayan men:

> Even though we have very important roles in the community, in the organizations, there are men who beat women. They think, "The man rules, it is my right to do whatever I want." Many men take advantage of women and leave them stuck with a child. They drink and they come home and fight in the house, in front of the children! I am separated from my husband because he abused me. I don't see any men now. I already have three children, and I don't need any more. My mother takes care of them so I can work and do my organizing work with women; I explain to the women that they don't have to endure these things, that they can participate. If I were still married, I could never do these things, be so involved. I think things are changing; some men are helping out more. What really makes a difference is when women have their own income. Then they don't have to sit through beatings. They can just leave.

A friend whose partner left her with a child after they returned from exile is enraged at Mayan male hypocrisy. She is struggling to make ends meet and to responsibly fulfill the demands of her job, her political commitments, and child care. The kinship ties that so many professional Mayan women depend on to help with raising children are not available to her, decimated by the violence that killed much of her family. On top of this, she is criticized by Mayan men for not being authentic because she has only one child!

Many women I interviewed would admit there were problems connected to alcohol consumption, violence, and abandonment in the communities they were bound to, but they would insist on the value of their culture: "Among the Maya, the man respects the woman. Men are our support; we must walk together."[36] Such statements are both about the heterogeneity of their identifications (see Moraga 1983; Mohanty, Russo, and Torres 1991; Spivak 1985 and 1988a) and about a strategic deployment of the discourses of equality intervening, *interdicta*, in practices of inequality. Just as the Maya movement as a whole appropriates nationalist discourses of unity and the glorious Mayan past for their own project, Mayan women are seizing hold of the memories of gender equality in the *Popul Wuj* to *formar* a more just future.

Part of this effort included the formation of the Seminar of Mayan Women. According to participants, about forty women first met in Antigua in 1987 to discuss the role of women in cultural and economic development. They decided that women are vital for development but tend to be marginalized and that they needed to work for more equality. Fifty women participated in the second meeting in 1989, where the emphasis was on the five hundred years of Conquest and its specific effects on women. They discussed spirituality, clothing, language, economics, and the general prejudice against Mayan women who are treated like slaves. A third seminar was held to discuss women's participation in the Quincentennial and how women could learn to value themselves as Maya and as women. Olga Xicox, one of the organizers said, "We have to fight against cultural patterns for women to participate. In the communities, women worked in the home. Also, before, if a woman began to emerge as a leader and the government noticed, she would suffer government repression, violence. Women are still afraid of participating." In addition to women's own reluctance, they have encountered problems with financing and with the suspicions of Mayan men:

> At first the men questioned our work. They were afraid we would tend toward feminism. Only women participate, but we are not feminist. We do not want a westernized organization. We are not against men. We do not say that women are better. We support the organizations of the men. Some men are afraid of competition, but it is not that. Women are the ones who have participated the least, who receive the least support. To be full partners for men and partners in the struggle to maintain our culture, we need to develop ourselves, create new ways of participating.

By 1993, the seminar seemed to have stopped meeting.

---

36. Eileen Maynard (1974), Lois Paul (1974), and Carol Smith (1995) all argue that Mayan women are comparatively better off than ladina women, at least as long as they perform their appointed roles in the community and gender system.

In 1989, I attended a two-day workshop in Mexico City of Guatemalan women; some were there in exile, and others had come in from Guatemala. About half the participants were Maya and half ladina. In the hours of lectures and discussion, the women explored the specificities of their situation as women. Like any "consciousness raising," there was a great deal of surprise and emotion, exclamations of "I never saw it that way before!" The subject of tortillas and the *nixtamal,* with cultural purity resting on the exploitation of women's labor, was ardently discussed, and several of the Mayan women vowed never to grind corn by hand again. In 1993, I ran into one of the participants in Guatemala City. She asked me if I were still involved in women's issues and said that she was not. "That feminism is all Western imperialism," she said. "I am a Maya before I am a woman."[37]

Such a statement makes perfect sense in a situation of intensely hostile markings of Mayan identity. However, the sorts of pressure from Mayan men that Ms. Xicox suggests were placed on the Seminar of Mayan Women also influence the conditions of possibility for Mayan women. Delia Tujab says she has found it impossible to work in the Mayan cultural rights movement and must find other venues to pursue her activism—in part through her law practice:

> When you look at the executive councils and boards, you see there are not any women participating. Some men are worse than others, but many can't stand for anyone else to be in charge—especially not when it is a woman. I've had big fights with some of them. We have become enemies. Some of it is just infighting and personal ambition, but there is a reason there are only men in the leadership. I've seen this happen. If there are any women who are starting to move up, then what the men do is seduce them, get them pregnant, and just leave them like that, so they won't get power, to shut them up. This happens a lot.

Apparently unaware of the inherent contradiction, Mayan men criticize women for being divisionary and at the same time reject similar criticism leveled against Mayan demands on the state for inclusion with a difference in the nation. For example, Dr. Demetrio Cojtí critiqued Mayan women for pushing for their issues to be addressed. "They are separatists! They can't have a separate space—don't they realize they are half of the Mayan movement? They are dividing us." Such comments parallel those ladino critiques of the Maya couched in terms of the heterosexual couple ("The Maya and the ladino are like a marriage. She can't just go off and leave her husband!"), which suggests the centrality of gender in the *formación* of both ladino and Maya bodies politic.

37. This comment suggests a fear similar to the ladinos' notion of the "gringoization" of the Mayan movement.

In the hybridity of postcolonial identity, narcissism and paranoia are not solely relegated to the colonizer. As Maxine Rodinson warns, "Direct or indirect narcissism takes over and the fact that the oppressed are oppressed becomes less important than the admirable way they are themselves. It becomes quite inconceivable that the oppressed might themselves be oppressing others" (in Harlow 1987, 29).[38] Mayan women who identify themselves as the ones who uphold tradition in a culture where "gender relations have always been equal among the Maya" are articulated contradictorily to a movement in which the majority of activist women are divorced or widowed. As one said, "I would never have been political if my husband were still around." Some of these limits are inherent to any project that is community-bound. Many Mayan women are struggling valiantly, inside and outside of the cultural rights movement, for inclusion with difference in both the nation-state and the Pueblo Maya. As Olga Xicox said, "I work a lot with women so that they are not so marginalized, so exploited, not taken as just a tourist attraction, but so they know how to defend themselves as women *and* as Maya." In 1997, some Mayan women who are community-bound but who refuse to be bound to motherhood and tortilla making are beginning to meet and discuss the specificity of women's issues. Just as the Maya are not withdrawing from the nation-state but struggling for representation there, these women do not want to contra-dict Mayan cultural rights activism. They are working interdicta.

When the president of the ALMG bawled me out for critiquing the Academy's gender politics—"Do people judge your work with how you live your life at home?"—he was clearly aware that gender is often a tool used to justify intervention in the lives of the less-powerful (white men—or feminist white women—saving brown women from brown men). In the next three chapters, I explore why gender is so important and its effects on Maya, ladino, Guatemalan (and in chapter 9, white feminist) body politics.

38. This narcissism may be similar to that which throws up the fetish when "throne and altar are in danger, and similar illogical consequences will also follow them" (Freud 1963a, 215), as described in the next chapter.

FIVE

Gendering the Ethnic-National Question

Rigoberta Menchú Jokes and the
Out-Skirts of Fashioning Identity

"Daddy, Why don't some people like Rigoberta?" "Because she's a woman and here we are machos, . . . because she's an Indian . . . and here we are racists, . . . and because she's intelligent and here we are a pack of mediocres."
FILÓCHOFO

Do they laugh?
Sixteenth-century criterion for defining Indians as human

INTRODUCTION: JOKES, THE *MUJER MAYA,*
AND THE ANXIETY OF CROSS-DRESSING

When the vice-minister of culture talks about "our cultural heritage as a major money-earner," he really means the Mayan woman. It is her incarceration in the highland villages that keeps them (and her) "traditional." Her ritual practices, the visual excitement of her colorful clothing, the commodification of her labor as weaver in the world-famous market towns, and her willingness to sit for photos are what attract tourists from all over the world.[1] When ladino candidates touring the country for votes think they've found "the real Guatemala" on the shores of Lake Atitlán, it is the traditionally costumed, dutifully worshipping Mayan woman they refer to. Mayan identity, too, leans heavily on the valiant Mayan woman who maintains her culture, reproduces the next generation of activists, and pats out tortillas for Mayan men. The Mayan woman (*mujer maya*) is an important support for national, ethnic, and class identifications and for the fashioning of both ladino and Mayan masculinities.

The orthopedics of the law, the labor market, and masculine body image—"men in *traje* are seen as 'less' masculine, serious, and competent" (Hendrickson 1996, 162)—make Mayan men "disappear" when they take off their *traje*. This process means that traditional clothing, which signifies

---

1. Carol Hendrickson estimates that Mayan women backstrap weavers earn "well under a dollar for an eight-hour day" (1996, 161).

indigenous identity in general, has become almost isomorphic with the Mayan woman who weaves it and wears it far more consistently than men. And *traje* brings with it the weight of tradition in general, condensing a whole range of affect-laden meanings about spirituality, community, food, language, children, the nation, and the past onto this fantasy construct of the *mujer maya* (a term I use to differentiate this smiling figure from real-life women juggling jobs, children, and "culture").[2] This is why she is so important to these different discourses. She joins the modern nation (and Mayan activists) with the contradictory need to be simultaneously traditional; she magically produces value with very little investment. And, as Jane Collier suggests, women's association with tradition is overdetermined. "Not only do the gender conceptions associated with modernity identify women with the emotion that is reason's opposite, but they also identify women's homes with leisure and desire. . . . Women are thus cast both as passive perpetuators of tradition . . . and as active guardians of the national culture" (1997, 210).

But what happens when the *mujer maya,* in *traje,* wins the Nobel Peace Prize? Well, it lands like a stick of dynamite among bodies politic that unthinkingly rely on her image for support. One way that Guatemalans reacted when Rigoberta Menchú Tum won in October 1992 was to tell jokes—silly, mean, ribald, clever, reassuring, stupid, smutty, *revealing* jokes. This chapter explores these jokes and the commentary circulating in response to Ms. Menchú's Peace Prize. Rigoberta Menchú is probably the best known Guatemalan in the world thanks, in part, to her testimonial *I, Rigoberta Menchú* (1984), which until recently was de facto banned in Guatemala. Ms. Menchú lost much of her family to Guatemalan army counter-insurgency violence in the late 1970s and early 1980s, was herself forced into exile, and finally returned to Guatemala in 1994. She won the Nobel Peace Prize in part for her decade of international work for human rights and the rights of the world's indigenous peoples.

Given the horrors of Guatemala's recent history, it may seem inappro-

---

2. The majority of monolingual speakers of Mayan languages are women. Uma Chakravarti points out that in the construction of the "new" woman for nineteenth-century nationalists in India from a past written by colonial Orientalists, a very specific woman was chosen to stand in for the whole: the romantic "Aryan woman (the progenitor of the upper caste woman). . . . It is no wonder then that the Vedic *dasi* (woman in servitude), captured, subjugated and enslaved[,] . . . disappeared" (1990, 28). Similarly, the *mujer maya* deployed to support national and ethnic identifications—as in the postcards scattered throughout this book— is always shown smiling, in blooming health, with full *traje* (sometimes even perfectly manicured); rarely is she shown as poor, desperate, or malnourished. Although it disappears their own experience, Chakravarti suggests that this image held affective power for women in India, and I would argue that this image of the *mujer maya* also has material effects on Mayan women.

Figure 11. *"Tres Razones"* (Three reasons). "Daddy, why don't some people like Rigoberta?" "Because she's a woman and here we are machos . . . because she's an Indian . . . and here we are racists . . . and because she's intelligent and here we are a pack of mediocres." Copyright Filóchofo. First appeared in *Siglo XXI,* 15 October 1992. Published with kind permission.

priate to look at jokes, but Guatemalans are actually quite famous for their macabre humor, and many take a national pride in it as a survival strategy. As one ladino anthropologist said, "It is our weapon, a tool to try to understand political relations." (This strategy can be seen in the popular early-eighties joke that attributed death and disappearance to OMNIs [Unidentified Military Objects]—from OVNI [UFO].) An example of just how macabre these can get was a very popular joke referring to the fact that Rigoberta's father, Vicente Menchú, was burned alive in the Spanish Embassy fire during a Campesino Unity Committee (CUC) action in 1980: "Rigoberta said she will create a foundation in honor of her father with the money from the Nobel Prize. The first thing they're planning to do in his memory is hold a big barbecue."

Horrific as the joke is, it functions as a tool wielded to recode and deflect, to make sense of the apparently irrational violence of the last thirty-five years. Jean Laplanche, following Freud, suggests that there is "reassurance implicit in any scenario (however scarifying) that structures anxiety" (in Hertz 1983, 31). The Rigoberta jokes are complex ways of structuring a variety of anxieties for many different Guatemalans whose national, ethnic, and gendered body images are wounded. Sigmund Freud suggests that there's always a kernel of thought buried in the "joking environment" that is revelatory, that what is comic is often about "self-betrayal" (1963b, 65). What Freud calls jokework may betray the ideological fantasies structuring these various identifications in Quincentennial Guatemala.

Just as, until 1994, Rigoberta Menchú was forced to live abroad and her book has only recently become available in Guatemala, until the Quincentennial the Maya tended to constitute an absent presence in public discourse. Not invited to the negotiating table, lumped together as "the poor" or "peasants," or enveloped in ethnostalgic discourses, the central but disavowed role of the Maya in national popular imaginings often slips out the back door in the form of jokes. Mayan absence from discourses about them parallels Freud's theory of the structure of dirty jokes, which are directed at women but should not be told in their presence. Instead, men tell jokes to other men, and this structures a relation between the men (helps them form an identification). In Guatemala, ladinos telling jokes about absent Indians may create a similar relation between ladinos who are, of course, "an ethnicity which is not one" (Irigaray 1985b), and the same goes for Mayan men telling each other these jokes in the absence of Mayan women. This is the ideal Freudian structure of the joke, a reason it may be, as Laplanche says, reassuring. It does not mean that ladinos don't tell jokes to Maya, or that men don't tell jokes to or in the presence of women, or that, after some coaxing, Guatemalans in general don't tell jokes to gringas. But through such absences, these jokes, like dreams, condense often contradictory fantasies and popular imaginings about the presence of indigenous peoples in the nation and in so doing help structure various bodies politic.

When I speak of popular imaginings, I am drawing on conversations, articles in the press, and lots of joke telling: in offices during formal interviews, in peoples' homes over dinner, on street corners and buses, and (where they flow most easily) in bars; and with men and women, Mayas, ladinos, and gringos, wealthy, middle-class, and poor people.[3] This means that the fantasies and anxieties I explore here not only apply to the "usual suspects" (rich ladino men) but are also expressed by ladinas and Mayan

---

3. I do not have the linguistic skills to analyze the entirely different class of jokes that Maya tell each other in their own languages.

men (I rarely heard Mayan women, besides Rigoberta, tell them)—although what they mean in each case may be different. This "popular imagination" is a complicated space, especially for an inquisitive outsider, but when you hear the same joke from a government official, a male Mayan activist, and the guy who sells you the paper, it seems to point to something worthy of exploration.

However, when I told Guatemalan friends that I was "working" on jokes, they weren't happy (you know feminists have no sense of humor!). They said things like "You have to remember that Guatemala is famous for its black humor. It's the only way we have of dealing with this terrible situation." That these concerns were ubiquitous and at times quite passionate (paralleling some responses in the United States to my critiques of gringa self-fashioning) suggests that there is a great deal of pleasure, and identification, at stake.

One way people seemed to fear I would take the fun out was by calling them racist, as did a *Prensa Libre* article on the jokes (24 January 1993). In fact, when Rigoberta Menchú came up in my interviews and informal discussions, many people (in particular, earnest supporters) would protest too much, insisting that they knew such jokes existed, but they had never heard one. "I leave the room when people start with that shit." Or, "My friends and family know me too well to say such things in my presence. They know I would yell at them." This symptomatic disavowal itself became a joke between me and my fellow joke collector José Fernando Lara. Invariably, a bit of grease in the form of us relating one of the more benign examples would open the floodgates. Freud notes that only jokes with a purpose risk meeting people who do not want to listen to them.

The jokes certainly lose in the translation and are diminished by the conditions of their retelling here. Ideally, rather than your reading them here, you and I would be telling them to each other over good food and drink shared with Rigoberta. Even though the jokes are racist and smutty, I'll admit that I laughed at most of them—as did Rigoberta Menchú when I gave her this paper.[4] In fact, she is quite adept at telling jokes about herself—one I heard her tell went: "I've been getting a lot of calls from Steven Spielberg. It seems he wants to make a movie called *Indio-na Jones.*" (This plays on the racist term *indio*, which is used to refer to the Maya.)

What is most intriguing to me about the jokes is their fascination with sexual difference in relation to ethnic and other identities. Similar to discussions of *mestizaje* (see chapter 6), analysis of these jokes in Guatemala has been completely indifferent to gender difference, despite, for example, the fact that several of the jokes cited in the *Prensa Libre* piece were explicitly

---

4. Many Guatemalans have asked for copies of this paper, although as one friend admitted, more for the joke collection than for any analysis I might offer.

about sexuality. Looking at the jokes from this perspective may help us understand the complex ways that ethnic and national bodies politic rely on gender.

Mayan women's traditional clothing figures prominently in the jokes and seems to mark a place of particular ambivalence or challenge to notions of ethnic-national identity. The *corte* (long, wrap-around skirt) is the subject of particular interest in the jokes, many of which seek to "unwrap" it. A joke I heard frequently (in fact, the first Rigoberta joke I heard) asks, "Why did Rigoberta really win the Nobel Prize? Because she is an *indita desenvuelta*" (*desenvuelta* means "articulate" or "well-spoken" as well as "unwrapped," which implies taking off the *corte*). Several jokes also suggest that male organs are hidden underneath: "Why won't Rigoberta wear mini-skirts? Because her balls would show." This has led me to the rather perverse reading that these discourses situate Rigoberta as a sort of transvestite who is not what she seems and therefore rips at the seams that are meant to bind identities. Indigenous clothing (*traje típico*), which is supposedly a "typical" and thus unproblematic marker of ethnic identity, is central to the jokes. But it is hiding something, problematizing identity, and is thus similar to the way drag problematizes the transvestite's identity. I do not in any way mean that Rigoberta is a transvestite, but that the logic of the jokes situates her that way. Like dreams, joke logic has little to do with actually existing people or objects and everything to do with the play of fantasy and anxiety. Thus I draw on Marjorie Garber's (1993) suggestion that the anxieties about authenticity that typically greet the cross-dresser are often about the lack of *any* solid identification. Similarly, Laura Kipnis suggests a "transcoding between bodily and social topography, a transcoding which sets up an homology between the lower bodily stratum and the lower social classes—the reference to the body being invariably a reference to the social . . . through which bodily grossness operates as a critique of dominant ideology" (1992, 376). So Rigoberta jokes help us read that cusp between the body and the body politic, and I suggest the transvestite metaphor as a way to talk about traveling over supposedly secure bodily and social category boundaries—which are actually rather fluid.

Thus the jokes open a window onto the Quincentennial because the Nobel Peace Prize for Rigoberta Menchú—an uncanny figure as a spokeswoman for people without a voice, clad in *traje* among the haute couture of international luminaries—served to articulate the many ambivalent feelings in Guatemala regarding the changing position of the Maya and of Mayan women.[5] The jokes are not only a "critique of dominant ideology" in the sense that they acknowledge the vital presence of the Maya, male and fe-

5. Florencia Mallon suggests that Rigoberta's mother, a healer, catechist, and political organizer who was denied a decent burial after her death, was also uncanny. She "transgressed

male, but also an attempt to deflect the anxieties that such acknowledgment creates.

Briefly, however, I want to stress that these responses were ambivalent. Just as state officials both resist and acquiesce to Mayan demands, the "hostile and cruel" (Freud 1963b) nature of many of these jokes should not obscure the fact that there was also great rejoicing about Rigoberta winning the Nobel Prize. Church bells rang, people set off firecrackers in the streets, and there were parades and parties and hearty congratulations in the newspapers. When I told the news to an indigenous woman who was cleaning a friend's house, she jumped up and down, clapping her hands and crying with joy. Because of Rigoberta's relation to the popular movement (she was a leader of CUC), many progressive ladinos saw her prize as vindication of their decades of struggle and an international acknowledgment of their suffering and the costs of the war. Even people who are fans of neither the indigenous nor the popular struggle said (in interviews and newspaper articles) that the prize made them proud as Guatemalans. Of course, the irony of Guatemala's two Nobel laureates was lost on no one: that a country with 70 percent illiteracy "has" a Nobel in Literature (Miguel Angel Asturias) and a country with over thirty-five years of civil war "has" a Peace Prize. Also ironic is the fact that both Asturias and Menchú were in exile when they won. I would suggest that these ironies and contradictions are part of what give the Rigoberta jokes their incredible force.

The jokes help us see the ambivalence created when someone like Rigoberta Menchú crosses those identity lines (of gender, nationality, locale, and ethnicity) that are taken for granted and assumed to be solid. She demonstrates how fluid they are. Though these border crossings clearly incite deep anxieties, we are reminded by Mary Douglas that the violation of such "pollution taboos" may produce pleasure. "It is not always an unpleasant experience to confront ambiguity. . . . There is a whole gradient on which laughter, revulsion, and shock belong at different points and intensities" (Douglas 1989, 37). The jokes themselves, in their very grossness, certainly seem to fit this description. I argue that the jokes provide a variety of complicated pleasures, but I do not claim to be able, in this short space, to address all the effects of the jokework. As Freud said, "Strictly speaking, we do not know what we are laughing at" (1963a, 102). I do, however, try to move beyond an easy dismissal of racism or sexism to suggest that they are meant to keep us in stitches as they attempt to suture the constitutive antagonisms of these identifications. In doing so, they are part of the contradictory process of creating a nation to suit all its inhabitants, cloaking hostility and unmasking desire.

---

boundaries by making women's 'proper' gendered spaces—motherhood, the kitchen—subversive" (1996, 78).

Figure 12. "Rigoberta Menchú Tum, Nobel Peace Prize 1992."
Postcard. Copyright Daniel Hernández Salazar. Published with kind
permission.

FASHIONING THE NATION

The Quincentennial has made it fashionable to talk about "The Nation" in
Guatemala. In newspaper editorials, paid ads, radio talk shows, speeches by
government officials, and general conversation, whether addressing the
Quincentennial or the peace process, the justice system, poverty indices,
bureaucratic corruption, or a former president's highly publicized trip to a

New York strip joint, "the nation" is a central theme. Or better put, the need to fashion a nation, to create a uniform identity, is seen as the only cure for this wounded body image, the basis for a true and lasting peace.

In 1992, the Mayan rights movement and Rigoberta Menchú's Nobel Peace Prize, joined with the continuing polemics over the drafting of the peace accords, forced the country's internal ethnic differences into the public consciousness and foregrounded what is seen as a failure of nation. For example, a text by Rigoberta Menchú, published in *Siglo Veintiuno* (11 December 1992) is entitled "The Challenge of Constructing National Unity."[6] As I explore in chapter 3, in much of this discussion the lack of a seamless national identity suited for participation in the "modern" international world is blamed on the survival of a premodern, locally based ethnic identity. In fact, some analyses see the "genocidal" counterinsurgency campaigns of the early 1980s as an attempt to force a national identity onto an apparently autonomous Mayan population. But just as tradition is not modernity's opposite, the Maya are not "outside" the nation: since the 1520s, the Maya have been subject to the attention of state orthopedics. In turn, there is increasing acceptance of the "politically correct" argument that Guatemala is a multicultural country. However, commentators from all parts of the political spectrum—including the popular movement—call for national unity, read as some sort of assimilation, to solve the ethnic-national question.

The calls for national unity over ethnic difference turn us to Benedict Anderson's "imagined community," with "a deep horizontal comradeship" (Anderson 1983, 16), clear borders with unproblematized state sovereignty, and marked by "that remarkable confidence of community in anonymity" (40). Perhaps we can imagine this ideal "modern nation" as a piece of clothing meant to cover all its inhabitants. And thus the goal of Guatemala's national project would be to stitch together the various materials—Mayan, ladino, criollo, *Garífuna*, German, and Chinese—to form a suitable outfit that would clothe and protect the "Guatemalan" as well as fashion (in the sense of *define* or *represent*) "Guatemalan-ness." If the clothes make the man, however, then this ideal nationalism may fit Guatemala like the camel hair suit of the joke: "A man has a camel hair suit made for him but the next day goes back to the tailor and says, 'The sleeve's too short.' The tailor replies, 'You can't recut a camel hair suit, but just hold your arm

6. She says, "The goal that confronts all Guatemalans is learning to construct a national unity in which Indians as well as mestizos can live together, respecting diversity and ethnic expression. . . . Those who have struggled against Army repression have learned through their long experience the need for everyone to be present in one unitary nation, without anyone having to renounce their traditions."

like this [over-extended] and no one will notice.' The man goes out with his arm like that, but the next day returns to say the right leg is too long. The tailor tells him to hold his leg like this [bent up] and no one will notice. Well, this goes on until the guy is walking around with his limbs every which way. A couple see him, and the woman exclaims, 'Look at the poor deformed man!' And her husband says, 'Yeah, but doesn't his camel hair suit fit great!'"

The camel hair suit of "modern nationalism" is not something that peoples can easily take off, despite its apparent ill-fit for Guatemala. Like the orthopedic techniques of the state, the suit of nationalism forms those who wear it—forming them by means that range from the pressures of international organizations like the United Nations and General Agreement on Tariffs and Trade (GATT) that take the nation for granted as the basis for participation, to struggles for human rights based on citizenship.[7] Nationalism is, as Eve Kosofsky Sedgwick says, "the overarching ideology of our age[,] . . . to the extent that one or another nationalism tends to become the form of last resort for *every* legitimizing political appeal—whether right or left, imperialist or anti-imperialist . . . elitist or populist, cynical or utopian" (Sedgwick 1992, 238). In turn, Anderson suggests that this "last resort" is not based on claims to "falsity/genuineness, but on the *style* in which it is imagined" (Anderson 1983, 15; emphasis added). In Guatemala, these differing styles, the varying alternative "political appeals," are clothed in the camel hair suit of nationalism, from the Guatemalan *National* Revolutionary Unity (URNG) to the Coordination of Organizations of the Pueblo Maya of Guatemala (COPMAGUA) and to former President Serrano Elías acting (in his words) as the "representative of national unity" as he gave Rigoberta a flag and a sheet of embroidered patriotic symbols to commemorate the Nobel Prize.[8]

ETHNIC DIFFERENCE

So, the current proliferation of discourses surrounding the nation in Guatemala may be said to be about contesting styles. The ideal style of a relatively uniform community, Luce Irigaray's "old dream of symmetry"

---

7. Cynthia Enloe makes a similar argument about the dual aesthetic and formative role of the military in her nicely polyvalent title "Does Khaki Become You?" (1983). A "becoming" suit is both suitable, an appropriate fit, and one that brings something into existence.

8. Serrano was full of symptoms that week. First, he claimed he could not congratulate Ms. Menchú because he had an earache and could not hear anything (a standard hysteric response to bad news). In his speech upon meeting with her several days later, he said, "I am giving you the national colors, the quetzal for the Maya and symbols of our *patria* to show our European descent; these are to show that *mestizaje* is the basis of our country."

(1985a), is voiced by many in the national political class and popular sectors in calls for ladino-indigenous unity or some form of *mestizaje*. This is brought into crisis by the ethnic "Other" (represented most explicitly in 1992 and 1993 by Rigoberta Menchú), who stubbornly resists integration (or sublation). A Guatemalan anthropologist said, "Ladinos reject Rigoberta's prize so strongly because she is a symbol of the unification of the Maya, that they are flourishing, strong, homogeneous, everything that the ladinos are not." The Maya are increasingly vocal and articulate in demanding the right to be different—and dressing differently, in the distinctive indigenous *traje,* is part of this claim.

The Mayan rights movement critiques the imagined uniform nation in favor of multiple styles (like *traje,* which is unique for each village). This critique in turn excites anxious reactions in some ladinos, who often reduce complex Mayan arguments to a simple binary between ladino and Indian and see this refusal of the same as totally destructive to the Guatemalan "nation." The often panicked discussion (see chapter 8) surrounding the Quincentennial as well as Convention 169, the UN International Year of Indigenous Peoples, the Accord on Indigenous Rights, and especially the Nobel Peace Prize usually culminates with the warning that Guatemala is on the verge of a race war that will make the previous thirty years of "class warfare" seem like child's play. As an editorial said, "One doesn't need to be an old Mayan witch [*brujo*] to realize that the consequences could be worse than in Yugoslavia" (Nájera 1992). In keeping with post-nineteenth-century theories of the nation, these suggestions presuppose an inherent contradiction between nation and varied ethnic identifications.[9] These positions also strangely resist the increasingly inexorable pulls toward peace rather than confrontation. In fact, the obsessive nature of these warnings suggests that titillation accompanies the vision of race war haunting these fantasies.

As I have been arguing, drawing on postcolonial critics like Homi Bhabha, Edward Said, and Gayatri Chakravorty Spivak, this ethnic "Other," far from being a straitjacket that limits national identity formation, is instead necessary for its very constitution—the loom on which it is woven. The nation in turn is productive of ethnic differentiations. At different historic moments, these differentiations are conjured up as self-constituting others (Spivak 1988a), as when ladinos define themselves against the hos-

---

9. This notion of nation was concretized in the nineteenth century but drew from a Platonic ideal of harmony couched, interestingly enough, in the language of clothing. Plato saw the role of politics as binding different virtues and contrary temperaments using the shuttle of popular opinion. The ruler gathered lives together into a community based upon concord and friendship, and so he wove "the finest of fabrics. The entire population, slaves and free men alike, were mantled in its folds" (in Foucault 1988, 66).

tile markings of the "Indian" who is "superstitious, fanatic, idolater, disrespectful, bestial, untrustworthy, apathetic, degraded, of impure blood, sick, lazy, lying, irresponsible, dirty, drunk, traitor" (González Ponciano 1991, 376). Despite a desire for the same (manifest, for example, in integrationist state policies and calls for *mestizaje* consciousness), there is a national need for difference, just as modernity needs tradition.

The editors of *Nationalisms and Sexualities* suggest that national identity is relational. It is "ineluctably shaped by what it opposes," and this relationality gives rise to "the nation's insatiable need to administer difference . . . and the nation's insatiable need for representational labor to supplement its founding ambivalence, the lack of self-presence at its origin or in its essence" (Parker et al. 1992, 5). Clothing is intimately linked to these processes. In terms of administering difference, *traje*'s identificatory features have been used in counterinsurgency (Simon 1987), and *traje* is a basic material for the nation's representational labor. Of course, *traje* also marks gender differences, allowing us to add another dimension to this warp and weft of nation and ethnicity.

GENDERING THE BINARY

In addition to dealing with internal difference, nation formation must be outfitted to differentiate an internal identity from an external other, to define what makes Guatemala special in the family of nations. Although there is a standard cut of the camel hair suit, each nation must find its own unique style for international representation. And here the out-*skirts* of the Maya-ladino and international-national binaries suggest that these identifications rely on gender. Just as Mayan-ness is often condensed into the *mujer Maya* in Guatemala, Guatemala is often differentiated on the international fashion-show runway by Mayan women in traditional clothing.[10] In international beauty contests, the pavilion in the Seville 1992 Expo, the Pasadena Rose Bowl Parade float, tourism propaganda, textile exports, and so on *traje* plays a major role in styling identity, affixing borders, and in knotting ambivalencies around nationalist representations. *Traje* is site-specific (and I'll revisit below the polemic over how it came to represent local differences, whether it's an authentic survival from the pre-Conquest period or was imposed during the Colony).

Traje is also sight-specific, apparently making identity completely available to the gaze: seeing *traje* means one is seeing an Indian; seeing a red *corte*

---

10. Landscape, a traditionally feminized trope, is also representative (especially Lake Atitlán), and the favorite scene is an indigenous woman *in* the landscape. The desire to denude the indigenous woman may parallel the deforestation carried out as part of the counterinsurgency campaign.

means the woman is Maya-Ixil. In fact, the army trains soldiers in how to identify people by their *traje,* and through the mid-1980s, Civil Patrollers were instructed by the military to detain anyone wearing certain *trajes.* If identity is constituted in difference—in other words, if difference is determinate—then that difference should be visible, unproblematically knowable. It should be a stable boundary marker. As the fabled men's room door apparently enshrines sexual difference (we know what the boy has that the girl doesn't), ethnic and national difference are supposed to be unproblematically visible and identifiable, solid, with clothing as the guarantee.[11]

This relation between the apparent obviousness of national and sexual identities is discussed by Benedict Anderson, who says, "In the modern world, everyone can, should, and will 'have' a nationality, as he or she 'has' a gender" (Anderson 1983, 14). In Guatemala, these various identities come together in *traje,* which is marked as a gendered category because many more Mayan women than men retain it. A hostile marking for this condensation is the generic (and disrespectful) term for indigenous women, *envuelta* (wrapped up), which refers to the way they wear their *corte. Traje* is also "ethnicized" by representing indigenous identity in general, and, by simultaneously marking these two differences, it genders ethnicity.

The Mayan in general are feminized vis-à-vis the ladino. For example, Mayan activists are imagined as the ungrateful wife who wants to leave the marriage. Mayan masculinity is disempowered in multiple ways by the disruptions of colonialism and by discourses of *blanquemiento* (whitening) that posit that any child born to a brown man is a stain on a lineage or a tainting, rather than improvement, of the race (see chapter 6, on discourses of *mestizaje*). Because *traje* marks the female Maya as ethnic (as Andrés Cus said, Mayan men tend to disappear), Mayan identity is gendered female. *Traje* as a gendered marker of ethnic identity is thus contradictory for Mayan men. As Carol Hendrickson suggests:

> The image of a Maya man in *traje* is categorically different from that of a Maya woman in *traje*. Women's indigenous dress is . . . painstakingly hand-crafted in a bright array of colors and complemented with jewelry, ribbons. . . . [It] conforms to . . . "Western" standards of femininity . . . and a nonproductive consumption of wealth. . . . Male *traje* on the other hand does not contain elements that resonate with the sartorial expression of masculinity. . . . The effect

11. The *Ladies* and *Gentlemen* written on the bathroom door appear to refer to the natural, stable identity differences of sex, but they are signifiers that create difference. As Jacques Lacan suggests, the words *Ladies* and *Gentlemen* create a distinction, "the image of twin doors symbolizing, through the solitary confinement offered Western Man for the satisfaction of his natural needs away from home, the imperative that he seems to share with the great majority of primitive communities by which his public life is subjected to the laws of urinary segregation" (1977, 151).

is not only to label a man in *traje* as "Indian" but also to see him as one who is less masculine (even less adult) in a world dominated by non-Maya values. (1995, 89)

But when I say that *traje* genders ethnicity, I also mean that gender identity is usually understood to revolve around the phallus, which we know is not supposed to be reducible to the penis, but in the most general sense to signal who has power—including the use of language—within patriarchal capitalist culture. It is supposed to be obvious, without anyone ever having to "unveil" the phallus, who has it and who does not. Thus *traje,* marking gender and ethnic difference, supposedly makes clear who has power in Guatemala and who does not. And, these differences being obvious, when a gringa solidarity activist or a ladina transvestites as an Indian in a beauty contest, we still know who has the power.

Traje is supposed to mark specific power differentials in Guatemala. It marks gender (woman versus man), ethnicity (Maya versus ladino), nation (Guatemalan versus foreigner) and class (bourgeois versus worker), as well as internal differences among Mayan peoples, rural people as opposed to urban, and authentic archaic culture as opposed to cosmopolitan modernity. Representations of Mayan women in *traje* almost invariably contain children and thus signal the safe channeling of their sexuality into reproduction. Additionally, women in *traje* (until very recently) have rarely been represented as talking or literate. We'll see in the following how the jokes about Rigoberta situate her as a transvestite who, by crossing all these borders, unravels the seams that hold together these "fabrications" of identity. The jokes in turn expend a great deal of psychic energy attempting to patch over these "un-seamly" gaps.

Though *traje* is supposed to do the work of administering and representing difference unproblematically, its role in the field of vision is ambivalent because it both displays and covers up. This covering up incites a desire to penetrate. The tourist desire to purchase souvenirs (made easy by currency differentials) and the incredible beauty of the pieces themselves surely incite the exquisite acquisitiveness that overcomes most visitors to Guatemala. However, having myself been a long-term and willing victim of "típica fever," I suggest that the almost overwhelming desire to begin one's own *traje* collection, to impress one's friends by being able to identify someone's town of origin by their clothing, or to apprentice oneself to a weaver to make the authentic article oneself (as many gringos do) all partake of this desire to penetrate, to understand, this apparently most available of signs.[12]

---

12. "Típica fever" is what I call the almost uncontrollable urge, experienced by tourists, anthropologists, and most other gringos, to buy handicrafts while in Guatemala. On my first trip to Guatemala, in addition to succumbing to the desires to buy textiles for gifts and for our-

The IIN attempts to regulate *traje* in the 1940s, and likewise, the extensive collections of textiles kept in trunks in the homes of ladino exiles in Mexico City, displayed in the homes of Guatemala's bourgeoisie, and housed in their very own museum (the lovely Museo Ixchel in an upscale neighborhood of Guatemala City) seem to express this desire to get a hold on something elusive, to fix it. Lectures at the military's Politécnico Institute on the geography of *traje* may merely be the most malignant end of this spectrum of fascination, which partakes of the pleasures of ethnostalgia and the magic of culture.[13]

This ambivalence inherent in the field of vision is expressed in an article in *Noticias de Guatemala*: "Clothes can reveal more than they conceal. . . . Textile art in Guatemala transmits the unwritten history of its peoples. . . . For thousands of years it has shielded, at times disguised, the most intimate aspects of those who inhabit it" (*Noticias de Guatemala* 1992).[14] In some ways, then, *traje* is like a hieroglyph, which, as Mary Ann Doan suggests, is the most readable of signs because it is writing in images and color (1991, 18). As *Noticias de Guatemala* puts it, it is the history of a people. For Mayan women, many of whom are still illiterate and Maya-monolingual, it serves as a signifying practice, a way of communicating.

However, *traje* and hieroglyphs may also constitute an indecipherable language: a signifying system that fails to signify anything to the uninitiated. And here *traje* may take on the attributes of the veil, as it has been analyzed by Edward Said (1978): of harboring mystery, of shielding what is most intimate, of inciting a desire to know what it means. This might explain the plethora of investigations into the meaning of *traje* by both national and international researchers and the fact that it has its own museum.

This ambivalent role of *traje* as both national signifier and intriguing unknown may have led the self-proclaimed "national corporation" Rubios, the cigarette manufacturer, to sponsor research into the meaning of *traje*. In full-page, color-print ads running from October through December 1992, the company proclaims: "Our textiles are not museum pieces, thanks to the

---

selves, my traveling companion and I were consigned the task of buying several *cortes* for Ms. Menchú, who was living in exile in Mexico City. On a routine army check of our bus, soldiers knifed through the brown paper wrapping the skirts and apparently decided we were simple consuming tourists. Once past the road block, we imagined with delight what the bastards would have thought if they had known that they let us slip past.

13. Of course, this fascination carries both material and symbolic advantages for Mayan peoples in the communities and for Mayan cultural rights activists. Selling *traje* to tourists and locals has kept thousands of indigenous communities afloat economically. The ethnostalgic valuation of *traje* is also a powerful tool for inciting interest in the rights of cultural survival. See Hendrickson (1995).

14. *Noticias de Guatemala* was published in Mexico City by Guatemalan exiles.

efforts of RUBIOS and of our artisans." Under this headline and a photo of a woman's hands weaving, the text reads:

> In 1992, the year when the rest of the world has begun to recognize the great values immersed in the autochthonous cultures of the Americas, RUBIOS presents the eighth monograph on the theme of Mayan textiles[,] . . . a series of facts and information that will enrich our understanding. . . . RUBIOS and the Ixchel Museum have helped keep this tradition alive. . . . Thanks to Tabacalera Centroamericana, through their product RUBIOS, our cultural values will never become museum pieces.[15]

A certain disavowal of this fascination with *traje,* mixed with the desire to find the "same" in this marker of difference, is evident in those theories that want to deny that *traje* signifies anything—theories such as Martínez Peláez's hypothesis that *traje* was entirely imposed by the Spanish as a way of identifying and controlling the colonized population. Although Linda Asturias de Barrios and other Ixchel curators have struggled to complicate this reading through lectures and publications, I found that many ladinos whom I interviewed shared the idea that "it doesn't mean anything, it was imposed by the Conquerors."[16] This ideological fantasy exists simultaneously with the apparently contradictory urge to collect, the many investigations of *traje* (like those sponsored by Rubios), and the popular imaginings echoed in the *Noticias* article that *traje* promises to reveal "the most intimate aspects of those who inhabit it."

This sense of unrevealed mystery is a sentiment echoed (and incited) by Rigoberta Menchú's autobiography, in which she states that "I'm still keeping my Indian identity a secret. I'm still keeping secret what I think no one should know. Not even anthropologists or intellectuals, no matter how many books they have, can find out all our secrets" (Menchú 1984, 247). This position seems to echo the situation of Woman as the object of scopophilia—both visually available and simultaneously inaccessible and mysterious. If *traje* is an ambivalent and thus fascinating boundary marker in general, it is especially so when it clothes Rigoberta.

15. The Rubios cigarette company exhibits an intriguing condensation of inclusion and exclusion in that their name means "light skinned" or "blonde" (as in the light tobacco, I assume), but their advertisements were the first to include indigenous people, and they use their support for the Ixchel Museum in their propaganda (see chapter 8).

16. This point is often raised in editorial polemics around Mayan organizing, Convention 169, the Accord on Indigenous Rights, and so on. Mario Alberto Carrera in *El Grafico* writes that *traje* is just a way to ghettoize Indian people and that it is nothing more than copies of Spanish colonial fashion (26 May 1995); in addition to being "hard to make and clean, it does not fulfill modern prerequisites for comfort and hygiene. It should remain in museums" (10 May 1995). Edgar Gutierrez in *Siglo XXI* says that *traje* is an imposition of the colonial period (30 June 1995).

Nuestros tejidos no son piezas de museo

Gracias al esfuezo de RUBIOS y de nuestros artesanos

Durante muchos años Tabacalera Centroamericana, a través de su producto RUBIOS, ha colaborado con el Museo Ixchel en su esfuerzo por conservar y perpetuar los tejidos de Guatemala, uno de los más bellos patrimonios de este país que, gracias a las nobles manos de artesanos guatemaltecos, constituyen una de sus más importantes riquezas. De esta manera, RUBIOS y el museo Ixchel han contribuido a mantener viva esta tradición, dándole todo el valor que se merece.

En 1992, año en que el resto del mundo ha empezado a reconocer los grandes valores inmersos en las culturas autóctonas de América, RUBIOS hace entrega de la octava monografía con el tema de los tejidos mayas

titulada "LA INDUMENTARIA Y EL TEJIDO MAYAS A TRAVES DEL TIEMPO", un acto de especial relevancia, fruto de el esfuerzo y el trabajo de un grupo de investigadoras que han sabido recopilar una serie de datos e informaciones que vienen a enriquecer los conocimientos sobre el tema que podrán tener ahora las actuales y futuras generaciones.

Gracias a Tabacalera Centroamericana, a través de su producto RUBIOS, nuestros valores culturales no se convertirán nunca en piezas de museo.

Figure 13. "Our weavings are not museum pieces. . . . Thanks to the efforts of Rubios and our artisans." Advertisement in *Siglo XXI*, 23 December 1992.

RIGOBERTA AS TRANSVESTITE

Now, finally, to the jokes![17] In *Jokes and Their Relation to the Unconscious,* Freud directly links "smut" or obscene jokes to sight, to wanting to see something that is prohibited. "It cannot be doubted that the desire to see what is sexually exposed is the original motive of smut" (Freud 1963b, 198). He holds that smut emerges from a sexual desire toward a woman that is blocked when she is unavailable; this desire then turns into a hostile impulse. "It becomes positively hostile and cruel. . . . By the utterance of the obscene words it compels the person who is assailed to imagine the part of the body or the procedure in question and shows her that the assailant is himself imagining it" (Freud 1963b, 98–99). If the woman is not available, the assailant calls on a third person as audience, who gets to imagine the exposure of the woman and thus satisfies his own libido: "The sexually exciting speech itself becomes the aim" (Gallop 1988, 33).

If the fashion choices of women in Latin America have been limited to a maternity gown, a nun's habit, and the sex worker's fishnets, Rigoberta in her *traje* blocks these fashion expectations. And, if gender and ethnic power differentials have meant that women in *traje* are traditionally supposed to be powerless and "available" for sex with ladino men—much of the vaunted *mestizaje* is based on rape—then *traje* signifies something else when it covers the body of Rigoberta Menchú, Nobel Peace Prize winner and United Nations ambassador. Perhaps to undermine this contradiction, I return to that popular joke that would like to see her unwrapped, disrobed: "Why did Rigoberta really win the Nobel Prize? Because she is an '*indita desenvuelta*' [both well-spoken and undressed]," playing on the slang term *envuelta* for indigenous women.

To return to Freud, sexual desire toward Rigoberta is blocked in several ways. As I discuss in the following chapter, ladino male desire is caught in a double bind toward indigenous women. Ladino men are both structurally encouraged to "whiten" the race through intercourse with Mayan women and imbued with a racist rejection of such women. Precisely following Freud's formulation, ladino men telling each other smutty jokes about (the absent) Rigoberta's sexuality allows this blocked investment to be released through laughter that simultaneously reinstates their relations to each other while excluding the indigenous woman.[18] Thus the jokework supports ladino male identification.

17. See the appendix for a full collection of the jokes.
18. Jane Gallop uses Jeffrey Mehlman's reading of this "ideal triangle" as oedipal, in which "the sexual joke that originates in a mythical scene between a man and a woman, never takes place except between two men." In the mythical scene of the "oedipal moment the boy gives up possession of the mother and gains identification with the father." Through Lévi-Strauss via Lacan, this posits the "supposedly heterosexual institution of marriage as actually an exchange

Sexual desire toward Rigoberta is also obviously blocked by her stature as an international celebrity. Even more transgressive, however, is her interstitial position of having been unmarried and unreproductive at the time of the prize, and also having renounced marriage in writing.[19] This official "prohibition" has incited a rather prurient interest in her sexuality that invades even black-tie events where no one would dare tell a smutty joke. Questions about her sexuality and reproduction plans took center stage in a forum she attended on "The Unknown Rigoberta" held in Guatemala City the week before the prize was announced, and she was constantly asked whether she retained this commitment in interviews. (Amazingly, she always responded in good humor, saying she was open to the idea of marriage, but no one had asked. Someone did, and Rigoberta married Angel Canil in March 1995.) This intense interest in the intimate, "unknown" Rigoberta in the context of forums in her honor or interviews on elite news programming reminds me of Steve Martin's joke: "We put women on a pedestal, and then we look under their skirts!"

The other side of this interest, the "positively hostile and cruel" reactions to being "sexually blocked," are obvious in the jokes that make her sexual availability their centerpiece and that simultaneously force us to imagine penetration into the "unknown Rigoberta." For example, "How do you know that Rigoberta is not a virgin? Because when she went to Mexico, President Salínas de Gortari gave her '*la vergue*'"—a play on the words *al-*

---

for the purpose of creating and strengthening bonds between men" (Gallop 1988, 33). Thus "men exchange women for heterosexual purposes, but the real intercourse is that exchange between men" (Gallop 1988, 37). The exchange of jokes about Rigoberta may suture many kinds of identifications, as they construct relations of "sameness"—not necessarily only between ladino men, but between Mayan men, or among ladinos with an indigenous person absent, or among gringos with Guatemalans absent (as in this book), and so on. When the jokes are told across these divides—say, by a ladino man to an Indian man, or a Mayan man to a Mayan woman—they may work to construct "difference" in a manner similar to the joke Freud analyzes: "A man says, 'I sat beside Salomon Rothschild and he treated me quite as his equal, quite famillionairely'" (Freud 1963b, 16). The joke plays on the similarities between familiar and millionaire, but the humor lies in the fact that these terms are precisely not the same—they emphasize the enormous class differences between the two that also inform many of the Rigoberta jokes.

Rigoberta, of course, bucks the tradition of Indians being poor. Because they're supposed to have a yen to ladinoize, once they acquire money they stop being Indians (like the joke: what is a ladino? An Indian with money). But then her sex intervenes to mark her as undesirable nonetheless: "They say that Rigoberta is a millionaire, but she is not rich"—*rica* (rich) meaning "delicious" or "sexually delectable."

19. See the chapter "Women and Political Commitment: Rigoberta Renounces Marriage and Motherhood" (Menchú 1984). Her marriage, adoption of a child, and subsequent pregnancy do not seem to lessen her political commitment.

bergue (place to stay, refuge) and *la verga* (penis). A very interesting joke that circulated during the May 1993 Serrano coup attempt posited that: "It seems President Serrano wants to see Rigoberta naked. Why? Because he is going around *quitando cortes*"—a play on *corte* as both "skirt" and "court of law": taking off skirts and disbanding the justice system. The cruelty is also apparent in the jokes about her supposed lack of sexual appeal. "How is Rigoberta like John Paul II? They both have the face of a *papa* [potato, or pope]." Or, "How is Rigoberta like a home run? They are both *incojible* [uncatchable and unfuckable]."[20]

Related to these jokes about her sexuality is a genre related to her reproductive capacity that addresses the anomaly of her childlessness through explanation or fantasized births. "Why does Rigoberta refuse to have children? Because she's from the *sierra* [mountains] and she's afraid she'll have *serranitos* [little Serranos, the former president]." Both her sexual availability and her reproductive unnaturalness are imagined in the joke that goes: "Rigoberta gave birth to a baby in Guatemala and when it came out it didn't look Indian at all. It had white skin, blue eyes, blonde hair, and looked very European. The doctor was shocked, and asked her how she had such a pretty baby when she was an *india*? She said, 'It is a baby *de probeta* of Mitterand, Clinton, and the Nobel Prize Committee'"—*probeta* suggests both a test tube baby and *probar* (to try something sexually). The way Rigoberta (and her unreproductive status) excites a category crisis in both ethnic and gender conceptions, as well as a common attempt to delegitimize her role as spokeswoman for indigenous causes, was expressed by a ladino priest who said, "There are so many jokes about Rigoberta because she is childless. Having children is what makes indigenous women legitimate. She has trouble speaking for the Indians because she is not married and has no children." Addressing this "unnatural" unreproductiveness while simultaneously disempowering Mayan men, a joke circulating since her marriage goes, "'They say Rigoberta is going to divorce her husband.' 'Why?' 'Because she found out he is *poco-man*.'" The joke is multilingual in that Pocomam is a Mayan ethnolinguistic community, and mixing it with the Spanish *poco* (little) and English *man* suggests he's not quite masculine enough for her![21]

---

20. A joke that I heard from Mayan leaders and various ladinos partakes of this insulting tone, as well as expresses frustration that this indigenous person rather than another was plucked from obscurity into international acclaim: "What does Rigoberta have in common with a zebra? For both *se rayó la mula*"—*rayar* means "to stripe" (a zebra is a striped mule, and thus Rigoberta is like a mule), and idiomatically the phrase means to get lucky.

21. I thank Charles Hale for passing that one on, although I later heard it told by Mr. Canil himself.

Although scopophilia (like the desire to see "the unknown Rigoberta") may be a basic drive of our libidos, it also contains a constitutive terror: castration anxiety, or, what if what you want to see is not there? In the classic psychoanalytic sense, the boy is terrified by seeing the girl's genitalia because if she doesn't have "one" then maybe his isn't as powerful as he thought. Rather than seeing the hoped-for "single" proud and solid organ of national unity, he may see the "open wound" of the nation constituted through ethnic, gender, and other divides. This is one site that state fetishism attempts to cover over.

Insofar as the phallus is not equal to the penis, castration anxiety should not be read literally but instead as a way of expressing real fears about the illegitimacy of power. Freud nods to the larger repercussions of castration anxiety—the link between body and body politic—when he says, "If the woman can be castrated then [the boy's] own penis is in danger; and against that there rebels parts of his narcissism. . . . In later life grown men may experience a similar panic, perhaps when the cry goes up that throne and altar are in danger, and similar illogical consequences will also follow them" (Freud 1963a, 215). Throne and altar are precisely the stakes (as well as the site) of the struggles in these Quincentennial times. An anxiety over losing such power seems expressed in the following joke: "What does Rigoberta have in common with Lorena Bobbitt? *El corte*"—*corte* here meaning both "to cut" and the traditional women's skirt.

The phallus is *supposed* to unproblematically mark gender differences that are hierarchical through the binary of one gender "having" the phallus and the other "being" the phallus (meaning that women cannot wield phallic power). But in Lacanian terms, "having" is always a fantasy, constantly haunted by the fear of losing. Marjorie Garber suggests that the figure of the transvestite, who rather than "having" or "being" (and who may or may not "have" a phallus) provides a third term, which is "to seem." In this way the transvestite marks a "category crisis, a failure of definitional distinctions, a borderline that becomes permeable, that permits of border crossings from one (apparently distinct) category to another" (Garber 1993, 16). It is in this sense that these jokes and comments fashion Rigoberta as a transvestite, as crossing borders. She represents a category crisis that is both already underway (in the vibrant Mayan rights movement, growing feminism, and popular and revolutionary organizations) but that is also always already there in the fluid constitutions of national, ethnic, and gender bodies politic in pre– and post–Quincentennial Guatemala. And I want to reiterate that I am not suggesting that this has anything to do with what or who Rigoberta *is*. Instead, I am trying to investigate the fantasies and anxieties, the regulatory norms and erasures, that structure these reactions to her.

One joke asks: "Why does Rigoberta refuse to wear patent leather shoes?

Figure 14. "Are you the government tailor? Then those pants fit us better." Copyright Fo. *Prensa Libre,* 26 October 1992.

Because they would reflect her balls."[22] Rigoberta seen as a "transvestite" in these jokes (a man masquerading as a woman) may also represent the opposite of castration anxiety (the fear of not seeing what you want to see), which instead might be the fear of seeing what you *don't* want to see. The deep anxiety expressed in these jokes is about a "phallic woman," a woman and a Maya wielding power that is supposed to be the property of men and ladinos. The intense reactions to "the surprise" of the film *The Crying Game* (that the "female" love interest had a penis) seems precisely about this anxiety. The nausea produced by the protagonist's shock at this unexpected and unwelcome sight was often paralleled in the audience.

This anxiety seems to inform the joke in which an airport guard asks Rigoberta what she has under her *traje.* She answers "missiles," and immediately all the alarms go off, guards come running, guns are drawn, and general panic ensues. The guard, breathless, asks again, "Madam, what do you have under there?" and Rigoberta answers, *"Mis hiles, mis tejeres, mis agujos."*

22. Of course, this is a one-size-fits-all joke about powerful women; it is recycled for Indira Gandhi, Margaret Thatcher, Hillary Rodham Clinton, CONAVIGUA President Rosalina Tuyuc, and so on.

The joke is that she has (like all stereotyped Indians who "can't speak Spanish") mispronounced *mis hilos* (my threads) and the names of other sewing implements like scissors and needles. Similarly, the covers of the weekly magazine *Tinamit* ("With Women Like These, Why Do We Need the Half-Men Who Govern Us?") and *La Hora*'s Supplemental Analysis ("In the Struggle against Impunity, Who Wears the Pants?"), as well as the cartoon from *Prensa Libre* in which Rigoberta says, "Are you the government tailor? I think those pants fit us better," also suggest that Rigoberta and Helen Mack are somehow transvestites—that they *should* wear pants.[23] Although seeming to compliment these incredible women, these examples actually demonstrate marked anxiety about them. The underlying message is that more manly men are needed, that the lack of secure phallic power has created the conditions for the "rise" of these uncharacteristic, indeed almost unclassifiable women (one columnist called Rigoberta *una india fuera de serie*, an Indian unlike the rest [Zarco 22 October 1992]).

In a letter to the editor, one man claims, "I'm a neighbor of Rigoberta because I'm from Chicamán and I knew this woman's entire family, so: Rigoberta was one of the first ones to get involved with the guerrillas. . . . One of her relatives, who still lives in Chicamán, once showed me a photograph of her where she was dressed in olive-green camouflage" (*Siglo,* 11 August 1992). Denunciations that link her to the guerrillas, though political in the obvious way of trying to discredit her as a "peace" prize winner, also seem to carry this charge: she is actually a rifle-woman, an armed guerrilla transvestiting as a humble (castrated) female. This anxiety fits in with relatively common stories told in Guatemala about male and female guerrillas transvestiting as indigenous women in order to enter towns under army control by hiding their weapons under the *cortes*. Similarly, one joke asks: "What is Rigoberta's blood type? URNG-positive."[24]

There is another element in the jokes that points to anxiety that a "transvestite" Rigoberta has a hidden phallus. This is in the sense that the phallus

23. The *Tinamit* cover photo, taken at the celebration party the night the Nobel Prize was announced, shows Rigoberta smiling with Helen Mack, who has tirelessly struggled for justice in the assassination of her sister, anthropologist Myrna Mack.

La Hora's cover shows Rigoberta and Helen Mack with Rosalina Tuyuc of CONAVIGUA and Ninéth de García, one of the founders of GAM.

24. The ambivalence of Rigoberta representing the Mayan movement come out in this joke, which I heard from several Mayan leaders as well as from ladinos. Even though she is working very hard to overcome such divisions, she has traditionally been much more linked to the popular, class-based struggle. This joke is intriguing in terms of the blood metaphors discussed in chapters 3 and 6, suggesting as it does that unlike ethnic or gender identity, which can change with one's dress, being a revolutionary is in the blood. The joke may unconsciously share the attitude behind the scorched-earth campaigns that held that killing children and babies was necessary because they would grow up to be subversives (Falla 1984).

also represents control of language. Men control high culture—the world of letters, politics, philosophy, modernity, and the universal—by reducing women to the body: women's form of contributing to culture is "natural"; they reproduce the species. The joke (she won the prize because she is *desenvuelta*), which links the sense of being *desenvuelta* (articulate) to being *desenvuelta* (unclothed), both reveals the anxiety that she is hiding a phallus under her *traje* and tries to assuage that anxiety by unwrapping her—reducing her to her body. The joke is smutty and degrading, implying that she slept her way to the prize, but it also marks anxiety about one of the important borders that Rigoberta crosses: the border that marks off women in *traje* as a silent ground on which national or ethnic identity can be fabricated. Rigoberta crosses that border in being an international spokeswoman for the poor, indigenous, and oppressed who is quoted in the world press and listened to on the floor of the UN General Assembly.

The dangers this crossing implies for exclusionary ladino and male power in Guatemala are acknowledged (bizarrely) in a letter to the editor that suggests Rigoberta kills people with her long, rapid-fire or heavy-duty *tongue* (*kilométrica lengua*). The letter seems to envision her as a transvestite wielding the phallic power of both a gun and language. A similar ambivalence, of course, surrounds another indigenous woman who crossed boundaries: la Malinche, who was also called "La Lengua." As translator and consort to Cortés, conqueror of Aztec Mexico, she has been a potent symbol of what Norma Alarcón (1989) calls "Traddutora-Traidora" (translator-traitor), scapegoated for the border crossings of colonial violence. La Malinche links power, sex, and language (see also C. Smith 1996; Cypess 1991). Similarly, Rigoberta is represented as a traitor to the nation who profits from her "unnatural" articulateness; we can see this representation in the common army and government refrain voiced by former Defense Minister General García Samayoa: "Certain people are earning well from speaking badly about Guatemala outside the country"—in which *speaking badly* has the double meaning "to speak ill of" and "to be a poor speaker" (*ganan bien por hablar mal*).[25]

If we accept that a certain anxiety about transvestitism marks a category

25. Another letter to the editor says, "I ran into the famous Rigoberta in the Chanel shop in Paris; she was wearing an exquisite yellow dress, elegant red shoes, a Cartier chain, and a seven-thousand-dollar Rolex Watch" (*Crónica*, 25 October 1992). This is similar to the many letters claiming that she lives in luxury while the poor of Guatemala suffer and suggesting, like General García Samayoa, that there's money to be made in denouncing Guatemala's human rights abuses—in other words, by speaking badly. To continue the double meaning, these comments reflect the shock many ladinos evince at the popularity of indigenous issues outside the country. Here are people who "speak badly" (don't even know Spanish) yet are feted by major foreign leaders and given cash prizes. For most ladinos struggling to make ends meet, it is hardly a laughing matter.

Guatemala, viernes 14 de mayo de 1993

Suplemento
Análisis

En la lucha contra la impunidad...
¿Quién lleva los pantalones?

La Hora
"TRIBUNA, NO MOSTRADOR" Clemente Marroquín Rojas
DECANO DE LA PRENSA INDEPENDIENTE

Figure 15. "In the struggle against impunity, who wears the pants?" *La Hora*, 14 May 1993.

crisis—in these cases, a crisis concerning gender characteristics—the jokes and comments might be seen as working to penetrate the masquerade to restabilize or fix those categories. Many of the jokes turn on a double meaning attached to the supposedly incorrect way that indigenous people speak Spanish (as in García Samayoa's comment). Significantly, this includes confusing the genders of nouns, as well as mixing up articles and conjugating verbs incorrectly. For example, "General García Samayoa and Rigoberta were at a cocktail party and he asked what her name was. 'Rigoberta,' she said. 'What a pretty name,' he said. 'Who gave it to you?' '*Mame me la pusa,*' she said"—mixing "*Mama me lo puso*" (my mother gave it to me) with "suck my pussy."[26] Thus, if Rigoberta seems to be an Indian woman who "has" the usually ladino male power of speaking well, we are reminded by the jokes' many plays on "speaking badly" or the way Mayans supposedly speak Spanish, and by the jokes' smuttiness, that she really is an Indian woman. (However, these attempts to fix her are bound to be frustrated. Rigoberta is *desenvuelta,* articulate or fluent, flowing easily.)

Though these jokes may seem rather pallid compensation for the anxieties Rigoberta as an internationally recognized figure causes, these at-

26. Interestingly, another version of this joke has a military commander overseeing the capture of Indians. The joke is much longer; he asks the names of various prisoners and makes an obscene or denigrating comment about each of them. Then Rigoberta is brought in and the same exchange transpires. He finishes by screaming, "Get this *indita* out of here, she is insulting me!" In a bizarre version of the cocktail party joke, García Samayoa follows up by complimenting Rigoberta on her hair braid and asks, "Who did your hair?" She says, "*Mame me la regla*"—mixing "My mother arranges it for me" (*Mama me la arregla*) with "Suck on my menstruation." The joke clearly raises a number of issues beyond the grammatical play!

Freud suggests that "the joker is a disunited personality, disposed to neurotic disorders" (1963b, 142), but that in telling jokes about other peoples—the example he uses are Jewish jokes told by non-Jews—"we are all able to feel that we are members of one people" (102). He differentiates these from Jewish jokes told by Jewish people: jokes from other sources "are for the most part brutal comic stories in which a joke is made unnecessary by the fact that Jews are regarded by foreigners as comic figures," whereas Jews "know their real faults as well as the connection between them and their good qualities" (111). Though ladino jokes told about the Maya are clearly about disunited personalities who hope to feel members of one people, my whole point here has been that the separations between Maya and ladino are not so clear. The jokes allow ladinos to satisfy their opposing instincts, including their fascination with the Maya. There is no better example than the sly mimicry ladinos practice of "speaking badly" (which entails an intimate "knowledge"). Most ladinos can slip into the stereotypes of Mayan grammar, and there are some who can talk for hours in this interdicta language, using the slippage among words and meanings to both reject and inhabit the place of otherness and in turn satisfy the sexual urge through the double entendres this wordplay allows. The most uproarious moment of the long-running play *Epic of the Indies* is when a Guatemalan indigenous Christopher Columbus goes to Spain and discovers the backward Isabel and Ferdinand speaking this tongue.

tempts to penetrate and expose—to counteract fears of phallic inadequacy by showing that Indian women don't "have" one—can be very material and malignant. I suggest that this desire to expose informed the direct reprisal against two young members of CONAVIGUA, the widow's organization that hosted Rigoberta in October 1992 when she won the Nobel. The day Rigoberta left the country, the teenage girls were stopped by security agents, stripped of their *traje,* and left naked on a busy street. This was a blatant reassertion of masculine power. The symbolics of stripping them seem to say, "Look, they don't 'have' one." The attack also attempts to reduce the threat of indigenous women who are *desenvuelta*—verbal and articulate— to women who are vulnerable, embodied, *desenvuelta*s.[27]

SKIRTING THE BORDER: TOPOGRAPHY AND IDENTITY

I have argued that the fantasmatic work of the jokes positions Rigoberta as a transvestite—exhibiting masculine characteristics although dressed in feminine garb—and in turn invites us to mentally undress her in order to be reassured that she doesn't "have" one (that she is solidly a powerless in-digenous female). I think these gender-intrigued reactions to the Nobel also attempt to contain anxieties about the crossing of ethnic identity boundaries occasioned by an indigenous woman who is a thoroughly mod-ern and well-spoken international celebrity. Thus, the jokes imagine Ri-goberta as a ladina transvestiting as a Maya. Because Mayan identity is so connected to *traje,* the *desenvuelta* joke—in which Rigoberta takes off her skirt—also suggests she is ladinoizing. The letter writer who claims to have seen her in a succulent yellow dress, the arguments that indigenous *traje* is a ladino invention imposed on the Maya, and frequent questions about whether she wears pants instead of *corte* when she's not in Guatemala point to worries about an ethnic masquerade. At some level, this may signal wish-ful thinking about ethnic difference being as easy to discard as a pair of clothes—underneath we're all ladinos. This is the assimilationist promise of *mestizaje* (explored in the next chapter), which has been so disrupted by the Mayan cultural rights efforts to fix and strengthen expressions of ethnic difference.

As I explore further in chapter 7, even though indigenous identity is of-ten defined as a special relation to a territory, in Quincentennial Guatemala activists insist they can be Maya without being bound to a rural landscape and increasingly assert their right to be modern without assimilating, or be-coming ladino. A certain recognition of Mayan claims to modernity seems

27. As Hendrickson points out, Mayan women usually appear in public completely cov-ered, except for the head, arms below the biceps, and ankles. She suggests that even seeing men and women together partially clothed (as at the beach) can result in the illness of *susto* "a disease characteristically brought on by violent transgressions of social norms" (1995, 168).

expressed in a joke that goes: "Rigoberta has decided to change her second last name to Fax.[28] Before it was Tum, like the old fashioned drum. But now that she is so modern she wants to send her messages by fax." This suggests uncertainty about the significance of the categories of ethnic identity, an uncertainty expressed by a ladino anthropologist who said of Dr. Demetrio Cojtí, "I don't know if he is an Indian dressed as a ladino, or a ladino dressed as an Indian." Such ambivalencies about what constitutes ethnicity in Guatemala come through in people claiming to have seen Rigoberta clothed in jeans when we know that genes don't determine difference in this very "racially" mixed society: in other words, ethnic difference is not necessarily visible when it is not marked by *traje*.

Rigoberta Menchú and the Mayan rights movement as a whole also cross the geographically symbolic borders meant to divide ladinos and Mayas between the national core and its periphery. In ladino eyes, Indians, especially Indian women, are bound to community; they are supposed to remain on the outskirts of national life. Thus *traje* is used to delineate internal boundaries between the local, rural, premodern, and poor, and the cosmopolitan, urban, modern, and wealthy—boundaries that have long stabilized many ladino identities. In the past, if indigenous people in *traje* were seen in Guatemala City, it was because they were in from the country to sell produce or crafts, or because they were performing some sort of labor, such as road construction, domestic work, or food preparation. In one joke, nostalgia for this moment is invoked through no less an authority than the Holy Gatekeeper: "They say that when Rigoberta died and went to Heaven, St. Peter opened the door and said, 'Hey! the tortillas are finally here!'"

Resorting to St. Peter's authority for reassurance suggests how frightening and eerie these boundary crossings are. In German this sensation is called *unheimlich* (uncanny), and Freud suggests it describes something cut off from intimacy, which was once one's own but is now alienated and returns to haunt the subject. *Heimlich* means "home," so the uncanny also means the loss of home—exactly what ladinos seem to be experiencing. In turn, home was an idiom frequently used in my interviews to deflect this discomfort by describing the (ideal) relation between the nation-state and indigenous peoples: "We all have to live in one house" or the Maya are "like a wife leaving her husband." Here, women's place is naturalized as being in the home and, as with *traje,* ethnicity is gendered female.

If the ladino body image has wanted to define itself as modern and urban in contrast to the Maya as traditional and community-bound, this image is also about class definitions. As Carlos Figueroa Ibarra said, ladino

28. This joke is similar to, if less smutty than, one that goes: "Rigoberta married a French man whose last name was Fas so now she is Rigoberta Menchú Fas" (*me enchufas* means "you turn me on," or "you rape me").

identity wants to be (at least) petit bourgeois. "I am ladino, petit bourgeois, and they tell me I have no culture! . . . We have our own Nobel Prize winner in Miguel Angel Asturias!" But it is the *mujer maya* as domestic worker, that smiling image of the Mayan woman, who supports this body image. She provides domestic labor in the ladino home: preparing food, caring for clothing, providing hospitality, raising children, supporting the leisure of others, and performing the innumerable tasks requiring nimble fingers and dexterous hands to maintain the bourgeois household.[29] A surprising number of ladino households employ Mayan women as domestic "help," in both the cities and rural areas. Most middle-class ladino families have a live-in domestic, and the upper classes often have several Mayan women living in their houses. This domestic support is structural: even extremely modest apartments in Guatemala City (with only a bedroom, living room, kitchen, and bath) have the expectation of domestic labor built in—a small room and separate bathroom for the *mujer maya*. Families who cannot afford full-time domestic labor often employ an indigenous woman to come in for one or two days a week to wash clothes, clean house, shop, cook food, and run errands.[30]

The naturalization of the *mujer maya* in the (even when someone else's) home undergirds what was far and away *the* most popular joke told about Rigoberta Menchú. Everyone who recounted a Rigoberta joke told this one: "Did you hear that Mattel is making a doll of Rigoberta? They say that Barbie is really happy because now she'll have a maid."[31] Ms. Menchú, of course, performed domestic labor for a ladino family in Guatemala City

29. Anne McClintock suggests that slaves, prostitutes, the colonized, and domestic workers in nineteenth-century England represent a similar paradox of abjection, that which is rejected but which imperial identity cannot do without. The "slum, the Victorian garret and kitchen . . . the bedroom. Inhabiting the cusp of domesticity and the market, industry and empire, the abject returns to haunt modernity[,] . . . that liminal state that hovers on the threshold of body and body politic" (1995, 72).

30. All but one of the foreigners I know who live in Guatemala City employ Mayan women to do housework, at least one day a week. At first I resisted doing this, remembering the snide remarks made in graduate seminars about Laura Bohannon and Hortense Powdermaker with their servants in the bush. Exploiting domestic labor was not my idea of doing the "new" ethnography, which would be painfully aware of power differentials. After several weeks of trying to wash my clothes by hand, fight the cockroaches, shop between interviews when the markets were open, and pay bills in person at distant offices when I had work to do, I followed in well-worn gringo footsteps and hired Isabel González to "enlarge my scope of operation" (Webster's) as my prosthetic. I'm still not comfortable with this decision, and it's embarrassing to admit to here, but it also suggests the systemic way that life in Guatemala and the production of this book depend on Isabel's labor and that of many other Mayan women.

31. A corollary to this joke went: "I hear that Mattel is discontinuing the Rigoberta doll. There are too many things disappearing from the Barbie house"—in other words, the indigenous maid is stealing things.

when she was a teenager. In her testimonial (1984), she denounces the in-humane treatment and horrifically low wages. Although she was spared, sexual abuse seems to be a common experience of young Mayan women working in ladino homes.[32]

Class categories are clearly about more than income. They are marked by hygiene, leisure practices, sumptuary codes, respectability, and other forms of cultural capital. As Ann Stoler describes in her work on Foucault and colonial biopower, bourgeois bodies are cultivated through certified knowl-edges and jurisdiction over how to live: "civilities, conduct, and competen-cies" (1995, 83) that are supported through discourses of race and in Gua-temala are made possible by the intensive labor of the *mujer maya.*

However, the ladino home (and urban public space) is increasingly less cozy. The jokes about Rigoberta Menchú are attempts to contain this inter-national celebrity, but it's not likely the Nobel Prize winner and United Na-tions ambassador will be mopping a ladino's floor any time soon. As a ladina state official said to Charles Hale, "The next thing you know they won't work for you either. It's hard to find good domestic help these days" (1996, 44). The rightful place for Indians in *traje* has been as servants, and "western" clothing was de rigueur for other employment. However, Rigoberta, along with thousands of indigenous women and some men, has crossed over into national life and retains (or has taken back) *traje.* Delia Tujab, in full *traje,* speaks at ESTNA, saying, "People say that they have no problems with Indi-ans . . . because they have Indian maids! . . . Valuing someone for their la-bor is not the same as valuing them as a full human being with respect for all the different aspects of their culture."

There is *traje* on the university campuses, in office buildings, in govern-ment bureaucracies, and on televised panel discussions. Thanks to Mayan organizing, the Accord on Identity and Indigenous Rights imposes sanc-tions against discrimination on the basis of *traje.* Even *muchachas,* the young indigenous women employed as domestic servants, are no longer shy about appearing radiant in their *traje* on their days off in the Central Square of Zone One. As one ladino friend said, "It's gotten so my family and friends call it 'the Reconquest'; the Indians are taking back the city. People used to love going to the cathedral on Sundays and spending part of the day in the park, but they don't go anymore because it is full of Indians."

Rigoberta Menchú also messes with internal boundaries and the at-tempts to pin down and identify difference in that she wears *traje* from all over the country rather than just the garb of her hometown of San Miguel Uspantán. This is part of a growing trend that seems to be a visible marker

32. To be fair, middle-class and upper-class Maya also employ Mayan women of lower classes to do domestic labor. I have also heard of cases of sexual abuse in these homes.

Figure 16. *Cholb'al Q'ij, Agenda Maya* (Mayan calendar). Cholsamaj 1995. Published with kind permission.

for both the violent displacement many Guatemalans have suffered with the war (transvestiting in other people's *traje* to hide dangerous regional identities from soldiers) and for the voluntary travel undertaken by indigenous women who increasingly move throughout Guatemala to buy and sell, to study and work, or simply to visit. In far-flung corners of the country like Cotzal in the Ixil area, women have several versions of their "own" *huipil* they have woven and always wear for special occasions and, in addition, several from other areas, bought with the proceeds from selling their own textiles. In August 1993, when I asked why she wasn't wearing a Cotzal *huipil*, one woman said, "I just like this. I bought it in Santa Cruz del Quiché when I was down buying thread. It is pretty. And Rigoberta has one like it." A woman from Patzún who is active in Mayan organizing wears a variety of *huipiles* as well, both because she thinks they are pretty and because to her they represent growing Mayan nationalism and unity. This woman, in addition to her law school studies and full-time job as a Congressional secretary, has created a Patzún *huipil* with the ancient Mayan calendar around the yoke, a design she learned through a Mayan cultural studies group.[33]

Many ladinos use this practice to discredit Rigoberta's "authenticity." A ladino government development official said, "I don't think of Rigoberta as an indigenous leader. She is very belligerent, and besides, one of our project leaders from the Ixil area says that he does not accept her because she changes her *huipil* every day. She is not one of us." The increase in the symbolic value of the *huipil* has raised peoples' consciousness about its material value, putting some ethnicist class categories (Indians are supposed to be poor) into crisis. A ladina woman who works cleaning offices complained to me several days after Rigoberta won the Nobel: "Do you know how much those shirts she wears cost!? Well, when she won, my sister in the United States wanted me to buy her one, so I went to the market to get it, and I couldn't believe it! I couldn't afford even one! And she has so many!"

Finally, just as Rigoberta models the fashions of increasing movement, interconnection, and articulation among Maya in Guatemala by crossing such internal boundaries, she also stands in for the international border crossings of the millions of Guatemalans who escaped violence and economic misery and now return to attempt reintegration into national life. Rigoberta's poem "Patria Abnegada" (Sacrificed homeland), which she recited the night she won the Nobel Prize, begins, "I crossed the border love and do not know when I will return." Although she now lives in Guatemala,

33. This *huipil* adorns the 1995 *Mayan Agenda* published by Cholsamaj. The artist said that many women have asked her for the pattern because they want to copy it. Hendrickson (1995) explores the multiple ways that *huipil* designs and *traje* practices in general change through time and with shifts in consciousness and identification.

for years crises attended her frontier crossings into Guatemala. For example, she was arrested the first time she returned to Guatemala in 1988, and numerous death threats greeted her arrival in October 1992.[34] These crises seem to condense the anxieties surrounding the porousness of national boundaries to refugees, exiles, economic migrants, and guerrillas, as well as transnational image repertoires, moral sanctions, economic pressures, and other threats to "national sovereignty" (see chapter 8). Rigoberta's accompaniment by international solidarity activists when she disembarked on national soil (including the former French first lady Madame Mitterand) levels an implicit critique of Guatemalan national civility. It also gives rise to the joke: "Why do they call Rigoberta a *chile relleno*? Because she always comes between two *francés*"—the stuffed pepper (*chile relleno*) sandwich is always served on French bread, and Rigoberta is always surrounded by French people; the joke also has sexual overtones as well as a subtle critique of her authenticity—bread as opposed to tortillas is a food associated with the ladino.

Ms. Menchú herself provided accompaniment and international attention for the first massive return of organized refugees from the United Nations High Commission on Refugees (UNHCR) camps in Mexico in January 1993. They refused to remain on the margins of national life by crossing directly from Mexico to their resettlement areas near the border. Instead, the refugees, with Ms. Menchú, insisted on trekking across the country, making a triumphant entrance into Guatemala City before turning north again toward their new lands.[35] These multiple border crossings are both resisted and acknowledged through the jokes. If indigenous people, and especially indigenous women, are supposed to be domestic and local, how are we to deal with one who is completely international? One way, of course, is to relocalize her by reducing her accomplishments to her body through degrading, smutty jokes. However, in the wash of current history, colors are bleeding through the ethnic, geographic, class, and gender boundaries hierarchically organized within the nation. Embroidered into the anxieties about Rigoberta's boundary transgressions of both internal and international borders is the constitutive anxiety of phallic inadequacy, of illegitimate power, and perhaps a growing recognition of the new articulations of

34. In a sorry attempt to undermine Ms. Menchú's Nobel chances, the Serrano government proposed their own ladina candidate for the prize, an upper-class philanthropist named Señora Molina Stahl. In addition, she was decorated with the country's highest honor, the Order of the Quetzal. This gave rise to a joke that played on the government's attitude toward Rigoberta: "When Molina Stahl met Rigoberta at a party, she said she had received the Order of the Quetzal and asked what order Rigoberta had received. Rigoberta replied, 'An order for my arrest.'"

35. The triumphal march was momentarily delayed when a baby was born en route!

the nation-state, in which women and the Maya are refusing to leave the room when the joke telling starts.

TRAJE AND THE CAMEL HAIR SUIT

Thinking about the way jokes situate Rigoberta fantasmatically as a transvestite and *traje* as multiply signifying helps us see how categories imagined as solid (like "gender," "ethnicity," and "nation") are instead in crisis. Identification itself is fluid, in ways both skirted and constantly reconfigured in the jokes—split by the catastrophic violence of the past thirty-five years, by class, by geography, by access to modernity, and by gendered, ethnic, and national identifications. Some of the pleasure of the jokes may come from the simultaneous confrontation with and the attempt to suture over these bursting seams. The jokes act as "weapons, tools for understanding political relations." As Mikhail Bakhtin suggests: "Things are tested and reevaluated in the dimensions of laughter, which has defeated fear and all gloomy seriousness. This is why the material body lower stratum is needed, for it gaily and simultaneously materializes and unburdens" (in Kipnis 1992, 377). The material body is needed here as jokes seize on its lower stratum to ground their metaphors, to solidify those uncannily fluid identifications. In some ways this is positive, as we can see that even those identities that seem to have the most coercive power, like the nation-state, are constitutively unstable, haunted, as Andrew Parker says, by definitional others. Of course, this also destabilizes the legitimation claims of the less powerful, which may be why Mayan men tell these jokes as well.

While keeping in mind that we may not know why we laugh, I've suggested that the jokework produces pleasure in part by creating links among the "same"—as in the "ideal" case of two ladino men telling each other smutty jokes meant to secure their shaky phallic power. But the jokes may be so engaging because "difference" is so unavoidable in the Year (and now Decade) of Indigenous People spearheaded by a Mayan woman. So even though the jokes want to cover over these differences, they also function as classic reaction-formations, not only allowing the expression of but also compelling the person to imagine that difference. Thus the jokes may offer consolation for the complexity of Quincentennial Guatemala that is constituted by the antagonism between the desire for the same and the need for difference. As Laura Kipnis suggests, "It's something of a Freudian cliché that shame, disgust, and morality are reaction-formations to an original interest in what is not 'clean.'"[36] One defining characteristic of a classic

---

36. Think of the clichés attached to the indigenous "other" listed in chapter 4, as well as the dependence on the *mujer maya* to maintain bourgeois ladino structures of hygiene.

reaction-formation is that the subject comes close to 'satisfying the demands of the opposing instinct while actually engaged in the pursuit of the virtue which he affects'" (Kipnis 1992, 381). Although the various *traje*-like styles of ethnic and gender difference are disavowed by the discourse of a uniform modern nation, these dirty, smutty, macabre jokes acknowledge and even allow a certain voluptuous wallow in those differences, suggesting that the uniform is instead a camel hair suit that changes the bodies politic it envelopes.

I think the jokes suggest the complexity of Quincentennial Guatemala, where boundaries are constantly violated and these various identities cannot be unwoven from each other. Though Freud's understanding of smut suggests that it functions to reinscribe power among the more powerful (among men), Bakhtin and others have read humor as the sly resistance of the underclass, a sort of weapon of the weak. The latter view informs the investment of many Guatemalans in their humor. Ladino men may have disproportionate power vis-à-vis, for example, indigenous women, but the majority also inhabit disempowered positions vis-à-vis Guatemala's extremely skewed economic system, vis-à-vis the historically violent government, and as citizens of a peripheral country in the new world order. Thus the jokes may offer a certain consolation regarding apparent changes in male-female and ladino-Maya relations. But they are also about the way those relations are crosscut with fears of violence: ladinos as well as Maya were burned alive in the Spanish Embassy massacre, ladinos as well as Maya are threatened when the president goes around *quitando cortes*—dissolving the justice system. The jokes also deal with the frustration and pain of identification with a nation that has been an international pariah and holds no foreign currency reserves.

Similarly, Mayan men are disempowered along national, ethnic, and gender lines. They disappear physically in government counterinsurgency and culturally through the orthopedics of military training and sartorial codes. They are discursively feminized vis-à-vis ladino men in a variety of ways and, as I explore in the next chapter, their sexuality is delegitimized through discourses of *blanquemiento* (whitening). Some of the jokes are about this frustration and pain and in turn attempt to fix or solidify the *mujer maya* as a support element in their *formación* of Mayan identity.

The jokes bespeak the contradictions of these various identifications and their relations to the structures that give them—and their boundary crossings—meaning. These meanings are in flux: for example, if the camel hair suit of national unity changes the body it covers, if it is hard to tell anymore what's under the *traje*, how can a nation be built? But perhaps boundary marking and building are not the most useful metaphors. Perhaps we should think instead of more flexible notions of identity, of the self as something fabricated, of fluidarity. This would signal an awareness of the fundamental insecurities of identity, based on differences that are not stable. Perhaps we can use as our model the changing forms of *traje* that retain difference but can mean various things, depending on how they are worn. *Traje* carries the marks of colonization (whether or not it was imposed, it is materially situated in Guatemala's history, having collected aspects from each historical period) but is constantly resignifying. Rather than cutting and stitching, it patiently weaves together different elements, designing ancient symbols in polyester. A *traje* metaphor helps us gender ethnic-national identities. It is antiessentialist, it can be ripped, it gets dirty, it can be changed. It is provisional and relatively temporary.

Ladino dreams of national unity transcending ethnic differences are troubled by the aspirations and demands articulated by Rigoberta Menchú (who represents Mayan cultural rights, returning refugees, and popular organizations); by the fluidity of *traje;* and by gender. As I explore in the next chapter, many ladinos attempt, at least fantasmatically, to deal with this uncanny shiftiness through dispensing with *traje* altogether and penetrating down to the solid body beneath it, which seems to offer a biological sameness: *mestizaje*. After all, just how far can a body contort to conform to the orthopedics of the "becoming" camel hair suit? Returning to the body from bodies politic offers the hope of stopping all that movement, getting down to the "natural," what really "matters." But just as modernity needs tradition and the state depends on "culture," *mestizaje* is constituted by gender and ethnic differentials and, like the identifications discussed here, leans on the *mujer maya*.

SIX

Bodies That Splatter

Gender, "Race," and the Discourses of Mestizaje

The only solution for Guatemala is to improve the race, to bring in Aryan seeds to improve it. On my finca *I had a German administrator for many years, and for every* india *he got pregnant, I would pay him an extra fifty dollars.*
Ladino plantation owner (in Casaus Arzú)

It is not simply a matter of honoring the subject as a plurality of identifications, for these identifications are invariably imbricated in one another. . . . [I]t is not a matter of relating race and sexuality and gender, as if they were fully separable axes of power. . . . What convergent set of historical formations of racialized gender, of gendered race, of the sexualization of racial ideals, or the racialization of gender norms, makes up both the social regulation of sexuality and its psychic articulations?
JUDITH BUTLER

Fantasies of "unwrapping" Rigoberta Menchú to find the body underneath the *traje* suggest the hope of grounding fluid bodies politic in a singular, solid body that is "Indian" or female, without a doubt. At the same time, the discourses of ladino identity posit that the body doesn't matter—because everyone is mestizo, biologically mixed. The process of ladinoization, whereby Indians assimilate to ladino culture, supposedly erases phenotypic (sight-specific) difference. Five hundred years of the interpenetration of boundaries means that all bodies are the same (that's why the clothes make the man, not the hair, nose, or skin color)—take off that colorful *traje* and the body will prove a national sameness. The *mestizaje* discourse of identity—that everyone is really the same underneath—makes liberatory promises: freedom from the horrors of essentialist racial difference and a unity that sublates—acknowledges yet transcends—difference (Anzaldúa 1987; Klor de Alva 1995; Hale 1996; C. Smith 1996; Mallon 1996). But the fact that it is Rigoberta Menchú's body that is being *desenvuelta* in the jokes suggests the racializing of gender and gendering of race (and class) that Judith Butler foregrounds, and it reminds us that the body as "ground" of the body politic is unstable.

This chapter explores the social regulation of race, gender, and sexuality in Guatemalan ladino discourse about Indians. I focus on the discourse of *mestizaje* and its apparent opposite—Indian-ness as a biological differ-ence instantly ascertainable because it is written on the body. Both dis-courses lean heavily on bodies to produce coherent identifications. But I ar-gue that identity categories splatter across the fault lines of gender and of sex, which link the body and the body politic. In turn, the instability of these categories may lead to the splattering of material bodies, as power attempts to fix them by imposing unitary meanings.

I can only go skin deep into the complex—and often repugnant—set of stereotypes, fantasies, ideals, and eroticized imaginaries that make up these ladino discourses. Just as Rigoberta jokes are only glancingly about the "real" Ms. Menchú, this chapter is not about actual indigenous people. Instead, it is about ladino understandings about Indians, and I echo la-dino use of the disrespectful term *indio* (Indian) to differentiate the views herein from the actual embodied lives of the Maya.[1] To look at discourses about identity and bodies in the Quincentennial, I lean on Marta Casaus Arzú's brilliant study *Guatemala: Linaje y Racismo* (Lineage and Racism), which looks at the imbrication of race and class through five hundred years of Guatemalan history—and which appeared in 1992.[2] Called "the book that unleashed a scandal" (*Crónica*, 30 April 1993, 16), it immediately be-came a best-seller in Quincentennial Guatemala. Drawing on Casaus Arzú's findings and my own interviews with ladinos in Guatemala City, I explore how bodies are marked by race in ladino discourse and ask what is erased as bodies are called upon to ground wounded ethnic and national body im-ages. To illustrate, I start with a story about my attempts to read a body that supposedly signified in completely obvious ways, an anecdote that "incor-porates" many of the complicated issues addressed here.

In 1988, I was living in Mexico City working with Guatemalan exiles when a friend connected with America's Watch invited me to go with him to inter-view a man who had been tortured by the military, an ordeal that included having acid poured on his body. At the interview, we were introduced by a nun, and then the three of us withdrew to a back room. There I watched with horror as the man took off most of his clothes to show us the new geo-graphies of his body, where the deltas and rivulets of acid had left their scars.

1. This echoes the diacritical distinctions that feminist scholars use between *Woman* (rep-resenting the idea of femaleness—its philosophical, cultural meanings) and *woman* (to repre-sent actually existing women). I use the term *Indian* (*indio*), like *mujer maya*, to refer to the ideas and stereotypes of a generalized indigenousness, and I use *Maya* to represent actually ex-isting indigenous peoples.

2. All translations in this chapter are by the author. The 1992 publication date of *Gua-temala: Linaje y Racismo* is four years before Marta Casaus Arzú's cousin Alvaro Arzú became president.

I had been involved for several years in human rights solidarity work, denouncing such abuses, describing them in detail, and leaning on the similarity of bodies (we can all imagine the pain of torture) to incite activism, but I had never seen an actual body that had been tortured. My friend took several rolls of film to document the man's story before we left. About a month later, I ran into the torture victim on the subway and we chatted for a while. Suddenly he began to talk about how he thought about me all the time and that he was in love with me. I looked at him amazed and tried to laugh it off, saying that I didn't even know him, what was he thinking? My stop came and I quickly got off the train, not giving him the phone number he asked for. I was intensely disconcerted by this "victim" talking back. He was not just testifying to his pain as in the torture reports I was so used to reading, not just denouncing state abuses through the immediately available signs on his body, but speaking a desire. This scene—the body I had seen, my body that he saw—was shot through with ambivalencies that disrupted the straightforward humanitarian and ethnographic gesture I thought I was involved in. It hadn't occurred to me to think I would be an object of desire, cloaked as I was in my concern; and I thought that concern should also cover over the privilege of my ethnic national identity, as well as any enjoyment I might take in the scene. In turn, the erotics of this man undressing in front of me would be blotted out by the singular meaning of his body as marked by pain and politics, a reading he shattered by invoking gender and sexuality.

Mestizaje is a ladino discourse about Indians and as such is in large part about ladino and national identification (C. Smith 1990b and 1996), an attempt to create a singular meaning out of bodies and the body politic. As I was reminded to my acute embarrassment on the train, sex is an interface that links these two forms of incorporation—the life of the individual and the life of the species (Foucault 1980). Despite going unremarked, gender and sexuality are constitutive of ladino discourses on the body—especially the unifying discourse of mestizaje. The anxieties I'm exploring here about the national body politic in Guatemala may result from the way bodies are constituted: bodies meant to mean one thing always signify too much.

In our commonsense notions about our bodies, they are the most material of things, the most tactilely and visually present aspect of ourselves and others. Like hieroglyphs, they seem the most readable of signs. Because of this, bodies are routinely called upon to materialize certain otherwise tenuous identities. But also like hieroglyphs, they may be indecipherable—an indecipherability that leads to the two apparently contradictory ladino discourses about Indian bodies. One discourse is that of explicit racial difference between Indians and non-Indians, which leans on tropes of blood purity and calls on "objective" phenotypic marks of difference like the *cara de indio* (face of the Indian) (Hale 1996, 44). An alternative to this overtly racist position is advanced by many progressive ladinos: the discourse of *mestizaje*. *Mestizaje* is supposed to solve the so-called ethnic-national question and the revolting racializing that undergirds Guatemala's system of inequality through claims that "really" all Guatemalans are the same, the body doesn't matter. The apparent differences between Indian and ladino are cultural, not genetic; ethnic, not racial; a question of equitable resource distribution rather than innate backwardness. Strip off that *traje* and everybody is pretty much the same.

I argue that these apparently opposed discourses are similar and may work simultaneously, like modernity and tradition, the similarity and difference that animate solidarity, or the state's paradoxical "fixing" of indigenous identity (both supporting Mayan culture and "repairing" it through ladinoization). Both discourses call on the body as proof, and both—as they "race" the body in different ways—simultaneously erase the constitutive gendering and sexualizing of those bodies. I foreground sexuality in analyzing these discourses of race in order to highlight the roles of pleasure and enjoyment in the production of both of these regulatory norms. Since "blood purity" and "interbreeding" are implicitly about sexual unions, discourses of racial difference and *mestizaje* are always actually "covert theories of desire" (Young 1995, 9). It was desire operating simultaneously with my rational ethnographic encounter that unsettled the identifications occurring in my relation with the body in pain. Similarly, although *mestizaje* discourse posits a clear teleology toward national unity—a body politic—the work of desire is not so disciplined. As Diana Fuss reminds us, "The form, strength or trajectory of a particular identification can never be foretold in advance" (1995, 8).

So rather than being a solid ground for bodies politic, bodies are produced (and aroused) in complex and often contradictory ways through desire and racial discourses like *mestizaje*. As Ann Stoler reminds us, such discourses derive "force from a 'polyvalent mobility,' from the density of discourses they harness, from the multiple economic interests they serve, from the subjugated knowledges they contain, from the sedimented forms of knowledge that they bring into play" (1995, 204–205). Raced (and sexed) bodies always carry more than their somatic markings. That is how, and why, bodies matter so terribly. In turn, this is why bodies have so much power in materializing "common sense" (Gramsci 1989; Hall 1986). Even those of us who think we know the difference between sex and gender or race and ethnicity tend to "really" believe that the body tells the truth in ways that dissimulating words may not. The problem is that bodies also splatter: they break apart wetly under the weight of signification they are meant to carry, and they overflow and obliterate the messages inscribed on them, messing up any clean, unified categories.

I chose the rather disgusting title "Bodies That Splatter" partly to play on

Judith Butler's *Bodies That Matter* (1993), which theorizes the processes and regulatory norms that materialize bodies. Rather than postulating an already existing body onto which racial, gender, sexual, or class identities are later inscribed, Butler argues that bodies are constructed (and undone) over time and through reiteration. "What constitutes the fixity of the body, its contours, its movements, will be fully material, but materiality will be rethought as the effect of power, as power's most productive effect" (Butler 1993, 2).[3] In attempting to parse how bodies matter in Guatemala—to read the "racial grammar" of a mestizo national project—I rely on Butler's strong constructivist argument, in her sense that "if certain constructions appear constitutive, that is, have this character of being 'without which' we could not think at all, we might suggest that bodies only appear, only endure, only live within the productive constraints of certain highly gendered [and raced] regulatory schemas" (Butler 1993, xi). Race, gender, sexuality, and other discourses make bodies matter differentially in Guatemala.[4] Speaking of bodies that splatter is an attempt to get away from the idea of either a primordial or a potential whole body—either of an individual or a body politic—and to focus attention on the wounded body, on constitutive differences and antagonisms.

Splattered bodies haunt the project of nation formation in Quincentennial Guatemala. The open wound in Tecún Umán's body is recalled in the splash of red on the breast of the quetzal bird, which circulates throughout the body politic in the nation's currency. Rumor has it that gringa baby-snatchers leave splattered bodies stuffed with dollar bills—the stolen organs magically reanimating other wealthier and lighter-skinned bodies. In the Rigoberta joke about having a cook-out to commemorate her father, killed in the Spanish Embassy fire, bodies are imagined spread out on the barbecue—an image that memorializes bodies destroyed in counterinsurgency. In the story "Peel Off Flesh, Come Back On" analyzed by Kay Warren (1993), Maya-Kaqchikeles tell of the *rajav a'a'*, a creature disguised as a normal human, one's wife for example, which leaves its splattered body by the door when it goes out at night in animal form.

3. "'Sex' is, thus, not simply what one has, or a static description of what one is: it will be one of the norms by which the 'one' becomes visible at all, that which qualifies a body for life within the domain of cultural intelligibility" (Butler 1993, 2). See also Halberstam 1995.

4. One important delineation that I can only briefly address is history and the way that practices and identities signify differently through time. Ann Stoler (1991 and 1995) makes this point forcefully in her rich discussion of the differing historic roles of concubinage, prostitution, and marriage in the sexual economies of colonialism in Asia. I thank Quetzil Castañeda for turning me on to Stoler's work. Although in my interviews I found echoes of many of the ideas described by Casaus Arzú, it should be pointed out that her fieldwork was undertaken in the 1970s and thus corresponds to a different moment in history than mine.

I invoke splattered bodies, like the graveyards in chapter 4, to fore-ground the threat of violence that continually surrounds bodies—Maya and ladino, rich and poor, and male and female—in Guatemala. As War-ren suggests, even the most intimate relations are untrustworthy, liable to split open and betray. This may be the result not only of civil war but also of the violence that governs the assumptions of gendered, racial, and other identifications (these are hostile markings). The term *splatter* emphasizes wetness and fluidity, insisting on the instability of bodies as carriers of mean-ing. A splatter leaves a wet spot, like blood, or "stains" on a lineage—an im-age that informs racist imaginings. Discourses of *mestizaje* seek to disavow the body by "raising" difference from the biological to the cultural level, but these "clean" discourses are also splattered by the weight of bodies that mat-ter in sexual and other ways. The term *splatter* both suggests the messiness of Guatemala's contemporary scene and works against the hygienic impulse of the erasures I am trying to mark. Finally, the splattered body with bleed-ing boundaries may help us think about bodies politic in Quincentennial Guatemala in a way useful for fluidary politics.

GENDER AND THE RACIALIZED BODY

As I explore throughout this book, the terms *Indian* and *ladino* are highly problematic and have long genealogies, the complexity of which I do not want to erase.[5] However, in the literature (both popular and "scientific"—see Rojas Lima [1990]; Rosada Granados [1987]), in the press, and in interviews, and despite the various identifications people might carry at different moments, the terms *Indian* and *ladino* function as operative categories, defined and produced in oppositional relation to each other (C. Smith 1990b; Watanabe 1992 and 1995; Hawkins 1984; Fischer and Brown 1996).

The standard understanding of indigenous and ladino identities I was taught when I first began to study Guatemala was that these are cultural categories, "ethnic" rather than "racial," marked by language, dress, cos-mology, and so on. Therefore they are, to some extent, a matter of choice and in fact thought to be so flexible as to be changeable by decree, as in the 1876 law that "declared ladinos the Indians of San Pedro Sacatepéquez." This was to be achieved by men and women wearing the *traje* that corre-sponded to the ladino class (see also Otzoy 1996).

Though it is popular in the United States to assume that racism is more retrograde in Guatemala than elsewhere, the notion of identity as "culture,"

---

5. Todd Little-Siebold (1997) has shown how contentious these terms were even at the be-ginning of the colonial period.

not as racialized bodies, is widely expressed. Such "politically correct" discourse is prevalent among the powerful ladinos I interviewed, who are well-educated and politically savvy people. Casaus Arzú also found that her informants dissembled on the issue of racism. "There is a deep anxiety to hide, distort, and mystify the existence of racism in all social classes. The silences in the interviews were often more revealing than the answers" (Casaus Arzú 1992, 301). However, I want to argue that in Guatemala, bodies do matter. Phenotype and blood, though not the "official line," figure largely in my interviews with Guatemalan state officials and in the research Casaus Arzú presents in *Guatemala: Linaje y Racismo.*

Casaus Arzú (in a book full of the detailed kinship diagrams that warm anthropologists' hearts) argues that twenty-two of the most important families of the Guatemalan oligarchy have retained political and economic power for close to five hundred years through strict endogamy sustained by racist ideology. Racism serves both to keep property in family hands and to legitimize the savage exploitation of the indigenous majority. She argues that these practices have created a "pigmentocracy" in which the macrosocioeconomic system is supported by the micropower networks of family ties constituted through race distinctions. Casaus Arzú's analysis is based both on painstaking genealogy work in archives and on interviews with members of Guatemala's elite—a privileged access made possible by her kinship ties with the oligarchy.

Casaus Arzú was active in the Left and since the early 1980s has lived in exile in Spain, where she received a doctorate in anthropology. Although she is still based in Spain, she has directed several follow-up research projects in Guatemala on lineage and racism. She has also been instrumental in pulling together a disparate group of influential ladinos for ongoing discussions of ladino identity, and she is frequently cited in the press. Attention to her ideas is vital because of her central role in articulating ladino and mestizo identifications and because her family romance has been enormously popular among Guatemala's (admittedly small) reading public. In the words of one avid reader, the book is "better than a *telenovela* [soap opera]," and during the Quincentennial it sold out as quickly as it could be printed. The book merited a front-page story in the weekly *Crónica,* which called it a scandal, "a burning stain for many Guatemalan families" (*Crónica,* 30 April 1993, 23).[6]

6. Many of these families were angry for being portrayed in an unflattering light or for not being mentioned. The *Crónica* article takes great pains to undermine Casaus Arzú's argument, accusing her of (undocumented) plagiarism, errors in her genealogies, and, worst of all, the use of Marxist methodology. It liberally quotes members of the families in question as they criticize the work. However, the *Crónica* piece ends by stating that people are upset about be-

The family, as metaphor and as practice, is far from innocent and cozy in Quincentennial Guatemala. Doris Sommer (1990) argues that the narrative of the family romance often attempts to bridge ethnic, geographic, and class differences in Latin American fiction by linking various members of the "nation" through the family structure. The nation as family is part of Guatemalans' body image, but for the protagonists in Casaus Arzú's melodrama, the body—in its blood and phenotypic markings—makes such reconciliation impossible. Instead, the family is shown to produce and maintain difference.

Casaus Arzú argues that purity of blood was and is a central concern in the identities of the elite. In matters of identification, bodies matter as "proof" of authenticity, of purity. When asked to define their ethnic background, many say, "white and with no mixing of Indian blood."[7] In her interviews, people would boast of their family's three hundred years of purity and thank their ancestors for their "ardor" in avoiding blood mixing. One family insisted that they "do not have even a drop of Indian blood. This is proved by our certificate of blood purity [*limpieza*] and the fact that all of us have blood-type O negative" (Casaus Arzú 1992, 118). When informants were asked to describe an "Indian," physical attributes—the color of the skin, height, facial features, and even smell—were central to their definitions. What are apparently nonphysical stereotypes of Indians as lazy, traditional, conformist, and submissive were also thought by many ladinos to be passed down in the blood, to be genetic traits. Casaus Arzú quotes a ladino who said, "Genes determine people's behavior and how they develop. Indians transmit an inferior race through their genes. The genes of the white race are superior, and this superior race produces great inventors and artists" (1992, 220). Her informants said that racial differences could also be discerned when they were mixed. One ladina said, "The mix of a German and an Indian is purer, more healthy, but because the Spanish race was not so pure, the Indian mixed with the Spanish is perverse, lazy" (1992, 220).

Historically, the identity categories of the national census were supposed to be based on "ethnic" or cultural criteria such as a person's language or

ing revealed as "members of a society considered racist and of a sector that has historically taken advantage of the domination of the indigenous people" (30 April 1993, 23).

7. I admit to a slippage between the use of *white* and *ladino* as identity signifiers. Most of Casaus Arzú's informants would not self-identify as ladino if asked, and neither would many of my contacts. However, even as "ladino" as a category is intricately split (making it an ethnicity that is not one), most of these people would identify as not-Indian. Because the race system is so polarized in Guatemala, I take the risk of oversimplifying by both using *ladino* as shorthand for this oppositional identity and, following Casaus Arzú, using it as a "social" category (Casaus Arzú 1992, 216–217).

whether they wore shoes, but in many cases the census taker (almost always ladino, and always male) decided for himself, based on his reading of their bodies.[8] Although the Indian-ladino division is in general understood as "ethnic," bodies as markers of difference also mattered to many people in my interviews. Even progressive ladinos, my friends, would remark on the physical characteristics that differentiate indigenous people from ladinos: "You can never tell how old they are; their faces always look so young;" or "that indigenous congressman is trying to hide behind his beard, but you can always tell who is an Indian." A number of people mentioned the (apparently mythic) ultimate bodily proof: "the Mongolian spot"—a birthmark on the lower back—which would prove that someone was an Indian "even if it didn't show up in their genealogy."[9] Attitudes are also thought to be related to blood. Alvaro Colón, who runs the government development agency FONAPAZ, told me, "We need to create a way for Indians to participate in decision making in this country. I don't have Indian blood, but I believe this anyway."

Embedded, so to speak, in the Guatemalan discourse of blood is the possibility of "whitening" or "improving" the race, a sense that is counterintuitive for many North Americans whose racist tradition has considered someone with as little as one one-hundredth part "black" "blood" to be black (B. Williams 1989; Klor de Alva 1995). In Guatemala and much of Latin America, despite the sense that a lineage can be stained by mixing blood, it is widely held that an influx of whiter blood can improve a "lower" race. R. Stutzman describes this process, known as *blanquemiento,* as "a putative lightening or 'whitening' of the population in both the biogenetic and cultural-behavioral senses of the term *blanco.* The cultural goals, the society, and even the physical characteristics of the dominant class are taken by members of that class to be the objective of all cultural, social, and biological movement and change" (1981, 49). This belief informs the practice of encouraging immigration from Northern European countries (supported by Guatemala's other Nobel Prize winner, novelist Miguel Angel Asturias) and asserts that the backwardness of the Indian, and thus of Guatemala, can be combated through importing superior races. As one of Casaus Arzú's informants said: "The only solution for Guatemala is to improve the race, to bring in Aryan seeds to improve it. On my *finca* I had a German adminis-

8. The ambivalence of the national census is discussed in Cojtí (1990) and manifested in the fact that the 1993 census, which was to have been the first to systematically ask people about their ethnic identification rather than relying on the bodily decodings of the census-takers, was postponed until after the Year of Indigenous Peoples, purportedly for lack of funds.

9. In her work on the Dutch colonial gynecologist C. H. Stratz, Stoler also found mention of a telltale "blue spot" at the base of the spine that "racially" marked native Javanese women—along with pigment variations in their vaginas (1995, 186).

trator for many years, and for every *india* he got pregnant, I would pay him an extra fifty dollars" (1992, 289).[10]

Although she cannot ignore the role of the exchange of women in maintaining the oligarchic networks, or the importance of their fecundity in assuring a lineage's success, Casaus Arzú is not attentive to the gender specificity of those "Aryan seeds" or who receives that fifty dollar inducement. Her family romance is primarily concerned with explaining how race functions in the service of maintaining unequal class relations, and she frequently states that among the ladino elite there are no differences in ideology based on gender. She says, "Racist attitudes are expressed equally by all members of the family, independent of sex, age, or occupation, because the ideology extends throughout the social system, and the family is the primary unit of socialization" (1992, 23). The reproduction of this system and the reproduction of individual subjects is naturalized in this analysis, which in turn erases the social system of gender difference (and how gender is racialized and classed) that makes it possible.

However, it is important to not just add gender to Casaus Arzú's rich mix. We must also interrogate its constitutive role in Guatemala's ethnic and national matrix. Whether a sexual liaison whitens a race or stains a lineage depends on the gender of the bodies so engaged. When white people "with no mixing of Indian blood" thank their ancestors' "ardor" for purity, they are referring to the violent policing of white women's sexuality. When white male members of their family tree rape the Indian maid, it is not seen as a breach of purity—they probably think he was doing her a favor. State eugenic prescriptions—like marriage, divorce, rape, and abortion laws, sanitation, and education practices—affect how "race and gender intertwin[e] to construct new images and social practices of the 'fit' nation" (Stepan 1991, 12).

In order to understand how bodies matter in Guatemala and why some matter less than others, we may need a unified analysis not just of kinship and gender, as Jane Collier and Sylvia Yanagisako have argued (1987), but of race, class, nation, and sexuality as well. A project of fluidarity must work in this single analytic field, and we must struggle to work there without, as Judith Butler says, merely juxtaposing "a list of attributes separated by those proverbial commas . . . that usually mean that we have not yet figured out how to think the relations we seek to mark" (Butler 1993, 167). One way to begin such an analysis is to suggest that within a kinship system predicated on maintaining "racial purity" for one group and instigating racial "im-

10. Though the efforts of such entrepreneurs in the whitening business would seem to fold into a mestizo project, the discourse of *blanquemiento* (also spelled *blanqueamiento*) posits a teleology toward white, rather than valuing a mixed, hybrid product. *Blanco* also means "target" in Spanish.

provement" in another, gender will be a constitutive category, even as it is differentially deployed.

White Women

In the system described by Casaus Arzú, white-ladina women's bodies are the site for maintaining difference. As one of Casaus Arzú's ladina informants said, "I would never allow my daughter to marry an indigenous man. Not because I don't like them, but because they are an inferior race and our obligation is to improve the race, not to make it worse" (Casaus Arzú 1992, 245).[11] Verena Stolcke describes a similar situation in slave society Cuba in which "male control of women's sexuality and the latter's consequent subordination was the result of the central role they played in reproducing family pre-eminence based so importantly on racial purity" (Martínez-Alier [Stolcke] 1989, xv).

The violence of the restricted economy of education, property ownership, and citizenship rights (all forms of state access to the life of the body and of the species), as well as multiple forms of domestic violence, are regulatory mechanisms that produce white women as subjects. *Marianismo,* as it has been analyzed by Tracy Ehlers in Guatemala (1990; see also J. Collier 1986), is another disciplinary technology that constitutes this "white woman" whose "ample capacity for reproduction ensured the survival of oligarchic families," according to Casaus Arzú (1992, 72). Another vital component in articulating ladina women's desires to the project of maintaining *sangre azul* ("blue" or pure blood) is the *principe azul* (fairy-tale prince), the intense and voluptuous romanticization of heterosexual love that saturates

---

11. The power of this model has recently been expressed in reactions to the marriage of the gringa Jennifer Harbury to the Mayan guerrilla commander Efraín Bámaca (see also A. Adams 1997). In addition to the severe political disruption that Ms. Harbury has engendered through her insistence on knowing the fate of her disappeared husband (unveiling the CIA money that supports the Guatemalan military responsible for his assassination), her sexual liaison with an Indian man has occasioned expressions of horror and repugnance in the Guatemalan press. José Eduardo Zarco, the editor of the nation's largest circulation daily, insisted that Ms. Harbury must be insane, insofar as "after graduating from one of the most expensive universities in the world[,] . . . eating caviar and hobnobbing with the rich and famous[,] . . . she would marry a third-world illiterate terrorist!" (*Prensa Libre,* 26 November 1994). (I thank Paul Kobrak for keeping me up to date on the rants.)

It is beyond the scope of this chapter to explore the contradictions in Guatemalan responses to the national allegory of the Harbury-Everado "romance," but anxiety surrounding the heterosexual matrix and international hierarchy also breaks through in the odd addenda Zarco added to this editorial in the form of a joke. "Given the choice of the Pope and Bill Clinton," he asks, "why does President Ramiro de León Carpio prefer that the Pope come to Guatemala? Because he would only have to kiss the Pope's hand."

their coming of reproductive age (as in the *telenovela*, pop songs, teen magazines, the parade of prepubescent boy stars, and the beauty and romance of the *quinceañeras* [coming-out parties]).[12] The point is not to suggest that women who buy into these fantasies are dupes but instead to gesture toward the complicated pleasures and imaginary work entailed in any identification. Casaus Arzú erases this process when she folds gender identity unproblematically into class position, but it is difficult and sometimes violent, what Judith Butler calls "the Girling of the Girl."[13]

Heterosexuality and its normativization through legal kinship constraints also figures in the differential deployment of race and gender. Non-reproductive individuals are accepted among the elite only if ensconced in the church, and the history of gays and lesbians in Guatemala remains an abjected, unwritten domain.[14] White-ladina women's sexuality will be force-

12. See also Maynard (1974). Rob Latham (personal communication) reminds me that the process of articulating subjects to the male-female dyad in the service of an historical eugenics project doesn't always reproduce heterosexual gender roles. For example, identifications with boy pop stars may have multiple gender effects. There are many sites of disarticulation in the production and interpellation of gender roles, and in turn race and other identities are mapped onto these in many different ways.

13. Butler is playing with the Heideggerian (1977) notion of the worlding of the world. By making the noun *girl* into a verb, Butler emphasizes the process by which a body is engendered, by which it is invested with history and given properties. A girl is never always already existing; she has to be made. Casaus Arzú suggests (but does not follow through with) the violence and alienation of this process of girling a white girl in her short reference to the conquistador Pedro de Alvarado, who boasted that he had received a shipment of Spanish women, "merchandise that will not sit for long in my store!" (Casaus Arzú 1992, 40).

14. Roger Lancaster (1992) offers a sensitive and insightful understanding for Nicaragua (and flags the issues at stake in enveloping a range of practices and meanings with the English term *gay*). Queer-safe spaces are developing in Guatemala, although class and ethnic privilege have always allowed some people more safety than others. Through enormous courage and dedication, gay men and lesbians (terms they use) are politicizing the identity, in part as a reaction to the AIDS emergency. For example, Guatemala's delegate to the international celebration of Stonewall 25 has been offering counseling on sexual identity in Guatemala City and elsewhere, including working with Maya-Tz'utujil in Solola.

One of the hostile markings of barbaric difference the Spanish conquerors deployed against the "natives" was sodomite. A strange analogy with the conquerors' hunger for gold seems expressed in the joke: "When the *conquistadores* came to Guatemala, all they wanted was gold, gold, gold. So they yelled and beat the Indians to make them bring gold, but the Indians didn't understand what it was. So they told them it was a yellow substance and sent them out to get some. Well, the Indians lined up with all the yellow stuff they could find, thinking it was gold. The first in line had a banana, but when he handed it over, the *conquistador* screamed, 'That's not gold you *indio bruto, estupido*! That's a banana. Stick it up your ass!' They sent the Indian away. The next in line had a mango, and the *conquistador* screamed at him, 'That's not gold! Stick it up your ass!' Then the Indian started laughing, and the Spaniard asked why. 'Because the next one has a pineapple,' he said."

fully channeled through reproduction sanctioned by state and church.[15] The elite family, with the wife and mother at the center, reproducing for the line, the class, and the nation, constitutes unequal gender roles and is in turn constituted by racial and gender inequalities. As Stolcke says, "Doctrines of biologically grounded inequality have served to consolidate the notion of the genetic family construed as the basic, natural and hence universal cell of society providing for the reproduction of socio-cum-racial preeminence" (Stolcke 1993, 35).

As the ladina woman's body becomes the site for this reproduction, it also forms the ground for ladino male fantasies of it as an object of desire and thus endangerment by Indian men.[16] Heated imaginings of the rape of white women have been important components of ladino calls to arms against supposed Indian uprisings, as in the case of Patzicia in the 1940s (R. Adams 1992) and more recent counterinsurgency. As with the horrifying history of "strange fruit" in the United States—state-supported lynchings of African American men because of their supposed desire for white women—the repetition and vehemence of these fantasies, joined with extremely limited evidence of their occurrence, is only explicable if we pay attention to white women's vital role in supporting the fantasmatic ladino body politic. As I suggested about the productive ways ladinos use jokes, white identity and solidarity cannot be assumed. It is an identity in pieces, a "self that is not one," dependent on historic processes of violence and fantasy, on gender, race, sexuality, and kinship configurations to materialize it, to make it matter. In the case of paranoia over Indian revolts, fantasies of the white female body splattered are instrumental in, at least provisionally, constituting this ladino identity.[17]

In Guatemala, the norms that supposedly regulate access to white women's bodies are deployed in many ways to race, class, and gender bod-

---

15. Though I cannot adequately explore this here, indigenous women's sexuality is also channeled into reproduction, although through different sanctions. The vitality of this demand is highlighted by the ambivalence surrounding an anomaly like Rigoberta Menchú, who was not reproductive in the Quincentennial years, and by the pressures Mayan men put on Mayan women explored in chapter 4. See also Ehlers's (1990) work on the way community organization of production supports women's desires for children.

16. In an interview, a progressive development professional criticized Dr. Demetrio Cojtí in a way that quilts these anxieties about ethnicity and sexuality. He explained that Dr. Cojtí had such a critical attitude toward Guatemalan ethnic relations—an attitude, he said, that verged on the racist—because when Cojtí was studying in Belgium he had been very lucky with the ladies there. It was because he was Maya—all the allure of his being so exotic. But of course, when he returned to Guatemala, he didn't get the same sort of attention, so he became bitter and jealous.

17. My argument dovetails in many aspects with Ann Stoler's rich analysis of the way sexuality maintained the internal cohesion of elites in colonial Asia (Stoler 1991, 69).

Figure 17. Debutante and father, Guatemala Club, Guatemala City. "'From what I have seen of the ruling class in Guatemala, they are people without very much in the way of redeeming features. . . . All they can talk about is how much it costs them to have a guard for their daughter, their sister.' Representative Clarence Long (D-Maryland) New York City, 1983" (Simon 1987, 67). Copyright 1998 Jean-Marie Simon. Published with kind permission.

ies. For example, a ladino man told me that he hated the indigenous Congressman Diego Velasco Brito because he drove a nice car, but mainly because he dated ladina women. On another occasion, a ladino government official echoed this opinion and seemed quite vexed that Congressman Brito had dated a ladina from a town where the women were reputed to be particularly beautiful. A ladino justice of the peace used the same argument to criticize Mayan leaders: "They are out of touch with their communities, they have abandoned their traditions, and worst of all, they are fascinated with white women."

Such boundary transgressions—at least in the fantasies of a powerful ladino man about indigenous men desiring white women—are laced with power and danger. And it is through such intersections of power and desire that bodies come to matter, that they are raced, gendered, and sexualized. In this process, the sexual desire of ladinoized male bodies may be directed toward any feminized body that may produce a white(r) offspring—namely, *all* women, within the logic of *blanquemiento*. Correspondingly, this ladino male desire and aggression may be directed at Indianized, (de)masculinized bodies whose sexuality is therefore limited.[18] Benigno Sánchez-Eppler makes a similar case around *blanquemiento* theory in nineteenth-century Cuba:

> All that has to happen to maximize whiteness is to inhibit any woman's potential to engender children darker than herself. This kind of reasoning, together with everything else that made it repugnant in the eyes of a slaveholding society for black males to engage in sexual coupling with white women—or with any woman capable of birthing a whitened child—forms the basis for what could be seen as the ideological inhibition of the black man's capacity to reproduce. Even if individual black men were not, in fact, castrated, even if slave marriage was practiced . . . nevertheless the doctrine of *blanqueamiento* depended primarily on the assertion of white male privilege and corresponding castration of blackness. (Sánchez-Eppler 1994, 80–81)

The joke that goes "Why is Rigoberta Menchú divorcing her husband? Because he is *poco*-man" links the indigenous Pocomam community with "little-man," or not being manly enough, and is similarly emasculating.

Another joke I heard many times in Guatemala envisions the "best-case scenario" for whitening: the case in which indigenous men have no access to any women. "A tourist went into an Indian town in the highlands and was hanging around when he noticed that there were no women. So he asked a passerby, 'What do you do here since there aren't any women? How do you make a couple?' And the native said, 'Well, we don't have any women so we make do with animals.' 'Oh!' said the tourist, 'I see!' The next day the Indian guy saw that the tourist was in the jail. He asked what had happened, and the tourist said, 'Well, when you said that you went to animals here, I went out and met a nice cow—I just didn't know she was the mayor's beloved!'" The "positively hostile and cruel" nature of this joke, the barely

18. Frantz Fanon (1967) and Albert Memmi (1965) eloquently address the demasculinization of the colonized male. In a similar vein, Octavio Paz (1961) reads the Malinche-Malintzin story as emphasizing the sexual violence of congress and conflating the rape of indigenous women with the emasculation of colonized males, expressed in part through the panic surrounding legitimacy, as Norma Alarcón argues (1989, 82). Florencia Mallon, citing Jeffrey Gould, suggests that in Nicaraguan indigenous communities "female sexuality was a principal site of anxiety and contention; for Indian men, too, saw *mestizaje* as the *ladino*/Spanish appropriation of Indian women's sexuality, and thus the breakdown of the system of indigenous patriarchy. . . . Masculinity was the political stock-in-trade among indigenous leaders fighting to claim authenticity for their faction" (Mallon 1996, 175–176).

concealed aggression, suggests ambivalence, an insecurity underlying the desire vectors of ladino men—who *is* the "*poco* or little-man"?

In turn, the limits on the sexuality of ladinoized feminized bodies produce certain pleasures for certain men. Doris Sommer suggests that white men are "seduced as much by the absolute power of their racial and sexual advantage as by their partner's sexual charms," steeped as they are in "a bastion of colonial custom where erotic protectionism nurtures desires in surplus of social needs" (Sommer 1991, 128). Again, these limits and desires, these pleasures and erotics, act as regulatory norms and are produced at the intersection of power differentials. These norms are what construct different bodies—construct not in the sense of making them artificial or dispensable, but in the sense of making them thinkable at all.

The discourse of Guatemalan elites explored in Casaus Arzú's book (and in much of the analysis of *mestizaje*) erases these constituting processes and situates the white female body or the Indian masculine body as singularly signifying, solid identities. Similarly, in my supposedly clean ethnographic encounter with the torture survivor, I thought his body meant one thing only—a solid testimony to the political abuse of power. But bodies are always overdetermined by legal norms of reproduction, violence, racial grammars, and male (and female) fantasies. Rather than assuming a unitary identity based on a body's phenotypic markings, a fluidary analysis needs to pay close attention to the materialization of those bodies.

Indigenous Women

Though ladina women are positioned to give proof of racial purity, in Guatemala the ideas of "whitening" and "racial improvement" situate indigenous women, legal kinship, and sexuality very differently. Under the terms of this racialist fantasy, indigenous women are to be impregnated by but never legally married to whiter men.[19] Thus Casaus Arzú reports that whites would allow their sons to have a sexual relationship with an Indian woman only if it were extramarital. They would never allow their daughters to have such a relationship. According to Casaus Arzú, "A fact admitted by the entire community . . . is the right of sexual access and the fact of rape

19. Though more a fascination in Mexico than Guatemala, the historico-symbolic position of La Malinche–Malintzin–Doña Marina as the indigenous mistress and thus as *La Chingada* (the fucked one) overdetermines this regulatory kinship category (Paz 1961). The relations among Malinche, the Virgen de Guadalupe, and La Llorona have been fruitfully explored by many in the context of Mexican nationalism and Chicana(o) identity. The semiotics of these mythic females are surely imbricated in Guatemalan imaginings of identity, but I'm not sure that they function in the same way. See Limón (1986), Anzaldúa (1987), Cypess (1991), and Alarcón (1989).

that plantation owners exercise over the indigenous women on their *fincas* [holdings]" (Casaus Arzú 1992, 242). A similar situation constrained the lives of women of color in Stolcke's study of Cuba: "Colored women were the prey of white men in non-legitimated sexual liaisons" (Martínez-Alier [Stolcke] 1989, xv). Stolcke suggests, however, that the women were often willing, because they hoped for material support and to improve their children's life chances through whitening—a sexual calculus that Ehlers (1990) also suggests may inform some women's choices in Guatemala. Although the girling of an indigenous girl is overdetermined by such constraints, and by the constant threat of sexual violence and rape, there are both symbolic and material supports for her interpellation into the position of white-man's mistress.

Thus, in Guatemala's ideal race-and-gender matrix, mestizos would only be born of indigenous women and out of wedlock. As Casaus Arzú mentions, as early as 1549 in Guatemala, *mestizo* and *illegitimate* were synonymous terms (1992, 40). Differently raced women produce different offspring, even when inseminated by the same man, an imbrication of race, gender, kinship, and state-regulated legitimacy codes that splatters any simple reading of those bodies or of the practices of sexuality. Ann Stoler emphasizes the ambiguity of physical, somatic properties produced by such splattered categories: "Social and legal standing derived from the cultural prism through which color was viewed, from the silences, acknowledgements, and denials of the social circumstances in which one's parents had sex" (Stoler 1991, 53). The Guatemalan historian Severo Martínez Peláez describes this perfectly in his *Patria del Criollo*: "The Spaniard—as well as the hispanic creole—carried out very different acts when he copulated with a Spanish woman and when he copulated with an Indian one" (1990, 355), a point that Carol Smith carefully analyzes (1995).

This suggests that gender is raced and race is gendered in particular ways in Guatemala. Bodies matter and are called upon to mark racial and other differences, but these categories of difference splatter with the contradictions I have been outlining. The ideological attempt to maintain these categories leans on a supposedly always already raced mother's body. This "race" is in turn supported by what Stolcke argues was the pre-Conquest Spanish notion of purity of blood: "A child's substance was provided by the mother's blood. Hence, purity of blood meant descent from Christian women" (Stolcke 1993, 32). And, hence, mestizo and "impure blood" mean descent from an indigenous woman. Raced identities thus are constituted through gendered differences that are themselves overdetermined by racialized regulatory norms governing sexuality. Judith Butler foregrounds these imbrications of race and gender in "the assumption of sexual positions, the disjunctive ordering of the human as 'masculine' or 'feminine' as taking place not only through a heterosexualizing symbolic with its taboo

Figure 18. *"Niña Cak'chiquel-Maya bañandose en las aguas cristalinas de lago Atitlán, Sololá, Guatemala"* (Kaqchikel-Maya girl bathing in the crystal waters of Lake Atitlán). Postcard. Copyright Thor Janson.

on homosexuality, but through a complex set of racial injunctions which operate in part through the taboo on miscegenation" (Butler 1993, 167).

As we have seen in Guatemala, the taboo on miscegenation applies differently to differently raced and gendered bodies. How, then, are we to understand the apparent shattering of that taboo, the urge to *mesticization?* *Mestizaje* emerges from a double bind of prohibition and incitement. The racist discourse that depicts Indians as ugly or smelling bad (one of the essentializing and hostile bodily markers differentiating Indians in ladino discourse), conjoined with the contradictory demand to "whiten" (extramaritally, of course) "the race"—powerfully influence both the racing and gendering of ladino men and indigenous women.[20] The race that is to be "whitened" are the Indians, who become strangely isomorphic with the nation, as this demand to whiten is braided into discourses of national progress. In turn, the demand may carry both a reassurance and an anxiety for the ladino men it leans on. The reassurance is that they are white enough themselves to "improve" the Indians; the anxiety, of course, is that they are never white enough.

In several of my interviews, ladino men told me that indigenous women are very sexually aggressive and that they want to sleep with white men in particular.[21] The justice of the peace mentioned earlier—a ladino who claims African ancestry but vehemently denies having even a drop of Indian blood—complained that Indian women are only interested in blond, fair-skinned men. "I took an American friend to Coban the other day, and the Indian women there were all over him. They would come up to him on the street and start flirting, but not one of them even looked at me!"

One friend of mine said that every ladino man he knows will insist that he has slept with an indigenous woman, and every one of them claims that the woman initiated it. "To be a man," he said, "they have to have had sex with an *india,* but they could never admit that they desired it. That would undermine their racism."[22] Many ladino men said that they had heard, and

20. As Butler suggests, "The enumeration of prohibited practices not only brings such practices into a public, discursive domain, but it thereby produces them as potential erotic enterprises" (Butler, 1993, 110).

21. José Limón (1985) cites Américo Paredes to link versions of the La Llorona story with this fatally seductive indigenous woman. The Siguanaba is a similar figure in Guatemala, an incredibly beautiful woman appearing to men when they are alone. In the stories, she inflames them with passion so intense that they pursue her, often over cliffs, or just as they reach her she turns, revealing a horse's head rather than a woman's face, sometimes killing them of fright. However, the stories I heard in Guatemala, both secondhand and from eyewitnesses, did not identify the Siguanaba as indigenous, a vital component of the La Llorona story.

22. In a case I discuss later, sexual relations between a ladino man and an indigenous woman were justified as the gentleman's empirical research into the nature-versus-nurture debate.

friends of theirs had suggested, that other men harbored a sexual fascination for indigenous women in traditional dress. This led, they said, to a booming trade for prostitutes who dressed that way. As my friend said, "But it has to be the really, real thing. The full *traje,* and the women have to look Indian." This does not mean that most prostitutes are indigenous. The emphasis on the "really real" here—on a cultural marker like clothing and the Indian "look"—suggests the slippage of identity and the crucial intervention of fantasy.[23] The boying of the ladino boy is itself incited through race, gender, and kinship regulations that offer different licit and illicit desires and pleasures—which in turn give rise to *mestizaje.*

Of course, the process of the boying of the ladino boy in Guatemala is also marked by anxiety. Indigenous women are reported to fiercely desire whiter men, but ladino boys are simultaneously afraid they are not white enough. The intervention of the more desirable "American friend" in Coban suggests a mapping of this anxiety onto the nation: the catastrophe of Guatemala's status in the global family romance is reinscribed by race and sexual desire as the whiter first worlder is preferred to the browner third worlder. These insecurities were reiterated in a satirical newspaper editorial on the 1992 Columbus Quincentennial. The author asked, "What if the English had discovered us?" The country would be much better off, he suggests, being named Guate-good rather than Guate-*mala* (Spanish for bad) and in part this would be because "the little Indian girls would have been so turned on by seeing those guys with the white faces that they would have begged to be fucked and from there would have been born a new race"

23. Foregrounding the ways identity is based in practice, Carol Smith suggests that no indigenous woman is a prostitute, because prostitution is by definition a "ladina" thing to do. She says that women who are *desenvuelta,* who take off their *traje* in exchange for western dress, thus signaling their sexual availability to nonindigenous men, are automatically recategorized as "whores" (Smith 1995). In her testimonial, Rigoberta Menchú says, "Anyone who doesn't dress as our grandfathers, our ancestors, dressed, is on the road to ruin" (Menchú 1984, 37).

Martínez Peláez cites as the "most ridiculous and pornographic genre of novel the countless fantasies in which 'the indigenous woman, trembling and curious, opened herself to the bearded semi-gods, overcome by the seduction of the victors, etc. etc.' (Such fantasies suit the tastes of many authors and readers with the most disgusting *criollo* mentality, of course)" (1990, 261). He expresses shock at how often he encounters such "paradisical fantasies" in books of history—where they have no place!

Anne McClintock (1995), Ann Stoler (1995), Cynthia Enloe (1990), Charles Bernheimer (1989), Nancy Leys Stepan (1991), and many others have mapped the way relations among paid sex work, marriage, and other forms of sexual intercourse are productive of colonial, gender, race, and class identifications. Many of my ladino male friends were taken, trembling and curious, by a male relative to a sex worker when they were young teenagers. These relations both transgress (in the pleasurable ways suggested by Douglas and Kipnis) and form boundaries between class, respectability, and hygiene (several told me the "Madame" squirted lemon juice on their private parts before they left, to cleanse them of any dirt or disease).

(*Prensa Libre,* 13 October 1992). The insecurities of masculinity embedded in this national allegory may be why sexual aggression is projected onto indigenous people: both the threat of Indian male desire for white women, and the fantasy of Indian female desire for white men.[24]

This projection of desire and aggression onto indigenous women allows ladino men to rape them and allows that rape to be described as desired by the woman: either because of her lust, or for material gain as a sex worker (and rape is also naturalized through the metaphor of the Maya as wife, therefore legally sexually available, in the national family). The particular way that a particular body is splattered in sexual violence is thereby erased to write a cleaner narrative of the "obvious" superiority and desirability of the ladino male. Of course, *mestizaje* is not only produced through rape and material violence, but neither is it always the product of love. Indigenous women are girled through contradictory norms and processes that sometimes lead them to love ladino men, but that also terrify them through reminders that there is a special place in the Mayan hell for indigenous women who sleep with ladinos.[25]

A grammar of respectability also links race, class, and the girling of different girls. Just as male and female ladino identification as bourgeois leans on the domestic labor of the *mujer maya,* so too stereotypes of her as sexually aggressive serve to discipline and *formar* the white woman. She is strongly encouraged to maintain her status as *gente decente* (decent people) by differentiating herself from the Indian woman (and from the stereotyped promiscuous gringa). This is the project Stoler describes as "the cultivation of the bourgeois self. It is through the technologies of sexuality that the bourgeoisie will claim its hegemony, its privileged position, its certified knowledge and jurisdiction over the manner of living, over the governing of children, over the civilities, conduct and competencies that prescribe 'how to live'" (1995, 83). The Mayan hell and the painful shunning practices that greet indigenous women who choose ladino partners suggest that Mayan communities also closely police "respectability" through technologies of sexuality that include differentiating Mayan and white women. In turn, Mayan women structure relations between Mayan and ladino men, as Florencia Mallon suggests, through a "gendered 'script' of *mestizaje:* . . . the

24. This is reminiscent of the colonial discourse of the cannibal. The fears of and fascination with being eaten that filled the colonial fantasy space are effective in producing the colonizer as tasty and delicious, the object of the colonizeds' desire.

25. I owe my knowledge of this special hell to Kay Warren, who described it in her discussion at the AAA 1994 panel "Fleshing Out the Bodies Politic: Re-Articulating and Engendering Ethnic, National, and Historic Identities in Contemporary Guatemala," where a preliminary version of this chapter was presented.

'sexual triangle' pits white or Spanish men in competition and struggle with Indian men over the sexual control or seduction of Indian women" (1996, 175).[26] In the blood analytics of *blanquemiento* and Mayan identity politics, the *mujer maya* is the universal donor.

All of these forces come into play as conditions of possibility for *mestizaje.* In the cultural logic set out here, a mestizo is a subject produced from a particular kind of relation—an illegitimate union between a ladino man and an indigenous woman—and the body of this mestizo could only materialize through the cultural symbolics encoded in those power differentials. Like the body of a torture victim, the "physical" features of the mestizo body don't stand alone but can only be read through this complex social regulation.

DISCOURSES OF THE MESTIZO

I have been arguing that attempts to delineate "racial" categories that lean on supposedly clearly visible embodied differences tend to fail. Because the body that is meant to anchor these differences between Indian and ladino is produced through contradictory and historically changing regulatory norms, it cannot exist outside those norms as their guarantee.

Too, just as gender is erased in Casaus Arzú's discussion of the discourses of racial differences, historic changes in the meaning of those categories and the norms that regulate them go unremarked. Bodies matter, but what they mean changes over time and as the result of political struggle. Before turning to Casaus Arzú's discourse of *mestizaje,* I want to relate a story that foregrounds the inherent and historic instability of categories like "white," "ladino," "Indian," and "mestizo" and the complicated ways these categories rely on gendered identities.

These matters inform a rumor that was recounted to me numerous times during my fieldwork. Because I was unable to meet the gentleman or the young lady in question, I will leave them anonymous, but almost everyone I interviewed had heard of this incident. The story goes that an important member of the government in the time of President Arévalo (early 1950s), who was also an anthropologist and well-known writer, decided to under-

26. Carol Smith proposes that "the next major identity movement in Latin America will almost certainly be some sort of feminist movement" (1996, 162), in part because both white and Indian women are in structurally similar positions: "The woman who makes sexual choices is dangerous to the system and the politics based upon it" (1996, 158). As a solidarity feminist, I find this prospect quite enticing (and I hope these analyses can in some small way support it). But as a fluidary feminist, I wonder if we might be hoping that race and class are as easy to take off as *traje*—underneath all women are the same and so can unite in a political project of liberation.

take an experiment regarding Indian blood.[27] At that time there was a lot of discussion about what the Indians "really" were and what should be done with them. For his experiment, he would have a child by an indigenous woman, but he would raise it as a ladino, sending it to all the best schools— even to Europe if need be—and see how it turned out. According to one version of the story, he said, "I am Guatemalan, but I have European blood, and I want to see the fruit of a union between the Indian and the European. Would it be as smart as a white or would it give proof of the backwardness of the Indian?" So he went to Lake Atitlán and found a pretty indigenous woman and made up a contract with her that apparently exchanged money for sexual favors and exclusive rights to any child she might have.[28] When the child, a girl, was born, he brought her to the capital and incorporated her into his "legitimate" family. When I asked about the wife's response, I was told that he was a famous *mujerriego* (ladies' man) and had had several wives. Apparently this one was willing to put up with an extra child in the house.[29] The girl grew up, got her French education, and is now an artist. According to friends who know her, she is competent at what she does, but no genius, and moves comfortably in the upper-middle-class ladino circles of the capital city. For all intents and purposes, they say, she is a ladina. I first heard this story, however, when a Guatemalan anthropologist told me excitedly that the man in question "finally admits he has an Indian daughter! Everyone knew, but he finally said it in public!" Apparently, at a forum on Mayan writers, the man had said he used to be embarrassed, but now he was proud that he had an "*hija india* [Indian daughter]."

The confession in 1993 that this white man had an indigenous daughter suggests the historic impact of the Quincentennial and the Mayan movement, which has made an Indian body signify differently. In 1993, he finally can be publicly proud of something that he kept secret for so long. The confession also points to the power of a particular "conception" of procreation, part of the "social regulation of sexuality." Rather than procreation understood as the active male seed and passive female soil that Carol Delaney (1991) has analyzed, a ladino man with an *hija india* suggests the continuing power of the Spanish purity-of-blood paradigm: the blood is passed

27. The gentleman in the government was also an early advocate of the National Indigenist Institute.

28. The various stories differed on the existence of this contract.

29. Casaus Arzú mentions other cases of this sort from the beginning of the Colony, in which the children of Spanish men and Indian women were accepted into the fathers' homes, and the wives, to cover their shame, accepted the children. Papal bulls could be dispensed to give these children their father's name, and here it is interesting how the "Name of the Father" is necessary to contradict the blood of the Indian mother. Casaus Arzú cites this as proof that "*mestizaje* has been a constant and common practice among the oligarchs" (1992, 240).

through the mother, and an Indian mother reproduces an *hija india*. However, Delaney's notion of the power of the seed also informs this rumored exchange of flesh in that the daughter belonged to the father, to be taken and raised by him. Her integration into white society suggests the power of "whitening": her father's seed, his "European blood," apparently saved her from "the backwardness of the Indian." The deeply contradictory significations carried by this daughter's body highlight the complexity of Guatemala's historic race-gender-class-sexuality matrix and would seem to undermine any attempts to rely on timeless, embodied racial difference.

Thus, the "racial" difference version of ladino discourse on Indians ("You can always tell") lacks a stable body in which to ground itself. Its physical properties, like hieroglyphs, are ambiguous. Its apparent opposite, *mestizaje,* is deployed as a progressive discourse against the oligarchic racializing of the indigenous body and relies instead on an undifferentiable body. Proponents of *mestizaje* argue that all bodies are the same; thus there had to be a "confession" of Indian identity because that identity was not apparent from the daughter's body. Similarly, Casaus Arzú says, "The self descriptions of the whites and ladinos interviewed do not correspond to the objective reality, given . . . the intrinsic difficulty of considering oneself white in societies that have suffered the process of *mestizaje.* Based on physical features, their genealogical charts, and historic anecdotes, not one of them could call themselves white" (1992, 212).

Casaus Arzú is clearly appalled at the racist discourses of the oligarchic families she interviewed—discourses that have had deadly effects in the counterinsurgency war of the early 1980s. Thus, in addition to the "objective reality" she finds based on physical features and genealogical charts, she is making a political argument both against the racialist differentiation that undergirds Guatemala's unjust class system and for the strengthening of something like a modern national identity. In language similar to the Mayan nationalist movement's, she describes the ladinos who so vehemently reject indigenous blood as lacking an identity of their own, as being defined only through negativity. "These oligarchs try to escape their own country. They desperately seek their roots elsewhere, outside their community of origin, in a heedless flight into emptiness, as they try to differentiate and separate themselves from anything that relates to the Indian" (1992, 214).[30]

Casaus Arzú would agree with Carol Smith (1990b) that these characteristics of the ladino—as ethnocentric, elitist, externally oriented, and racist—work against a unifying national identity. In contrast, she finds that among those who call themselves "mestizo" "their identity seems more con-

---

30. Casaus Arzú also quotes Guzmán Böckler's (1975) work on the emptiness of ladino identity, which he calls *ningunidad* (nobody-ness).

solidated and their consciousness of being mestizo is fully assumed" (Casaus Arzú 1992, 216). The mestizos in her study would even accept their daughter marrying an indigenous man, saying that it was a question of her own free will. The families she dubs "modernizers," the Castillos and the Loves, are those whose "marriages are about improving their economic networks more than about blood purity. . . . They have a more pragmatic view of society" (1992, 188).[31] Thus, in addition to seeing mestizo identity as bodily "true," she differentiates that identity from the negative aspects of ladino identity. "I have found the oligarchy to be mestizo in origin, [but] ladino and ethnocentric in their conceptions of the world" (1992, 21). For her, the mestizo is a socioracial product in which Indian blood is mixed with other ethnic groups. Thus, it is a category of "biological origin" that she suggests includes most Guatemalans, although "*socially* it fits between the Indian and the ladino" (1992, 216; emphasis added).

This mestizo pragmatism resonates with modernization narratives and the revolutionary claim that the "real" divide in Guatemala is between classes. Ancient race prejudice weighs on the minds of the living but can be shucked off in favor of more "modern" sensibilities. In this sense, Casaus Arzú's categories of "ladino" and "mestizo" take on a temporal bias. The ladino is an older, less efficient mode of being in the world, caught up in an outmoded "symbolics of blood." The mestizo appears more modern, flexible on personal choice (the daughter can marry an Indian if she really wants to), adept at maximizing economic networks, and rational regarding romantic entanglements, more in the mode of an "analytics of sexuality." Of course, Foucault, from whom I draw these categories, sees them as superimposed. "Sexuality" does not displace the "blood" in a progress narrative of history—instead, body discipline works with mass regulation, the deployment of alliance works with that of sexuality, and the symbolics of blood work with the analytics of sexuality.

Casaus Arzú advocates the embodied "truth" of *mestizaje,* which is not to be confused with strategies of ladinoization or assimilation, which she harshly critiques. She sternly takes to task those Marxists who view indigenous cosmology and traditions as petit bourgeois and thus push for full proletarianization. She sees this attitude stemming from racist and classist prejudices (1992, 229).[32] She also criticizes the government's "integration" strategies as "counterinsurgency," linking them to U.S. imperialism through

---

31. This pragmatism includes listing indigenous forebears in their genealogical charts, as opposed to some families (like the Duráns) who left blank spaces where a woman of probable indigenous background produced legitimated offspring—who in turn carried only one last name, (e)racing the maternal line (120).

32. Héctor Díaz-Polanco (1987) makes a similar critique from within a Marxist framework.

AID funding and the theories of "Adamcismo" (1992, 285) (from the "ladino continuum" theory of Richard Adams).[33] However, she also seems suspicious of the indigenous rights movements. In her rather cryptic conclusion, she warns that the future may bring "powerful socio-political explosions through nationalist social movements linked to international powers and with strong fanatical and fundamentalist characteristics that would revitalize the ethnic-national problem and reinforce authoritarian racist movements like in Europe. . . . The most lucid members of Guatemalan society must be aware of the need to deal with this problem" (1992, 305). Embracing an undifferentiated mestizo body seems to be the solution she offers, a third term between (and beyond) "ladino" and "Indian," whose radical differences have so divided the country.

Casaus Arzú draws on a physical "truth" of *mestizaje:* that it is hard to tell the difference. Contradicting the many ladinos who say that they can "always tell" an Indian by their phenotypic characteristics, everyday ladino practice suggests the terror of not being able to tell. One young ladino man (to my eyes, quite light-skinned) told me that his mother instructed him to never sit next to an indigenous woman on the bus because she might be taken for his mother, and thus he would be misrecognized as Indian. The nonobviousness of these purportedly "racial" differences means that many ladinos rely on "cultural" markers to identify Indians—markers such as clothing, language, relations to technology, and occupation. In terms of occupation, indigenous people are again relegated to the body, because Indians are supposedly best suited for physical labor. The Maya are not supposed to have access to technology without becoming ladino, a stereotype I explore in the next chapter. Ladinos in turn avoid manual work when at all possible, especially on the land, because they are "afraid to be taken for an Indian" (Casaus Arzú 1992, 263).

Such everyday practices regarding the mestizo body also inform the political discourses of *mestizaje* in Quincentennial Guatemala, which are linked to calls for national unity. When I asked a Christian-Democrat congressman about the future of Guatemala, he replied, "We must get ready for the future. This means accepting that we are all mestizos. We are part ladino and part Indian. There are no Maya, they were tribes of long ago. Guatemala is a mestizo nation." Similarly, Mario Sandoval, an editor at *Prensa Libre* (Guatemala's largest circulation daily) and press secretary for former President

---

33. Probably unfairly, and primarily because of a mid-1970s denunciatory book edited by Humberto Flores Alvarado, Richard Adams has been forever identified in Guatemala with his early work on the ladino continuum, which is understood to advocate assimilation. "*Adamcismo*" has become something of a catchall phrase for imperialist intellectual intervention. Charles Hale (1996) addresses this polemic.

Ramiro de León Carpio, wrote regarding the Quincentennial: "The national question must be analyzed by those who, because they represent the racial and cultural mix between ladinos and Indians, have a foot in each of Guatemala's racial worlds and through this privileged position can become true leaders for the future. . . . We need to create the Guatemalan ethnicity" (4 November 1992). Mario R. Morales outlined this hybrid becoming-Guatemalan ethnicity in public talks and a Quincentennial-year-long series of articles in *Prensa Libre*. In poetic language informed by postmodern theory, the novelist and political activist describes a world of tamales made from the sacred corn of the Maya and cooked in microwave ovens, and pop songs sung in the language of the *Popul Vuh*, as an invitation to unity, "the need to recognize ourselves as one people, a necessary *mestizaje*" (*Prensa Libre*, 20 January 1993).[34]

A similar discursive move informs comments like that of Edmund Mulet, former president of the Congress and then ambassador to the United States, who said, "Guatemala is not racist. Not like in the United States. It is not racism based on race; instead it is discrimination on the basis of economic and social standing. It is Guatemala's disgrace that Indians tend to be poor." This sort of class reductionism, as Stolcke calls it, in which race conflicts are understood as ideological expressions of class struggle (Stolcke 1993, 29), has largely informed Marxist analyses of Guatemala's situation, as Carol Smith (1992) has pointed out.[35] It also informs a popular joke about the difficulty of distinguishing between ladino and Indian: "What is an Indian? A ladino with no money."

---

34. Mario Roberto Morales is an intriguing figure, an armed insurgent in the late 1970s and early 1980s and a well-known novelist, he lived for years in exile and returned to Guatemala in 1992. He says that he writes the *mestizaje* series as a way to get Guatemalans to imagine a different future:

> I'm trying to translate García Canclini's notion of hybridity into the context of Guatemala, to deal with the much larger issue of the mestizo. I would like to open up a debate on the issue, about where the nation is going, but no one is responding to me at all! It just shows how backward Guatemala is in terms of political culture. People who like it will tell me, and people who don't just talk behind my back. There is no dialogue, no public space in Guatemala.

(He is referencing Néstor García Canclini's 1989 work on hybrid cultures.) Despite this disappointment, I would argue that discourses of *mestizaje* are very much in circulation. Morales received an undesired response to his work a month after we spoke of this—a death threat (*Prensa Libre*, 16 April 1993). In the past few years, his columns have become increasingly mean-spirited and acerbic, projecting racism onto the Maya because they don't accept his version of mestizo unity. In response, the Mayan activist and columnist Estuardo Zapeta has engaged Morales in a furious and productive public debate through the newspapers and public forums, including the August 1997 Mayan Studies meetings.

35. For a forceful exposition of this sort of class reductionism, see Immanuel Wallerstein (1992).

The conviction that it's about class, not race, where race is seen as a brutal and antiquated ideological formation, offers a powerful unifying promise.[36] In fact, its almost magical power may explain the anger many progressives feel when Mayan cultural rights activists resist their invitation to class-based unity.[37] As I discuss in chapter 2, the Maya appear divisionary, blind to the links of poverty and *mestizaje* that unite the majority of Guatemalans, and all this just in the name of some esoteric "feathers and flourishes" cultural effluvia that is rapidly becoming extinct in any case (B. Williams 1989, 435). These arguments draw on Martínez Peláez (in C. Smith 1991) to suggest that Indians will be freed from their chains when they unite behind the battle fatigues of the guerrilla (or for neoliberal ladinos, behind a three-piece Armani business suit).

This "antiracist" denial of racial difference in support of class (and incipient national) unity is widespread in Guatemala and draws on deep-rooted lexicons of progress and modernization condensed in the hopes for *mestizaje*. These discourses are "not only righteous because they profess the common good; they are permeated with resurrected subjugated knowledges, disqualified accounts[,] . . . preserved possibilities" (Stoler 1995, 69)—possibilities of, for example, a unified *pueblo* purified of the vampiric elites and transnational baby snatchers. The idea that all Guatemalans are the same and mainly divided by class standing, and even that "racial" divisions are actually the effects of government counterinsurgency, was expressed by a leader of the labor federation Guatemalan Union of Labor Unions (UNSITRAGUA). "The confrontation between the Indian and the ladino is about other things. It is encouraged by the system, provoked. There are those who are opposed to our search for unity; they send in external agents. This is a conscious policy, there are both Indian and ladino provocateurs. There are no objective differences between the Indian and the ladino. We are all proletariat. We all need to eat." As the justice of the peace mentioned earlier (who as a student leader barely escaped the death squads of the late 1970s) put it, "These Indian intellectuals are all talking about cosmology and stuff, but if you ask people at the grassroots about their beliefs, this cosmology, even what *traje* means, they know nothing.

36. Part of the power of this promise resides in the fact that class, unlike race, is scientifically calculable—a question of poverty indices, life expectancies, infant mortality rates, and income differentials: in other words, statistics. Karl Marx, of course, understood quite well that these rational, pragmatic, scientific projects were thoroughly shot through with magic and irrationality (1977).

37. As discussed in chapter 2, the Sandinista experience with the Miskitu contra (see Hale 1994), particularly the CIA support for armed indigenous counterrevolutionaries, has caused many Guatemalan leftists to view Mayan nationalism with alarm. This might in part explain Casaus Arzú's warning about fanatical nationalist social movements with links to international powers.

They are all illiterate and their grandparents didn't tell them anything. What they care about is economics, how to survive!"[38] These analyses, of course, are true to some extent. The majority of Guatemala's population, ladino and Maya, are extremely poor, and hundreds of thousands of indigenous people have joined hundreds of thousands of ladinos in the revolutionary and in the popular struggles for land and labor rights, economic justice, and civil liberties.

Given Guatemala's extremely disadvantageous position in the world system and its history of external intervention (including the promised package of one billion dollars now that the peace agreement is signed), an analysis that highlights this antagonism in order to empower resistance is a good thing. The body image of the mestizo body politic is formed in relation to the image other bodies politic have of it, and Latin American nationalist discourses have traditionally deployed a notion of *mestizaje* in order to differentiate themselves as peoples of color against white aggressors, internal and external (Vasconcelos 1944; Knight 1990; Anzaldúa 1987; Klor de Alva 1995).

External aggression does not only take the form of military, political, and economic intervention. It also impacts the national body image with the hostile markings of aesthetico-scientific criteria. For example, the social Darwinist biopolitical economy developed in Europe and the United States in the late 1800s blamed Latin American backwardness on the degeneracy caused by mixed unions or "miscegenation" (a term invented in the United States in 1864) and by the tropical climate (Young 1995).[39] "As evidence that 'half-breeds' could not produce a high civilization, anthropologists pointed to Latin Americans who, they claimed, were now 'paying for their racial liberality.' . . . The 'promiscuous' crossings . . . had produced a degenerate, unstable people incapable of progressive development" (Stepan 1991, 45). The neo-Lamarckian eugenics developed in Latin America, partly in response to these racist dismissals, emphasized nurture rather than nature (because acquired traits could be passed on) and the importance of

38. I have to admit that this attitude informed my own introduction into Guatemala studies in 1985. The attention that earlier anthropologists had paid to calendrics, festivals, shamans, and mountain shrines, to the detriment of economic exploitation, land loss, forced labor on lowland plantations, and to the later indigenous consciousness-raising and revolutionary activity, to me smacked of a New Age romanticism and even a sort of complicity with centuries of violence. If any of that stuff was left, it would be fine to look at it after the extent of the genocide and counterinsurgency had been documented. Needless to say, I have learned a great deal from patient Mayan friends. The discourses of manipulation and duping also resonate with gringa responses to the baby snatching rumors and signal similar disavowals of the complexities of identifications.

39. Of course, this parallels the way ladinos blame indigenous people for national "backwardness."

state intervention. By improving living conditions (through sanitation, physical fitness, and antialcohol campaigns), the stock of the nation could in turn be improved and head toward that goal (*blanco*) of *mestizaje*. This neo-Lamarckianism is a "preserved possibility" that animates the righteousness of class struggle—which also refuses to view misery and poverty as genetically determined. Just as eugenicist notions are retained in the Ministry of Culture and Sports, progressive discourses of *mestizaje* that posit a collective antidote may (unconsciously) partake of this science of national progress.[40]

But nation building is deeply ambivalent. Its deployment against an external other mandates erasure of internal heterogeneity—at the same time that those internal differences are being produced. It is not already existing racial divisions that limit national unity, but instead injunctions and incitements around kinship and miscegenation norms that produce categories of race (and gender). Similarly, discourses of national unity arise simultaneous to the consolidation of capital, which produces antagonistic class relations. Verena Stolcke argues that the discourse of nation, with its attendant notions of equality among all citizens, inherently contradicts the inequality of capitalist relations of production. Thus, she argues, racial inequalities are naturalized as "an ideological subterfuge intended to reconcile the irreconcilable, namely a pervasive ethos of equality of opportunity of all human beings born equal and free with really existing socio-economic inequality" (Stolcke 1993, 19).[41] Thus, racism is an aspect of class exploitation, as Casaus Arzú's book powerfully argues.

However, race relations in Guatemala do not merely reflect the class structure. Cultural markings are not just "feathers and flourishes" blinding the Maya to the "bricks and mortar" of real power relations (B. Williams 1989). A discourse that links class struggle to the promise of a modern mestizo nation is not wrong, per se. But a fluidary analysis suggests that just as tradition is not modernity's opposite, class and national unities are not the opposites of race and "cultural" identifications. In turn, the race and class inequalities that Stolcke examines must be understood as constituted by the social regulation of gender and sexuality. Ignoring this runs the risk of falling victim to "an ideological subterfuge" blinding us to the centrality of gender in the production of race, class, and national identification in Guatemala. What do these overdetermined differences do to the body, especially the gendered body, when it is called on to mark "the same" in the proliferation of discourses of *mestizaje* in Quincentennial Guatemala?

40. On the relation of dependency theory to *mestizaje* discourses, see also Klor de Alva (1995).

41. This is similar to the utopic discourses surrounding cyberspace and the liberatory potential of information technologies, which I explore in the next chapter.

"Mestizaje Cultural"

The term *mestizaje* received a lot of play in 1992 and 1993 with the exhibition "Mestizaje Cultural" mounted by the internationally recognized Guatemalan photographer Diego Molina and supported by major businesses and national banks.[42] The exhibition was held in a large gallery adjacent to the National Palace (and the military intelligence office) that was donated by the government, and it was widely publicized through frequent full-page color advertisements in the national newspapers throughout its several-month run. Diego Molina has mounted a series of exhibitions in this space, including "Guatenfoto" (Guatemala in photographs), "The Agony of the Jungle" on ecological issues, and the follow-up to Mestizaje Cultural entitled "The Guatemalans," which all included high-quality large-scale mounted photographs, dioramas, and 3-D exhibits (Mestizaje Cultural included a six-foot-tall scale model of Columbus's ship), potted plants, a twenty-minute video, and frequent wall-plaque reminders to "Show your culture: do not litter; do not spit; do not play or make noise." These exhibits, which are free, have been extremely popular: entire schools come to view them, families of all social classes bring their children, and people crowd the halls even on weekdays. Molina claims that on one day alone over seven thousand people viewed the exhibit.

In addition to these exhibits, Diego Molina publishes a series of postcards and an oversize occasional magazine called *Guatemala Facil* (Guatemala made easy) with photos and short articles. In an interview, he described his goal:

> to show what is beautiful about Guatemala, the things no one pays any attention to. Too many people make their living off of the crisis, but that is not all there is to Guatemala. The root of our situation, our crisis, is that we have two origins, and that cannot be erased. These two origins come out everywhere, in people's names, their hair, how they think. But this is not a question of guilt, what it means is that we all have a mestizo origin. We want to confront this shared past. This is a people with many cultures, and we can live in peace. It is part of a nationalist essence that is positive; we want the Guatemalan public to find a new way of appreciating the national. We are trying to create a family album for Guatemala, full of what is beautiful and positive. We have had a marvelous response to this work.

Though several reviews of the *Mestizaje* exhibit criticized its lack of attention to poverty and violence, in general it was well received in the cultural pages of the newspapers and magazines, and the comment books at the exit

---

42. I thank José Fernando Lara for introducing me to Mr. Molina and accompanying me several times to exhibits and interviews.

were filled with enthusiastic responses (nearly twenty large books were filled with the responses of viewers). Reading over people's shoulders, I saw comments such as "Thank you so much for this wonderful exhibit! This is the national project that Guatemala needs," "You are giving us back our nation, thank you!" and "Every Guatemalan should see these photographs!"

Diego Molina said:

> Some people thought we did Guatemala an injustice with this show by focusing on the Indian past. They said we were dirtying history, devaluing our roots. But what I have tried to do is dignify the two roots of the country, without confrontation. All of these things, bread, tortilla, cattle, literature, science, clothing, food, these things are Guatemalan and based in both groups. I am very proud of this project. . . . Others objected that there weren't enough Indians in the show. The work is full of Indians, but without their *traje* no one notices them. That is the importance of *mestizaje*. I am trying to help people know themselves. This experience helps to form [*formar*] them, to make Guatemalans.

Molina says that he tries to stay away from polemical issues but that some people have accused him of being left-wing for highlighting the indigenous population and for criticizing the rich. As he said in our interview, "Our youth are lost . . . in the movies, in consumption, in status symbols, cassettes. Look at these rich kids on their motorbikes who talk down to the Indian [*tratan de vos a los indios*]. This is a time bomb." However, like Casaus Arzú, he is not a supporter of the Mayan movement. "The indigenous movements are extremist, they are trying to vindicate a cause that is lost in time, from another epoch, it is absurd." What the country needs, he said, "is a collective, massive, and immediate nationalist education project, like Mexico has. We need to create an absolute patriotism. We are becoming more and more divided. What is sure is that the only hope for Guatemala is national socialism. We need to attack poverty and work to create a unified nation." He did not use the term *national socialism* lightly: he had a swastika flag displayed in his office.

The national unity Diego Molina posits seems based on a physical identification that all Guatemalans share ("without their *traje* no one notices"), an identification that allows cultural differences such as clothing, food, music, and language to be valued as part of "national" identity. Much of his work positively portrays indigenous lifeways—enough to get him in trouble with some sectors—and although it falls within familiar exoticizing parameters, his political project is clearly opposed to the racist paradigm that wants nothing to do with the Indian. He has found broad acceptance from the government and private sector as well as the viewing public for a representation of Guatemala that includes indigenous cultural difference. His postcards of indigenous couples are very popular among Guatemala

City's lower-class to upper-middle-class population, who send them to friends and family inside and outside of the country. Like Casaus Arzú, whose work denounces policies of assimilation, Diego Molina suggests that as long as a "racial" *mestizaje* is accepted (a fundamental embodied sameness), the Guatemalan nation can deal with cultural difference (it does not need to fully assimilate the Indian).

These discourses of *mestizaje* are different from those of ladinoization or *blanquemiento* as cultural or "racial" assimilation. "Cultural" difference does not need to be erased in this model. Charles Hale and others have suggested that the current emergence of *mestizaje* discourse is simply a counterattack on the Maya movement. "Dominant actors appropriate the discourse of multiplicity, but then smuggle the unified subject back in" (Hale 1996, 41). Though many who deploy it are anti-Maya, *mestizaje* discourse may also resonate with the demands of Mayan activists, who carefully distance themselves from racializing notions of difference and concentrate instead on cultural rights and the *formación* of activists.[43] It is also important to remember that, given the massive wounding of the civil war, *mestizaje* discourse minimizes "racial" difference, making the politically vital argument that "cultural" difference should not signify a threat and that struggles for cultural rights do not merit a violent response. Rather than dismiss these claims as racist, we need to think of them as articulations: they change as they are spoken and as they are joined to (and against) Mayan projects. And, as Fuss suggests, they are identifications that cannot be foretold in advance.

Although I'm suspicious of its liberatory claims, *mestizaje* discourse may be a tool in fluidary politics—as long as we examine the regulatory norms and erasures that structure it (and make a unified subject, unchanged by its articulations, difficult to smuggle back in). I am highly sympathetic to Casaus Arzú's approach and do not suggest that her notion of *mestizaje* is the same as Diego Molina's (whose project is complex, but who expresses sympathies for fascism). Indeed, the deployment of *mestizaje* discourse by government officials, by an artist heavily supported by private enterprise, and by their antagonists in the popular sectors suggests both that politics are complex in Guatemala and that the discourse is rich enough to be articulated to quite different projects. Perhaps this fluidity exists because, as Klor de Alva puts it, *mestizaje* is "an internal frontier in a perpetual state of creation and decomposition" (1995, 243), somewhat like Timothy Mitchell's (1991) description of the state-civil society divide, which, I have suggested, animates the "piñata effect" of the state.

43. For example, an emphasis on identity as cultural informs the category some Mayan activists have begun to deploy of "Maya-ladino"—which is a discourse of hybridity but with a different emphasis than *mestizaje*.

I have been suggesting, in fact, that discourses of *mestizaje,* like "culture," and like the state, accrue fetishlike magical powers both from what they try to cover over (that "polyvalent mobility") and from the identification work they do. They mobilize energies in defense of the promises of renewed life and unity. Stoler, discussing Foucault's notion of racism as a positive power over life and death, suggests that class struggle and "the fight of races" "both emerged out of an earlier binary conception of the social body as part of the defense of society against itself, out of a shared vision of a deeper biologized 'internal enemy' within" (1995, 130).

If these projects for Guatemala's future share a reliance on the mestizo body for their force and possibility, what does this image of the split social body suggest? The discourses of *mestizaje* posit the physically same body as the ground for class struggle and national unity, a "Guatemalan ethnicity," often viewed as lacking in the wounded body politic of Quincentennial Guatemala. This sense of the unified nation is similar to Benedict Anderson's "deep horizontal comradeship," with clear borders and state sovereignty "fully, flatly, and evenly operative over each square centimeter" (1983, 26). But the desired unity of Anderson's and ladinos' body image is fictitious, and positing such unity covers over the differences that are constitutive to it. The category of "mestizo" *needs* difference—between Indian and ladino, between men and women, and between legitimate kinship and illegitimacy. The category of "mestizo" can only materialize through the differences and asymmetries produced through the intersections of Guatemala's kinship, gender, sexuality, class, and race systems. These constitutive differences are both excluded from the discourses of similar mestizo bodies and simultaneously necessary for them to exist (just as gender difference is often erased from Mayan cultural rights discourse and yet remains central to it). This is why I disagree with Carol Smith, who sees nation-building *mestizaje* as suppressing already existing "race, ethnicity, religion, gender" identities (1996, 161). Robert Young suggests instead that discourses about race hybridity like *mestizaje* "circulate around an ambivalent axis of desire and aversion: a structure of attraction, where people and cultures intermix and merge, transforming themselves as a result, and a structure of repulsion, where the different elements remain distinct and are set against each other dialogically. The idea of race here shows itself to be profoundly dialectical: it only works when defined against potential intermixture, which also threatens to undo its calculations altogether" (1995, 19). *Mestizaje* only works through producing differential (although never clearly foretold) identifications, not through suppressing them.

In Guatemala the lack of a seamless national identity suited for participation in the "modern" international world is often blamed on the survival of the "Indian," but this "other" is necessary for the very constitution of the nation. This is an identity that is in part produced through exclusion and in part through fundamental contradictions like those described by Stolcke, including the constitutive role of gender and sexuality. To return to Andrew Parker et al.:

> Like gender, nationality is a relational term whose identity derives from its in-herence in a system of differences. In the same way that "man" and "woman" define themselves reciprocally (although never symmetrically), national iden-tity is determined not on the basis of its own intrinsic properties but as a func-tion of what it (presumably) is not. Implying "some element of alterity for its definition," a nation is ineluctably "shaped by what it opposes." . . . If the ob-sessive representation of the nation as a community forms one of the most persistent responses to this ambivalence, such "unity" has been modeled in a wide variety of national cultures on gender and sexual norms. (Parker et al. 1992, 5)

"Obsessive" claims that everyone in Guatemala is mestizo echo an old dream of symmetry (Irigaray 1985a), but such claims are constitutively un-stable.[44] They attempt to solve the problem of difference by leaving the raced body behind—in other words, if ethnic difference is about culture not race, because we are all racially mestizo, then we can escape racism. Verena Stolcke argues that the move from race to ethnicity is not so easy, that "race and ethnicity are not independent elements of social stratifica-tion, but must be understood in terms of the systems of domination which they endow with meaning" (Stolcke 1993, 25). She suggests that similar feminist attempts to escape the sexed body by assigning gender difference to culture also founder because "social and gender inequalities are con-strued and legitimized by rooting them in the assumed biological 'facts' of race and sex differences" (1993, 19).

These "facts" support both the racializing that Casaus Arzú and I found in interviews, and *mestizaje* discourse. The contradictory moment in which a ladino is afraid to be taken for an Indian, even though they "can always tell the difference," points to the difficulty of finding any "objective" sameness or difference. Casaus Arzú grounds her antiracist and modernizing mestizo discourse in the body and relegates the racism of the oligarchs to a "ladino and ethnocentric world view." Although she argues that racism is structural in maintaining Guatemala's unequal class system, she also seems to relegate racism to an epiphenomenal position. She suggests that the difference the ladino elites "see" between white and Indian bodies is a false consciousness that hides the (embodied) truth that the ladino oligarch refuses to "see"—that he is really mestizo. Casaus Arzú and many other ladino nationalists

---

44. *Dream of symmetry* is Luce Irigaray's term for the patriarchal positioning of woman as "the same" as man, only deficient, as castrated males, the representation of lack.

would argue that transforming the class structure would be the best way to eradicate racism and thus reveal the racial unity hiding behind the ideologies of class. When enunciated by presidential advisors and congressmen, the discourse of *mestizaje*—that difference is "cultural," not "real"– also promises national unity. Through education, photo exhibitions, newspaper editorials, Civil Patrolling, belt tightening, and structural adjusting, these cultural limits can be overcome to create the "Guatemalan ethnicity."

But, as Stoler suggests, it is this "combined palpability and intangibility that makes race slip through reason and rationality. For it, like nationalism, is located in 'invisible ties' and hidden truths. . . . Invoked as common sense knowledge, these hidden truths are rarely identifiable; but because they are hidden they can be explicitly enumerated by those with expert . . . knowledge—and just as quickly regrouped and subject to change" (1995, 206).

BODIES THAT SPLATTER

The unified "national" ethnicity of *mestizaje* leans as heavily on the body as the elites' racializing discourse. It obsessively covers over the rapes that initiated *mestizaje* and ignores the splattering of gendered and ethnicized bodies that are supposed to support rational national identifications—but that so often slip through reason. As Parker et al. suggest, "Nations are forever haunted by their various definitional others" (1992, 5). In Guatemala, these constitutive violences return, in Tecún Umán's blood circulating on the quetzal and in the many Guatemalans haunted by La Llorona, a creature of legend who cries in the night—mourning her children and possibly stealing those of others. Guatemalan folklorist Celso Lara Figueroa suggests that La Llorona was an indigenous woman who drowned her mestizo children, products of the union with a Spanish conqueror.[45]

If we are to understand ladino discourses about Indians in Guatemala and the effects of these discourses, we must heed this haunting of identity categories by an indigenous woman—that universal donor—and we must investigate how gender, sexuality, race, ethnicity, class, and nation are mutually constituting. These power-infused vectors are not artificially imposed on bodies, but instead are "norms which govern the[ir] materialization" (Butler 1993, 3).[46] And these processes by which bodies are made to mat-

45. I thank Abigail Adams for this reference.
46. Kaja Silverman, working from a similar theoretical base as Butler, says that "while human bodies exist prior to discourse, it is only through discourse that they arrive at the condition of being 'male' or 'female'—that discourse functions first to territorialize and then to map meaning onto bodies" (Silverman 1989, 324). She uses the notion of *anaclisis* as a way to understand the articulation between real and constructed bodies. The term comes from Freud's notion of the leaning or propping of the erotic drive upon the self-preservation in-

ter also splatter the predicated unity of the mestizo national body politic, just as La Llorona's cries shatter the night.

In fact, La Llorona's story may be the most adequate founding myth of identity based on catastrophe, lack, and loss. Bess Lomax-Hawes reads La Llorona as existing in a "state of disequilibrium," and for women who tell her story, La Llorona "signal[s] the essential unwholeness of their condition" (Lomax-Hawes in Limón 1986, 73).[47] La Llorona may be a symptom of the way "woman," "Indian," "white," "mestizo," and so on are bodies politic that splatter, and her drowned children may represent the violence of loss, the founding lack that splatters national "unity." La Llorona's constant search, her cries of pain, are emblematic of national identity in Guatemala, haunted by the unwholeness it seeks to disavow.

The tendency to lean on a material body—the desire to find an absolute, "natural" difference (in racialist discourse) or sameness (the mestizo)—seems born of these contradictions, an attempt to counter the ambivalence in the very formation of the nation.[48] But bodies cannot prove such absolutes, and this may be one reason that states attempt to violently inscribe one singular meaning on them through torture, wounding, and death. The splattered body—as the photographed torture victim, and as the cadaver left by counterinsurgency on the side of the road—is deployed to ground these identifications. For the army, that body is meant to clearly signify the danger of resisting the government and its neoliberal economic policies, and wounded bodies are still quite material in Guatemala where human rights abuses continue even as peace is declared.[49]

Of course, these splattered bodies, like the vacillating racial discourses that lean on them, are as polyvalent as hieroglyphs. For human rights activists, these bodies are evidence against the regime. For communities that

---

stincts. Silverman says, "In an analogous way discursive bodies lean upon real ones—lean both in the sense of finding their physical support in, and of exerting their own pressure upon real bodies. . . . The body is charted, zoned, and made to bear meaning . . . which proceeds entirely from external relationships, but which is always subsequently apprehended both by the female subject and her 'commentators' as an internal condition or essence" (1989, 325). I have been leaning on this concept throughout this book.

47. In "La Llorona in Juvenile Hall," Bess Lomax-Hawes describes the incarcerated girls as "children of loss, children of need, children of lack" (in Limón 1986, 73).

48. As Duncan Earle reminds me (personal communication), a belief in strict community endogamy means that Mayan identity is seen to have a physical, biological component—a certain pureness that the ladino (as bastard) lacks. In my experience, the Maya cultural rights organizers have been extremely cautious in playing the race card. Their strategic responses to critiques of their "authenticity" include insisting on difference as cultural and often the function of conscious choice. This "strict endogamy," like any ardor for purity, is often based on violent erasures, as indigenous women who are raped by or who sleep with nonindigenous men are automatically recategorized as not indigenous.

49. On the role of torture in making and unmaking the world, see Elaine Scarry (1985).

have survived massacre, they signify injustice and governmental illegitimacy, as Victoria Sanford (1994) has shown in her work on the exhumations of clandestine cemeteries. Perhaps this insecurity of even so legible a bodily sign as torture and death may lead the state to disappear bodies in an attempt to remove them from signifying systems where they mean too much. Like La Llorona's missing children, the forty thousand disappeared in Guatemala form a wound that will not heal.

The splattered body is also a way that Guatemalans imagine themselves.[50] When *Lineage and Racism* was published, it was called "a finger in the wound" (*Crónica*, 30 April 1993, 18), a metaphor frequently used to describe ethnic relations in Guatemala. The Mayan activist Pop Caal also sees the nation as a wounded body politic: "The ladino tries to erase and put a veil over the problem, not because he is convinced that discrimination does not exist, but because he is afraid that putting a finger in the national wound will stir up conflicts between both groups" (in Bastos and Camus 1993, 27).

Thus, Guatemala is a nation which is not one—a term I borrow from Luce Irigaray's polysemous notion of "the sex which is not one" (1985b). This pun suggests, among other things, that the feminine is not "a sex" at all, and that it is not "one" in that it is multiple, composed of many erogenous zones as opposed to the singleness of the phallus. This may be another way to think of the ethnic-national issue in Guatemala, as in "This Race Which Is Not One." This suggests that neither ladinos, whites, or mestizos are a "race" biologically speaking, and it reminds us that all of these categories are multiply split, shot through with contradictions and variously articulated identifications.

The wounded body politic of the Guatemalan nation (which is not one) may also correspond to Jacques Lacan's (1977) notion of the child's "body in pieces"—the way a child experiences the world—which is territorialized in different ways as the child becomes a gendered, raced, and sexualized subject. This may help us think about Anderson's imagined communities as

50. Sexta Avenida, the main thoroughfare in Zone One, Guatemala City, is lined with movie theaters that show mostly B movies and lower-grade films of violence, gore, and soft-core sex—similar in content to the U.S. genre known as splatterpunk. *Cannibal Holocaust*, prison films, schlock horror, the complete Chuck Norris oeuvre, and other blood and guts movies are standard fare at most cinemas outside the central zones of the city; they fill the video stores of department capitals and are the stock of traveling video shows. Many people—gringos, ladinos, and educated Maya—shudder at these low culture tastes of the masses. "How can they watch that stuff with all the *real* violence around them?" is a standard question. Though the theme merits an entire book, I wonder if such representations perform critical fantasy work for the splattered imaginary of the Guatemalan body politic? As Carol Clover (1992) points out, slasher film is deeply concerned with the repetition effects of dysfunctional family romances, the way people and places are haunted by the "terrible family," and how we learn (through the struggles of the Final Girl) to repeat with a difference and survive the killer.

Imaginary in the psychoanalytic sense—as always lost, irrecuperable, like the children of La Llorona, once the subject has entered the Symbolic. In the next chapter, I look at ways the nation is being reterritorialized by the Maya-hacker and becoming a differently "raced" and gendered subject in the process.

The Guatemalan national project is seen as a failure—either because Indians who are supposedly too physically different are thought to hold it back, or because a unifying mestizo physical identity is not yet acknowledged. I have tried to find the wet spot in both these discourses that lean on the body: the spot, I argue, is the way these bodies are only intelligible through the production of difference. But thinking of bodies as discursively produced does not mean that they do not matter. Instead, it means that identity is radically contingent—open to articulation and reterritorialization. Thus, with Butler, I resist the claim that feminism or nationalism or ethnic mobilization is being "'ruined' by its fragmentations, a position that implicitly or explicitly establishes the dispensability of some crucial constituency, and the claim that fragmentation ought to be overcome through the postulation of a phantasmatically unified ideal" (Butler 1990a, 124).

I began with a story of how I took a detour through the other (Fuss 1995, 3) to define myself as a concerned gringa by looking at a torture victim's body. I erased his body of any meaning beyond what the state had marked there. He reminded me that we were structured by gender and often unconscious desire as we looked at each other and that both pleasures and dangers were involved in that relation of identification. I have tried, in a fluidary and contingent way, to explore how ladino identification is always a detour through others. It is immaterial without those articulations and the regulatory norms that constitute them—including the incitements and pleasures involved. *Mestizaje* discourse is powerful because it allows desire to slip through rationality, carrying inchoate yearnings for the swell of music and that final kiss that clinches the family romance. It allows us to long for an end to the painful processes of girling and boying, racing and classing, to dissolve in the climax of seduction, the Maya as woman melting into the oceanic embrace of the ladino man.

Mestizaje discourse is also powerful because it is implicitly about the future (Klor de Alva 1995). Though the nation suffered a catastrophic origin, *mestizaje* carries the subjugated eugenic promise that through the collective management of life a more fit nation will triumphantly emerge. Flaunting its feathers and flourishes but armed with modern rationality, pragmatism, and science, it will magically progress and take its rightful place in the family of nations. It is precisely on this terrain of the modern and of science (fiction) that the Maya-hacker is contesting what this future will look like.

SEVEN

Maya-Hackers and the Cyberspatialized Nation-State

Modernity, Ethnostalgia, and a Lizard Queen in Guatemala

The Maya give thanks for food, for air, for the tools that serve us, the office machines, and the computers.

Leader of the ALMG

Science fiction is generically concerned with the interpenetration of boundaries between problematic selves and unexpected others and with the exploration of possible worlds in a context structured by transnational technoscience.

DONNA HARAWAY

ALIEN ENCOUNTERS

I'm going to jack you into this chapter with a third world arrival scene.[1] It is 1985 in Nebaj, Guatemala, under a military government. I am on my first research trip, investigating the effects of civil war on highland indigenous communities, and Nebaj is famous for its traditionalism. Most women and many men wear the *traje* distinctive to the town, and, although not as robust as before, the civil-religious cargo system functions, and the yearly titular festival is intensely colorful, with saints' processions, fireworks, the Dance of the Conquest, and all-night revelry. Day keepers still practice their craft, giving readings of the present based on the Mayan calendar (Colby and Colby 1981). In other words, the town offered all the exoticism my recently conferred bachelor's degree in anthropology had incited me to desire. Nebaj, however, had also been one of the towns hardest hit by the government's counterinsurgency campaign, which leveled all twenty-six surrounding villages. In addition to the dancers, weavers, and shamans, Nebaj was a town of refugees, survivors, and soldiers.

In 1985, the journey to Nebaj took twelve hours in an extremely cramped

---

1. This chapter has benefited especially from discussions with Warren Sack, Rob Latham, Scott Mobley, Marcia Klotz, Christa Little-Siebold, Jane Collier, and Mario Loarca.

Figure 19. Cofradía procession, Nebaj, August 1985. Photo by author.

Bluebird school bus (twelve people in my row!) that groaned its way over the spine of the Cuchumatanes mountains to finally drop down into the remote valley centered on its colonial-era church. After the ride, while I was walking around the garrison town to stretch my legs, a group of children surrounded me, asking if I'd buy stuff or wanted my shoes shined. They asked me my name, and when I said "Diana," they all started yelling: "Queen of the Lizards! Queen of the Lizards!"

I was stumped. I knew this town had been pretty strongly proguerrilla, and I wondered if the kids, in calling a gringa a lizard, were displaying the effects of anti-imperialist education imbibed while the town was "liberated."

Figure 20. *V.* The bottom photo shows the Lizard Queen's minions in human form with the center front alien unmasked, revealing the scaly truth beneath the façade. Copyright 1983 Warner Bros. All Rights Reserved. Published with kind permission.

But this was not the case. On the contrary, it turns out that they had been sneaking into the cantina with the town's one TV to watch a U.S. science-fiction series called *V.* The show dealt with the arrival on earth of an advanced and apparently benevolent group of aliens who promise all sorts of techie wonders as well as world peace. Most humans willingly accept their offerings and presence. Only a small group of hearty souls realize that they are actually lizards disguised as humans and that they are on earth to rape and pillage her natural resources—including harvesting humans for snacking on back home.[2] Those who refuse to be duped fight a valiant guerrilla

2. The similarities to the organ-stealing rumors that incited the beating of June Weinstock are striking.

struggle against both their own kind, who refuse to see the exploitative relationship they have entered, and the lizard aliens led by their queen, Diana.

Telling this story of science fiction in Nebaj tends to excite a giddy sensation in audiences, who usually laugh and exclaim, "How postmodern!" They aren't very interested, however, in stories of Guatemalan leftists exiled in Mexico City who planned their study groups around the TV schedule of *V.* These urbanized, politicized (ladino and indigenous) Guatemalans liked the show because it faithfully represented their own problems of intracell tensions, the dangers of living underground, and the difficulties of fighting an increasingly hegemonic power structure.[3] This is not as intriguing as the boundary transgression between the supposedly "premodern" Maya-Ixil Indians of Nebaj and the postmodern of science fiction. Encountering kids in a backwater town who were sophisticated in the ways of Lizard Queens was something of a shock.

THE MAYA-HACKER

This shock comes from the sense that science fiction is about the future, whereas Guatemala's indigenous highlands tend to represent the past. This colonial binary of the modern cosmopolitan west opposed to the archaic indigenous, which Johannes Fabian (1983) has explored, is precisely the predicament faced by the growing Mayan cultural rights movement.[4] The assimilationist discourse of Guatemalan nationalism has proposed that the majority indigenous population is inappropriate for modern nationalism. The "cultural treasures" of the glorious Mayan past of Tikal and traditional practices of clothing and ritual are appropriated to represent the nation in tourist literature, beauty pageants, or a float in the 1993 Pasadena Rose Bowl Parade. However, for full representation in the nation, the Maya have

3. *V* is explicit about its relation to revolutionary Central America. The miniseries opens in El Salvador, where our intrepid heroes, a journalist and photographer, are covering what seems to be an FMLN-held village. When the Salvadoran military attacks in U.S.-supplied helicopters, the heroes barely escape with their lives. Later, as they latch on to the aliens' counterinsurgency plans, the photographer remarks, "This is just like El Salvador!"

4. Hendrickson suggests that, in fashion at least, going to the United States from Guatemala is a trip into the future. Even passé items in the United States can be transformed by a trip back across the border into "scarce luxury goods . . . the products of Guatemala's future" (1995, 71). This power accorded the north resonates with Charles Hale's notion of "Anglo affinity" in Nicaragua (1994). The popularity of cast-off clothing from the United States can create gross ironies (a child with parasite-distended belly wearing a "We Are the World" T-shirt) and hilarious transvestisms (a burly, macho dude whose shirt proclaims, "It's not PMS, I'm just a bitch!"). Of course, the reasons people wear these clothes—that they're the cheapest thing available, in part because of NAFTA with its attendant changes—is far from hilarious.

been expected to put aside their indigenousness: to learn Spanish, dress in western clothes, and so on.

In fact, the binary semiotics of identity in Guatemala mean you cannot simultaneously be Indian and modern. Ladino identity is defined as modern in terms of technology and lifeways. Because centuries of *mestizaje* have made it difficult to tell an indigenous person from a non-Indian, the categories are culturally marked (although "culture" is clearly a contested category). Thus, any indigenous person who speaks Spanish, has earned an academic degree, or holds a desk job has historically been redefined as ladino. I argue, however, that Mayan cultural rights activists are refusing ladinoization and instead are "Maya-hackers." Like computer hackers, who do not control the systems they work in but intimately understand their technologies and codes, the Maya are appropriating so-called modern technology and knowledges while refusing to be appropriated into the ladino nation, becoming what Trinh Minh-ha has called "the inappropriate(d) other" (Trinh 1986).[5]

The incongruity of my term *Maya-hacker* tends to occasion chuckles, which I think highlight the continuing power of the primitive-modern divide. So I deploy the term as a caution against ethnostalgia—the romance of tradition, modernity's longing for sincerity, for a link to the ardor and mystery of the past.[6] Ethnostalgia is also my frisson of exoticism that was so rudely disrupted when my cover as solidary gringa anthropologist was blown by a positive ID as a Lizard Queen.

Ethnostalgia is a powerful contradiction for Mayan activists. It empowers their work and wins them allies among the ladino elites and foreigners. Links to the Mayan past are necessary to legitimate their demands, but ethnostalgia also limits them to the past side of the binary that defines ladinos as modern.[7] I argue that Maya-hackers are decoding and reprogramming such familiar binary oppositions as those between past and future, between being rooted in geography and being mobile, between being traditional as opposed to being modern, between manual labor and white collar technol-

5. Deborah Heath makes a similar argument around women's dance in urban Senegal. She seeks a way to analyze practices as more complex than just resistance and finds dance (as I argue for "hacking" in the largest sense) to be "a resource put to various, often contradictory uses in the production of meaning and power" (1994, 89).

6. Like jokes, ethnostalgia is ambivalent. Though at one level it is about the comfort of a self-consolidating other (we're modern, they're traditional), it is also more fluid. The suffix *algia* means to feel pain, reminding us of the finger in the wound of these various bodies politic (including Lizard Queens).

7. Estuardo Zapeta, the enfant terrible of the Mayan movement and columnist for *Siglo XXI*, peevishly reminds readers that Mayas drive, own Mercedes-Benz, watch TV, and have money. He's tired of always being represented as a "cosmological esoteric hippie" (1 June 1995).

ogy and informatics manipulation, between mountain shrines and mini-malls, and between unpaved roads and the information superhighway. Continuing with the modern metaphors, I suggest we should also think of the site of this reprogramming work as the cyberspatialized nation-state. This foregrounds the importance of information and representation in the work of the Mayan activists and in producing an imagined community like the Guatemalan nation. The cyberspatialized nation-state is a site of articulation in two senses. First, and just as Rigoberta Menchú is portrayed as *desenvuelta* (articulate, or well-spoken), the Maya-hacker is a skilled user of language and information. Second, these information technologies are deployed in *articulation with*—linking the Maya to—the nation-state. Here I mean *articulation* in the recombinant sense of "any practice establishing a relation among elements such that their identity is modified as a result of the articulatory practice" (Laclau and Mouffe 1985, 103). Both the Maya-hacker and the nation-state are constantly being constituted through these doubled articulations.

My designation as Lizard Queen, like the term *Maya-hacker,* is also an articulation meant to suggest the incongruous juxtaposition of science fiction and the social science of anthropology.[8] I would suggest that this juxtaposition is increasingly the standard fieldwork experience. It is both about being hailed by science fiction in a place I had assumed was backwards and traditional and about how to write about boundary crossings—ours and others'. Science fiction (SF) metaphors help us articulate this historic moment when the natives are writing back and anthropology must creatively confront that "interpenetration of boundaries" that Donna Haraway suggests defines SF and the postmodern condition. A fluidary response must draw on anthropology's tradition of self-reflexive double vision that makes the strange familiar and the familiar strange—a project in which science fiction is an ally.[9] Science fiction has been described as "a thesaurus of themes . . . a body of privileged allegories . . . to cope with the drastic transformations that technology has wrought on life" (Csicsery-Ronay 1991, 305). These drastic transformations constitute the conditions of possibility for both Guatemalan nation formation and Mayan organizing in the context of an evolving global political economy of information technologies (Castells 1989). I hope that science fiction terms like *Maya-hacker* and *cyberspatialized nation-state* help us resist an ahistorical vision of either the Maya or Guatemala as outside of these global trends, because the terms mess with the boundaries between what Haraway calls "problematic selves and unex-

8. I borrow the notion of social science fiction from Stephen Pfohl (1992), a companion in exploring this very productive interpenetration of boundaries.

9. In fact, there's more than fictive kinship there, as embodied in science fiction writer Ursula Kroeber Le Guin, daughter of anthropologist Alfred Kroeber.

pected others." I hope that anthropology can be grafted with science fiction that, as Csicsery-Ronay suggests, "names the gap between . . . belief in the immanent possibility (and perhaps inexorable necessity) of [scientific-technological] transformations and . . . reflections about their possible ethical, social, and spiritual interpretations (i.e., about their embeddedness in a web of social-historical relations)" (1991, 387).

I also like the way that the science fiction of Lizard Queens in Nebaj interrupts my ethnostalgic notions of an authentic indigenous village, my assumption that I would be welcome there, and the attempt of this book to say something about the vertiginous experience of Guatemala. It firmly situates me, the gringa anthropologist-as-Lizard-Queen, as a border-crosser rather than a "solid" identity. I don't know if those kids really thought scaly lizard flesh hid behind my sunburned cheeks, but gringas are ambivalently marked when we enter highland communities, especially those ripped open by violence. June Weinstock was almost killed in the belief that she was a gringa stealing baby organs—a rather Lizard Queen–like project. Being designated Diana, Queen of the Lizards, forces me to consider the sorts of fantasy spaces that I inhabit for those I am "studying" and how my fantasies and romances inflect how I study them. This consideration is increasingly important to address because Mayan organizing calls into question the representational work of anthropologists and asks how much of our fieldwork makes it back to the fields we harvest it from. Although much ethnographic work done by gringos has been useful for Mayan projects, we must not disavow the often alien anthropological cyberproject of harvesting information for intellectual snacking on back home.[10]

Keeping this ambivalent Lizard Queen position in mind, in this chapter I continue to describe the work of the Mayan cultural rights activists in Guatemala (with emphasis on the centrality of information technologies to their work and the effects of their struggles over representation) and the responses of nonindigenous state sectors. By drawing parallels between cyberspace and the nation-state, I hope to keep "the context structured by transnational technoscience" on our viewscreens (Haraway 1992, 300).

THE MAYAN CULTURAL RIGHTS MOVEMENT AND INFORMATION TECHNOLOGIES

In 1993, on my sixth sojourn in Guatemala, I was sitting in an upscale Guatemala City steak house with the Mayan activist Dr. Demetrio Cojtí. We were talking about the politics of creating a pan-Mayan identity out of the many

10. In turn, understandings gleaned from Mayan experience are also useful for gringos (an identity that is not one, of course) who attempt to analyze and struggle with transnational power relations.

divided community and linguistic groups, as people begin to self-identify as Maya-Ixil, Maya-K'iche', Maya-Q'eqchi', and so on. One strategy has been to reverse the standard appropriation of indigenous people to ladinoiza-tion by calling the mestizo population "Maya-ladino"—a reprogramming of the premodern and modern that has shocked many ladinos.[11] Planning for our next meeting, Dr. Cojtí pulled out one of those amazing computerized agendas that hold thousands of names, addresses, dates, world time zones, telephone numbers, and even maps. I said, joking, that they should invent a new identity term, the *Maya-hacker.*

We both laughed, but I came to think this *could* describe Dr. Cojtí—a man with a Ph.D. in communications, very technologically literate, who is a vital presence on the national Internet, accessing the burgeoning Mayan cultural rights movement as well as the government, nongovernmental organizations (NGOs), and international networks through his job at UNICEF. He also maintains connections in the rural and urban matrix through contact with his small-town home and with many rural-based Mayan organizations, and he frequently contributes to the national press and indigenous publications. As I discussed in chapter 1, in its short his-tory the Guatemalan indigenous rights movement has been split between what are known as the "popular" indigenous organizations—like Rigoberta Menchú's Campesino Unity Committee (CUC) and other human rights groups who identify with class issues—and the more culturally active Mayan movement—which insists that racism is not reducible to capitalist exploita-tion. Dr. Cojtí, however, is becoming a vital node in the conciliation process between these two positions, which has been energized by national and in-ternational events like the Quincentennial, Rigoberta Menchú's peace prize, and the international summits she convened during the UN Year of Indigenous Peoples, and by the process leading up to the December 1996 peace treaty. Dr. Cojtí also functions as the modem used by anthropolo-gists, journalists, state bureaucrats, and Lizard Queens to log on to the in-digenous rights bulletin boards.[12]

Why Hacker?

The term *hacker* originated at the Massachusetts Institute of Technology (MIT), the primordial soup of computing, as a term of respect and ac-

11. Though Kay Warren reports from the field that this term does not seem to have caught on, the anxiety that it instills has. Post-Quincentennial Guatemala is buzzing with discussions, public and private, of the suddenly problematized category of ladino identity.

12. Tragically, modernity's destructive tendencies also affect the Maya-hacker. When I showed Dr. Cojtí a version of this paper, he laughed and said, "And now I am suffering from a disease of modernity!" He had recently been diagnosed with stress-related diabetes, as a result of which he was having to curtail his work.

knowledgment for extraordinary competence in the manipulation of hardware and software.[13] A hacker is defined (in *The New Hackers Dictionary*) as "a person who explores the details of programmable systems and how to stretch their capabilities . . . who enjoys the . . . challenge of creatively overcoming or circumventing limitations" (Raymond 1991, 191). Bruce Sterling defines the term *to hack* as to work on something, to explore, to be "determined to make access to computers and information as free and open as possible" (1992, 51). Thus hacking is about the understanding and control of information technology and, most important, the ability to form networks for communication and information sharing.

When I joke about the Maya-hacker, I am thinking about the vital importance of information and networking to the political strategies of the indigenous cultural rights movement in Guatemala. Information, of course, has been an essential orthopedic tool in the colonial and postcolonial history of Guatemala and as a hostile marker of bodies politic. Knowledge of the Indians, especially their divisions, facilitated the Conquest. The Colony was instituted through the sword and the cross, a combination of violence and ideology, deployed mostly through the *formación* of indigenous middlemen and middlewomen—as soldiers or cannon fodder for the violence of the equation, and as lay church workers, document translators, and later bilingual school teachers, health workers, and agricultural extensionists, exactly in the mode of Macauley's Minute discussed in chapter 4. "We must render [interpreters] by degrees fit vehicles for conveying knowledge to the great mass of population" (in Spivak 1988a, 282). These translating roles offered *mestizaje cultural*—entry into the cash economy and access to signs of "modernity," which promised that with a generation or two of speaking Spanish and dressing "up," their children might escape the stigma of indigenous identity. However, it is precisely these middlemen and middlewomen who have begun to appropriate these information technologies and deploy them for alternative aims. They are using literacy, desktop publishing, linguistic theories, radio, and computers to promote cultural survival. Rejecting the Macauley role of being destroyers of their own culture, they say that the "decolonization of the Maya begins with knowing how to use technology and not being used by it" (ALMG 1990, 42).[14]

Public indigenous organizing around cultural issues like the survival of Mayan languages—what Edward Fischer calls the "tripartite relationship

---

13. Jean Jackson (personal communication) reminds me that a hack is also a technologically complex but harmless practical joke. As must be evident by now, I am fascinated with the disruptive and revealing power of jokes.

14. The Maya-hackers are seizing the possibilities generated by these new technologies to learn and educate differently, similar to the way Andrew Ross characterizes computer hackers: the "development of high technology has outpaced orthodox forms of institutional education

between language, culture, and politics" (1996, 57)—began in the 1940s with the work of Adrián Inés Chávez, who argued for a new K'iche' alphabet. In the 1950s, the Summer Institute of Linguistics (SIL), contracted by the National Indigenist Institute (IIN), began intensive linguistic and bilingual education work in the highlands, founding the Guatemalan Mayan Writers Academy (AEMG) and training indigenous linguists as middlemen (Fischer 1996, 58). Combined with the efforts of Catholic Action, the Francisco Marroquín Linguistic Project (PLFM), and UN-supported bilingual education (Richards and Richards 1996), among other factors, by the 1970s there was a critical mass of indigenous men and women working throughout the highlands in churches, schools, agricultural cooperatives, nongovernmental development agencies, and medical services, who began to meet and discuss issues of indigenous empowerment (for a fuller discussion, please see Falla 1978; Pop Caal 1981; Fischer 1996; Arias 1990; Richards and Richards 1996; CECMA 1992; and Englund 1992).

Mayan leaders say that in the 1970s they began to understand the importance of language: of the indigenous languages as both a symbol and ongoing practice of indigenous identity, and of language and information as a way to contest racism and economic and political oppression. They began to discuss how ladino control of the representation of indigenous peoples in history, education, and the media determined how the Maya saw themselves, in turn making them unwitting allies in this process. As Narciso Cojtí, the activist who had worked as a Catholic catechist with his father, now says, "I spoke against the traditional religion. We were the worst destroyers of our own culture. Now that I am more involved, I understand the barbarity I've committed and the need to support our traditions."

In the 1970s, with increasing poverty, many of those who are now Mayan activists were influenced by Liberation Theology and other social movements of the time (often working closely for the first time with different ethnic-linguistic groups and ladinos) and were then radicalized by the military governments' violent suppression. Rigoberta Menchú's testimonial vividly recounts the journey from nonviolent social activism to armed resistance (1984). Though some indigenous activists took this route, thousands of educators, catechists, and development workers were killed for their roles as middlemen and middlewomen. As I discuss in chapter 4, the catastrophic violence of the civil war and continuing human rights violations limit political organizing around taboo subjects like land reform, but the 1986 inauguration of civilian rule and contestations around the Quincentennial have created a space for survivors and a new generation to under-

---

[, allowing] . . . them to maintain fronts of cultural resistance and stocks of oppositional knowledge as a hedge against a technofascist future" (Ross 1991, 81–82).

take different kinds of political struggle, to engage in the dreamwork of the state. The massive violence has convinced many of the need for new strategies and careful organizing, a "working differently."

Thus, contrary to fears that thirty-five years of ethnocidal civil war would destroy the Maya, in the past ten years, hundreds of indigenous-identified groups have emerged. These Maya-hackers are not challenging state and ladino power directly, nor do they accept the fetishized division between state and society. They are sharing information and creating networks. They are concentrating on education; rural development; research and support for languages and other cultural practices (such as religious, sartorial, and artistic expression); on the creation of libraries and literatures devoted to indigenous issues; on publishing and radio broadcasting; lobbying Congress with information and well-crafted arguments (often in collaboration with international organizations kept in touch through e-mail and faxes); and participating in the peace process (see also Fischer and Brown 1996; Warren 1992; Bastos and Camus 1995).

These modes of "working differently" are tactical responses to violence, but they also reflect a global historical shift. In part, as R. McKenna Brown suggests, as a result of urbanization, industrialization, the massive displacements caused by the 1976 earthquake and the civil war, and the way higher education and employment opportunities are concentrated in Guatemala City, "growing numbers of Maya now lead, at least temporarily, urban lives" (1996, 170). Though many indigenous people are small farmers, agricultural peons, textile producers, or workers in Guatemala's industries and *maquila* production, increasing numbers are employed in service and information-management jobs—teachers, lawyers, bureaucrats, merchants, and so on. Thus the conditions of possibility for the Maya-hacker include the emergence of a critical mass of educated people, shifts in transnational organization that increasingly emphasize the information economy, and the technological changes that have made the relevant hardware and software increasingly available.[15] These technologies include not only the computer but also low-cost publishing and reproduction technologies, video recording and playing equipment, cassette technology, radio equipment, and even simple telecommunication grids through which to keep in touch. For example, it was not until 1993 that Nebaj received telephone service.

The ALMG and other Mayan groups create and distribute videos and cassettes with linguistic, historical, and anthropological information, lec-

15. There is a growing literature that attempts to name and analyze these "New Times" (Hall and Jacques 1990), which are variously characterized as post-Fordist, postindustrial, disorganized capital, or the new international division of labor, as I discuss in chapters 8 and 9.

tures by members of the movement and other researchers, and scenes from the ALMG investiture of their executive council with the accompanying rituals and prayers. Given Guatemala's high levels of illiteracy, radio has traditionally been an important medium and message, both in the sort of ideological work on passive listeners that some media critics have warned of (Adorno 1993; Bukatman 1993; Debord 1983) and as a carrier of other messages—in Mayan languages, for example (A. Adams 1997; Wilson 1995)—or of official messages that can be decoded (Cojtí 1990; Hall 1993). I am not arguing that the Mayan cultural rights activists have complete control over these technologies; I am arguing that the hacker mode is an appropriate tactical response to what Rob Latham calls "the real ambiguities of information society, whose promise of technological empowerment bears with it the threat of increasing politico-economic surveillance and control" (Latham 1995b, 10).

One expression of this "working differently" (what might be thought of as a synergistic milieu of hackers in Manuel Castells's sense) is the ALMG.[16] As I discuss in chapter 4, member organizations work in Mayan-controlled grassroots development projects and research, documentation, and education. They sponsor conferences and seminars and publish economically and intellectually accessible materials—what I call "shareware."

The ALMG's first hacking project was to create a unified alphabet for the different Mayan languages through linguistic research and painstaking negotiations, and then to lobby the national Congress to make this alphabet official for use in school texts and government publications.[17] In pursuing this goal, they have used the 1984 Constitution, which, although it enshrines Spanish as the official national language, does recognize the existence of indigenous languages. Strategically deploying the embedded code of this national operating system, the ALMG won official recognition for their new alphabet, thereby joining in the struggle for representation in its double sense. First, this effort to control how their languages and thus how they themselves are represented—in the sense of their portrayal, the information about them that circulates in the national media (*darstellung*, as Gayatri Spivak says)—is directly linked to the ALMG's struggle to win representation—in the sense of speaking for themselves (*vertretung*) in the state (Spivak 1988a, 276). Through tenacious lobbying and strategic use of

16. It is a synergistic milieu in the sense that it is a space of innovation, where views and ideas are exchanged, an "overall social milieu that constantly produces and stimulates its intellectual development . . . where social reproduction becomes a direct productive force" (Castells 1989, 351).

17. For a detailed history of the project to create a unified alphabet, see the essays in Edward Fischer and R. McKenna Brown (1996).

ladino internal divisions and ladino allies, in 1990 the ALMG won recognition as a government-funded but autonomous organization in charge of linguistic and educational research, the development of curriculum materials, and training of teachers, among other things. Like hackers who work in the interstices of computer networks, the Maya-hackers are creating spaces for themselves inside the state—they are speaking in between, interdicta. Thus, rather than the state being a "thing" to be smashed, the Maya see the post-1985 Guatemalan government as a site for their work.

The ALMG plays a major role in Mayan organizing (Bastos and Camus 1995) and is a nodal point for many of the Mayan organizations based in the countryside.[18] The flow of information through this node was clear to me in the hours I sat in their waiting room until someone had time to be interviewed. The building was filled with a procession of indigenous people from all over the country, who came in for training, to turn in vocabulary lists from their linguistic areas, to ask for a job, to confer about curricula for their Mayan schools (see Richards and Richards 1996), or to gather up people to take a request to the Congress or the press. My interviews were constantly postponed as ALMG members left town to run a seminar in some small town or to do computer training.

Thus, although these Mayan groups make political and economic demands, they are keenly aware of the power of discourse and representation—that the production and deployment of information and knowledge is a potent form of power—in both the *formación* of Mayan activists and in gaining representation in the state. For five hundred years, the killing fields have been controlled by those with superior hardware. Now, with a radio transmitter, a computer and printer, a modem, or a chip-run agenda, the Maya-hackers are reprogramming from the bottom up.

This is also the position of many U.S. hackers—such as Phiber Optik,

18. This central role has also made it a site of struggle, in part around representation of (in the sense of "speaking for") the different linguistic communities, in part around individual power, and in part around "bureaucratic tangles" (Fischer 1996) such as labor demands and how to form a new organization. The ALMG has been embroiled in a union struggle that involved the national courts and made for sensationalist accounts in the ladino press. The boom in organizing around the Quincentennial has also produced many sites of Mayan activism, somewhat displacing the ALMG from its central position in coordinating the cultural rights movement. The Guatemalan Council of Mayan Organizations (COMG) began to take on this role in 1990, and the Assembly of the Pueblo Maya (APM), founded during the Serrano "coup" of 1993, and the Coordination of Organizations of the Pueblo Maya of Guatemala (COPMAGUA), created in 1994 to participate in the peace process, are also functioning as Maya umbrella organizations (Bastos and Camus 1995). Because of the ambivalent position of the ALMG as an autonomous but state-backed agency, its leaders have decided not to participate actively in COMG or the APM, although they have been very active in COPMAGUA (Bastos and Camus 1995).

who was recently released from a year in jail for computer trespassing. *Time* magazine describes Optik as "raised in a working-class neighborhood. . . . He used his $300 Radio Shack computer like a magic carpet to cyberspace, staying up all night to explore the mysteries of the worldwide telephone grid . . . and he was happy to share his knowledge" (Quittner 1995, 61).[19]

Similarly, using the tools at their disposal and without large financial reserves, Mayan activists are insisting on the appropriateness of their presence in the postmodern world by appropriating such technology for their own ends. One Mayan leader told me, "The Maya give thanks for food, for air, for the tools that serve us, the office machines, and the computers."[20] Generations of indigenous struggle, the tools of the information revolution, and the historic reconfiguration of the Guatemalan state have opened up a new arena where Mayan activists can hack the ladino power structure. By *hack* I mean that they are overcoming system limitations, decoding and reprogramming postcoloniality, and pressing "enter" on the keyboard of the Guatemalan nation.

The Hacker as Cowboy and Indian

A second meaning of the term *hacker* is "romantic outlaw." In *The Hacker Crackdown,* Bruce Sterling describes "hackers of all kinds [as] absolutely soaked through with heroic antibureaucratic sentiment. Hackers long for recognition as . . . the postmodern equivalent of the cowboy" (Sterling 1992, 51). This is the heroic protagonist in such films as *War Games, TRON, Max Headroom, Hackers,* and *Johnny Mnemonic,* and the "console cowboy" in the genre of science fiction known as cyberpunk. This hacker, almost always male, surfs through the military-industrial cyber-networks, laughing at their security systems and every once in a while leaving a clever clue to his passing.[21] These in general lighthearted break-ins, however, often lead to paranoid warnings that a hacker will start World War III, which in turn jus-

19. Kevin Mitnick, a recent hacker cause célèbre, was also from a "disadvantaged" beginning—the child of a divorced waitress, he never finished high school (Quittner 1995, 61; Markoff 1995, A1).

20. Similarly, Irma Otzoy reports that women are incorporating "alphabetic writing and machines" in their weavings (1996, 149).

21. One exception to the rule that in popular representations the hacker-cowboy is really a boy was Sandra Bullock's character in *The Net.* However, unlike most hacker-SF films and cyberpunk fiction in which the boy gets the trophy-girl but retains his fascinating isolation, the entire point of *The Net* was to punish Bullock's character for being too isolated. Her denouement is not satisfied heterosexuality with the promise of more adventures to come; instead, she returns to the home and cares for her childlike mother. Thanks to Scott Mobley for discussions about this.

tify periodic hacker crackdowns and punishments wildly disproportionate to the "crimes."

I argue that the Guatemalan state may think of the Maya as hacker in this paranoid sense. Decades of antiracism work in Guatemala have driven most (but not all) overtly anti-indigenous remarks out of public discourse (and into jokes). Most ladino state functionaries are publicly very pro-Maya: some most sincerely, whereas others are clearly attempting to appropriate this vibrant new social movement to their own ends. However, there are suggestions that ladinos feel the Maya are invading a space that is inappropriate for them—the urban, literate, mediatized state. This space of the nation-state, the hackers' topos and the ground of contention in Guatemala, can be visualized as cyberspace.

THE CYBERSPATIALIZED NATION-STATE

Cyberspace is a utopia in two senses. Many proponents excitedly proclaim that you can be anything you want to be there. It is unlimited information and communication: the ultimate public sphere. In this way, it is similar to the hopes surrounding democratization and the peace process in Guatemala, hopes that may fuel fascination with and love for the state. However, it is a utopia as well in the etymological sense of a no-place. In this sense it is also similar to the state, a notoriously difficult entity to pin down, as Timothy Mitchell (1991) and Philip Abrams (1988) remind us. Of course, the nation-state and cyberspace are both expressions of Foucauldian power-knowledge. Cyberspace is where computer information "is," where your money "is" when you think it's in the bank, where people "are" when they gather in multiple-user dimensions. The term was coined by the science fiction writer William Gibson in the 1984 novel *Neuromancer,* who calls cyberspace "a graphic representation of data abstracted from the banks of every computer in the human system. Unthinkable complexity. Lines of light ranged in the nonspace of the mind, clusters and constellations of data . . . a consensual hallucination" (Gibson 1984, 51). Sound like Benedict Anderson's "imagined community?" I think it does, and I think the science fiction of the cyberspatial nation-state may be productive for thinking about Guatemala and the Maya, just as Guatemala may be productive for thinking about cyberspace.

I am not saying that the nation-state is exactly like cyberspace, of course, but both are communities formed through asymmetrically shared information. Discussing the importance of print capital to the development of nationalism, Benedict Anderson says, "Fellow readers to whom [the citizen is] connected through print, formed, in their secular, particular, visible invisibility, the embryo of the nationally-imagined community"

(1983, 47). Like print, cyberspace is both the informational computer codes of its infrastructure and the active and constant creation of shared "space" and subjectivity as people write themselves into being on the net. Both the democratizing Guatemalan nation-state and the technologically emerging cyberspace are sites for active negotiations about their future configurations.

Economically, the nation-state and cyberspace are ways of organizing material production. Nationally organized regulation determines the mode of development of capital in specific areas (Boyer 1990), and the informatic possibilities of cyberspace make possible flexible accumulation and just-in-time production, hallmarks of current post-Fordist economic development. As Manuel Castells argues, we seem to be entering an informational economy in which the "production of surplus derives mainly from the generation of knowledge and from the processing of necessary information" (Castells 1989, 136).

Politically, through the nation, liberal discourses of universal citizenship offer the ideological fantasy of total inclusion, and the proponents of cyberspace offer a dream similar to *mestizaje:* that you can be whoever you want to be, that all the limitations of gendered, racialized, or otherwise "disabled" physicality will fall away.[22] It is in part because of such promises that we feel love and fascination for both sites. If the nation is understood as the space in which "state sovereignty is fully, flatly, and evenly operative over each square centimetre" (B. Anderson 1983, 26), cyberspace is described by "silicon positivists" (Ross 1991, 94) in similar terms—only better. It is "a world in which the global traffic of knowledge, secrets, measurements, indicators, entertainments . . . take on form, [and] can be . . . accessed from anywhere. . . . Suddenly cultural knowledge, collective memory, technological advances [become] the object of interactive democracy" (Benedikt 1991, 7). Andrew Ross also finds democratic, even socialist possibilities: "Information technology involves processing, copying, replication, and simulation, and therefore does not recognize the concept of private information property" (Ross 1991, 80). In language reminiscent of the colonial basis of the nation-state, but without the pesky natives, cyberspace is seen to "represent a continent about which we have hitherto communicated only in sign language, a continent 'materializing' in a way" (Benedikt 1991, 17).

22. The "Conscience of a Hacker" in *Phrack,* a hacker manifesto, claims: "We seek after knowledge . . . and you call us criminals. We exist without skin color, without nationality, without religious bias . . . and you call us criminals. You build atomic bombs, you wage war . . . yet we're the criminals. Yes, I am a criminal. My crime is that of curiosity. My crime is that of judging people by what they say and think, not what they look like. My crime is that of outsmarting you, something that you will never forgive me for" (Sterling 1992, 83). Jaron Lanier is perhaps the most ecstatic of these proponents. Allucquere Rosanne Stone (1991), Chris Gray and Mark Driscoll (1992), Anne Balsamo (1996), and Donna Haraway (1991) address this trick of erasure.

However, both cyberspace and the nation-state are founded on exclusions hostilely marked by race, gender, sexuality, and class: the nation-state through restrictive citizenship laws (Maurer 1997), and cyberspace through educational and financial limits on who has access to the Internet. Verena Stolcke (1993) has argued that the nation-state is fundamentally unstable as a result of the inherent contradictions between liberal humanism and capitalist antagonisms. Similarly, Castells reminds us that in the new informational mode of development, "knowledge mobilizes the generation of new knowledge as the key source of productivity" (Castells 1989, 10), and, despite utopic promises, not everyone starts out with the knowledge that generates new knowledge: we are already on an uneven playing field. As with *mestizaje* discourse and its constitutive divisions, gender specifically structures access to these forms of power-knowledge, as I explore in the conclusion to this chapter.

Thus, there seem to be similar contradictions inherent to the nation-state and to cyberspace. I would suggest that the Maya-hackers work precisely on these faultlines, or "wounds." In their quest for cultural and human rights for indigenous peoples and in their appropriation of information technologies to make knowledge "as free and open as possible" (especially knowledge about these contradictions), they both deploy the utopic promises and highlight the deeply problematic imagined community and economic organization of the cyberspatialized nation-state. This may explain in part the ferocious violence of the counterinsurgency war, as well as the paranoia surrounding hackers.

In addition, I deploy the cyberspace metaphor to unsettle certain ethnostalgic tendencies, such as the New Age search for modernity's antidote in archaism and the hopes of those working in political solidarity who want the Maya to form the ethnicity-for-itself that will end Guatemala's long calvary.[23] Thinking of political work as interventions in information flows (like the social science fiction of this book) is a component of my project of fluidarity. The science fiction of the cyberspatialized nation-state may also be useful to grasp a democratizing Guatemala in which the stock market booms and 80 percent of the population live in extreme poverty, and which, as a nation-state, is both powerful and a site of struggle. The Maya are hacking a world deeply structured by transnational technoscience—whether it is the Israeli computers that allowed Guatemalan army intelligence (known as the "Archive") to track guerrilla safe houses through tiny increments in electricity use, or the faxes and e-mail that regulate the flows of just-in-time

23. The obsessive interest in this supposed beginning of a new age, which gripped large portions of North America in 1987, with people flocking to "spiritual" sites—many in Guatemala and Mexico—to experience it, was lampooned by Gary Trudeau as the "Moronic Convergence" and has been insightfully analyzed by Quetzil Castañeda (1996).

production that determine the daily lives of young Mayan *maquila* factory workers (Goldin 1996; Peterson 1992; Oglesby 1997).[24]

Nation-States and Cyberspace in the Cold Embrace of Military Systems

The nation-state and cyberspace as environments are also similar in that both are the monstrous spawn of the military-industrial matrix: gridded and programmed in accordance with the demands of C3I (command-control-communication-intelligence). Both are concerned with mapping territories, policing boundaries, and charting population movements, as well as constituting identities and determining potential risks—the aims of governmentality, as Foucault (1991) suggests. In *Neuromancer*, Gibson describes cyberspace as the visualization of maps of data organized by corporate conglomerates: "The unfolding of his distanceless home, his country, transparent 3D chessboard extending to infinity. Inner eye opening to the stepped scarlet pyramid of the Eastern Seaboard Fission Authority burning beyond the green cubes of Mitsubishi Bank of America, and high and very far away he saw the spiral arms of military systems, forever beyond his reach" (Gibson 1984, 52). This cold reminder of the military presence emphasizes the origins of actually existing cyberspace in army simulation tanks, Defense Advanced Research Project Agency (DARPA) funding, and its current use in smart bombs.[25] Turning to Guatemala (which has had barely twenty years

24. Elizabeth Oglesby describes scientific management, the new cyber-orthopedics of labor discipline, on Guatemala's sugar plantations:

> Computerized data bases now record daily worker productivity and the year-to-year labor history of each cane cutter. Cane cutters receive a weighted score based on productivity (40%), work quality (40%), and "attitude" (20%), and these records are used to recontract with only the most productive and cooperative workers. Pantaleón [the country's largest sugar mill] keeps files on workers' marital status, ethnicity, religion, land tenure relations and off-season occupation in an on-going effort to develop a profile of the "ideal" worker. (1997, 12)

25. "The Defense Advanced Research Project Agency (DARPA), famed for its managerial flexibility and its bold understanding of scientific research, has launched a number of ambitious programs, connecting leading universities and high-technology companies in defense-targeted research programs. . . . The acceleration of the technological revolution and its particular emphasis on information technologies represents a qualitatively different stage in the close interaction among the military, technological change, and industrial development" (Castells 1989, 267). Castells also discusses the role of the Pentagon in developing the ADA computer language that allows different software systems to communicate, as part of the Strategic Defense Initiative. Intriguingly, gender surfaces here: the language is named after Ada Lovelace, "the world's first programmer." The child of Lord Byron, she collaborated with Charles Babbage in the creation of the first computer, known as the Analytic Engine (Balsamo 1996, 207). She also figures in the cyberpunk collaboration *The Difference Engine* by William Gibson and Bruce Sterling (1990). Required reading on war and intelligent machines includes Manuel de Landa (1991), Paul Virilio (1990), and Chris Gray (1997).

of civilian government in the past 150 years) while keeping in mind the history of the military foundations of the cyberspatialized nation-state, we recall that the spiral arms of military systems always embrace the hardware and software that Maya-hackers and sympathetic Lizard Queens are trying to reprogram—in other words, there is *always* danger involved in this work.

Guatemala's virtual nation-state seems deeply ambivalent about its Indians and their supposed embeddedness in premodernity. For example, the Maya are expected to lack access to technology, and when they appropriate info tech, that appropriation is a shock and viewed as a threat. Former Defense Minister José García Samayoa seemed unable to believe that Maya would have access to modern reproduction techniques: "It is strange that Indians from the highlands have at their disposition dossiers of more than two thousand photocopies," he exclaimed (*Crónica,* 5 February 1993). The fact that these were copies of denunciations of army abuses made this even more of a problem for the general.

Modernity and Ethnostalgia

In interviews and other public statements, ladino state officials espouse the politically correct vision of an inclusive Guatemala, of *mestizaje cultural* where unity is strengthened by diversity and everyone partakes equally in rights and responsibilities. In unguarded moments, however, they suggest that the Maya are obsolete—after all, they express themselves through handwoven cloth in the age of the microchip and satellite transmission. In this stereotype, the Maya are defined by their commitment to tradition and hence by their lack of modernity. This commitment is signified through the very things that drew me (and that draw thousands of tourists) to Nebaj— their traditional clothing, noncapitalist relationship to the land, Catholicism, illiteracy, and their inability to speak Spanish, which is seen to limit them to the local and the past. A newspaper editorial argued that Mayan languages should not be taught at the elementary level because they are "stuck in the middle of the sixteenth century" (*La Hora,* 11 August 1990). The former vice-minister of culture said, "Demetrio Cojtí wants to go back five hundred years to before the suffering of the Conquest!" A former Finance Ministry official said, "How is a modern nation possible if we have people speaking twenty-three different languages? How can you translate Shakespeare into K'iche'? How will they have access to universal culture if they are isolated in their different languages?" Newspaper editorialist Mario Roberto Morales jokes that they want to live in "Mayassic Park,"and others more ominously declare that the Maya are falling into fascist nostalgia.[26]

---

26. Though this joking insult seems compensatory—like the Rigoberta jokes and most attempts to relegate the Maya to the past and thereby ensure a ladino hold on the future—it also

Mario Alberto Carrera asserts that, like the Italians under Mussolini or the Spanish under Franco (who wanted to return to the times of Julius Caesar or Carlos V), the Mayas want to return to their old empire (*El Grafico,* 21 January 1995).

And yet these same people often laud this resistance to modernity. The vice-minister of labor spoke approvingly of "the amazing valor of these people—they have almost been genocided, but they maintain their culture, they do not forget their origins. Even when they migrate to other places to work, they do not change. And the women especially, they are the most resistant to foreign values. They reproduce their culture." The head of a government development agency expressed awe at the Indians' different sense of time: "This is a distinct advantage. They do not think about progress in one year or five years—they think in terms of hundreds of years! They are in no hurry."

The sense of the Maya as outside history, locked in tradition, informs the popular notion of the indigenous community as naturally equal, solid, and inherently resistant to army counterinsurgency measures like the Civil Defense Patrols; it represents a wholeness that national culture has lost. A member of the government's human rights office remarked that "indigenous communities are horizontally organized. The Civil Patrol is vertical and destructive to traditional community life. In the communities, people are respected for contributing to the community, for their skills and their knowledge." Another government development official said, "Indigenous social structure is very complete and democratic and functional. It is better than the national structure. Their system is very rich, but they are very jealous of it. They will not let us enter. Their elders and *principales* [community leaders] are very powerful and there is a deep mysticism they will not share with us." Following Partha Chatterjee (1990), I suggest that these ideas of tradition and of a rural communitarian past have been vital in propping up Guatemalan national modernity.

Such forms of ethnostalgia and fascination are also important for the high-tech imagi-*nation* of cyberspace, from the tribal subcultures and totem identifications of hackers and Silicon Valleyites, to total-immersion games like Dungeons and Dragons. Similar visions of tradition and community hold romantic power for Lizard Queens involved in writing scientific fictions and for Mayan nationalists working to make such fictions into science. Much of the work of Maya-hackers in documentation, publishing, and education has been aimed at rescuing or even recreating tradi-

---

bespeaks anxiety. Invoking the massive strength of the dinosaurs brought to life in Steven Spielberg's film *Jurassic Park,* it acknowledges the power the Maya draw from their claims on the past, a power also used to prop up the "modern" Guatemalan nation but now problematized by the Maya-hacker.

tional indigenous lifeways. The ALMG says, "We seek to affirm our identity through strengthening the values of the Mayan culture through the research, institutionalization, and systematization of a desire to be different in language, external identification (clothing), cosmology, and other factors" (ALMG 1990, 41).[27] However, most Maya-hackers are quite explicit about their appropriateness in the modern world. For ALMG founder Guillermo Rodriguez Guajan, "Mayan Nationalism means combining 'modern' science and technology with 'traditional' Mayan knowledge of language, medicine, farming know-how, and community life in order to develop new forms of Mayan knowledge." This is precisely what many ladinos try to delete from their screens.

In interviews, most ladinos do not deny that the Maya have a right to inclusion, but they insist that the access code is in Spanish and English, not Kaqchikel or K'iche'. To log on to the modern, the Maya must ladinoize, acquiesce to *mestizaje cultural*. Speaking Spanish, wearing western clothes, being literate, and having technical expertise: these are, by definition, ladino. The colonial binary that consigns the Indians to the premodern and defines *ladino* as those with access to the "modern" has worked in Guatemala to redefine as ladino, in both the census and in popular understanding, any indigenous person who spoke Spanish or wore western clothes. As Andrés Cus said, without their *traje*, Mayan men tend to disappear. For example, a government development official said, "The leaders of the Indian movement are not Maya. They do not come from the communities, and they all have a book under their arm"—in other words, if they read, they are not Maya.

This mutually exclusive and solid binary informs and shores up many of the negative reactions of state sectors and ladinos in general to the Mayan rights movement. A ladino researcher who identifies as a Marxist said, "This cultural rescue work denies the Indians the possibilities of enrichment from other cultures. . . . They are very closed. Their work is motivated by resentment, and I think it is dangerous because it has no future. They care more about what they were than what they will be."[28]

27. This is very much the hacker mythos as well. The hacker 'zine *2600* describes a world in which the "tiny band of techno-rat brothers (rarely sisters) are a besieged vanguard of the truly free and honest. The rest of the world is a maelstrom of corporate crime and high-level governmental corruption, occasionally tempered with well-meaning ignorance" (Sterling 1992, 64). Sterling calls them a subculture: "Undergrounds by their nature constantly must maintain a membrane of differentiation. Funny/distinctive clothes and hair, specialized jargon, different hours of rising, working, sleeping. . . . The digital underground, which specializes in information, relies very heavily on language to distinguish itself" (1992, 72).

28. Another common trope for consigning the Maya movement to the past is to accuse them of merely retreading the 1960s arguments about *indigenismo*. I have heard many leftist ladinos exclaim with disgust after hearing a Mayan speak, "This is like going back in time! They

Those Maya who choose to jack in, read, live in cities, do intellectual work, and carry computerized agendas—those who snarf or appropriate anything "modern"—will themselves be appropriated, automatically becoming ladinos.[29] Those who remain in the premodern countryside and maintain "real" indigenous lifeways will be appropriated as well—as the tradition that props up modern national identity, and as tourist commodities for the pomo world eagerly seeking an "island in the net" for a quick vacation getaway.[30]

THE INAPPROPRIATE(D) OTHER

To many ladinos, the Maya-hacker is inappropriate to the cyberspatialized nation-state. The Maya-hackers themselves, however, are staking out an alternative position as inappropriate(d) others, which Trinh Minh-ha describes as the "historic positioning of those who cannot adopt the mask of either 'self' or 'other' offered by modern Western narratives of identity and politics. To be an 'Inappropriate/d Other' means to be in a critical, deconstructive relationality" (in Haraway 1992, 299).

In this critical relationality, the Maya-hacker is always already inside the machine; their traditions are not modernity's opposite. As the Mayan Congressman Claudio Coxaj said, "We are inside the State. We have adopted the modern." Demetrio Cojtí said, "'Modernity' is not the property of anyone. It is universal, no one can lay claim to it. . . . Everyone is always trying to say that we are inauthentic. But their ideas of indigenous people are very stereotypic, very rural. We are trying to mix things up."[31] In fact, this "mixing up" might be the Maya-hacker ethos. As cyberpunk writer Neal Stephenson puts it in his science fiction novel *Snowcrash*, "A truly advanced hacker comes to understand the true inner workings of the machine—he sees through the language he's working in and glimpses the secret func-

---

are making the same arguments that Guzmán Böckler [a ladino] made thirty years ago!" The trope is sometimes turned around, however. After the public presentation of a new study on the indigenous movement by Humberto Flores Alvarado, a Mayan activist said, "The presentation was boring, but it was worth it to go, if only to see that they are in the same position as in the 1960s; they have the same colonial attitude." Richard Adams's work (1990) on ladino representations of indigenous people between 1944 and 1954 reveals an almost uncanny resemblance to Quincentennial ladino discourses, more of which are explored in the next chapter.

29. *To snarf* is "to grab, especially to grab a large document or file for the purpose of using it with or without the author's permission. . . . To acquire, with little concern for legal forms or *politesse* (but not quite by stealing) . . . with the connotation of absorbing, processing, or understanding" (Raymond 1991, 326).

30. This is a reference to Sterling's 1986 cyberpunk novel, *Islands in the Net*. Even those of us enthralled by postmodern possibilities often long for an escape.

31. R. McKenna Brown also addresses these charges of inauthenticity (1996).

tioning of the binary code" (1993, 279). I argue that the advanced Maya-hacker is reading the binary codes of ladino-Maya and modern-premodern that structure the Guatemalan cyberspatialized nation-state, and they are decoding, reprogramming, and then networking to train others to do it.

In addition to the networking I describe earlier, the Maya are intervening in these contests through their publications, which act as shareware and include *Rujunamil Ri Mayab' Amaq* (Specific rights of the Mayan people) (COMG 1991); the proceedings from the Forum of the Mayan People and the Presidential Candidates (CEDIM 1992); Dr. Cojtí's *Configuración del Pensamiento Político del Pueblo Maya* (The political thought of the Mayan people) (1990 and 1995); the Mesa Maya's document entitled *Identity and Indigenous Rights: Statements and Demands in the Negotiating Process between the Government-Army and the URNG* (1993); *Derecho Indígena: Sistema Jurídico de los Pueblos Originarios de América* (Indigenous law) (CECMA 1994); the *Cholb'al Q'ij Agenda Maya* (Cholsamaj 1994, 1995, and 1996), a calendar paralleling Gregorian and Mayan dates and full of information about traditional practices; and COMG's "Análisis Evaluativo Sobre el Acuerdo de Paz" (Analysis of the Accord on Indigenous Rights) (1995). The effects of this shareware have been extraordinary, despite the resistances I explore in the next chapter. The Accord on Identity and Indigenous Rights, part of the 1996 Peace Accords, is almost identical to these Mayan demands for specific rights (COPMAGUA 1995; Bastos and Camus 1995). Along with the ILO Convention 169, these documents are tools for reprogramming work, manuals for writing a new DOS system that will read commands in indigenous languages, and they lay out a menu of demands for cultural, educational, health, territorial, and human rights for the Maya, rights that are becoming national law.

Of course, such science-fiction boundary crossings by unexpected others tend to problematize the self—to show up the bugs in the way the programs run. Through the work of the Maya-hackers, the cyberspatialized nation-state is shown to be itself divided and unsure, forced to question its own hold on "modernity."[32] The Maya are appropriating not only the markers of "modern" ladino identity (technological expertise and international networking skills—in which gringas and Lizard Queens play a role), they are hacking ladino identity itself (forced to question its self-definition as modern and universal); as a result, many binary codes begin to misfire, scrolling up as jokes and general anxiety about bodies politic.

Functionaries in the Guatemalan nation-state are much like computer

32. For an example of such questioning, see an essay by Dr. Cojtí entitled "Problems of Guatemalan 'National Identity'" (Rodriguez Guajan 1992). The tenuousness of ladino modernity was also nicely evoked during the Serrano attempted coup d'etat when the daily paper *Siglo Veintiuno* (Twenty-first century) was published as *Siglo Quatorce* (Fourteenth century).

executives and other postindustrial capitalists. They have developed and used the state or cyberspace primarily for personal profit and believed it to be a clean and secure workplace. But now they are confronted with the traces and long-lasting effects of hackers in the system.[33] Through the "Archive" and highly developed surveillance, filing, and information recall technologies, they were accustomed to being the ones with the data on diskette, the ones who represented (in the sense of forming and controlling an image) those excluded from cyberspace and the nation-state. As I discuss in chapter 5, the border crossings of unexpected and inappropriate(d) others, like Rigoberta Menchú and the Maya-hackers, who insist on representing (speaking for) themselves is highly problematic. In the United States, paranoia about similar "intrusions" was expressed in the "Hacker Crackdown" that followed the 1990 crash in AT&T's system (Sterling 1992).[34] This crash was blamed on "hackers" and led to a nationwide mobilization of law enforcement personnel and the trampling of multiple civil rights (Sterling 1992, 101–107, 147–164). The crash was actually caused by an internal software flaw, paralleling the internal contradictions of Guatemala's ex-

33. The anxiety surrounding such "inappropriate" access to technology is expressed in a genre of jokes about Indians' inability to use or even appreciate it. Many jokes about Rigoberta at the time of the Nobel Prize hinged on her sudden ability to buy newfangled machines that she could not understand; the jokes imagined her looking under the hood of her new Mercedes-Benz to find the "horses" she had heard were there, or driving it in first gear around the country because she couldn't understand the clutch. As Enrique Anleu, a Guatemalan anthropologist who told me some of these jokes, explained, "Social position is important here, and ladinos want to prove that they know about cars, laser discs, cable TV, that they are modern, part of the twentieth century. The joke would be that, even if she has money, Rigoberta is Indian, she is a brute, she doesn't know how things work. The opposite is that we're not Indians, so we do know." Celso Lara recounted an older series of jokes about the indigenous Don Chevo with similar themes. For example, Don Chevo watched them install the first telegraph line and asked what it was for. They told him that on the wire you could send a message from one place to another. So the next day they came back and he had tied his shoes to the wire. They asked why he had done that, and he said that he was waiting for the shoes to be taken to his brother's house.

34. Discursively, the crackdown was swiftly and brutally effective, creating a major shift in the U.S. popular definitions of *hacker* in the time it took this piece to go from a steakhouse conversation (with Dr. Cojtí in 1993) to a public talk (1995). From the heroic (see Levy 1984) or at least benign (Raymond 1991), the term is now coded almost entirely as negative, thanks in part to sensationalist reporting—"Outlaws on the Cyberprairie" (Evenson and Quinn 1995), and "Internet Is Becoming a Dangerous Road" (Quinn 1995)—and to best-selling books on the Kevin Mitnick affair (Shimomura 1996; Goodell 1996). This shift marks the now-naturalized but actually quite recent capitalist takeover of the Internet, as cyber-Enclosure Acts privatize terrain previously inhabited by low-rent academics and pranksters. Of course, I'd like to resist this counterinsurgency prose (Guha 1988), which demonizes the hacker in the United States and in Guatemala.

clusionary nationalism, which has led to civil war.[35] Similarly, as I suggest in the next chapter, Maya-hackers are being "framed," blamed for creating the wounds in the national body politic that they are merely pointing out.

I am thankful that there has so far been no crackdown on the Maya-hackers, who have been extremely careful in their dealings with the cold embrace of the spiral arms of military systems.[36] However, ambivalence and creeping paranoia about their border crossings do come on-line. A staff member of the presidential secretary for political affairs said, "The government thinks the Indians are not capable of anything. They are ignorant and dependent. But they also say that the Maya are our competition for the future." Despite the vocal distancing by Mayan activists from much of the URNG revolutionary movement's politics and methods, official discourse attempts to link them, a strategy that has had bloody consequences in the past. Even powerful ladino state officials say that they have been accused of being guerrillas because they express sympathy for the Mayan position. Former Defense Minister General Enríquez does not directly accuse the Maya of subversion but warns that their demands may be "appropriated and taken advantage of by the URNG. God willing, the ideological use, the interested use, of the issues of the indigenous peoples will not drive us to a national division. This is perhaps our greatest concern."

As I discuss in chapter 4, this fear of the "interested use of the issues of the indigenous peoples" colors other reactions to the Maya-hacker. Leftist

---

35. In Bruce Sterling's words:

The stuff we call "software" is not like anything that human society is used to thinking about. Software is something like a machine, and something like mathematics, and something like language, and something like thought, and art, and information . . . but software is not in fact any of those other things. The protean quality of software is one of the great sources of its fascination. It also makes software very powerful, very subtle, very unpredictable, and very risky. . . . There is simply no way to assure that software is free of flaws. Though software is mathematical in nature, it cannot be "proven" like a mathematical theorem; software is more like language, with inherent ambiguities, with different definitions, different assumptions, different levels of meaning that can conflict. (Sterling 1992, 31–32)

Sterling makes software sound very fluidary indeed, not unlike the Maya-hacker body politic.

36. However, indigenous activists with more popularly identified organizations like the National Indigenous and Campesino Coordinator (CONIC, a Mayanist offshoot of CUC) and the New Guatemalan Democratic Front (FDNG, a left-of-center political party) have been killed (GHRC/USA 1996 and 1997). United Nations human rights monitors from MINUGUA report that "On 6 November [1995], a member of the Fundación Myrna Mack who was holding a workshop on human rights in Santa Barbara, Huehuetenango, was summoned to the mayor's office [and] . . . accused of belonging to URNG because he was carrying a book on the rights of the Maya people and a copy of the Agreement on Indigenous Rights" (MINUGUA 1996, 7). He was beaten and threatened with death, as were MINUGUA personnel who later tried to intervene.

ladinos and U.S. academics have suggested that the Maya-hackers are co-opted by the state, or even by the very technologies they are appropriating.[37] Such concerns, well intentioned I know, insist on viewing the authentic Maya as traditional by definition. They reify either-or categories imbued with an ethnostalgia that posits some pure, true space of indigenousness that is outside of "the state," technological degradation, and history itself. Again, these imaginaries are powerful for both the Maya and those who seek to support their goals, but (besides the way they echo ladino state functionary discourse) they are too *solid*. They refuse the "mixing up" that Maya-hackers feel is so necessary.

Jane Collier has suggested that it may be less useful to investigate the authenticity, or lack thereof, of any cultural expression than it is to interrogate modernity itself as a condition of possibility, including its engendered categories (1997; and J. Collier, Maurer, and Suarez-Navaz 1995). This has been my goal in investigating the work of the Maya-hacker in the cyberspatialized nation-state—to suggest that it is a very scary place as well as a site for struggle. As Haraway says, we should view the "daily sphere of human-machine interface not only as a product of power relations but also as a potential site for contesting and redefining those relations" (in Ross 1991, 161). Most important, there is no outside to this interface between humans and machines, humans and the state, and humans and the transnational information economy. Despite past and present attempts to exclude them, Guatemala's indigenous peoples have always been deeply imbricated in the "modern" nation-state: as laborers, as symbolic markers for national identity, and as tourist commodities. The tradition they represent is not modernity's opposite (J. Collier 1997, 215); it is a necessary part of the operating system, always already "mixed up."

Perhaps modern nationalism's disavowed dependence on the Maya is what feeds a paranoic ambivalence about the Maya-hackers' new ways of articulating with the cyberspatialized nation-state. Haraway describes cyberspace as a "consensual hallucination of too much complexity, too much articulation. It is the virtual reality of paranoia . . . the belief in the unrelieved density of connection, requiring, if one is to survive, withdrawal and defense unto death. . . . Paradoxically, paranoia is the condition of the impossibility of remaining articulate" (Haraway 1992, 325). Articulation with the environment that is cyberspace and the nation-state is "terminal"—where could one withdraw to?

I borrow the notion of terminal identity from Scott Bukatman's epony-

37. I am thinking of questions raised passionately during presentations of this work at the University of California, Davis, and Yale University. I thank those colleagues for helping me think through this issue.

mous book to mean "a new subject that can somehow directly interface with . . . the cybernetic technologies of the Information Age, an era in which, as Jean Baudrillard has observed, the subject has become a 'terminal of multiple networks'" (1994, 2). This identity is "an unmistakably doubled articulation in which we find both the end of the subject and a new subjectivity constructed at the computer station or television screen" (Bukatman 1994, 9). But "terminal identity" is not the end of the subject. Instead, it describes fluidary identifications that rely on connective devices: there is no identity outside of those articulations mediated by various information technologies—from the Macauley Minute to the TV show *V.* Terminal identity is another way to eschew the binary opposition between being inside or outside of the nation-state, between ethnostalgia and modernity, and to resist assigning a third-world country like Guatemala to some pre–Information Age moment.

Just as Rigoberta stands in for the Maya as articulate (*desenvuelta*), the Maya-hacker is articulated to the cyberspatialized nation-state, creating a relation in which, despite paranoia, there is room for contestation. God*s* willing (as the Maya might say), the Maya-hackers' reprogramming is re-articulating the Guatemalan nation-state, and further genocidal attempts at a hacker crackdown will come up as a systems error.

GENDER AS THE MAYA-HACKER'S PROSTHETIC

pros-the-sis (präs'the sis) *n.* [NL. fr. Gr. addition, fr. *prostithenai* to add to, fr. *pros-*, in addition to +*tithenai,* to place, DO] 1:   MED. (a) the replacement of a missing part of the body, as a limb, eye, or tooth, by an artificial substitute CORP. (b) tool, support, fantasmatic structures   BODY POLS. (c) a foreign element that reconstructs that which cannot stand up on its own . . . establishing the place it appears to be added to   FEM. (d) overcoming a lack of presence, the site of pleasure and pain—n. prosthetic sociality (medium of connection) [38]

I chose the metaphor of the Maya-hacker as a countermeasure to the ethnostalgic trope of consigning them to the romantic premodern in both anthropological and popular discourses. But I also want to resist technostalgia—another form of romance. What do I, as a Lizard Queen, hope to find in the Maya, and why is it so easy to transfer the metaphor of the rebellious hacker cowboy to the Mayan Indian? Steve Levy's book *Hackers: Heroes of the Computer Revolution* calls hackers "a unique new breed of American hero," and the book is described as "fascinating, inspiring, here is the

---

38. This cyborg definition leans on Webster's; Gray, Figueroa-Sarriera, and Mentor (1995); Wigley in Jennifer González (1995); and Stone (1995b).

splendid epic of . . . the hackers, people whose brilliant thinking has created the future—the ultimate triumph of man and machine" (1984, jacket copy). Clearly, romance is an important part of political work, but as class-based revolutions in Central America grind down, with no ultimate triumph in sight, I have to wonder about my own need for a "new breed" of hero and about the celebratory tone of this chapter.

I do believe that the work of the Maya-hacker is heroic, and I am quite partial to their project. But pushing the science-fiction hacker metaphor a bit further returns me to the gender politics of heroism and to the exclusions and double binds discussed at the end of chapter 4. In the Mayan cultural rights movement, as in hackerdom, cyberpunk, and the control of high tech in general (Pfeil 1990; Ross 1991; Balsamo 1996), women are almost completely absent from decision-making positions. Similarly, as SF-writer Joanna Russ writes, "There are plenty of images of women in science fiction. There are hardly any women" (1970, 37).[39] Here I return to the image of women in the Mayan cultural rights movement to suggest that "she" functions as a prosthetic that supports the work of the Maya-hacker and the wounded Maya body politic. Again, I use the term *mujer maya* to describe this fantasy construct as distinct from actually existing Mayan women.

As usual, it was a joke that got me thinking about this—one of the more macabre I've heard in many years of working in Guatemala. It goes something like this: an anthropologist had lived in a highland Mayan village for several years but left when the civil war got bad in the early eighties. When he returned in the early nineties, he noticed a remarkable change and mentioned it to an informant: "You know," he said, "when I lived here before, the women always walked ten steps behind the men. No matter what I would say, they wouldn't change. But now they walk ten steps in front! It seems like you are finally catching up with the times. Before, women would never walk in front of the men." The informant said, "Before there were no land mines."

I think this joke captures the extremely fraught relation between Mayan men and women and between Mayan women and modern technology. Told, ruefully, by Mayan men, it may express their terror at living in the aftermath of civil war, and it suggests an awareness of the utility of Mayan women in their survival strategies (the hope that brown women will save brown men from counterinsurgency).[40] When I recount it in print and

39. I thank Jean Jackson for connecting me with this piece! As I was reminded by SF fan Carolyn Hill, this situation is changing for women in science fiction (and, I hope, in the Mayan movement).

40. Discussing the colonial discourse of *sati*, in which the British circulated horrendous tales of widow burning in order to justify intervention in India, Gayatri Spivak suggests the formula of "white men saving brown women from brown men" (1988a, 297). She models this on Freud's analysis of the rather slippery sentence: "a child is being beaten" (Spivak 1988a,

other gringas read it, we may laugh guiltily and grimace in horror. But we feel that, as offensive as the joke is, it captures something about the continuing power of patriarchy. It may also justify an intervention (like this book), because we hope that somehow we can change that situation (white women saving brown women from black humor).

Much of the work on gender in relation to colonialism, nationalism, and ethnic mobilization posits women as the ground or site on which such bodies politic stand (Mani 1990; A. McClintock 1995; Chatterjee 1990; Rajan 1993). The landmine joke suggests, instead, that Mayan women are prosthetics. As minesweepers, they serve as tools, as bodily extensions in desperate attempts to survive, and they bear the often excruciating weight of these survival strategies. Fittingly, the ground in this joke is a space of violent fragmentation.

Mark Wigley describes a prosthesis as an "element that reconstructs that which cannot stand up on its own, at once propping up and extending its host. The prosthesis is always structural, establishing the place it appears to be added to" (in J. González 1995, 135). The *mujer maya* as prosthetic, as an active connection that constitutes the elements involved, helps us understand the double bind of gender in the Maya-hacker body politic: "she" (the fantasy construct), and the effects this construct has on actually existing women, is no passive ground. Like the Maya-hacker who is seeking inclusion with some autonomy (rather than acquiescence to *mestizaje cultural* or total independence in a solely Mayan state), the metaphor of the *mujer maya* as prosthetic does not offer transcendence or even hope of steady ground to stand on (such as Mayan women acquiescing to the erasure of gender difference or Mayan women's liberation separate from Mayan men). Instead, both extend what the editors of *The Cyborg Handbook* playfully describe as

296). This sentence describes a patient's fantasy, which, under the pressure of analysis, reveals that it is actually a reversal—the sentence suffered a history of repressions that changed it from its original form, which was "*I* am being beaten" (Freud 1955). In other words, the child's own fantasy of being beaten (which is about the domestic space as a site of seduction and victimization) is displaced onto another child being beaten (suggesting the interchangeability of subject-positions in fantasy). These shifting identifications reveal a slippage between who is being beaten and who is being saved (like a possible slip from "she is being blown up" to "I am the victim of violence"). Such slippages may inform the fantasmatic figure of the *mujer maya* in the landmine joke and in my playful reversals of Spivak's sentence—a slip that acknowledges the incorporation of the *mujer maya* into various body images. For example, told by ladinos, the landmine joke is compensatory—by demonstrating the venality of Mayan men, it allows them to feel superior. Articulated with development and modernizing discourses, it legitimates "protective" intrusion into Mayan life, allowing for "white(r) men saving brown women from brown men." But it may also suggest ladino anxiety, a slippage in identification from the powerful to the victim. Government counterinsurgency shocked many ladinos because it treated them like Indians—expendable, worthless, and bereft of civil and human rights.

the cyborg dialectic—thesis, antithesis, synthesis, prosthesis. This dialectic is "different than a synthesizing [process]. . . . Enhancements and replacements are never fully integrated into a new synthesis, rather they remain lumpy and semi-autonomous" (Gray and Mentor 1995, 466).

Mayan body politics need prosthetics because, as the ALMG says, the *pueblo Maya* is "not only oppressed, but mutilated and atomized" (ALMG 1990). Pan-Mayan organizing entails the formation of a body politic from the stumps and wounded body images left by conquest and civil war, and as such, it depends on the prosthetic support of the *mujer maya*. This emerging identity, like national and ladino bodies politic, must prove itself appropriate to modernity (appropriating markers like science, rationality, technology, and organization [Chatterjee 1990], as well as speaking Spanish, dressing "professionally," and living in the city) while at the same time the Maya-hackers must show that they are inappropriate(d) by modernity. Otherwise they would just be ladinos, without a valid claim for a separate cultural existence. As Jane Collier says, "Modern nationalists have to find traditions that distinguish them from other nations without marking them as traditional or backward. This task is ultimately impossible . . . but the impossibility of the task does not relieve modern nationalists from the obligation to attempt it" (1997, 207).

Maya-hackers deploy the *mujer maya* as prosthetic to overcome this impossibility. I suggest that Maya-hackers can be modern because Mayan women represent tradition. The *mujer maya,* who lives in the rural villages, raises children, is Maya-monolingual and illiterate, weaves her own clothing, retains the Mayan calendar, pats out tortillas by hand, and maintains the *milpa* (corn crop) while her husband, brother, or son is in the city agitating for indigenous rights, represents the living link to the past, to the Classic Maya. She is the prosthetic that extends across historical distance, making the past present, and thus she legitimizes the urban-based Maya-hacker claim that as Maya they are both appropriate to the modern nation and inappropriated by the corruption of current events. Some Mayan activists even claim that because Mayan women stayed in the villages and their homes during the Conquest and colonization, they did not interact with the damaging effects of Spanish rule. Thus, they claim, she has never been conquered and so retains a direct link with the cultural past.[41]

This story resonates strongly with Partha Chatterjee's discussion of na-

41. Though meant to be empowering, this story strongly parallels the theory expressed by many ladinos that the Maya have been left out of History's onward march and that they must be brought up to speed if Guatemala is to enter the modern world. Similarly, Blanca Muratorio suggests that anthropologists have frequently represented women as "people without history" (in Schneider and Rapp 1995).

tionalism in India and its "resolution of the women's question." Nationalists in India dealt with the impossible demand of being both modern and traditional by setting up barriers between the inner and outer, the home and the world. "As long as we take care to retain the spiritual distinctiveness of our culture, we could make all the compromises and adjustments necessary to adapt ourselves to the requirements of a modern material world without losing our true identity. . . . The world is a treacherous terrain of the pursuit of material interests. . . . The home in its essence must remain unaffected by the profane activities of the material world—and woman is its representative" (Chatterjee 1990, 238–239).

In strikingly similar ways, the Maya-hacker (though not nationalist in the sense of working for independence) leans, often quite heavily, on the *mujer maya* who is produced through the same fantasmatic split between public and private that supported nationalists in India. Many male activists commute weekly or monthly to highland villages and towns to be with their families, but their claim to identity seems dependent on the women's territorial incarceration. Mayan men put intense pressure on Mayan women to resist "feminism," as Olga Xicox suggested (see chapter 4), and other markers of the "modern" such as urban living, public outspokenness, living single rather than married, having fewer children, wearing jeans, and cutting their hair. I suggest that this is why many women have found it impossible to work in the Maya-hackers' synergistic milieu.[42] The story about Mayan men seducing and abandoning Mayan women as a way to short-circuit their access to power is just one way Mayan women make sense of their lack of presence in leadership positions. Many Mayan women find that they cannot have both a husband and a career, a fact that points to the way this fantasmatic split between public and private is maintained through often violent exclusions. Mayan men's reluctance to allow Mayan women to become Maya-hackers (and the enjoyment many of them take in jokes about the unsettling Rigoberta Menchú) suggests their dependence on the *mujer maya* as prosthetic, the need for her to act as a legitimizing link to the land, to the past, and to tradition.

A recent issue of the magazine *Iximulew,* produced by the Center for the Study of Mayan Culture (CECMA) and Cholsamaj (both Maya-hacker milieus where Mayan women work only as secretaries) and published in *Siglo*

---

42. Other examples include the pressures put on the Tujab sisters for their work on Convention 169 (see next chapter), the intense frustrations increasingly voiced by Mayan women intellectuals, and the courageous admission in the 1996 annual report of the National Indigenous and Campesino Coordinator (CONIC) that "despite our efforts we continue to fail in our work with women. We continue to suffer deficiencies in terms of the remarks made at last year's assembly, which argued that men are refusing to allow women to increase their participation."

XXI, strikingly deploys this prosthetic. Their August 9, 1996, issue was dedicated to "Mujeres Mayas" and repeats tropes I heard over and over in interviews with Mayan male activists. The opening editorial states:

> As we reach the millennium, we must remember and recognize the decisive and fundamental role played by *la mujer maya* throughout time, as the guardian of life, wisdom, knowledge, and the reproduction of our ancestral culture. We must contemplate this millenarian aspect of *la mujer maya,* to revalorize and revitalize her role in the framework of complementarity and duality inherited from our ancestors. Especially now when feminist movements from other cultures, foreign to our own, attempt to divide indigenous peoples. (CECMA 1996, 1)

The editorial is followed by an article on *traje* and tradition that argues that "although some details have changed, the weavings worn by *mujeres mayas* today are almost exactly like the clothing seen in the stela and codices of the Classic Mayan civilizations" (CECMA 1996, 2). In other articles and interviews with Mayan men, *Iximulew* repeatedly connects the *mujer maya* to the past, to tradition, and thus to culture. "She is just now waking up to modernity," says an interviewed Mayan leader. "She is valued in the communities as priestess, midwife, and mother," says another leader (1996, 3). Similarly, my interviews with Mayan activists are full of remarks like "It is the women who retain their Mayan culture." By *culture* they seem to mean values, community, the "mother tongue," foods, *traje,* customs, and traditions—all of which are maintained by the *mujer maya* and her labor.

Remember the leader of the ALMG who said, "A Mayan woman is not a woman unless she makes tortillas. . . . My wife would be too ashamed if she did not make tortillas." Similarly, Richard Wilson suggests that the Mayan Qawa Quk'a movement in Alta Verapaz, which seeks to boycott national and international products in favor of traditional and locally made goods, leans most heavily on women's labor. "Men's clothes and agricultural tools (especially machetes) are two types of goods that involve participation in the market, yet they are excluded from the boycott. . . . The boycotting of foodstuffs, manufactured soap, and plastic vases is likely to affect women's labor more than men's" (Wilson 1995, 287).

Joanna Russ suggests that a central image of women in science fiction is that "women's powers are passive and involuntary—an odd idea that turns up again and again. . . . If female characters are given abilities, these are often innate abilities which cannot be developed or controlled, e.g. clairvoyance, telepathy, hysterical strength, magic. The power is somehow IN the woman" (1970, 36).[43] Mayan women's labor is similarly naturalized in Maya-

---

43. As an SF (and Maya-hacker) fan and a feminist, it's hard to know how to deal with this irritating idea, an issue I return to in the book's conclusion. As Russ (1978) and Penley's

hacker discourses about the *mujer maya*. Performed in the private space and because she wants to—because, as Jane Collier (1997) reminds us, the home is a place of freedom so no one is making her do it (otherwise she would be "too ashamed")—it becomes part of her essence. Hendrickson suggests that women's weaving ability is also simply assumed by Mayan men. The verve, color, and beauty are spontaneous manifestations of her soul, produced by "unschooled automatons with clever hands" (1995, 151). Men can weave if they want to, but they tend to work with technology (foot loom as opposed to back strap) that makes the work less wearisome and more lucrative. Men's weaving tends to be seen as a learned skill and a profession (modern), whereas women's weaving is performed as free expression and in her "free" time (while she simultaneously cares for children, tends animals, and cooks food).[44] The fact that most Mayan women are Maya-monolingual is similarly naturalized as the *mujer maya's* "valiant" commitment to maintain her language and heritage (rather than being seen, for example, as an effect of gendered schooling practices that more frequently pull girls than boys out of school to work at home or for wages [Pérez Sáinz, Camus, and Bastos 1992]). Also naturalized is the hard work of saving money, preparing for, and cleaning up after festivals and *cofradía* rituals, which "naturally" falls to the *mujer maya* (Stephen 1991; J. Collier 1997).

The pronatalism discussed in chapter 4 also suggests that Mayan body politics lean on the naturalized reproductive capacities of the *mujer maya* and her domestic role, which supports the spiritual superiority of the Mayan home ("You have the children God gives you" and "Abortion is a sin"). This powerful image of the Mayan home as separate and better than the ladino world is evoked in the claims to gender equality drawn from stories of the *Popul Wuj* (where, unlike in the Christian Bible, men and women are created at the same time from the same substance). This discourse of gender complementarity, central to the paeans in *Iximulew* (CECMA 1996), separates the Mayan home, represented by the *mujer maya*, from the outside world and legitimates the demands of the Mayan body politic.[45]

(1997) work on slash fiction reminds us, however, fans have their own fluidary ways of dealing with such contradictions.

44. Maria Mies (1991) writes that women's creative labor is often coded merely as "handicrafts" and "supplemental" to household production, a leisure-time activity. This dichotomy between men who have and use technology and women who *are* the technology clearly resonates with Lacan's reading of the gender of the phallus.

45. Once again, the *mujer maya* prosthetically supports Mayan identity by defining it against ladino identity (brown women saving brown men from ladinoization). Much of the limited ethnography of Guatemala that deals with gender at all also leans ethnostalgically on this serenely complementary *mujer maya* to describe Mayan communities as different from ladinos. (Richard Wilson [1995], who admits that gender segregation did not allow him to speak with many women, relies heavily on this trope.) Eileen Maynard (1974), Lois Paul (1974), and

This public-private boundary is often cruelly policed by Maya-hackers, using precisely the notions of authenticity they resist so fiercely when used to mark the Maya-ladino frontier. The same men who are "mixing up" the stereotypes and too solid hostile markings projected on to them, who insist that there is no one way to be Maya so long as one identifies with the cause, are telling Mayan women that they are not "really" Maya if they work outside the home or have too few children. They (unconsciously I assume) mimic ladino discourse about claims for rights being divisionist, like a wife leaving her husband: Dr. Cojtí, commenting on Mayan women, said to me, "They are separatists! They can't have a separate space—don't they realize they are half of the Mayan movement? They are dividing us!" In turn, attempts to inoculate indigenous women against the divisive effects of foreign feminism (which in the *Iximulew* editorial is linked to Protestant sects and the Guatemalan army as threats to the integrity of the Mayan community) suggest an awareness that the prosthetic is lumpy, semiautonomous, and may have a mind of her own.

Similarly, when I suggest that the *mujer maya* is produced as "traditional" through various orthopedics, this is not to say, as Jane Collier (1997), Lois Paul (1974), Lynn Stephen (1991), and others point out, that women do not enjoy a great deal of satisfaction from performing this work well, or that these discourses of the home and of ethnic pride do not move them powerfully and allow them to articulate a range of meanings to their labor. As a prosthetic, the *mujer maya* is always more than an exploited victim. This is another reason I like the metaphor. It is ambivalent and allows for play (as bloody as it is, the landmine humor is a joke, a way both brutal and silly to deal with almost unrepresentable violence). Here I'd like to strap on Allucquere Rosanne Stone who describes falling in love with prostheses—her

---

Carol Smith (1995) all argue that Mayan women are comparatively better off than ladina women, at least as long as they obey the rules of the community's gender system. Kay Warren describes Maya-hackers who search their histories for stories of complementarity. Though she implies that all is not hunky-dory in the here and now, she gives few details beyond the intriguing remark that at culturalist conferences "flashes of female anger have jolted audiences, only to be swallowed up by the dynamics of Maya consensus making" (Warren 1996, 96). Carol Delaney (1991) has beautifully untangled the gendered power differentials in systems of apparent complementarity, as has Lynn Stephen (1991).

Carol Hendrickson (1996) suggests that studies of women's issues are in general devalued, both in Guatemala activist circles and U.S. academia, which may be why anthropologists lean on this already constituted image of the complementary *mujer maya*. Given the metonymic link between feminism and the Guatemalan army as threats to Mayan survival in *Iximulew*, it's not easy for fluidary feminists to deal with this anger and this devaluation. However, this is a prosthetic relationality and as such may have strange and transformative effects. I thank Erich Fox Tree for discussion of this complex topic.

own and others'.[46] Stone writes of such interactions as "couplings," with all the affect that implies, and she insists that "the structure of pleasure and play . . . is the heart and soul of prosthetic sociality" (Stone 1995a, 397).

So, to address gender in the Mayan cultural rights movement, I tender the metaphor of prosthetic rather than ground for its flexibility in evoking the active and deeply affecting possibilities in these relations. With the notion of prosthetic as somewhat active, lumpy, and productive of pleasure, we may be able to distance ourselves from the "pessimistic functionalism" (Lipietz 1987) inherent in the notion of Woman as ground—in other words, a feminist Lizard Queen's concern that Mayan women are trampled on. For example, Stone describes hir voyages in cyberspace: "Some of the interactions are stereotypical and Cartesian, reifying old power differentials whose workings are familiar. . . . But some of the interactions are novel, strange, perhaps transformative, and certainly disruptive of many traditional attempts at categorization" (Stone 1995b, 36). Stone suggests that this is because there are people in the box and in the tool. This is a complex relationality with a somewhat active participant—not fully synthesizable, not a passive ground, and also not the rational free agent of liberal humanism—but a semiautonomous prosthetic in intimate connection with the self.[47]

Mayan Women

Intriguingly, in the intimate connection between body politic and prosthesis, sandwiched in the *Iximulew* supplement between the editorial and Mayan men musing about her new awakening to modernity, is a centerfold of notable Mayan women, where a different voice momentarily breaks through. Here are professionals, congresswomen, linguists, professors, journalists, engineers, and researchers—educated, sophisticated, and articulate.

This different voice suggests Mayan women find themselves in an ambivalent position, a double bind: incorporated and essential to a Mayan body politics that is community bound, but also leaned on and only semiautonomous. This position is familiar to women working in nonfeminist

46. Stone, who is transgendered (and I hope that's not too restrictive a term!) writes movingly in *The War of Desire and Technology at the Close of the Mechanical Age* of her intimate relations with various prosthetics—from music equipment, surgical materiél, and Stephen Hawking's vocal aids, to cyberspace.

47. Even Claude Lévi-Strauss acknowledges this special affect, reminding us that at that quintessential site of men forming a relation with each other through the exchange of women, "even in a man's world she is still a person, and in so far as she is defined as a sign she must be recognized as a generator of signs. . . . This explains why the relations between the sexes have preserved that affective richness, ardour, and mystery" (1969, 496).

popular or revolutionary movements, and to women of color working in white feminist organizations where their claims, like the Maya-hacker's, too often evoke paranoiac responses. For example, it is stunningly easy to lay Barbara Smith's "myths to divert Black women from our own freedom" next to the reactions to Mayan women's organizing discussed in chapter 4. First: The Black woman is already liberated. "The Mayan woman has never been conquered." Second: Racism is the primary (or only) oppression Black women have to confront. "That feminism is all western imperialism; I am a Maya before I am a woman." Third: Feminism is nothing but man-hating. "At first the men questioned our work. They were afraid we would tend toward feminism. Only women participate, but we are not feminist." Fourth: Women's issues are narrow, apolitical concerns. People of color need to deal with the larger struggle. "They are separatists! . . . Don't they realize they are half of the Mayan movement? They are dividing us!" (B. Smith 1981, xxvi–xxix).

Smith says that "the concept of the simultaneity of oppression is still the crux of a Black feminist understanding of political reality" (B. Smith 1981, xxxii). Mayan women, too, must figure out how to support Mayan activism and the way it is denaturalizing various power-drenched body images in Quincentennial Guatemala at the same time that it leans on the naturalized prop of the *mujer maya*. Many Mayan women are active in the movement and find that it incorporates quite nicely with their body image. The home as free from colonial disfiguration, stories of gender complementarity backed up by the authority of the *Popul Wuj,* and the spiritual power of the *mujer maya,* these are empowering discourses for Mayan women. In various ways Mayan women may also lean on the *mujer maya*—her image, her naturalized labor, her free time in the village, and class differentials—to construct their own visions of the Mayan body politic, although for them she is a less wieldy prosthetic.

Mayan women—like Guatemalan nationalists, ladinos, and Mayan men—are caught between the simultaneous modernity and tradition demanded by nationalist politics, bourgeois law, and their male companions in struggle. Just as tradition is not modernity's opposite but is modern as well (J. Collier 1997, 215), the *mujer maya* is not opposed to modernity but is part of it, produced by it, and productive of it. As a lumpy, semi-autonomous prosthesis, she sustains modernity and is in turn changed by it, made problematic. The struggles that create the conditions of possibility for the Maya-hacker (Catholic Action, the bilingual education system, peasant organizing, development programs, and the war) have not left Mayan women untouched—more and more Mayan women are leaving their villages and pursuing education, holding information-service jobs, and getting involved in Mayan activism.

Those who stay are doing very different things in their villages, like work-ing for export production plants and sustaining the tourism industry, or driving pickup trucks and watching V. Many of these women do not have time to weave or make tortillas.[48] Claudia Dary found that modern nontra-ditional export production in Chimaltenango has contradictory effects on Mayan women. Though the crops provide employment in their communi-ties so the women are less likely to migrate (and thus more likely to retain their *traje* and language), these women found it harder to participate in community life, primarily because they lacked the time. Women are also los-ing the financial autonomy that allowed them to buy thread, contribute to festivals, and participate in "tradition," because their vegetable plots (for which they controlled the earnings) are now devoted to export crops whose earnings tend to be controlled by the husband or father (Dary 1991). Be-cause they're too tired, they have no time, or they never learned, only 9 per-cent of the women Dary canvassed weave for sale, and only 20 percent for their own use (1991, 79).[49] This means that more of these professional Mayan women lean on the labor of other *mujeres mayas* to be both mod-ern and traditional (Ms. Menchú certainly does not have time or energy to weave all of her beautiful *huipiles*).

The body image of Mayan women who identify themselves with the *mu-jer maya*—as the ones who uphold tradition in a culture where "gender re-lations have always been equal"—is in complex relation with a body politic in which Mayan women are deeply engaged in "modern" forms of produc-tion and in which the majority of activist women are divorced or widowed, and excluded from positions of power. As one said, "I would never have been political if my husband were still around." But as Olga Xicox said, "I work a lot with women, so that they are not so marginalized, so exploited, not taken as just a tourist attraction, but so they know how to defend them-selves as women, *and* as Maya." In 1997, Mayan women activists are again addressing gender issues more directly, in part through the Peace Process and going public with their demands. As in the *Iximulew* supplement where the prosthetic of the *mujer maya* as tradition rubs in both irritating and ex-citing ways with images of Mayan women as engineers and lawyers, the *mu-jer maya* is always more than passive ground.

48. Hendrickson writes that women active in the revitalization movement felt they had to choose as girls between weaving and their schoolwork. They now express interest in learning to weave but often cannot find the time (1996, 161).

49. In addition, many indigenous communities are now both disrupted and sustained by the emigration of young women and men, many to the capital or areas with *maquila* employ-ment (Goldin 1996). Tracy Ehlers (1990) also documents how women weavers in Totonicapan are becoming more dependent on male wage earners because their daughters' unpaid labor, which once sustained their production, is lost to education and paid work.

SYNNERS

As an end note, I would like to proffer one more strand of science fiction—another shading to the promising monsters of inappropriate(d) others like Maya-hackers and the *mujer maya* as prosthetic—through the work of the woman cyberpunk writer Pat Cadigan (1991). She develops the notion of Synners, people who must synthesize the individual with the corporation and the state, the self with its embodiment and incorporation, the body with machines and information technology, and oneself with one's community. As Anne Balsamo points out, *Synners* pays close attention to the embodiment of laboring bodies, marked bodies, and the "constitution of the informed body" (1996, 140). Cadigan's book offers girl hackers, people laboring under hostile markings, and most vitally, bodies in connection. The term *Synners* also carries the older notion of sinner as well. Cadigan's characters, who come in all shapes, sizes, ages, colors, and orientations, aren't always particularly good at what they do, their situated knowledges are extremely limited, they are dependent on multiple prosthetics, and they are often powerless. But they are able to articulate, to connect, and to link culture, language, and politics: like Maya-hackers, men and women, they are community-bound.

Thinking of the Maya-hacker as Synner in this sense—not as hero but not as co-opted either—may capture the fluidary and hopeful possibilities of doing political work in the cyberspatialized nation-state and the prosthetic relations among gender, ethnicity, and activism. It may also open a point of articulation with another kind of synner—the Lizard Queen. In the context of transnational technoscience, it is important to find ways to work together to reprogram the binaries of either-or into both-and. Perhaps in a more fluidary relation, we would be reprogrammed as both a Lizard Queen and a gringa anthropologist in fluidarity, as the Maya (men and women) both retaining indigenous identity and participating fully in the Guatemalan nation-state, the nation state as both a site and a stake in the struggles over representation, and the Maya as both appropriate to and inappropriate(d) by the modern, transnational world.

In the next chapter I explore Mayan strategies for articulating with the nation-state and with transnational actors through legal means that allow them to be both included and different. I argue that just as the information technologies imposed as an orthopedics of power have been appropriated by the Maya-hackers, the law can also be a site for rearticulations. However, strategies of articulation also provide the space for countermoves, and I explore the way the Guatemalan state is responding to these appropriations.

EIGHT

A Transnational Frame-Up

ILO Convention 169, Identity, Territory, and the Law

Guatemala is socially, culturally, economically, politically, and religiously multiply fragmented. Of what unity do they speak, those who say they fear Mayan secession? There is no unity, and they proclaim its existence. Where there is so much cultural diversity, they deny that it exists. It would be far easier to reverse the situation, denying that unity exists in order to find it, and recognizing diversity in order to make unity possible. We must stop discrimination and pass 169!

RIGOBERTO QUEMÉ CHAY

Juridical notions of power appear to regulate political life in purely negative terms— that is through limitation, prohibition, regulation. . . . But the subjects regulated by such structures are, by virtue of being subjected to them, formed, defined, and reproduced in accordance with the requirements of those structures.

JUDITH BUTLER

INTRODUCTION: MULTIPLY LINKING LOCAL, NATIONAL, AND TRANSNATIONAL

Throughout this book, I try to keep the links among the Maya, the Guatemalan nation-state, and the world system (including Lizard Queens) in view. In this chapter, I turn more specifically to these interconnections, exploring the struggles over the drafting and ratification of the United Nations International Labor Organization's Convention 169 on the Rights of Indigenous and Tribal Peoples in Independent Countries, which became an important site of struggle in Quincentennial Guatemala. I am particularly interested in the role of a law like Convention 169 in constituting "subjects before the law" within the national and international frame.[1] The "rule of law" is a quintessential sign of modernity. As such, it functions as a prosthetic to prop up transnational, nation-state, and ethnic bodies politic. Struggles over the meaning of territory for subject-formation (access to ancestral land claims, and who belongs where) figure prominently in indigenous claims before such laws and in the reactions of states and the suprastatal United Nations. The state and the UN are spaces (like the cyberspatial

---

1. My understandings of law and society are deeply indebted to Bill Maurer.

nation-state) currently being territorialized by indigenous organizations—if only interstitially, as hackers tend to do—and this territorialization is a process of articulation that produces different national and transnational identifications.

My investigation into the relations of the Guatemalan state with the Maya takes place in a complex field of transnational, national, and local relations. Though I argue here for intense interconnectedness among the indigenous peoples, the Guatemalan nation-state, and the UN as a transnational actor, I also argue against evacuating the nation-state of autonomous effects and reducing it to a submissive comprador state, a pathetic lackey in the world system. This chapter attempts to elucidate the multiple and at times contradictory effects of a struggle to define and legalize indigenous identity and territorial rights within nation-state and transnational frames that are themselves in crisis.

The United Nations, the transnational vector I explore here, is deeply imbricated in Guatemalan national life and in popular and Mayan organizing. The UN moderated the six years of negotiations that finally yielded the Peace Accords of December 1996, with Jean Arnault, the UN representative, co-signing each of the intermediary accords along with the Guatemalan government, army, and guerrilla representatives. UN resources and clout are perhaps most visible on the ground through the United Nations Mission to Guatemala (MINUGUA), which has peacekeeping and agreement verification teams posted throughout the country, and which publishes frequent reports on peace treaty implementation.

In addition, each year the Guatemalan government nervously awaits the verdict of the UN Human Rights Sub-Commission, and it underwrites costly international propaganda campaigns and diplomatic missions in attempts to avoid a punitive verdict on its rights record.[2] Simultaneously, exile groups like the United Representation of the Guatemalan Opposition (RUOG; of which Rigoberta Menchú was a member), international solidarity, and the national popular movement lobby the UN in favor of sanctions. The government's efforts and the ensuing international judgment are always front-page news in Guatemala.

The UN also has a very high public profile through its High Commission on Refugees (UNHCR), which is overseeing the repatriation of the more than forty thousand refugees (who are primarily indigenous) returning from Mexico. In coordination with national agencies, the UNHCR is settling land disputes, buying land for resettlement, and providing protection and physical infrastructure. UN resources are also funneled into com-

---

2. The United Nations has a series of levels to mark increasingly heinous human rights abuses; each level carries a different degree of international oversight and corresponding political and economic isolation.

munities through its Development Program (UNDP) and Children's Fund (UNICEF), agencies that also provide an economic and social base for Guatemalan intellectuals (including Maya like Dr. Demetrio Cojtí), many of whom are between jobs in the state structure. It was a 1965 UN-sponsored seminar that led to bilingual education in Guatemala (Richards and Richards 1996), and UNICEF is currently funding Mayan Schools (Bastos and Camus 1995). UNESCO is developing and promoting the "Maya Route" tourism project in conjunction with the government Tourism Institute. This project, in turn, is being contested by Mayan cultural rights groups. The UN has also provided Rigoberta Menchú with funding and institutional backing by naming her Goodwill Ambassador for the International Year (and Decade) of Indigenous People.[3]

Here I examine the interactions of the UN, the Guatemalan state, and local, national, and international indigenous organizations in one long-term process: the struggle for ratification of ILO Convention 169. I argue that the ratification process of this international legal instrument quilts the state's relations with indigenous people in ways that reveal both the discontinuities in state and suprastate power and also the role of the state and law in producing "sanctioned identities" (J. Collier, Maurer, and Suarez-Navaz 1995). Unlike, for example, the Nobel Prize for Ms. Menchú, to which the state could only react, ILO Convention 169 is something the Guatemalan state has to act on. The ratification process was long and complex and has given rise to shifting investments and identifications for and against the Convention amongst ladino state officials, CACIF (the private business lobbying organization), in the press, and among indigenous organizations.

In a case like Convention 169, Guatemalan national debates around ethnic identity and indigenous participation must be viewed in a transnational frame—but a frame is also an internal structure that gives shape and support. So, although it may appear that Mayas and ladinos come "as they are" to dispute the Convention at the national level, or that indigenous activists and government officials represent unchanging positions in struggles in the ILO, I argue that, like the Quincentennial, the process of drafting and then ratifying—of disseminating and discussing, of constituting positions and developing arguments for or against—is a process that constitutes identities such as Maya, ladino, and Guatemalan. Within the ILO, debates surrounding the definition of indigenous peoples, their relation to territory, and their role as subjects before the law are also struggles about what con-

3. This is an intriguing institutionalization of her complex relation to space and territory. As an exile at the time of the Nobel Prize (she returned to live in Guatemala in 1994) and "international citizen," she is a boundary crosser, as I explore in chapter 5. The United Nations also provided material and symbolic support for the three international indigenous summits convened by Ms. Menchú.

stitutes a nation-state and its boundaries, including the entire concept of sovereignty.

The legal framework of Convention 169 radically challenges ideas of a homogeneous nation through its emphasis on indigenous rights to territory, to self-determination through educational, legal, and cultural institutions, and to full representation in state decision-making that affects indigenous peoples. Thus the Convention 169 ratification process has incited people of diverse sectors to frame an answer, to put into words and actually utter their positions on what the Guatemalan nation should be, how citizens should relate to each other and govern themselves, what an Indian is, and the relationship between people and place. At the same time that naturalized notions of nation, state, territoriality, ethnicity, and self are being challenged by a number of historic processes, the international and local pressure to ratify Convention 169 is pushing people to articulate—and in doing so, constitute—such identities.

For example, in 1991 the Guatemalan state, with UN support, organized forums throughout the indigenous highlands to discuss Convention 169. In these meetings the Maya "were informed of" their (internationally recognized) rights to ancestral territories, bilingual education for everyone (ladinos would have to learn a Mayan language as well as Mayans learning Spanish), and limited autonomy. As a result of these meetings, the Labor Ministry took responsibility for the Convention, fashioning itself as representing indigenous interests. Another result was the *formacion* (creation) of Mayan activists out of delegates to these meetings, who were often schoolteachers and local development workers. These newly active Maya—made into Maya-hackers through a relation with the state—formed the Delegation for the Ratification of Convention 169 and began to learn how to lobby Congress, get press attention, and form alliances with international organizations through foreign travel and fax machines.

Territory is a central theme in the struggles over Convention 169 at the international and national levels. Here I explore the ways that international law has linked states as subjects before the law to territorial sovereignty and the resistance of these "subjects" to the contemplated indigenous autonomy. Indigenous representatives argued vigorously for language in the Convention that acknowledges the special importance of traditional territories for their material, cultural, and spiritual survival. This survival is a function of constantly producing identities, in part through interaction in new territories, including the corridors of the state and the United Nations.[4]

---

4. Bill Maurer's brilliant book (1997) charts the construction through the law of territory as a "natural" category and the effects of this move on the constitution of differently empowered subject-positions.

Though I have discussed a range of ambivalent reactions to Maya organizing—the jokes, *mestizaje* discourse, as well as various sorts of state acquiescence—the ratification process in Guatemala, especially this idea of territorial autonomy for the Maya, called out especially powerful reaction-formations. In interviews and in the press, reactions were alarmist: "It will destroy the nation!" "It will create a state within a state, or worse yet, twenty-three little states!" "What sort of antipatriot would even suggest such a thing? It will bring the dismemberment of our beautiful nation; it will create a race war that will make Yugoslavia look like child's play!" "Indians will invade our best lands, and the sacred right to private property will be abolished! It is state-sanctioned idolatry. Guatemalan sovereignty is at risk!"

These heartrending cries see the state, and by extension the nation, as under attack from two directions—internal divisionism and external impositions (with the Maya seen as maneuvering international support against the state).[5] These reactions echo claims that the rise of transnationalism is accomplishing the withering away of the state: as multinational capital and suprastatal organizations (such as the EC, GATT, and NAFTA) gain in power, they limit the control of individual nation-states (a philosophy apotheosized in the neoliberal policies exported by the IMF). Some of this anxiety may be produced by the ambivalence at play between the argument that Guatemala must join the "modern" family of nations—by ratifying international conventions and achieving "sustained development" through neoliberal models—pitted against the view that foreign influences are undermining national sovereignty. Simultaneously, objections to the autonomy provisions of Convention 169 reveal the fear that, given the opportunity, each ethnic group would declare independence, forming "twenty-three little states." As such, these reactions may also acknowledge that the state, and by extension, the nation, are wounded bodies politic.

In this chapter, I address these "threats" to national identity and explore

5. Similar anxieties surround Guatemala's international image as a human rights "pariah nation," an image that has been only somewhat dispelled by the return to civilian government. Such anxieties are expressed in the similar vitriol of official attacks on human rights monitors and exiles (who "earn well for speaking badly" of Guatemala in the international arena). In addition to Rigoberta Menchú's Nobel Peace Prize (acknowledged as a response to army violence in the joke that goes: "The army is claiming half the Peace Prize money because they say they did all the work"), through 1992 and 1993 Guatemala's self-image was shaken by the assignment of a UN special rapporteur to monitor human rights abuses, Helen Mack receiving an international human rights prize known as the "Alternative Nobel," U.S. State Department condemnation of the Michael Devine murder case, and threats to their standing in the General System of Preferences trade agreements because of labor-law violations. Jennifer Harbury's efforts to learn the fate of her husband, which revealed ongoing human rights abuses (funded and supported by the CIA), and the Truth Commission agreed to in the peace treaty stoke these anxieties.

the apparently contradictory fact that Convention 169 was supported by many sectors of the Guatemalan state. What sorts of reconfigurations are shaping the responses of the "democratizing" Guatemalan state? I draw on the political economic theories of the Regulation School to read these contradictory responses as symptoms of the crisis that Guatemala, like many nation-states, is experiencing as a peripheral country in a rapidly changing world system and to show that relations between the Maya and the state in Quincentennial Guatemala are dialectical, that changes occur on both sides in recombinant articulations.

The chapter is divided into two sections: the first examines the process of drafting Convention 169 in the UN's International Labor Organization, and the second addresses how the legal definitions of identity contained in the Convention articulate with Guatemalan public discourses concerning cultural self-determination, customary law (*derecho consuetudinario*), and territorial autonomy. In this second section, I explore both the "ancient fears" of those who oppose Convention 169 and the governmental rationality underlying support for its ratification, which occurred in March 1995. I argue that the transnationally overdetermined moment of what has been termed "post-Fordism" is part of the conditions of possibility for the production of Mayan and Guatemalan bodies politic.

PART ONE: INTERNATIONAL LAW, TERRITORY, AND INDIGENOUS PEOPLES
The UN "Family" and the International Labor Organization

The International Labor Organization (ILO), founded in 1919, was the first international agency devoted to standard-setting and enforcement surrounding labor practices and human rights. It emerged from the Second International and predates the League of Nations. Within the UN "family," the ILO boasts a unique structure in that it is tripartite, with representatives of governments, employers, and workers from each member country.[6] This structure allows for multiple alliances (among progressive governments and workers, among workers and employers against governments, and so on), which in turn allow the ILO a wider range of action than most UN organizations.

---

6. The employer and worker representatives come from national organizations and trade union federations in each country, and each party has equal voice and vote in standard drafting. However, in the annual decision-making conference, each member state has two voting representatives, whereas the workers and employers have only one. Likewise, the governing body is composed of rotating memberships of twenty-eight government and fourteen representatives each of workers and employers (UN 1992).

After World War II, the ILO was incorporated into the UN along with the newly formed autonomous agencies, the International Bank for Reconstruction and Development and the International Monetary Fund (IMF). It is recognized as a specialized agency that deals with labor issues and retains reciprocal representation in the General Assembly and in the Economic and Social Council (ECOSOC, which coordinates the work of the UN and its specialized agencies a.k.a. the "UN Family"). The ILO is financially independent from the General Assembly (which is made up only of government representatives), but ECOSOC and the General Assembly must include ILO recommendations on their agendas.

Law and Indigenous Peoples

The ILO produced the first international legal instrument to address indigenous rights: ILO Convention 107 Concerning the Protection and Integration of Indigenous and Other Tribal and Semi-Tribal Populations in Independent Countries, which was adopted in 1959 and ratified by twenty-eight countries. Though undeniably assimilationist and primarily concerned with the labor issues affecting indigenous peoples, the Convention was the first and (to date) only binding international standard on indigenous land rights. It guarantees the right to ownership, customary law regarding land use and inheritance, and the right to compensation if land is appropriated by the state or private interests. Even now, as its replacement (Convention 169) is slowly ratified around the globe, Convention 107 is being used to support indigenous claims against governments.

The differences between the two conventions grow out of competing theories of how best to address the "problem of indigenous peoples" through legal means, which in turn parallel arguments internal to nations like Guatemala. Russel Barsh, a lawyer, member of the Mikmaq people, and permanent observer at the UN for the Four Directions Council, suggests these two opposing positions have yet to be resolved. One position argues that the "problem" is based in discrimination (the lack of equality). The other position blames assimilation (forced equality with the population of the administering state). The provisions of Convention 107 are meant to address the former: they seek to overcome discrimination by mandating equal access to health, education, employment, and so on (Barsh 1990, 377). Nonetheless, Convention 107 has been described as "repugnant," "an embarrassment to the ILO" (Berman 1988, 49), and "destructive in the modern world" (Anaya 1994, 43), because of its ethnocentric bias and program of directed integration. The ILO Meeting of Experts decided to update Convention 107 in 1986; in 1989, they adopted Convention 169. In the following, I explain how, as the result of an historic change in which the UN became a site for indigenous struggle, self-determination—rather than discrimination or assimilation—became the guiding principle of Convention 169, which includes protection of territorial rights. In addressing the ILO adoption procedure, I describe the reterritorialization of indigenous struggle in the 1970s and 1980s, as demands were made within the UN framework to constitute a new international indigenous subject.

Pushing into the Legal Frame   With the colonization frenzy of the nineteenth century, the law of nations changed, making states (newly the incarnation of nations) the only subjects of international law, as opposed to the "natural rights" that had previously upheld indigenous claims to lands. This new position was articulated in 1894 by the British John Westlake, who claimed that international law only applies to relations between "civilized" states, defined by their European forms of government (Poggi 1978). As Leo Gross describes it, this emerging Euro-state was defined by its position within a new interstate system, produced through struggles and compromises that culminated in "the coexistence of a multiplicity of states, each sovereign within its own territory, equal to one another, and free from any external earthly authority" (Gross, in Poggi 1978, 89).

Thus, by the nineteenth century, sovereign control over territory became definitive of the state, as was the state's monopoly over law. Indigenous land was declared *terra nullius,* and the force of earlier indigenous claims under the "laws of nations" was diluted because these laws were recast as moral issues. As theories of law and society have described, this opened a new way for European and Latin American nation-states to assert their sovereignty and enlightenment: as the paternal addressee for these indigenous claims. This process of recasting the relation of the state to indigenous peoples as a moral "responsibility," rather than a relation between two sovereign subjects, was a piece of the constitutive work of differentiating "civilized" (a.k.a. modern) nation-states from the "others" who would be subject to them (a philosophy guiding the work of Guatemala's National Indigenist Institute [IIN]; see chapter 3). Law became the "possession" of the colonizer states, and in a perfect double bind, law came, in itself, to represent the "civilization" necessary for the self-definition of that state, the legitimating mark of modern statecraft (Chatterjee 1990). Thus law became "the gift that we gave them," in Fitzpatrick's phrase (1990, 22), the doubly binding circular "truth" of state constitution that secured the boundary between state sovereignty and its subjects.

This ontology of the modern world system was recapitulated in the constitution of the United Nations, in which decision making is the singular right of territory-governing states, and in turn, membership is definitive of full and mature statehood. *Basic Facts about the United Nations* says that "membership is open to all peace-loving nations which accept its obligations and which, in the judgment of the Organization, are willing and able to carry out these obligations" (UN 1992, 7).[7] Paralleling anthropological practice as it is critiqued by Gupta and Ferguson (1992), the UN looks like it bridges the "natural" gaps between the "peoples of the world," but the UN is actually a vital site for the production and maintenance of such differences (namely, the way states are defined as international actors).

For example, even though a great deal of UN policy is made in practice by the burgeoning bureaucracy and experts, drafting and voting are reserved for states.[8] The only voice available to anyone not representing a "government" is through formal Non-Governmental Organization (NGO) status recognition from ECOSOC. These NGOs occupy an interstitial space among the "united" nations. Because they are considered subjects of the settler states administering their territories, indigenous representation before the UN has been limited to NGO status.

Indigenous struggles at the UN have focused on territory and status—both vis-à-vis their position within the UN system and vis-à-vis their national states. In the UN, territory and status are intimately linked. UN membership bestows legitimacy on governments, constituting them as sites on the global map of territorially defined "peace-loving nations." It simultaneously consigns other entities to simple NGO status (defined through what they are not, even when they may have territory, as in the U.S.). The drafting and ratification process of Convention 169 has been rife with dissension regarding land claims and who may make them. Similarly, the UN as a site has itself been a ground of contention concerning who may make a legitimate claim to be there—and whether they will be in a conference room, the mythic General Assembly chamber, or in the hallway (working and hacking in the interstices).

In the early 1970s, with the drive for decolonization, the rise in indigenous organizing, and the increasing international acceptance of human rights discourses, the UN began to address indigenous issues more directly.[9]

7. In turn, the role of the UN in binding these identities is suggested in *Basic Facts about the United Nations,* which makes explicit the doubly bound relation of nation and state by using the terms interchangeably: "The UN is today an organization of 179 nations—nearly every State on the planet—legally committed to cooperate in supporting the principles and purposes set out in its Charter" (UN 1992, 3).

8. In representations of UN functioning, the ideal, unified collective of each nation-state is momentarily made real as it is magically and unproblematically spoken for through their representatives. See reports on the debates over Convention 169 in which "the United States objects" or "Australia supports."

9. This work began in 1949 at the beginning of the cold war, when the General Assembly had invited the subcommission to study general conditions in the Americas, including the indigenous situation, in the hopes that "the material and cultural development of these popula-

As Russel Barsh put it, indigenous peoples became "an emerging object of international law."[10] In 1971, ECOSOC commissioned Ambassador Martínez Cobo to study the situation of indigenous populations worldwide, a study that resulted in a report finished in 1983. However, by the mid-seventies, this objectification of indigenous peoples, with the UN's apparently self-contained framework of states investigating their "situation," was pushed to include indigenous peoples themselves, if only in the margins as "consultants." Working through the 1970s, eleven indigenous organizations have won NGO status. The first time indigenous representatives participated directly in a UN gathering was the NGO International Conference on Discrimination against Indigenous Peoples of the Americas, held in Geneva in 1977, where they called for recognition of indigenous peoples as the subjects of international law.

In 1982, ECOSOC established the Working Group on Indigenous Populations composed of five nonindigenous experts, and in 1985 the Voluntary Fund for Indigenous Populations was established to provide material support for indigenous presence at the UN offices in Geneva.[11] Indigenous peoples, with and without consultative status, have also struggled to participate in the drafting of Convention 169, with commentators disagreeing on their degree of success.

I suggest that the formal mechanisms of winning status, making declarations, forming representatives, and writing up proposals both shape indigenous participation (in the sense of *formar*) and are shaped by it. The Native American legal scholar Robert Williams suggests that indigenous peoples have found an hospitable environment in international human rights work: "The highly formalized standard-setting activities of the human rights process have provided a sanctuary for indigenous peoples to . . . raise

---

tions would result in a more profitable utilization of the resources of America to the advantage of the world" (Barsh 1990, 370). In the early 1950s, the ILO instituted a program to improve the social and economic conditions of the Andean Indians, "with the objective of integrating them into the social, economic, and cultural life of their countries, while preserving their own way of life" (Alcock 1970, 251). More sustained attention to indigenous issues began in the 1970s.

10. Indigenous struggles at the international level have a long history, including the conferences at Patzcuaro, Barbados, and the Inter-American Indigenous Institute.

11. The five nonindigenous experts, one from each of the UN regions, were to gather information on the conditions of indigenous peoples. In 1985, their mandate was expanded to drafting a Declaration on the Rights of Indigenous Peoples, a process completed in 1993. As part of the drafting process, the working group created a space for the participation of indigenous groups without formal NGO status, despite initial disapproval by governments. Though designation with "expert" status means that these people do not represent their governments, the fact that the working group contains representatives of the UN's five regions seems to acknowledge a certain territorially linked identity, despite their status as "impartial."

consciousness and redefine the terms of their own survival in the world" (Robert Williams 1990, 662). A great deal of indigenous work at the UN is still confined to lobbying in the corridors, but they now have a presence in the UN landscape.[12] Julian Burger, secretary of the working group, heralded as an historic moment Rigoberta Menchú's address to the General Assembly in 1993 and the fact that indigenous leaders spoke to the Commission on Human Rights. "Such access to the world's governments and the international press would have been unthinkable a decade ago" (Burger 1994, 36). These international spaces—the corridors, and for limited periods the podiums of the UN—are being reterritorialized as resources for indigenous work, as landscapes charged with symbolic meanings, and as spaces for indigenous peoples to inhabit. Like Maya-hackers in the Guatemalan state, these peoples are working to speak in-between, to speak *interdicta*—lobbying among governmental representatives, in the hallways, on the outskirts, trying to get a word in edgewise between the speeches of the "nation-states."

The Indigenous Summit convened by Rigoberta Menchú in 1993 (where I volunteered as a translator [Nelson 1995]) was the culmination of these decades of struggle, as Ms. Menchú acknowledged in her opening speech in which she thanked her predecessors (several of whom were at the summit). In her speech, she remembered that this was a *struggle:* that in 1977, indigenous peoples had organized a march in Geneva to open up room at the UN, and their rallying cry, she said, was: "We have come to Geneva in peace and we want to be received peacefully, but if they don't open the door we will push it down and force ourselves in!"[13] She emphasized the importance of having constituted a space in the UN, in terms of opening a territory, and she remembered the aid she had received from indigenous leaders when she arrived there, to work, as she said, "in the corridors. I want to thank the many Indian leaders who, when I first arrived in 1982, taught me how to work in this field, who taught me how to struggle and not lose myself in frustration in these areas, in the hallways, where indigenous peoples had come to ask for a signature, to ask for a meeting, to ask for a little bit of space." She also lauded the Guatemalan ladino Agosto Willensen, who had worked for nearly thirty years in the UN on indigenous issues and who struggled to create an international juridical framework for the indigenous cause.[14] She reiterated that "indigenous peoples need to have a place, a space that is

12. However, this is a site strewn with landmines from previous warlike engagements, fraught with painful experiences such as hearing others debate one's fundamental rights.

13. Welcoming speech by Rigoberta Menchú, UN Goodwill Ambassador, First International Indigenous Summit, May 24, 1993. Translation by author.

14. Agosto Willensen began this work when he was exiled from Guatemala in 1954 after the overthrow of the Arbenz government. In 1993, he returned to his native land to take up a

more than a moment, in which to speak, a moment at a conference." The summit was also planned as a beginning in a new phase of struggle to create a permanent site for indigenous representation at the UN and thus to create new territories and new statuses before international law.

The Drafting of Convention 169   In the UN, organizing around Convention 169 has been both an impetus to and an effect of this process of indigenous territorialization. Robert Williams says that "the sudden emergence of indigenous peoples' human rights in international law is documented in official texts of the international legal system, most notably by the June 1989 adoption of Convention 169" (Robert Williams 1990, 663).[15]

The ILO adopted Convention 169 in two years (compared to ten years for the Draft Declaration on the Rights of Indigenous Peoples), and indigenous representatives were present as both nonvoting observers and as represented by the Workers' Caucus. Convention 169 constitutes a powerful tool in international law because, unlike a declaration, the ILO views nonratification as a potential human rights violation, and member countries are closely monitored on their ratification status. States must submit progress reports to the Committee of Experts on the Application of Conventions and Recommendations, and complaints of nonobservance can be made by any ILO member state or by associations of workers. If such complaints are not resolved through the ILO system, they can be referred to the International Court of Justice. Thus indigenous people, through their trade unions or in cooperation with workers, have access to the Committee of Experts to challenge their state governments, and they can receive ILO technical and financial assistance in filing claims (Barsh 1994, 46).

Although the ILO procedure has been harshly criticized for marginalizing indigenous voices, many commentators suggest that it is useful as a minimum standard, to be defined and expanded through use.[16] Robert

---

position in the Human Rights Ombudsman Office under Ramiro de León Carpio, with a mandate to deal with indigenous rights. I return to this work at the end of the chapter.

15. The Convention has been unfavorably compared with the Draft Declaration on the Rights of Indigenous Peoples recently completed by the working group (which grants much broader rights), but the Draft Declaration is also limited. It has taken close to ten years to write and must still pass through consideration by four more levels of the UN hierarchy (from the Sub-Commission on the Prevention of Discrimination and Protection of Minorities to the Commission on Human Rights, then through ECOSOC and finally to the General Assembly). Though wide-ranging commentary has been accepted from indigenous peoples, the Declaration was drafted in secret by five nonindigenous experts. Additionally, as a Declaration of Rights, it is not legally binding. Although it contains implementing language, it is merely a statement of values, and the UN has little authority to push for ratification or to act on individual complaints of violations.

16. Other critiques view the Convention as a cynical move by the ILO to expand its mandate. Howard Berman (1988), analyzing the revision of Convention 107 at the halfway point,

Williams insists that such international conventions have "demonstrated efficacy. Moral suasion, shame, and the simple capacity to appeal to an internationally recognized legal standard for human rights have all done much to undermine the legitimacy of state-sanctioned dominating practices that deny human rights" (Robert Williams 1990, 69). Wilton Littlechild, who represents the Great Council of the Cree (Quebec, Canada—an NGO that holds consultative status before the UN) and who was a delegate to the indigenous summits, said that he was in general satisfied with Convention 169. "We spent a lot of time and energy lobbying the ILO on that Convention. We submitted a series of draft proposals, and I think they really listened to us—surprisingly so, in fact. When we saw the final document, there were a lot of our own proposals incorporated into it."[17]

So what will be the object of the moral suasion Williams finds in Convention 169? What were the sticking points, the moments of opposition between indigenous aspirations and what Robert Coulter calls the "ancient fears of governments worldwide" (Coulter 1994, 37)? In general, the sites of struggle were similar at the international level as in Guatemala: the definition and thus status of indigenous peoples, which in turn influences their struggles for self-determination and territory.

The Legal Status of Indigenous Peoples   There is no commonly accepted definition of the term *Indian* in contemporary international law. In UN debates, the American states have frequently insisted that Indians are assimilated (*mestizaje* discourse) and already an integral part of the nation. This position parallels arguments made in Guatemala that deny ethnic and other differences by insisting that Guatemala is composed of "the same." In most UN deliberations, however, the 1983 Martínez Cobo report is used as a base.[18] This "Study of the Problem of Discrimination" loosely defines in-

---

charged that "no small element of bureaucratic territoriality [was] a prime motivating factor. . . . The process was entirely internally generated as part of the promotional activities of the bureaucracy" (Berman 1988, 49). He also criticizes the process by which the only direct input of indigenous peoples was limited to a ten-minute presentation for each category of articles placed before the committee. He quotes the director of the International Working Group on Indian Affairs (one of the eleven NGOs with consultative status), saying, "They were relegated to the rim of the conference hall, looking on aghast as their fundamental rights were discussed, debated, horse traded, and more often than not, thrown out" (Berman 1988, 52).

17. Author interview, Mexico City, May 1994. The contradictions, or perhaps better said, the dialectics of the struggle, are clear in the final version, which Aamir Ali, speaking for the ILO director-general, admits represents the "opposing pressures on the Committee of the desire to develop an instrument consonant with the aspirations of indigenous peoples and UN developments while at the same time not wishing to jeopardize ratifications by going too far beyond existing national legislation" (in Berman 1988, 52).

18. The report concludes that self-determination "must be recognized as the basic precondition for the enjoyment by indigenous people of their fundamental rights and the deter-

digenous people as exhibiting historic continuities with preinvasion societies that developed on their territories and who consider themselves distinct from other sectors. These continuities may include occupation of
lands, a common ancestry with the original occupants, and specific manifestations of their culture including religion, a tribal system, membership in
the community, dress, language, and life-style (thus the importance of the
mujer maya). In this definition, "Indians" form nondominant sectors of society and are determined to preserve, develop, and transmit to future generations their ancestral territories and their ethnic identity as the basis of
their continued existence as peoples. The distinction between *indigenous*
people and *minorities* has been highly contested in the UN, threatening a
superpower confrontation at one point.[19]

Clearly aware of the power of representation to form an image (*darstel-*
lung), indigenous delegates argued before the ILO that state power to clas-
sify groups as nonindigenous, through purportedly objective or extrinsic
criteria such as genealogy and behavior, is actually the power to extinguish
legal rights. They also claim a different status than merely "minority." In response to these indigenous arguments represented, or spoken for (*vertre-*
tung), by the Workers' Caucus in discussions, Convention 169 makes self-
identification fundamental to the definition of *indigenous,* which is a major
change from previous UN documents.

A great deal of the extremely heated controversy that surrounded this
definition during the drafting of Convention 169 centered on three apparently simple terms: *people, peoples,* and *populations.*[20] *Populations* (used in the
official title of the working group) and *people* (used in designating the International Year) do not signify official status, because international law recognizes only *peoples* and *minorities.* Use of the term *peoples* in the plural
signifies the status of having a collective identity, and governments were
fearful that this would imply the right to self determination, as defined in
the Charter of the UN: the right to autonomy, up to and including inde-

---

mination of their own future." However, the report concludes that self-determination does
"not necessarily include the right to secede from the State in which they may live and to set
themselves up as sovereign entities. This right may in fact be expressed in various forms of autonomy within the State" (quoted in Barsh 1990, 371).

19. Similar to some in Guatemala, the (former) USSR insisted that it has no indigenous
people, only minorities, and therefore is not regulated by such law. In this definition, indigenous identity is equated with the specific colonial history of the Americas and Australasia.

20. The controversy over these terms has been bitter in the Working Group and around
the declaration of an International Year. As overworked translators at the Indigenous Summit,
unfortunately clueless regarding these long-standing debates, we were often chided for mis-
translating and mixing these terms, whose long histories make them potent and overdetermined symbols for the indigenous delegates to the summit.

pendent statehood. According to Robert Williams, international law recognizes that "peoples" are a kind of collectivity, whereas a state is a kind of governing and administrating apparatus. However, the law has

> delicately avoided defining what is to count as a people that will distinguish "people" from other "lesser" kinds of collectivities for whom it is felt that the right to self-determination cannot reasonably be applied. States have been naturally fearful of calls for self-determination from groups that might meet some definitional test of peoplehood and therefore claim a collective right of secession. Such fears have found their embodiment in international human rights legal instruments, which, it should be remembered, are approved, ratified, and made effective by states in the international legal system. (Robert Williams 1990, 685)

Thus, the word *peoples* led several speakers to warn that use of the term would lead inexorably to the dismemberment of states (Berman 1988, 53).

The claims by indigenous representatives that they are "peoples"—which Williams sees as the most significant challenge to present conceptions of international law—has generated a great deal of compensatory discourse from UN officials in attempts to reassure states anxious about their territorial sovereignty. At present, international law does not contest unilateral assertions of state sovereignty that limit or completely deny the collective rights of indigenous peoples (Robert Williams 1990, 664). Erika-Irene Daes, chairperson of the working group, says that "where there is an existing state, constituent peoples must act through that states' political system and government unless the system is so exclusive and non-democratic that it no longer can be said to represent the whole of the population. . . . The international community discourages secession as a remedy for the abuse of fundamental rights" (in Coulter 1994, 39). Asbojørn Eide, former chair of the working group, writes that "conceptually and institutionally, world order is founded on the system of nations organized in states. [Though] state sovereignty is becoming increasingly more porous as international organization and trans-border cooperation advance[,] . . . the state will maintain its paramount role . . . as the organizing framework for law and order, and to a lesser extent for economic and social activity. Human rights require a functioning legal order, and states will remain the main framework for this" (Eide 1994, 62).[21] The legal scholar Hurst Hannum says that "self-determination does imply the right, although not the necessity, of inde-

---

21. The Declaration of the Granting of Independence to Colonial Countries and Peoples states, "Any attempt at the partial or total disruption of the national unity and the territorial integrity of a country is incompatible with the purposes and principles of the charter of the UN" (in Robert Williams 1990, 685).

pendent statehood, and governments tend to equate all demands for self-determination with independence and secession. . . . Negative government reactions to indigenous demands for self-determination are not surprising" (Hannum 1988, 672). I return later to these reactions as expressed in Guatemala and explore the surprising find of government support for decentralization and possible autonomy.

According to Coulter, practically no indigenous representatives have ever spoken of a right to secede from an existing country. In their written and oral presentations to the ILO, indigenous representatives explain that their understanding of self-determination means freedom from political and economic domination by others; self government and management of their own affairs; the right to their own governments and laws; free and agreed-upon political and legal relationships with the government of their country; the right to participate in the international community; and the right to control their economic development. As the discussions raged in the ILO over the terms, assurances by several indigenous organizations that they were not seeking secession did little to alleviate governmental unease. The matter was only resolved in 1989 in a complex off-record agreement to use the term *peoples* but with a disclaimer to make clear that "the use of the term 'peoples' in this Convention shall not be construed as having any implications as regards the rights which may attach to the term under international law" (Barsh 1990, 233).[22]

The weak resolution of this issue has led some international indigenous groups to in turn disclaim the Convention. Howard Berman insists that "the debate over terminology revealed that governments would resist any incorporation of principles of indigenous self-determination into the Convention. . . . Governments retained unilateral power over all aspects of indigenous life" (Berman 1988, 53). Yet Barsh, who participated in the debates, claims that although the Convention makes no direct reference to self-determination, "it plainly achieves the same result indirectly" (Barsh 1990, 215). Through respect for indigenous institutions, and by acknowledging rights to collective action and to control of economic development and cultural, linguistic, legal, and religious life, the Convention recognizes indigenous peoples as distinct societies possessed of their own representative institutions and identity. Convention 169 codifies the rights of indige-

---

22. The chairman said, "In my opinion . . . the ILO's mandate and scope of action does not enable the Organisation to define, grant or restrict the right to self-determination, a responsibility which belongs in other fora" (in Barsh 1990, 233). Also included was a separate section on Canada's objections and a personal explanation by the chairman that the ILO did not have the jurisdiction to decide on such a matter. In Guatemala, the Arzú government also added riders insisting that national law would always trump the Convention. Hotly contested by Maya groups, the riders certainly eased ratification but ironically may not be constitutional.

nous peoples to active participation in national decision-making. Though it does not establish full autonomy, it devolves management and policy control in health, development, and education (while not relieving the state of financial responsibility) and discourages interference in customary law. Additionally, recognition of an international legal personality is contained in the Convention stipulations that governments must facilitate contacts and cooperation among indigenous peoples across borders.[23] Barsh insists that, like many international obligations, the wording of Convention 169 is relatively imprecise, which makes its application vital in determining its scope. Through frequent invocations and rigorous claims based on the Convention at the national and international levels, he believes that an effective instrument can be forged.

Space, Identity, and the Politics of "Territory"   The debate over land rights in Convention 169 was as heated as that over status, and was also informed by government fears of a "loss of sovereignty."[24] One bone of contention was whether the term *land* would be used, or *territory*, a term that carries broader political, geographical, and ecological implications. Rather than indicating mere proprietary possession, it was felt that the term *territory* would best ensure the complex interrelation between peoples and the land, waters, plants, animals, and other natural resources that indigenous representatives claim. Indigenous claims to traditionally held lands were also viciously contested by the Government and Employer Caucuses, as were claims to the use of land owned by others and the ownership of subsoil resources. The committee deadlocked on the land issue until, in the final days of the 1989 session, the chair personally negotiated off the record with all three caucuses and devised a land package that was still so controversial that government abstentions almost broke quorum.

Article 14 now reads, "The rights of ownership and possession of the peoples concerned over the lands which they traditionally occupy shall be recognized" (with *lands* defined as the total environment of the areas occupied or in use). The claims to traditional occupation do not appear strong, however, and the Convention generally calls on national legal systems to resolve land claims. Convention 169 does not guarantee indigenous peoples' control of subsoil resources but maintains that their development should

23. This provision was apparently too radical for inclusion in the Working Group's draft declaration. Though Rigoberta Menchú under the aegis of the UN has been able to gather indigenous activists from many nation-states, the contacts and cooperation envisioned are limited to those allowed by national immigration authorities. For example, Mayan Guatemalans studying hieroglyphic writing were denied visas for travel to Palenque, Mexico. (Schele and Grube 1996, 135)

24. I borrow this section's title from Gupta and Ferguson (1992).

require consultation with indigenous peoples, impact assessment, benefit sharing, and damage compensation. Barsh describes the land-rights provisions of the Convention as complex and problematic but suggests that they respect indigenous systems of land tenure, emphasize the collective aspects of land rights, and "generally support the maintenance of a distinct regime respecting the conservation, allocation, and use of resources" (Barsh 1990, 226). Additionally, land claims based in the Convention are subject to enforcement by the ILO—the only international site where such issues can be addressed directly.

The Convention's other provisions contain the following: states must settle historical land claims, cannot remove people without their informed consent, must strengthen traditional subsistence activities, must support community-controlled education, employment, and health programs, must ensure fluency and literacy in indigenous languages, and must protect workers from coercive recruitment and hazardous working conditions. The Convention requires states to combat prejudices among nonindigenous citizens and to ensure that history textbooks and other educational materials provide a fair, accurate, and informative portrayal of indigenous societies and cultures.

In advocating strenuous use of the Convention, Barsh argues that international standards tend to begin weak and get stronger if they are used. Anaya seems to agree that Convention 169 reflects an emergent customary international law in which a certain common ground has been reached on minimum standards. "The existence of customary law concerning indigenous peoples is significant: states generally are bound to follow customary international law whether or not they have taken some formal action assenting to it" (Anaya 1994, 44).

Though indigenous peoples have pushed the frame of the UN to include them, their participation as "nongovernmental" is still limited. In the debates over Convention 169, only accredited indigenous NGOs were allowed to speak, and then for only one ten-minute presentation per category of articles. Although the Voluntary Fund is designed to materially support indigenous presence at the UN, such limitations reflect government anxiety that indigenous peoples who push into the international frame are out of place. They need to be "fixed" through a cordon sanitaire that limits their privileges in terms of when they may speak and for how long.

These anxieties may reflect the fact that the UN is not as all-powerful as it would seem. The UN itself disavows its powerful position in *Everyone's UN,* insisting that it is an organization of independent sovereign nations but has no sovereignty of its own. Its function is to harmonize, encourage, and initiate (UN 1986, 2). Additionally, NGOs have been less effective than framers planned because the ECOSOC, through which they work, has been overshadowed by the Security Council.[25] UN observers argue that the speeches and position papers of NGOs, and of many countries, are easily ignored, because global inequalities are recapitulated within the General Assembly.

Even the spaces opened up by indigenous organizing as NGOs are extremely limited within the larger UN organization. The Third International Indigenous Summit in May 1994 drafted a plan for the UN Decade of Indigenous Peoples that called on the Human Rights Group to take the lead in improving indigenous access to the UN. However, Ms. Helen McLaughlin, a member of the UN Working Group on Indigenous Populations, shocked the delegates when she explained how little infrastructural support the working group receives and how understaffed and underpaid the Human Rights Office is in general: except for her, there was only one other person, and they worked without so much as a secretary or a computer.

Additionally, the weapons in the UN human and indigenous rights arsenal appear rather weak, consisting primarily of the threat of placing a human rights violator in a shameful light in the eyes of world public opinion. Unless such censure is backed up by material sanctions, an approach which tends to be rare, the mobilization of shame must rely on the highly problematic assumption of a shared interiority and moral code across international lines (in other words, that they'll *care*)—hardly something you'd want to bet your life on![26]

Philosophical Limits: Identity "before" the Law   The issue of indigenous identity and status (and of the UN as a space to be territorialized) is raised when the "authenticity" of indigenous representation before the UN is questioned. Berman argues that indigenous NGOs with consultative status tend to be advocacy groups and international in scope, rather than representing grassroots activists who have closer ties to local or regional issues. He and observers of the indigenous summits criticize what they see as the formation of an international Indian elite that spends its time traveling and in meetings and thus loses touch with the conditions "on the ground" they supposedly fight for.

---

25. The Security Council, in turn, is often seen as ineffective in the wider world, as "rogue states" defy the "blue helmets" sent to keep peace. Like Rigoberta jokes, a recent cartoon relies on gender stereotypes to represent these power differentials in the case of the former Yugoslavia but reverses the depictions of Rigoberta Menchú as a phallic woman by representing the UN as a dried-up schoolmarm preparing to slap the wrist of the brutish soldier twice her size (which represents Serbia).

26. Rey Chow suggests that international attention actually incited Chinese government violence against the protesters in Tiananmen Square (1993).

These critiques suggest that indigenous insistence on having a space and status in the international arena encounters similar reactions in the UN as the Maya-hackers confront in Guatemala. The difficult and somewhat successful work of indigenous organizing at the UN has been "to convince the world that indigenous peoples are proper legal subjects of international concern or sanction"—that they are subjects before international law (Robert Williams 1990, 69). In order to do this, indigenous representatives argue (and official definitions like the Martínez Cobo Report concur) that they are subjects "before" the law in the sense of being temporally anterior to that law. This argument posits that before the conquest and through the ensuing upheavals, a collective identity with a specific relation to land and something called "culture" existed and still exists. The discourse of rights that is being deployed demands an essence, an unchanging identity that remains identifiable today. This is the power of tradition carried by ethnostalgia and described by Jane Collier (1997) and Partha Chatterjee (1990) as impossibly necessary for modern bodies politic. And this is precisely the site of struggle, as evidenced in the ILO controversies over the definition of *indigenous peoples*.

The perilousness of this site (which evokes the dangers of a landmined territory) has led some indigenous leaders to repudiate Convention 169. Similarly, this ground could not support "Identity in Mashpee" (Clifford 1988).[27] James Clifford describes how, through the disciplinary technologies of the U.S. legal system, the Mashpee Wampanoag were called out to prove their difference, to demonstrate their timeless essence as "indigenous" if they were to win land rights (which they were unable to do)—just as indigenous representatives before the ILO have to define their identity if they are to have access to rights. The demand to prove that they are different is also encoded in the Martínez Cobo definition of indigenous peoples: they must exhibit an historical continuity with preinvasion societies and preserve, develop, and transmit to future generations their ancestral territories and their ethnic identity. The claims to an identity before—anterior to—the law, which grounds the special claim to "ancestral lands," thus

---

27. James Clifford describes the Mashpee Wampanoag Tribal Council's attempts to *formar* an identity before the law in Cape Cod, Massachusetts, in 1976:

> The plaintiffs could not prevail in court because their discourse and that of their attorneys and experts was inevitably compromised. It was constrained not simply by the law, with its peculiar rules, but by powerful assumptions and categories underlying the common sense that supported the law. Among the underlying assumptions and categories compromising the Indians' case three stand out: (1) the idea of cultural wholeness and structure, (2) the hierarchical distinction between oral and literate forms of knowledge, and (3) the narrative continuity of history and identity. (Clifford 1988, 337)

places indigenous peoples in the double bind that in order to sue for land they must be "Indians" (or a tribe, or peoples), and to be "Indian" they must have land. This suggests the enormous weight carried by the prosthetic of the *mujer maya* with her links to the past and to rural life. The added double bind (precisely that affecting the Maya-hacker) is that the presence of indigenous peoples in the UN or the courtroom, in suits and ties, speaking "legalese" and organized in international NGOs, undermines their claims to traditional authenticity, which are definitionally based on "traditional" clothing, means of livelihood, language, and the ties to a particular locale. Again, this suggests the prosthetic importance of Rigoberta Menchú in her *traje* as the first indigenous person to speak before the General Assembly. Her power in this transnational site flows from her articulateness, her personal dignity and political astuteness, and also from the fact that she is a *mujer maya* and carries all of those fantasmatic condensations.

This is precisely the terrain of struggle for those governments that insist on solid identities, who claim that there is no difference there, that everyone is mestizo, assimilated into national and, now, international identity. Alternatively, the claim to an identity "before" the law enables a discourse of governmental paternalism that posits that indigenous identity is shaped exclusively outside of, and thus it is inappropriate to, the modern nation state.[28] This is the cyberspatial terrain of the Maya-hacker, the inappropriate(d) other; this is why the notions of *formación* are so vital and why the inclusion of self-definition in the Convention is such an important political victory.

However, as the struggles over this position suggest, there is no subject "before" the law (temporally anterior) because the law is instrumental in producing the subject. Judith Butler reminds us that "Foucault points out that juridical systems of power *produce* the subjects they come to represent. Juridical notions of power appear to regulate political life in purely negative terms—that is through limitation, prohibition, regulation. . . . But the subjects regulated by such structures are, by virtue of being subjected to them, formed, defined, and reproduced in accordance with the require-

28. Similarly, Vicki Schultz argues that women appearing "before" the law (as in a courtroom when they sue for equal rights) are undermined by notions of women being temporally "before" the law—notions that envision their identities and aspirations as preexisting, formed completely in the private realm. This temporal notion of "before" the law then justifies legal rejection of their claims against sex segregation in the workplace. By rejecting an historical version of subjectivity formed "within the context of, and in response to, structural features of the workworld . . . shaped in the context of what larger institutional and legal environments define as possible" (1992, 299 and 303), these notions of women before the law allow employers and judges to blame the victim (for example, for choosing low-paying, dead-end jobs).

ments of those structures" (Butler 1990b, 2; emphasis in original). Though this is one way of understanding individual subject construction, I suggest that "indigenous peoples" as a category did not exist as such until so defined by conquest and colonial law—including laws governing who must live in *pueblos de indios* (Indian towns segregated from the Spanish), the theories of just war and the doctrine of discovery, and the violent enforcement of "the iron law of wages" or the "laws" of capitalist underdevelopment. This is recognized (if problematically) by the school of thought (represented by Severo Martínez Peláez in Guatemala) that suggests that indigenous identity is economically determined—that it is nothing more than lower-class identity in a colonial setting, which will thus disappear once colonial relations are superseded. More nuanced accounts see all identity as historically constituted, as in Carol Smith's (1990b) or Ralph Woodward's (1987) work on the nineteenth-century mutual constitution of indigenous and ladino identities in Guatemala.

Additionally, the claim that indigenous peoples may be defined (in part) by a special relationship to the land, and that such a relation further defines them as a "people" or as a "nation," is only intelligible through eighteenth- and nineteenth-century laws of nation formation. The invention of tradition, including a timeless and natural connection to land, is a central strategy of constituting a national culture (Foster 1991). In part, such claims by indigenous peoples may be seen as a resistive move that articulates demands (for land, for sovereignty) in a shared language—one that the oppressor will understand. As Sally Merry points out, "Ironically, as aboriginal peoples living in developed independent nations governed by people of European ancestry make claims for the land and its products, they must argue these claims in the terms provided by the legal systems of these European nations" (Merry 1992, 368). Of course, land ownership and the very idea of sovereignty, notions of resistance, and an agency that would make it possible (as well as our ability to study those things) are historically specific; they do not exist "before" the law. Additionally, the process of articulating such political positions modifies the nature of what is articulated, leading, as Merry suggests, to the need for an analytical framework that can account for "dynamic, interactive, and historically formed relations between indigenous peoples and land" (Merry 1992, 368).

These suggestions concerning the historically constituted relations of indigenous peoples to the land are not meant to undermine the validity of claims to territory, but to point out the contingency and historical production of the agents that make such claims before the law and the danger in acquiescing to definitions that posit Indians as inappropriate to the modern, transnational world. To take these suggestions seriously questions the possibility of any existence "before" the law and in turn problematizes all foundationalist discourses. Thus, when representatives of the "international system of states" contest the "truthfulness" of indigenous identities and claims to land as constituted by (and therefore assimilated to) the (western, capitalist) law, their claims are equally open to contestation, because their political prerogative is constituted through the exclusion of such claims. I suggest that it is precisely these contestations that are at play around Convention 169 in the UN and in Guatemala. Antifoundationalism, as suggested by Judith Butler and others, is not necessarily about delegitimizing the claims of the less powerful but about interrogating and contesting power wherever it is deployed. "For if the subject is constituted by power, that power does not cease at the moment the subject is constituted, for that subject is never fully constituted, but is subjected and produced time and again. That subject is neither a ground nor a product, but the permanent possibility of a certain resignifying process . . . which is power's own possibility of being reworked" (Butler 1992, 13).

Such an understanding of the contingency of identity, its fluidity, may be contained in those indigenous claims to land that posit a "special relation" (Watanabe 1992; Wilson 1995). Such claims indelibly link indigenous identity to their environment, to their context. Thus, as they move into new environments—like the cyberspatialized nation-state and the corridors of the UN—identifications will change correspondingly. Through the process of contestation, the law constitutes these subjectivities of new territories.

For example, indigenous peoples appearing before the UN to argue this claim of a special relation to territory represent a diverse array of subjectivities, along both the continuum of indigenous experience within their own nation-states and of differences among those living in nation-states with varied political and economic systems. Think of the young, barely bilingual recent exile from civil war, Rigoberta Menchú, arriving at the UN in the early 1980s and meeting Wilton Littlechild, the strapping, confident, well-traveled, long-term bureaucracy warrior of Canada's sovereign First Nations. As they and hundreds of others arrive at the UN, interact with other indigenous delegates, are treated as representing indigenous claims, and are "hailed" as "international representatives," new sorts of identity positions are formed and inhabited.[29]

Thus those critics who complain of the formation of an international elite in this work on international law are right to some extent. There are new positionalities forming through the articulations of indigenous demands and governmental and international prohibition and acquiescence. For Mayas, their interactions with indigenous peoples with very different miens and experiences, and with governments and NGOs that treat them respectfully because they are indigenous, serve to form different aspira-

---

29. They were "hailed" in the Althusserian sense of *interpellated* (1971).

tions and models for identification. As a Mayan Indian chats with a representative of the Confederation of Indigenous Nationalities of Ecuador (CONAIE) and learns that their protests shut down all of Ecuador for weeks, or talks (through a translator) to someone from the First Nations of Canada and learns that they own their own airline, the resulting compare-and-contrast exercises serve to frame (in the double sense) their own identities. International indigenous organizing is a terrain in which men and women experience "becoming Indian" in the same way that leaders of the ALMG came to recognize themselves as Maya (see chapter 4). For example, the increasing emphasis in Ms. Menchú's public discourse on her indigenous identity, including references to "Grandmother Moon" and so on, and a more combative attitude toward the URNG on indigenous issues, may be another manifestation of this. Though some critics snipe that this change is opportunistic, others, including Ms. Menchú herself, suggest that the identity has taken on new meaning and power for her through her international work, as she focuses on indigenous rights at the global level, as well as on human rights in Guatemala.

Just as Guatemalan state and ladino body images are changing, indigenous identities are not the only things transformed by the articulations occurring around the international work of drafting Convention 169. Hannum suggests that indigenous peoples and their representatives have been in the vanguard of attempts to deal with ethnic and other conflicts by invoking or creating international norms (Hannum 1988, 700). Also, as Ms. McLaughlin of the working group reminded indigenous delegates to the summit called by Ms. Menchú, the UN—as powerful as it seems—is also a limited arena, fissured and contradictory. This in turn makes it a ground of hegemonic struggle.

Clearly, the UN has powerful effects, justifying struggles for indigenous representation there, but such power is not always where it might appear to be. Looking for power, even in institutions like the UN or the state, reminds us that it is hard to find a "there" there. Instead, power is constituted in relation: through articulations and continuing struggles over hegemony. This is why the UN is valuable as one front in the indigenous war of position. The indigenous work in the corridors, on the sidelines, attempting to speak in-between, is all hegemony work. As Robert Williams argues, this work in the UN with the project of defining indigenous peoples' rights is transforming discourse. "Rights discourse has functioned effectively in generating a shared, empowering vocabulary and syntax for indigenous peoples. [It] has enabled [them] to express their oppression in terms that are meaningful to them and their oppressors . . . [and] has organized indigenous peoples on a global scale to combat their shared experiences of being excluded and oppressed" (Robert Williams 1990, 701). As Merry argues, UN declarations "have substantially shaped the discourse and the politics of indigenous groups" (Merry 1992, 367). In turn, however, indigenous groups have shaped the UN through conventions like 169.

The State, Indigenous Peoples, and the International Frame

Nation-states are formed in relation, framed through international law and through relations with indigenous "others," in part through legalized exclusions. As Eide of the working group said, "Human rights require a functioning legal order, and states will remain the main framework for this." The nation-state is power-laden and yet its power is also diffuse, governmental (Foucault 1991), formed through articulations around a nodal point like Convention 169. Its frame of reference is also constituted through the exclusions of certain identities

The international frame in which, beginning in the nineteenth century, nation-states are the only active subjects was constituted by the exclusion of indigenous peoples as subjects from international law. The exclusionary framework of the "doctrine of discovery" allowed indigenous lands to be occupied as *terra nullius,* the inhabitants relegated to passive aspects of the landscape, as subjects of and subjected to the "civilized," "peace-loving" state. American (and European) nation-states, born in conquest, fashioned through "Indian wars," sustained through Indian (and other) labor in mines, on plantations, and in the household, are constituted through these relations, which become historically erased to leave the twentieth century's autonomous, "civilized" state as the sole subject of international law. Just as modernity conceals the tradition it relies on and apparently excludes, the frame of the UN, "the moral consciousness of the world" (Robert Williams 1990, 69), conceals such exclusions and naturalizes states as ready-made autonomous subjects acting on the world. Judith Butler describes this process:

> the subject is constituted through an exclusion and differentiation, perhaps a repression, that is subsequently concealed, covered over, by the effects of autonomy. In this sense, autonomy is the logical consequence of a disavowed dependency, which is to say that the autonomous subject can maintain the illusion of its autonomy insofar as it covers over the break out of which it is constituted. This dependency and this break are already social relations, ones which precede and condition the formation of the subject. The subject is constructed through acts of differentiation that distinguish the subject from its own constitutive outside, a domain of abjected alterity conventionally associated with the feminine, but clearly not exclusively. (Butler 1992, 12)

The fetishized position of an autonomous nation-state, acting in the international field ("The United States objected strenuously"; "Brazil argued that") is predicated on such exclusions, such attempts to cover over these wounds. It sets up a hierarchized binary relation (civilized state versus subject populations; international subject versus object of concern or protection; nation versus ethnic group; modernity versus tradition; and so on). But this binary is in turn disrupted by "fingers in the wound": by the reliance of each term on its "other" and by the refusals of Nobel Prize winners, Maya-hackers, *mujeres maya*, and Lizard Queens to accept these hierarchies. As Andrew Parker says, "The very fact that such identities depend constitutively on difference means that [they] are forever haunted by their various definitional others" (Parker et al. 1992, 5). In the case of the UN, this identity is haunted by indigenous peoples insisting on acting in—and thus reterritorializing—the international field. In turn, gringas writing social science (fictions) are pushed to make our frame of reference more fluid as the fields we describe are reterritorialized. See Gupta and Ferguson (1997).

The issue of autonomy is closely linked to sovereignty, which is both a universalized "right"—as enshrined in the laws accompanying the decolonization drive—and a jealously guarded component of the definition of nation-states as the subjects of international law.[30] A fear of indigenous claims for sovereignty, accompanied by the threat of dismembering the nation-state, informs the resistance of governments and employers to the provisions of Convention 169 dealing with definition, the limits on indigenous participation in the drafting process, and the panic expressed by some Guatemalan ladino state officials quoted earlier.

Yet the ILO has drafted a Convention that contemplates indigenous self-determination. This has led some Guatemalan officials to fear not only internal dissolution but also a loss of nation-state sovereignty to foreign intervention. Such anxieties would appear to be rational responses to the goals of the IMF and the World Bank (the ILO's brother organizations in the UN "Family of Nations"), whose structural adjustment packages do systematically undermine the power and efficacy of state structures, especially in small peripheral countries like Guatemala. Thus, despite the UN's investment in states, it is tempting to argue that the nation-state is obsolete and that its continuing existence in "false and frenetic nationalisms" is

30. In fact, some analysts, swept up in colonial nostalgia, would still like to deny full sovereignty to many "third-world" nation-states. Robert Jackson suggests the term *quasi-states* to describe those poor and violent third-world countries, which he claims are propped up by an international security net, just like individuals on welfare (1990). The symbolic divide setting off "first-world" from "third-world" nation-states is in large part mapped by the unevenness of "degrees" of sovereignty, and Guatemala's position in this system clearly influences both its relations with the Maya and in the international arena. However, evacuating the Guatemalan nation-state by suggesting that its power resides elsewhere—for example, somewhere in the international system—does not adequately explain the fetish effects of the state.

merely a convenient cover for "real social purposes" (Raymond Williams 1983, 197)—in other words, the perfectly realized power of transnational capital.

When I insist that indigenous struggles and the national-state must be viewed in an international frame, I am clearly indebted to the immensely important work on world systems, dependency, and uneven development. Colonialism, imperialism, and the extremely unequal power relations that retain within the global system, and the fissured, discontinuous nature of the state, must be acknowledged. However, we must also be wary both of overvaluing the power invested in the global system and of evacuating the nation-state of its power to create effects. It is dangerous to rely on a model of false consciousness that displaces such power to some more "real," other site (it is "really" international capital, it is "really" bourgeois interests, and so on). Similar to representations of Mayan activists as manipulated, duped, a *costal de papas* (bag of potatoes), or of the Mayan woman as ground rather than a lumpy, semiautonomous prosthetic, this model both suggests these identities are too solid and paternalistically consigns them to eternal victim status.

This is the trap of what Alain Lipietz, following Bourdieu, calls "pessimistic functionalism": "It is tantamount to saying that every compromise and every shift in the balance of power at any given point on the surface of the earth corresponds to the need to adjust a totally adaptable and perfectly homeostatic cybernetic system" (1987, 19). In order to avoid confusing the fact that the world is interdependent with the assumption that the world, or at least the "third world," is becoming completely homogenized, Lipietz and other analysts of the Regulation School urge us to look closely at "each national social formation in its own right . . . [to understand] the social and political struggles which stabilize to form a hegemonic system" (Lipietz 1987, 20).

In analyzing the tendencies in "post-Fordism" toward the simultaneous increase in globalization and localization—which some see as doing away with the nation-state (Robins 1989, 149)—the Regulationists suggest we keep in mind the role of the state as "the archetypal form of all regulation. It is at the level of the State that the class struggle is resolved; the State is the institutional form that condenses the compromises that prevent the different groups making up the national community from destroying one another in an endless struggle" (Lipietz 1987, 19). In thinking about Convention 169 in Guatemala (as in the UN), it may be most suggestive to see the state as a productive site, a terrain of struggle and compromise inundated with power but subject to unintended results, rather than as a lapdog of transnational interests. We need to look at the conditions of possibility for state action on the Convention and the effects of those actions, including those that simultaneously support the interests of Mayan activists, ladino elites, and multinational capital. Though always "partial," this is all part of a fluidary analysis, which I hope will inoculate us against "pessimistic functionalism."

Turning to the history of Convention 169 in Guatemala, I review the resistances to it but also ask, without presuming any preordained outcome, why there has been state support for it. How is the state framed, in the sense of supported, by Convention 169? Would increased indigenous autonomy necessarily undermine the nation-state? Is the model of the hegemonizing, homogenizing state, repressing all difference, the most useful to understand the changing relations of nation-states to indigenous peoples? How are we to understand "the peculiar sacred and erotic attraction, even thralldom, combined with disgust, which the State holds for its subjects" (Taussig 1992, 111)—which draws Maya and ladino to fight with such passion on its terrain?

For now I want to suggest that the framework of the nation-state itself, in the UN and at the national level, constitutes the terms of struggle and in turn is constituted through such struggles. For example, the nation-state is reinscribed in the battles over Convention 169 in various ways: indigenous delegations are identified by their nation-state (delegates are Guatemalan not Maya-Q'eqchi', Ecuadoran not Quichua), state institutions are the guarantors for most of the Convention's provisions, and the Convention must be ratified by the state, which focuses the struggle within that framework. The Convention's caveats that compliance occur only where compatible with national laws shows that it envisages a very active and legitimate national state.

PART TWO: ILO CONVENTION 169 IN GUATEMALA

With these questions, I now turn back to Quincentennial Guatemala, where the relations between ladino and Maya, the nation-state and its ethnic others, tend to be viewed, for both historical and strategic reasons, as the imposition of the unnatural and illegitimate frame of the Euro-derived nation-state onto indigenous communities. I suggest a more complex reading of this state framework, with an emphasis on the work, or the production, that occurs as the Guatemalan state becomes the site for the competing power vectors of international organizations, Mayan lobbying, and internal contentions along its own fissured grid.

It may seem a contradictory enterprise to argue that the state is both a discontinuous, somewhat open terrain for hegemonic struggle (especially given its brutal counterinsurgent history in Guatemala) and the site of power that is far from reaching its planned obsolescence. Michel Foucault warns us not to overvalue the state, not to become paralyzed by "the fascination which the love or horror of the state exercises today. . . . Maybe the state does not have this unity, individuality, rigorous functionality, nor this importance" (Foucault 1991, 103). Clearly, I do not want to underestimate the power of the once and possibly future genocidal Guatemalan state, but it is important to transform pessimistic functionalist notions of the Guatemalan state as all-powerful and yet retain an awareness of its magical effects. Despite tremendous losses, the Mayan and popular movements clearly find hegemony work within the state possible. As argued in chapter 3, state power (see Balibar 1992) cannot be reduced to the centralized apparatus, the National Palace, or the army high command. Instead, support for Convention 169 suggests that we may need a different model of the state, one in which the moves toward decentralization contained in the Convention's provisions may not necessarily be disempowering. I hope the following analysis of the ratification process (finalized in 1995, although debates over implementation continue to rage) contributes to understanding current struggles over implementing the peace treaty's Accord on Identity and the Rights of Indigenous Peoples and attempts to reform the Constitution, in which these same issues are at stake. The content of the Accord on Identity, which incorporates almost entirely the framework suggested by the Coordination of Organizations of the Pueblo Maya of Guatemala (COPMAGUA) and which in some cases is more radical than the Convention, points to the success of this framework—the productivity of the struggles—around Convention 169.

Convention 169: Contents

To quickly review what all the fuss is about: in an explanatory publication, the Guatemalan Delegation for the Ratification of Convention 169 (hereinafter called the Delegation) stresses that the Convention recognizes the enduring existence of indigenous peoples defined as those whose social, economic, and cultural conditions distinguish them from the rest of the nation, who are descended from pre-Conquest populations and conserve their own social institutions, and who are conscious of their indigenous identity. The document says that the Convention stipulates indigenous participation in the development and implementation of laws that will affect them and promulgates more general participation in national life, whereas the state must actively promote the maintenance and development of their difference. The national government must respect *derecho consuetudinario* (customary law) and take indigenous culture into account in seeking alternative punishment for infractions of national law. Convention 169 also calls for recognition of the special importance and spiritual relationship that indigenous peoples have to the land, which will include lands they occupy or use in other ways (ceremonial, and so on). The government should ensure the right to land traditionally occupied by indigenous peoples. Additionally, it calls for protection against discrimination in labor, sanctions against sexual harassment, protection of religious freedom, equality in education, and access to health services and the mass media.

The National Consultation   In addition to the full text of the Convention and this introduction that emphasizes its main points, the Delegation document includes the articles of the 1984 Constitution of Guatemala that pertain to indigenous communities, a brief history of the Delegation and of the Convention in Guatemala as of July 1992, and the text of President Jorge Serrano Elías's speech at the closing ceremonies of the National Consultation held to discuss the Convention.[31] There, Serrano congratulated everyone involved and said that he was

> extremely satisfied with the explanations of the Convention. . . . They are mature, clear, and simple, and prove that as Guatemalans we can agree to deal with issues that have been taboo in our history for many years. . . . Contrary to those who claim that the Convention will cause a national disintegration, we have seen that there is a clear desire to support the consolidation of our State as a nation and, moreover, to establish the ways in which we can make ourselves more Guatemalan with those multicultural characteristics we share, with the multiethnic formation of our nationality. This project has failed since the Conquest, but it is never too late to take the first step. (Delegación 1992, 28)

Serrano Elías became the president of Guatemala in January 1991 with what he termed a "government of national unity." Winning unexpectedly, Serrano had little in the way of a party infrastructure or the vital relations of graft and patronage that oil the political machine.[32] Thus *unity* referred to both his hopes of going down in history as the man who brokered peace in the thirty-year war (this would have to wait until 1996, with the government of Alvaro Arzú) and to being forced to share the treats in the state's piñata

31. The Delegation document also includes a note reminiscent of the Situationists (Debord 1983): "It is vitally important to reproduce this document by any means, so there is no limit on doing so" (Delegación 1992, 2).

32. Serrano won on the coattails of General Ríos Montt, who, because he took power in a coup in 1982 (not because he oversaw some of the worst of the counterinsurgency violence) was not permitted to run, despite a very popular campaign. In the 1994 elections, Alfonso Portillo (like Serrano before him) ran as Ríos Montt's "beard" and lost to Arzú in the run-off by only 3 percent of the votes. For many extremely complex reasons (see D. Stoll 1993), despite his role in the most violent years of highland counterinsurgency, Ríos Montt has done well electorally, including in indigenous areas. Jorge Serrano Elías, who had been in charge of the State Councils (which included indigenous representatives) under the military dictatorship, won with votes meant for Ríos Montt.

A similar lack of party infrastructure and political relations confronted Serrano's successor, Ramiro de León Carpio.

with other parties in hopes of constructing a minimally functioning government with some counterweight to the bloated army. Through this power sharing, the Labor Ministry came to be headed by members of the Social Democrat Party, recently returned from exile, who were entrusted with the ratification process for Convention 169.[33]

Through the ratification process, ILO member states are supposed to dialogue with the populations affected, so in February 1991 the Labor Ministry, through Gloria Tujab, a Maya-Q'eqchi' woman and head of their Office on Women, began to organize the National Consultation on the Convention.[34] To coordinate the work, the ministry hired a Mayan activist who had worked with the ALMG. He resigned just days before the inauguration, and Tujab's sister, Delia Tujab (see chapter 4), was hired as national coordinator.

The National Consultation was inaugurated in May 1991 by President Serrano in the luxury hotel El Dorado and attended by government ministers, the diplomatic corps, and representatives of churches, the private sector, labor, and international NGOs. Though some Mayan activists, including Dr. Cojtí, objected that few Maya were invited, Delia Tujab insisted that this was the fault of her predecessor and not a rebuff from the Labor Ministry. Things were off to a rollicking start.

The inauguration was followed by two training sessions held in Guatemala City, run by Jorge Dandler of the regional ILO and attended by Labor Ministry personnel, lawyers, members of the research institute ASIES, and representatives of the urban indigenous rights groups. A team of lawyers was set up to study the relation between the Convention and national laws, and a support team composed of academics, development professionals, Labor Vice-Minister Aura Azucena Bolaños de Aguilera, and Delia Tujab was formed to recruit regional indigenous support. The Convention was translated into four Mayan languages and published by the government.

Four regional workshops, each with a local coordinator, were held in Quetzaltenango, Tecpan Chimaltenango, Chajul Quiché, and Tactic Alta Verapaz. The meetings were facilitated by representatives from the UN, the

33. The Labor Minister was Mario Solórzano, the Social Democrat presidential candidate in 1985. The personal experience of Vice-Minister of Labor Aura Azucena Bolaños de Aguilera is an interesting example of the interconnections among local, national, and transnational circuits. Before becoming vice-minister, she worked for UNICEF with indigenous women in the highlands. She says that this was a breakthrough experience for her in understanding the situation of the rural areas and the importance of the work of Mayan intellectuals which, she claims, made her an eager supporter of Convention 169.

34. The ministry worked with representatives of and funding from the ILO disbursed through the Italian development group PRODERE (Program for the Displaced, Refugees, and Returnees) and in coordination with the World Council of Indigenous Peoples (WCIP), which is a recognized NGO before the UN.

ILO, the World Council of Indigenous Peoples, the government, ladino NGOs, and, in Alta Verapaz, the commander of the local army base. Each workshop lasted for three days of explanations and discussions of the Convention, and representatives from a total of ninety-six Mayan organizations participated. Fifteen representatives were elected from the workshops to attend a national meeting, which wrote up the final conclusions presented to the president at the national forum held on November 29, 1991. Twenty Mayan representatives were elected in this meeting to become the National Delegation for the Ratification of Convention 169, representing the ninety-six participating organizations. Government support for these representatives was not unanimous, however. Ixil delegates on their way to the capital for a meeting were stopped by the army and accused of being "neocommunists." According to Alfredo Copil, president of the Delegation in 1993, when members complained to President Serrano he denounced the threats, and since then the Delegation has had no security problems.

Concurrent with the regional workshops, the Convention was discussed in cabinet meetings and in every government ministry, as well as in professional associations like CACIF and the academic sectors, who were all asked to study it and submit a document outlining positions and policy recommendations. These documents, as well as the conclusions from the four regional workshops, were presented at the national forum in November, which was attended by representatives of the government and the private and popular sectors. All of the participants except CACIF supported the Convention, and the government made a public commitment to actively pursue ratification.

In retrospect, Labor Vice-Minister Bolaños, like Serrano in his speech at the national forum, expressed great satisfaction with the process as a whole:

> We encountered some divisions, we found a lack of real discussion of the role of the Guatemalan state regarding the indigenous people, but this was a way of beginning this discussion. There is a serious problem here and we must reflect on it carefully. The president understands this; that is why we consulted with everyone—the cabinet, research centers like FLACSO and ASIES, and working with the press. It has been excellent for those of us in the state. We are openly discussing these issues, through the forum, through the dialogue, using the television. It is important for people to see this, that they not be misled by rumors. This has been a great success for the government.

Regional Forums   Although they were considered successful by participants, the regional forums also revealed local rivalries. The National Coordinator Delia Tujab complained that many Mayan leaders tried to twist the forums to their advantage and excluded positions they did not agree with. She said she was surprised at the "paranoia. In Quetzaltenango they are convinced that everyone else is sold out, that people are spies. It is all a result of the violence, of course, but it made it very hard to do this work."[35]

Many participants, however, agreed that the workshops were extremely useful in bringing people together to discuss issues of cultural, political, and economic rights and in educating them in the national and international laws governing (and thus partially constituting) such rights. Delia Tujab said that, despite the problems, she was amazed at how productive the discussions of the Convention were, as people talked for days about how it could be used as a tool and how it created a new way of envisioning their relation to the nation-state.

Each workshop was the responsibility of a local Mayan organization. Ms. Tujab said:

> What really amazed me was the workshop in the Ixil region. It was incredible what happened up there. With the counterinsurgency and the war, with all the repression and violence, they were the most open and the best organized. For example, the groups in Nebaj recognized that they were always the center of such things and decided that Chajul should have the opportunity to organize and learn how to host a meeting like this.[36] The people in Chajul didn't want to at first, I think they felt insecure, there are no hotels there, no facilities. But they pulled it off wonderfully, hiring the parish hall, and everyone pitched in to help, making food, doing things. No "Doctór this" and "Señor that." Everyone was treated equally. We all stood in line for food, we all drove together over those terrible roads. But most important, we all listened to each other!

Several people I interviewed about the process said that they had never thought about their position in terms of such rights before these meetings, and that the workshop discussions of self-determination had been eye opening.[37] As a result, many Mayan organizations took on the Convention

---

35. She recounted how groups in Quetzaltenango refused to allow the labor minister into the closing ceremonies of their workshop, arguing that they had made the Convention their own, whereas he just wanted to use them for political gain. So Minister Solórzano and his full entourage of aides and TV crews were made to wait, after traveling several hours out from the city, until Ms. Tujab could convince the delegates that it was to their advantage to let him in. Ms. Tujab thought this was also meant to embarrass her, because she had undermined the attempts by leaders there to exclude local Mayan organizations that were not within their fold and had openly challenged Mayan men who treated her in a sexist manner. She said, "It really pissed them off when they tried to take over and I told them, 'You are a participant like anyone else. I am the coordinator. The only man who can tell me what to do is my husband, and you are certainly not my husband!' I sure made some enemies that day!"

36. The three municipalities of the Ixil area (known in military parlance as the "Ixil Triangle") are Nebaj (the first town reached by road), Cotzal, and furthest north and most inaccessible, Chajul.

37. Of course, these discussions all took place in the presence of state officials like Ms. Tujab and ladino researchers from government-identified think tanks like ASIES and INIAP,

as their own, publishing copies and commentaries for use by their members. An officer in the ALMG said, "The Academy supports the Convention. We have sent many telegrams to the Congress in favor of it. The people understand how important it is. We were involved with the consultations, and now it is accepted. When we go home, we take copies of 169 and people say, 'What's this?' and we explain. It is important that people know about these laws." The Maya, *Garífuna,* and Popular National Resistance Movement's illustrated pamphlet on Convention 169 (Movimiento Nacional 1993) suggests how productive the process of discussing the Convention has been in creating new realities and new activists. It reads, "We believe that it is important that our communities know, discuss, and exchange views on international laws with the goal of creating a deeper understanding of our life, our national and international rights, and to take the corresponding role in the political, social, economic, and cultural life of our country."

Alfredo Copil, president of the Delegation in 1993, said that the National Consultation marked his entrance into the Mayan movement:

> Before I had worked with a Mayan mayoral candidate in Quetzaltenango because he was a family friend. He proposed me for work on the Convention. Before I started planning for the workshop, we had not even heard of the Convention. Everything was new. They told us about the ILO and how they were interested in the indigenous people. I never thought I'd be at the front lines in working with them. For us, the Convention seemed like an opportunity to say I am here, I am alive, I am present, you cannot erase me. Historically we have been trampled on, in the national panorama we have been smashed down, but this Convention reasserts that no one can erase us—even with all the death they have handed out. If we ask for different treatment, they won't walk all over us now. The Convention reflects this—and knowing about it gave us proof of our culture, and we immediately decided to take it and make it ours. We made copies, to help people think about it; we handed out copies, and we studied it. Now we know.

In an interview in the summer of 1993, Mr. Copil eagerly tells stories of meetings with congresspeople and government officials, verbal sparring with the heads of political parties, arguments that convinced members of the Catholic hierarchy of the validity of the Convention, and negotiations with the owners of the country's newspapers. He has gone from a self-described apolitical man at the time of the Quetzaltenango workshop to an articulate figure on the national scene. Like many Mayan organizations, the Delegation has been criticized as opportunist. However, I think it is more

---

although most of the dignitaries—like the Alta Verapaz army representative or Labor Minister Solórzano—only made an appearance for the photo-op opening and closing ceremonies.

interesting to explore how certain bodies politic are being constituted through articulation with national and international actors and law.

The Work of the Delegation

This section looks in some detail at the relations between a Mayan organization and the state to give a flavor of how they work together. Though I cannot describe it here, these relations closely parallel Maya participation in the Association of Civil Sectors (ASC) and the process of working toward and now implementing the peace treaty.

Following the national forum, the Labor Ministry transferred responsibility for ratification to the Delegation, which set up base in the offices of a development NGO in the capital. The Delegation has labored under economic duress, but they managed to meet with many officials and to expound on the Convention before various groups.[38] They collected official support for the Convention from various government officials, including two congressional presidents (Mulet and Lobos Dubón), former Defense Minister García Samayoa, and many others.[39]

At what came to be a rather famous forum sponsored by the Delegation, one of the heads of CACIF, Reyes Mayén (who became Arzú's minister of agriculture), came out strongly against the Convention. His complaints concerned the same problem the ILO encountered in drafting: the issue of defining the "indigenous." According to Mr. Copil, who was on the panel, one of Reyes Mayén's main complaints was the section that linked identity to consciousness: he did not see how it could be applied. Mr. Copil says that he explained that the Delegation is fighting for people to be conscious of their identities, so that anyone "who has defended us, who has come to identify with us through this struggle—well, many Mayas are not conscious of their identity—but if you join us, if you are conscious of the Maya, then the Convention applies to you.' So then Reyes Mayén said to me, 'If so, then I am Maya. If it is not about the color of your face, then I can say that I feel Maya. It excites me to be in Tikal. I feel a strong presence there.' After that we became friends." This led other people to say about the head of CACIF, "He didn't know if he was Mayén or Maya."

---

38. These groups included the National Forum on Indigenous Rights organized by the Human Rights Ombudsman's Office (headed at the time by Ramiro de León Carpio).

39. Other officials and agencies included President of the Supreme Court Juan José Rodíl Peralta, President of the Congressional Commission of Indigenous Communities Claudio Coxaj, the Congressional Commission on Human Rights, the Ministry of Foreign Relations, and the Indigenous Parliament of America. In fact, several of these officials and agencies tried to claim responsibility for the Convention, saying they had fought for it when no one else was interested.

Though some dismiss this as simple opportunism, I suggest that such public statements do reveal a shift, a modification resulting from new articulations among different historically situated subject-positions (a newly formed Mayan activist like Mr. Copil, or Reyes Mayén, an obscenely wealthy ladino, called upon to take Mayan identity seriously because of international pressure). Clearly, there is no set outcome for these always contingent and overdetermined positions. They will not necessarily lead to the "consolidation of our state as a nation . . . [or] establish the ways in which we can make ourselves more Guatemalan," as Serrano Elías said in his speech on the Convention, but they will not necessarily give CACIF or the ladino government more power that they can wield unproblematically.

The Work in the Congress   Despite all this support, Serrano did not sign the Convention for almost nine months after the national forum. However, with the hoopla surrounding the exhibition for the Quincentennial in Seville, Spain, Serrano made an extremely proindigenous speech in Guadalajara, Mexico, speaking of Guatemala as an "Indian country" and promising to work hard for indigenous rights. The Delegation used this speech to pressure him to finally send the Convention to Congress for approval in July 1992. With it they submitted a "Petition to the Honorable Congress of the Republic of Guatemala," stating that the Maya were tired of war and of the racist positions that had left thousands of Mayan dead and tens of thousands refugees and that allow increasing poverty in the countryside. They also pointed out that although the Convention seems to exclusively favor the Mayan People, it is an international law that benefits the Maya, the *Garífuna,* the Xinca, and the ladino peoples of Guatemala because it "contributes to creating a democratic, participative, and pluralist system that will lead to unity and the solution to the country's socioeconomic and cultural problems because it respects and accepts the cultural diversity of these peoples" (Delegación 1992, 4).

The Congress passed the Convention through the first three phases of ratification so quickly, according to Mr. Copil, that he's not even sure many of the congresspeople read it. In the Quincentennial year of 1992, the Convention had a high public profile. The Five-Hundred-Years March through Guatemala City on October 12 stopped at the doors of the Congress and the National Palace to deliver a petition demanding its prompt ratification. There was thus political work going on in the streets as well as the kinds of lobbying that surrounded the writing of the Convention in the UN: the work in between (*interdicta*), in the hallways, on the phone, and through telegrams and other circuits in the cyberspatialized nation-state. In December 1992, independent Maya-Kaqchikel Congressman Guillermo Nicolás was optimistic about the effects of indigenous organizing around the Quincentennial in general and regarding the Convention in particular. "We're taking advantage of the political space this gives us. . . . The Convention is excellent; it would bring many benefits, and we are very interested in getting it passed."

However, in the final stage of write-up, all hell broke loose. CACIF began a negative publicity campaign claiming that the Convention would destroy private property rights and state sovereignty; the army reversed its support and reportedly "lobbied" congresspeople to do the same, Ms. Tujab, the national coordinator, was fired and her family suffered personal attacks, and the editorialists of the major newspapers began to warn of race wars, which led the Congress to put the Convention "in the freezer."

Part of this sudden chill in government support included naming staunch defender Congressional President Mulet as ambassador to the United States and postponing indefinitely the publication of various ministries' supporting documents, which disappeared into the bowels of the Foreign Ministry. Additionally, once the frisson of the Quincentennial and Nobel Prize had passed, Delegation members complained that the press was no longer interested in covering Mayan issues and that they in turn didn't have the funds to pay for *fafa* (bribes to get your story published). In mid-1993, Mr. Copil said, "The indigenous situation is out of fashion now. It's different for someone like Rigoberta; everything she does is news. But for the rest of us, we have to do something explosive, sensationalist, to get attention. If we sit down and carefully explain our positions, they are not interested." In turn, just as members of the press wanted something in return for coverage, in meetings with congresspeople the Delegation found that the political parties wanted them to declare party membership in return for their support.[40]

Resistance to the Convention

Despite the kid glove treatment that the Convention gives to state sovereignty, its provisions for indigenous rights to "traditional territories," local autonomy, consultation on development, and fair wages seem suited to give Guatemala's traditional elites well-deserved apoplexy. Despite the interest it generated, timing also had an impact on transforming the gentlemanly approval of the November 1991 national forum into the shrill headlines that abounded in late 1992: "Demagogues on the Left, Fear and Emptiness on the Right: Convention 169"; "We Must Prevent an Ethnic Explosion";

---

40. Many congresspeople also questioned them sharply on whether they planned to start their own Indian party. This is a contentious issue among the Maya.

"Autonomy for the Ethnics? Smashing Guatemala's Geographic Unity?" Final approval of the ratification was planned for October 1992, with the combination of the commemoration of the 1944 Democratic Spring, the Quincentennial, the first massive refugee return (later postponed), peace talks with the guerrilla, and the Nobel Peace Prize awarded to Rigoberta Menchú.[41]

Thus one explanation for the sudden reversal in the Convention's fortunes may be the way it stimulates Guatemala's founding trauma of colonization, its wounded body image, and induces the familiar reaction formations of fantasmatic paranoia. In the historic overdetermination of 1992, the basic injustice of the postcolonial mode of regulation, in which a tiny class and ethnic minority controls the wealth, becomes problematized—the sutures holding together national-ethnic identity start to give way. The antagonism of that relation breaks through centuries of wealthy ladino hegemony work attempting to naturalize indigenous subordination, and elites are reminded (again) of the relative precariousness of their position.[42] The refugee return coalesces the trauma of the counterinsurgency war and the attending international disapproval with anxieties regarding territory, including the porousness of national boundaries and fears of indigenous autonomy. The first organized, massive return was rescheduled for January 1993. As part of the return agreement, the settlement area in the Ixcán region of northern Guatemala was to be demilitarized: the army was not welcome there, and the returnees refused to participate in the Civil Patrol. In April 1993, the national press was complaining that the indigenous former refugees were creating an "autonomous territory." "Soon you'll need a visa to go to *Victoria 20 de Enero* [Victory January 20; the settlement's name, memorializing the date of the return]. It is like a state within a state" (*Crónica*, 16 April 1993).

The issues surrounding "identity" and status that wracked the ILO debates also inform reactions against Convention 169 in Guatemala, where a special emphasis on the definition of *Indian* and how many of them there are highlights the precariousness of the elite minority. The official statistic of the indigenous population as 40 percent and declining places the Maya in a minority and has been used to claim the success of ladinoization and to justify the attitude of "Why give them rights when they will disappear in a

41. The 1944 Democratic Spring is when the dictator Jorge Ubico was overthrown, an event that ushered in the ten years of elected governments of Presidents Arévalo and Arbenz, which were ended by a CIA-backed coup followed by decades of military rule.

42. Ernesto Laclau and Chantal Mouffe suggest that resistance exists wherever there is power, but that this resistance is only sometimes openly antagonistic and thus political (Laclau and Mouffe 1985, 142).

couple of generations anyway?"[43] However, with the Convention, the Maya suddenly become a menacing majority, with some opponents asserting that they are 80 percent of the population. CACIF's Reyes Mayén talks of being outnumbered in his own country. "Convention 169 is supposed to protect minorities, but here *we* are the minority—how will it protect us?" (*El Grafico,* 14 October 1992).[44] Editorialist Alvaro Enrique Palma warned: "We must remember that the *indios* of this country are the majority. Today they are extremely conscious, and what they want is to rule. If these *indios* one day take power—which they will do legitimately, because they have the most votes— then these majorities will decide our fate" (*Prensa Libre,* 31 August 1992). The opposite argument is also used against Convention 169 (although somewhat halfheartedly): there are no Indians, so the Convention is not appropriate for Guatemala. Congressman Mérida Mérida said, "In Guatemala we are all mestizos, part Indian, part ladino. There are no 'Maya.' There might be ethnic groups here, but Convention 169 is for indigenous peoples and tribes, so it doesn't apply here." Serrano's Presidential Secretary Juan Daniel Alemán said, "Our Indians have TVs, wear shoes, and are fully participating in the society of consumption. They are not really different from any other Guatemalan, so they don't need some different regime. There is no need to construct an other Guatemala inside Guatemala."[45]

The Role of Law against Convention 169   The framework of the law both outlines and structures the various reactions against Convention 169. Congressional opponents of the Convention carefully couched their objections in the staid terms of legality, questioning the Convention's relation to national sovereignty as framed in the Constitution. Diego Velasco Brito, a Maya-Ixil congressman and supporter, said, "They say they have constitutional questions. *Now* they are Constitutionalists! Just as an excuse to keep 169 from being discussed, they send it to the Constitutional Court for a study." The claim that the Convention was not constitutionally valid has been an effective stalling device. Given the importance of the notion of the "rule of law" for progressive organizations, it was difficult to refute such objections.

The legalist position is also a response to the "dread" of foreign intervention. The Convention is portrayed as introducing the cancer of national disintegration, as I explore later, whereas the Constitution is represented as a protective membrane, legally protecting the national body politic.

43. Dr. Demetrio Cojtí has called these low numbers a "statistical genocide."

44. As Carol Smith has shown, however, this is not a terror confined to right-wing ladinos (C. Smith 1992).

45. This is precisely the digital binary (same-different, modern-traditional) that the Mayas are hacking.

A constitutionally sanctioned go-ahead for ratification did not stop opponents from insisting that the Convention be sent to the Constitutional Court for further (extended) study. However, when the Delegation tried to set up a forum in the Congress to address constitutional issues, Mr. Copil recounts that many congresspeople became flustered and insisted that this was not necessary. "They keep saying that they need to discuss it more, but when we become serious and offer to bring in lawyers and to discuss the position of the Pueblo Maya calmly, they get scared and run away. They will not listen because they are afraid of being convinced." The fluster of the congresspeople when the Delegation became more legalistic than they, and the recourse to national law to contain them, suggests consternation about the Maya territorializing this (previously ladinos-only) legal terrain.

The legal counterargument insists that the issues addressed by the Convention would be better resolved through national legislation. When I asked him about Convention 169, Serrano's Presidential Secretary Alemán picked up the Constitution on his desk and read aloud all of the articles regarding indigenous peoples, to prove that ratification was extraneous (although he supported the Convention, he assured me). Intriguingly, though the 1985 Constitution is one of the first to directly address the indigenous situation, the articles that "protect ethnic groups, their lands and agricultural cooperatives, and communal lands" circle around a central lack. Rather than address the specifics of these issues, the framers of the 1985 Constitution literally left it for later. Article 70—the "specific law" meant to address the indigenous population—reads merely, "A law will regulate the materials in this section." Guatemalan patriots say there is no need to use external regulations to deal with the indigenous situation, when they have Article 70. This argument convinced CACIF's Reyes Mayén, who, according to Mr. Copil, had been a friend to the Delegation after coming out as a Maya at the November 1992 forum. But "he was turned around. He says personally he supports the ideas in Convention 169, but that we should make *national* laws, reform the civil code."

However, national law and the Constitution (despite its lacks) are a double-edged tool that may also work for Mayan interests. Mr. Copil said, "We have Mayan lawyers and ladino lawyers working on 169. The legal arguments have sustained us. Congresspeople may not understand our cosmology, but the legal factor is understood. We have been praised for basing all our arguments in the Constitution." In a newspaper editorial on Convention 169, Rigoberto Quemé Chay, a Maya-K'iche' researcher (and in 1996 the first Mayan mayor of Quetzaltenango), said, "Laws have always maintained discrimination. . . . They may make the state look benevolent, like it is giving the indigenous people privileges, but their true goal is to maintain the exploitation of cheap Mayan labor. Convention 169 promotes the participation of those excluded from the system and puts new social actors on the stage who are seeking new spaces for their own development" (*Siglo XXI,* 3 July 1993).[46]

Effects of the Serrano Coup and the de León Carpio Government

Ratification, already stalled in legalistic arguments, was further set back by Serrano's illegal auto-coup in May 1993. Dissolving the Congress during the state of siege created legislative mayhem, and after the de León Carpio government was installed, a campaign began to purge the Congress. In July and August 1993, as human rights groups occupied the Congress and demanded the resignation of corrupt legislators, that discredited body turned to Convention 169 and promised final approval. This move was denounced by the press, and Mayan organizations were divided on whether the general chaos symbolized an opportunity or a danger.[47] Members of the Delegation suggested that "running water is good for fishing," that it didn't matter why they ratified the Convention as long as it was legally on the books.[48] Dr. Cojtí, however, said, "The parties are using the Indians for legitimacy at the same time that the people are calling for them to be purged. This makes the Delegation look like it is selling out, and there has been a strong reaction against them. Of course, you can see the racism in that reaction too." By September 1993, President de León Carpio called for a referendum to purge the Congress, and the Delegation gave up hope of passing Convention 169 through the lame-duck institution. It stayed "in the freezer" until August 1994, when new members of Congress were finally elected.

Mayan lobbying for the Convention did not stop, however. After taking office, de León Carpio undertook a sort of postpartum electoral campaign, and at many of his whistle-stops, village leaders called on him to ratify Convention 169. In her welcoming speech, Quetzaltenango's indigenous queen insisted that to make Guatemala a unified nation would require more than the faith in democracy that resisted the Serrano coup. Instead there had to

---

46. See Kay Warren's book (1998), which deals with the formation of Mayan lawyers.

47. Marta Altolaguirre said in September 1993, "This use of 169 (which of course we support as long as it is not used to violate the human rights of private property, legitimately acquired), this use of indigenous rights and talk of distributing land, is a clumsy attempt to gain the sympathy of the dispossessed classes, revealing an extravagant cynicism" (*Siglo XXI,* 3 September 1993).

48. Mr. Copil said that the May 1993 state of siege helped him make the legal argument for Convention 169 when he lobbied congresspeople. "I would say that the ladinos only had to bear five days of the lack of constitutional guarantees that the Maya have endured for centuries, and they couldn't stand it. We live with this situation all the time, but they experience it for five days and everyone is mobilized—the church, CACIF, the army, all the ladinos were out there protesting. When I say this, people say they finally understand what we've been talking about all this time."

be real support for indigenous demands, including ratification of Convention 169, and the creation of a National Indigenous Fund to support the democratic participation of the Maya in the country's future. de León Carpio, who had supported 169 in his work as human rights ombudsman, cited ratification as an immediate goal in his "180 Days Plan," the framework for his new government.

Land   The polemics surrounding land and territory that so divided the ILO not only resonate in Guatemala; they are amplified and structure intense reactions to Convention 169. In Guatemala's agricultural economy, the most entrenched antagonism is grounded in skewed patterns of landholding. The Convention is seen by opponents as threatening land "rights," private property in general, and even the state's control of territory—calling up what many commentators call "ancestral terrors" of land invasions and other porous boundaries.[49] It is precisely the land issue that most people blame for the sudden chill around ratification in the Congress, specifically caused by CACIF's pressure. Congressman Paíz Hernández, a member of the Christian Democrats, said that they were having trouble fighting CACIF. "Land is a problem. People think that it will create invasions. . . . Landowners are saying that they will arm their people on the *fincas* and shoot anyone who comes near. We are afraid that it will lead to more violence—that it will push these people to invade." Supporters of the Convention, such as Labor Vice-Minister Bolaños, deny that it will result in radical redistribution. "People are afraid the Convention will make the Indians demand land. But the Convention does not say this. It must correspond with national laws. There will be nothing like Arbenz's Article 90. We've advanced. Too many years have gone by to return to that time."[50]

Such assurances notwithstanding, reactions against the Convention's land rights reveal the assumption that land rightfully belongs to ladinos. Although the Convention's opponents deny that land should belong to the Indians, they see Indians as belonging to the land, both in the romantic ethnostalgic sense of a special bond with nature, and in the sort of spatial

49. A popular Rigoberta joke played on this fear: "Rigoberta does not want to invest the Nobel Prize money in buying land because she's afraid that Indians will invade it."

50. The 1952 Article 90 on land reform empowered the government to expropriate holdings greater than 674 acres, or 224 acres if the land were not cultivated. Expropriated lands were paid for at the value assessed by the owner. More than 1.4 million acres were expropriated (one-quarter of Guatemala's arable land), including 372,000 acres of the United Fruit Company's fallow holdings. The Dulles brothers' personal holdings in the United Fruit Company led, in part, to the U.S.-backed overthrow of the Arbenz government (Sinclair 1994; Handy 1984; Gleijeses 1991).

incarceration that makes rural life and the peasantry equivalent to "Indian."[51] For example, members of PAN (represented by current President Arzú), an urban-based based political party, told the Delegation that they did not need to support 169 because they did not represent areas with an indigenous population. Mr. Copil responded that the city is full of Maya and that there are indigenous people in every party.[52] Many seem to retain the sense, however, that indigenous people belong elsewhere, whereas the land belongs to ladinos.

This refusal to acknowledge indigenous territorialization throughout the country accompanies increasing attempts by ladinos to territorialize the country's interior. The "laboratories of modernity" created by the war's militarization of the countryside, and the plans for bureaucratic decentralization, are examples of this ladino territorialization. The double sense that identifies Indians as passive objects attached to the land rightfully owned by ladinos because they actively interact with it is expressed thousands of times a day in the ubiquitous print, billboard, radio, television, and movie preview ads for Rubios cigarettes. The slogan for Rubios, "This is my land" (*Esta es mi Tierra*), always accompanies the image of a buff ladino man. The ads' narrative sequences show an indigenous person in distress: an elderly man falls in a pothole-strewn street, a dock collapses into Lake Atitlán, or a shepherd boy loses his black sheep. They are rescued by the Rubios-smoking white man, who, to the swell of music, fixes the road or dock lickety-split, or restores the black sheep to the *traje*-dressed child. At the fade out, the ladino enjoys his cigarette and the thankful and admiring gazes of the townsfolk as a manly voice-over intones "This is my land."[53]

This image of a white man saving brown people from a brown landscape is echoed in ladino claims that Convention 169's land articles will hold indigenous peoples back. A Guatemalan analyst at the UNDP, who had served in the Finance Ministry during Cerezo's government, said, "This part of the Convention confounds me, as an economist. I understand that people want

51. The USAC historian Edeliberto Cifuentes suggested that the current system is still mired in the feudal practices of the *encomienda,* in which land, including its complement of indigenous workers, was partitioned among the Spaniards.

52. Despite such comments, the Delegation spoke of PAN as a friend of Convention 169 in general (they had also supported the ALMG legalization). Perhaps PAN listened to Mr. Copil because they have begun to extend their reach into indigenous areas, winning the congressional seat for the Ixil area in the August 1994 elections and the 1995 presidential campaign. For indigenous experiences in the city, see AVANCSO (1991), and Pérez Sáinz, Camus, and Bastos (1992).

53. Rumor had it that Rubios, touted as a "national product," used the second-best, cast-off tobacco (as well as the image) from the Marlboro factory. This placed it in a category similar to that of Coca-Cola, known as the *aguas negras del imperialismo* (imperialist sewage).

Figure 21. "This is my land." Billboard for Rubios cigarettes. Photo by Lois Nelson. Published with kind permission.

land, I respect their cultural values, that it makes them feel secure to be cultivating a parcel, but giving one hundred tiny parcels to one hundred families is not going to solve the problem. It is to condemn them to be poor. It is a way of stigmatizing people . . . a return to the past, going back to primitive relations. Instead, we need to bring people into the larger economy, make them into entrepreneurs."

An official in the Culture Ministry said, "The question of lands in 169 concerns me a great deal. Look at the case of Cajolá [an indigenous land invasion]. They say they want a particular piece of land because of their cosmology, that their roots are in that little space. But they do not understand that the land has another owner now. It would be beautiful if 169 were complied with—it would be another world! But we can't go back in time. We must go forward."

Many derided any notion of returning traditional lands, suggesting that the gringos should first return Manhattan to the Indians! This antagonism was enunciated during the Quincentennial protest march on October 12, 1992. As the march wound its way through the close streets of Zone One in

Guatemala City, marchers' chants called for land: "Guatemala is our land too!" A ladina woman in a housewife's apron and slippers started screaming from among the sparse onlookers, "It WAS your land! It WAS your land!" Then she muttered to the people around her, "I don't like it. They want to take the land away from the rich people." I said, "You're not rich, why do you care?" And she responded, "The land does not belong to them. I don't like it."[54]

Sovereignty and the Contradictions of the Nation-State as "Autonomous" Subject

At the national as at the international level, land issues are clearly linked to concerns about sovereignty. Congressman Paíz Hernández complained about the external pressures on Guatemala to ratify the Convention. "They are pressuring Guatemala about tariffs and the General System of Preferences. But Washington has signed fewer ILO conventions than we have. Who are they to pressure us?" Buried in the land issue are also fears about the loss of territorial integrity. A member of the Agricultural Chamber denounced Convention 169 in a public forum because it would lead to "Indians overrunning the best lands, the country becoming ungovernable, and Guatemala turning into Yugoslavia." In fact, Yugoslavia serves as a master trope in the reactions against the Convention, raising the specters of race war linked to territorial dismemberment. Oscar Clemente Marroquín, editor of the daily La Hora, warns against the Convention on the grounds that "the greatest danger confronting humanity, worse than class war, is race war, and the Yugoslavia case is a clear demonstration that if anything can take men to the extremes of savagery and ferocity, it is racial differences" (23 February 1993). Fear of further territorial divisions is informed by a nostalgia for some former "Greater Guatemala" sliced down over time to the present sorry rump, the final indignity the recent (and still unreconciled) loss of Belize.[55] In response to 169 and the idea of indigenous au-

---

54. Her response recalls Charles Hale's work on "resistance and contradiction" among the Miskitu and Sandinistas on Nicaragua's Atlantic coast in which "conjugated oppressions" (economic exploitation, ethnic identifications) make for what appear to outsiders as strange alliances (1994).

55. In 1986, I worked in Guatemala with a Mexican colleague who was shocked at the number of Guatemalans who blamed him personally for the "loss" of Chiapas.

The deep ambivalence about Belize merits much closer scrutiny than I can afford it here. Serrano Elías was vilified (and some blamed the failure of his auto-coup on this residual hatred) for bowing to history and publicly acknowledging the independent status of Belize (in return for British financial assistance). On many official Guatemalan maps, Belize still appears as a department rather than a neighboring country (Suzana Sawyer [1997] explores a similar official reaction in Ecuador). A letter to the editor on the occasion of the Quincentennial suggested that the Maya could prove their appropriateness to the nation by reconquering Belize

tonomy, a Finance Ministry official invoked the old home and family metaphor once again: "The state and the people are like a man and a woman
who have been married. They cannot just go off with someone else! They
have a legal union, a relationship!"

Mario Antonio Sandoval, editor of *Prensa Libre* and later presidential
press secretary for de León Carpio, was one of the most committed Convention opponents. He fulminated against it in a series of articles over several months in 1992 and 1993, drawing together many of the criticisms discussed here:

> The Convention violates eighteen constitutional articles [and] gives interna-
> tional law preeminence over national law. The ILO will control the Guatema-
> lan political regime and affect the unity and sovereignty of the state. Conven-
> tion 169 affects the territorial integrity of this country and constitutionally
> establishes discrimination among Guatemalans by benefiting indigenous
> groups in complete opposition to legally guaranteed equality. . . . If we accept
> the existence of a "people" with their own "territory" all they need is political
> organization to transform themselves into a state. The Kekchi [*sic*] state, let's
> say. And along with that, the twenty-two states of Guatemala's Indian ethnici-
> ties. This will be the real result of the application of Convention 169, the
> Yugoslavization of Guatemala. But the Indian ethnicities are divided among
> themselves, as in their languages, and the principal ethnicities will try to
> dominate the rest, and all of them will try to dominate the ladinos and the
> ladinoized Indians. The concept of the ladino will no longer be a social dis-
> tinction, but will become cemented into an ethnic differentiation. We are, my
> friends, on the threshold of allowing the slow but inevitable disintegration of
> Guatemala. And this will be the result of applying in our country a plan con-
> ceived for other places, places with minority indigenous and tribal people.
> (*Prensa Libre,* 26 October 1992)

Not only is the nation's territorial integrity threatened by fevered imaginings of parallel Mayan and ladino states or even twenty-plus ethnic
nation-states—with all the ladinos forced to move to the arid southeast—
but, in the words of Congressman Juan Francisco Reyes, the Maya are leaving an "open door, an unprotected entryway through which who knows

---

for Guatemala. A thoughtful ladino who I had not read as particularly "nationalist" surprised
me during one interview by going off for almost half on hour on what he called the "open
wound" of the loss of Belize and how this affected every single Guatemalan. Finally, the National Theater's popular musical comedy *Bye Bye Belize* (performed in black face and partially
sponsored by the Defense Ministry) enacted the contradictory feelings regarding Belize. In
part a denunciation of divisionary British colonialism and broken treaties, in part a critique of
the Guatemalan government ("Belizians may be poor but they don't have to suffer counterinsurgency and death squads"), in part a racist caricature suggesting it's just as well they're not
Guatemalans, the show ran for over a year.

what may enter" (*Siglo XXI,* 3 July 1993). This trope posits indigenous rights as a deadly virus and the nation-state as a vulnerable body. *Prensa Libre*'s Sandoval, rejecting international pressures to "atomize this already small country into a series of mini-quasi-states with no possibility of surviving in this world of major blocs," calls on all Guatemalans to protest the Convention. "Guatemala should not make the mistake of introducing into its laws the cancer of its assured disappearance as a country" (*Prensa Libre,* 2 November 1992).

International intervention into the internal affairs of the nation-state threatens to enter through this unprotected opening. In interviews, ladinos on both ends of the political spectrum suggested that Convention 169 was an international plot to divide Guatemala and keep it weak within the world system. Juan Francisco Reyes said during a televised debate, "Convention 169 will divide the country in two parts and will make ladinos into second class citizens. This is a clear instance of outside interference, the desire to divide and conquer the nation." It is also seen as an opening for subversive penetration. Defense Minister General Enríquez warned that the URNG is taking advantage of the discourse of indigenous rights. "Now that the ideology that gave the subversives power is invalid, they are looking to this other contradiction in order to divide the nation. This is what I fear. . . . I know many Indians. I love them, I admire them, but I am personally very worried, institutionally we are very worried, about the ideologically interested manipulation of this issue."[56]

The Maya are clearly being framed here, assigned the guilt for the unjust resource distribution that has fanned over thirty-five years of war and for foreign intervention that began long before the CIA coup in 1954 and continues through imposed World Bank structural adjustment packages and CIA "assets" (Harbury 1997). This returns me to the central tension I am exploring here, in the sense that the autonomous bounded Guatemalan nation-state is a frame in two senses: in that it both really exists as a site that produces effects, a frame in the sense of a support, and is an empty space, determined by its inclusions and exclusions. Inasmuch as the nation state is an autonomous "subject," it is, to return to Judith Butler, the product of "exclusion and differentiation. . . . Autonomy is the logical consequence of a disavowed dependency" (Butler 1992, 12).

Regarding these anxieties about autonomy, Rigoberto Quemé Chay makes a similar point: "Guatemala is socially, culturally, economically, politically, and religiously multiply fragmented. Of what unity do they speak, those who say they fear Mayan secession? There is no unity, and they pro-

---

56. Speech at the Annual Seminar of the Business Association of Guatemala: "Does Guatemala Have a National Strategy?" October 30, 1992.

claim its existence. Where there is so much cultural diversity, they deny that it exists. It would be far easier to reverse the situation, denying that unity exists in order to find it, and recognizing diversity in order to make unity possible. We must stop discrimination and pass 169" (*Siglo XXI*, 3 October 1992).

Given the framework of Guatemala's imperiled postcolonial nationalism and its disadvantageous insertion in the global system, it makes sense that ladino elites would find Convention 169 somewhat threatening. What is perhaps odder is why anyone would support it. Quemé Chay suggests that Guatemala is a nation that is not one, a splattered body politic, and to my surprise I found that many ladinos agreed. Many Guatemalans acknowledge that their nation is a wounded body and echo the Maya in a call to recognize diversity and support the ratification of Convention 169.

Support for the Convention

Despite disappointment in the slowness of ratification, Delia Tujab, members of the Delegation, and other supporters said that they were surprised and pleased at the support they encountered. For example, Ms. Tujab said, "We've always had a very good response. It's just a question of explaining what the Convention is about and why it is important. You can't just force it on people. But when we've explained it, we find that even unexpected people, like at the Military Center for Strategic Studies [CEEM], have supported us."[57]

Mr. Copil, president of the Delegation, said that through his work on the Convention he had seen a marked change in ladino attitudes: "People are becoming more respectful now. When we started, they would say, 'Oh you, the *inditos*.' Rather than get mad we would just say, 'You, the *ladinitos*,' and they would understand what they had said. Now they speak of the *Maya*. I think we have won something with that. We talk about these issues seriously, but if they make a joke, then we can joke along with them."

Despite negative reactions, there was strong support at the highest levels for ratification; Serrano and de León Carpio both supported Convention 169, and the presidents of the Supreme Court and Congress openly pro-

---

57. In their position paper for the national forum in November 1991, the Defense Ministry had supported ratification. In mid-1992, they began to express reservations. According to Delia Tujab, a series of unfortunate incidents occurred following the national forum, when she was abruptly relieved of her post as national coordinator. Among the personal attacks that she and her sister suffered during 1992 and early 1993 were rumors concerning their sex lives, including an anonymous call to Gloria Tujab's husband. The caller claimed that Gloria was having affairs with military men—that she had sold out and was sleeping with an officer and that the army supported the Convention because of that. These stories play on the same issues raised in the jokes about Rigoberta Menchú and are similarly hostile and cruel.

moted it. As the new Congress took office in September 1994, Congressman Ríos Montt said, "Convention 169 must be included in our new agenda. We should undertake this, we must" (*El Regional*, 16–22 September 1994).[58] The Christian Democrat Congressman Alfonso Portillo, emphasizing his party's support for Convention 169, said, "Many countries have already ratified the Convention, and we have got to get ourselves up to date with what is happening in the world. If the world today is demanding modernity, and this Convention will lead us into modernity, then we have to support it" (*El Regional*, 16–22 September 1994). So, despite the resistances explored above, Convention 169 and the rights of indigenous peoples do not terrify everyone. How to account for ladino support of 169, the presidential signatures, and public displays of approval?

Perhaps the most obvious reason, and what many Guatemalans believe is the case, is that any support is pure demagoguery, a mask.[59] Indigenous issues are fashionable, so politicians are getting on the bandwagon and currying favor. The government is weak, so it needs the Indians. An anthropologist at the National University accused the government of "trying to woo the Indians with this work, but it is only for their own benefit." A Finance Ministry official said, "The Indians are the most vital, organized sector in Guatemala today, and the government needs them for legitimacy. They don't really care about the Indians." A metaphor frequently deployed for this state use of the passive indigenous population was that the Maya are a *costal de papa* (a bag of potatoes) that can be picked up, albeit with some effort, and manipulated.

The paternalism of such a critique is clear, positioning the Maya as easily duped, like a naive girl seduced by a callous suitor who wants one thing, and one thing only. In many of my interviews, these complaints took on the tone of a jilted suitor, especially with ladinos on the Left, who seemed to feel that their offers of true love were rejected.[60] This gendered trope of the

58. I thank Paula Worby for keeping me in touch!

59. The seeming support may also be corruption. Although I was unable to determine how much money was invested by the UNDP and PRODERE in the ratification campaign, there was a general sense that people were taking advantage of it. Delia Tujab complained that the Labor Ministry had expected her to allocate them large sums of the money meant for the workshops (for example, Mr. Solórzano wanted reimbursement for his entire party for the nearly aborted trip to Quetzaltenango for the closing ceremonies of the workshop there). In turn, several Maya and ladinos interviewed made unsubstantiated comments about the Tujabs and members of the Delegation making a profit out of their work for the Convention. Corruption is certainly rampant throughout the Guatemalan state. However, neither the lifestyles of people working for ratification nor the funding premises of the United Nations suggest that great fortunes are being amassed.

60. Within Guatemala, these metaphors suggest that the Indians, usually gendered female, have been seduced by the state, an inappropriate mate. The powerful affect of romantic fan-

Maya as the object of (not always respectable) attentions was often used in conversation, like the Finance Ministry official who likened indigenous autonomy to a wife jilting her legal husband.These metaphors condense discourses of affect that surround reactions to the Convention. Claims that ladino state officials are using the Maya, trying to "woo" them, without really caring about them, are probably true in many cases. However, such an analysis hinges on a desired authenticity of ladino feeling for the Indians— as if it is not enough for them to say they "love the Indians" as General Enríquez does, they must truly feel it as well.

What is perhaps more interesting than an investigation of, say, Serrano's true feelings is to look at the frame around his support for the Convention, the conditions for its possibility. This support reveals a shift in ladino-Maya relations, a small change in the hegemonic framework of how the state relates to those it governs. Here I view hegemony in the Gramscian sense— not just as some more effective control of better-duped citizens (imagined as a sack of potatoes or inexperienced naïf)—but as a process by which ruling power must concede to alternative power blocs. It is historically novel for state elites to not only give lip service to Mayan issues but to make temporal, financial, and legislative investments in them. If they are trying to woo the Indians, it is relatively new that they even care. That state bureaucrats, including the presidents of the Congress, Supreme Court and the country, have some sense of being held accountable to the Pueblo Maya *is* about demagoguery, but saying that it is *only* about demogoguery erases the sacrifices, struggles, and small triumphs of decades of the coalescing Mayan movements. State "concessions" (such as support for Convention 169 and the Accord on Identity) both respond to Mayan political work and open up space for continued struggles, as Quemé Chay suggested. As one ladino in the government said, laughing, "We got way more than we bargained for with 169! It really brings together a large number of otherwise chaotic positions among the indigenous groups with an internationally recognized legal basis. They got a foot in the door, and now we can't close it." Gabriel Aguilera of FLACSO said, "The National Consultation on 169 really snowballed! The government doesn't know what to do with it now."

We might ask if the Maya are indeed like a sack of potatoes or a woman

---

tasies in which Prince Charming saves the damsel in distress is laid over progress narratives in which revolutionary change saves the people. These emotions, these subjugated hopes and fears that I associate with eugenics discourse (see chapter 6), may animate the jilted tone of Left reactions to Mayan organizing. Similar feelings are expressed about the inappropriate (sexual) nature of the relations between international actors and the indigenous population, as in the jokes about Mexican President Salínas de Gortari giving *la vergue* (refuge and penis) to Rigoberta Menchú, or about making a sandwich with Rigoberta between two *francés* (French bread and French solidarity activists).

easily seduced and abandoned, or whether a more fitting metaphor might be the transvestite suggested in jokes about Rigoberta Menchú. Here are historically disempowered people wielding phallic power encoded in the law, international support, and articulate arguments on nation-state terrain. Similarly, notions of the prosthetic dependency and interactive relation of the state and the Maya give us more fluidary models and help us resist this dominator-victim dichotomy. Several Maya I interviewed, including Gloria Tujab, forcefully reject the paternal implications of another affect-laden metaphor used to describe state support of Convention 169: "They can't feed us *atol* with their finger." *Atol* is a corn-based drink fed to babies this way, and Tujab means that they aren't children to accept anything the state gives them. Instead, Tujab said, the "Maya will fight for ratification and full compliance with the Convention. If the politicians think they can take advantage of the Maya, they will learn that the Maya know how to use politicians to our advantage as well!"

Thus, partial government support for Convention 169 may be seen as both a result and a cause of ongoing struggles that have changed the ways indigenous peoples are treated in national discourses. A leftist Guatemalan who had recently returned from exile said:

> I think the years of work at the local level are really paying off. I see an enormous change since when I left. The government, businessmen, everyone, is having to take the Maya into account. In fact, a group of businessmen invited me to give them a course on ethnic issues! I couldn't believe it when they asked me, they know my political history. But I am from one of the big old families, we grew up together, and they know they need to understand these things. Pressure from the local sectors is strong.

One of the Delegation's trump cards is the claim to represent 96 Mayan organizations throughout the country. The weight of so many "potatoes" seems to have impressed many government officials. Alvaro Colón, the director of the National Peace Fund (FONAPAZ), said that he approached the Delegation to administer the new Guatemalan Indigenous Fund (FODIGUA) because of this national coverage.[61]

> They have perhaps the best representation of the diversity within the Mayan population. There are members from many of the different ethnic groups, and from many different tendencies within the movement. There are some more radical groups represented there, people who are filled with resentment, but I think that is justified. The worst of this war fell on the indigenous

---

61. The FODIGUA, set up in 1994 to contribute technical and financial assistance to programs that improve the quality of life of the Mayan population, has been somewhat hamstrung by insufficient funds, but Santiago Bastos and Manuela Camus (1995) see it as an important "new field of action" for Mayan work within the state.

people; they have suffered discrimination, poverty, abandonment by the state, violence. They can't stand it anymore, and I agree. It is they who have to decide what is going to happen in this country. I wouldn't say this in public, of course, they would kill me, and I wouldn't have said it in private ten years ago, but now I am sure, the ladinos are the minority here and the Indians should make the decisions on the politics of this country.

This is an example of the sort of careful discourse that is increasingly prevalent in Guatemala, discouraging the more egregious public displays of racism that were once common. Even though such discourse may hide "real" feelings that emerge elsewhere (in the form of jokes, for example), it is more than "just words." The discussion of Mayan rights and the emerging organization (which can field hundreds of Mayan delegates to the National Consultation) surrounding the ratification process are changing the nature of the struggle and the framework of state-Maya relations, as was clear in the ASC and peace negotiations.

Convention 169's supporters say that it is precisely this shift that makes the implementation of the envisioned changes not only possible but also inevitable. A common response was, "You can't block the sun with just your finger." Edmund Mulet, former president of the Congress and later ambassador to the United States, said in October 1992,

> I think 1992 is a real step forward. Guatemala is becoming aware of what we really are. We cannot block the sun with a finger. We can't continue efforts to assimilate the ethnic groups into the western plan. Now we can see that assimilation lost and in the process limited the possibilities for national development. It became a battle with one side trying to assimilate the other by force and the other half living in full resistance. They are committed to conserving their identity. . . . I've said many times that the only way to maintain unity is to recognize diversity. If we don't recognize this reality now, we face a century of ethnic confrontation.

Though opponents warn that ratifying Convention 169 will lead to race war, proponents insist that only by responding to indigenous demands, including ratification, can a race war be avoided.

Again, this may seem to be just p.c. b.s. (politically correct bologna), but it marks a shift in the conditions of possibility for Mayan struggle and for national strategy—the emergence of a different, historically specific, Guatemalan body image. These conditions not only allow Mulet to represent himself as a friend of the Maya to me as a gringa researcher but also lead him (and others) to publicly stake out this position, enduring the calumny of their fellow ladinos. For example, in August 1992, *Prensa Libre*'s Alvaro Enrique Palma took Mulet to task. "What is this, Mulet, about destroying the unity of Guatemala?! It is not just, it is not patriotic, it is not politic, it is not practical, and moreover it is an error. You must be desperate to propose this extraordinary abuse and heresy against the Guatemalan nation, especially because you are a high member of the STATE and your obligation is to care for, defend, and protect all Guatemalans" (*Prensa Libre,* 31 August 1992).[62]

The Role of Law in Support of Convention 169   Just as official concern for Mayan issues seems strange given Guatemala's racist history, the effort put into ratifying Convention 169 as a law seems strange given that legal precedent has rarely had much force in a country where death squads operate out of the National Palace. A newspaper poll taken in early 1993 found that only 20 percent of the population surveyed expressed faith in the country's legal system.

However, with civilian rule and the new Constitution of 1985, the legal arena has become a vital site of struggle—much like the UN—in which various sectors are articulating the law into different configurations. Though such work is not always successful and relies heavily on international pressure, for the first time in decades members of the military are being charged with their crimes (for example, in the Myrna Mack and Michael Devine assassination cases), popular sectors have maintained an anti-impunity campaign since 1990, and the Council of Ethnic Communities "Everyone United" (CERJ) and other human rights groups have successfully fought for indigenous peoples' constitutional rights to refuse military and civil patrol service.

So, despite the continuing human rights violations, the discourse of legality has attained a special resonance in Guatemala. Similar to the way law marks a colonial boundary between the "civilized" world and those who need to receive the law, legality symbolically marks the emergence from the dark days of military rule pre-1985. Though many in the state willingly admit that the "rule of law" (*estado de derecho*) remains a horizon rather than a reality, for many it represents a shift in the conditions of possibility for political work. "It's not like it was before" was a refrain of my interviews. For example, former Vice-Minister of Culture Estuardo Meneses said, "We have suffered a great deal in the war, but the Constitution has created a new framework. We can work within it, we can begin to fulfill our duties as citizens, to learn to respect each other."

After the Serrano coup, this discourse of legality was deployed with spe-

---

62. This diatribe is worth quoting at length, in part because he made similar points repeatedly during the Quincentennial years in which 169 was debated. He goes on:

The Constitution says that the state has sovereignty over national territory. . . . The Constitution would never, ever allow something so illogical as you are seeking, to tear to pieces, to make a mockery of the country. You must be after something, maybe it is propaganda among the indigenous sectors, but credibility there is not worth very much. . . . You should be taken to court for even suggesting something like this. Things will not, nor should they, go in this direction. It is insane and imprudent. (*Prensa Libre,* 31 August 1992)

cial vigor (verging on a repetition compulsion), especially by the army as it represented itself as the savior of the Constitution. In his speech at the Army Day celebrations of June 1993, Defense Minister Enríquez spoke of the historic moment in which the army (unlike in the past) followed the Constitution as its supreme mandate. "The Constitutional order was broken, but the army refused to allow this violence against the Guatemalan family. The people cried out for their rights during the crisis and the army heard them. . . . The army is a constitutional institution just like other state powers. All the actions of the army as an institution fall within this constitutional mandate."[63]

Law as a category that distinguishes "democratic" regimes from their violent military predecessors is clearly a legitimation tool for the army and government. But this concept of legality also supports struggles for justice against the army and the state, ranging from CONAVIGUA's legal campaign against forced recruitment to the efforts to ratify Convention 169. This is the ambiguous relationship described by Sally Merry, in which colonial law is both a weapon for expropriation and provides a language in which the colonized can resist (Merry 1991, 891). This ambiguity or "double move" of "law" as a concept also defines how law is made and deployed in struggles to articulate the law's content, interpretations, and execution with competing and even antagonistic projects.[64] Through these struggles, the state is

---

63. Although incredibly complex power-plays lay behind the Serrano coup and its subsequent failure, the discourses of legality—especially rejecting the suspension of the Constitution and the dissolution of the courts (*quitando cortes*)—mobilized those who resisted, including, it appears, the army factions that supported the return to institutionality. These in turn were supported by international conditions that frowned on the specter of lawlessness and by economic incentives that encouraged the return to civilian rule. Similar forces created the conditions of possibility for signing the peace treaty.

64. Law is always produced through struggle, concession, strategic self-interest, and lobbying, as with the framing of Convention 169 in the ILO and the recent reforms of Guatemala's penal code, which dovetail with Mayan demands and with the contents of the Convention. The new code institutes oral arguments (more appropriate for those with limited literacy), translation for non-Spanish speakers, and respect for customary law.

A federal judge said that part of the reason the (former) president of the Supreme Court (Juan José Rodíl Peralta) was on the list to be purged after the Serrano coup was his role in instituting these changes:

> They want Rodíl out because the new penal code is very pro-Indian and the people in power don't want it to happen. With oral arguments, the Indians will be much better represented, and there will be translators, a prosecutor, and a jury, instead of the secrecy we have now. We also need to pay attention to the way people solve conflicts in their communities—we need to use the traditions that exist. The courts have been holding workshops so people are aware of their rights, and the old-timers don't like that at all. They are mad that it is giving power to the Mayan people.

Part of the reform also includes assigning justices of the peace to every town. This positions a state representative and outsider in far-flung areas, making it possible for the state to be both

both reinscribed as a site and guarantor of rights and revealed as fissured, wounded, and open to contestation.[65]

Derecho Consuetudinario—Customary Law   Customary law plays an integral role for Maya and ladinos in the emerging hegemony work around the "rule of law." The juridical section of COMG's "Specific Rights of the Pueblo Maya," incorporated almost exactly into the Accord on Identity, demands legal recognition of Mayan languages, the administration of justice in those languages, and recognition, respect, and promotion of *derecho consuetudinario,* which "regulates the daily lives of the Maya today." Majawil Q'ij published similar demands on October 12, 1992, calling for "state recognition of our laws, but recognition through respect, not with pity or paternalism" (*La Hora,* 12 October 1992). Convention 169 reads, "In applying national laws and regulations to the peoples concerned, due regard shall be paid to their customs or customary laws. These peoples shall have the right to retain their own customs and institutions, where these are not incompatible with fundamental rights defined by the national legal system and with internationally recognized human rights. . . . The methods customarily practiced by the peoples concerned for dealing with offenses committed by their members shall be respected" (Art. 8).

Guatemala's new penal code contemplates customary law and FLACSO, INIAP, and ASIES, as well as CECMA, are studying its practice at the local level and its national ramifications. The results of such studies have been publicized through public forums, newspaper coverage, editorials, and even cartoons, and ASIES is lobbying for legislative reforms that include customary law.[66]

---

more diffuse and more present. It also provides an alternative for people to go over the heads of the entrenched local power, who may be ladinos in a primarily indigenous area, the civil patrol leader, and so on. One recently installed ladino justice of the peace bragged that he had taken away 99 percent of the power of the town's mayor. "He had been in charge for twenty years and was so corrupt. These people can do whatever they want, they were way too powerful!" The implementation of this code and its differing local effects deserve much fuller study. Here I merely point out the possibly productive contradictions in state legal interventions at the local level—interventions that simultaneously open a space for Mayan participation and for increased state surveillance. Parallels can be found with UN intervention in national affairs: is it unconscionable meddling, or a way to effect change in otherwise unyielding local power structures? Far more research is necessary on the effects of these changes in different locales, but I would assume that the answer, as always, is both-and.

65. For example, a federal judge defies death threats, some of them certainly emanating from people on the state's payroll, to find an army officer guilty of assassinating Myrna Mack, and this judge agrees that the case points to higher ups, who in turn must be judged by members of the state.

66. In one cartoon, standing next to a sign advertising the ASIES forum on customary law, two caricatured Maya, with buck teeth and ragged *traje,* are talking. One says, "Did you hear

These supporters admit that attempts to fully assimilate the indigenous population have failed and that attention to and juridical legitimation of "their way of doing things" is merely accepting the reality of the multicultural country.[67] The introduction to the ASIES study, "Basic Investigation of Customary Law in Three Maya-Speaking Communities of Guatemala," admits that it is a response to the international situation and to Mayan organizing. "At this time, the dynamism of the country's indigenous sectors is impressive, creating and fortifying grassroots organizations, formally demanding social, economic, political and cultural rights, removing their ancestral practices from the semiclandestinity in which they have languished, and reactivating their customs" (ASIES 1993, 3). These internal and external pressures "demand the systematic study of the legal and protolegal systems of the indigenous cultures and societies and of their knowledge and understanding in order to coordinate it with the 'national legal system' in ways that are less ethnocentric and more just" (ASIES 1993, 3). The study was presented as vital for all members of the legal, legislative, executive, academic, bureaucratic, and public servant communities as well as the population at large, in order to create "a juridical system congruent with the cultural, linguistic, and ethnic diversity of the country and that restores justice to interethnic relations in Guatemala" (ASIES 1993, 4).

The ASIES forum where the study was presented was a formal affair with government officials, including Ramiro de León Carpio (then human rights ombudsman), the culture minister, and the upper echelons of the academic, development, progressive, and Mayan communities in attendance, as well as students, members of grassroots indigenous organizations, and a smattering of gringos. The lecture hall was overflowing, the aisles full of people. During the break (over wine and hors d'oeuvres), people gathered excitedly to discuss the presentations (by ASIES investigators and international experts, including Agosto Willensen, but no Maya). The people from the Mayan cultural organizations were animated, almost exuberant, as they analyzed the forum. The study itself, the feel of the evening, the national and international luminaries in attendance and those discussing indigenous rights, seemed to act as a powerful reinforcement of their work and their communities. This wasn't a small Mayan organization begging for attention. This was ASIES, the think tank organized by the major political parties, whose founders included top state officials and whose re-

---

that they are insulting the *indígena*?" The other responds, "Yes, they even say that our law wears an ordinary sweater" (*derecho* [law] *con sueter ordinario* [with an ordinary sweater]) (*El Grafico*, 18 February 1993). I thank Pepe Lara!

67. This attitude is suggested in the name of ASIES, which is both the acronym for the Association for Social Investigation and Studies and means *así es* (that's the way it is), similar to the common refrain of "You can't block the sun with your finger."

searchers were presidential and congressional advisors. The parallels between the speeches on the stage and their own discourses were felt as a triumph. My party-pooper suggestions that this interest in customary law might be simply counterinsurgent, an invasion of the last redoubt of Mayan self-determination, were quickly dismissed.[68] Even Dr. Cojtí seemed jovial and supportive of the study. In interviews, many of the Maya were willing to contemplate a pernicious reading of ladino interests in customary law, but they thought I was missing the point of how productive this interest was for their work at the national level. Powerful ladinos were validating the importance of indigenous communities and lifeways, calling for justice in interethnic relations, and demanding the ratification of Convention 169. "The more information that exists about this, the better!" I was told at the forum. "Especially if it is based in these kinds of scientific studies. This work is good and very useful."

In addition, these studies are productive in the sense of recruiting and reinforcing Mayan scholars and activists, of *formando* (creating) Maya-hackers, similar to the work of the ALMG and the ratification process of Convention 169. Both ASIES and FLACSO hired and trained Mayan researchers to do fieldwork in indigenous communities. One Kaqchikel university student conducted interviews in his home community for the FLACSO study, including with members of his family:

> I began to talk to my mother, my grandmother, my aunts and uncles about these laws, these customs. They were so excited that anyone cared, that I was showing interest in their lives, in the village. I had been so eager to get out, to come to the city for school. This was the first time I really listened to what they had to say. Before I had just ignored them. I didn't think there was anything interesting there until I started this work.

Now, in addition to his university studies, he is an active member of CEDIM (Mayan Center for Research and Documentation) and supports the Delegation's work for Convention 169. He is continuing his work on customary law for his own thesis.

A great deal more should be said about the productivity of and contradictions surrounding work on customary law. George Collier (1994) has explored the deeply complicated deployment of "custom" in Zinacantán, Mexico, in which it is a tool used internally by members of the community to constitute and maintain class differentials, at the same time that it is used by the community to deflect state and national intervention into local affairs. Official support for Convention 169 and this interest in customary law

---

68. This was before I had the full and complex grasp of hegemony that I am developing here (!). I was thinking only of Foucauldian disciplinary technologies without any notion of counterpower.

parallels the government "decentralization" project, which national and international sectors are attempting to articulate into a hegemonic project

Decentralization

Similar sectors of Guatemala's state officials support Convention 169 and the current discourse of "decentralization." Decentralization is being pursued in a number of ways and claims to be a discourse of empowerment and democracy. Based in a neoliberal philosophy of "freedom," it posits a limited state, decision making from the ground up, local autonomies, and self-management (or *autogestión* in the developmentalist discourse [Turbyne 1995]). The incipient practices are varied, including the reform of the penal code, the deployment of justices of the peace, and support for customary law. Many ministries and state agencies are "regionalizing," which means that they are setting up offices outside the capital (like the Human Rights Ombudsman office in Nebaj, Quiché). The constitutionally mandated 8 percent of the national budget that is allocated for the municipalities is meant to increase local autonomy in decision making and project implementation. The new Funds—for social investment (FIS), peace (FONAPAZ), housing (FONAVIVIENDA), and indigenous needs (FODIGUA)—are meant to supply economic support for more locally based initiatives by bypassing the corrupt and inefficient bureaucracy.

Decentralization is also termed "modernization," and as such contemplates privatization for increased efficiency, meant to make the state more responsive. In the Business Association of Guatemala (AGG) forum on October 30, 1992, entitled "Does Guatemala have a National Strategy?" Richard Aitkenhead, then the minister of finance and later a key advisor on the peace process, said:

> The state must be reformed administratively. Historically the state has been most active, with most presence in urban areas. You could even call it a 'city-state.' In order to confront the future, we must make the state less bureaucratic, more disciplined, more decentralized. It should be a state that is closer to the population, much closer to their necessities. Not so that the state becomes the executor, or the one that carries out these projects aimed at fulfilling basic needs.[69] No, it should furnish the necessary resources so that people can respond to their own necessities.

69. The double meaning this term carries of "executor" and "executioner" may not have been consciously deployed by Mr. Aitkenhead. A similar double entendre appeared in the military's Army Day float in 1993. The point of the float was that the army was in the countryside, aiding with development at the local level. With a mise-en-scène of a rustic house, corn, and children dressed in *traje,* a soldier pumped real water. The caption for this tableau: *El Ejército da agua al pueblo* (the army brings water to the people). However, to *dar agua* is also slang for "to kill." Accidental? A Freudian slip? A not-so-subtle warning?

A blueprint for these changes entitled *Decentralization and Popular Participation in Guatemala* (Amaro 1990) maintains that decentralization is the necessary precursor to stabilizing the democratic regime in Guatemala. Nelson Amaro, the author, formerly the vice-minister of development (under Cerezo) and then an advisor for the World Bank, claims to be particularly concerned with encouraging indigenous participation in nation building through local development and respect for their cultural differences.

When I asked Dr. Amílcar Burgos of ASIES (and a Serrano advisor) about the state's indigenous policy, rather than talking about Mayan demands per se he described efforts to reform the municipal code to devolve more power to the towns and villages. This legislation follows Amaro's blueprint for decentralization closely and consists in creating "municipal councils" in every population—from towns (*municipios*) to villages (*aldeas*) and hamlets (*caserios*). Burgos said:

> We want these areas to participate in the decisions of the municipal government. A council would be selected from each village, to deal with education, or other issues. They would work with the heads of families, teachers, NGOs, and the government to address the specific problems occurring there. This would change the flow of decision making in the towns. This would revalorize all that is indigenous, as opposed to the centralized laws that are imposed by the ladinos. Communities have long traditions for resolving complex problems; we must use this resource to reinforce horizontal organization at the subregional level. For a political evolution based in municipal autonomy, we must regenerate the country from below.

The Congress did not pass this reform in 1993, but ASIES continues to refine the legislation and lobby congresspeople. The peace treaty incorporates many of these ideas, and the Party of National Advancement (PAN) government is moving eagerly to implement similar decentralization policies.

These neoliberal discourses around decentralization, which accompany state sector support for Convention 169, parallel Mayan demands for autonomy at the local level and participation at the national level. In fact, at a televised forum (the weekly *Libre Encuentro* talk show) on October 11, 1992, the vice-rector from the conservative Francisco Marroquín University went one better than Edmund Mulet and Dr. Cojtí, who were both present supporting the Convention. Dr. Cojtí spoke of the importance of 169 in terms of the outside impetus needed to create change in Guatemala, and Mr. Mulet mentioned other advances for the Pueblo Maya, including the new penal code. Vice-Rector Rigoberto Juarez said, "What I want to see is a radical change in the Constitution. We need a new state divided into autonomous regions, like Spain and many other countries. This solution has been talked about for years, but as Guatemalans we show a lack of character, a lack of courage. We must face reality. The only solution to the current situation is autonomy. The ILO Convention is good, but it is only superficial."

This caused a general hubbub. After a hasty commercial break, the discussion resumed, with Mr. Mulet insisting on the integrity of the state. "We have a lot of problems here, but when I think about ten years ago, I am very satisfied with the way the country is evolving. . . . We need more changes, of course, but the state was destroyed. We may look toward autonomy in the future, but we must maintain the unity of the state or we will enter a very dangerous situation. We have the Constitutional Court, we have the Human Rights Ombudsman, we are conscious of what Guatemala is as a country." Dr. Juarez replied, "The state has not allowed the country to develop. It does not trust its citizens. It tries to control everyone. Autonomy must be about empowering ordinary citizens." Dr. Cojtí said, "I agree. There are demands for regional autonomy, this will help to increase participation, decentralize the state." Congressman Juan Francisco Reyes, a firm opponent of the Convention, said, "OK, but why autonomy just for the Indians? Decentralization is good for all Guatemalans. We don't need to let outside influences like the ILO address the problems that we can all recognize. Regional autonomy would allow decisions to be made from the bottom up. We need people like Demetrio Cojtí here, who go from the university into politics, people who are willing to take responsibility." The discussion continued on the show, in the streets, in the hallways, and continues still, often in outright antagonism.

Decentralization, the Mode of Regulation, and the Governmental State   So here is an apparent contradiction. The emotional outbursts against Convention 169 seem explicable, almost inevitable, but how to reconcile Dr. Cojtí on network TV agreeing with the vice-rector of the country's most conservative university? Strange bedfellows indeed? But there are multiple contradictions showing up here—fissures among state sectors about the future of the state and a breakdown in the usefulness of labels like "conservative" and "progressive." Although Mr. Mulet and Dr. Juarez seem to disagree on the role of the state in a country divided into autonomous zones, they apparently agree with each other and the growing chorus of decentralizers, that some form of autonomy, like that envisioned in Convention 169, is necessary to save the state—albeit a very different state than the classic model that assimilates and homogenizes.

Perhaps the work for ratification of Convention 169, which incites discourse concerning Mayan rights, the Constitution, and the role of the state, does productive work for certain sectors of the state, which may explain the conundrum of official support. Part of what constitutes the fissures between supporters and opponents of Convention 169 may be grossly characterized as a struggle over modes of regulation. I borrow this term from the Regulation School of political economy to talk about the overdetermination of social, political, and economic struggles while suggesting ways to go beyond a base-superstructure explanation for something as complicated as this shift in theories and practices of the state.

Robert Boyer defines *modes of regulation* as procedures and behaviors that reproduce fundamental social relations through the combination of historically determined institutional forms. The mode of regulation ensures the compatibility over time of a set of decentralized decisions, without the economic actors themselves having to internalize the adjustment principles governing the overall system (Boyer 1990, 44). The notion of regulation insists on the "tangled connections between institutionalized compromises whose consequences are sometimes contradictory" and rejects the "seductive but fallacious hypothesis that social relations always ultimately adapt themselves to categorical imperatives represented by the growth of the productive forces" (Boyer 1990, 48). In other words, regulation eschews pessimistic functionalism. As such, "regulation" is concerned with crises, with the contradictory character of the long-term reproduction of the system. In fact, the Regulation School is perhaps best known for theorizing the crisis of Fordism, the previously prevailing regime of accumulation based on mass production and consumption.[70]

Guatemala is clearly in crisis. The sense is widespread that, despite the gains of "democratization," the state is not working, the nationalist project is in disarray, it is a catastrophe, a wounded body politic. The debates around Convention 169 crystallize more general contestations over the compromises needed to adjust to this crisis.[71] Additionally, responses to this crisis are both specific to Guatemala and closely linked to the crisis in the international sphere. One way of mapping the different positions toward the Convention within the Guatemalan state is along the lines of landhold-

---

70. The regime of accumulation may be understood as the set of regularities that ensure the general and relatively coherent progress of capitalist accumulation, allowing for the resolution or postponement of distortions and disequilibria to which the process continually gives rise. An analysis of the regime of accumulation would include the form of competition, the wage relation, and the insertion of each country in the existing international relations (Boyer 1990, 35).

71. Though most people hope for a resolution of the crisis, the contradictory and overdetermined nature of any mode of regulation suggests there is no such resting place:

The idea of regulation is inseparable from the idea of contradiction. . . . Regulation is the regulation of contradiction by contradictions. In other words, capitalist regulation is a contradictory process of regulation. It combines social practices which are contradictory (not simply incoherent or incompatible) into a single set, and it bears within itself the conditions which give rise to crisis. The social procedures of regulation are the historical forms of the articulation of competition and the class struggle. (Fortune Di Ruzza, quoted in Boyer 1990, 122)

ing oligarchs versus the neoliberals and the ways their personal accumulation depends on different relations to international capital. The scoundrels of the more traditional oligarchs find refuge in nationalist patriotism—suddenly seeing unacceptable international intervention in Convention 169. In turn, many who support the Convention see the international arena as a sort of ideal ego, and Guatemalan acceptance there (into the family of nations) would be a sign of acceptance into modernity (and markets), part and parcel of more efficient, flexible, and lucrative capital accumulation.[72]

This is one aspect of the conditions of possibility for support, but there are also internal reasons: the neoliberal model has different interests in indigenous populations than the plantation system, perhaps freeing this elite from the "ancestral terror" of the Indian and allowing them the apparently progressive stance of supporting Convention 169. (Of course, the plantation system is also having to change and adapt to these new times; see Oglesby 1997.) Cultural difference and "ethnic identity" articulate differently with shifts in the mode of regulation. Perhaps the cultural differences (hostile markings) defining Guatemala's twentieth-century stereotype of the "Indian"—backward and tied to the land but not owning it—were articulated to the extreme exploitation of the mass labor of the export economy, which supported Guatemala's insertion into global Fordism. These cultural differences are (re)markable in the move to flexible specialization, which is one of the markers of post-Fordism. To read the "difference" of the Maya as only a barrier to development is to miss both the nation's dependence on them historically and the complex changes in Guatemala's relations of production in the past decade (Peterson 1992; Goldin 1996; Oglesby 1997). To read elite support for Convention 169, decentralization, and a discourse of "unity with diversity" as pure demagoguery is to miss how productive such differences are when articulated in new ways. Thus, these elites may support the Convention because it can be articulated with their struggles over an emerging mode of regulation that includes a different vision of the state and of the Indian.

Despite the contentions of opponents, the provisions for autonomy in Convention 169 and in decentralization plans will not necessarily create a weaker state. In fact, the Delegation and other Mayan proponents insist that the point of the Convention is to increase Mayan participation in the state. As Agosto Willensen, longtime indigenous rights advocate said, "Autonomy, or self-government as you say in English, is based in the continuing exis-

72. As Elizabeth Grosz (1994) suggests for neurophysiology, the body image is linked to the model the subject has of other bodies and that other bodies have of the subject's body. Guatemala's body politic is clearly formed in relation with the UN and other transnational actors, which influence its body image.

tence of the state to in turn affirm that autonomy. Autonomy is based in the desire for participation in political power, so it must, as a project, affirm the existence of the state . . . but of a different kind of state. One that shares power."

The ratification process and the discourses of legality legitimate and strengthen the state. Despite its emphasis on local decision-making and limited autonomy, Convention 169 reinstates the state as the guarantor of these "rights," as the privileged site for maintaining and even developing indigenous identity markers, and as the central subject of demand. Like Willensen, supporters of Convention 169 seem to agree that it affirms the existence of the state. Though Mayan friends dismissed my concerns that state interest in customary law and other aspects of decentralization might have pernicious effects, I argue that the decentralized, or what Foucault might call the governmental, state can be very powerful indeed.

Foucault speaks (all too briefly) of an historical shift to the "governmental state"—a state involved with different institutions, procedures, analyses, and tactics from the state that must impose itself on a recalcitrant territory. As I suggest in chapter 3, the governmental state is engaged in a productive relationship with a population. It works through discourse and differentiation rather than imposition and homogenization. Like the orthopedics of the school and the prison, the governmental state is productive. It produces subject-effects and as such is far more lithe and flexible than the repression of military dictatorship.

Carol Smith describes this shift in Guatemalan state practices as "counterinsurgency." She suggests that the Guatemalan army of the mid-1980s was aware that the highlands would not be secure without the end of extreme exploitation, and that the state would have to increase the incorporation of indigenous populations through investment and development at the local level, building nationalism by encompassing the different levels of national life (C. Smith 1990a, 273).

The plans for decentralization would certainly seem to fit this notion of counterinsurgency. Though Dr. Burgos of ASIES describes revisions in the municipal code as supporting democratization and participation (which they might very well do), he also admits that the Maya are increasingly organized, that "more and more municipal governments are occupied by the Indians." Decentralization would both accept this "reality" and create more concrete networks through which surveillance and Foucault's "pastoral" control could be enacted. The prototype of Nelson Amaro's decentralization plan (1990) is the Interinstitutional Coordinators, created in the mid-1980s under the military governments to oversee rural development, that "laboratory of modernity": to coordinate reconstruction work in areas decimated by army scorched-earth practices.

An advisor to Serrano put it quite plainly:

There needs to be a place for the indigenous issues within the state. In the last few years, we have all seen a major increase in indigenous organizing around a whole set of demands, and it is getting stronger and stronger. Now, I studied at the CEEM. I have studied strategies. And anyone who has studied that kind of social movement can see that what is happening is really important and the government needs to respond. We need to channel what is happening, to control it, to make sure it doesn't get out of hand. Otherwise who knows what will happen: look at Bosnia. I talked about this to a friend of mine in the army, we were together at CEEM, and I told him this and he said, "You know, you're right. We do need to pay attention to it."

I am arguing here that state responses to indigenous demands are both important gains for the Maya and possibly counterinsurgent. I do not, however, want to "frame" the state, to make it guilty of crimes of omnipotence so that even when it seems to be acting for good it is truly the handmaid of Satan. For one thing, state schemes are dependent on hegemony work, replete with concessions, multiple armistices, unintended consequences, and overdeterminations. Many of them do not work. People hit the piñata as well as expecting sweets. The army's Interinstitutional Coordinators were a flop, the municipal code did not pass, and many state officials admit that they are making things up as they go along. Dr. Burgos said, "The Serrano government never left off improvising, it was jumping from one crisis to another." Serrano's advisor complained that his warnings about indigenous organizing needing to be challenged fell on deaf ears. "I don't think they take this as seriously as they should. I've said this to many people, but I don't think the government is really dealing with it. Of course, with the chaos that's happening [post-coup, 1993] they won't do anything for a long time." This returns us to Foucault's injunction that we not overvalue the problem of the state. Nor should we underestimate the multiple ways that this fissured, fluid space is productive for Mayan demands—and of Mayan subjects. The competing discourses over Convention 169 also show the resonances between the indigenous rights contained in the Convention and the interests of some of the Guatemalan elite, as well as the ongoing hegemony struggles among Mayan organizations, state sectors, and international institutions.

Agosto Willensen suggests that the forms of autonomy contemplated in Convention 169 both strengthen the state and may force it to share power. Moves toward decentralization may be attempts to counter an insurgency understood to be occurring at the local level through indigenous organizing. But they are also concessions, retorts to consolidating local power, acquiescence to international pressures, and responses to demands enunciated in a legal language that the state can and must understand. Counterinsurgency is not a foregone conclusion. As I discuss throughout this book, the brutality and disciplinary technologies of the civil war developed and deployed against the indigenous population, although undeniably destructive, have also produced new forms of Mayan identification and struggle. Various state orthopedics, including the law, are part of the conditions of possibility for the *formacíon* of Maya hackers, who are opening up new terrains of struggle.

I think we have to see the state as a frame that cannot be escaped. For late-twentieth-century patriarchal capitalism, it is the frame for all political work, even as it exists within an international frame. The most radical movements are still framed by the state model, which becomes the privileged site to be occupied (smashing the state is no longer the avowed goal of most revolutionary groups). This double sense of *frame* as defining a site of struggle but also as a support for antagonistic identities may mimic the notion of the camel hair suit of nationalism that fashions the body it covers. The nation-state may have been imposed historically, but in Guatemala today it is a space of productive power that makes it impossible to frame any other response.

NINE

Global Biopolitical Economy
Prosthetics and Blood Politics

They couldn't kill all the Indians. Then who would do all the work?
Guatemalan ladino

Given the capacity of identifications continually to evolve and change, to slip and shift under the weight of fantasy and ideology, the task of harnessing a complex and protean set of emotional ties for specific social ends cannot help but to pose intractable problems for politics. . . . [Yet] there can be no politics without identification.
DIANA FUSS

FLUIDARITY AS PRACTICE AND ANALYTICS

This conclusion will remain somewhat open, like a wounded body, just as this book is concerned with the processes of being "community-bound" without a clear arrival and with writing in "fluidarity" rather than assuming a solid space or identity from which to act. Fluidarity is a practice and an analytics. Gringas in solidarity are practicing a politics critical of their own privilege, but we are also attempting to solidify our own identifications in a detour through the other. The analytic categories that such a practice afforded me were hard pressed to contain Mayan villagers recognizing a gringa as baby snatcher and my witnessing of a body wounded by a *pueblo* I thought was solid. This is also the shock of the Lizard Queen, who cannot solidly extricate herself from the many boundary-transgressing flows she is a part of—tourists and counterinsurgency specialists, science fiction shows and sexualized imaginaries of white women's bodies, Mayan anthropologists and the pangs of ethnostalgia. As I discuss in this chapter, the gringa is also a wounded body and relies prosthetically on her relation with Guatemala, and with the *mujer maya,* in order to function. Thus fluidarity mournfully renounces solid identifications while vigilantly investigating the investments and conditions of possibility for such identification-effects. It painfully acknowledges that bodies and bodies politic are not cleanly demarcated entities in the world but instead are wounded: they suffer bleeding boundaries and are constantly threatened by fingers in the wound. Fluidarity is not about withdrawing from the complexities of this scene to nurse these ferocious aches. It is about trying to find a way to ethically articulate these relations: to articulate in the sense of writing and speaking about (producing the book you hold in your hands), in the sense of paying attention to those strange and transformative connections that make identities, and in the sense of constituting and being constituted by those very connections.

I argue in this book that Maya and ladino, rich and poor, men and women, and North Americans and Guatemalans do not come already constituted to struggle over the state. Those identifications are fluid because they are formed through their articulations, through their interactions, and in that struggle. I suggest the metaphor of the camel hair suit that, like the orthopedics of the school, the law, and the church, transforms the body that wears it in often unexpected ways. Mayan middlemen and middle-women were trained as translators to keep the boundaries clear between languages and were expected to ladinoize and become "the worst destroyers of their own culture." But through their articulation with those sites of power, by putting on the camel hair suit of nationalism, they are transformed into activists, Maya-hackers, and articulate women like Rigoberta Menchú wielding phallic power. They are speaking between (*interdicta*) the repetitions and interdictions (prohibitions) of power, making those very places where power seemed to work most directly—the school, the bourgeois home, the court, the chapel, the cyberspatialized nation-state, and the United Nations—suddenly uncanny, unhomelike. In turn, ladinos and transnational elites, including gringa anthropologists, find their own identifications decidedly less solid.

Mayan activists call this experience *formación,* with the sense of being made by practices of articulation. Fluidarity explores the *formación* of ethnic, gender, and national identifications in contexts ranging from the local to the transnational and maps the limits and conditions of possibility for bodies politic such as Mayan cultural rights organizing and Quincentennial Guatemala. These are not identity decisions that people make when they get up in the morning. As Judith Butler says, "Bodies only appear, only endure, only live within the productive constraints of certain highly gendered [and raced] regulatory schemas" (Butler 1993, xi). The nation-state is a body politic materialized through just such schema—it appears and endures through dreamwork, through taking on impossible tasks such as being simultaneously modern and traditional. State policies toward the Mayan cultural rights movement appear contradictory, caught in the apparent double bind of "fixing," where assimilationist policies work simultaneously with support for cultural and political difference. So, too, the transnational frame-work (like the dreamwork of the state, and jokework surrounding Rigoberta Menchú) both constrains and supports a new flexibility in national and ethnic incorporations. This is not a cause-and-effect relation. Dreamwork helps us think between and beyond the manifest content of the powerful, hegemonic state that has material effects on everyone's lives and between and beyond the latent content of its multiple sites of power, the corruption, and seat-of-its-pantsness—in other words, the complexities of state relations that I'm calling the piñata effect. Framework (like the camel hair suit and the prosthetic) is about thinking of our politics as always networked into multiple sites and understanding identifications as recombinant and mutually changing—even when it's seemingly powerless Mayan women interacting with the apparently invincible World Bank. In this conclusion, I explore briefly how even transnational processes like neoliberal structural adjustment policies are articulations that change—to varying degrees—those involved.

A joke about Rigoberta Menchú reminds us that articulation is also about "coupling," about sexuality and desire. "Why did Rigoberta really win the Nobel Prize? Because she is an *indita desenvuelta.*" She is *desenvuelta:* both articulate and "unwrapped," stripped of her *traje* and sexually available. The joke is gender-specific because only Mayan women wear the wrapped skirts that make the pun possible. Fluidarity has renounced last instances or final "grounds" on which other identifications are superstructured, but it is also deeply cognizant of the vital role of gender. A central argument of this book is that none of the identifications under study can be understood without taking gender into account. Fantasies of the *mujer maya;* of white women's bodies; of ladino boys heroically whitening the race and improving the nation; of tradition and a millenarian link to the ardor and mystery of the past that anchors the scientific rationalism of ethnic and national mobilization; utopic visions of gender complementarity in the Mayan home or as metaphors for Maya-ladino relations in the nation-state; and the incitements, pleasures, and violences that boy the boy and girl the girl: these are all ways that gender works to frame identifications.

In the previous chapter, I suggest that transnational frame-work (processes sometimes called post-Fordism) contributes to the conditions of possibility for changes in relations of production in Quincentennial Guatemala—which in turn let ladinos in the state support Convention 169. If "they couldn't kill all the Indians" because Indians do all the work, then new products, new demands from international lenders, and new ways of producing traditional crops affect how work is organized and what *Indian* means. Of course, these are never just rational economic calculations. Like ratification of Convention 169, they depend on state regulation, on the outcomes of struggles on a multitude of terrains, and on the articulation of identifications in those processes, including, as I suggest in this chapter, a prosthetic dependence on gendered bodies.

White women trying to understand brown body politics amid a sea of red ink and black humor may need a "Pink Freud" analytics. With apologies to the rock bank Pink Floyd, but with a nod to the power and pleasures of popular culture, we might think of fluidarity as "pink" in the sense of Marx-ist, with close attention to class relations, but also as "Freudian," attune to the work of desire and the unconscious. We might also call this biopolitical economy, the way gender and sexuality link body and body politic (as I sug-gest in chapter 6). These may be first steps in understanding the relations among the international regime of accumulation, the Mayan cultural rights movement, gender, the Guatemalan nation-state, and the hopes surround-ing the implementation of the peace treaty. I can only briefly address these issues here. But if we are to promote peace in Quincentennial Guatemala, we must deploy a fluidary analysis that can articulate these multiple rela-tions together, interpenetrating traditionally solid categories like econom-ics, politics, statistics, and denunciations of human rights abuses with more fluid understandings of governmental states, fantasy, desire, dreams, jokes, and identification as a detour through the other (Fuss 1995).

TOWARD A BIOPOLITICAL ECONOMY
OF STRUCTURAL ADJUSTMENT

Body images are formed in relation to images of other bodies. As a result of its catastrophic third-world status (crumbling infrastructure, massive pov-erty, civil war, and ongoing human rights abuses), many Guatemalans im-age their body politic as wounded, in painful contrast to the fantasmatic im-ages of the sleek and whole body politic of core or "first-world" countries. Such bodies beautiful are represented in ubiquitous ads for first-world products and function as ideal others in much Guatemalan nationalist dis-course—as melting pots that have successfully homogenized the popula-tion. Liberal economic theory promised that underdeveloped countries like Guatemala were "'behind the industrialized countries in the same way that children are 'behind' adults" (Lipietz 1987, 2), but with integration into the world market, they would soon "take off" and grow up. Like indi-vidual maturing, the development of the body politic into its modern, postindustrial adulthood promised to bring sovereign autonomous subjec-tivity with complete control of the lower bodily strata (often mapped, as Laura Kipnis [1992] and Mary Douglas [1989] suggest, onto socially "lower" groups such as Indians and the poor). Mayan culture—as unho-mogenized, inappropriate—has traditionally functioned as a "therapeutic myth" to explain the painful symptoms of Guatemala's stunted moderniza-tion. The lack of a healthy "grown-up" body politic is blamed on the major-ity indigenous population, and the failure to modernize is ascribed to the weight of tradition-bound Indian communities mired in their twenty-one different languages and antiquated mode of production. The Mayan body functions to fetishistically cover over the lack that structures Guatemala's relations with the transnational economy (and, as many Mayan activists have pointed out, magically hides the fact that what access ladinos have to the commodity-driven international economy is based on indigenous labor).

Uneven development and dependency theory (S. Amin 1974; Cardoso and Faletto 1979; Gunder Frank 1967; Rhodes 1970; Palma 1978) long ago challenged the assumption that a peripheral country like Guatemala would motor down the royal road to metropole status once internal differences were assimilated; these theories suggest instead that it is relations of dependency that hemorrhage off the vital components necessary for integral development (the north sucks out first the south's natural resources and then its financial reserves by selling it back the finished product). These theories powerfully legitimate revolutionary organizing by showing that the body politic will not naturally mature and that poverty is not the result of inherent weakness—stunted growth, perennial childhood, or in the Social Darwinist sense, degeneracy based on interbreeding. Instead, "backwardness" is caused by Guatemala's unnatural, alien insertion into world systems of unequal exchange that can be changed through struggle. This unequal relation is condensed, perhaps, in the nightmare vision of gringas as baby snatchers.

Alain Lipietz suggests that, despite its undeniable superiority over liberal economics, dependency theory indulges in "pessimistic functionalism" (1987, 4), insofar as it posits imperialism as a totally powerful "Beast of the Apocalypse." This pessimistic functionalism underwrites the Left's imperative for unity. The enemy is so strong that, in order for resistance movements to survive, internal differences must be overcome—even violently, because unity is necessary for the greater good. Similarly, Carol Smith (1992) suggests that even though they reject liberal modernization theory, many Guatemalan leftists retain its notion of stages: the Maya must unify with poor ladinos (in other words, proletarianize) before Guatemala can successfully resist dependency. So the praxis accompanying dependency theory is animated by "subjugated knowledges" similar to the Lamarckian eugenics that make *mestizaje* discourse so powerful, an argument I return to later. Antidependency praxis acknowledges that the body politic is wounded, not merely immature, and also promises a way to heal it through unifying mass struggle against the first world. So leftists may also deploy Mayan "divisionism" (cultural rights activism instead of class struggle) to magically explain the failure of this struggle (as liberals do to explain stunted growth). This may be why ladinos of both the liberal Right and Marxist Left tell jokes about Rigoberta Menchú and view Mayan organizing as a finger in the wound, a deadly virus that threatens to Yugoslavize Guatemala's body politic.

Despite its explanatory power, dependency theory is limited, according to Lipietz, because it "paid little attention to the concrete conditions of capitalist accumulation either in the center or on the periphery. It therefore could not visualize that transformations in the logic of accumulation in the centre would modify the nature of centre-periphery relations. Nor could it see, in consequence, that transformations in the basis of that logic within the peripheral countries would lead to nothing less than the fragmentation of the 'Third World'" (1987, 2). This fragmentation at the transnational level undermines both the analytics and practices that view the world as rigidly divided into solid blocs. This makes for a dangerous and anxious time for liberation struggles, especially those that try to cover their wounds with a fetishized Mayan body that is increasingly articulate. But these are also times of crisis for nation-states, transnational capital, and other apparently powerful actors, and perhaps, as we saw with the ratification of 169, these are times of opportunity.

One response to the global crisis of debt and accumulation has been neoliberalism. Carlos Vilas describes these attempts, usually deployed through the World Bank and the International Monetary Fund, as "deregulation of the economy, trade liberalization, the dismantling of the public sector, and the predominance of the financial sector of the economy over production and commerce" (1996, 18). The price for countries receiving international financial support is compliance with "structural adjustment packages," a bundle of policies aimed at stabilization and structural reform. Lael Parish describes the aim of these measures as "to get foreign debt payments under control by reducing government expenditures, raising taxes, tightening the money supply, and devaluing the currency (an important move that serves to encourage exports and discourage imports). Structural reform measures work to reduce the size and change the role of government, particularly through privatization of state-run enterprises and services" (1996, 8). These policies have violent material effects that resemble the handiwork of Lipietz's "Beast of the Apocalypse": downsizing, unemployment, drastic reductions in state services, increased infant mortality, and dire poverty.

The bundle of policies, decisions, individual particularities, and material effects that we fetishistically call the World Bank, the United Nations, or the State have awful power. But in arguing against pessimistic functionalism ("that the world is as it is because it was designed to serve 'the interests of the powerful'" [Lipietz 1987, 4]), Lipietz (and I in his footsteps) refuses to give these sites *all* the power:

> I have no intention of exonerating Great Satans like America . . . or more abstract Great Satans such as Capitalism. . . . I am simply saying that *results* should not be confused with *causes of existence:* that a body of partial regularities which "forms a system" is not the same thing as a system which "unfolds." The formation of the international division of labour cannot be regarded as the deliberate or functional organization of a system. Quite apart from the freedom

of history, the class struggle and competition between capitals, we also have to take into account the way in which the existences of nations and of State sovereignty compartmentalize the reproduction of social relations. (Lipietz 1987, 18–19)

For example, when the World Bank attempts to deliberately organize a system through structural adjustment packages, it confronts internal contradictions as well as class (and other) struggle on many fronts. The emphasis on finance rather than production makes this system particularly vulnerable to body image (think of the intensely magical anxieties of the U.S. fetish-ridden finance markets, with their totem animals of bull and bear and jittery investors awash with portents) and to the threat of social unrest causing perceived instability (see Maurer 1997). Vilas suggests that "neoliberals fear that such problems would create a climate of instability that might negatively affect the inflows of foreign capital, putting the whole economic model at risk. In this sense, social policy becomes closely linked to the politics of the moment" (1996, 18). Partly for this reason, the World Bank and IMF have been unable to force structural adjustment down the throats of Latin American bodies politic. Sustained and heroic resistance has forced the implementation of the social investment funds in various countries, aimed at alleviating the poverty and dislocation caused by privatization, downsizing, and belt-tightening (see Parish 1996; NACLA 1996a and 1996c). Though definitely counterinsurgent, such funds both channel money and provide opportunities for activists that may be used in unexpected ways and remind us that even such powerful actors as the World Bank must acquiesce and frame a reply. Similarly, when asked to explain the implementation of structural adjustment in Guatemala, state officials said that many of their efforts were stymied—by public protest, bureaucratic inertia, congressional resistance, competing interests among the elites, counterpressures from international human rights groups and the UN, and, some admitted, by their own reluctance to employ certain policies.[1] Although "the state" promises to limit spending in order to receive financial support, export processing zones have opened, currency stabilization has been made a priority, and privatization and decentralization efforts are underway, officials said they were hard pressed to explain how any single policy handed down by the World Bank was directly implemented in Guatemala. The process, like any articulation, is characterized by contradictions, compromises, and an "infinite number of divergent interests which, intellectually, we group into force fields, but which are in fact simply pursuing local or locally materialized interests. In reality they are no more than

1. These comments are based on interviews and information presented by state officials invited to AVANCSO over six months in 1993. I and most of my colleagues there were quite surprised by the mounting evidence that the World Bank did not always get what it wanted.

partially integrated, and it is through the State that they find their overall expression" (Lipietz 1987, 22). Compromises occur at different levels including the state and World Bank (as in being forced to implement the funds) and have unintended consequences, including the mobilization of powerful resistances. All of which offers further evidence against pessimistic functionalism. Just as Guatemala may help us think about cyberspace, gringos may also learn from these responses as we too face violent globalizing adjustments.

"Post-Fordism" is a name for transformations in transnational political economy, and like the unintended consequences of neoliberal reform, these processes help form the conditions of possibility for Maya-hackers, state support for Mayan cultural rights, and Guatemala's peace process. Post-Fordism is defined by changes in information technologies, flexible accumulation strategies, and just-in-time production (A. Amin 1994; Boyer 1990; Hall and Jacques 1990; Harvey 1989; Lipietz 1987; O'Connor 1984). Fordism was named for Henry Ford's assembly-line factories, which were based on Taylorist principles where workers were interchangeable and production was based on homogenized labor and consumption (you could build and buy any kind of car, as long as it was a black Model-T). Post-Fordism, on the other hand, is characterized by close attention to minute differentiations in constructing consumer preferences and in positioning workers for flexibility. At least since the "democratic opening" of 1985, Guatemala has become increasingly imbricated in a transnational system in crisis as Guatemala attempts to find a place in the "new international division of labor." These "new times," as Stuart Hall calls them, involve "a shift towards a more flexible, specialized and decentralised form of labor process[:] . . . the hiving off or contracting-out of functions and services[,] . . . greater emphasis on choice and product differentiation[,] . . . on the 'targeting' of consumers by lifestyle, taste and culture, [and] the rise of the service and white collar classes . . . with the 'feminization' and 'ethnicisation' of the work force" (Hall 1990, 118). And, just as Mayan culture played a role in liberal and dependency models of national development (explaining backwardness and the failure of revolution), it also helps structure Guatemala's participation in global post-Fordism.

Guatemala and Structural Adjustment

In relating to international finance, Guatemala's body image is compared with the model of other bodies (Guatemalan state officials look at "first-world" economies and sign up for drastic surgical measures hoping to become that). In turn the images other bodies have of the subject's body (the IMF and World Bank triage procedures put Guatemala at the front of the line) deeply affect the subject's body image. Both processes emphasize Guatemala as wounded—as Willy Zapata, president of Guatemala's Central Bank, said, "The medicine must be taken" (Forster 1996). The treatment regime negotiated with international lenders (during which only "white" men were present at the table), termed "structural adjustment," aims to lower inflation, drastically reduce public spending, and increase foreign reserves (AID 1982; Barry 1987; Poitevin 1993). The means chosen to pursue these ends are *las exportaciones no tradicionales* (nontraditional exports) that include out-sourcing (*maquila* production), primarily of textiles (Peterson 1992); new crops like snow peas, broccoli, and flowers (Castellanos de Ponciano, González, and Poitevin 1992; Dary Fuentes 1991; Pérez Sáinz, Camus, and Bastos 1992); and Guatemala's image as a sort of premodern island in the net for tourist consumption. These new exports lean heavily on the Mayan body as a source of labor and site of "culture." Rather then holding it back, in government plans for the future this body now promises to magically develop, energize, and heal the wounded nation.

Thus, rather than trumpeting the traditional goal of assimilation (although many still seem to desire it), current government policy—modeled in the rural Development Poles, deployed through the Ministry of Culture and Sports, and instituted and legalized with the ALMG, Convention 169, the Accord on Identity, and Constitutional amendments—now includes "the right to culture." As official documents declare, "culture" (indigenous identity) is part of integral development and democratization, and the right to culture will allow the "people of Guatemala to be able to say with pride, 'I am part of this nation'" (Ministry of Culture 1988, 2). In official discourse, culture (ethnic identity) is now seen as integral to the existence of the state, to identity, and to national defense, in part because when the Guatemalan man feels part of the nation, the "transformative energy of his creativity begins to surge" (Ministry of Culture, 1988, 2). Concomitantly, the loss of his heritage weakens him.

Of course, not everyone agrees with this new valorization of culture. Michel Foucault argues that the governmental state does not transcend body discipline, nor does the deployment of sexuality overcome that of alliance, but instead these regimes work together, simultaneously. Similarly, if we want to connect the changes in attitude and practice described in chapter 8 with transnational transformations called post-Fordism, we must remember this is not the next step beyond Fordism in a progress narrative, but instead the two regimes interpenetrate on every side. Groups with different economic, familial, and political interests will have different (and sometimes contradictory) reactions to Mayan organizing and to the nation's insertion into the global economy. If traditional power was in the hands of the army and agroexport sectors whose profits relied on undervalued labor, control of public finance, the customs system, and outright corruption, the next generation of those families, modernizing army officers, and a new class of urban technocratic managers may find their profits in competitive markets, free access to the factors of production, a functional judicial system, and representative democracy (GNIB 1996a)—and probably drug trafficking. The technocrats, represented by the Party of National Advancement (PAN), which won the 1996 elections and signed the peace treaty, seem to be gaining acceptance. This does not mean that traditional power structures have been transcended or that they are not adjusting themselves. But we do need to understand contradictory responses to Convention 169, the ALMG, and so on both as the effect of Mayan organizing and as imbricated in national and transnational compromises and struggles over power.

These struggles have resulted in the Guatemalan state (since 1988) declaring its role to be promoting all cultural expressions, with "culture" understood as market value rather than political problem. Government documents now extol the rich and ancient multiplicity of cultures that configure the ethnological map of Guatemala. In turn, this change in policy has had material effects, including funding dispersal through the Social Investment Fund (FIS), the National Peace Fund (FONAPAZ), and the Guatemalan Indigenous Fund (FODIGUA); a historic peace treaty that recognizes indigenous rights; state funding of the ALMG, bilingual education, and municipalities increasingly controlled by indigenous people; and plans to decentralize government and turn some power over to Mayan communities. A state official cited two major reasons for this increase in government interest in the Maya, reasons that are worth repeating. First is the impact of indigenous organizing—as I argue, Maya articulation with the state is a recombinant relation that changes both sides. "In the last few years we've seen a major increase around a whole set of demands, and it is getting stronger and stronger. . . . We can't stop it. But the government needs to respond, to channel it." Second, he said, some people are finally beginning to realize that indigenous culture is a "productive resource." "The major money maker for Guatemala now is tourism. . . . Our cultural heritage could be our entry into the global economy."

Of course, this industry that will save Guatemala in the new international division of labor includes several double binds—for the state and for the Maya. First, it leans on a very specific Mayan body: not the inappropriate(d) Maya-hacker but a "Mayan" body in traditional clothing and settings (which in turn carries heavily gendered affect). Though government valorization of traditional indigenous "culture" legitimates the demands of Mayan cultural rights activists, it simultaneously resists their claims to represent the Maya: because most activists hold service-sector jobs (one of the effects of Post-Fordism) as teachers, development workers, lawyers, and so on, they are considered inauthentic, or ladinoized, by many ladinos. Urban, educated, articulate Maya are not "Indians" in this symbolic economy. However, in the image of the authentic "Indian" produced as a nontraditional export for tourist consumption, the Maya belongs on the land, doing their traditional thing, an image that supports Mayan demands for the right to own and control ancestral territories. Many ladinos are caught in the bind of denying that land should belong to the Indians, whereas Indians are seen as belonging to the land, both in the ethnostalgic sense of a special bond with nature and in the sort of spatial incarceration that makes rural life and the peasantry equivalent to "Indian."

The state simultaneously militarizes the countryside and plans for bureaucratic decentralization, which would, to some extent, devolve power to local, indigenous organizations. As such, these initiatives not only seem to respond to Maya demands for increased indigenous autonomy and power but also open up new terrains for the *formación* of Mayan activists.

According to its theorists and practitioners, decentralization is the necessary precursor to nation building in Guatemala, which will lean on local development and respect for Mayan cultural differences. Again, these neoliberal discourses of decentralization both respond to the demands of a post-Fordist regime of accumulation and parallel Mayan demands for autonomy at the local level and participation at the national level. Cultural difference and "ethnic identity" articulate differently with shifts in the mode of regulation. In my fluidary analysis, which tries to articulate these shifts with the power of images and imagi-nations, I suggest that state responses to indigenous demands are both counterinsurgent and important gains for the Maya. Articulation with the transnational post-Fordist scene is the condition of possibility for both Guatemalan national projects and Mayan cultural rights activism, but this work is overdetermined by racism, fantasies of whitening, contradictory deployments of gendered bodies, and struggles over identifications that lean on the phenotypically marked body. These often frustrate attempts to transform the Maya into entrepreneurs (and thus ladinos). State schemes are dependent on hegemony work, replete with unintended consequences. Many of them do not work. In turn, this fissured space can also be productive for Mayan demands.

PROSTHETICS

Here I want to again strap on the notion of prosthetic—that medium of connection that supports and makes possible bodies politic (Gray, Figueroa-Sarriera, and Mentor 1995) and that establishes the place it appears to be added to (Wigley in J. González 1995). If you remember the joke from chapter 7, the anthropologist sees Mayan women walking in front of men as a sign of progress because they always walked behind before. The anthropologist is rudely surprised at the reason: before there were no land mines. The violences of civil war, fantasmatic self-fashioning, and national and transnational biopolitical economy make the ground that identification attempts to rest on a site of danger. Maya and ladino, rich and poor, the state and the *pueblo,* men and women, modernity and tradition, none of these identifications are possible on their own. Instead, that which seems added on—the nation-state imposed on primordial ethnicity; the feathers and flourishes of indigenousness on the bricks and mortar of class relations; backward-looking Indians on modern rational statecraft; embarrassing ladino racializing stuck on to the liberation promised by *mestizaje cultural;* or the divisiveness of Mayan women on pan-Mayan identifications—these actually establish those sites. These are prosthetic relations, active articulations, intimate incorporations, and "strange, perhaps transformative" linkages (Stone 1995b, 36). As Gray and Mentor suggest, prosthetic connection is "different than a synthesizing [process]. . . . Enhancements and replacements are never fully integrated into a new synthesis, rather they remain lumpy and semi-autonomous" (Gray and Mentor 1995, 466).

All of these boundaries are interpenetrated in Quincentennial Guatemala (race, ethnicity, class, gender, national, sexual, modern, tradition, solidarity, gringa, and so on). The *mujer maya* has a special relation to all of these identifications, as universal donor to the blood politics of *mestizaje* discourse, as prosthetic support for ladino bourgeois domesticity, and as that link to the past that legitimates the inappropriate(d) Maya-hacker. She is also a vital prosthetic in producing Guatemalan prosperity in the dangerous terrain of global post-Fordism. Without her, it wouldn't have a leg to stand on.

Prosperity

Just as the landmine joke posits the *mujer maya* as a prosthetic that bears the brunt of historic violence, she has been deployed to face the toxic conditions of Guatemala's front lines in its articulations with transnational capital. *Exportaciones no tradicionales* such as the new crops of snow peas and flowers, *maquila* production, and tourism all lean heavily on the *mujer maya.*

Throughout the world, as Aihwa Ong (1987), Maria Mies (1991), Cynthia Enloe (1990), and others have demonstrated, women's labor makes possible the new international division of labor, in part through what Mies calls the housewivization of women. Because women's work is supposedly supplemental to family income—she is "helping out" a father or husband— her wages are much lower than men's. Nations attract foreign investment with an "attractive labor pool," and indigenous (and ladina) women, displaced by war and willing to work for one or two dollars a day, are extremely attractive. Studies of the *maquila* and new crops in Guatemala have found that many employers prefer to hire young, unmarried women and insist on intrusive, violent means to ensure that they remain productive (and not reproductive).[2] Kurt Peterson, working in Guatemala, reports that "owners almost unanimously desire young, unmarried women in order to capitalize on their availability, youthfulness, and endurance" (Peterson 1992, 42). He quotes the personnel manager at a Korean *maquila* as saying: "My ideal worker is young, unmarried, healthy, thin and delicate, single, and does not have previous experience. If they have experience they come with many vices. They do not like to follow orders" (Peterson 1992, 43). Over four-fifths of the workers in Guatemala's *maquila* factories are women, and most of these are indigenous. Women are also understood to be naturally doc-ile, dexterous, nimble, and genetically programmed to sew and process food—unlike men, whose labor takes strength and effort (Pérez Sáinz, Ca-mus, and Bastos 1992; Castellanos de Ponciano, González, and Poitevin 1992). Claudia Dary found that most men and women working in the new industries in Chimaltenango, Guatemala—both workers and employers—accept these stereotypes and the resulting wage differentials (1991, 69).

Jane Collier suggests that the enlightenment division between private (the home as space of leisure and desire) and public (the world of labor and alienation), and the ideals and institutions of citizenship and bourgeois law that facilitate Guatemala's incorporation into transnational markets, de-pend on this idea of women's natural predilections—the *mujer maya* as pros-thetic housewife. These institutions require people to have natural charac-teristics, to obey inner voices. "[T]he ideal of a free market for jobs and commodities—that accompanied, and was made possible by, the spread of bourgeois legal concepts and institutions—required competitors for em-ployment and sales to have inner capacities and desires that distinguished them from rivals" (1997, 207). The "inner capacities" Mayan women deploy in export processing, in turn, are linked to the home and to women's incar-ceration there as housewife—an unpaid laborer because she does it for love. In women's "hearts and homes rational men can seek the 'inner voice' that speaks their cultural heritage" (J. Collier 1997, 210), and in turn, be-cause this is a modern home and no one is forcing women to cook and clean, they must do it because they want to.

Working in textile-manufacturing *maquilas* and with new crops, Mayan

2. Guatemala's "traditional" exports also rely on the "housewivization" of Mayan women's labor in various ways. Labor on coffee, sugar, and cotton plantations is often not waged but paid by amount harvested, so entire families will work together for one payment. In cases where men alone undertake seasonal migration to the coast (or Mexico, or the United States—remittances are an increasingly important basis for the Guatemalan economy), women's labor maintaining crops and household production, as well as raising children, is also unpaid. Lynn Stephen (1991) documents the way Zapotec women's labor is a prosthetic for men's migration from Mexico.

women are seen to be doing what comes naturally in the home—weaving, food preparation, and gardening—while simultaneously participating in modern production methods and the production of modern selves. Of course, Mayan women's decisions to participate in these activities are complex, responding to economic and familial pressures as well as hopes and dreams of their own, which often include both pride in their Mayan identity and the desire to be modern. So, though the Mayan home may seem vestigial to the national political economy and overarching transnational markets, these new industries lean on the interplay of modernity, tradition, nature, and home that coalesce in the *mujer maya* at work on the assembly line.

Similarly, tourism in Guatemala is deeply dependent on the ardor and mystery of the *mujer maya*—as condensation of indigenous culture—as well as on her underpaid labor. When the vice-minister of culture says, "Our cultural heritage is a major money-earner," he means the *mujer maya,* because she keeps highland villages "traditional" and her production and deployment of *traje* mark Guatemala as indigenous and therefore "attractive" to hard-currency bearing tourists. I was told, "No one comes here to see the pollution and traffic in Guatemala City! . . . They come to see Indians," and as I argue, Indianness itself is condensed on to the *mujer maya.*

So, although ladino men may imagine themselves as white men saving brown women through "structural adjustment" and "national development," it's a joke. With tourism, *maquila* production, the new crops, and women's underpaid labor on plantations and in the service industries, actually, brown women are saving white men and women from red ink.

Peace

The *mujer maya* also figures prominently in coverage of the biggest news event of recent times: the peace treaty signed in December 1996, which in turn is related to transnational biopolitical economy. As long as Guatemala was still embroiled in "the longest-running civil war in Latin America," it didn't look very modern and proved a rather embarrassing member of the global "family of nations." Not only did all the spilled blood make it harder for governments and corporations to do business there without looking complicit, but also the country was rife with that instability so unattractive to the foreign capital needed for neoliberalism to function. Enormous international pressure, from the threat of sanctions to the promise of a billion dollars, helped create the conditions of possibility for peace.

Most Guatemalans are enthusiastic about the Peace Accords, but many have deep reservations. For one, the process itself has been exclusionary: the only people present at the negotiating table have been ladino men (even for the accord on indigenous rights), most of whom seem convinced that they are saving their white and brown fellow citizens.

Allucquere Rosanne Stone (1995b) suggests that prosthetics are about overcoming a lack of presence, and in Guatemala's peace process the *mujer maya* as image is deployed to bridge the span between those speaking and those spoken for. Frequently used to represent the peace process as a whole for national and international audiences, she works to cover over the gap, to bandage the wounded national body politic so that those excluded feel they have a stake. For example, the government pamphlet "Peace Has Arrived," designed for mass distribution, describes the accords in cartoons and simple language and prominently displays the *mujer maya*. Rigoberta Menchú, although an ambiguous figure because of her international power, is also deployed as a quintessential *mujer maya* in front-page stories in Guatemalan newspapers and the *New York Times* that trumpet the signing of the accords (where she is shown hugging government representatives) (Preston 1996).

In turn, Rigoberta Menchú has been a vital prosthetic for the organization of the URNG and for their participation in the peace talks. This is in part through the power of her testimonial (Menchú 1984). As I discuss in chapter 2, although the revolutionary organizations have worked hard to theorize the relations among class, ethnicity, and nationalism, and despite the large numbers of Mayan combatants, many Maya feel they are not represented in the URNG, in part because there were no indigenous commanders representing the guerrillas in the peace talks. Just as for the nation, the *mujer maya* in the form of Rigoberta Menchú prosthetically overcomes this lack of presence. Although she has distanced herself from them, Ms. Menchú is popularly understood to be, if not part of, then quite sympathetic to the URNG.[3] She was the only indigenous person in the United Representation of the Guatemalan Opposition (RUOG), an exile group that spoke for a range of opposition organizations before the UN, foreign governments, and solidarity groups. Her testimonial, *I, Rigoberta Menchú* (1984), which makes clear her family's connections to the guerrillas, was produced in collaboration with the revolutionary organizations and Elizabeth Burgos-Debray as part of a public relations campaign. Her powerful and poignant story, chosen from many others, was deployed prosthetically

3. Criticized for inviting Rodrigo Asturias, one of the three commanders of the URNG, to the Nobel Prize ceremonies in Oslo, she said it was because of his relation to Guatemala's other Nobel Prize winner (Miguel Angel Asturias, Rodrigo's father), not to the revolution. A popular joke at the time of the Nobel asked, "What is Rigoberta's blood type? URNG-positive." Prosthetic support, as I hope is clear, is not the same as saying nice things about the guerrillas in public or raising money for them. Ms. Menchú does not publicly claim to have been an official member of the URNG, and she has strongly criticized them in public.

to explain to world opinion why a people would justly rebel against their government. Ms. Menchú is an extraordinary woman whose personal skill, grace, and gravitas have all contributed to the position she holds today, but many Mayan men, ladino men, and ladina women have similarly powerful and poignant experiences, many of which are published and available. I think the condensations that create the *mujer maya* have also combined to make this particular story known worldwide and Ms. Menchú an international symbol of resistance and survival. She is both a Mayan woman, acting on the national and transnational stage, and a *mujer maya,* propping up the wounded body politic of a revolutionary movement that was militarily defeated.

Among some Mayan activists there is understandable resentment of her fame and of the way she prosthetically supports the guerrillas by whom many feel betrayed.[4] Several times after the Nobel Prize was awarded, I heard Mayan activists complain that the URNG was using Ms. Menchú as a mop to clean up their messes, which include a history of racist exclusion.

Ms. Menchú as United Nations goodwill ambassador prosthetically supported the peace process, shuttling among the various participants (representatives of the URNG, the Guatemalan government, the UN, and international supporters like the United States), several times jump-starting stalled negotiations. Her presence also helped forestall increasingly bitter critiques from the popular and Mayan movements about their lack of access to the process. Though her incorporation was semiautonomous, she was a brown woman saving white men from red-faced embarrassment at these exclusions. But prosthetic sociality also helps us understand the *mujer maya* as a medium of connection among all these sites. She props up stumped bodies politic that could not exist on their own; she extends their scope of operation through international representation, or as a mop; but she is incorporated in intimate, complex ways into these body images; and she is lumpy, semiautonomous. Rigoberta Menchú's story may be an ideal prop for extending revolutionary consciousness (which, like national identity, must be both modern and traditional), but she in turn has extended herself in surprising, transformative ways. As for the Mayan movement described in chapter 7, for national, ladino, and revolutionary identifications the prosthetic of the *mujer maya* as tradition rubs in both irritating and exciting ways with her as an absolutely constitutive aspect of their incorporations.

4. Exiles like Ms. Menchú are often resented by those who stayed in Guatemala, because the exiles missed some of the worst of the counterinsurgency and later consolidation activities (like forced participation in the Civil Patrols). These feelings are encouraged by government propaganda that denounces guerrilla leaders and other exiles for living in five-star luxury while people in Guatemala starve.

Feminist Prosthesis

I was trained as a feminist anthropologist to seek out these irritations and excitements, to aggressively listen for the way different voices sometimes break through, because they are a site of articulation where I can connect in transnational solidarity. I love it when the *mujer* speaks as a woman, saying what I want to hear. Mayan women complaining about sexism in the cultural rights movement resonates with my own experiences of misogyny, a wounded place we seem to have in common. In turn, the *mujer maya* gets to function as my prosthetic as I speak for her here against venal national elites, the violence of transnational capital and structural adjustment, Mayan men who don't appreciate her the way I do, and other anthropologists who ignore gender in their analyses. But with the slight twist of gender in the first term, we are right back to Gayatri Spivak's original calculation of white women saving brown women from brown (and whiter) men and women. This is kind of a sick joke, because brown women are really supporting the wounded body image of gringa middle-class feminist anthropology, stuck with our phantom limbs of racism, classism, homophobia, and colonizing erotic investments. Like all of the bodies politic examined here, we are in a seemingly impossible situation where we must simultaneously respond to the modern demand to think for ourselves, by performing critical analysis (objectivity), and hold on to the discipline's tradition of being in solidarity with the people we work with.

Jean Jackson (1989) and Jane Collier (1997) have eloquently explored the difficulty of how to talk about the nationalist traditions that legitimate struggles over rights, when to the long-term ethnographer those traditions are clearly invented. As Jackson says, the stakes over "culture" in the Vaupés of Colombia are so high that it's easy to make enemies when she talks about it. Collier notes that, regardless of academic theories about hybridity, identity as constructed, and the dangers of essentialism, for many people identity is not negotiable: "Nationalists have to be right. . . . Scholars, too, have to be right" (1997, 204).

Gringo scholars whose body image includes being in solidarity with a people in struggle often find ourselves stumped by how to conduct a friendly critique (see Hale 1994; Warren 1992). Well aware of the colonizing nature of salvation discourses, roundly critiqued both at home and abroad for unwanted interventions, self-reflexive about the systems of transnational privilege that allow us to even be there, and cognizant of the disempowerment of people who have suffered ethnocide and neoliberal "adjustments," who are we to criticize? In many field sites, anthropologists have decided to remain silent rather than risk neocolonialism (and maybe losing informants—especially on the issues of feminism, often so vehemently resisted by male nationalists). The intense violence of the civil war in Guatemala has made it especially hard to make friendly critiques of the exclusions practiced by the Left and the Mayan movements.

Just as ladinos think of Mayan organizing as "a finger in the wound," gender seems to be an especially fraught issue for the Mayan movement, for all the reasons I have been discussing here. The Mayan magazine *Iximulew* in its issue on the *"Mujer Maya"* links feminism with the army as a danger to Mayan community, and the prominent Mayan intellectual Dr. Demetrio Cojtí critiques Mayan women who push for their issues to be addressed. Ms. Xicox says that Mayan men "were afraid we would tend toward feminism" and insists that Mayan women have not. When I first ventured a query about the lack of women in leadership positions in the ALMG, the president bawled me out for half an hour, saying, "Who are you to judge? Do people judge your work with how you live your life at home?" His comments express both the impossible divide between modernity and tradition that the Mayan body politic must cover over and the importance of the *mujer maya* to do that. He is also expressing a keen understanding of context, of the way Mayan body image is formed in relation to other body images and to the (often negative) images those bodies politic have of the Maya. As he is well aware, ladino and gringo racisms have historically leaned on colonized women to justify often violent interventions.

Mayan body image, however (like Guatemalan nationalist and revolutionary bodies politic), is also formed in relation to positive images that other bodies have of it. Though Mayan activists work to both salvage and maintain cultural practices in their communities, a great deal of their energy is addressed to non-Maya: writing and publishing studies of Mayan practices and carefully argued treatises on their historical and legal rights in Spanish; reporting and opining in the national radio and print media; skillfully lobbying the Guatemalan government for legislative and financial support for their initiatives; holding seminars and forums open to the public; touring the United States and Europe to present their case; and granting thousands of interviews a year to national and foreign scholars. The value placed on the image held by non-Maya, especially foreign scholars, is clear in the immense amount of time devoted to these interviews—some leaders may give two or three a day![5] Kay Warren (1992) and the contributors to the anthology edited by Edward Fischer and R. McKenna Brown (1996) sensitively address the intricate relations among scholars and Mayan activists, the exchanges of information, money, suspicion, and recrimina-

5. A similar relation obtains between popular or revolutionary organizations and international solidarity, as well as between the representatives of the Guatemalan nation-state and international representatives of governments, finance capital, business, the United Nations, and so on.

tion, as well as support and friendship that occur there.[6] Gringo scholars, of course, lean on the Maya as subjects of analysis and supports for our careers, but the Maya body image in turn incorporates the transnational authority bestowed by this interest, some security from state violence through contacts outside Guatemala, the financial support it may provide, and the scholarly legitimation of being written about. As Jane Collier reminds us, "Current nationalists live in a world where powerful interlocutors associate 'truth' with the kind of 'objectivity' that social scientists claim" (1997, 204).

Mayan men and women so graciously and generously give their time and energy to gringos in part because they are acquiescing to the demands of the scholarly body politic that leans on them across a transnational power differential. (State officials also generously gave their time to me, and the reasons are probably similarly complex.) This relation *can* be understood as neocolonial—our search for the scoop on an exotic other, our excitement at seeing a new historical actor emerge, or our desire to find women organizing for their rights, even if they "are not feminist." But even though this characterization certainly rings true, it also returns us to the already constituted solid first-world scholar who produces her professional and political subjectivity over the ground of Mayan organizing. I have been arguing that the *mujer maya* is more lumpy, semiautonomous, and the gringa more open, wounded. Feminist scholars may not be able to hear this "subaltern speak," as Spivak reminds us (1988a), on a distortion-free channel, but we cannot help but be in intimate, irritating, and exhilarating prosthetic contact. Gender can be a medium of connection, the straps that hold body to prosthesis. It does not make us the same, but this may be so cyborg a relation that differences between body and prosthetic become unclear. Perhaps she also uses me to extend her scope of operations, to overcome distance and be represented here on these pages. Gringo anthropology and solidarity are partially, lumpily incorporated into the Mayan body image—through the prosthetic joinings I have been discussing and through Mayan men and women becoming anthropologists. Similarly, Quetzil Castañeda critiques "the insidiously pompous concern of the field-worker" over their "impact" on the other, which "implicitly and explicitly argues that the society or culture being impacted is a static, ahistorical, agencyless, solidly bounded,

6. Through these hours of interaction, over time and in ways colored by both resentment and interest, scholars are partially incorporated into these body images. In later conversations with members of the ALMG, Dr. Cojtí, and others (and through presentations at Mayan studies conferences), we discussed issues of gender in changing ways. Rather than seeing their comments as knee-jerk machismo, I began to understand the complexities of gender for wounded bodies. As I shared my changing views with them (not merely publishing critiques in English and in foreign journals), what had been antagonistic discussions became much more civil. Overcoming distance (as in between where we gather information and where we present analysis) is an integral part of prosthetic sociality and fluidary practice for Lizard Queens.

noninteractive object. . . . Rather, 'impact' consists of multiple reworkings and contestations of the ways collectivities imagine the contours of the social forms they inhabit" (Castañeda 1996, 7 and 9).

This is prosthetic sociality in Stone's terms (1995b), in which the Maya are not only victim or ground for the formation of feminist anthropology's body politic. Both body and prosthetic change as they are joined. Rather than reified nationalist, ethnic, or first-world feminist identities (the latter an unintended effect of a guilt-tinged refusal to engage), these are cyborg body politics, wounded and constitutively leaning on their prosthetics. These are stumped identities—open, bewildered, and political. Though Jane Collier is right when she says that "nationalists have to be right" (1997, 391), at some level the identities under discussion acknowledge this contingency. Perhaps the brutal violence of Guatemala's thirty-five years of civil war makes explicit the fact that nation, ethnicity, gender, and even scholars in solidarity are wounded bodies politic.

A POLITICS OF BLOOD

This book tries to cast suspicion on any explanation of Quincentennial Guatemala that relies on a notion of "duped-ness" for its power: that Mayan villagers are deceived by army propaganda that gringas are baby snatchers; or that Mayan activists are taken advantage of by the co-opting state that distracts them by legalizing the ALMG; or that state workers who devote their energies to "culture" are victims of false consciousness that it will actually do some good; or that taking the state as the site and stake of struggle is to be fooled by a mask, when analysts know that real power lies elsewhere. I also try to cast aspersions on any language of "waking up," as in the Maya as a sleeping giant waiting for the revolutionary cock's crow to roust them from slumber, or Mayan women just now opening their eyes to modernity. Without positing an autonomous sovereign subject, I try to represent ladinos, Mayas, and gringos as deciding to struggle on certain terrains, as actively articulating demands, and as daring to participate in the strange and transformative practices of *formación*, the complex processes of identification.

To conclude, I want to return to my ladino friend's plea to refrain from caricatures. The Maya are not particularly powerful vis-à-vis ladino elites, but they are hacking away at the power structure and have made amazing gains in the last ten years. They are skillfully articulating their struggles with local, national, and transnational forces, and it is easy as a fluidary gringa to feel excited at their prospects. The Left faces a far greater challenge, attempting to articulate identifications in the midst of post-Fordist adjustments where flexibility undermines clear-cut enemies and the willingness to sacrifice for future goals. Rather than victory, they must make do with a negotiated peace and with the dirt and general unpleasantness of electoral politics. To many Maya and outside observers, they appear to have less finesse dealing with emerging identity positions articulated around ethnic and gender demands than the traditionally far more rigid state sectors.

But it was too simple to say that the state wants to assimilate the Indian, or even that many ladinos now want to harness the magic power of indigenous culture and the *mujer maya* as resources needing no investment. Instead, they find themselves in an uncanny, prosthetic relation with the Maya—men and women.

And it is equally too simple to say that the Guatemalan Left is duped by economic reductionism and thus unable to think beyond class divisions, falling unawares into unthinking racism. Though resistance to Mayan claims from many leftists—indigenous and ladino—may disappoint solidarity gringos (like myself) who want everyone we like to just get along, we must understand these reactions as the result of identifications that are shifting and multiply determined. For one thing, as Carol Smith (1990b) argues (and Charles Hale [1994] suggests about Sandinista resistance to Miskito demands), the Guatemalan Left is nationalist, and the nation faces the impossible task of being both modern and traditional at the same time. The Maya are thus both necessary and highly problematic, because they symbolize the backwardness the nation struggles against (paralleling the contradictory relations of Mayan "nationalists" to gender issues).

Too, as with all of the bodies politic examined in this book, blood is a central axis of these identifications and thus of politics. In Quincentennial Guatemala, spilled blood takes on special meaning. For many leftists, it is a shock to hear the Maya claim that they were victims of genocide in the civil war, because most do not see the war as being about race—it was about an historically unjust mode of production that mercilessly exploited the majority of Guatemalans, regardless of their skin color, the clothes they wear, or the number of gods they worship. In turn, Maya denunciations of genocide, especially when echoed internationally around the Quincentennial and Nobel Peace Prize, seem to denigrate the enormous loss of ladino blood, shed in the hopes of winning economic and political justice and of improving the body politic as a whole. When the Maya claim that their bodies fill the graveyards, that their blood has been sacrificed more than any other, they are making a claim on the nation, on rights to citizenship and to have a say in the future, as Brackette Williams suggests. Many on the Left soldiered on through years of agonizing defeat, expecting that their blood had spilled "on fertile ground destined to produce lasting and worthy contributions" (B. Williams 1989, 436). Men and women returning from the mountains and from exile, venturing into public life in a move that only a short time ago would have left them tortured and dead, find themselves called racist, whereas indigenous militants are suddenly not Maya enough. Their already tenuous stake to the future is threatened by Maya

claims to have bled more—in part at the hands of the revolutionaries—
which reduces their own suffering to a "spoiled sacrifice" (B. Williams 1989,
437). Charges of genocide are particularly galling because there are more
Maya now than there have been since the Conquest—in part as a result of
formación.

This is in part why Carlos Figueroa Ibarra, visiting from exile in October 1992, might say that "the worst part of all this five-hundred-years stuff
is the Maya saying that the ladinos have no culture. How ignorant! I am
ladino, petit bourgeois, and they tell me I have no culture! We have our literary tradition and a history of resistance! Without us, there would have
been no 1944, or the resistance of the 1960s. We have a valiant history. We
have our own Nobel Prize winner in Miguel Angel Asturias!" This may be
why the journalist Mario Roberto Morales wants to relegate indigenous
claims to the past of "Mayassic Park." But what sound like knee-jerk reactions must be understood in the larger context of painfully wounded body
politics and the politics of blood.[7]

To return to my arguments in chapter 6, these blood politics are also
transfused with a grammar of race in Foucault's sense, which provides the
moral authority to defend the social body. Part of the grid of intelligibility
that sustained the "longest-running struggle in Latin America" was the righteousness instilled through the struggle for the common good, the "resurrected subjugated knowledges[,] . . . the manifestation of preserved possibilities, the expression of an underlying discourse of permanent social war,
nurtured by the bio-political technologies of 'incessant purification.' Racism does not merely arise in moments of crisis, in sporadic cleansings. It
is . . . woven into the weft of the social body, threaded through its fabric"
(Stoler 1995, 69). This is not racism as unthinking abjection of a phenotypically marked body; it is a grammar of folding and vacillating differentiations, a discursive tactic that can map on to social classes and nations, as
well as "races." In all those divisions it "establishes a *positive* relation between
the right to kill and the assurance of life" (Stoler 1995, 84).

If and when the guerrillas murdered indigenous people, they probably
did not do it because they hated Indians per se (many of them are indigenous themselves), but because particular indigenous people became identified with an other enemy, like the state and the dominant elite. Killing,
within the "permanency of war-like relations inside the social body" was
seen as contributing to a greater good (Stoler 1995, 84). This is in *no*
way meant to exonerate these murders—they are horrifying and must be
judged by the Guatemalan Truth Commission—but this positive relation

7. Of course, blood is a symbol (D. Schneider 1980; Collier and Yanagisako 1987). It does
not "really" link people through kinship or by itself give anyone a claim to the future. It is a way
of talking about larger structures of meaning—about *mestizaje,* identifications, and sacrifice.

may explain the apparently ingenuous response of guerrilla leaders to charges of insensitivity to ethnic issues. Their actions were not understood to be racist, but on the contrary, to ensure life.

Similarly, drawing on Nancy Leys Stepan (1991), I suggest that Lamarckian eugenics is a subjugated knowledge that animates this struggle to ensure life (among the Left, the Right, and the Maya).[8] It holds that the collective body should manage life and thereby legitimates interventions that improve social conditions and strengthen both individual and social bodies (because advances are passed on through the blood). The whole point of taking the state is to more effectively perform such interventions, but improvements are produced along the way, through that very struggle.

For example, eugenic hopes are condensed into the revolutionary figure of the "New Man," produced through physical fitness training, literacy campaigns, self-criticism, and the rationalization of gender roles and sexuality, both as part of everyday practice in the guerrilla organizations and as part of their plans for the future. Hygiene and literacy campaigns in liberated territories and pressure on plantation owners to improve wages and living conditions are also eugenic interventions that set the stage for taking state power. Basic nutrition, better health and well-being, clearly contribute to better citizens and to improving the nation, phenomena verifiable through statistics. Eugenics, even as a preserved possibility rather than an explicit discourse, carries this added allure of science—verifiability, a truth outside politics—a powerful tool for overcoming the irrational racism and class bias of bourgeois society. These dreams of progress are further supported by the "dismal science" of economic theory: through a mix of the liberal notion of underdeveloped countries as immature children and dependency theory that claims that only through the Oedipal move of revolt will the child ever actually grow up. As the revolutionary poet Otto René Castillo put it, "*Vamos patria a caminar* [Let's begin walking, my country]."

The revolution brought together a variety of dreams and sentiments and shed an enormous amount of blood. Some of its hopes were sharply delineated and fiercely demanded, others remain inchoate longings, potent mixtures of ethnostalgia, technophilia, moral transcendence, and fantasies of conjugal love, "a range of desire that articulated unevenly with the multiple hierarchies of nation, gender, race, and class" (Stoler 1995, 188). And there is still much mourning to be done. Post-1996 Quincentennial Guate-

8. The term *eugenics* is rarely used now without conjuring the Nazis' racial cleansing through the "final solution" of wholesale murder. Stepan, however, argues that the meaning of *eugenics* in Latin America in the early twentieth century was very different and primarily about positive, productive interventions, much in the sense of a Foucauldian biopower (Foucault 1980; Stoler 1995). I am suggesting that these positive meanings continue to work as preserved possibilities, animating the blood politics of both the Guatemalan Left and the state.

mala, with the signing of the peace treaty, is reincorporating. It is demilita-
rizing thousands of fighters from both sides of the war, supporting Mayan
"culture," and struggling to find new ways to articulate these desires and
longings and to make the ground fertile on which so much blood has fallen.
The state, site and stake of struggle, the "institutional form which condenses
the compromises which prevent the different groups making up the national community from destroying one another" (Lipietz 1987, 19), reeling
from the "piñata effect," is awash with all these dreams and sentiments.
Considering such emotions as duped or a form of false consciousness will
not support peace. I hope that acknowledging the grid of intelligibility, the
conditions of possibility—which always include gender and sexuality—for
these emerging body politics will.

Through the alchemy of articulation, neither subjects nor conceptual
tools are unproblematically either liberatory or pernicious. As the state becomes reterritorialized, as previously excluded subject-positions push into
its frame, the state changes, as do the "Indians." Mayan attempts to work
within the state, to petition and demand of it, are not only co-optation but
can be strategic interventions with powerful results, at the same time that
they may exclude Mayan women. State responses, both paranoic rejection
and strategic support, may be concessions in hegemony work. If nothing
else, they expose the fissures and nonunitariness of the fetishized state. In
the struggles over the meaning of the Quincentennial, the effects of the war,
the content of Mayan identity, and the future of the Guatemalan nation,
each decision, each discursive strategy, incites counterstrategies and multiple possibilities. Power is deployed by international figures, government
employees, and Mayan organizations, and it simultaneously works on them,
like a camel hair suit.

I suggest that these bodies politic are gendered in specific ways and intimately related to each other, so that we cannot understand the relations
among the imagined and lived body of the bleeding nation (revolutionary
or counterinsurgent), the relation between indigenous rights and the project of nation building, the simultaneity of modernity and tradition, and the
theoretical problems of the relation between real bodies and social fantasy,
solidarity and critique, without thinking them all together. Disconnecting
from these complex relationalities does not seem to be an option. I've suggested fluidarity as an appropriate mode of prosthetic relationality—a
practice of necessarily partial knowledge, in both the sense of taking the
side of, and of being incomplete, vulnerable, and never completely fixed.
Fluidary anthropology needs to remember that articulation is two-way, that
the late capitalist cyborg body politic is about connection, as well as wounds,
about wetware and not very solid identities, about desire and jokes (laughter is a most necessary ingredient), and that maybe salvation is not the
point.

APPENDIX

SELECTED RIGOBERTA MENCHÚ JOKES
What's Under There?

¿Por qué verdaderamente ganó Rigoberta el premio Nobel (o en otra versión, ¿por qué ya no se pone un cinturón/faja con su corte la Rigoberta)? Porque ya es una indita muy desenvuelta.

Why did Rigoberta really win the Nobel Prize (or, why doesn't she wear a belt with her skirt)? Because she's a little Indian who is very articulate/ unwrapped. (Because of the way the traditional skirt [*corte*] is worn wrapped around the body and held in place with a belt, indigenous women are often called *envueltas*. *Desenvuelta* also means to speak easily, to be verbally articulate.)

Rigoberta llegó al aeropuerto de Italia para regresar a Guatemala y en la entrada el guardia le tocó su blusa y le dijo "¿Qué lleva allí, señorita?" "Ella le dijo 'Misiles.'" El guardia inmediatamente llama a todos los policías; y llegan todos corriendo con sus pistolas. Cuando le preguntan de nuevo, "¿Qué lleva allí?" Dice Rigoberta: "Mis hiles, mis tijeres, mi aguje."

When Rigoberta was leaving Italy to go back to Guatemala, the guard at the terminal asked her what she had in her blouse, and she said, "Missiles." He immediately called all the other guards, who came running with their pistols drawn. Then he asked her again what she had, and she said, "*Mis hiles* [from *mis hilos* (my threads)], my scissors, my needles." (As with many of the jokes, this one makes fun of the way indigenous people supposedly speak Spanish by mixing up articles and not knowing how words end, so that *mis hilos* becomes *mis-hiles* [missiles]—thus "my threads" become missiles, and *mi aguja* [my needle] becomes *mi aguje*.)

¿Por qué no usa Rigoberta Menchú zapatos de charol? Porque le reflejan los huevos.

Why doesn't Rigoberta wear patent leather shoes? Because they reflect her balls.

¿Qué tienen Rigoberta Menchú y Lorena Bobbit en común? El corte.

What do Rigoberta Menchú and Lorena Bobbit have in common? The cut/skirt.

Dicen que Rigoberta va a divorciar a su marido. Se dió cuenta que es Poco-man.

They say that Rigoberta is going to divorce her husband. She found out that he is Poco-man. (Pocomam is one of the Mayan ethnolinguistic groups, but *poco* means "little," so the suggestion is that she's too much woman for this little man.)

Smut: She's Sexually Available

¿Cómo sabemos que la Rigoberta no es virgen? Porque cuando se fue a México, Salínas le dio al vergue (albergue/la verga).

How do you know that Rigoberta is not a virgin? Because when she went to Mexico, Mexican President Carlos Salínas de Gortari gave her a place to stay/his penis. (This mixes up articles and word endings so that *albergue* [housing, refuge] sounds like *la verga* [dick].)

Cuando Rigoberta conoció al General García Samayoa le preguntó a ella: "¿Cómo se llama?" "Rigoberta," dijo ella. "Bonito el nombre," dijo García Samayoa. "¿Quién te lo puso?" "Mama me la pusa," dijo Rigoberta.

When Rigoberta met Defense Minister General García Samayoa, he asked her what her name was, and she said, "Rigoberta." "That's a pretty name," he said. "Who gave it to you?" "My mother gave it to me/suck my pussy." (This dirty joke plays on Spanish grammatical mistakes between *mama me lo puso* [mother gave it to me] and *mama me la pusa*.)

Rigoberta Menchú dio luz a un bebé muy canche y visitó con su hijo al presidente Serrano Elías. El le preguntó, "¿Cómo se llama tu hijo?" Ella dijo, "Probeta." "¿Probeta? y ¿por qué así?" dice Serrano. "Porque probé ta-lega en México, en Italia, en Noruega."

Rigoberta gave birth to a very blonde baby and went to visit President Serrano Elías. He asked her what she called it, and she said, "Test-tube/tried out." "And why do you call it that?" he asked. "Because I tried out men in Mexico, Italy, Norway."

Rigoberta tiene miedo que Serrano Elías la va a desnudar. Porque anda quitando cortes.

Rigoberta is afraid that Serrano Elías is going to take her clothes off (also, Serrano wants to see her naked). Because he is going around taking off skirts/dissolving the courts.

Rigoberta Menchú se casó con un francés de apellido Fas. Ahora se llama Menchú Fas.

Rigoberta Menchú married a Frenchman with the last name of "Fas," so now she is Menchufas. (*Me enchufas* means "you rape me" or "you assault me.")

Un acto de teatro. Primera escena—está Rigoberta de pie, sin su huipil o sea desnuda arriba del corte. Segunda escena—está Serrano con ella, con su cabeza entre sus pechos. ¿Cómo se llama la obra? Gallo en chicha.

This is a play. In the first scene Rigoberta is seen standing without a shirt; she is naked from the waist up. In the second scene we see Serrano with his head between her breasts. What is the name of the play? *Gallo en chicha.* (*Gallo en chicha* is a traditional chicken dish, but this also plays on the symbol for Serrano's party [the rooster] and a slang term for breasts [*chiches*].)

A la Premio Nobel de la Paz no le gustaría tener hijos, porque como ella es de la sierra, le podrían salir "serranitos."

The Nobel Prize winner doesn't want to have children. Because she comes from the mountains, she is afraid they would come out little Serranos. (This plays on *sierra* [mountain] and the name of former president Serrano.)

Rigoberta se fue a Nebaj, entre los Ixiles, y puso sus jeans de marca Lee. Fue a caminar por el pueblo y todos la miraron desde atrás. Por fin un hombre le dijo, "¿Si lee su culo escribe mi pene?"

Rigoberta went to Nebaj among the Ixiles, and she was wearing her Lee brand jeans. She took a walk around the town, and everyone was looking at her behind. Finally a man said to her, "If I read your ass, will you write with my dick?"

Insulting: She's Not Sexual

¿Qué tiene que ver Rigoberta con Juan Pablo II? (o en otra versión, ¿por qué quiere Rigoberta que la llamen "Su Santidad")? Porque los dos tienen cara de papa.

Why is Rigoberta like John Paul II (or, why does Rigoberta insist that people call her Your Holiness)? Because they both have the face of a potato/pope.

¿Qué tiene que ver la Rigoberta con un jonrón? Los dos son incojibles.

How is Rigoberta like a home run? Both are uncatchable/unfuckable.

¿Qué tiene que ver la Rigoberta con una cebra? Con los dos se rayó la mula.
What does Rigoberta have in common with a zebra? They both are mules with stripes. (*Rayar* means "to stripe," and "to stripe the mule" is a colloquial expression for getting lucky or standing out.)

Rigoberta es millonaria, pero no es rica.
Rigoberta is a millionaire, but she is not rich. (*Rich* here means "delectable," in the sexual sense.)

Class Transgressions

Mattel is now making a doll of Rigoberta, which makes Barbie and Ken happy because now they'll have a maid.

They say that Mattel is discontinuing its line of Rigoberta Menchú dolls. Because it turned out that too many things were disappearing from Barbie's house.

Rigoberta will not invest the Nobel Prize money in buying a plantation because she's afraid Indians will invade the land.

I heard that Rigo is buying a house in Zone Fourteen, and she's put out word that she's looking for a *muchacha* among the ladino girls who live there. (Zone Fourteen is Guatemala's richest area, and a *muchacha* is a domestic servant.)

Rigoberta Menchú dies and goes up to heaven and knocks at the gate. When St. Peter opens the door he says, "Who are you?" "The Nobel Prize winner," she says, and he says, "We don't have anyone by that name in the book." Rigoberta Menchú taps her foot and says, "I'm the UN Special Ambassador." And Peter says, "I'll look in the book, but I don't see anyone by that name." So Rigoberta says, "I am Rigoberta Menchú Tum, Nobel Peace Prize winner and UN Ambassador, let me in." So Peter goes to take another look at the book. As she's standing there waiting, Saint Thomas comes by and sees her standing there and says, "The tortillas are finally here!"

¿Cuál es la parte más rica del cuerpo de Rigoberta? Los pechos.
What is the richest/most delicious part of Rigoberta's body? Her breasts. (The joke, like the following one, refers to indigenous women's practice of keeping their money tucked inside their bras.)

When Rigoberta won the Nobel Prize, she begged them not to give it to her in cash because it wouldn't all fit.

They say that now Rigoberta doesn't want to be called "Rigo" but Reebok instead.

When Rigoberta won the Nobel Prize, she went out and bought a big Mercedes Benz. A friend went to visit her and found her peering under the hood looking very puzzled. "What's wrong, Rigo?" he asked. "I can't find the horses," said Rigoberta.

Others

The Guatemalan army is claiming half the Nobel Prize money because they say that they did all the work.

What type blood is Rigoberta? URNG positive. (The URNG is the Guatemalan National Revolutionary Unity, the umbrella group for the armed movement.)

¿Por qué a la Rigoberta no le gusta el futból? Porque su papá se murió de chamusca.
  Why doesn't Rigoberta like soccer? Because her papa was killed in a *chamusca*. (*Chamusca* refers both to a friendly pick-up game and to being burned, like a barbecue or the Spanish Embassy fire where Vicente Menchú died.)

They say that Rigoberta wants people to remember her father through the foundation in his name, but she also wants people to remember the other side of him—the fun side—so she's using some of the Nobel money to hold a big barbecue in his memory.

Rigoberta Menchú Tum se cambió su apellido "Tum" y se puso "Fax" para ser Rigoberta Menchú Fax porque ya pasó la epoca del tum tum tum—el sonido de los tambores y el fax es lo más moderno.
  Rigoberta changed her last name "Tum" to "Fax" to be Rigoberta Menchú Fax, because the time of the old fashioned tum-tum-tum of the drum is over and the fax is the most modern.

¿Por qué le llama a Rigoberta Menchú chile relleno? Porque siempre anda entre dos franceses.
  Why do they call Rigoberta Menchú a chile relleno? Because she's always between two French people. (*Franceses* refers to slices of bread and to French solidarity activists accompanying her.)

They say that Rigoberta is getting calls from Steven Spielberg because he wants to make the movie *Indio-na Jones.*

Rigoberta was with Señora Molina Stahl, the government's "alternative" Nobel candidate, who told her that she received the Order of the Quetzal. She asked Rigoberta what Order she had received, and Rigoberta said, an Order of Capture [an arrest warrant].

Rigoberta Menchú dice que está enojada con el Papa. ¿Por qué? Es porque a el no le gusta la gente de caites, solo de botas (devotos).
    Rigoberta says she is angry with the Pope. Why? Because he doesn't like people who wear sandals, only people who wear boots. (This plays on her mixing up *de botas* [people who wear boots] with *devotos* [pious people].)

COMMENTS FROM LETTERS TO THE PRESS

"¿A cuántos de sus compatriotas mató ella personalmente, no sólo con el fusil sino con la kilométrica lengua que posée?"
    How many other Guatemalans did she kill personally, not just with a gun, but with that long, rapid-fire tongue of hers?

"Tropecé con la famosa Rigoberta en la tienda Chanel en Paris, tenía puesto un suculento vestido amarillo y unos elegantes zapatos rojos, su cadena Cartier, y su muy elegante Rolex con date de siete mil dólares."
    I ran into the famous Rigoberta in the Chanel shop in Paris. She was wearing an exquisite yellow dress, elegant red shoes, a Cartier chain, and a seven thousand dollar Rolex watch.

"Soy paisano de Rigoberta porque soy originario de Chicamán y conocí a toda la familia de esta mujer, pues bien: Rigoberta fue de las primeras involucradas en la guerrilla junto a toda su familia y cuando se involucró venía amenazando a toda la población. Hay un pariente que todavía vive en Chicamán y en una ocasión me mostró una fotografía de ella donde estaba de verde olivo."
    I'm a neighbor of Rigoberta because I'm from Chicamán, and I knew this woman's entire family. Rigoberta was one of the first ones to get involved with the guerrillas, together with her whole family, and when they got involved, they came around threatening everyone. One of her relatives, who still lives in Chicamán, once showed me a photograph of her where she was dressed in olive-green camouflage.

GLOSSARY

Blanquemiento	the process of whitening, understood as a genetic process whereby white or European "blood" is added to the brown, Indian, or black population to gradually "improve" the succeeding generations.
Campesino	someone who works the land, a farmer, or peasant.
Cofradía	brotherhood or saint society, organized to sponsor village festivals, often part of the civil-religious hierarchy system of cargos or increasing responsibilities.
Compañero or Compañera	companion or comrade, often used to mean an ally in struggle or in the revolution.
Corte	the long wrap-around skirt worn by many Mayan women. It is part of *traje típica,* or the traditional clothing that marks one as indigenous.
Criollo	designates the Spaniards born in Guatemala who oversaw the colonial political economy, and describes a continuing attitude and historical legacy derived from the Colony.
Derecho consuetudinario	customary law, the usually unwritten, community-specific processes that deal with local wrongdoers. It functions outside the national legal system.
Desenvuelta	unwrapped, often it means naked in reference to the disrespectful term for indigenous women as *envueltas,* or wrapped. It also means articulate, or well spoken. Many of the jokes about Rigoberta Menchú depend on this double entendre. Because the *corte* is a central marker of indigenous identity, it also refers to ladinoization.

379

Formación	the process of creating activists. It has the sense of consciousness raising, or taking on a commitment.
Formar	to form, or create, often to make activists out of formerly uninvolved people.
Güera	foreign woman, blond, or lighter-skinned. Often used as a cat call.
Indígena, Indio, Maya	are highly contested terms in Guatemala for indigenous people, who themselves use many different words to self-identify, depending in part on the context and the interlocutor. These words include identification by village or hamlet, town, linguistic group, and family. Many use the term *natural,* meaning native to a place (Carlsen 1993; Falla 1978), although I seldom heard this used among the urban Maya. The term *indigenous people* is closest to a generic, and I use it when I hope to avoid more political overtones. I employ *Indian* for the disrespectful term *indio* when I write of ladino racist attitudes. There has been a conscious political strategy of taking back the term *indio* in Mexico and among Guatemalans in exile there, some of whom have attempted to incorporate the term as they return to Guatemala. This has met with little success and has led to tense moments when people felt insulted by Mexican activists or returnees. The term *Maya* has come to signify an indigenous person who consciously takes on this identity and struggles for Mayan rights. Just as the terms are problematic and in flux, so are the identities they seek to name, because both Maya and ladino are identities in formation.
Kaxlan	indigenous term for foreigner, or outsider. Wilson (1995) translates it literally as chicken, a bird brought to Guatemala by the Spanish.
Maquila	export processing plants. Usually owned by transnational capital (in Guatemala, primarily U.S. and Korean) and operated by foreign-born overseers. Workers often perform piecework in textile manufacture, or sort and package specialty crops.
Mestizaje	has complex meanings of "racial" and cultural mixing that entail both a miscegenation fear of "mongrelization" and a hope for postcolonial unity in the creation of a "new race."
Milpa	corn or a patch of land planted with corn and beans.

Mujer Maya	Mayan woman. I use the term to refer to the fantastical woman who supports the tourism industry, the *mestizaje* project, and Mayan gender practices. Different than actually existing indigenous women.
Pueblo	is often translated from Spanish as "people," but this translation misses the term's powerful *gemeinschaft* qualities. Though the old-fashioned organic community sense of *nation* informs the use of *pueblo* in Guatemala and in solidarity discourse, in discussions of rights and even of autonomy projects it is carefully distinguished from *nation*. When people use the term in this sense, I have retained *pueblo*.
Traje	traditional indigenous clothing, usually hand-made. For women, who wear it far more regularly than men, it usually includes an ankle-length wrap-around skirt (*corte*), woven shirt (*huipil*), an apron, and a shawl or a head covering. For men, usually knee-length pants, a woven shirt, open-toed sandals (*caites*), and often a coat or woolen poncho.
Tzuultaq'a	the mountain spirits among the Maya-Q'eqchi' of Alta Verapaz, known as the earth owner in other Mayan areas.

WORKS CITED

Abrams, Philip. 1988. "Notes on the Difficulty of Studying the State." *Journal of Historical Sociology* 1, no. 1.

Adams, Abigail E. 1997. "Organ Harvesters and Harbury: Transnational Narratives of Impunity and Accountability in Postwar Guatemala." *Mesoamerica* (summer).

———. 1998. "Word, Work, and Worship: Engendering Evangelical Culture in Highland Guatemala and the United States." Ph.D. diss., University of Virginia.

Adams, Richard. 1956. "Cultural Components of Central America." *American Anthropologist* 58.

———. 1970. *Crucifixion by Power.* Austin: University of Texas Press.

———. 1990. "Ethnic Images and Strategies in 1944." In *Guatemalan Indians and the State, 1540–1988.* Ed. Carol Smith with Marilyn Moors. Austin: University of Texas Press.

———. 1992. "Las Masacres de Patzicia de 1944: Una Reflexión." *Winak: Boletín Intercultural* (June 1991–March 1992).

Adorno, Theodor, and Max Horkheimer. 1993. "The Culture Industry: Enlightenment as Mass Deception." In *The Cultural Studies Reader.* Ed. Simon During. London: Routledge.

AID (U.S. Agency for International Development). 1982. *Land and Labor in Guatemala: An Assessment.* Guatemala: Ediciones Papiro.

Alarcón, Norma. 1989. "Traddutora, Traditora: A Paradigmatic Figure of Chicana Feminism." *Cultural Critique* (fall).

Alcock, Anthony. 1970. *History of the International Labour Organization.* London: MacMillan Press.

ALMG (Academia de Lenguas Mayas de Guatemala). 1990. *Documentos del Seminario: Situación Actual y Futuro de la ALMG.* Guatemala: Patrocinio del Ministerio de Cultura y Deportes.

———. 1991. *Ley de la Academia de Lenguas Mayas de Guatemala y sus Reglamientos.* Guatemala: Editorial Maya Wuj.

Althusser, Louis. 1971. "Ideological State Apparatuses (Notes towards an Investigation)." In *Lenin and Philosophy and Other Essays*. New York: Monthly Review Press.

Amariglio, Jack, and Antonio Callari. 1993. "Marxian Value Theory and the Problem of the Subject: The Role of Commodity Fetishism." In *Fetishism as Cultural Discourse*. Ed. Emily Apter and William Pietz. Ithaca: Cornell University Press.

Amaro, Nelson. 1990. *Descentralización y Participación Popular en Guatemala*. Guatemala: Instituto Centroamericano de Estudios Políticos (INCEP).

Amin, Ash. 1994. *Post-Fordism: A Reader*. Oxford, U.K.: Blackwell.

Amin, Samir. 1974. *Accumulation on a World Scale: A Critique of the Theory of Underdevelopment*. New York : Monthly Review Press.

Amnesty International. 1987. *Guatemala: The Human Rights Record*. London: Amnesty International Publications.

Anaya, S. James. 1994. "International Law and Indigenous Peoples: Historical Stands and Contemporary Developments." *Cultural Survival* (spring).

Andersen, Nicolás. 1983. *Guatemala: Escuela Revolucionaria de Nuevos Hombres*. Mexico City: Editorial Nuestro Tiempo.

Anderson, Benedict. 1983. *Imagined Communities: Reflections on the Origin and Spread of Nationalism*. London: Verso.

Anderson, Marilyn, and Jonathan Garlock. 1988. *Granddaughters of Corn: Portraits of Guatemalan Women*. Willimantic, Conn.: Curbstone Press.

Annis, Sheldon. 1987. *God and Production in a Guatemalan Town*. Austin: University of Texas Press.

Anzaldúa, Gloria. 1987. *Borderlands/La Frontera: The New Mestiza*. San Francisco: Spinsters/Aunt Lute.

Apter, Emily. 1993. Introduction to *Fetishism as Cultural Discourse*. Ed. Emily Apter and William Pietz. Ithaca: Cornell University Press.

Arias, Arturo. 1990. "Changing Indian Identity: Guatemala's Violent Transition to Modernity." In *Guatemalan Indians and the State, 1540–1988*. Ed. Carol Smith with Marilyn Moors. Austin: University of Texas Press.

Arriola de Geng, Olga. 1991. *Los Tejedores en Guatemala y la Influencia Española en el Traje Indígena*. Guatemala: Litografía Modernos.

ASIES. 1993. *Investigación Basica Sobre Derecho Consuetudinario en Tres Comunidades Mayahablantes de Guatemala, Informe Final*. Guatemala: ASIES (January).

Asturias de Barrios, Linda, and Dina Fernández García. 1992. *La Indumentaria y el Tejido Maya A Través del Tiempo*. Guatemala City: Ediciones del Museo Ixchel.

AVANCSO. 1988. *La Política de Desarrollo del Estado Guatemalteco, 1986–1987*. Guatemala: AVANCSO.

———. 1991. *Vónos a la Capital: Estudio sobre la Emigración Rural Reciente en Guatemala*. Guatemala: AVANCSO.

———. 1992. *¿Dónde Está el Futuro? Procesos de Reintegración en Comunidades de Retornados*. Guatemala: AVANCSO.

Bacal, Joey. N.d. "Judaism and 'Jewishness' as Other in Nineteenth Century Russia: The Conscription/ Conversion Policy of Nicholas I." Senior thesis, Lewis and Clark College.

Balibar, Etienne. 1992. "Foucault and Marx: The Question of Nominalism." In *Michel Foucault Philosopher*. Trans. Timothy J. Armstrong. New York: Routledge.

Balsamo, Anne. 1996. *Technologies of the Gendered Body: Reading Cyborg Women.* Durham: Duke University Press.

Barry, Tom. 1987. *Roots of Rebellion: Land and Hunger in Central America.* Boston: South End Press.

Barsh, Russel Lawrence. 1990. "An Advocate's Guide to the Convention on Indigenous and Tribal Peoples." *Oklahoma City University Law Review* 15.

————. 1994. "Making the Most of ILO Convention 169." *Cultural Survival: A Wave of Change; The United Nations and Indigenous Peoples* (spring).

Bastos, Santiago, and Manuela Camus. 1993. *Quebrando el Silencio: Organizaciones del Pueblo Maya y sus Demandas, 1986–1992.* Guatemala City: FLACSO.

————. 1995. *Abriendo Caminos: Las Organizaciones Mayas desde el Nobel hasta el Acuerdo de Derechos Indígenas.* Guatemala City: FLACSO.

Bell, Diane, Pat Caplan, and Wazir Jahan Karim. 1993. *Gendered Fields: Women, Men, and Ethnography.* London: Routledge.

Benedikt, Michael, ed. 1991. *Cyberspace: First Steps.* Cambridge, Mass.: MIT Press.

Benjamin, Walter. 1969. *Illuminations.* Ed. Hannah Arendt. Trans. Harry Zohn. New York: Schocken Books.

Berman, Howard. 1988. "The International Labour Organization and Indigenous Peoples: Revision of ILO Convention No. 107 at the Seventy-Fifth Session of the International Labour Conference, 1988." *The International Commission of Jurists, The Review,* no. 41.

Bermúdez, Lilia. 1987. *Guerra de Baja Intensidad: Reagan contra Centroamérica.* Mexico City: Siglo XXI.

Bernheimer, Charles. 1989. *Figures of Ill Repute: Representing Prostitution in Nineteenth-Century France.* Durham: Duke University Press.

Beverly, John. 1989. "The Margin at the Center: On *Testimonio* (Testimonial Narrative)." *Modern Fiction Studies: Narratives of Colonial Resistance* (spring).

Beverly, John, José Oviedo, and Michael Aronna, eds. 1995. *The Postmodernism Debate in Latin America.* Durham: Duke University Press.

Bhabha, Homi. 1984. "Of Mimicry and Man: The Ambivalence of Colonial Discourse." *October* 28.

————. 1985. "Signs Taken for Wonders: Questions of Ambivalence and Authority under a Tree outside Delhi, May 1817." In *Race, Writing, and Difference.* Ed. Henry Louis Gates Jr. Chicago: University of Chicago Press.

Borch-Jacobson, Mikkel. 1996. *Remembering Anna O: A Century of Mystification.* Trans. Kirby Olson. New York: Routledge.

Bowman, Glenn. 1989. "Fucking Tourists: Sexual Relations and Tourism in Jerusalem's Old City." *Critique of Anthropology* 9, no. 2.

Boyer, Robert. 1990. *The Regulation School: A Critical Introduction.* Trans. Craig Charney. New York: Columbia University Press.

Brintnall, Douglas E. 1979. *Revolt against the Dead: The Modernization of a Mayan Community in the Highlands of Guatemala.* New York: Gordon and Breach.

Brown, R. McKenna. 1996. "The Mayan Language Loyalty Movement in Guatemala." In *Maya Cultural Activism in Guatemala.* Ed. Edward F. Fischer and R. McKenna Brown. Austin: University of Texas Press.

Brown, Wendy. 1995. *States of Injury: Power and Freedom in Late Modernity.* Princeton: Princeton University Press.

Bukatman, Scott. 1993. *Terminal Identity: The Virtual Subject in Postmodern Science Fiction.* Durham: Duke University Press.

Burchell, Graham, Colin Gordon, and Peter Miller, eds. 1991. *The Foucault Effect: Studies in Governmentality.* Chicago: University of Chicago Press.

Burger, Julian. 1994. "A Project for the Decade." *Cultural Survival: A Wave of Change; The United Nations and Indigenous Peoples* (spring).

Burns, Allan F. 1993. *Maya in Exile: Guatemalans in Florida.* Philadelphia: Temple University Press.

Butler, Judith. 1990a. "The Force of Fantasy: Feminism, Mapplethorpe, and Discursive Excess." *Differences: A Journal of Feminist Cultural Studies* 2, no. 2.

———. 1990b. *Gender Trouble: Feminism and the Subversion of Identity.* New York: Routledge.

———. 1991. "Imitation and Gender Insubordination." In *Inside/Out: Lesbian Theories, Gay Theories.* Ed. Diana Fuss. London: Routledge.

———. 1992. "Contingent Foundations: Feminism and the Question of 'Postmodernism.'" In *Feminists Theorize the Political.* Ed. Judith Butler and Joan W. Scott. New York: Routledge.

———. 1993. *Bodies That Matter: On the Discursive Limits of "Sex."* London: Routledge.

———. 1994. "Gender as Performance: An Interview with Judith Butler." By Peter Osborne and Lynne Segal. *Radical Philosophy* 67 (summer).

Cadigan, Pat. 1991. *Synners.* New York: Spectra.

Cancian, Frank. 1965. *Economics and Prestige in a Maya Community: The Religious Cargo System in Zinacantan.* Stanford: Stanford University Press.

Cardoso, Fernando Henrique, and Enzo Faletto. 1979 [1971]. *Dependency and Development in Latin America.* Berkeley: University of California Press.

Carlsen, Robert. 1993. "Discontinuous Warps: Textile Production and Ethnicity in Contemporary Highland Guatemala." In *Crafts in the World Market: The Impact of Global Exchange on Middle American Artisans.* Ed. June Nash. Albany, N.Y.: SUNY Press.

Carmack, Robert M. 1981. *The Quiché Mayas of Utatlan: The Evolution of a Highland Guatemalan Kingdom.* Norman: University of Oklahoma Press.

———. 1988. *Harvest of Violence: The Mayan Indians and the Guatemalan Crisis.* Norman: University of Oklahoma Press.

———. 1990. "State and Community in Nineteenth-Century Guatemala: The Momostenango Case." In *Guatemalan Indians and the State, 1540–1988.* Ed. Carol Smith with Marilyn Moors. Austin: University of Texas Press.

———. 1995. *Rebels of Highland Guatemala: The Quiché-Maya of Momostenango.* Norman: University of Oklahoma Press.

Carrillo Ramírez, Alfredo. 1971. *La Evolución Histórica de la Educación Secundaria en Guatemala, 1831–1969.* Vol. 1. Guatemala City: Editorial José de Pineda Ibarra.

Casaus Arzú, Marta. 1992. *Guatemala: Linaje y Racismo.* San José, Costa Rica: FLACSO.

Castañeda, Quetzil. 1996. *In the Museum of Mayan Culture: Touring Chichén Itzá.* Minneapolis: University of Minnesota Press.

Castellanos de Ponciano, Eugenia, Carlos González, and René Poitevin. 1992. *Mujeres, Niños y Ajuste Estructural.* Guatemala City: FLACSO.

Castells, Manuel. 1989. *The Informational City: Information Technology, Economic Restructuring, and the Urban-Regional Process.* Oxford, U.K.: Basil Blackwell.

CECMA (Centro de Estudios de la Cultural Maya). 1992. *Hacía una Educación Maya: Encuentro Taller de Escuelas Con Programas de Cultura Maya.* Guatemala City: Cholsamaj.

———. 1994. *Derecho Indígena: Sistema Jurídico de los Pueblos Originarios de América.* Guatemala City: Serviprensa Centroamericana.

———. 1996. "Mujeres Mayas." *Iximulew* in *Siglo Veintiuno,* 9 August.

CEDIM (Centro de Documentación e Investigación Maya). 1992. *Informe: Foro del Pueblo Maya y los Candidatos a la Presidencia de Guatemala.* Guatemala: Cholsamaj.

CEIDEC (Centro de Estudios Integrados de Desarrollo Comunal). 1992. *Guatemala: Seminario Estado, Clases Sociales, y Cuestión Etnico-Nacional.* Mexico: Editorial Praxis.

Chakravarti, Uma. 1990. "Whatever Happened to the Vedic *Dasi?* Orientalism, Nationalism, and a Script for the Past." In *Recasting Women: Essays in Colonial History.* Ed. Kumkum Sangari and Sudesh Vaid. New Brunswick, N.J.: Rutgers University Press.

Chatterjee, Partha. 1990. "The Nationalist Resolution of the Women's Question." In *Recasting Women: Essays in Colonial History.* Ed. Kumkum Sangari and Sudesh Vaid. New Brunswick, N.J.: Rutgers University Press.

Cholsamaj. Published annually. *Cholb'al Q'ij Agenda Maya.* Guatemala: Cholsamaj and Maya Wuj.

Chomsky, Noam. 1985. *Turning the Tide: U.S. Intervention in Central America and the Struggle for Peace.* Boston: South End Press.

Chow, Rey. 1993. *Writing Diaspora: Tactics of Intervention in Contemporary Cultural Studies.* Bloomington: Indiana University Press.

Clendinnen, Inga. 1987. *Ambivalent Conquests: Maya and Spaniard in Yucatan, 1517–1570.* Cambridge: Cambridge University Press.

———. 1991. *Aztecs: An Interpretation.* Cambridge: Cambridge University Press.

Clifford, James. 1986. "Introduction: Partial Truths." In *Writing Culture.* Ed. James Clifford. Berkeley: University of California Press.

———. 1988. *The Predicament of Culture: Twentieth-Century Ethnography, Literature, and Art.* Cambridge: Harvard University Press.

———. 1997. *Routes: Travel and Translation in the Late Twentieth Century.* Cambridge: Harvard University Press.

Clover, Carol. 1992. *Men, Women, and Chainsaws: Gender in the Modern Horror Film.* Princeton: Princeton University Press.

COCADI (Coordinadora Cakchiquel de Desarrollo Integral). 1985. *El Idioma, Centro de Nuestra Cultura.* Guatemala: Editorial Kamar.

Coe, Michael. 1993. *The Maya.* New York: Thames and Hudson.

Cojtí Cuxil, Demetrio, a.k.a. Waqi' Q'anil. 1990. *Configuración del Pensamiento Político del Pueblo Maya.* Part 1. Quetzaltenango, Guatemala: AEMG.

———. 1994. *Políticas Para la Reivindicación de los Mayas de Hoy (Fundamento de los Derechos Específicos de los Pueblos Maya).* Guatemala City: Cholsamaj.

———. 1995. *Ub'anik Ri Una'ooj Uchomab'aal Ri Maya' Tinamit: Configuración del Pensamiento Político del Pueblo Maya.* Part 2. Guatemala City: Cholsamaj.

Colby, Benjamin N., and Lore M. Colby. 1981. *The Day Keeper: The Life and Discourse of an Ixil Diviner.* Cambridge: Harvard University Press.

Collier, George. 1994. "The New Politics of Exclusion: Antecedents to the Rebellion in Mexico." *Dialectical Anthropology* 19, no. 1.

Collier, Jane Fishburne. 1986. "From Mary to Modern Woman: The Material Basis of Marianismo and Its Transformation in a Spanish Village." *American Ethnologist* 13, no. 1.

———. 1997. *From Duty to Desire: Remaking Families in a Spanish Village.* Princeton: Princeton University Press.

Collier, Jane Fishburne, Bill Maurer, and Liliana Suarez-Navaz. 1995. "Sanctioned Identities: Legal Constructions of 'Modern' Personhood." *Identities: Global Studies in Culture and Power* 1, no. 2.

Collier, Jane Fishburne, and Sylvia Yanagisako. 1987. "Towards a Unified Analysis of Gender and Kinship." In Collier, Jane Fishburne, and Sylvia Yanagisako, eds., *Gender and Kinship: Essays toward a Unified Analysis.* Stanford: Stanford University Press.

COMG (Consejo de Organizaciones Mayas de Guatemala). 1991. *Rujunamil Ri Mayab' Amaq* (Specific rights of the Pueblo Maya). Guatemala City: Cholsamaj.

———. 1995. "Análisis Evaluativo Sobre el Acuerdo de Paz: Identidad y Derechos de los Pueblos Indígenas." *B'oko'* (April).

Concerned Guatemala Scholars. 1982. *Guatemala: Dare to Struggle, Dare to Win.* San Francisco: Solidarity Publications.

COPMAGUA (Coordinación de Organizaciones del Pueblo Maya de Guatemala), a.k.a. Saqb'ichil. 1995. *Acuerdo Sobre Identidad y Derechos de los Pueblos Indígenas.* Guatemala City: Cholsamaj.

Coulter, Robert T. 1994. "Commentary on the UN Draft Declaration on the Rights of Indigenous Peoples." *Cultural Survival: A Wave of Change; The United Nations and Indigenous Peoples* (spring).

Csicsery-Ronay, Istvan Jr. 1991. "Science Fiction and Post Modernism." *Science Fiction Studies* 18.

Cypess, Sandra Messinger. 1991. *La Malinche in Mexican Literature: From History to Myth.* Austin: University of Texas Press.

Dary Fuentes, Claudia. 1991. *Mujeres Tradicionales y Nuevos Cultivos.* Guatemala City: FLACSO.

Dean, David J., Lt. Col. USAF. 1986. *Low Intensity Conflict and Modern Technology.* Maxwell Air Force Base, Ala.: Air University Press.

Debord, Guy. 1983 [1967]. *The Society of the Spectacle.* Detroit: Black and Red.

De Landa, Manuel. 1991. *War in the Age of Intelligent Machines.* Cambridge, Mass.: Zone Press.

Delaney, Carol. 1991. *The Seed and the Soil.* Berkeley: University of California Press.

de Lauretis, Teresa. 1987. *Technologies of Gender: Essays on Theory, Film, and Fiction.* Bloomington: Indiana University Press.

Delegación Guatemalteca Pro Ratificación del Convenio 169 de la Organización Internacional del Trabajo. 1992. *Derechos Indígenas: Convenio 169 de O.I.T. Sobre Pueblos Indígenas y Tribales en Paises Independientes 1989.* Quetzaltenango, Guatemala: Lito Marco.

Díaz-Polanco, Héctor. 1985. *La Cuestión Etnico-Nacional.* Mexico City: Editorial Linea.

———. 1987. *Etnia, Nación y Política.* Mexico: Juan Pablo Editorial.

Dibbell, Julian. 1994. "Profiles in Lameness." *The Village Voice,* 15 February.

Dirks, Nicholas B., ed. 1992. *Colonialism and Culture*. Ann Arbor: University of Michigan Press.

Doan, Mary Ann. 1991. *Femmes Fatales: Feminism, Film Theory, Psychoanalysis*. New York: Routledge.

Douglas, Mary. 1989. *Purity and Danger*. New York: Ark Paperbacks (Routledge).

Dreyfus, Hubert L., and Paul Rabinow, eds. 1983. *Michel Foucault: Beyond Structuralism and Hermeneutics*. Chicago: Chicago University Press.

Driscoll, Mark. 1988. "Count Zero Goes to Guatemala: Baudrillardian Magical Resistance and a Colonial Cyber-Discourse." Paper presented at the Strategies of Critique conference, York University.

———. 1992. "Point Me in the Direction of Albuquerque: Virtual Space and Boeing and Nothingness." *Semiotext(e)/Architecture*. New York: Semiotext(e).

———. 1994. "Apoco-Elliptic Japan." Paper presented at the Themes in East Asia conference, Monterey Institute.

———. 1998. "Erotic Empire, Grotesque Empire." Ph.D. diss., Cornell University.

D'Souza, Dinesh. 1991. *Illiberal Education: The Politics of Race and Sex on Campus*. New York: Free Press.

Dujovne Ortíz, Alicia. 1987. "Buenos Aires." *Discourse* 8.

EAFG (Equipo de Antropología Forense de Guatemala). 1995. *Las Masacres en Rabinal*. Guatemala City: EAFG.

Ehlers, Tracy Bachrach. 1990. *Silent Looms: Women and Production in a Guatemalan Town*. Boulder, Colo.: Westview Press.

Eide, Asbjørn. 1994. "New Approaches to Minority Protection." *Cultural Survival: A Wave of Change; The United Nations and Indigenous Peoples* (spring).

Englund, Nora. 1992. *Autonomía de los Idiomas Mayas: Historia e Identidad*. Guatemala: Cholsamaj.

———. 1996. "The Role of Standardization in Revitalization." In *Maya Cultural Activism in Guatemala*. Ed. Edward F. Fischer and R. McKenna Brown. Austin: University of Texas Press.

Enloe, Cynthia. 1983. *Does Khaki Become You? The Militarization of Women's Lives*. Boston: South End Press.

———. 1990. *Bananas, Beaches, and Bases: Making Feminist Sense of International Politics*. Berkeley: University of California Press.

Evenson, Laura, and Michelle Quinn. 1995. "Outlaws on the Cyberprairie." *San Francisco Chronicle*, 2 April.

Fabian, Johannes. 1983. *Time and the Other: How Anthropology Makes Its Object*. New York: Columbia University Press.

Fabri, Antonella. 1994. "(Re)composing the Nation: Politics of Memory and Displacement in Maya Testimonies from Guatemala." Ph.D. diss., SUNY, Albany, New York.

Falla, Ricardo. 1978. "El Movimiento Indígena." *Guatemala: Drama y Conflicto Social*, special edition of *Estudios Centroamericanos* (June–July). Central American University, José Simeon Cañas.

———. 1980. *Quiché Rebelde: Estudio de un Movimiento de Conversión Religiosa, Rebelde a las Creencias Tradicionales, en San Antonio Ilotenango, Quiché, 1948-1970*. Guatemala City: Editorial Universitaria de Guatemala.

————. 1984. "We Charge Genocide." In *Guatemala: Tyranny on Trial. Testimony of the Permanent People's Tribunal.* Ed. Susanne Jonas, Ed McCaughan, and Elizabeth Sutherland Martínez. San Francisco: Synthesis Publications.

————. 1988. "Struggle for Survival in the Mountains: Hunger and Other Privations Inflicted on Internal Refugees from the Central Highlands." In *Harvest of Violence: The Mayan Indians and the Guatemalan Crisis.* Ed. Robert Carmack. Norman: University of Oklahoma Press.

————. 1992. *Masacres de la Selva: Ixcán, Guatemala, 1975–1982.* Guatemala: Editorial Universitaria.

Fanon, Frantz. 1967. *Black Skin, White Masks.* New York: Grove Press.

Fauriol, Georges A., and Eva Loser. 1991. *Guatemala's Political Puzzle.* New Brunswick, N.J.: Transaction Publishers.

Ferguson, James. 1990. *The Anti-Politics Machine: "Development," Depoliticization, and Bureaucratic Power in Lesotho.* Cambridge: Cambridge University Press.

Figueroa Ibarra, Carlos. 1991. *El Recurso del Miedo: Ensayo Sobre el Estado y el Terror en Guatemala.* San José, Costa Rica: Editorial Universitaria Centroamericana.

Fischer, Edward F. 1996. "Induced Cultural Change as a Strategy for Socioeconomic Development: The Pan-Maya Movement in Guatemala." In *Maya Cultural Activism in Guatemala.* Ed. Edward F. Fischer and R. McKenna Brown. Austin: University of Texas Press.

Fischer, Edward F., and R. McKenna Brown, eds. 1996. *Maya Cultural Activism in Guatemala.* Austin: University of Texas Press.

Fitzpatrick, Peter. 1990. "Custom as Imperialism." In *Law, Society, and National Identity in Africa.* Ed. J. M. Abun-Nasr et al. Hamburg: Helmut Buske Verlag.

Forché, Carolyn. 1981. *The Country Between Us.* New York: Perennial (Harper and Row).

Forster, Cindy. 1996. "The Neoliberal Assault Begins: Guatemalan Labor Confronts Free Trade." *Report on Guatemala* (fall).

Foster, Robert J. 1991. "Making National Cultures in the Global Ecumene." *Annual Review of Anthropology.*

Foucault, Michel. 1970. *The Order of Things: An Archaeology of the Human Sciences.* New York: Vintage Books.

————. 1979. *Discipline and Punish: The Birth of the Prison.* New York: Vintage Books.

————. 1980. *The History of Sexuality, Volume I: An Introduction.* Trans. Robert Hurley. New York: Vintage Books.

————. 1988. "Politics and Reason." In *Michel Foucault: Politics, Philosophy, Culture. Interviews and Other Writings, 1977–1984.* Ed. Lawrence D. Kritzman. New York: Routledge.

————. 1991. "Governmentality." In *The Foucault Effect: Studies in Governmentality.* Ed. Graham Burchell, Colin Gordon, and Peter Miller. Chicago: University of Chicago Press.

Frank, Luisa, and Philip Wheaton. 1984. *Indian Guatemala: Path to Liberation: The Role of Christians in the Indian Process.* Washington: EPICA Task Force.

Freidel, David, Linda Schele, and Joy Parker. 1993. *Maya Cosmos: Three Thousand Years on the Shaman's Path.* New York: William Morrow and Co.

Freud, Sigmund. 1955. "'A Child Is Being Beaten': A Contribution to the Study of the Origin of Sexual Perversions." In *The Standard Edition of the Complete Psychological Works of Sigmund Freud.* Vol. 17. Trans. James Strachey et al. London: Hogarth Press.

———. 1963a. "Fetishism." In *Sexuality and the Psychology of Love.* New York: Collier Books.

———. 1963b. *Jokes and Their Relation to the Unconscious.* New York: W. W. Norton.

———. 1963c. "On the Mechanism of Paranoia." In *General Psychological Theory: Papers on Metapsychology.* New York: Collier Books.

Fried, Jonathan L., Marvin E. Gettleman, Deborah T. Levenson, and Nancy Peckenham. 1983. *Guatemala in Rebellion: Unfinished History.* New York: Grove Press.

Friedlander, Judith. 1975. *Being Indian in Hueyapan: A Study of Forced Identity in Contemporary Mexico.* New York: St. Martin's Press.

Fuss, Diana. 1995. *Identification Papers.* New York: Routledge.

Gallop, Jane. 1988. *Thinking Through the Body.* New York: Columbia University Press.

Garber, Marjorie. 1992. "The Occidental Tourist: M. Butterfly and the Scandal of Transvestitism." In *Nationalisms and Sexualities.* Ed. Andrew Parker, Mary Russo, Doris Sommer, and Patricia Yaeger. New York: Routledge.

———. 1993. *Vested Interests: Cross-Dressing and Cultural Anxiety.* New York: Harper Perennial.

García Canclini, Néstor. 1989. *Culturas Híbridas: Estrategias para Entrar y Salir de la Modernidad.* Mexico City: Grijalbo.

García-Ruiz, Jesús. 1991. *Historias de Nuestra Historia: La Construcción Social de las Identificaciones en las sociedades Mayas de Guatemala.* Guatemala: IRIPAZ.

Geertz, Clifford. 1973. *The Interpretation of Cultures.* New York: Basic Books.

Gelbspan, Ross. 1991. *Break-Ins, Death Threats, and the FBI.* Boston: South End Press.

Gerth, H. H., and C. Wright Mills, eds. 1958. *From Max Weber: Essays in Sociology.* New York: Oxford University Press.

Gettleman, Marvin E., Patrick Lacefield, Louis Menashe, and David Mermelstein. 1986. *El Salvador: Central America in the New Cold War.* New York: Grove Press.

Gewertz, Deborah, and Frederick Errington. 1991. *Twisted Histories, Altered Contexts: Representing the Chambri in a World System.* Cambridge: Cambridge University Press.

GHRC/USA (Guatemala Human Rights Commission/USA). 1996. *Guatemala.* (Bulletin of GHRC/USA) (spring–summer).

———. 1997. *Guatemala.* (Bulletin of GHRC/USA) (spring–summer).

Gibson, William. 1984. *Neuromancer.* New York: Ace.

Gibson, William, and Bruce Sterling. 1990. *The Difference Engine.* New York: Bantam Books.

Gleijeses, Piero. 1991. *Shattered Hope.* Princeton: Princeton University Press.

GNIB (Guatemala News and Information Bureau). 1995. *Report on Guatemala* (summer).

———. 1996a. "Update on Guatemala." (February).

———. 1996b. "Update on Guatemala." (October).

Goldin, Liliana. 1996. "Maquila Age Maya: Assessing Our Theories, Methods, and Choices of Anthropological Socioeconomic Analysis." Paper presented at the American Anthropology Association meetings, San Francisco, Calif.

Goldman, Francisco. 1992. *The Long Night of White Chickens*. London: Faber and Faber.

Gómez-Peña, Guillermo. 1987. "Border Culture and Deterritorialization." *La Linea Quebrada* (March).

González, Jennifer. 1995. "Autotopographies." In *Prosthetic Territories*. Ed. Gabriel Brahm and Mark Driscoll. Boulder, Colo.: Westview Press.

González, Nancie. 1989. *La Historia del Pueblo Garífuna: Pasado y Presente*. Tegucigalpa, Honduras: ASEPADE, IHAH, COSUDE.

González Ponciano, Jorge Ramon. 1991. "Guatemala, la civilización y el progreso. Notas sobre Indigenismo, Racismo e Identidad Nacional, 1821–1954." In *Anuario: Inst. Chiapaneco de Cultura*. Tuxtla Gutierrez, Mexico: Dept. de Patrimonio Cultural e Investigación.

Goodell, Jeff. 1996. *The Cyberthief and the Samurai*. New York: Dell.

Government of Guatemala. 1985. *Polos de Desarrollo y Servicios: Historiografía Institucional*. Guatemala: Editorial del Ejército (Army Press).

Gramsci, Antonio. 1989. *Selections from the Prison Notebooks*. Ed. and trans. Quintin Hoare and Geoffrey Nowell Smith. New York: International Publishers.

Gray, Chris Hables. 1996. "Manplus: Enhanced Cyborgs and the Construction of the Future Masculine." Paper presented at the American Anthropological Association meetings, San Francisco, Calif., November.

———. 1997. *Postmodern War: The New Politics of Conflict*. New York: Guilford Press.

Gray, Chris Hables, and Mark Driscoll. 1992. "What's Real about Virtual Reality? Anthropology of, and in, Cyberspace." *Visual Anthropology Review* 8, no. 2.

Gray, Chris Hables, with Heidi J. Figueroa-Sarriera and Steven Mentor, eds. 1995. *The Cyborg Handbook*. New York: Routledge.

Gray, Chris Hables, and Steven Mentor. "The Cyborg Body Politic Version 1.2." In *The Cyborg Handbook*. Ed. Chris Gray, with Heidi Figueroa-Sarriera, and Steven Mentor. New York: Routledge.

Green, Linda. 1995. "Living in a State of Fear." In *Fieldwork under Fire: Contemporary Studies of Violence and Survival*. Ed. Carolyn Nordstrom and Antonius C. G. M. Robben. Berkeley: University of California Press.

Grewal, Inderpal. 1996. *Home and Harem: Nations, Gender, Empire, and the Cultures of Travel*. Durham: Duke University Press.

Grosz, Elizabeth. 1994. *Volatile Bodies: Toward a Corporeal Feminism*. Bloomington: Indiana University Press.

Guaman Poma de Ayala, Felipe. 1980 [1650]. *Nueva Crónica y Buen Gobierno*. Ed. Franklin Pease. Caracas: Biblioteca Ayacucho.

Guha, Ranajit. 1983. *Elementary Aspects of Peasant Insurgency in Colonial India*. Delhi: Oxford University Press.

———. 1988. "The Prose of Counterinsurgency." In *Selected Subaltern Studies*. Ed. Ranajit Guha and Gayatri Chakravorty Spivak. Oxford: Oxford University Press.

Guidieri, Remo, Francesco Pellizzi, and Stanley J. Tambiah, eds. 1988. *Ethnicities and Nations: Processes of Interethnic Relations in Latin America, Southeast Asia, and the Pacific*. Austin: University of Texas Press through Rothco Chapel Books.

Gunder Frank, Andre. 1967. *Capitalism and Underdevelopment in Latin America*. New York: Monthly Review Press.

Gupta, Akhil, and Jim Ferguson. 1992. "Beyond 'Culture': Space, Identity, and the Politics of Difference." *Cultural Anthropology* (February).

————, eds. 1997. *Anthropological Locations: Boundaries and Grounds of a Field Science.* Berkeley: University of California Press.

Guzmán Böckler, Carlos. 1975. *Colonialismo y Revolución.* Mexico City: Siglo XXI.

Guzmán Böckler, Carlos, and Jean-Louis Herbert. 1970. *Guatemala: Una Interpretación Historico-Social.* Mexico City: Siglo XXI.

Halberstam, Judith. 1995. *Skin Shows: Gothic Horror and the Technology of Monsters.* Durham: Duke University Press.

Hale, Charles R. 1994. *Resistance and Contradiction: Miskitu Indians and the Nicaraguan State, 1894–1987.* Palo Alto: Stanford University Press.

————. 1996. "*Mestizaje,* Hybridity, and the Cultural Politics of Difference in Post-Revolutionary Central America. *Journal of Latin American Anthropology* 2, no. 1.

Hall, Stuart. 1985. "Signification, Representation, Ideology: Althusser and the Post-Structuralist Debates." *Critical Studies in Mass Communication* 2, no. 2.

————. 1986. "Gramsci's Relevance for the Study of Race and Ethnicity." *Journal of Communication Inquiry* 10, no. 2.

————. 1990. "The Meaning of New Times." In *New Times: The Changing Face of Politics in the 1990s.* Ed. Stuart Hall and Martin Jacques. London: Verso.

————. 1993. "Encoding, Decoding." In *The Cultural Studies Reader.* Ed. Simon During. London: Routledge.

————. 1996. "The Problem of Ideology: Marxism without Guarantees." In *Stuart Hall: Critical Dialogues in Cultural Studies.* Ed. David Morley and Kuan-Hsing Chen. London: Routledge.

Hall, Stuart, and Martin Jacques. 1990. *New Times: The Changing Face of Politics in the 1990s.* London: Verso.

Handy, Jim. 1984. *Gift of the Devil: A History of Guatemala.* Boston: South End Press.

Hannum, Hurst. 1988. "New Developments in Indigenous Rights." *Virginia Journal of International Law* 28.

Haraway, Donna. 1991. *Simians, Cyborgs, and Women: The Reinvention of Nature.* New York:. Routledge.

————. 1992. "The Promises of Monsters: A Regenerative Politics for Inappropriate/d Others." In *Cultural Studies.* Ed. Lawrence Grossberg, Cary Nelson, and Paula A. Treichler. New York: Routledge.

————. 1996. *Modest Witness@Millenium Meets OncoMouse®.* New York: Routledge.

Harbury, Jennifer. 1994. *Bridge of Courage: Life Stories of the Guatemalan Compañeros and Compañeras.* Monroe, Maine: Common Courage Press.

————. 1997. *Searching for Everardo: A Story of Love, War, and the CIA in Guatemala.* New York: Warner Books.

Harlow, Barbara. 1987. *Resistance Literature.* New York: Methuen.

Harnecker, Marta. 1984. *Pueblos en Armas: Guatemala, El Salvador, Nicaragua.* Mexico City: Serie Popular Era.

Harvey, David. 1989. *The Condition of Postmodernity: An Enquiry into the Origins of Cultural Change.* Oxford: Basil Blackwell.

Hawkins, John. 1984. *Inverse Images: The Meaning of Culture, Ethnicity, and Family in Postcolonial Guatemala.* Albuquerque: University of New Mexico Press.

Hayles, N. Katherine. 1990. *Chaos Bound: Orderly Disorder in Contemporary Literature and Science.* Ithaca: Cornell University Press.

Heath, Deborah. 1994. "The Politics of Appropriateness and Appropriation: Re-contextualizing Women's Dance in Urban Senegal." *American Ethnologist* 21, no. 1.

Hegel, Georg W. F. 1977. *Phenomenology of Spirit.* Oxford: Oxford University Press.

Heidegger, Martin. 1977. *The Question Concerning Technology and Other Essays.* Trans. William Lovitt. New York: Harper Torchbooks.

Hendrickson, Carol. 1995. *Weaving Identities: Construction of Dress and Self in a Highland Guatemala Town.* Austin: University of Texas Press.

———. 1996. "Women, Weaving, and Education in Maya Revitalization." In *Maya Cultural Activism in Guatemala.* Ed. Edward F. Fischer and R. McKenna Brown. Austin: University of Texas Press.

Hertz, Neil. 1983. "Medusa's Head: Male Hysteria under Political Pressure." *Representations* 4 (fall).

Hill, Robert M. 1992. *Colonial Cakchiquels: Highland Maya Adaptation to Spanish Rule, 1600–1700.* Fort Worth, Tex.: Harcourt Brace, Jovanovich.

Hill, Sarah. 1992. "'Don't Be an Indian': Conflicting Ethnic and National Identities in Contemporary Guatemala." Paper presented to the Program in Atlantic History, Culture, and Society, Johns Hopkins University.

Hinshaw, Robert E. 1988. "Tourist Town amid the Violence: Panajachel." In *Harvest of Violence: The Mayan Indians and the Guatemalan Crisis.* Ed. Robert Carmack. Norman: University of Oklahoma Press.

Hobbes, Thomas. 1985 [1651]. *Leviathan.* New York: Penguin Books.

Hobsbawm, Eric, and Terence Ranger, eds. 1983. *The Invention of Tradition.* Cambridge, U.K.: Cambridge University Press.

Hooks, Margaret. 1991. *Guatemalan Women Speak.* Washington, D.C.: EPICA.

INFORPRESS Centroamericana. 1996. *Compendio del Proceso de Paz II: Análisis, Cronologías, Documentos, Acuerdos.* Guatemala: INFORPRESS.

INGUAT (Instituto Guatemalteco de Turismo). N.d. *Maya World: Where Man, Nature, and Time Are One.* Brochure. Guatemala City: INGUAT.

INIAP (Instituto de Investigación y Autoformación Política). 1992. *Movimiento Indígena en Guatemala: Diagnóstico y Movimientos de Unidad* (December).

Instituto Indigenista Interamericano. 1954. *Legislación Indigenista de Guatemala.* Ed. Jorge Skinner Klee. Mexico: Instituto Indigenista Interamericano.

International Labor Organization. 1989. *Convention 169 on the Rights of Indigenous and Tribal Peoples in Independent Countries.* Geneva: United Nations.

Irigaray, Luce. 1985a [1974]. *Speculum of the Other Woman.* Trans. Gillian C. Gill. Ithaca: Cornell University Press.

———. 1985b [1977]. *This Sex Which Is Not One.* Trans. Catherine Porter. Ithaca: Cornell University Press.

Jackson, Jean. 1989. "Is There a Way to Talk about Making Culture without Making Enemies?" *Dialectical Anthropology* 14.

Jackson, Robert. 1990. *Quasi-States: Sovereignty, International Relations, and the Third World.* Cambridge: Cambridge University Press.

Jameson, Frederic. 1991. *Postmodernism, or the Cultural Logic of Late Capitalism.* Durham: Duke University Press.

JanMohammed, Abdul R. 1985. "The Economy of Manichean Allegory: The Function of Racial Difference in Colonialist Literature." In *Race, Writing, and Difference.* Ed. Henry Louis Gates Jr. Chicago: University of Chicago Press.

Jonas, Susanne. 1991. *The Battle for Guatemala: Rebels, Death Squads, and U.S. Power.* Boulder, Colo.: Westview Press.

Jonas, Susanne, Ed McCaughan, and Elizabeth Sutherland Martínez, eds. 1984. *Guatemala: Tyranny on Trial.* San Francisco: Synthesis Publications.

Jonas, Susanne, and David Tobis, eds. 1974. *Guatemala!* Berkeley: NACLA.

Kadetsky, Elizabeth. 1994. "Guatemala Inflamed: Accused of Stealing or Murdering Babies, American Women Are Attacked by Hysterical Mobs." *Village Voice,* 31 May.

Kearney, Michael. 1996. *Reconceptualizing the Peasantry: Anthropology in Global Perspective.* Boulder, Colo.: Westview Press.

Kinzer, Stephen, and Stephen Schlesinger. 1983. *Bitter Fruit.* New York: Doubleday Books.

Kipnis, Laura. 1992. "(Male) Desire and (Female) Disgust: Reading *Hustler.*" In *Cultural Studies.* Ed. Lawrence Grossberg, Cary Nelson, and Paula Treichler. New York: Routledge.

Klare, Michael T., and Cynthia Arnson. 1981. *Supplying Repression: U.S. Support for Authoritarian Regimes Abroad.* Washington, D.C.: Institute for Policy Studies.

Klor de Alva, Jorge. 1995. "The Postcolonization of the (Latin) American Experience: A Reconsideration of 'Colonialism,' 'Postcolonialism,' and 'Mestizaje.'" In *After Colonialism: Imperial Histories and Postcolonial Displacements.* Ed. Gyan Prakash. Princeton: Princeton University Press.

Knight, Alan. 1990. "Racism, Revolution, and *Indigenismo:* Mexico, 1910–1940." In *The Idea of Race in Latin America, 1870–1940.* Ed. Richard Graham. Cambridge: Cambridge University Press.

Kondo, Dorinne K. 1990. *Crafting Selves: Power, Gender, and Discourses of Identity in a Japanese Workplace.* Chicago: University of Chicago Press.

Kulick, Don, and Margaret Willson. 1995. *Taboo: Sex, Identity, and Erotic Subjectivity in Anthropological Fieldwork.* New York: Routledge.

Lacan, Jacques. 1977. *Ecrits: A Selection.* Trans. Alan Sheridan. New York: W. W. Norton.

Laclau, Ernesto, and Chantal Mouffe. 1985. *Hegemony and Socialist Strategy: Towards a Radical Democratic Politics.* London: Verso.

LaFarge, Oliver. 1940. "Maya Ethnology: The Sequence of Cultures." In *The Maya and Their Neighbors.* Ed. Clarence Hay et al. New York: D. Appleton Century.

Lancaster, Roger. 1992. *Life Is Hard: Machismo, Danger, and the Intimacy of Power in Nicaragua.* Berkeley: University of California Press.

Latham, Robert. 1995a. "Consuming Youth: Technologies of Desire and American Youth Culture." Ph.D. diss., Stanford University.

———. 1995b. "Review of Terminal Identity: The Virtual Subject in Postmodern Science Fiction by Scott Bukatman." *New York Review of Science Fiction* (April).

Lévi-Strauss, Claude. 1969. *Elementary Structures of Kinship.* Boston: Beacon Press.

———. 1973. *Tristes Tropiques.* New York: Washington Square Press (Pocket Books).

Levy, Steve. 1984. *Hackers: Heroes of the Computer Revolution.* New York: Dell.

Lewin, Ellen, and William L. Leap. 1996. *Out in the Field: Reflections of Lesbian and Gay Anthropologists.* Urbana: University of Illinois Press.

Limón, José. 1986. "La Llorona, the Third Legend of Greater Mexico: Cultural Symbols, Women, and the Political Unconscious." *Renato Rosaldo Lecture Series Mono-*

graph no. 2, 1984–1985. Tucson: Mexican American Studies and Research Center, University of Arizona.

Lipietz, Alain. 1987. *Mirages and Miracles: The Crises of Global Fordism.* Trans. David Macey. London: Verso.

Little-Siebold, Christa. 1997. "Una Chapina Gringa en Un Pueblo Donde el Indígena No Existe: Análisis del Espectro Etnico." Paper presented to the Latin America Studies Association, Guadalajara, Mexico, April 19.

Little-Siebold, Todd. 1997. "Rendering Diversity: Local and Imperial Discourses of Identity on Guatemala's Eastern Periphery." Paper presented to the Latin America Studies Association, Guadalajara, Mexico, April 19.

Lorde, Audre. 1984. *Sister Outsider.* Freedom, Calif.: The Crossing Press.

Lovell, George. 1985. *Conquest and Survival in Colonial Guatemala: A Historical Geography of the Cuchumatan Highlands, 1500–1821.* Montreal: McGill-Queen's University Press.

Luera, Fernando. 1997. "Integrating Literatures: From Incest to Hybridity in Faulkner, Barnes, Hinojosa, and Castillo." Ph.D. diss., Stanford University.

MacCannell, Dean. 1976. *The Tourist: A New Theory of the Leisure Class.* New York: Schocken Books.

———. 1994. "Cannibal Tours." In *Visualizing Theory.* Ed. Lucien Taylor. New York: Routledge.

Majawil Q'ij. 1992. "500 Años: Despojo, Destrucción, y Discriminación y las Raices de la Resistencia, Vida, y Futuro de Nuestros Pueblos." *La Hora,* 12 October.

Malinowski, Bronislaw. 1967. *A Diary in the Strict Sense of the Term.* Stanford: Stanford University Press.

Malkki, Liisa. 1992. "National Geographic: The Rooting of Peoples and the Territorialization of National Identity among Scholars and Refugees." *Cultural Anthropology* 7, no. 1.

———. 1997. "News and Culture: Transitory Phenomena and the Fieldwork Tradition." In *Anthropological Locations: Boundaries and Grounds of a Field Science.* Ed. Akhil Gupta and Jim Ferguson. Berkeley: University of California Press.

Mallon, Florencia E. 1996. "Constructing *Mestizaje* in Latin America: Authenticity, Marginality, and Gender in the Claiming of National Identities." *Journal of Latin American Anthropology* 2, no. 1.

Mani, Lata. 1990. "Contentious Traditions: The Debate on Sati in Colonial India." In *Recasting Women: Essays in Colonial History.* Ed. Kumkum Sangari and Sudesh Vaid. New Brunswick, N.J.: Rutgers University Press.

———. 1992. "Cultural Theory, Colonial Texts: Reading Eyewitness Accounts of Widow Burning." In *Cultural Studies.* Ed. Lawrence Grossberg, Cary Nelson, and Paula Treichler. New York: Routledge.

Manz, Beatriz. 1988a. *Refugees of a Hidden War: Aftermath of Counterinsurgency in Guatemala.* Albany, N.Y.: SUNY Press.

———. 1988b. "The Transformation of La Esperanza, an Ixcán Village." In *Harvest of Violence: The Mayan Indians and the Guatemalan Crisis.* Ed. Robert Carmack. Norman: University of Oklahoma Press.

———. 1995. "Reflections on an *Antropología Comprometida:* Conversations with Ricardo Falla." In *Fieldwork under Fire: Contemporary Studies of Violence and Survival.*

Ed. Carolyn Nordstrom and Antonius C. G. M. Robben. Berkeley: University of California Press.

Markoff, John. 1995. "A Most-Wanted Cyberthief Is Caught in His Own Web." *New York Times,* 16 February.

Martínez-Alier (Stolcke), Verena. 1989 [1974]. *Marriage, Class, and Colour in Nineteenth-Century Cuba: A Study of Racial Attitudes and Sexual Values in a Slave Society.* Ann Arbor: University of Michigan Press.

Martínez Peláez, Severo. 1990 [1970]. *La Patria del Criollo: Ensayo de Interpretación de la Realidad Colonial Guatemalteca.* Mexico: Ediciones en Marcha.

Marx, Karl. 1977. *Capital.* Vol. 1. Trans. Ben Fowkes. New York: Vintage Books.

Maurer, Bill. 1997. *Recharting the Caribbean: Land, Law, and Citizenship in the British Virgin Islands.* Ann Arbor: University of Michigan Press.

Maynard, Eileen. 1974. "Guatemalan Women: Life under Two Types of Patriarchy." In *Many Sisters: Women in Cross Cultural Perspective.* Ed. Carolyn Matthiasson. New York: The Free Press.

McClintock, Anne. 1995. *Imperial Leather: Race, Gender, and Sexuality in the Colonial Contest.* New York: Routledge.

McClintock, Michael. 1985. *State Terror and Popular Resistance in El Salvador* and *State Terror and Popular Resistance in Guatemala.* Vols. 1 and 2 of *The American Connection.* London: Zed Books.

Meisch, Lynn A. 1995. "Gringas and Otavaleños: Changing Tourist Relations." *Annals of Tourism Research* 22, no. 2.

Melville, Marjorie, and Thomas Melville. 1971. *Guatemala: The Politics of Land Ownership.* New York: Free Press.

Memmi, Albert. 1965. *The Colonizer and the Colonized.* Boston: Beacon Press.

Menchú Tum, Rigoberta. 1984. *I, Rigoberta Menchú: An Indian Woman in Guatemala.* Ed. Elisabeth Burgos-Debray. Trans. Ann Wright. London: Verso.

———. 1992. "The Challenge of Constructing National Unity." *Siglo Veintiuno,* 11 December.

Merry, Sally Engle. 1991. "Law and Society." *Law and Society Review,* no. 4.

———. 1992. "Anthropology, Law, and Transnational Processes." *Annual Review of Anthropology.*

Mesa Maya. 1993. *Identity and Indigenous Rights: Statements and Demands in the Negotiating Process between the Government-Army and the URNG.* Guatemala: Cholsamaj.

Mies, Maria. 1991. *Patriarchy and Accumulation on a World Scale: Women in the International Division of Labor.* London: Zed Books.

Ministry of Culture. 1986. "Políticas, Objetivos, Estrategias, Metas: Periodo, 1986–1990." Pamphlet. Guatemala City.

———. 1988. "Democrácia Cultural y Deporte para Todos: ¿Por qué, para qué y cómo?" Pamphlet. Guatemala City.

Ministry of Education. 1981. "Primer Encuentro de Coordinación Cultural: Informe Especial." Pamphlet. Guatemala City.

MINUGUA (United Nations Mission to Guatemala). 1996. "Fourth Report of the Director of the United Nations Mission for the Verification of Human Rights and of Compliance with the Commitments of the Comprehensive Agreement on Human Rights in Guatemala." New York: United Nations General Assembly.

Mitchell, Timothy. 1991. "The Limits of the State: Beyond Statist Approaches and Their Critics." *American Political Science Review* 85 (March).

Mohanty, Chandra Talpade, Ann Russo, and Lourdes Torres, eds. 1991. *Third-World Women and the Politics of Feminism*. Bloomington: Indiana University Press.

Moraga, Cherrie. 1983. *Loving in the War Years: Lo que Nunca Pasó por sus Labios*. Boston: South End Press.

Morley, David, and Kuan-Hsing Chen. 1996. *Stuart Hall: Critical Dialogues in Cultural Studies*. London: Routledge.

Movimiento Nacional de Resistencia Maya, Garífuna, y Popular. 1993. "Año Internacional de los Pueblos Originarios: Resumen y Taller Sobre el Convenio 169." Guatemala.

Mulvey, Laura. 1989. *Visual and Other Pleasures*. Bloomington: Indiana University Press.

NACLA (North American Congress on Latin America). 1996a. "In Pursuit of Profit: A Primer on the New Transnational Investment." *Report on the Americas* 24, no. 4.

———. 1996b. "An Interview with Rigoberta Menchú Tum." *Report on the Americas* 24, no. 6.

———. 1996c. "Rhetoric and Reality: The World Bank's New Concern for the Poor." *Report on the Americas* 24, no. 6.

Nájera Saravía, Antonio. 1992. "Desde la Montaña, A Dos 'Mayas' Cordialmente." *Siglo XXI,* 14 October.

Nelson, Diane M. 1987. "Poverty and Despair Prevail in Guatemala's 'Model' Villages." *The Guardian,* 16 September.

———. 1990. *Guatemala Polos de Desarrollo: El Caso de la Desestructuración de las Comunidades Indígenas*. Vol. 2. Mexico City: CEIDEC. (Published anonymously for political reasons.)

———. 1991. "The Reconstruction of Mayan Identity." *Report on Guatemala* (summer).

———. 1995. "Gringas, Baby Snatching, and 'Partial' Anthropology in Guatemala." *Anthropology Newsletter* (May).

———. 1997. "Crucifixion Stories, the 1869 Caste War of Chiapas, and Negative Consciousness: A Disruptive Subaltern Study." *American Ethnologist* 24, no. 2.

New York Times. 1997a. "Investigation Blames Rebels for Massacre of 120 in a Guatemalan Village." 4 September, A8.

———. 1997b. "Maya Dress Tells a New Story, and It's Not Pretty." 13 June, A4.

Noguera, Francisco. 1993. "¿Qué Reflejan los chistes sobre Rigoberta Menchú?" *Prensa Libre; Domingo,* 24 January.

Nordstrom, Carolyn, and Antonius C. G. M. Robben, eds. 1995. *Fieldwork under Fire: Contemporary Studies of Violence and Survival*. Berkeley: University of California Press.

Noticias de Guatemala. 1992. "La Herencia de Ixmucane: Notas sobre arte textil en Guatemala." January–February.

Oakes, Maud. 1951. *The Two Crosses of Todos Santos: Survivals of Mayan Religious Ritual*. New York: Pantheon.

O'Connor, James. 1984. *Accumulation Crisis*. Oxford: Basil Blackwell.

Oglesby, Elizabeth. 1995. "Myrna Mack." In *Fieldwork under Fire: Contemporary Studies of Violence and Survival.* Carolyn Nordstrom and Antonius C. G. M. Robben. Berkeley: University of California Press.

———. 1997. "Labor and the Sugar Industry: Scientific Management on the Plantation." *Report on Guatemala* 18, no. 1.

Ong, Aihwa. 1987. *Spirits of Resistance and Capitalist Discipline: Factory Women in Malaysia.* Albany, N.Y.: SUNY Press.

O'Rourke, Dennis. 1987. *Cannibal Tours.* Los Angeles: Direct Cinema. (Film, 70 minutes).

Otzoy, Irma. 1991. "Maya Clothing and Identity." Paper presented at the American Anthropology Association meeting, Chicago, Ill.

———. 1996. "Maya Clothing and Identity." In *Maya Cultural Activism in Guatemala.* Ed. Edward F. Fischer and R. McKenna Brown. Austin: University of Texas Press.

Painter, James. 1987. *Guatemala: False Hope, False Freedom.* London: Latin America Bureau.

Palma, G. 1978. "Dependency: A Formal Theory of Underdevelopment, or A Methodology for the Analysis of the Concrete Situation of Underdevelopment." *World Development* 6 (July–August).

Pancake, Cherri M. 1988. "Nuevos Métodos en la Interpretación de textos graficos: Aplicaciones de la 'teoría del lenguaje' a los tejidos autóctonos de Guatemala." *Mesoamerica* 16 (December).

———. 1992. "Fronteras de Género en la Producción de Tejidos Indígenas." In *La Indumentaria y el Tejido Maya a Través del Tiempo.* Ed. Linda Asturias de Barrios and Dina Fernandez. Guatemala: Museo Ixchel del Traje Indígena de Guatemala.

Pancake, Cherri M., and Sheldon Annis. 1982. "El Arte de la Producción: Aspectos socio-economicos del tejido a mano en San Antonio Aguas Calientes, Guatemala." *Mesoamerica* 3, no. 4.

Parish, Lael. 1996. "Social Funds to the Rescue: The World Bank Manages Guatemala's Poor." *Report on Guatemala* 17, no. 2.

Parker, Andrew, Mary Russo, Doris Sommer, and Patricia Yaeger, eds. 1992. *Nationalisms and Sexualities.* New York: Routledge.

Paul, Benjamin, and William Demarest. 1988. "The Operation of a Death Squad in San Pedro la Laguna." In *Harvest of Violence: The Maya Indians and the Guatemalan Crisis.* Ed. Robert M. Carmack. Norman: University of Oklahoma Press.

Paul, Lois. 1974. "The Mastery of Work and the Mystery of Sex in a Guatemalan Village." In *Women, Culture, and Society.* Ed. Michelle Zimbalist Rosaldo and Louise Lamphere. Stanford: Stanford University Press.

Payeras, Mario. 1983. *Days of the Jungle: The Testimony of a Guatemalan Guerrillero, 1972–1976.* New York: Monthly Review Press.

Paz, Octavio. 1961. *The Labyrinth of Solitude: Life and Thought in Mexico.* Trans. Lysander Kemp. New York: Grove Press.

Pedro González, Gaspar. 1992. *La Otra Cara.* Guatemala City: Editorial Cultural (Ministry of Culture and Sports).

Penley, Constance. 1997. *NASA/TREK: Popular Science and Sex in America.* New York: Verso.

Perera, Victor. 1994a. "Behind the Kidnapping of Children for Their Organs." *Los Angeles Times,* 1 May.

———. 1994b. *The Cross and the Pear Tree: A Sephardic Journey.* New York: Knopf.

———. 1995. "Political Violence Finds a New Cover." *Los Angeles Times,* 17 December.

Pérez Sáinz, Juan, Manuela Camus, and Santiago Bastos. 1992. *Todito, Todito es Trabajo.* Guatemala City: FLACSO.

Peterson, Kurt. 1992. *The Maquiladora Revolution in Guatemala.* New Haven: Orville H. Schell Jr. Center for International Human Rights at Yale Law School, Occasional Paper Series 2.

Pfeil, Fred. 1990. *Another Tale to Tell: Politics and Narrative in Postmodern Culture.* London: Verso.

Pfohl, Stephen. 1992. *Death at the Parasite Cafe: Social Science (Fictions) and the Postmodern.* New York: St. Martin's Press.

Pietz, William. 1993. "Fetishism and Materialism: The Limits of Theory in Marx." In *Fetishism as Cultural Discourse.* Ed. Emily Apter and William Pietz. Ithaca: Cornell University Press.

Poggi, Gianfranco. 1978. *The Development of the Modern State: A Sociological Introduction.* Stanford: Stanford University Press.

Poitevin, René. 1993. *Guatemala: La Crisis de la Democracia—dudas y esperanzas en los golpes de estado de 1993.* Debate No. 21. Guatemala City: FLACSO.

Pop Caal, Antonio. 1981. "Réplica del indio a una disertación ladina." In *Utopia y Revolución: El Pensamiento Político Contemporaneo de los Indios en America Latina.* Ed. Guillermo Bonfil Batalla. Mexico City: Editorial Nueva Imagen.

———. 1992. *Li Juliisil Kirisyaanil ut li Minok ib': Judeocristianismo y Colonización.* Guatemala City: Nawal Wuj.

Prakash, Gyan. 1992. "Writing Post-Orientalist Histories of the Third World: Indian Historiography Is Good to Think." In *Colonialism and Culture.* Ed. Nicholas B. Dirks. Ann Arbor: University of Michigan Press.

Pratt, Mary. 1985. "Scratches on the Face of the Country; or, What Mr. Barrow Saw in the Land of the Bushmen." In *Race, Writing, and Difference.* Ed. Henry Louis Gates Jr. Chicago: University of Chicago Press.

———. 1989. "Women, Literature, and National Brotherhood." In *Women, Culture, and Politics in Latin America.* Berkeley: University of California Press.

———. 1992. *Imperial Eyes: Travel Writing and Transculturation.* London: Routledge.

Preston, Julia. 1996. "Guatemala and Guerrillas Sign Accord to End Thirty-Five-Year Conflict." *New York Times,* 20 September.

Quinn, Michelle. 1995. "Internet Is Becoming a Dangerous Road." *San Francisco Chronicle,* 24 January.

Quittner, Joshua. 1995. "Hacker Homecoming." *Time,* 23 January.

Rabinow, Paul. 1977. *Reflections on Fieldwork in Morocco.* Berkeley: University of California Press.

———. 1984. *The Foucault Reader.* New York: Pantheon Books.

———. 1991. *French Modern.* Berkeley: University of California Press.

Rajan, Rajeswari Sunder. 1993. *Real and Imagined Women: Gender, Culture, and Postcolonialism.* London: Routledge.

Raymond, Eric, ed. 1991. *The New Hackers Dictionary.* Cambridge Mass.: MIT Press.

Reyes Illescas, Miguel Angel. 1985. "Guatemala: En el Camino del Indio Nuevo." *Boletín de Antropología Americana* (July).

Rhodes, Robert I., ed. 1970. *Imperialism and Underdevelopment: A Reader.* New York: Monthly Review Press.

Richards, Julia Becker, and Michael Richards. 1996. "Maya Education: A Historical and Contemporary Analysis of Mayan Language Education Policy." In *Maya Cultural Activism in Guatemala.* Ed. Edward F. Fischer and R. McKenna Brown. Austin: University of Texas Press.

Robins, Kevin. 1989. "Reimagined Communities? European Image Spaces, beyond Fordism." *Cultural Studies* 3, no. 2.

Robles, Lorena. 1995. "Marching in the Streets Is Not Enough: Lorena Robles Discusses Women's Role in Civil Society." *Report on Guatemala* (winter).

Rodriguez Guajan, Demetrio (Raxche'). 1992 [1989]. *Cultura Maya y Políticas de Desarrollo.* Guatemala: COCADI.

Rojas Lima, Flavio. 1988. *La Cofradía: Reducto Cultural Indígena.* Guatemala City: Seminario de Integración Social (reprinted 1992).

———. 1990. *Etnicidad: Teoria y Praxis. la Revolución Cultural de 1990.* Guatemala City: Serviprensa.

Rosada Granados, Héctor Roberto. 1987. *Indios y Ladinos: Un estudio antropológicosociológico.* Guatemala City: Editorial Universitaria.

Rosaldo, Renato. 1988. "Ideology, Place and People without Culture." *Cultural Anthropology* 3, no. 1.

Ross, Andrew. 1991. *Strange Weather: Culture, Science, and Technology in the Age of Limits.* London: Verso.

Rothenberg, Daniel. 1994. "Heeding a Grotesque Morality Tale from Latin America." *Chicago Tribune,* 8 July.

Ruiz Franco, Arcadio. 1972. "La Contradicción en la Problematica Indígena." *América Indígena* 32, no. 2.

Rus, Jan. 1983. "Whose Caste War? Indians, Ladinos, and the 'Caste War' of 1869." In *Spaniards and Indians in Southeastern Mesoamerica: Essays on the History of Ethnic Relations.* Ed. Murdo Macleod and Robert Wasserstrom. Lincoln: University of Nebraska Press.

Russ, Joanna. 1970. "The Image of Women in Science Fiction." *Red Clay Reader,* no. 7 (November).

———. 1978. "Pornography by Women for Women, with Love." In *Magic Mommas, Trembling Sisters, Puritans, and Perverts: Feminist Essays.* Trumansburg, N.Y.: The Crossing Press.

Said, Edward W. 1978. *Orientalism.* New York: Vintage.

Sam Colop, Enrique. 1991. *Jub'aqtun Omay Kuchum K'aslemal, Cinco Siglos de Encubrimiento.* Guatemala City: CECMA.

Sánchez-Eppler, Benigno. 1994. "Por Causa Mecánica: The Coupling of Bodies and Machines and the Production and Reproduction of Whiteness in *Cecilia Valdés* and Nineteenth-Century Cuba." In *Thinking Bodies.* Ed. Juliet Flower MacCannell and Laura Zakarin. Stanford: Stanford University Press.

Sanford, Victoria. 1994. "Buried Secrets: Truth and Human Rights in Guatemala." Paper presented at the American Anthropological Association meetings, Atlanta.

Sangari, Kumkum, and Sudesh Vaid, eds. 1990. *Recasting Women: Essays in Colonial History.* New Brunswick, N.J.: Rutgers University Press.

Sawyer, Suzana. 1996a. "Indigenous Initiatives and Petroleum Politics in the Ecuadorian Amazon." *Cultural Survival* (spring).

———. 1996b. "Marching to Nation across Ethnic Terrain: The 1992 Indian Mobilization in Lowland Ecuador." *Latin American Perspectives.*

———. 1997. "Marching to Nation across Ethnic Terrain: The Politics of Identity, Territory, and Resource Use in the Ecuadorian Amazon." Ph.D. diss., Stanford University.

Scarry, Elaine. 1985. *The Body in Pain: The Making and Unmaking of the World.* Oxford: Oxford University Press.

Schele, Linda, and Nikolai Grube. 1996. "The Workshop for Maya on Hieroglyphic Writing." In *Maya Cultural Activism in Guatemala.* Ed. Edward F. Fischer and R. McKenna Brown. Austin: University of Texas Press.

Schele, Linda, and Mary Ellen Miller. 1986. *The Blood of Kings: Dynasty and Ritual in Maya Art.* New York: George Braziller, Inc.

Schneider, David. 1980 [1968]. *American Kinship: A Cultural Account.* Chicago: University of Chicago Press.

Schneider, Jane, and Rayna Rapp. 1995. *Articulating Hidden Histories: Exploring the Influence of Eric R. Wolf.* Berkeley: University of California Press.

Schultz, Vicki. 1992. "Women 'Before' the Law: Judicial Stories about Women, Work, and Sex Segregation on the Job." In *Feminists Theorize the Political.* Ed. Judith Butler and Joan W. Scott. New York: Routledge.

Sedgwick, Eve Kosofsky. 1992. "Nationalisms and Sexualities in the Age of Wilde." In *Nationalisms and Sexualities.* Ed. Andrew Parker, Mary Russo, Doris Sommer, and Patricia Yaeger. New York: Routledge.

Shimomura, Tsutomu, with John Markoff. 1996. *Takedown: The Pursuit and Capture of Kevin Mitnick, America's Most Wanted Computer Outlaw—By the Man Who Did It.* New York: Hyperion.

Silverman, Kaja. 1983. *The Subject of Semiotics.* New York: Oxford University Press.

———. 1989 [1984]. "Histoire d'O." In *Pleasure and Danger: Exploring Female Sexuality.* Ed. Carole S. Vance. London: Pandora.

Simon, Jean Marie. 1987. *Eternal Spring, Eternal Tyranny.* New York: W. W. Norton.

Sinclair, Minor. 1994. "Guatemalans Reclaim the Vision of the Decade of Spring." EPICA pamphlet (October).

Sklar, Holly. 1988. *Washington's War on Nicaragua.* Boston: South End Press.

Slack, Jennifer Daryl. 1996. "The Theory and Method of Articulation in Cultural Studies." In *Stuart Hall: Critical Dialogues in Cultural Studies.* Ed. David Morley and Kuan-Hsing Chen. London: Routledge.

Smith, Anthony. 1986. *The Ethnic Origins of Nations.* New York: Basil Blackwell.

Smith, Barbara. 1981. *Home Girls: A Black Feminist Anthology.* New York: Kitchen Table, Women of Color Press.

Smith, Carol A. 1984. "Local History in a Global Context: Social and Economic Transitions in Western Guatemala." *Comparative Studies in Society and History* 26, no. 2.

———. 1988. "Destruction of the Material Bases for Indian Culture." In *Harvest of*

Violence: The Mayan Indians and the Guatemalan Crisis. Ed. Robert Carmack. Norman: University of Oklahoma Press.

———. 1989. "Survival Strategies among Petty Commodity Producers." *International Labour Review* 128.

——— 1990a. "Failed Nationalist Movements in Nineteenth-Century Guatemala: A Parable for the Third World." *Nationalist Ideologies and the Production of National Cultures.* Ed. Richard G. Fox. American Ethnological Society Monograph Series, No. 2.

———. 1990b. *Guatemalan Indians and the State, 1540–1988.* Austin: University of Texas.

———. 1991. "Maya Nationalism." In *NACLA Report on the Americas.* Washington, D.C.: NACLA.

———. 1992. "Marxists on Class and Culture in Guatemala." Paper presented at the Latin America Studies Association, Los Angeles, Calif.

———. 1995. "Race-Class-Gender Ideologies in Guatemala: Modern and Anti-Modern Forms." *Comparative Studies in Society and History* 37, no. 4.

———. 1996. "Myths, Intellectuals, and Race/Class/Gender Distinctions in the Formation of Latin American Nations." *Journal of Latin American Anthropology* 2, no. 1.

Solares, Jorge, ed. 1993. *Estado y Nación: Las Demandas de los Grupos Etnicos en Guatemala.* Guatemala City: FLACSO.

Sommer, Doris. 1990. "Irresistible Romance: The Foundational Fictions of Latin America." In *Nation and Narration.* London: Routledge.

———. 1991. *National Romance, Foundational Fiction.* Berkeley: University of California Press.

Soyinka, Wole. 1996. *The Open Sore of a Continent: A Personal Narrative of the Nigerian Crisis.* Oxford: Oxford University Press.

Spivak, Gayatri Chakravorty. 1985. "Women's Texts and a Critique of Imperialism." In *Race, Writing, and Difference.* Ed. Henry Louis Gates Jr. Chicago: University of Chicago Press.

———. 1988a. "Can the Subaltern Speak?" In *Marxism and the Interpretation of Culture.* Ed. Cary Nelson and Lawrence Grossberg. Urbana: University of Illinois Press.

———. 1988b. *In Other Worlds: Essays in Cultural Politics.* New York: Routledge.

Stavenhagen, Rodolfo. 1968. "Classes, Colonialism, and Acculturation." In *Comparative Perspectives on Stratification: Mexico, Great Britain, Japan.* Ed. J. A. Kahl. Boston: Little, Brown.

Stepan, Nancy Leys. 1991. *"The Hour of Eugenics": Race, Gender, and Nation in Latin America.* Ithaca, N.Y.: Cornell University Press.

Stephen, Lynn. 1991. *Zapotec Women.* Austin: University of Texas Press.

Stephenson, Neal. 1993. *Snow Crash.* New York: Bantam.

Sterling, Bruce. 1986. *Islands in the Net.* Berkeley: Berkeley Press.

———. 1992. *The Hacker Crackdown: Law and Disorder on the Electronic Frontier.* New York: Bantam.

Stolcke, Verena. 1993. "Is Sex to Gender as Race Is to Ethnicity?" In *Gendered Anthropology.* Ed. Teresa del Valle. London: Routledge.

———. 1995. "Invaded Women: Sex, Race, and Class in the Formation of Colonial Society." In *Ethnicity, Gender, and the Subversion of Nationalism.* Ed. Fiona Wilson and Bodil Folke Frederiksen. Portland, Ore.: Frank Cass and Co.

———. N.d. "The 'Right to Difference' in an Unequal World.' Unpublished manuscript.

Stoler, Ann. 1991. "Carnal Knowledge and Imperial Power: Gender, Race, and Morality in Colonial Asia." In *Gender at the Crossroads of Knowledge: Feminist Anthropology in the Postmodern Era.* Ed. Micaela di Leonardo. Berkeley: University of California Press.

———. 1995. *Race and the Education of Desire: Foucault's History of Sexuality and the Colonial Order of Things.* Durham, N.C.: Duke University Press.

Stoll, Clifford. 1989. *The Cuckoo's Egg.* New York: Pocket Books.

Stoll, David. 1982. *Fishers of Men or Founders of Empire? The Wycliffe Bible Translators in Latin America.* London: Zed Press.

———. 1988. "Evangelicals, Guerrillas, and the Army: The Ixil Triangle under Ríos Montt." In *Harvest of Violence: The Mayan Indians and the Guatemalan Crisis.* Ed. Robert Carmack. Norman: University of Oklahoma Press.

———. 1990. *Is Latin America Turning Protestant? The Politics of Evangelical Growth.* Berkeley: University of California Press.

———. 1991. "I, Rigoberta Menchú vs. I, David Stoll." Paper presented at Stanford University.

———. 1993. *Between Two Armies in the Ixil Towns of Guatemala.* New York: Columbia University Press.

———. N.d. "Guatemala: Solidarity Activists Head for Trouble." Unpublished manuscript.

Stone, Allucquere Rosanne (Sandy). 1991. "Will the Real Body Please Stand up? Boundary Stories about Virtual Cultures." In *Cyberspace: First Steps.* Ed. Michael Benedikt. Cambridge, Mass.: MIT Press.

———. 1995a. "Split Subjects, Not Atoms; or, How I Fell in Love with My Prosthesis." In *The Cyborg Handbook.* Ed. Chris Hables Gray, with Heidi J. Figueroa-Sarriera and Steven Mentor. New York: Routledge.

———. 1995b. *The War of Desire and Technology at the Close of the Mechanical Age.* Cambridge, Mass.: MIT Press.

Stuart, George E., and Gene S. Stuart. 1977. *The Mysterious Maya.* Washington, D.C.: National Geographic Society.

Stutzman, R. 1981. "*El Mestizaje:* An All-Inclusive Ideology of Exclusion." In *Cultural Transformations and Ethnicity in Modern Ecuador.* Ed. N. E. Whitten Jr. New York: Harper and Row.

Taller J'a C'amabal I'b (Casa de la Unidad del Pueblo, House of the People's Unity). 1986. Presentation at the States, Autonomy, and Indigenous Rights Symposium, Managua, Nicaragua, July.

———. 1989a. "La Civilización Maya y la Lucha de Clases." Pamphlet, Popular Education Series 2. Mexico City: Taller J'a C'amabal I'b.

———. 1989b. "La Guerra de Conquista." Pamphlet, Popular Education Series 4. Mexico City: Taller J'a C'amabal I'b.

Taussig, Michael. 1987. *Shamanism, Colonialism, and the Wild Man: A Study in Terror and Healing.* Chicago: University of Chicago Press.

————. 1992. *The Nervous System*. New York: Routledge.

Tax, Sol. 1937. "The Municipios of the Midwestern Highlands of Guatemala." *American Anthropologist* 39.

Tedlock, Barbara. 1992 [1982]. *Time and the Highland Maya*. Albuquerque: University of New Mexico Press.

Trinh T., Minh-ha. 1986. "She, the Inappropriated Other." *Discourse* 8.

————. 1989. *Woman, Native, Other: Writing, Postcoloniality, and Feminism*. Bloomington: Indiana University Press.

Tsing, Anna Lowenhaupt. 1993. *In the Realm of the Diamond Queen: Marginality in an Out of the Way Place*. Princeton: Princeton University Press.

Turbyne, Judith. 1995. "Auto-Gestion in Guatemala." Ph.D. diss., University of Bath, England.

United Nations Department of Public Information. 1986. *Everyone's UN*. New York: UN Publishing.

————. 1992. *Basic Facts about the United Nations*. New York: UN Publishing.

United States State Department. 1994. "Guatemala—Travel Warning." 24 June.

Vasconcelos, José. 1944. *La Raza Cósmica: Misión de la Raza Iberoamericana*. Paris: Agencia Mundial de Librería.

Vilas, Carlos M. 1996. "Neoliberal Social Policy: Managing Poverty (Somehow)." *NACLA Report on the Americas* 24, no. 6.

Virilio, Paul. 1990. *War and Cinema*. New York: Semiotext(e).

Visweswaran, Kamala. 1994. *Fictions of Feminist Ethnography*. Minneapolis: University of Minnesota Press.

Vogt, Evan Z. 1990 [1970]. *The Zinacantecos of Mexico: A Modern Maya Way of Life*. Fort Worth, Tex.: Harcourt Brace Jovanovich College Publishers.

Wallace, Michelle. 1992. "Negative Images: Towards a Black Feminist Cultural Criticism." In *Cultural Studies*. Ed. Lawrence Grossberg, Cary Nelson, and Paula A. Treichler. New York: Routledge.

Wallerstein, Immanuel. 1974. *The Modern World-System I: Capitalist Agriculture and the Origins of the European World-Economy in the Sixteenth Century*. New York: Academic Press.

————. 1983. *Historical Capitalism*. London: Verso.

————. 1992. "The Construction of Racism, Nationalism, Ethnicity." In *Race, Nation, Class: Ambiguous Identities*. Ed. Immanuel Wallerstein and Etienne Balibar. London: Verso.

Walsh, Janet. 1996. "Truth, Justice, and Human Rights in Guatemala's Transition to Democracy." Working paper no. 1, Institute of International Studies, University of California at Berkeley.

Warren, Kay. 1989 [1978]. *The Symbolism of Subordination: Indian Identity in a Guatemalan Town*. Austin: University of Texas Press.

————. 1992. "Transforming Memories and Histories: The Meaning of Ethnic Resurgence for Mayan Indians." In *Americas: New Interpretive Essays*. Ed. Alfred Stepan. New York: Oxford University Press.

————. 1993. "Interpreting *La Violencia* in Guatemala: Shapes of Mayan Silence and Resistance." In *The Violence Within: Cultural and Political Opposition in Divided Nations*. Ed. Kay Warren. Boulder, Colo.: Westview Press.

————. 1996. "Reading History as Resistance: Maya Public Intellectuals in Guatemala." In *Maya Cultural Activism in Guatemala.* Ed. Edward F. Fischer and R. McKenna Brown. Austin: University of Texas Press.

———. 1998. *Indigenous Movements and Their Critics: Pan-American Activism in Guatemala.* Princeton, N.J.: Princeton University Press.

Watanabe, John M. 1992. *Maya Saints and Souls in a Changing World.* Austin: University of Texas Press.

———. 1995. "Unimagining the Maya: Anthropologists, Others, and the Inescapable Hubris of Authorship." *Bulletin of Latin American Research* 14, no. 1.

Weiner, Tim. 1995. "In Guatemala's Dark Heart, CIA Tied to Death and Aid." *New York Times,* 2 April.

———. 1996. "Records Tie CIA Informer to Two Guatemala Killings." *New York Times,* 7 May.

Whitehead, Tony Larry, and Mary Ellen Conaway. 1986. *Self, Sex, and Gender in Cross-Cultural Fieldwork.* Urbana: University of Illinois Press.

Williams, Brackette F. 1989. "A Class Act: Anthropology and the Race to Nation across Ethnic Terrain." *Annual Review of Anthropology* 18.

Williams, Raymond. 1983. *Towards 2000.* London: Chatto and Windus/Hogarth Press.

Williams, Robert A. 1990. "Encounters on the Frontiers of International Human Rights Law: Redefining the Terms of Indigenous Peoples' Survival in the World." *Duke Law Journal,* no. 4.

Wilson, Richard. 1995. *Maya Resurgence in Guatemala: Q'eqchi' Experience.* Norman: University of Oklahoma Press.

Wolf, Eric R. 1957. "Closed Corporate Peasant Communities in Mesoamerica and Central Java." *Southwestern Journal of Anthropology* 13, no. 1.

———. 1986. "The Vicissitudes of the Closed Corporate Community." *American Ethnologist* 13.

Woodward, Ralph Lee. 1987. *Central America: A Nation Divided.* New York: Oxford University Press.

Young, Robert J. C. 1995. *Colonial Desire: Hybridity in Theory, Culture, and Race.* London: Routledge.

Zizek, Slavoj. 1989. *The Sublime Object of Ideology.* London: Verso.

INDEX

Page numbers followed by "n" or "nn" refer to material in notes. Illustrations are denoted by page numbers in *italics*. Abbreviations are listed by initials only.

Columbus, Christopher, 195n26
COMG (Guatemalan Council of Mayan Organizations), 20–21, 126, 161, 257n18, 337
Commander Benedicto (Mario Payeras), 58
Commander Everado (Efraín Bámaca Velásquez), 10n14, 46, 59n29
community-bound identification, 128–136; as definition of Maya, 37, 128–133; double bind of, 163–169; as goal of Maya organizing, 49, 136–143. *See also* territory; *traje*
computers. *See* cyberspace; Maya-hacker
CONAVIGUA (National Coordinating Committee of Guatemalan Widows), 16n20, 20, 196, 336
CONDEG (Guatemalan Council for the Displaced), 20
Conference on Culture, 111–112
CONIC (National Indigenous and Campesino Coordinator), 269n36, 275n42
Constitution (1985), 82, 114, 239, 312, 321–323, 335
contact zones, 50n14
Convention 107, 289
Convention 169, 7, 126; ALMG support for, 316; Article 14 of, 299; Congress and, 318–319; contents, 39, 298–299, 298n22, 299n23, 300, 311–314; decentralization and, 340–347; drafting of, 294–295; effect on state, 39–40, 345; *formación* and, 286, 303; land issues in, 299–307, 324–327; law and, 321–323, 335–337; National Consultation, 312–314, 316; National Delegation for the Ratification of, 314, 316, 317–319, 322, 330; "peoples" in, 295–299; ratification of, 104, 122, 286–287, 313–317; regional forums on, 314–317; resistance to, 18n21, 298, 298n22, 308, 317, 319–323, 327–328, 334; self-determination in (*see* self-determination, in Convention 169); sovereignty and autonomy issues in, 327–330; state effects on ratification of, 323–327; support for, 21, 24, 317, 317n39, 330–340; territory as issue in, 286–288; transnational framework of, 285–286; workshops for, 313–314, 315
Copil, Alfredo: on Constitution, 322, 323n48; on identity consciousness, 317;

influence of, 325n52; on ladino attitudes toward Indians, 319, 330; on National Consultation, 316; on security threats against Delegation, 314
COPMAGUA (Coordination of Organizations of the Pueblo Maya of Guatemala), 179, 257n18, 267, 311
corruption, 112n42, 331n59
corte, jokes about, 38, 175, 204. *See also traje*
cotton, 360n2
Coulter, Robert, 295, 297, 298
counterinsurgency, 85n10, 150, 269n36, 345; Civil Defense Patrols in, 27n28, 48n9; effect on FAR, 9; effect on URNG, 10, 59–60; fantasmatic paranoia as, 11, 320; as genocide, 91; indigenous participation in, 95; against ladinos, 91n20; military propaganda in, 59; in relation to Belize, 16n19; state response to Mayan demands as, 230–231, 345, 346; *traje* as colonial, 130, 185, 185n16; transnational organizations as, 354. *See also* Civil Defense Patrols (PAC); Development Poles; military; model villages
CPR (Communities of the Population in Resistance), 20, 97, 98n28
CUC (Campesino Unity Committee), 20, 48n10, 144, 172
cultural rights groups, 20–21. *See also* Mayan organizing; *names of specific groups*
culture: as commodity, 114, 118–119, 125, 357; as ethnic identity, 356; fixing of, 108n39, 125; gender differences in, 240; "high," 25, 26n27, 78, 108, 110, 116, 117–118, 193; hybridity of, 232n34; identity as, 211–212; Mayan male notion of, 276; Mayan organizing and, 80, 131–132; meaning of, 78, 80; military use of, 90–94, 108; in Quincentennial, 78, 80; right to, 356–357; state use of, 109, 113n43, 122–127; URNG use of, 125n53. *See also* Mayan culture; Ministry of Culture and Sports
Cus, Andrés, 146–147, 152, 159n30, 161, 265
customary law (*derecho consuetudinario*), 39, 89n18, 300, 311, 336n64, 337–340. *See also* law
cyberspace, 235n41, 258, 261–266; articulation and, 250, 270–271; ethnostalgia and, 261, 263–266, 270; gender and,

cyberspace (*continued*)
271–272; as imagined community, 250;
mestizaje and, 260; military-industrial
complex and, 262–263, 262n25; as parallel to nation-state, 259–262; paranoia
and, 270; transnational flows and, 261–
262. *See also* Maya-hacker
Cypess, Sandra Messinger, 193

"Dance of the Conquest," 15–16
Dandler, Jorge, 313
DARPA (Defense Advanced Research Proj-
ect Agency), 262, 262n25
Darwinism, 110
Dary Fuentes, Claudia, 281, 356, 360
DC (Christian Democrats), 103, 105, 112–
115, 153
decentralization, 340–347, 358. *See also*
autonomy
Declaration of the Granting of Independence to Colonial Countries and
Peoples, 297n21
Declaration on the Rights of Indigenous
Peoples, 292n11, 294n15
Delaney, Carol, 228–229, 278n45
democracy, 82, 102
"Democratic Spring," 88–90, 320, 320n41.
See also Arbenz, Jacobo; Arévalo, Juan
José
democratization, 68, 74, 81–82, 102, 343
dependency theory, 352–353
derecho consuetudinario. See customary law
(*derecho consuetudinario*)
desenvuelta, meaning of, 38, 175, 187, 193,
195, 250. *See also* articulation; *traje*
determination, 73n
development: eugenics and, 234–235;
government financial support for, 82;
gringo(a) involvement in, 100, 100n30;
military involvement in, 99–100. *See also*
Development Poles; model villages
Development Poles, 32, 45; creation of, 91–
92; definition of, 97; Peace Accords and,
96n26; progress in, 99; right to culture
and, 356. *See also* military; model villages
Devine, Carol, 45
Devine, Michael, 45, 157n27, 287n5, 335
Día de la Raza, 13
Díaz-Polanco, Héctor, 59, 60n30, 130,
230n32
Doan, Mary Ann, 184

domestic labor: housewivization of Mayan
women and, 359–361, 360n2; impact of
nontraditional exports on, 281; Indian
maids and, 199; Mayan woman and,
276–277, 277n44; *mujer maya* as, 198,
198nn30,31, 226
double binds, in Maya versus state, 27–31,
163–169, 279, 290, 303, 349; for Mayan
women, 163–169
Douglas, Mary, 176, 225n23, 351
drug trafficking, 81n6; 157
D'Souza, Dinesh, 48n10
Dujovne Ortíz, Alicia, 56

EAFG (Guatemalan Forensic Anthropology
Team), 10, 53
Earle, Duncan, 242n48
EC (European Community), 74n2, 287
economics: identity and, 304; state and, 74;
structural adjustment, 351–358; trade,
139, 357–358. *See also* biopolitical economy; dependency theory; Regulation
School
ECOSOC (Economic and Social Council),
289, 291, 292, 300–301
education, bilingual. *See* bilingual education
EGP (Guerrilla Army of the Poor), 9, 58, 59,
59n29, 97n27
Ehlers, Tracy, 216, 222, 281n49
Eide, Asbojørn, 297
elites, *219;* ALMG and, 154; on culture, 110;
decentralization and, 344; Indian, 301;
Maya power relationship to, 367; purity
of blood and, 213; racism of, 212–213,
212n6, 215, 229, 230n31; resistance to
Convention 169 by, 320; sexuality and,
217–218; "wooing" of Indians by, 331–
332. *See also Guatemala: Linaje y Racismo*
(Lineage and Racism) (Casaus Arzú);
oligarchy
El Salvador, 44n6, 248n3
Englund, Nora, 159, 254
Enloe, Cynthia, 91, 139, 179n7, 225n23, 359
Epic of the Indies, 26n27, 195
ESTNA (School for Strategic National Studies), 101–102, 131, 196
ethnicity, 57; versus class, 60n30, 77–78; as
cultural identity, 356; gendering of, 181,
183, 197; ladino, 78 (*see also* ladino(s));
mestizaje and, 2, 38; nation and, 27, 179–
181; versus race, 38, 240

patriarchy, metaphors of, 26, 168, 197, 213, 240n44, 331–332
Patzcuaro Accords (1938), 88
Paul, Lois, 167n36, 277n45, 278
Payeras, Mario (Commander Benedicto), 57, 58, 60n30
Paz, Octavio, 220n18
Peace Brigades, 45n7
Peace Corps, 53
peace process (treaty, accords): The Left and, 367–368; provisions of, 114n44, 142n19; role of *mujer maya* in, 361–363; supporters of, 10n15; URNG role in, 10. *See also* Accord on Identity and Indigenous Rights
Pedro González, Gaspar, 116, 120
Penados de Barrios, Prospero, 13
penal code, 336n64, 337
Penley, Constance, 276n43
peoples, definition of, 296–297, 298. *See also* Convention 169
Perera, Victor, 7n9, 65, 66n40, 101n32
pessimistic functionalism, 30, 279, 309, 310, 311, 343, 352–353, 355
Peterson, Kurt, 344, 356, 360
Pfohl, Stephen, 250n8
PGT (Guatemala Workers' Party), 9
phenotype, identity and: body and family, 213; *cara de indio* and, 208; erasure by *mestizaje*, 206; meaning in transnational political relations, 45; oligarchy and, 229; racialization of, 94, 134, 231; use in solidarity, 52
Pietz, William, 127
piñata effect. *See* state: piñata effect of
pleasure: pollution taboos and, 176; role in identification, 30; in solidarity, 55–57; white men and, 221
PLFM (Francisco Marroquín Linguistic Project), 156, 254
Poggi, Gianfranco, 74, 75, 290
Poitevin, René, 356, 360
Poma de Ayala, Guaman, 165n35
Pop Caal, Antonio, 1, 254
popular sector, 19–20, 148–149, 164n34, 335
populations, definition of, 296
Popul Wuj, 23, 23n25, 92, 161, 164, 167
Porras Castejón, Gustavo, 60n30, 92–93
postcolonial theory, 3, 180–181

post-Fordism, 40, 288, 309, 344, 350, 355, 356
Prakash, Gyan, 70
Pratt, Mary, 50n14, 55, 56, 128n1
pre-Colombian peoples. *See* Mayan culture: classic ruins
Prera Flores, Anaisabel, 112, 120
PRODERE (Program for Displaced, Refugees, and Returnees), 313n33, 331n59
pronatalism, 166
PRONEBI (National Program of Bilingual Education), 115n46, 143, 156
prosthetic(s), 358–367; body image and use of, 30; definition of, 271; dependency on, 333; gender as, 271–281; *mujer maya* as (see *mujer maya*); Rigoberta Menchú as, 303, 362
prostitution, 225n23. *See also* sexuality
Protestant churches, 65, 140–141
psychoanalysis, 29. *See also* fetishism; Freud, Sigmund
pueblo: anthropologists as shield for, 45; divide between state and, 46, 84; heterogeneous, 37, 57, 68; military and, 94; organizations for, 45, 121n49, 179, 257n18, 267, 311

queen contests, 93, 183
Quemé Chay, Rigoberto, 147n21, 322–323, 329–330, 332
quetzal bird, symbolism of, 13, 16, 210
Quincentennial (Five Hundred Years), 1, 4; discourse on, 13, 15–16, 266n28; effects of, 61, 77–78, 162; government response to, 12–13; indigenous responses to, 21–24; ladino responses to, 18n22, 25–27; meaning of culture in, 78, 80; press response to, 13, 18, 18n22; procession banner, 23; URNG response to, 18–19. *See also* jokes
Quittner, Joshua, 258

race, 77–78; versus class, 233–235; concept of, 239; as difference, 240–241; versus ethnicity, 38, 240; eugenics tie with gender, 110; gendering of, 222, 224; inequality and, 235; Mayan organizing on, 242n48; *mestizaje* on, 38, 239 (See also *mestizaje*); national identity and, 110. See also *blanquemiento;* racism

Compositor:	G&S Typesetters, Inc.
Text:	10/12 Baskerville
Display:	Baskerville
Printer and Binder:	Thomson-Shore, Inc.